MORE NAMES
AND NAMING

Recent Titles in
Bibliographies and Indexes in Anthropology

Hispanic First Names: A Comprehensive Dictionary of 250 Years of
Mexican-American Usage
Richard D. Woods, compiler

Ecce Homo: An Annotated Bibliographic History of Physical
Anthropology
Frank Spencer, compiler

Personal Names and Naming: An Annotated Bibliography
Edwin D. Lawson, compiler

The Arapaho Indians: A Research Guide and Bibliography
Zdenek Salzmann, compiler

Micronesia 1975–1987: A Social Science Bibliography
Nicholas J. Goetzfridt and William L. Wuerch, compilers

Indigenous Navigation and Voyaging in the Pacific:
A Reference Guide
Nicholas J. Goetzfridt, compiler

The Bibliography of Human Behavior
Hiram Caton, editor and compiler

The Sioux and Other Native American Cultures of the Dakotas:
An Annotated Bibliography
Herbert T. Hoover and Karen P. Zimmerman, compilers

MORE NAMES AND NAMING

An Annotated Bibliography

Compiled by

EDWIN D. LAWSON

Bibliographies and Indexes in Anthropology, Number 9

GREENWOOD PRESS
Westport, Connecticut • London

Library of Congress Cataloging-in-Publication Data

Lawson, Edwin D.
  More names and naming : an annotated bibliography / compiled by
Edwin D. Lawson.
    p. cm.—(Bibliographies and indexes in anthropology, ISSN
0742–6884 ; no. 9)
  Includes bibliographical references and index.
  ISBN 0–313–28582–9 (alk. paper)
  1. Names, Personal—Bibliography. I. Title. II. Series.
Z6824.L38 1995
[CS2305]
016.9294—dc20   95–31626

British Library Cataloguing in Publication Data is available.

Library of Congress Catalog Card Number: 95–31626
ISBN: 0–313–28582–9
ISSN: 0742–6884

First published in 1995

Greenwood Press, 88 Post Road West, Westport, CT 06881
An imprint of Greenwood Publishing Group, Inc.

Printed in the United States of America

The paper used in this book complies with the
Permanent Paper Standard issued by the National
Information Standards Organization (Z39.48–1984).

10 9 8 7 6 5 4 3 2 1

To the memory of Florian W. Znaniecki
and
In honor of Ross Stagner

My two great professors at the University of Illinois,
Urbana-Champaign

CONTENTS

Preface   xiii
Sample Entries   xvii
Citation Abbreviations   xix
1. Names, General Works   1
2. Bibliographies   6
3. Address, Forms of and Names   8
4. Affectionate Names   12
5. The Bible and Names   13
   5.1. Bible Figures: General   16
   5.2. Bible Figures: Moses   16
   5.3. Bible Figures: Jesus   17
6. Cataloging and Names   18
7. Change of Name   19
   7.1. Entertainers   22
8. Computers and Names   22
   8.1. Soundex   23
9. Ethnic, National, and Cultural Names   24
   9.1. African: General   24
      9.1.1. Miscellaneous Groups 25
      9.1.2. Bini   29
      9.1.3. Ghana   29
      9.1.4. Igbo   30
      9.1.5. Republic of South Africa 31
      9.1.6. Swahili   32
      9.1.7. Zimbabwe   32
      9.1.8. Zulu   33
   9.2. African American   34
      9.2.1. Change of Name   36
      9.2.2. Slave Names   36
   9.3. American Indian   38
   9.4. Ancient Middle East   44
      9.4.1. Akkadian   48
      9.4.2. Aramaic   48

9.4.3. Assyrian   48
9.4.4. Egypt   49
9.4.5. Hittite   52
9.5. Arabic   52
9.6. Baltic   54
9.7. Brazilian   55
9.8. Bulgarian   56
9.9. Canadian   56
        9.9.1. Change of Name   58
        9.9.2. Law and Names   59
        9.9.3. Naming Patterns   59
        9.9.4. Nicknames   60
9.10. Celtic   60
9.11. Central American   61
9.12. Chinese   62
        9.12.1. Surnames   64
9.13. Classical Greek   65
9.14. Classical Roman   68
9.15. Danish   71
9.16. Dutch   74
9.17. English   74
        9.17.1. Address, Forms of   78
        9.17.2. Alias Names   80
        9.17.3. First Names   80
        9.17.4. Middle English Names   82
        9.17.5. Nicknames   85
        9.17.6. Old English   85
              9.17.6.1. Coins   89
        9.17.7. Population Structure and Names   90
        9.17.8. Scandinavian Names in England   93
        9.17.9. Surnames   93
              9.17.9.1. Specific   100
9.18. Ethiopian   101
9.19. Faroese   102
9.20. Finnish   102
9.21. French   104
9.22. German   105
9.23. Greek (Modern)   107
9.24. Hawaiian   109
9.25. Hispanic   109
9.26. Huguenot   109
9.27. Hungarian   110
9.28. Icelandic   111
9.29. Indo-Pakistani Sub-Continent   111
9.30. Iranian   113
9.31. Irish   113
        9.31.1. First Names   116
        9.31.2. Gaelic   116
        9.31.3. Population Structure and Names   117
        9.31.4. Stereotypes and Names   117
        9.31.5. Surnames   118

Contents   ix

9.31.5.1. Specific   120
9.32. Islamic   121
9.33. Italian   122
   9.33.1. Nicknames   123
9.34. Japanese   124
9.35. Jewish   125
   9.35.1. Ancient Israel   129
   9.35.2. Change of Name   130
   9.35.3. Chinese   131
   9.35.4. First Names   131
   9.35.5. Naming Patterns   132
   9.35.6. Surnames   132
9.36. Lappish   135
9.37. Maltese   135
   9.37.1. Nicknames   136
9.38. Manx   137
9.39. Mexican   137
9.40. Miscellaneous   139
9.41. Norwegian   142
9.42. Oceania   144
   9.42.1. Australian   144
   9.42.2. New Zealand   145
      9.42.2.1. Maori   145
   9.42.3. Papua New Guinea   146
9.43. Peruvian   147
9.44. Philippine   147
9.45. Polish   148
9.46. Portuguese   148
9.47. Russian   148
9.48. Scandinavian   150
9.49. Scottish   150
   9.49.1. First Names   151
   9.49.2. Nicknames   152
   9.49.3. Population Structure   153
   9.49.4. Surnames   153
      9.49.4.1. Specific   155
9.50. Slavic   156
9.51. South American   156
   9.51.1. Indians   157
9.52. Spanish   158
   9.52.1. First Names   158
   9.52.2. Nicknames   159
   9.52.3. Surnames   160
9.53. Swedish   161
   9.53.1. Change of Name   164
   9.53.2. First Names   165
   9.53.3. Law and Names   165
   9.53.4. Nicknames   166
   9.53.5. Runic Names   166
   9.53.6. Surnames   169
   9.53.7. Theoretical Aspects   169
9.54. Swiss   170

    9.55. Turkish   170
    9.56. Ukrainian   171
    9.57. Welsh   172
        9.57.1. First Names   174
        9.57.2. Surnames   174
    9.58. West Indian   176
10. Education   176
11. First Names   178
    11.1. Baby-Names   179
    11.2. Specific   181
    11.3. Unisex   182
12. God   182
    12.1. Bible   185
    12.2. YHWH   185
13. Gods   186
14. Graffiti   188
15. Humor and Names   188
16. Indexing and Names   190
17. Influence of Names   190
18. Junior and Names   192
19. Juvenile Level: Books and Articles on Names   192
20. Law and Names   193
    20.1. Name Change   194
    20.2. Women and Surnames   195
21. Middle Names   195
22. Miscellaneous Aspects of Names   196
23. Naming Process: Historical Patterns   199
24. Naming Process: Patterns and Practices   201
25. Naming Process: Theoretical and Linguistic Aspects   204
26. Nicknames   205
    26.1. Blues Singers   211
    26.2. Presidents   212
    26.3. Sports   212
27. Numerology and Names   214
28. Popular Names   214
29. Population Structure and Names   217
30. Pronunciation and Names   219
31. Proverbs and Names   221
32. Pseudonyms   222
33. Psychology and Names   222
    33.1. Clinical Psychology   223
    33.2. Learning and Names   223
    33.3. Perception and Names   225
    33.4. Physiological Psychology and Names   226
34. Public Health and Names   226
35. Recreational Aspects of Names   227
36. Religious Figures and Names   229
37. Same Name   230
38. Sociological Aspects of Names   231
39. Sound and Names   231
40. Spelling and Names   232

Contents

41. Statistics and Names   232
42. Stereotypes and Names   233
    42.1. First Names   235
43. Style and Names   236
44. Surnames   237
    44.1. Specific   239
45. Unique Names   239
46. Women and Names   243
    46.1. Birth Names   243
    46.2. Law and Legal Aspects   245
    46.3. Surnames   245
47. Words from Names   245
    47.1. Medical   248
    47.2. Recreational Aspects   252
    47.3. Science   253
    47.4. Slang   253
Author Index   255
Subject Index   279

PREFACE

Onomastics is the area of study concerned with the content and meaning of all types of naming. Among its major concerns, along with literary names and placenames, is personal names. Personal names are the labels or tags used in identifying people or groups of people. We use first names, middle names, surnames, many types of nickname, and even numbers as names!

The reader of this volume will see that the subject of personal names involves many disciplines from music to medicine, from cultures as diverse as Australian and Zulu. Not only is there a wide range in the disciplines that the study of names touches on but there are also wide cultural, ethnic, and geographical variations in how names are selected and bestowed.

To address these and other concerns, Elsdon C. Smith in 1952 published his *Personal Names: A Bibliography* which has over 3400 entries. The impact of this bibliography, his contributions as a founder and first president of the American Name Society, and his many publications, was to stimulate scholarly work on names. In the 40 years since the original bibliography was published there has been a tremendous number of books and articles published on personal names.

When my 1987 bibliography *Personal Names and Naming* came out, it was thought to be current to that time and that it would stand for a number of years. However, an explosion of research dealing with names accompanied by newer methods of retrieval of new books and articles led to the decision to do a second completely new volume

One of these new retrieval methods was the ability to use OCLC searches to locate books that had been published before the advent of modern retrieval services. Related to this is that in evaluating current books and articles, we were able to identify items that were published in the past but never listed anywhere. An example would be a chapter in a book that would not show up in a catalog entry. The 1987 bibliography had approximately 1200 items. This one has close to 2200.

Scope and Coverage

What I have tried to do here is to supplement the earlier Smith volume and my 1987 book. Not included are items already in either of these bibliographies, some of which have been reprinted since 1952 by Gale Research and other publishers. In general, if an item was unavailable through Inter-Library Loan or was very expensive to borrow, it also was not included (this happened in only about a dozen cases).

Regrettably, non-English research contributions were not included. However, where there was an English summary, it is included. This is particularly true of Scandinavian contributions. There are thousands of valuable contributions in other languages but due to space and language limitations, it was not possible to include them. For further information, the interested reader should consult *Onoma,* which has bibliographic materials from all over the world.

In order to build the bibliography of approximately 2200 items, numerous sources were consulted. Among these were: *Names, Nomina, Onoma,* and *Onomastica Canadiana,* and the following abstracts sources: *Arts and Humanities Citation Index, ERIC, MLA International Bibliography, Psychological Abstracts, Religion Index, Social Citation Index,* and *Sociological Abstracts.* It might be mentioned that at least 400 additional items which seemed to be appropriate by title turned out on inspection not to be suitable. Some dealt with placenames or literary names. Some were non-English. About 50 books or articles were unavailable either because no library was willing to loan them or the charge for photocopying was judged prohibitive for most researchers.

Arrangement

The entries are grouped alphabetically in the 47 major subject categories shown in the Table of Contents. Within each subject category, or sub-category, the items are listed alphabetically by author. The category for an item was chosen on the basis of what appeared to be the most salient feature relating to onomastics. However, since most entries have more than one possible category, cross-references are provided in the Subject Index.

Entries

For books, the entry includes: author, date, title, edition, place of publication, total pages or specific pages related to annotation, and references, tables, or figures, if any.

For journals, the entry includes: author, date, title of article, name of journal, pages, annotation, and references, tables, figures, and a foreign language summary, if any.

Acknowledgments

Appreciation is expressed to the following libraries in Canada for assistance, especially with British items: University of Guelph Library, Niagara Falls Public Library, and St. Catharines Public Library.

In England: the British Museum, the University Library at the University of Cambridge; in Wales, the National Library at Aberystwyth; in Scotland, the Mitchell Library in Glasgow; and in Ireland, the National Library in Dublin.

Tony Carr of the Local History Department and members of the staff in the Reference Department of the library in Shrewsbury, England were most helpful. David Schoen of Niagara University ran OCLC searches.

Many, many other libraries contributed to the success of this project by making available books and journal articles through Inter-Library Loan.

Four editors of journals, Göran Hallberg of *Sydsvenska ortnamnssällskapet årsskrift,* Joanna Kolléca of *Onomata,* Lena Peterson of *Studia Anthroponymica Scandinavica,* and Willy Van Langendonck of *Onoma,* contributed in different ways.

A number of other individuals were also very helpful: Margaret E. Pabst, Inter-Library Loan and her two associates Janet I. Ferry and Rhona M. O'Connell who were so patient with all my requests; Gary D. Barber, who answered numerous questions on all kinds of matters; Sandra A. Lewis, Computing Services, who guided me through complicated computer programs; Thomas E. Morrissey, Department of History, who found a number of onomastic items and sent them along to me; Norwood J. Barris of Dunkirk, NY and Richard F. Sheil of Fredonia, NY who got me through perilous situations with WordPerfect; Jerome Jacobson who provided advice in the early stages of the book; and to the staff at WordPerfect who were so patient with my questions. Finally, I would like to thank my wife, Irene Kentner Lawson, for checking the entries in their final form.

EDWIN D. LAWSON
State University of New York
   at Fredonia

SAMPLE BOOK ENTRY

1   2   3   4   5

[1.11] Dunkling, Leslie (Alan). (1993). *The Guinness book of names,* 6th ed. Enfield,

                    6   5   6   7   8

Middlesex [England]: Guinness Publishers; New York: Facts on File, 255p. Refs.

9

Expansion over previous eds. Wide coverage of many aspects of names and naming. Includes 1st name origins, fashions, nicknames, and trade names. Listing of the 50 most popular 1st names in England and Wales, the US, and Australia for boys and for girls over time; list of the frequencies of 1100+ names in England and Wales at 12 intervals from 1900-1990.

1. Entry number
2. Author
3. Year of publication
4. Title of book
5. Place of publication
6. Publisher
7. Number of pages (or specific pages referred to)
8. References present
9. Annotation

SAMPLE JOURNAL ENTRY

1   2   3   4

[9.9.9] Lapierre, André. (1991). When *Auclair* becomes *O'Clair*: Some remarks on

                          5   6 7   8   9

Franco-American surnames. *OnoCan, 73*, 49-56. Refs. French summary.

10

Description of how French-Canadian surnames were modified in the 2nd half of the 19th cent. when 1000's of Quebecers moved to New England. Topics include: translation of name (Boisvert to Greenwood) and modification (Barrette > Barrett; Deveaux > Devoe).

1. Entry number
2. Author
3. Year of publication
4. Title of article
5. Name of journal
6. Volume number
7. Pages
8. References present
9. Foreign language summary
10. Annotation

CITATION ABBREVIATIONS

DissAbstrIntl = *Dissertation Abstracts International*
ICOS = International Congress of Onomastic Sciences
OnoCan = *Onomastica Canadiana*
StudAnthroScan = *Studia Anthroponymica Scandinavica*
SydOrtÅrss = *Sydsvenska ortnamnssällskapet årsskrift*

1. NAMES, GENERAL WORKS

[1.1] Aristides, Nikolai. (1980-1981). Onomastics, You and me is quits. [Life and Letters]. *American Scholar, 50,* 15-24.
General on several aspects of names: 1st names, surnames, initials, and change of name. Has a light touch.

[1.2] Aron, Michael. (1976, Jan.). What's in a name? [Wraparound]. *Harper's Magazine, 52,* 3-10. Refs. Illus.
Intro. to names followed by quotes from a number of names authorities including Rennick, Elsdon Smith, and Hendrickson.

[1.3] Ashley, Leonard R. N. (1989). *What's in a name...Everything you wanted to know.* Baltimore, MD: Genealogical Publishing, 265p.
General. Chs. 1-10 deal with 1st name, surnames, changes, and other general aspects of personal names; Ch. 20 covers names that became words; Ch. 23 is on fortune-telling with names; and Chs. 24-25 are on naming the baby.

[1.4] Barnhart, Clarence L. (1975). The selection of proper names in English dictionaries. *Names, 23,* 175-179.
Makes a case for the inclusion of proper names in dictionaries. Shows pronunciation of names.

[1.5] Barnhart, Clarence L. (Ed.). (1954). *The New Century cyclopedia of names.* New York: Appleton-Century-Crofts, 3 vols., 4342p.
Entries for 100,000 proper names of all times including personal names.

[1.6] Boulanger, Jean-Claude. (Ed.). (1990). *Le nom propre au carrefour des études humaines et des sciences sociales: actes du XVI congrès international des sciences onomastiques* [Proper Names at the Crossroads of the Humanities and Social Sciences: Proceedings of the 16th ICOS, Québec, Université Laval, 16-22 Aug. 1987]. Québec: Les Presses de l'Université Laval, 591p.
Has 53 papers. Among these are 6 in English dealing with some aspect of personal names. Among these are: Eichler [23.5], Embleton [9.9.3.2], Hengst [47.15], McGregory [9.2.7], and Nogrady [9.27.6].

[1.7] Bryant, Margaret F. (1976). After 25 years of onomastic study. *Names, 25,* 30-55.
Reviews the activities of the American Name Society from its founding in 1951 to 1976. While much attention is given to placenames, there are descriptions of work on personal names.

[1.8] Clark, Cecily. (1991/1992). Personal name studies: Bringing them to a wider audience. *Nomina, 15,* 21-34. Refs.
Wide-ranging in approach to different areas of onomastics. Asks for more scholarship and accuracy in research.

[1.9] Dickson, Paul. (1986). *Names: A collector's compendium of rare and unusual, bold and beautiful, odd and whimsical names.* New York: Delacorte, 282p. Refs. Illus.
Popular presentation of the world of names, many of which are personal names.

[1.10] Dorff, Daniel. (1984). The meaning of personal names. *Verbatim, 10(3),* 3-4.
General on 1st names. Attention to diminutives and affectionate forms.

[1.11] Dunkling, Leslie (Alan). (1993). *The Guinness book of names,* 6th ed. Enfield, Middlesex [England]: Guinness Publishers; New York: Facts on File, 255p. Refs.
Expansion over previous eds. Wide coverage of many aspects of names and naming. Includes 1st name origins, fashions, nicknames, and trade names. Listing of the 50 most popular 1st names in England and Wales, the US, and Australia for boys and for girls over time; list of the frequencies of 1100+ names in England and Wales at 12 intervals from 1900-1990.

[1.12] Dunn, R(obert). D. (Ed.). (1984). *William Camden: Remains concerning Britain.* Toronto: University of Toronto Pr., 576p. Refs. Portrait.
The *Remains* was originally published in 1605, then revised in 1614 and 1623. Pp. 45-154 include 1st names, surnames, allusions to names, and name anagrams. Camden's work is considered by many the most important early source on names in English. In the light of modern scholarship, care should be exercised.

[1.13] Friend, J(ohn Albert) Newton. (1957). *Words: Tricks and traditions.* New York: Scribner's, 184p.
Has some information names. Ch. 3 (pp. 32-33) has 3 anagrams, example, Florence Nightingale = Flit on Cheering Angel; Ch. 10 covers nicknames including the longest one, given by Sir Walter Scott to his printer, Aldiborontiphoscophornio (p. 122); Ch. 11 (pp.127-139) does surnames and baptismal names and includes this inscription from Nantucket:
>   Under the sod, under these trees
>   Lies the body of Jonathan Pease.
>   He is not here, but only his pod,
>   He has shelled out his peas and gone to his God.

[1.14] Gasque, Thomas J. (1990). Names: Four decades of contributions to international onomastics. *Proceedings of the 17th ICOS, Helsinki, 13-18 Aug. 1990, 1,* 354-361. Refs.
Names, the quarterly journal of the American Name Society, has always had an international outlook and has published many articles focused on areas outside of the Americas. Some of these are described.

[1.15] Gersuny, Carl. (1974). Occupations, occupational names and the development of society. *Journal of Popular Culture, 8,* 99-106. Refs. Table.
Shows how the development of society from agricultural to nonagricultural influenced surnames. Shows a table of 12 occupations in 9 European languages where 93 out of 96 of the cognates appear. Occupations shown include: baker, cooper, mason, and shoemaker.

[1.16] Hanks, Patrick & Hodges, Flavia. (1986). *The Oxford minidictionary of first names.* Oxford: Oxford University Press, 288 p.

Has entries for almost 2000 1st names used in the English-speaking world. Gives pronunciation according to the International Phonetic Alphabet. Indicates variants, short forms, and affectionate forms. Gives stories about people who bore famous names. Glossary.

[1.17] Hanks, Patrick & Hodges, Flavia. (1988; 1989). *Dictionary of surnames*. David L. Gold, special consultant for Jewish names. New York: Oxford University Press, 840p. Refs.
Covers 60,000 surnames with about 10,000 entries (many names are grouped into a major entry) from the English-speaking world and Europe. Lengthy intro. describes naming practices in various cultures. Probably the 1st systematic survey of surnames. Entries contain varying amounts of information depending on the name. These include: roots and meanings; peculiarities of regional distribution; information about the language and region where the surname originated; grouped together with the main entry are variants, diminutives, and other related names. There is also mention of major events in the history of some famous names.

[1.18] Hanks, Patrick & Hodges, Flavia. (1990). *A dictionary of first names*. Supplement on Arab names by Mona Baker. Supplement on names from the Indian subcontinent by Ramesh Krishnamurthy. Oxford: Oxford University Press, 433p. Refs. Contains about 4500 entries which with variants are probably considerably more. Entries for the main section give language, cultural origin, meaning, variants, some historical notes, and in some cases, level of popularity.

[1.19] Harder, Kelsie B. (Ed.). (1986). *Names and their varieties*. Lanham, MD: University Press of America, 317p. Refs.
This collection of articles from *Names* includes 5 on personal names: Smith [87:12.11], Straubinger [87:31.2], Brender [87:25.2.3], Rennick [87:28.1], and Davis [87:8.55.6].

[1.20] Harder, Kelsie B. (1986). Towards a history of onomastics. *Publications of the North Central Name Society,* No.1, pp. 1-10. Refs.
Brief history of personal name and placename research. Mention of better standard sources of information on personal names.

[1.21] Hazen, Barbara Shook. (1979). *Last, first, middle, and nick: All about names*. Englewood Cliffs, NJ: Prentice-Hall, 131p. Illus. by Sam Weissman.
General intro. to many aspects of names. Juvenile level.

[1.22] Hitt, Roberta Frissell. (1984). *What does your name mean?* Parsons, WV: McClain Printing, 241p.
Listing of approx. 10,000 1st names, alphabetically listed and grouped according to meaning. No specific derivations or sources given.

[1.23] Hook, J. N. (1991). *All those wonderful names: A potpourri of people, places, places, and things*. New York: Wiley, 317p. Refs.
About 1/2 of this book is devoted to personal names. Among the topics on personal names are: most popular names in various categories, unusual names, traditional names, naming children, surnames and their meanings, unusual surnames, and changes of name.

[1.24] *Information please almanac: Atlas and Yearbook*. (1994), 47th ed. Boston: Houghton Mifflin, 1024p.
Pp. 537-544 contain a list of approx. 175 Bible figures with 1-line descriptions. Other lists show kings of Judah and Israel, figures in Greek & Roman mythology, Norse mythology, Egyptian mythology.

[1.25] Jennings, Gary. (1965). *Personalities of language*. New York: Crowell, 282p. Refs(pp. 269-274).
The ch. "Our shining names are told" (pp. 134-154) deals with many aspects of personal names, patronyms, residence names, change of names, and others.

[1.26] Jobes, G. (1961). *Dictionary of mythology, folklore, and symbols*, New York: Scarecrow, 2 vols. 1759p.
Names of men, women, gods, and goddesses included among the 1000s of items, example, Maia was a Greek mountain nymph (p. 1046), the Maid of Saragossa was Augustina Zaragoza, "famous for her heroism during the siege of Saragossa, Spain, by the French in 1808 and 1809" (p. 1046).

[1.27] Kraft, Charles E. (1986, Dec.). The romance of names. *Antiques & Collecting, 91,* 80-84.
Reactions to Mencken's *The American language* with a discussion of unusual surnames and 1st names.

[1.28] Laird, Helene & Laird, Charlton. (1957). *The tree of language*. Cleveland: World, 233p.
Ch. 9 (pp. 77-83), *Names and how they began* has material on surnames for the beginner in onomastics.

[1.29] Lawson, Edwin D. (1989). Social psychological aspects of personal-naming. ERIC Document Reproduction Service No. ED 298 570. Summary in *Resources in Education*, 1989, *24(2)*, 51. Refs.
Review over the past 90 years of the contributions of social psychology to the science of names. Historical review, description of research on 1st names, hypcoristic names, affectionate names, nicknames, and unique names. Recent research has focused on theoretical approaches, stereotypes, popularity, school achievement, and other aspects.

[1.30] Lawson, Edwin D. (1990). For editors, authors, and readers: What we need to do to improve our journals. *Proceedings of the 17th ICOS: Helsinki, 13-18 Aug. 1990, 2,* 95-102. Refs.
Suggestions involving indexing, journal deposits, 2nd language abstracts, more reprints, and others.

[1.31] Lawson, Edwin D. (1992). Onomastics journals: How many and where? *Serials Librarian, 21,* 99-138. Refs. Tables.
Follow-up to Lawson [1.30]. Reports on a survey of 32 onomastic journals world-wide. Topics include: area of onomastics covered, editorial policy, where indexed/abstracted, and languages acceptable for publication.

[1.32] Martin, Charles B. (1987). New international names on the campus. *Names, 35,* 86-94. Refs.
Increase in international students on American campuses has brought new names. Description and discussion of naming customs from Chinese, Nigerian, Middle Eastern, Korean, Japanese, and Thai cultures. 100+ names listed, many of whose meanings are given.

[1.33] Meltzer, Milton. (1984). *A book about names*. Illus. by Mischa Richter. New York: Crowell, 128p. Illus.
Popular presentation about many aspects of names, i.e., surnames descriptive of physical appearance (Short, Stout, Longfellow), variations of Smith (Smyth, Smits, Schmidt), post-Revolutionary Russian names (Utopiya, Genii, Ninel), and others. Each page has text and drawing(s). Suitable for younger readers.

[1.34] Mezes, Basileios. (1989-90). The origin of family names in Europe and the genealogical research on them. *Onomata, 13,* 176-187. Refs. Greek. English summary. General on surnames in Europe.

[1.35] Names. (1991). *NewEncyBrit, 8,* 493.
Brief entry. Gives basic definitions of types of name. Includes personal names and quasi-personal names. For extended entry also in *NewEncyBrit,* See: Zgusta [1.49].

[1.36] Närhi, Eeva Maria. (Ed.). (1990). *Proceedings of the 17th ICOS: Helsinki 13-18 August 1990.* 2 vols. Helsinki: University of Helsinki and the Finnish Research Centre for Domestic Languages. Vol. 1, 501p.; Vol. 2, 494p. Refs. Tables. Figs. Maps.
Contains 120+ papers from all areas of onomastics. Languages include: English, French, German, and Russian. 18 of the papers are abstracted in this bibliography.

[1.37] Nuessel, Frank. (1992). *The study of names: A guide to the principles and topics.* Westport, CT: Greenwood, 152p. Refs.
A general view of onomastics. One section covers a great many aspects of personal names.

[1.38] *Oxford English dictionary.* (1933). Edited by James A. H. Murray & others. Oxford: Clarendon, 13 vols.
Has entries for *name, nickname, surname,* and other concepts useful for those interested in onomastics. Many individual names are also listed and defined.

[1.39] Pulgram, Ernst. (1951). What's your name? *Michigan Alumnus Quarterly Review, 57,* 303-309. Refs.
General intro. to surnames. Sympathy expressed to immigrants who change their names.

[1.40] Raphael, Frederic. (1976, Oct. 28). Remaking a name. *The Listener,* p. 549.
General discussion on names. Then focuses on an individual's "making a name" and being distinctive.

[1.41] Rule, La Reina & Hammond, William K. (1973). *What's in a name? Surnames of America.* New York: Jove (Harcourt Brace Jovanovich), 445p.
Contains 5000+ entries for surnames + a number of variations. Example, "Ashley, (English) root word Aesc-leah (Old English) ash-tree meadow. Shield: Silver background, three black bulls."

[1.42] Scheetz, George H. (1988). *Names' names: A descriptive and prescriptive onymicon,* rev. & enlarged. Sioux City, IO: Schuetz Verlag, 20p. Refs.
Defines terms which refer to types of name. Gives sources. Expansion from [87:1.11] to include approx. 130 entries, some of which refer to personal names, example, "Filionym--a name derived from that of a son," "Maritonym--a wife's name derived from that of her husband."

[1.43] Shoumatoff, Alex. (1988;90). *The mountain of names: A history of the human family.* New York: Vintage, 318p. Refs. (Originally published by Simon & Schuster in 1988).
The "mountain of names" refers to the repository outside Salt Lake City where the Mormons have collected a billion and 1/2 names. The book is devoted to the history and kinship relations of the human family and has some information on naming practices and surnames in different sections. Most appears to be from 2ndary sources.

[1.44] Smith, Elsdon C. (1953). Personal Names. [Collector's Choice]. *Antiquarian Bookman, 11,* 1879-1880.
Reminiscences of a famous onomatologist on collecting books on names.

[1.45] Stern, Gladys B. (1953). *A name to conjure with.* London: Collins, 223p.
The author describes her associations with various aspects of names and naming. Topics include her own name, Beethoven, James, and saints' names. Comment is wide-ranging and literary.

[1.46] Stewart, George R. (1952, Apr. 20). 'Iron-Hewer' or 'Man of Toft.' *New York Times Magazine,* p. 17.
Popular article introducing names to the lay public. Uses the PLON (patronym, location, occupation, nickname) scheme. Examples include: Stevenson, patronym; Warren, location; Eisenhower, occupation (blacksmith); and Russell, nickname.

[1.47] Wagner, Geoffrey (Atheling). (1968). *On the wisdom of words.* Princeton, NJ: Van Nostrand, 345p.
Ch. 5 (Pp. 172-187) is devoted to names. It is wide-ranging and inveighs against the often semantically incorrect current use of names. Topics include: numbers as names, the meaning of X in Malcolm X, sound names, names of entertainers, and other aspects of names.

[1.48] Walker, Barbara G. (1983). Name. In *The woman's encyclopedia of myths and secrets.* San Francisco: Harper & Row, pp. 708-716. Complete refs. pp. 1105-1118.
Survey of many ancient cultures, Egyptian, Babylonian, Scythian, Celtic, Germanic, Greek, Italian, Roman, and Japanese. Emphasis on the role of motherhood and women. Information on mother-names before the transition to father-names. See Also: Motherhood, pp. 680-695 for more on ancient name rites.

[1.49] Zgusta, Ladislav. (1991). Names. *NewEncyBrit, 24,* 728-733. Refs.
Wide-ranging concise description of onomastics. Topics include: forms of personal names in different cultures, choice of personal names, legal aspects of names, family names, and theophoric names.

[1.50] Zonabend, Françoise. (1980). Le nom de personne. *L'Homme, 20(4),* 7-23. Refs. French. English summary.
General survey of classification and research on 1st names, nicknames, and surnames. Emphasis on anthropological frame of reference. Refs. from many parts of the world.

2. BIBLIOGRAPHIES

[2.1] Alston, R. C. (1977). *A bibliography of the English language from the invention of printing to the year 1800, Vol. 11, Place names and personal names.* Printed for the author, Ilkley, England: Grove Press, 148p. Plates.
In addition to placename material lists 20 items on personal names (some represent different editions of the same work; some are included in Elsdon Smith's 1952 bibliography [87:6:16], example, "K'eogh John *A vindication of the antiquities of Ireland.* Dublin, 1748." Alston also has a number of plates of title pages and 1st pages. Also gives location of these books in public libraries.

[2.2] Arney, Roberta. (Ed.). (1993). *The Lurline H. Coltharp collection of onomastics: A bibliography.* El Paso, TX: University of Texas at El Paso Library, 74p.
Listing of this extensive collection of onomastic material by author, title, and LC call number.

[2.3] Bates, D. (1986). *A bibliography of Domesday book.* Woodbridge, Suffolk [England] & Dover, NH: For the Royal Historical Society by Boydell Press, 166p.
Includes 10 or more publications that relate directly to personal names in England. All in English are included in Elsdon Smith (1952) [87:6:16], Lawson (1987) or this vol.

[2.4] British Library. (1984). *Reader Guide No. 8: Family and personal names: A brief guide to sources of information,* 7p. Department of Printed Books, Reference Division, British Library.
Lists a number of basic reference materials for English and non-English names.

[2.5] Crammer, Marjorie. Compiler. (1975). *Bibliography of American folklore: Index to materials in books on select American folk characters.* Hyattsville, MD: Prince George's County Memorial Library System, 22p. (ERIC Documentation Reproduction Service No. ED 117 727)
Lists books in children's literature related to 200 real or imagined characters in American folk culture. Real nickname characters included are: Peter Stuyvesant (Peg Leg Peter),Annie Oakley (Little Sure Shot), and William F. Cody (Buffalo Bill).

[2.6] Lawson, Edwin D. (Compiler). (1987). *Personal names and naming: An annotated bibliography.* Westport, CT: Greenwood; London: Westport Publications, 185p. Refs.
Contains almost 1200 annotated bibliographic entries on all phases of personal naming. Some entries in this vol. refer to the 1987 bibliography.

[2.7] Lawson, Edwin D. (1988/89, Winter). *Personal names and naming: A new annotated bibliography. Journal of the North Central Name Society,* pp. 43-61. Refs. Tables.
Comparison of the major categories for entries in 2 bibliographies Elsdon C. Smith's 1952 *Personal names: A bibliography* [87:6.16] that of Lawson's 1987 *Personal names and naming: An annotated bibliography* [2.6]. Among the differences reported: the 1987 bibliography had proportionately fewer entries dealing with General Works, Bible,God(s), First Names, Law, and Surnames; there were more items in the Ethnic Groups, psychological, and Nicknames categories.

[2.8] Lawson, Edwin D. (1990). Nicknames: An annotated bibliography. *Names, 38,* 323-363. Refs.
Draws on Elsdon Smith [87:6.16], Lawson [2.8] and search of the more recent literature to compile about 320 entries.

[2.9] Names. (1979, Aug.). *Dictionary catalog of the Research Libraries: A cumulative list of authors, titles, and subjects representing materials added to the collections beginning January 1, 1972, Vol. MUT-NEW,* pp. 116-113. New York Public Library. Refs.
Has references for names.

[2.10] Nicknames. (1979, Aug.). *Dictionary catalog of the Research Libraries: A cumulative list of authors, titles, and subjects representing materials added to the collections beginning Jan. 1, 1972, Vol. NEW-NZZ,* p. 283. New York: New York Public Library. Refs.
Has references for nicknames.

[2.11] Pentland, David H. & Wolfart, H. Christoph. (1982). *Bibliography of Algonquian linguistics.* Winnipeg, MB, Canada: University of Manitoba Press, 333p.
Includes scattered refs. on personal names. Some are included in Elsdon Smith [87:6.16], the rest are included in this vol.

[2.12] Roberts, R. J. (1961). Bibliography of writings on English place- and personal names. *Onoma, 8(3),* 1958/59, 1-82. Refs.
Some general personal name entries are on p. 9. Pp. 63-71 have over 270 additional items. Many are in Smith [87:6.16] or in Lawson (1987). However, there are a number

in English not included in either previous vol. but are included here.   There are
additional non-English refs., mostly German.

[2.13] Taylor, Archer & Mosher, Fredric J. (1951). *The bibliographical history of
anonyma and pseudonyma.* Chicago:University of Chicago Press, 289p. Refs.
Extensive and detailed coverage of the entire field from classical times. Included along
with anonyms and pseudonyms are homonyms & latinized names. Hundreds of refs.
The 17th cent. is well covered. Dictionaries of anonyms and pseudonyms described.
Annotated biblio. of approx. 400 entries also extensive and indexed.

3. ADDRESS, FORMS OF AND NAMES
(See Also: 9.17.1. ETHNIC NAMES: *English: Address*; 43. STYLE AND NAMES)

[3.1] Anderson, Lynn R.; Finn, Martha; and Leider, Sandra. (1981). Leadership style
and leader title. *Psychology of Women Quarterly, 5,* 661-669. Refs. Tables. Fig.
Investigation of democratic and authoritarian leadership style with form of address (Mr.,
Ms. Miss, Mrs.) in men and women. Results show that the democratic style is preferred
but for women in the authoritarian condition the title *Ms.* carried desirable connotations.

[3.2] Aristides, Nikolai. (1977-1978). Greetings and salutations. [Life and Letters].
American Scholar, 47, pp. 16, 18-20, 22-24.
Responding to the shift in forms of address, especially the ms. designation, decries some
forms of address intimacy as used by salesmen and others.

[3.3] Atkinson, Donna L. (1987). Names and titles: Maiden name retention and the use
of Ms. *Journal of the Atlantic Provinces Linguistic Association, 9,* 56-83. Refs. Tables.
Extensive investigation of stereotypes associated with Ms. and birth name retention,
concludes there is a strong correlation between the 2. Description of stereotypes.

[3.4] Braun, Frederike. (1988). *Terms of address: Problems of patterns of usages in
various languages and cultures. Contributions to the sociology of language, 50.* Berlin:
Mouton de Gruyter, 372p. Refs.
While the focus of the book is on forms of address often directed at T (intimate form of
address) vs. V (the polite form of address), there are many references to the proper title
and form of the person's name when being addressed. Teknonyms also mentioned.
Several languages discussed including Portuguese, Georgian, Norwegian, Arabic, and
German. Extensive biblio. and refs.

[3.5] Brown, Roger & Gilman, Albert. (1960). The pronouns of power and solidarity.
In Thomas A. Sebeok (Ed.) *Style in language* (pp. 253-276); refs. pp. 435-449).
Cambridge, MA: M.I.T. Press.
Similar to Brown & Ford [87:2.2].

[3.6] Cantwell, Mary. (1983, Oct.). Call me Madam, Mrs...or Miss. First-name
dropping: Liberty, equality...or effrontery? *Vogue,* p. 178.
Discusses the emerging practice of 1st-naming new acquaintances. Resents being
1st-named by strangers.

[3.7] Chadwick, Nora K. (1961). Bretwalda, Gwledig, Vortigern. *Bulletin of the Board
of Celtic Studies, 19,* 225-230. Refs.
Evaluation concludes that these 3 terms were used as titles for English kings in the
5th-8th cents.

[3.8] Connor, Jane; Byrne, Fiona; Mindell, Jodi; Cohen, Donna; & Nixon, Elizabeth. (1986). Use of the titles Ms., Miss, or Mrs.: Does it make a difference? *Sex Roles, 14,* 545-549. Refs.
Measurement of stereotypes of hypothetical women on 16 personality scales showing the effect of using Miss, Mrs., Ms., or no title. The only significant difference was that the Ms. title was rated as less honest by both sexes.

[3.9] Croft, Bernard. (1976, Jan. 22). The naming game. *The Listener,* p. 78.
Deplores casual use of 1st names on radio and TV shows.

[3.10] Dabbs, Jack A. (1971). *Dei Gratia in royal titles.* The Hague: Mouton, 280p. Refs. Plates.
Scholarly systematic approach. Shows how rulers through the ages from the pharaohs on have used this title meaning "Grace of God" or something similar to validate their rule. This continues to this day with Elizabeth II. 1000+ rulers and titles listed in extensive appendices of Roman, Merovingian, English, Spanish, and other rulers. Extensive refs.

[3.11] Dunkling, Leslie (Alan). (1990). *A dictionary of epithets and terms of address.* London & New York: Routledge, 268p.
The intro. defines the whole world of types of address including those of: endearment, the family, polite, neutral, and insults. The book is written for: (1) native speakers of English in the US, Britain, Canada, Australia, and New Zealand so they can better understand one another's culture, and (2) for students of English from other countries. There are 2000 entries such as, Your Eminence, loon, Buttinsky, boychick, and mater, each with an explanation. Many have literary refs.

[3.12] Ervin-Tripp, Susan. (1969). Sociolinguistics. In Leonard Berkowitz (Ed.) *Advances in experimental social psychology, vol. 4,* pp. 91-165. Refs. Diagrams. New York: Academic Press.
Sets up a system for forms of address. Comparison of American system with that of other cultures.

[3.13] Ervin-Tripp, Susan. (1972). On sociolinguistic rules: Alternation and co-occurrence. In John Gumperz & Dell Hymes (Eds.) *Directions in sociolinguistics (pp. Refs. Figs.* 213-269; 555-581). New York: Holt, Rinehart & Winston.
A longer version of Ervin-Tripp (1969) above.

[3.14] Ervin-Tripp, S. M. (1972). Sociolinguistic rules of address. In J. B. Pride and J. Holmes (Eds.) *Sociolinguistics* (pp. Refs. Figs. 225-240). Hammondsworth, England: Penguin.
Also a version of Ervin-Tripp (1969) above.

[3.15] Feinsilver, Lillian Mermin. (1983). Speaking of the clergy. *American Speech, 58,* 114-125. Refs.
After referring to a number of sources, recommends that Christian clergy on formal occasions be introduced as Rev. Mr. (Ms. or Miss or Mrs.) Jones. Informal use of Reverend discussed. Use of appropriate title for rabbis also described.

[3.16] Gruita, Mariana. (1984). Address in American English: Diminutives and nicknames. *Studia Universitas Babes-Bolyai, Philologia, 29,* 47-51. Refs. Rumanian summary.
Systematic description of the American style of address drawn from the work of Brown & Ford [87:2.2] and others.

[3.17] Hamblen, Carol Howe. (1979). The married woman's name: A metaphor of oppression. *Et cetera (ETC), 36,* 248-256. Refs.
Influenced by Roger Brown's *Words and Things* [87:22.4], traces the use of the title Mrs. (as in Mrs. Donald Spencer). Points out that there have been major changes in society in recent years and that a woman who retains her birth name is preserving her identity.

[3.18] Heilman, Madeline E. (1975).   Miss, Mrs., Ms., or none of the above. *American Psychologist, 30,* 516-517.
In 2 investigations, 1 at Yale, 1 at a New York City high school, male students rated college courses with instructor listed as Miss, Mrs., Ms., Mr., or no title plus initials and surname. Results depend somewhat on the level of the course.

[3.19] Hook, Donald D. (1984).   First names and titles as solidarity and power semantics in English. *International Review of Applied Linguistics in Language Teaching, 22,* 183-189. Refs. Charts.
Power differences exist in all societies. In some, degrees of power and intimacy are shown by the use of personal pronouns. English lost this in the 18th cent. when *thee, thou,* and *ye* were dropped. Instead, titles are used. Charts show types of pattern currently used.

[3.20] Humbert, Marc. (1993, Aug. 10). Officials get to play the name game. *Buffalo News* [Sunrise Edition], p. 1.
New York State legislation allows officials in local or state government the right to insist on specific or gender neutral forms of address. A woman elected to a city council can ask to be addressed as councilwoman or councilperson; to the Assembly as Assemblywoman.

[3.21] Kendall, Martha B. (1981). Toward a semantic approach to terms of address: A critique of deterministic models in sociolinguistics. *Language & Communication, 1,* 237-254. Refs.
Evaluation of several approaches to forms of address. Also covers humor and sarcasm in connection with use of or lack of use of title and name.

[3.22] Kivi, Dolores. (1985, Apr.).   Did he say it was ok to use his first name? [Patient's Advocate] *RN,* p. 13.
Points out that while many patients like to be addressed by their 1st name, others do not.

[3.23] Konigsberg, Evelyn. (1957). The fallacy of the first name. *Today's Speech, 5,* 2.
Raises question as to whether schoolchildren should address their teachers by 1st name. A similar point of view is raised with regard to the industrial worker. Concludes that use of 1st names may send out false signals.

[3.24] Krauthammer, Charles. (1981, Sept. 16). Seamless vocatives. *New Republic,* p. 43.
Reacts negatively to mail advertising where the person addressed is referred to in the body of the letter as "for the first time, Charles Krauthammer, at an affordable rate?"

[3.25] Lakoff, Robin. (1973). Language and woman's place. *Language in Society, 2,* 45-80. Refs.
Pp. 68-73 have a discussion of forms of address.

[3.26] Leeds-Hurwitz, Wendy. (1980). *The use and analysis of uncommon forms of address: A business example.* Austin, TX: Southwest Educational Development Lab., 20p. (ERIC Document Reproduction Service No. ED 200 049).

Description of the forms of address in an industrial setting. Has the case history of a female executive. Includes use of the 1st name, nickname, title and last name.

[3.27] Lewis, Lionel S. (1963). Kinship terminology for the American parent. [Brief Communications]. *American Anthropologist, 65,* 649-652. Refs.
232 students at the University of Nevada responded on terms of address for parents under different conditions. Males tend to use the term "dad" more often; females "dad" and "daddy." Discussion of use of "mother" and "mom." Results compared with Schneider & Homans [3.34].

[3.28] Lewis, Lionel S. (1965). Terms of address for parents and some clues about social relationships in the American family. *Family Life Coordinator, 14,* 43-46. Refs.
College students were asked their form of address in 4 types of family situation. Results indicate differences by sex, situation, and parent concerned.

[3.29] Murphy, Cullen. (1991, July). Dear me: The end of a beginning. *Atlantic,* p. 32. Illus.
On how salutations in letters have changed. With gender-ambiguous 1st names, letters are addressed with 1st name and surname and no Mr., Mrs., or Ms., example, Dear Robin Leach.

[3.30] Nemy, Enid. (1987, Jan. 18). First names: Too much and too soon. [New Yorkers, etc.]. *New York Times,* Section I, p. 46.
On the pattern of calling people by their 1st names. Some negative comments.

[3.31] Pfaller, Benedict. (1966). Designating Benedictine names in documents of appointment. *Names, 14,* 184-185.
Usage depends on whether the appointee works within the order, or outside. If inside, reference is made to religious and family name. If outside, "prominence is given to the baptismal name."

[3.32] Pine, Leslie Gilbert. (1970). *The story of titles.* Rutland, VT: Charles E. Tuttle, 176p.
Scholarly discussion of titles throughout the ages in many countries.

[3.33] Robinson, Matthew. (1970, May 31). Not strictly entitled. *Sunday Times Magazine* [London], pp. 8-15. Illus.
Description of a man (in England) who changed his name from Peter Robinson to Lord Robinson. Anecdotes of some titled individuals.

[3.34] Schneider, David M., & Homans, George C. (1955). Kinship terminology and the American kinship system. *American Anthropologist, 57,* 1194-1208.
Results from informants on forms of address in the kinship system show 3 types: (1) kinship terms ("father"), (2) variants on 1st name ("Uncle Ben"), and terms of endearment ("honey"). Some others also reported.

[3.35] Sequeira, Debra-Lynn Marie. (1988). Personal address in American culture. *DissAbstrIntl, 48,* 2666A.
Based upon participant observation and interviews, analyzed 20 forms of personal address. Conclusion supports a revision of Brown & Ford [87:2.2] and Ervin-Tripp (1972) models.

[3.36] Smithers, Janice A. (1977). Institutional dimensions of senility. *Urban Life, 6,* 251-276. Refs.
Sociological description of the patterns of social control in a convalescent home. P. 259 describes staff members' use of 1st names with patients as one of the strategies that,

"reinforce the status differences between staff and patients and encourage dependent, childlike behavior in aged patients."

[3.37] Spender, Stephen. (1981, Oct. 25). "Hi Steve, meet Joe." Stephen Spender defends the use of surnames. *Observer* [London], p. 35. Photo.
Comment by a well-known English author on current 1st-naming practice carried on by individuals who are not really close friends is seen as showing hypocrisy and false familiarity.

[3.38] Super, D. E. (1985). Nicknames in professional writing: An admonition. *Journal of Counseling & Development, 63,* 631. Refs.
Protest against the use of short names (Bob, Don) or affectionate names (Annie, Davy) in professional publications.

[3.39] *Titles and forms of address: A guide to correct use,* 18th ed, London: A & C Black, 212p.
Includes justification for use of a hyphenated double name, correct use of title and other marks of honor or office (King, Queen, knights, bishops, etc.). Also gives correct pronunciation of about 1000 names including Chalmondeley (chum-li), Bois (Boyce), and Munzie (Mun-ee).

[3.40] Vanek, Anthony L., & Darnell, Regna. (1977). Direct discourse as interactional reality. *International Review of Slavic Linguistics, 2,* 189-214. Refs.
Extensive discussion of you in forms of address with emphasis on Slavic languages. Background of the Russian-speaking Doukhobors in Canada especially with reference to generational differences in the use of pronouns. Pp. 207-208 describe the use of "nicknames" [actually affectionate forms of 1st names] that are considered appropriate for a specific age level, example, Mitika (for a child), Mit'ka (between infancy and teens), Mitro (young man), Mitja (married man), and Dmitri (old man, respectful). If not used appropriately, the term is considered an insult. Diminutives are also used in different forms to show levels of intimacy.

[3.41] Yo, Mary! Hey Dave! [Editorial]. (1988, June 3). *New York Times,* P. A30.
Deplores casual 1st-naming; praises use of courtesy titles Mr., Miss, Mrs., or Ms.

4. AFFECTIONATE NAMES

[4.1] [Kjellmer, Göran. (1987). Larry. *Neophilologische Mittelungen, 88,* 218-220. Refs.
Gives 2 explanations for the name *Larry* which comes ultimately from the Latin *Laurentius:* 1, the direct ancestor is the French *Lorence* and 2, *Lorry,* the affectionate form of Lorence, underwent a Middle English vowel change to the *a* sound.

[4.2] Nicknames for ancestors. (1985). *Connecticut Nutmegger, 18,* 138.
List 61 hypocoristic or affectionate (not nickname) forms of 1st names that might be encountered in genealogical work. For example, Rye, < Zechariah, Neva < Genevieve, & Donia < Fredonia.

[4.3] Susman, M. E. Stewart. (1976). The parental /ij/. [Miscellany]. *American Speech, 51,* 283-285.
Discussion and classification of 5 categories of 1st name with the bound morpheme /ij/. Group 1 includes names like Louie; Group 2, like Mary; Group 3, like Lee; Group 4, no *ij*; Group 5, names that could take *ij* but do not normally, Bruce, Ralph. When added to Group 5 names, suggests intimacy or immaturity. Contrast between baseball players

and football players in use of Group 1 names (baseball players do, football players do not).

[4.4] Tavris, Carol. (1983, May). What's in a nickname? *Vogue,* p. 94.
Reports a study by Von O. Leirer et al. [42.1.7] which found that men tend to drop the adolescent form of their names (Eddie, Ronnie).

5. THE BIBLE AND NAMES

[5.1] Barr, James. (1969-70). The symbolism of names in the Old Testament. *Bulletin of the John Rylands Library, 52,* 11-29. Refs.
Examination of naming patterns. Points out that while the meaning and origin of many names is clear, for others it is not. Nabal, the husband of Abigail, whose name is usually interpreted as "churlish fool," is really open to more than one interpretation.

[5.2] Beegle, D. M. (1953). Proper names in the Dead Sea Scroll (DSIa). [Proceedings]. *Journal of Biblical Literature, 72,* pp. xiii-xiv.
The Scroll has added to the knowledge of Semitic linguistics, especially with regard to *waw* and *yod* in proper names.

[5.3] Cadbury, Henry J. (1962). A proper name for Dives: Lexical notes on Luke-Acts VI. *Journal of Biblical Literature, 81,* 399-402. Refs.
The Bodmer Papyrus of Luke shows the name Neues as a proper name for Dives in the rich man in the Lazarus story.

[5.4] Daniel-Rops, Henri. (1962). *Daily life in the time of Jesus.* Trans. from the French by Patrick O'Brian. New York: Hawthorn Books, 512p.
Pp. 124-127 have a description of Jewish naming practices at the time of Jesus. Points out that while many Jews had biblical names, half the people in the NT had Greek names. Greek names were especially common with important people. Examples.

[5.5] de Fraine, J. & Hartman, Louis. (1963). Personal names. In Louis F. Hartman *Encyclopedic dictionary of the Bible: A translation and adaptation of A. van den Born's Bijbels Woordenboek,* 2nd. rev. ed, 1954-1957. New York: McGraw-Hill, columns 1810-1812. Refs.
Description of forms of name (simple word vs. sentence). Sentences can be: (1) nominal, (2) participial, or (3) verbal. Meaning can be secular or religious. Examples.

[5.6] Eybers, I. H. (1971). The use of proper names as a stylistic device. *Semitics, 2,* 82-92. Refs.
Uses about 10 examples from the Prophets to show how names can be interpreted in terms of historical references or literal meaning. One example is Hosea 2:24-25 where Hosea names his son Jezreel "God sows" and is preaching against the sins of the house of Jehu. However, in Jeremiah 31:27-28, the same name carries the connotation that God would bless Israel.

[5.7] Fee, Gordon D. (1971). The use of the definite article with personal names in the gospel of John. *New Testament Studies, 17,* 168-183. Refs.
Systematic examination of the instances where the use of the definite article was used with names, and where it was not. Rules formulated.

[5.8] Fuller, J. William. (1983). "I will not erase his name from the book of life." (Revelation 3:5). *Journal of the Evangelical Theological Society, 26,* 297-306. Refs.
Discussion and analysis of the meanings of *onoma* in various passages of Revelations.

[5.9] *Geneva Bible, The: A facsimile of the 1560 edition.* (1969). Intro. by Lloyd E. Berry. Madison: University of Wisconsin Press, n. p.
After the Bible itself "The first table" lists recommended biblical names to be used as 1st names to replace "the signes and badges of idolatries." Approx. 700 names given (including alternate spellings), with meaning, and Bible citation. Examples include: Gamaliel ("God's reward"), Talmon ("dew"), and Uzzi ("my strength").

[5.10] Gibson, J. C. L. (1962). Light from Mari on the Patriarchs. *Journal of Semitic Studies, 7,* 44-62. Refs.
As part of a larger article on the origin of the patriarchs as members of a Proto-Aramean tribe, gives some attention to the meaning of the names in the light of the Mari findings (pp. 51-52).

[5.11] Grabbe, Lester L. (1988). *Etymology in early Jewish interpretation: The Hebrew names in Philo.* (No. 115, Brown University Judaic Studies). Decatur, GA: Scholars Press, 268p. Refs.
Philo Judaeus (30 BC to 45 AD) gave etymologies in his allegorical use of 166 Hebrew names. These are systematically evaluated using a number of sources. Example, No. 122 (pp. 197-198) Reuben ("look, a son") is symbolically interpreted by Philo as, "natural excellence (*euphuias*) because the man who enjoys facility of apprehension and natural excellence is endowed with sight (*horatikos*)."

[5.12] Hanson, R. P. C. (1956). Interpretations of Hebrew names in Origen. *Vigiliae Christianiae, 10,* 103-123. Refs.
Analysis of the etymologies by Origen of 112 names from the Old Testament concludes that Origen owed more to Rabbinic literature than has generally been acknowledged.

[5.13] Hastings, James. (Ed.). rev. ed. by Frederick C. Grant & H. H. Rowley. (1963). *Dictionary of the Bible.* New York: Scribner, 1059p. Refs.
Well-known authoritative source on the Bible. Has many entries relating to the names of biblical figures (although not all). See separate entries on God by James Barr [12.1] and Names (in NT times) by John Taylor [5.25].

[5.14] Heath, D. I. (1855). *The Exodus papyri.* London: Parker, 240p.
Pp. 31-32 describe a priest in Ancient Egypt named Osariph who changed his name to Moses. Further mention of Moses on pp. 163-165.

[5.15] Hunsberger, David Ritchie. (1971). Theophoric names in the Old Testament and their theological significance. *DissAbstrIntl, 30,* 2607-A. (University Microfilms No. 69-19,957) Unpublished doctoral dissertation. Temple University, Philadelphia, 407p.
Comprehensive systematic examination of major aspects of theophoric names. 100s of refs.

[5.16] Ingholt, Harald. (1953). The surname of Judas Iscariot. In *Studia orientalia Ioanni Pedersen septuagenaria, A. D. VII Id. Nov. anno MCMLIII a collegis discipulis amicis dicata* (pp. 152-162). Refs. Copenhagen: Einar Munksgaard.
After examination of available evidence, concludes that Iscariot means "of ruddy complexion."

[5.17] Lockyer, Herbert. (1967). *The women of the Bible.* Grand Rapids, MI: Zondervan, 321p. Refs.
Entries for 400+ Bible women. Entries include meaning and scriptural ref. as well as other material. Examples Hannah, I Samuel 1, < Hebrew ("gracious"); Dorcas, Acts 9:36 < Greek ("gazelle"); Salome, Mathew 14:6, feminine form of the Hebrew of Solomon ("peaceful").

[5.18] Lussier, Ernest. (1956). 'Adam in Genesis: 1,1-4,24. *Catholic Biblical Quarterly, 18,* 137-139. Refs.
Points out that 'Adam is used with 4 meanings in the 28 places in these passages. These are: (1) a man, (2) as a referent, i.e., wife of the man, (3) mankind, and (4) a proper noun, the name of the 1st man.

[5.19] McCarter, P. Kyle, Jr. (1888). The historical Abraham. *Interpretation, 42,* 341-352. Refs.
Gives sources for approx. 50 Bible names. Many are from Genesis, others from other parts of the OT. Citations are given. Included are: Nahor, Abraham's grandfather and brother < Nakhur, a city southeast of Haran; Terah, Abraham's father < Tilsha-Turakhi, a city.

[5.20] Meek, Theophile S. (1939). Moses and the Levites. *American Journal of Semitic Studies & Literature, 56,* 113-120. Refs.
Comment on 6 OT names that Meek considers of Egyptian origin: Moses, Assir, Pashhur, Hophni, Phinehas, and Merari.

[5.21] Motyer, J. A. (1962). Name. In J. D. Douglas (Ed.) *The new Bible dictionary* (pp. Refs. 861-864). Grand Rapids, MI: Eerdmans.
Names from a Bible orientation; the giving of a name; the relationship of a name to a person; and name theology (the name is the person).

[5.22] Odelain, O., & Séguineau, R. (1981). *Dictionary of proper names and places in the Bible.* Garden City, NY: Doubleday, 481p. Map. Also published in 1982 by Robert Hale in London.
2 French theologians have provided this dictionary of 3500 entries which includes all names in the Old and New Testaments. Each has appropriate citations. Some of the personal names were held by more than one individual. Each individual is described, e.g., there are 12 Obadiahs.

[5.23] Skinner, Mary Ann Long. (1994). Onomastics: Some biblical and literary examples. *Nexus* [Boston]: *11,* 25-28. Refs.
Description and discussion of 13 biblical names (with pronunciation) from colonial Massachusetts with many examples from historical records. Names included are: Abel, Abigail, Abishai, and Abner.

[5.24] Steinmueller, John E. & Sullivan, Kathryn. (1950). *Catholic biblical encyclopedia: Old Testament.* New York: Joseph F. Wagner, 1163p.
Has a number of entries for Old Testament personalities. Pp. 756-761 have entries for "Name" and "Names of God."

[5.25] Taylor, J. (1963). Personal names. In James Hastings (Ed.) *Dictionary of the Bible* (pp. 687-688), rev. ed., by Frederick C. Grant & H. H. Rowley. New York: Scribner.
Concise description of personal names in NT times. A number of examples, some with meaning, some with Bible citations. Names mentioned include: Balaam, Abijah, Judas Maccabeus, and Jason.

[5.26] Thompson, David W. (1962). *A Bible who's who.* London: Hodder & Stoughton, 64p. Illus.
Entries for 620 personalities in the Old and New Testaments. Each listing includes pronunciation, description, and biblical citations. Items also include names of groups such as Ammonites and Colossians.

[5.27] Tuland, C. G. (1958). Hanani-Hananiah. *Journal of Biblical Literature, 77,* 157-161. Identifies Hanani as a hyocoristic form of Hananiah. Hananiah was a brother of Nehemiah (Book of Nehemiah), governor of Judah. Suggests that Hananiah was a negotiator for the Jewish community of Elephantine (Egypt), 445-415 BC.

[5.28] van Huyssteen, P. J. J. (1988). Daniel 1 vers 6-7: Die naamverandering van Daniel en sy vriende [The name of Daniël and his three friends]. *NomAfr, 2,* 337-347. Refs. Afrikaans. English summary.
Comment and evaluation on these figures from the Book of Daniel: Daniel, Hananiah, Mishael, and Azariah and their Babylonian names: Belteshazzar, Shadrach, Meshach, and Abednego.

[5.29] Zadok, Ran. (1977). On five biblical names. *Zeitschrift für die Alttestamentliche Wissenschaft, 89,* 266-268. Refs.
3 of these are personal names, 'Eliqa (II Samuel), Silo (various places), and Zaeraes (Book of Esther).

5.1. THE BIBLE AND NAMES: *Bible Figures: General*

[5.1.1] Freedman, D. N. (1963). The original name of Jacob. *Israel Exploration Journal* [Israel], *13,* 125-126. Refs.
States that Jacob is really a hypocoristic [shortened] form of *ya'qub-'el* meaning "May (the god) El protect."

[5.1.2] Lockyer, Herbert. (1958). *All the men of the Bible.* Grand Rapids, MI: Zondervan. 381p. Refs.
Main section contains 3000+ entries for biblical figures, 350 of these are extended. Entries give pronunciation, meaning, biblical refs. and historical summary. Includes both Old and New Testaments.
[5.1.3] Steinmueller, John E. & Sullivan, Kathryn. (1956). *Catholic biblical encyclopedia: New Testament.* New York: Joseph F. Wagner, 702p.
Entries for New Testament Bible personalities. Includes items for Jesus, God, Jehovah, Jahweh, and Mary.

5.2. THE BIBLE AND NAMES: *Bible Figures: Moses*

[5.2.1] Griffiths, J. Gwyn. (1953). The Egyptian derivation of the name Moses. *Journal of Near Eastern Studies, 12,* 225-231. Refs.
After examination of a number of sources, concludes that the name *Moses* came from Egyptian through Greek into Hebrew.

[5.2.2] Josephus, Flavius. (1958). *Jewish antiquities,* Vol. 4, trans. by H. St. J. Thackeray, 649p. London: William Heinemann; Cambridge, MA: Harvard University Press, 649p.
P. 268, similar to the Bible (Ex. 2:10), explains the derivation of Moses' name as being the one who was saved from the water.

[5.2.3] Oesterly, W. O. E., & Robinson, Theodore H. (1932). *A history of Israel,* Vol. 1. *From the Exodus to the fall of Jerusalem, 586 B. C.* (Vol. 1 by Robinson). Oxford: Clarendon Press, 296p.
P. 81 has reference to Moses' name being of Egyptian origin; that Moses means "son of" and was a suffix. One speculation is that it was originally Ahmose.

[5.2.4] Reisner, George Andrew; Fisher, Clarence Stanley; & Lyon, David. (1924). *Harvard excavations in Samaria, 1908-1910*, Vol. 1, Text. Cambridge: Harvard University Press, 416p. Plates.
Results of an expedition begun in 1908 to Sebastia, near Nablus. Studied coins, lamps, amphora handles, stone objects, metal objects; extensive inscribed materials. Included are 67 Israelite inscriptions (pp. 229-246). Other inscriptions are: Greek, Latin, cuneiform, hieroglyphic, and Aramaic. Israelite inscription No. 24 (pp. 234-235) is cited by William F. Albright [*American Journal of Semitic Languages and literatures, 41*, 83f. (1925)] and J. Gwyn Griffiths [5.2.1] as relating to the root of Moses' name.

[5.2.5] Towers, John Robert.(1935). The name Moses. *Journal of Theological Studies, 36*, 407-412. Refs.
Suggests that the name Moses (Moshe) is, "the Hebrew form of the Egyptian *mi* or *ma* Shu and means 'like the sun.'"

5.3. THE BIBLE AND NAMES: *Bible Figures: Jesus*

[5.3.1] Chaplais, Pierre. (1987). The spelling of Christ's name in medieval Anglo-Latin: 'Christus' or 'Cristus'? *Journal of the Society of Archivists, 8*, 261-280.
Extensive, detailed examination with comments of a number of medieval mss. with the 2 different spellings. Evaluation of the influence of Greek on the spelling along with the tendency not to spell out sacred names in full.

[5.3.2] Gariepy, Henry. (1974). *Portraits of Christ: Devotional studies of the names of Jesus.* Old Tappan, NJ: Fleming H. Revell, 128p.
Discussion and comment on 52 names & titles of Jesus. Included are: Seed of the Woman, Emmanuel, The Light of the World, and The Nazarene.

[5.3.3] Hahn, Ferdinand. (1969). *The titles of Jesus in Christology: Their history in early Christianity.* Trans. from the German by Harold Knight and George Ogg. New York: World Publishing Co., 415p. Refs.
Has 5 major chaps. devoted to each of the 5 titles: Son of Man, Kyrios, Christos, Son of David, and Son of God.

[5.3.4] Irvin, Maurice R. (1975). *Eternally named.* Harrisburg, PA: Christian Publications, 117p.
Each of the chs. focuses on one of the names of Jesus. These include: Son of God, the Nazarene, King of Kings, and Lord of Lords.

[5.3.5] Rolls, Charles J(ubilee). (1953; 1984). *The indescribable Christ, A-G,* rev. ed. Neptune, NJ: Loizeaux Brothers, 215p. (First published by Zondervan in 1953).
Presentation of 12 names for Jesus for each letter A-G. These include: The Author of Salvation, The Beloved Son, The Creator, The Deliverer of Zion, The Eternal God, The Firstborn, and The Glory of God. This book and the 4 following develop names for Jesus for each letter of the alphabet. The letter I has 21 names, X has none, Y has 1, and Z has 1. All the others have 12. Examples include: the Author of Salvation, the Beloved Son, the Creator, etc. Bible citations are given.

[5.3.6] Rolls, Charles J(ubilee). (1956). *The world's greatest name: The names and titles of Jesus Christ,* (H-K). Grand Rapids, MI: Zondervan, 185p.
Continues the series with several names for each letter. Among these: for H, The Highest, Himself; for I, The I Am, Immutability; and for J, The Jasper Stone.

[5.3.7] Rolls, Charles J(ubilee). (1958). *Time's noblest name: The names and titles of Jesus Christ: L through O.* Grand Rapids, MI: Zondervan, 217p.

Gives 12 names for each letter covered. Among these are: Lord of the Harvest, Lord of Lords, Lion of Judah, Messenger of the Covenant, and Offerer.

[5.3.8] Rolls, Charles J(ubilee). (1965; 1985). *The name above every name: The names and titles of Jesus Christ (P-S).* Neptune, NJ: Loizeaux Brothers, 255p.
Continues the series with 12 names for each letter. Examples include: for P, The Priest; for Q, The Questioner; and for R, The Redeemer.

[5.3.9] Rolls, Charles J(ubilee). (1975; 1985). *His glorious Name: The names and titles of Jesus Christ (T-Z),* 2nd ed. Neptune, NJ: Loizeaux Brothers, 267p.
Presentation of 12 names for Jesus for each letter T-W. These include: The Teacher, The Urim, The Victor, The Witness, The Yokefellow, and Zaphnath-Paaneah.

[5.3.10] Sabourin, Leopold. (1967). *The names and titles of Jesus: Themes of biblical theology.* Trans. from the French by Maurice Carroll. New York: Macmillan, 334p. Refs.
Examination of 50 names and titles of Jesus which were grouped into 5 categories. Some names have lasted, others have not. Examples include: the Master, the Good Shepherd, the Bridegroom, and the Amen. The Appendix has an additional listing which is a translation by Father Diekamp of a 7th cent. Greek work by an anonymous author. Examples from this list include: the Chosen Arrow, Bread of Life, Stag. Most have sources in either the OT or the NT.

[5.3.11] Taylor, Vincent. (1953). *The names of Jesus.* New York: St. Martin's Press, 179p. Refs.
Description of 80 names of Jesus in the New Testament. Includes: the King, He That Cometh, the Vine, the Way, and the Alpha & the Omega.

6. CATALOGING AND NAMES
(See Also: 16. INDEXING AND NAMES)

[6.1] *Names of persons: National usages for entry in catalogues,* (1977). 3rd ed., Compiled and edited by Tom C. Clarke with Rosamond Kerr (names are not shown on title page). Compiled by the International Federation of Library Associations for UBC. London: International Federation of Library Associations International Office for UBC, 193p.
Contains description of the naming systems and name elements for the world's cultures that are in print; also the proper order of the elements for cataloging. Patterns are as varied as those of the Canadian Inuit who only used the surname before the 1960s to those of Brazilians who have as many as 15 types of name elements in catalog entries.

[6.2] Names of persons: Notes on African names. (1972). *International Cataloging, 1,* 4-5. Refs.
Recommendations for the cataloging of African names from conferences at Lusaka in 1969, Addis Ababa in 1971, Mauritius (no date), and Uganda (no date).

[6.3] Rait, S. K. (1984). *A dictionary of Punjabi name elements.* Leeds: School of Librarianship, Leeds Polytechnic, 461p. Refs.
Includes about 4600 items, phonetic transcription, and glossary for understanding names of this region. Information helpful to catalogers on titles, surnames, clan, and given names.

[6.4] Ranganathan, S(hiyali). R(amamrita). (1988). Assisted by A(rashanpalai) Neelameghan. *Classified catalogue code: With additional rules for Dictionary Catalog Code,* 5th ed. Bangalore: Sarada Ranganathan Endowment for Library Science, 644p.

General on library cataloging. Names are covered on pp. 110-113; 205-245. Special emphasis on East Indian names.

[6.5] Sharify, Nasser. (1959). *Cataloging of Persian works*. Chicago: American Library Association, 161p.
Chs. 5-6 (pp. 65-95) deal with types of name and entry procedure. There is a systematic description of 25 types of name category. Examples.

7. CHANGE OF NAME
(See Also: 20.1. LAW AND NAMES: *Name Change,* 46.2. WOMEN AND NAMES: *Law and Legal Aspects)*

[7.1] Brown, Rusty. (1983, Apr. 7). What's in a name? A lot (column). *Evening Observer* [Dunkirk-Fredonia, NY], p. 6.
Problems of women involving change of name at marriage and divorce, retention of birth names.

[7.2] Bumppo, Natty. (1975, June). Why I'd rather be *Natty. Esquire,* pp. 110ff.
Humorous account of a change of name. The author's original name was James Dean but after Watergate and being associated by the public with James W. Dean, III, he decided to change it to Natty Bumppo, a character in James Fenimore Cooper's *Leatherstocking Tales.*

[7.3] DelaBarre, D. M. (1961). Names--change--rights of petitioner and sufficiency of reason. *North Dakota Law Review, 37,* 119-120. Refs.
Comment and discussion on a Massachusetts case in which the petitioner's wife did not like his Italian surname. One court upheld denial of the name change because the reasoning was "un-American." However, the Supreme Court of Massachusetts upheld the right of the petitioner to change his name. Further discussion on fraud as being the main reason to deny a name change.

[7.4] Dralle, Penelope Wasson & Mackiewicz, Kathelynne. (1981). Psychological impact of women's name change at marriage: Literature review and implications for further study. *American Journal of Family Therapy, 9,* 50-55. Refs.
Literature review and discussion of problems with regard to social and legal aspects of name alternatives in marital relationships.

[7.5] Duckert, Audrey. (1964). Notes and queries. *Names, 12,* 130-133.
Contains information purportedly from Philip L. Forstall listing 4 categories of singers who changed their name. Examples include: Frances Saville, Rosa Ponselle, and Jenny Tourel.

[7.6] Ellwand, Geoff. (1986, Mar. 24). Name dropping: It isn't easy being a Tit. *Alberta Report,* p. 25.
A Polish refugee family changed their surname from Tit to Tilstone. Possible legal problems.

[7.7] Fayer, Joan M. (1988). First names in Puerto Rico: A change in progress. *Names, 36,* 21-27. Refs. Table.
Students at the University of Puerto Rico completed questionnaires on 1st names over 4 generations. For both sexes 96% of the 1st generation has Spanish 1st names; 3%, English; 1%, Other. The 4th generation showed shifts away from Spanish and also sex differences. Explanations offered.

[7.8] Glenn, Menahem G. (1961). Name, please? *Recall* [Los Angeles], *2* (Winter), 15-19.
Popular article describing trends in adoption of new names (1st names and surnames) by Jewish immigrants to the US, apparently before 1920.

[7.9] Horsley, G. H. R. (1987). Name change as an indication of religious conversion in antiquity. *Numen, 34,* 1-17. Refs.
While many of the changes in the ancient world were due to religious conversion, many were not. Other reasons were: recruits going into the Roman army, adoption into a Roman family, and, in one case, a dream. Name changes were made by Egyptians, Jews, and Christians.

[7.10] How to change your name. (1957, June). *Good Housekeeping, 144,* p. 53.
Brief description of how to change a name legally. Suggests that the person 1st use the name for awhile.

[7.11] Irving, Ronald. (1973, Dec. 3). The names that people call themselves. *Times* [London], p. 16.
Brief review of British legal practices with regard to name change by: (1) British common law, (2) deed poll, and (3) High Court. Also points out that Hawaii is the only jurisdiction that requires a married woman to assume her husband's name at marriage.

[7.12] Kaplan, Justin. (1987, May 7). Tune that name: An honorable American tradition. *New Republic, 190,* pp. 10-11.
Response to criticism of presidential candidate Gary Hart's change of surname from Hartpence points out that many prominent individuals have also changed their names. These include: Sigmund Freud (from Sigismund), Walt Whitman (Walter Whitman, Jr.), Gerald Ford (Leslie Lynch King, Jr.), and Ulysses S. Grant (Hiram Ulysses Grant).

[7.13] Kirk, Matthew. (1979, June 1). Heil, Schickelgruber? [Personal View]. *Daily Telegraph* [London], p. 16.
Speculates whether some prominent people would have been so prominent with other names, as Hitler with Schickelgruber, or if William Shakespeare were named Thomas Bastard. Notes prominent people who have changed their names.

[7.14] Marshall, Arthur. (1977, Mar. 5). Smelling as sweet. [First Person]. *New Statesman* [London], p. 397.
Comments on name change and mention of entertainers who changed their names, examples, Joanne Dru (Joanne la Cock), Clifton Webb (Parmalee Hollenbeck).

[7.15] Massotty, Karen A. (1974, Sept.). Name change game; with transcript of court proceedings. *Mademoiselle, 36,* 39.
A Colorado woman who wished to legally retain her birth name at marriage ran into unpleasantness in the court proceeding that eventually resulted in her getting that right.

[7.16] McLaughlin, M. (1974, May). My maiden name...Till death do us part. *McCall's,* p. 49.
Describes the procedure for women wishing to keep their birth name at marriage. Story of a prime minister of Japan who legally adopted his daughter's husband so she could keep her birth name.

[7.17] Morgan, Ted. (1978). *On becoming American.* Boston: Houghton Mifflin, 336p. (pp. 75-96).
Contends that name-changing is an old American custom, examples, Rockefeller < Rogenfelder, Hoover < Huber, Mondale < Mundal. Mention of prominent people who

have changed their names.   Stories include artist, Arshile Gorky, and Whittaker Chambers.

[7.18] Mr. Coke-Is-It--He's the real thing. (1985, Mar. 25). *Newsweek*, p. 74. Photo. Frederic Karel Koch of Guilford, Vt. has petitioned for a legal name change to Coke-Is-It.

[7.19] Nurnberg, M. (1966). Cohen-Kagan. [Letter]. *Names, 14,* 192.
Robert Rennick [87:20.9] quoted a judge who refused a change-of-name on the grounds that Kagan was a different name than Cohen. Far from being a variation of the Irish name of Keegan, it is a well-documented Russian form of Cohen. There is no 'h' sound in Russian and the 'g' is usually substituted.

[7.20] Rennick, R. M. (1969). Editor's correspondence. *Names, 17,* 315-316.
Reactions of Rennick to comments on his article on name change [87:20.9].

[7.21] Scadding, Henry. (1868?). *On metonmyms, or translated and quasi-translated personal names.* Toronto: no publisher listed, 24p.
Metonyms here refer to those names taken by scholars and others and which appear to be Latin or Greek forms of the original name from about the 15th cent. on. Thus, Conrad Rauchfuss ("hairy-foot") became Conradus Dasypodius; Krushner became Pellicanus. The language groups doing this include: German, French, Italian, Spanish, Portuguese, Greek, Hebrew, Slavonic, and Chinese. Hundreds of examples [May be of interest to those involved with medieval mss. and research].

[7.22] Scherr, Arthur. (1986). Change-of-name petitions of the New York courts: An untapped source in historical onomastics. *Names, 34,* 284-302. Refs.
Description of a nonprofit organization in New York City which has collected civil court records of the city from 1674-1910. These records have information on name-change petitions which are an opportunity for onomastic research on the evolution of the city. Examples.

[7.23] So the name has been changed. (1986, Apr.). *Ebony, 41,* pp. 46, 50. Photos. Background information on 14 people who changed their names. Includes Mr. T, Nat King Cole, Muhammad Ali, Flip Wilson, and Della Reese.

[7.24] Spitzer, Neil. (1988, Aug.). What's in a name. [Notes]. *Atlantic,* pp. 14, 16. Illus.
Spitzer apparently perused *Personal names and naming* and concluded that name changing is not really abnormal but does have advantages.

[7.25] Tooker, Dorothy Thomasina. (1953, Jan. 17). Taking of Thomasina. *Ave Maria* [Notre Dame, IN], pp. 79-82.
An adult new convert to Catholicism explains her choice of Thomasina as her confirmation name.

[7.26] Trujillo, Nick. (1984, July). Comment: On male maiden names. *Working Woman, 9,* p. 42.
Experiences of a man who changed his name to a joint one on marriage (O'Donnell-Trujillo) and then, after divorce, went back to his original name.

[7.27] Van Doren, Barbara. (1953, Oct.-Nov.). A new name for the child? *Life Today,* 47-49.
Popular article on the changing of a child's surname when the mother remarries.

[7.28] What's in a name? (1960, Feb. 13). *Economist* [London], *194*, 602-603.
Support for the Queen's proposal to change the family name to Mountbatten-Windsor.

7.1. CHANGE OF NAME: *Entertainers*

[7.1.1] Barnes, Clive. (1989, May). The naming of names. [Names]. *Dance Magazine*, p. 4.
At the beginning of this century, ballet dancers with Anglo-Saxon surnames russified their surnames, thus Hilda Munnings > Lydia Sokolova; [Lillian] Alice Marks > Alicia Markova. Now it is the custom to keep non-Russian names.

[7.1.2] Carlinsky, D. (1973, Apr./May). What's in a name? *Modern Maturity*, p. 30.
Popular presentation of prominent personalities who have changed their name. Quiz.

[7.1.3] Egos melting the pot. (1962, Mar. 23). [Show Business]. *Time*, p. 73.
Popular presentation on approx. 75 entertainers who changed their names. Before and after names are shown.

[7.1.4] Walsh, Jim. (1970, June). Real names of Edison cylinder performers. *Hobbies* [Chicago], *75*, 37-39.
Edison cylinders were early versions of the phonograph. 25+ names of performers from the 1889-1912 period are listed. Many show alterations rather than real changes. Most of the names would be unfamiliar today. Examples include: Thomas Chalmers > Thomas Hardie Chalmers, Bessie Abbott > Bessie Pickens.

[7.1.5] Whatever happened to Aaron Chwatt? (1964, Sept.). *Esquire*, pp. 128-129.
Cartoons of 72 individuals (without faces), presented on one page with the person's original name, on the 2nd with the current name. Examples include: Aaron Chwatt = Red Buttons, Margie Yvonne Reed = Martha Raye.

8. COMPUTERS AND NAMES

[8.1] Boot, M., Lourens, P., & Lucassen, J. (1983). A linguistic preprocessor for record linkage in socio-economic historical research. *Computers & the Humanities, 17*, 45-64. Refs. Tables. Figs.
Description of a linguistically-based computer program (KLANKBAS) for the study of historical records of German migrant workers who went to Holland in the 19th cent. The program deals with German names and the difficulties of reading German handwriting.

[8.2] Borkowski, Casimir. (1977). Automatic identification of personal titles and personal names in computer-readable natural language texts. *Onoma, 21*, 144-156. Refs. Figs.
Description of a system for computer identification of names and titles in newspaper texts such as the New York Times for preparation of an automatic index.

[8.3] Davidson, Leon. (1962). Retrieval of misspelled names in an airlines passenger record system. *Communications of the Association for Computing Machinery, 5*, 169-171. Refs.
Description of the rationale for a computer search system for locating misspelled surnames. Also uses 2ndary search procedures such as telephone numbers.

[8.4] Everett, David & Pilachowski, David H. (1986, Oct.). What's in a name? Looking for people online--humanities. *Database, 9(5)*, 26-34. Figs.

Description of databases of books and articles in the humanities with some studies of their efficiency. *MLA International Bibliography* included.

[8.5] Why, O why, doesn't that name compute? (1991, Aug. 28). *New York Times,* national ed., A13.
Difficulties of a South Korean in the US whose surname is O. How he resolved problems with computers and credit cards.

[8.6] Wrigley, E. A., & Schofield, R. S. (1973). Nominal record linkage by computer and the logic of family reconstitution. In E. A. Wrigley (Ed.), *Identifying people in the past* (pp. 64-101; 151-154). Refs.
Reports on a computer program that uses 1st names and surnames to identify records of individuals.

8.1. COMPUTERS AND NAMES: *Soundex*

[8.1.1] Bouchard, Gérard & Pouyez, Christian. (1980). Name variations and computerized record linkage. *Historical Methods, 13,* 119-125. Refs.
Extensive detailed description of computer programs used to study surnames in a large investigation of the Saguenay region of Quebec from 1842-1951. The acronym for this program with French names is FONEM.

[8.1.2] Clarke, David. (1984, Feb.). Sounds familiar. *Practical Computing, 7(2),* 90-92.
Description and listing for a Soundex program to search & index surnames.

[8.1.3] Gillen, John. (1984, Aug.). The "Soundex" routine. *Data Based Advisor,* pp. 46-47.
A computer program for converting names to the Soundex system.

[8.1.4] Guth, Gloria J. A. (1976). Surname spellings and computerized record linkage. *Historical Methods Newsletter, 10,* 10-19. Refs. Figs.
Description of computer programs with advantages over Soundex. These new programs are designed to match historical records of individuals even though the name for the same individual has been spelled differently on a different record.

[8.1.5] Hershberg, Theodore; Burstein, Alan; & Dockhorn, Robert. (1976). Record linkage. *Historical Methods Newsletter, 9,* 137-163. Refs. Tables. Figs.
Extensive, detailed description of the Philadelphia Social History Project which uses record linkage of individuals by surname, 1st name and other available information in order to study patterns of residential, occupational, and economic mobility. Development of a new soundex/viewex coding system. Description of how adjustments are made to the processing procedure.

[8.1.6] Madron, Thomas W. (1985, Apr.). Searching with soundex. *PC Tech Journal, 3(4),* 163-164. Refs.
Presents a computer program in BASIC which the author feels is an improvement over the original Russell method.

[8.1.7] Munnecke, Tom. (1980, May). Giving your computer an ear for names. *Byte,* pp. 196, 198, 200. Refs. Tables. Fig.
Description of the Soundex system which can be used to store and retrieve names.

[8.1.8] Roughton, Karen G., & Tyckoson, David A. (1985, June). Browsing with sound. *Information Technology & Libraries, 4(2),* 130-136. Refs.

Oriented toward librarians who want to locate authors regardless of the spelling of the name. Comparison of Soundex with the Davidson Consonant Index [8.3]. Suggestions for librarians include a catalog based on sound.

[8.1.9] Stephenson, Charles. (1974). Tracing those who left: Mobility studies and the Soundex Indexes to the US Census. *Journal of Urban History, 1,* 73-84. Refs.
Description of success in tracing the mobility of people using the Soundex system on families from Albany County, New York in the years 1875 and 1905. Belief that the system can succeed in tracing people anywhere in the US.

[8.1.10] Winchester, Ian. (1970). The linkage of historical records by man and computer: Techniques and problems. *Journal of Interdisciplinary History, 1,* 107-124. Refs.
Record linkage refers to bringing information from different sources for a given individual. Evaluation of the Soundex system in matching historical records in 3 investigations, 2 from other reseachers. Explains development of a computer system for adding scoring weights to improve accuracy.

9. ETHNIC, NATIONAL, AND CULTURAL NAMES

9.1. *African: General*

[9.1.1] Asante, Molefi Kete. (1991). *The book of African names.* Trenton, NJ: Africa World Press, 64p. Illus.
Popular presentation. The book has a Pan-African orientation and does not give language or tribal classifications. Thus, the names are presented for five African regions: Southern, Central, Eastern, Western, and Northern. The entries (roughly 1200) give each name and its English meaning, example, Kwaku is a male name from the Western Region and means "Born on Wednesday"; Fatimah is a female name from the Northern Region and means "Daughter of the prophet."

[9.1.2] Che-Mponda, Aleck H. (1973). *Soul by name: Book of African names.* Gary, IN: NIMM Educational Media Service, 16, 24p. Illus.
After a historical background and description of Pan-Africanism, lists approx. 300 names showing that orientation. Listings include: Chema ("the good one") and Chicha ("one who loves children") for females and Mboto ("good-looking one") and Mponda ("creator") for males.

[9.1.3] Kiteme, Kamuti. (1972). What is our name in Africa? *Negro History Bulletin, 35,* 80-83.
The 1st section describes how African culture is perceived through European eyes. The 2nd section deals with African names, especially under the influence of Western culture on naming. Praises American blacks for adoption of African names and calls for the adoption of African names in Africa.

[9.1.4] Pedersen, Birte Hjorth. (1986). Havad skal barnet hedde? --i Afrika [What is the baby to be called? --in Africa]. In Vibeke Dalberg & Gillian Fellows-Jensen (Eds.) *Mange baekke små* (pp. 195-213). Copenhagen: Reitzels. Danish. English summary. Refs. Map.
Examination of naming in Nigeria, Zimbabwe, Lesotho, Kenya, and Ethiopia. Topics are: naming practices, naming motives, and the structure of names including phrase names.

[9.1.5] Stewart, Julia. (1993). *African names: Names from the African continent for children and adults:* New York: Citadel, 171p. Refs. Maps. Illus.

Background on African languages. Suggestions on how to change a Western name to an African (Barbara, "strange, foreign" to Baraka, "blessing"). Main section has 1500 entries. Entries show pronunciation of each name, meaning, and, in some cases, historical information.

9.1.1. ETHNIC NAMES: *African: Miscellaneous Groups*

[9.1.1.1] Berry, J. (1960). Some preliminary notes on Ada personal nomenclature. *African Language Studies* [London], *1*, 177-184. Refs. Tables.
The Adali are a tribe in present Ghana. Description of their naming system with examples. There are Tiwi and Ewe elements in their names. Types of names include: theophoric, toponymic, patronymic, birth-names, nicknames, clan-names, pet-names, and phrase names.

[9.1.1.2] Boahen, A. Adu. (1964). *Britain, the Sahara, and the Western Sudan 1788-1861,* Oxford Studies in African Affairs. Oxford: Clarendon Press, 268p.
Appendix I, p. 235, lists 7 explorers of this period with their Western surnames and the Arabic names they assumed, examples, (James) Richardson was known as Ya'qub; Gordon Laing as Al-Ra'is.

[9.1.1.3] Chaplin, J. H. (1959). A note on some Central African forenames. *Africa, 29,* 384-390. Refs. Tables.
Names from about 1000 men in Lusaka, Zambia were obtained in 2 samples, 1 urban, 1 at a high school. Responses were classified by tribe, religion, year of birth, and educational level and as Biblical, vernacular, European, noun, and invented. Largest category was Biblical. Just a few examples.

[9.1.1.4] Cornevin, R. (1954). Names among the Bassari. *Southwestern Journal of Anthropology, 10,* 160-163. Table.
The Bassari live in northern Togo, West Africa. The table shows how children are named in each of 13 clans. Some clans have 5 names for boys; 5 for girls. Others fewer. Comment on twin names.

[9.1.1.5] Evans-Pritchard, E. E. (1948). Nuer forms of address. *Uganda Journal, 12,* 166-171. Refs.
The Nuer live in Sudan. Description of naming customs and patterns including these types of name: (1) personal or birth, (2) twin, (3) honorific or praise, (4) ox, and (5) patronyms and teknonyms. Appropriate forms of address also described.

[9.1.1.6] Finnegan, Ruth H. (1970). *Oral literature in Africa.* London: Clarendon Press, 558p. Refs.
Has a section on names pp. 470-480. General on type and function of African names. Includes discussion of proverb and praise names. Material drawn from several investigators. Examples.

[9.1.1.7] Fortes, M. Meyer. (1955). Names among the Tallensi of the Gold Coast. *Deutsche Akademic der Wissenschaften zu Berlin. Institut für Orientforschung, Nr. 26. Afrikanische Studien,* pp. 337-349. Refs.
The Tallensi, a preliterate people, live in the Northern Territories of the Gold Coast, West Africa. Description with examples of their naming practices which are closely related to their religion. People have 2 major names, (1) a public everyday name, and (2) a private name, *segher,* which is known only to the family.

[9.1.1.8] Gulliver, P. H. (1952). Bell-oxen and ox-names among the Jie. *Uganda Journal, 16,* 72-75.

The Jie (pop. 18,200 in 1948) live in the Karamoja district of Uganda. Oxen are important in this culture and a man takes his name from that of one of his favorite oxen. A man may change names over the years. Approx. 20 names are listed. Among them: Apa-longor ("greyish-brown hide"), Apa-loputh ("grey hide"). Women also have ox-names.

[9.1.1.9] Herskovits, Melville Jean. (1938). *Dahomey: An ancient West African kingdom,* Vol. 1. New York: Augustin, 402p. Refs. (Complete ref. citations are in Vol. 2, pp. 373-376).
Dahomey is a West African country bordering Nigeria in the East, Togo on the west. Pp. 149-150 gives the forms of address for spouses. Teknonymy is followed. Pp. 263-268 give further information on child-naming.

[9.1.1.9A] Huntingford, G. W. B. (1951). The social institutions of the Dorobo. *Anthropos, 46,* 1-48.
The Dorobo are [were?] a hunting people of the high forest lands of Kenya. Pp. 47-48 have some information on names. A Dorobo male has 4 names: (1), a spirit name, (2), a porridge-name (given when the child is 1st fed), (3), a nickname (Parngetuny, "lion-killer"), and (4), a patronym.

[9.1.1.10] Innes, Gordon. (1966). A note on Mende and Kono personal names. *Sierra Leone Language Review, No. 5* [journal refers to number], 34-38.
Among the Mende, there are 2 types of personal name. One type is that of Arabic or English usage, the 2nd type refers to the birth circumstance(s) or personal appearance. Many examples. Among the Kono, name is determined by sex and birth order. Examples.

[9.1.1.11] Jeffreys, M. D. W. (1963). Mumbo Jumbo, or Mambo, the heart eater. *NADA (Native Affairs Department Annual)* [Salisbury, Rhodesia], *40, 74-83.* Refs.
Traces the title "The Heart Eater" used by East African chiefs as recently as the 19th cent. to the ritual murders of the pharoahs of Ancient Egypt which was linked with the heart of a sacrificial bull. Reports indicate that in recent Africa the new king would eat the heart (or powders made from it) of his predecessor.

[9.1.1.12] Kimenyi, Alexandre. (1978). Aspects of naming in Kinyarwanda. *Anthropological Linguistics, 20,* 258-271.
"Kinyarwanda is a Lake Bantu language spoken in Rwanda." Discussion of how personal names are formed and naming practices. There are no family names. Several examples given including: Kimenyi ("the 1 who has knowledge"), Muhandwa ("the 1 who receives"), and Maguru ("legs").

[9.1.1.13] Kruger, F. (1937). Tlôkwa traditions. *Bantu Studies, 11,* 85-115. Refs.
This tribe is from Transvaal province of the Republic of South Africa. Description of their tales and traditions. Pp. 107-110 explain 10 names of women [no similar section on men].

[9.1.1.14] Lewis, I. M. (1961). Force and fission in Northern Somali lineage structure. *American Anthropologist, 63,* 94-112. Refs.
Mostly devoted to family lineage. However, p. 98 does have a description of the naming pattern where a son or daughter "is given a first name and takes as surname the first name of the father. So that each generation bears a new name."

[9.1.1.15] Marapara, Malakia. (1954). Wazezuru names and their meanings. *NADA (Native Affairs Department Annual)* [Rhodesia], *31,* 7-9. Refs.

Lists 21 boys' names and 7 girls' names. Included are: Marapara ("Sable antelope: His father is a hunter of wild beasts") and Njodozi ("Disaster: The mother experienced great troubles during her confinement").

[9.1.1.16] Markwei, M. (1966). Naming a child among the Sherbro. *Sierra Leone Bulletin of Religion, 8,* 1-6. Refs.
Describes special greetings and other ceremonies for the naming of a child (usually on the 8th day). Listing of standard birth names for boys and girls by ordinal position.

[9.1.1.17] Munday, J. T. (1948). Spirit names among the Central Bantu. *African Studies, 7,* 39-44.
The Central Bantu at the time of this study lived in Northern Rhodesia (now Zimbabwe) and that part of the Belgian Congo (now Zaire) which it surrounded. Africans of this area have 2 names: (1) a spirit name and (2) a name of manhood or womanhood. Extensive description of these types of name and naming patterns. Spirit names are given for a dead person and do not change; 2nd names do change.

[9.1.1.18] Munday, J. T. (1956). Bantu name difficulties. *Northern Rhodesia Journal, 3,* 8-13. Refs.
Explanation of the cultural and religious background for Bantu naming customs in which individuals may have several names. These include spirit names, father's given name as a surname, post-infancy names, and Christian names.

[9.1.1.19] Nemer, Julie F. (1987). Phonological stereotypes and names in Temne. *Language in Society, 16,* 341-352.
Temne is a Mel language spoken in the Sierra Leone republic on the west coast of Africa. Examination and classification of sounds from other languages that appear in Temne personal names. Discussion of phonological stereotyping. Examples.

[9.1.1.20] Nsimbi, M. (1949). African surnames. *Makere* [Kampala], *3,* 17-20.
Naming among the Baganda of Uganda. Brief description of 8 types of names: proverbial and nicknames, titles, automatic (for twins, 1st-born), romantic, locative, derived from gods and goddesses, royal clan, and clan. Examples.

[9.1.1.21] Nurse, G. T. (1976). Isonymic studies on the Griqua of the North Cape province of South Africa. *Journal of Biosocial Science, 8,* 277-286. Refs. Table. Map.
The Griqua are a mixed ancestry people. Their surnames were studied to supplement a sero-genetic study. Analysis of their surname structure shows British, Northwest European, Khoisan, Sotho/Tswana, other Negro origins, slave origins, and even Ashkenazi Jewish origins which help to understand their ethnic mixture.

[9.1.1.22] Raum, O. F. (1940). *Chaga childhood: A description of indigenous education in an East African tribe.* London: Oxford University Press, 422p. Refs.
The Chaga (also Chagga) are a Bantu-speaking tribe who live on the southern slopes of Mt. Kilimanjaro in Tanzania. Raum has several comments on naming customs, terms of address, rituals, and honorary names. Index shows the pages.

[9.1.1.23] Rici, Julien. (1967). Blessing. Jeffrey C. Haight & Annie S. Mahler (Trans.). In Mircea Eliade (Ed.), *The encyclopedia of religion, vol. 2,* pp. 247-253. Refs.
Among the Rundi people of Burundi in east central Africa, the child at birth is placed under the blessing of Imana, the supreme god. The father names the child at the 8th day. There are many theophoric names, examples, Haremimana ("God creates"). Four other examples.

[9.1.1.24] Ruud, Jørgen. (1961). *Taboo: A study of Malagasy customs and beliefs.*
Oslo: Oslo University Press; New York: Humanities Press, 325p.
This report is from Malagasy, formerly Madagascar. Among the taboos, a guest must
never ask the name of a person in the house (p. 12); a child must not ask the name of
its father (p. 15). Ch. 10 (pp. 171-180) deals with posthumous names. A person has
a new name after death. Many examples.

[9.1.1.25] Sakah, B. T. (1963). Nso magico-religious practices. *Abbia, 2,* 67-70.
The report is based upon customs of the Nso tribe of Cameroon, a country located
between West and Central Africa, bordering Nigeria. Description of magico-religious
naming of children. Children who are twins, born with the umbilical cord around their
necks, or are sickly have special rites.

[9.1.1.26] Schonenberger, Paul. (1961). Names for "God" known and used by the
Wanyamwezi. *Anthropos, 56,* 947-949. Refs.
The Wanyanwezi are an African tribe of about 500,000 who live around and near Tabora
in Tanzania. After evaluation of possible origins concludes that the meaning is not clear.
Other words for God also discussed include: Limi ("the Sun"), Likubala ("the Great
Counter"), and Matunda ("the Creator").

[9.1.1.27] Stayt, Hugh A. (1931). *The BaVenda.* Oxford: University Press, 392p.
The BaVenda (at the time of the study) lived in the Zoutpansberg district of the Northern
Transvaal of South Africa bordering on what is now Zimbabwe. Pp. 88-89 have a
description of naming customs.   Seven names are listed including: Takalani
("happiness"), Mutshinya ("mistake"), and Ratshivhadela ("block of wood").

[9.1.1.28] Thipa, H. M. (1983). By their names you shall know them. *Proceedings of
the 2nd Southern African Names Congress, Pretoria,* pp. 286-291. Refs. Tables.
Describes 3 aspects of naming in the Sesotho and Xhosa tribes.   These are: (1)
Reincarnation (Kwame Nkrumah, Steve Bikol, (2) Historical (Mantwa for Sesotho;
Nomfazwe for Xhosa, "war"); and (3) Death (Puseletson for Sesotho; Mbyiselo for
Xhosa, "recompense.") where the child is a reward for previous dead children.

[9.1.1.29] Timpunza-Mvula, Enoch. (1984). Nicknaming in conversational context
among the Chewa of Malawi. *Folklore Forum, 17,* 134-143. Refs. pp. 230-238.
The Chewa compose over 50% of Malawi. Their nicknames function as a form of social
control. Among the types are: personal characteristics (Kamtedza, "groundnut lover"),
proverbs (Kadyankena mbiri ya kheswe, "whenever someone else has eaten the food the
mouse is always the villain"), and anatomical characteristics (Kamkwara, "giraffe").

[9.1.1.30] Waters, Tony. (1989). Some practical notes on a names taboo in Western
Tanzania. *Disasters, 13,* 185-186.
Experience as a relief worker with the Waha people shows there is a names taboo. A
parent avoids mentioning a child by name since it is believed that this makes the child
more visible to evil spirits.

[9.1.1.31] Willis, Roy. (1982). On a mental sausage machine and other nominal
problems. In David Parkin (Ed.), *Semantic anthropology* (pp. 227-240). London:
Academic Press. Refs. Figs.
Information on the Bantu-speaking Fipa of southwest Tanzania. They have 5 types of
name: (1) a secret name known only to the parents & the child, (2) nicknames, (3)
teknonyms, and two types of descent names. The descent names indicate a person's
social identity and are linked to both sides of one's family.

[9.1.1.32] Willoughby, W. C. (1905). Notes on the totemism of the Becwana. *Addresses & Papers Read at the Joint Meeting of the British & South African Associations for the Advancement of Science, 3,* 263-293,
At the time the article was written the Becwana lived north of the Vaal River in what is now the Republic of South Africa. While the presentation deals mostly with totems, pp. 264-265 touch on proverb names. Thus a man known as Modimoecho ("God of our fathers") is showing the short form of *Modimoecho ga a laolwe* ("the God of our fathers is not restrained").

[9.1.1.33] Wilson, Monica. (1951). *Good company: A study of Nyakyusa age-villages.* Boston: Beacon Press, 278p. Refs.
The Hyakusa are a Bantu-speaking tribe on the slopes of Mt. Kilimanjoro in Northern Tanzania. Their customs include one in which a betrothed girl is allowed to look at her prospective father-in-law once. After that she is to avoid him and even avoid pronouncing his name (p. 83).

9.1.2. ETHNIC NAMES: *African: Bini*

[9.1.2.1] Omijeh, M. E. (1968). Bini proverbs. *Nigeria Magazine, 96,* 40-44. Refs.
Description of 8 types of proverb names that involve: (1) predestination, (2) individual responsibility, (3) self-assertion, (4) hope for the future, (5) indifference of "outsiders," (6) conduct, (7) general values, and (8) human behavior. Examples of a self-assertion proverb name: Udin-yiwe (Udiniwe), "The palm tree does not shed its leaves." Meaning, "I am invulnerable."

[[9.1.2.2] Wescott, Roger W. (1974) Bini names in Nigeria and Georgia. *Linguistics, No. 124,* 21-32. Refs. Tables.
The Bini live in Nigeria. Relationship of Bini names to Gullah-speakers in Georgia. Extensive analysis of current Bini names in various type categories. Many examples such as, *èbhúù* ("mist"), *àmèn'igbàárlò* ("rain-hat," lit. "water won"t strike the face"). Attention also to nicknames, examples, *ùbébè* ("scamp"), *émìtè* ("shorty").

[[9.1.2.3] Wescott, Roger W. (1975). Nicknames in Bini and English: A comparative study. *Folklore Forum, 8,* 148-149. Refs.
Compares similarities (such as phoneme repetition, hypocoristic affixation, and word length) and differences with Bini (such as no monosyllabic nicknames, and no hypocoristic suffixes). About 12 examples.

9.1.3. ETHNIC NAMES: *African: Ghana*

[9.1.3.1] Antubam, Kofi. (1963). *Ghana's heritage of culture.* Leipzig: Koehler & Amelang, 222p.
Pp. 56-61 deal with names. Ghanians have 2 names, the 1st is "the name of the tutelar deity of the day on which one is born," the 2nd is given by the father. Several examples Nicknames (called fond names or names that make a person great) are also given. Nicknames are derived from 2nd names, examples, Obrisii (the dark-hearted) is derived from Kwaku.

[9.1.3.2] Grottanelli, Vinigi L. (1977). Personal names as a reflection of social relations among the Nzema of Ghana. *L'Uomo, 1,* 149-175. Refs. Italian summary.
The Nzema represent the southernmost group of the Akan nation of Ghana, West Africa. Systematic description of the complex system of 8 categories (+ subcategories) of names used. These include: soul name, birth name, patronymic, given name, nickname, baptismal name, surname, and praise appellation.

[9.1.3.3] Nunoo, Ebenezer. (1971, Dec./1972, Jan.). More African names: The Akan (Ghana) way. *African Progress, 1,* pp. 37, 52.
70% of the people in Ghana, West Africa speak Akan. Brief description of naming customs and listing of day-names [children named after the day of the week they are born], names for ordinal position of birth, and names for twins.

9.1.4. ETHNIC NAMES: *African: Igbo*

[9.1.4.1] Ezeanya. S. N. (1967). *A handbook of Igbo Christian names.* Port Harcourt, Nigeria, 48p. Refs. Illus.
Intro. Has 650+ entries. Each shows all or one of the following: Igbo name, English version, biblical or Christian version, and the feast day. Examples, Chukwuamaka (Igbo), "God is extremely good" (English), Tobias (biblical version), Nov. 2 (feast day).

[9.1.4.2] Jell-Bahlsen, Sabine. (1989). Names and naming: Instances from the Oru-Igbo. *Dialectical Anthropology, 13,* 199-207. Refs.
Description of the naming customs of the Igbo tribe of Nigeria. Topics include: naming a child, boys' names, children's names, adult greeting names, elders and titles, and changing names.

[9.1.4.3] Kraft, Charles H. (1976, Nov.). An ethnolinguistic study of Hausa epithets. *Studies in African Linguistics, Supplement 6,* 135-146. Refs.
Description and classification of 521 epithet names collected by R. C. Abraham in 1949. Among the 10 classifications are: simple nicknames ("1 with an elephant harpoon"), occupations ("daybreaker"), and personal characteristics ("a crow"). Many examples.

[9.1.4.4] Nwachukwu-Agbada, J. O. J. (1991). Aliases among the Anambra-Igbo: The proverbial dimension. *Names, 39,* 81-94. Refs. Tables. Map.
The Igbo (formerly Ibo) are concentrated in Anambra State in southern Nigeria. They have a special kind of alias which is used in address. The aliases derived from proverbs involve a call and response. An example (translated) on truth: Call: "Beat truth to a pulp", Response: "...it floats still." Meaning: truth cannot be buried. 32 proverbs are given.

[9.1.4.5] Okediji, F. Olu & F. A. (1966). The sociological aspects of traditional Yoruba names and titles. *Odu, 3,* 64-79. Refs.
Presentation of the organization and rationale of Yoruba names. Many examples.

[9.1.4.6] Oseni, Z(akariyau) I(drees-Oboh). (1981). *A guide to Muslim names: With special reference to Nigeria.* Lagos, Nigeria: Islamic Publications Bureau, 99p. Refs.
Comprehensive discussion of the rationale behind Muslim names. Relevant quotes from the Koran. Includes 66 names for Muhammed with meanings, and Nigerian variations, examples, Kamil means "The Perfect Prophet." Nigerian variations are Kamilu and Kaminu. Names also given for other categories (prophets from the Bible, angels, Islamic heroes and heroines) with Nigerian variations. Approved Nigerian Muslim day-names also listed. Total of over 250 names given.

[9.1.4.7] Sofola, J. A. (1970). "What's in a name?": The sociological uses of names and naming among the Yoruba and the Ibo ethnic groups of Nigeria. *Ibadan, 28,* 43-48. Refs.
Both groups believe that there is "an agreement between the name given a child and that child's soul." Types of name described.

[9.1.4.8] Umunna, Ifekandu. (1968). Ibo names and the concept of death. *African Scholar, 1,* 28.

The Ibo of Nigeria show their reactions to death with the names *onwu* ("death") as either a prefix or suffix. These include: Onwuke ("death is greater than man") and Jideonwu ("death, forbear!").

[9.1.4.9] US. Central Intelligence Agency. (1965). *Hausa personal names.* 49p. Microfilm by Library of Congress, 1970.
Hausa is a major African language and is concentrated in northern Nigeria but extends to other countries. There are no hereditary surnames. A man named Ibrahim Musa Abu Bakar would have Ibrahim as his given (our 1st) name; Musa, that of his father; and Abu Bakar, his grandfather. Description of naming patterns and customs. Approx. 378 names listed with pronunciation, some with meaning. Types of titles also described.

9.1.5. ETHNIC NAMES: *African: Republic of South Africa*

[9.1.5.1] Combrink, Johan. (1990). Die Vroee Stamboom van *Alewyn* en *Alwyn* [The family tree of Alewayn and Alwyn]. *NomAfr, 4(2),* 21-34. Refs. Afrikaans. English summary.
Traces the 1st name and its variant Alwyn to Alewyn Smith in 1695. Shows how Alewyn became a surname out of families with different previous surnames, examples, Smits, Kruger, Ras.

[9.1.5.2] Herbert, Robert K. & Bogatsu, Senna. (1990). Changes in Northern Sotho and Tswana personal naming patterns. *NomAfr, 4(2),* 1-19. Refs.
Investigated Northern Sotho and Tswana-speaking urban residents. The 50 families showed 113 (1st names) of 3 types: (1) emotion-related (Tshepo [hope], "because I love him very much"); (2) religious-oriented (Tebogo [gratitude], "I thank God because I got baby boy"); and (3) family continuity (Asser. "from the great-grandfather"). Mothers gave the largest percentage of names.

[9.1.5.3] Jacobs, J(ohan) U. (1991). A proper name in prison: Self-identification in the South African prison memoir. *NomAfr, 5(1),* 4-14. Refs. Afrikaans abstract.
Examination of the role of one's name in the identity crisis faced by political prisoners in South Africa as seen through the autobiographies of Ruth First and Albie Sachs.

[9.1.5.4] Nathan, Carmen. (1990). Names and the law. *NomAfr, 4(1),* 49-65.
Description of naming laws in the Republic of South Africa. Topics include: choice of 1st name (relatively free), legitimacy (a posthumous child takes the mother's surname), change of name (difficult in South Africa), and marital name (a wife can assume her husband's name, hyphenate or keep her birth name).

[9.1.5.5] Neethling, S. J. (1988). Voorname in Xhosa. *NomAfr, 2,* 223-238. Refs. Afrikaans. English summary.
Current naming practices of Xhosa students at the University of the Western Cape.

[9.1.5.5A] Neethling, S. J. (1990). Iziteketiso. [Call names]. *NomAfr, 4(1),* 11-33. Refs. Tables. Afrikaans. English summary.
Describes 5 types of Xhosa nickname: (1) shortening to one syllable (Nomonde > Monde), (2) shortening to an affectionate form (Lindiwe > Lindie), (3) modification of one syllable (Nosipho > Sposh), (4) one syllable kept and letters added (Nomonde > Simono), and (5) others, (Zolani > Z).

[9.1.5.6] Neethling, S. J. (1991). Proper names in some Nguni idioms and proverbs. *NomAfr, 5(1),* 65-77. Refs. Afrikaans summary.

Discussion of 12 proverbs, 3 Zulu, 9 Xhosa, each with onomastic content. Example, no. 3, Kukusa kukaNxele [Xhosa] ("It is the coming of Nxele") means a forlorn hope. Nxele was a leader captured by the British who never returned.

[9.1.5.7] Thipa, H. M. (1987). What shall we name him? *NomAfr, 1(2),* 107-119. Refs. Tables.
Intro. to Sesotho and Xhosa culture followed by discussion of naming categories for children and adults. For children, those relating to: (1) the supernatural (examples, Sesotho, *Mpho;* Xhosa, *Sipho* "gift", (2), rocking the boat (Xhosa, *Nomfazwe,* "mother of war"), and (3) great expectations (Sesotho, *Katleho,* "success"). For parents: (1) parental status (Basotho, *Mmamohau,* "mother of mercy"), (2) compliance with cicumcision (*Rotholwana* [language and meaning not shown]), and (3), traders' names (Xhosa, *Sompempe,* "father of whistles").

9.1.6. ETHNIC NAMES: *African: Swahili*

[9.1.6.1] Buhlmann, Walbert. (1953). Principles of phonetic adaptation in Swahili applied to Christian names. *Africa, 23,* 127-134. French summary.
Rules for names based upon Swahili phonetic laws, examples, 'x' is not used in Swahili, so Alexius > Alesi; Latin names ending in -er tend to drop the 'r', so Silvester > Silivesta.

[9.1.6.2] Dammann, Ernst. (1954). The translation of biblical and christian names to Swahili. *Bible Translator, 5,* 80-84. Refs.
Description of the difficulties involved with the translation of biblical names into Swahili. Favors the translation of a name directly from Hebrew or Greek rather than through Latin. Also reports the difficulty of Bible names that came through Arabic.

[9.1.6.3] Zawawi, Sharifa. (1993). *What's in a name? Unaitwaje? A Swahili book of names.* Trenton, NJ: African World, 86p. Refs. Illus.
Background on the Swahili (East African) language and culture. Part I lists with meaning approx. 150 Swahili names found in the US (Juma [male], "born on Friday"; Sharifa [female], "honorable"). Part 2 lists approx. 500 male and 500 female names with their meanings (Badru [male], "full moon"; Rafiya [female], "dignified").

9.1.7. ETHNIC NAMES: *African: Zimbabwe*

[9.1.7.1] Berlyn, Phillippa. (1965). Traditional religion of the MaShona. *NADA (Native Affairs Department Annual)* [Salisbury], *9,* 94-96. Refs.
The MaShona live in what is now Zimbabwe. In their religion the supreme being is Mwari, other names include Nyadenga, Musiki, and others. Some origins of the names explained.

[9.1.7.2] Doke, Clement M(artyn). (1931). *The Lambas of Northern Rhodesia: A study of their customs and beliefs.* London: Harrap, 407p. Refs.
The Lambas live in what is now Zimbabwe. In a normal birth, the child is named by the maternal grandmother for a dead relative or ancestor. In a difficult birth, the child is named by the doctor (p. 135). Later at 10-12, there are youth names, example, Ntambika ("offerer of food") and later in life, praise-names, example, Konibwile ("I've no fear of night") (pp. 146-147).

[9.1.7.3] Hemans, T. J. (1968). A note on Amandebele names. *NADA (Native Affairs Department Annual)* [Salisbury, Rhodesia], *9(5),* 74.

The Amandebele tribe has 3 types of name: (1) the *ibizo,* similar to the Western 1st name, example, Ndhlalami ("bad hunger-drought"); (2) the *isibongo,* a hereditary surname, example, (Ngwenya ("crocodile"); and (3) isitemo, an hereditary name, related to marriage rules. Nicknames are also common.

[9.1.7.4] Jackson, S. K. (1957). Names of the vashona. *NADA (Native Affairs Department Annual)* [Salisbury, Rhodesia], *34,* 116-122.
Describes names of the Shona tribe of what now is Zimbabwe in East Africa. Their names recall events. 80% of the names recall family quarrels (Hamumdidi, "You do not love me") or death (Mhute, "Mist, this baby will vanish as the mist"). Other types of name are descriptive or religious. Many examples.

[9.1.7.5] Jeffreys, M. D. W. (1956). Origin of the name "Wankie." *African Notes & News, 12,* 17-18. Refs.
Concludes that Wankie was (is) the name of a ruling Barotse dynasty in what is now Zimbabwe.

9.1.8. ETHNIC NAMES: *African: Zulu*

[9.1.8.1] Koopman, Adrian. (1979). The linguistic difference between nouns and names in Zulu. *African Studies, 38,* 67-80. Refs.
The Zulu have 5 types of name: (1) a personal name, (2) a town name, (3) a nickname, (4) a clan-name, and (5) a clan praise-name. The article is directed at the personal name and involves systematic analysis of several types of noun, inflected and non-inflected, as well as those types derived from other parts of speech. Many examples.

[9.1.8.2] Koopman, Adrian. (1979). Male and female names in Zulu. *African Studies, 38,* 153-166. Refs.
Continuation of article above.

[9.1.8.3] Koopman, Adrian. (1987). Zulu names and other forms of address. *NomAfr, 1(1),* 136-162. Refs. Tables.
Description of various types of address associated with type of name. Includes title + clan-name, kinship term, descriptive name, football-name, 'christian' name, and pet name. 24 types of name defined with examples

[9.1.8.4] Koopman, Adrian. (1989). The aetiology of Zulu personal names. *NomAfr, 3(2),* 31-48. Refs.
Describes 5 major types of 1st name in this tribe. These refer to: (1) family structure (uMfanafuthi, "another boy"), (2) role of God in the birth (uNkosinathi, "the Lord is with us"), (3) relationship between parent and child (uThandiwe, "loved one"), (4) family circumstances (uMfanakayise, "son of his father"), and (5) the wider clan (uPhasizwe, "support the clan"). Several examples of each.

[9.1.8.5] Turner, Noleen S. (1992). Zulu names as echoes of censure, discontent and disapproval within the domestic environment. *NomAfr, 6(2),* 42-58. Refs.
Description of the social function of derisive names in a closed society. There are 4 types of these names which can show conflict between: (1) spouses or lovers, (2) in-laws, (3) family members, and (4) family and neighbors. Example of a parental conflict name, Mphikeni ("the denial"). "This boy was given the name by his mother to reflect the father's refusal to accept the child as his." 50 other examples.

[9.1.8.6] Ungerer, H. J. (1988). Die rol van samestelling in Zulu-naamgewing. *NomAfr, 2,* 323-336. Refs. Afrikaans. English summary.
Systematic description of Zulu name-bestowal.

9.2. ETHNIC NAMES: *African American*

[9.2.1] Armstrong, Orland K. (1931). *Old Massa's people: The old slaves tell their story*. Indianapolis, IN: Bobbs-Merrill, 357p.
P. 62 has a short statement on baby-naming by slaves in the tidewater area, "When a baby was born the day an important ship arrived, the port from which it sailed or the destination of the cargo it was to carry back were drawn on for a name."

[9.2.2] Brickell, John. (1737; 1911; 1968). *The natural history of North Carolina*. Murfreesboro, NC: Johnson, 424p. Originally published in 1737, republished in 1911 and again in 1968.
An early acct. Gives early comments on African American names (p. 274). Lists 10 names including: Jupiter, Mars, Venus, Drunkard, Piper, and Fiddler. Indian naming mentioned (p. 308) "some being called Eagle, Tyger, Panther...or some other wild creature." Bird, fish, and other wild animals also used.

[9.2.3] Burton, Orville Vernon. (1985). *In my father's house are many mansions: Family and community in Edgefield, South Carolina*. Chapel Hill, NC: University of North Carolina Press, 450p. Refs.
Pp. 166-167 (refs on p. 386) describe naming patterns among slaves. About 1/3 of slaves were named for fathers, < 1/10 for mothers. Slaves were also named after other relatives. Also points out that in 1860 there were 695 black surnames vs. 1254 in 1870. Thus, "Blacks had created and maintained their own family identities through their surnames."

[9.2.4] Harder, Kelsie B. (1990). Some implications arising from Black names found in Colonial Connecticut. *Connecticut Onomastic Review, No. 3*, pp. 48-52. Refs.
Suggests that the origin of 15+ names thought to be classical in origin may be derived from West African languages. These classical names were given because they sounded similar to African names. Example, *Cato*, probably < Hausa *Ketto*.

[9.2.5] Jackson, Edward M. (1990). Black Americans: The naming of themselves: A historical and literary approach. *Connecticut Onomastic Review, No. 3*, pp. 60-71. Refs. Table.
General on naming in Africa. Table shows types of name held by African Americans in the 18th-19th cents.

[9.2.6] Johnson, Thomas A. (1977, Mar. 19). Harlem baby named Kunta Kinte, for 'Roots' hero. *New York Times*, p. M36. Photo.
Children in New York, Los Angeles, Atlanta, and Cleveland are being named after Kunta Kinte (central character of Roots) or his daughter Kizzy.

[9.2.7] McGregory, Jerrilyn. (1990). Aareck to Zsaneka. *Proceedings of the 16th ICOS, Laval University, Quebec, 1987*, 389-396. Refs.
Data from birth records of African American children born in 1970, 1975, and 1980 in Gary, Indiana. Beginning in 1965 there were new trends in naming. One of these was the -La prefix (Latanya, example, for girls; LaBraun for boys). Other types also described. Considerable increase in middle names 1945-1980. "These new names can be attributed to important societal changes in the 1960's."

[9.2.8] Morrison, Lemuel & Speed, Anoona. (1980). C'est toi qui l'a nommé (You have named him, not I). *Clinical Pediatrics, 19*, 267-270. Refs.
Interviews of a sample of 70% black mothers and 30% white mothers in south Alabama indicates that 3/4 of the mothers named the children. For 40% of the 1st-born and 26% of the later-born, non-traditional names were bestowed (a non-traditional name is one not

found in a traditional baby-name book or occurred only once in the study). Non-traditional names include: Aladra Zakie, Toiya Yaskika, and Laquonda Lashaye.

[9.2.9] Muhammad, Wallace D. (1976). *Book of Muslim names*. Chicago: Elijah Muhammad Mosque No. 2, 40p.
Directed to African American Muslims. Includes the 99 names of Allah (Al-Malik, "the King"); 55 of Muhammad (Mansour, "victorious"); surnames (Ashraf, "most noble"); approx. 300 male 1st names (Sabir, "patient"); and approx. 280 female names (Nida, "voice, call").

[9.2.10] Old slave names. [Contributors' Club]. (1890, Sept.). *Atlantic Monthly, 66,* p. 428.
Anecdotal reports of several black names such as, Junniper Buzby, Reason Hinton, and July Grey.

[9.2.11] Terrell, Francis; Terrell, Sandra L., & Taylor, Jerome. (1988) The self-concept level of Black adolescents with and without African names. *Psychology in the Schools, 25,* 65-70. Refs. Tables.
Black males who had African 1st names and who were in a predominantly black high school in the Southeast scored significantly higher on self-esteem with the Black Ideology Scale. The Coopersmith scale did not show significant differences.

[9.2.12] Walker, Sheila. (1977). What's in a name? Black awareness keeps the African tradition of 'meaningful' names alive. *Ebony, 32(8),* p. 74ff.
Popular article on sources for surnames for blacks in the US. Points out the impact on Africans when on arrival as slaves they were renamed by their masters. Listing of 75 female and 75 male Euro-American names used by blacks. Additional lists of 33 female and 45 male African names. All names show meaning and language of origin. African names show pronunciation.

[9.2.13] Williamson, Joel. (1965). *After slavery: The Negro in South Carolina during Reconstruction, 1861-1877.* Chapel Hill, NC: University of North Carolina Press, 442p. Refs.
Pp. 309-311 provide an overview of the patterns of adoption of surnames by ex-slaves following the Civil War. One point made is that the adoption by many of the surnames of their ex-masters is evidence of a respect for the masters.

[9.2.14] Wood, Peter. (1974). *Black majority: Negroes in Colonial South Carolina from 1670 through the Stono rebellion.* New York: Knopf, 346p. Refs.
Pp. 181-186 deal with naming patterns. Description of West African day-names and how they were modified to English names which sounded similar. Examples include Cudjo ("Monday") to Joe; Abba, a female name ("Thursday") to Abby. Discussion of changes in original meaning and influence of Gullah.

[9.2.15] Woodson, Carter G. (1925). *Free Negro heads of families in the United States in 1830.* Washington, DC: Association for the Study of Negro Life & History, 296p. Tables.
Extensive intro. Listing of all free "Negro Heads of Families" living apart from whites in 1830. Listing by state and county. There is also a general alphabetical listing. First names included.

9.2.1. ETHNIC NAMES: *African American: Change of Name*

[9.2.1.1] Hare, Nathan (1962). Rebels without a name. *Phylon, 23,* 271-277. Refs.
Mostly on the term Negro and alternatives to it. Some mention (p. 274) of personal
name changes by followers of Father Divine and Black Muslims.

[9.2.1.2] Litwack, Leon. (1979). *Been in the storm so long: The aftermath of slavery.*
New York: Knopf, distributed by Random House, 651p. Refs.
Pp. 176, 228, 247-251, 454 deal with names. Reports on interviews with ex-slaves
conclude that after emancipation 1st names were not changed but surnames often were.
Ref. on p. 586.

[9.2.1.3] New dignities. (1882, Oct.). [Studies in the South, VIII]. *Atlantic Monthly,*
50, 476-488.
P. 477 makes reference to changes. Some African Americans under new conditions
[1882] changed their names. Examples include: Romeo Jones > Romey O. Jones;
Pericles Smith > Perry Clees Smith; and Polly's Jim > Apollos James.

9.2.2. ETHNIC NAMES: *African American: Slave Names*

[9.2.2.1] Cobb, Joseph B. (1851). *Mississippi scenes; Or, sketches of Southern and*
Western life. Philadelphia: Carey & Hart, 250p.
Passing ref. (pp. 173-174) to 4 slaves, recently arrived (at that time) from Africa and
who bore the names, Capity, Saminy, Quominy, and Quor.

[9.2.2.1A] Cody, Cheryll Ann. (1987). There was no "Absalom" on the Ball
plantations: Slave-naming practices in the South Carolina low country, 1720-1865.
American Historical Review, 92, 563-596. Refs. Tables. Figs.
A comprehensive description of the Ball family and its emphasis on perpetuation of kin
names is followed by a description and analysis of slave naming patterns showing the
transformation from the dominance of day-names and placenames, to classical, common
English, and biblical names. Points out that the slaves also perpetuated kin names.

[9.2.2.2] Escott, Paul D. (1979). *Slaves remembered: A record of twentieth-century*
slave narratives. Chapel Hill, NC:
Pp. 50-51 state that most slaves had a name different than that of the master. P. 51 has
a table showing surnames of 2036 male and female slaves. Ref. is on p. 203.

[9.2.2.3] Genovese, Eugene D. (1974). *Roll, Jordan, roll: The world the slaves made.*
New York: Vintage, 823p. Refs.
Pp. 443-450 (refs. pp. 756-757) deal with slave names and give refs. to other sources.
Some mention of post-Emanicipation influence.

[9.2.2.4] Gudeman, Stephan. (1979). Herbert Gutman's *The Black family in Slavery*
and Freedom, 1750-1925: An anthropologist's view. *Social Science History, 3,* 56-65.
Refs.
Pp. 59-61 explain why slave surnames were not the same as those of the master and why
there was a shift from matronyms to patronyms after emancipation. Comment also on
1st names.

[9.2.2.5] Inscoe, John C. (1983) Carolina slave names: An index to acculturation.
Journal of Southern History, 49, 527-554. Refs. Tables.
Systematic, comprehensive presentation of several aspects of slave names in the
Carolinas. Covers African, classical, biblical, and puritanical origins of 1st names;

influence of slave owners and their wives on naming practices; surnames; and effects of the end of the Civil War on naming.

[9.2.2.6] Joyner, Charles. (1984). *Down by the riverside: A South Carolina slave community.* Urbana, IL: University of Illinois Press, 345p. Refs. Tables.
The chapter on Gullah has several pages (pp. 217-222; 236; 329-330) describing African names among slaves of All Saints Parish. Listing of 40+ day names with English and African equivalents. Other types of naming also described. Many examples.

[9.2.2.7] Kulikoff, Allan. (1986). *Tobacco and slaves: The development of Southern cultures in the Chesapeake, 1680-1800.* Chapel Hill, NC: University of North Carolina Press, 449p. Refs.
Pp. 325-326 describe the renaming of Africans brought to the Chesapeake area as slaves. Most were given English names although some had day names such as, Cuffy (for Friday), Juba (female name for Monday).

[9.2.2.8] Lyell, Charles. (1849). *A second visit to the United States of North America,* Vol. 1. New York: Harper & Brothers; London: John Murray, 273p.
Lyell was a famous visitor to the US. In a passage on slaves at the Hopeton estate in Georgia, mentions slave names January, Monday, Hard Times, Old Bacchus, Quash, and Bullaly.

[9.2.2.9] Meaders, Daniel E. (1975). South Carolina fugitives as viewed through local Colonial newspapers with emphasis on runaway notices 1732-1801. *Journal of Negro History,* 60, 288-319. Refs. Tables.
Along with other material, names of slaves are included. Examples include Cuffe, Wiley, Serva, and Ben.

[9.2.2.10] Norton, Mary Beth. (1980) *Liberty's daughters: The revolutionary experience of American women, 1750-1800.* Boston: Little, Brown, 384p. Refs.
Pp. 85-87 (Refs. pp. 332-333) describe slave naming-patterns. In the Jefferson family records, more sons were named after fathers than daughters after mothers. More Virginia black families named their children after grandparents than white New Englanders.

[9.2.2.11] Rawick, George P. (Ed.). (1972). *The American slave: A composite autobiography.* Westport, CT: Greenwood, 19 vols.
The Federal Writers' Project of the Works Progress Administration (WPA) conducted 2000 interviews with ex-slaves in the 1930s. The interviews were conducted in 17 states. Unfortunately, there is no index but from some sources (Genovese [9.2.2.3], Litwack [9.2.1.2]), some specific pages referring to names have been identified and confirmed. Most refer to how slaves or ex-slaves acquired their surnames.
2(1), 14, 66, 327; 2(2), 117, 233, 238, 266;
3(3), 24, 59-60; 3(4), 44, 256;
4(1). 51, 54, 137; 4(2), 192, 237;
5(3), 5;
8(1), 296;
9(3), 105;
11(7), 10, 245.
11(7), 10, 245.

[9.2.2.12] Rogers, George C. (1970). *History of Georgetown County, South Carolina.* Columbia, SC: University of South Carolina Press, 565p. Refs.
Pp. 439-441 describe choice of surname by ex-slaves. Many choices were names of planters who were their masters. First names also described. Categories include: common names of the white population, biblical names, classical names, months of the

year and days of the week, African, non-African geographical, names of rank ("Prince"), historical figures, hope and awe names. Examples.

[9.2.2.13] Yetman, Norman R. (1970). *Life under the "Peculiar Institution": Selections from the slave narrative collection*. New York: Holt, Rinehart & Winston, 368p.
Composed of 100+ narratives drawn from the Federal Writers Project of the 1930s. There are some references to how names of slaves were derived. Some are on pp. 11-12, 27, and 175. There are probably more but there is no index.

9.3. ETHNIC NAMES: *American Indian*

[9.3.1] Barnes, Robert B. (1982). Personal names and social classification. In David Parkin (Ed.), *Semantic anthropology* (pp. 211-226). London: Academic Press.
After a review of philosophical approaches to names (Mill, Frege, Lyons), analyzes naming patterns in American Indians. Among the tribes discussed are the Sioux, Omaha, Mohawk, and Hidatsa.

[9.3.2] Barnes, Robert H. (1980). Hidatsa personal names: An interpretation. *Plains Anthropologist, 25,* 311-331.
Systematic description and explanation of the naming patterns of this tribe especially as contrasted with the Omaha.

[9.3.2A] Boas, Franz. (1932). Current beliefs of the Kwakiutl Indians. *Journal of American Folklore, 45,* 177-260. Refs.
The Kwakiutl Indians (often associated with the potlatch custom) live on Vancouver Island. In this collection of 759 superstitions, there are several relating to names (the index gives the pages). Some relate to twins.

[9.3.3] Braroe, Niels Winther, & Braroe, Eva Ejerhed. (1977). Who's in a name: Identity misapprehension on the Northern Plains. *Diogenes* [Florence, Italy], *98,* 71-92.
Examination of an isolated Cree Indian community of 100 persons in Western Canada from an anthropological point of view. Description of naming customs. This group has a sacred name, a nickname, and a white name. Description of several social customs about names.

[9.3.4] Burgesse, J. Allan. (1943). Montagnais-Naskapi nomenclature. *Primitive Man, 16,* 44-48.
The Montagnais-Naskapi are a Canadian Indian tribe of Algonkian stock historically from the region on the north shore of the St. Lawrence to Labrador. Surnames are relatively recent and are perceived as being the caprice of traders.

[9.3.5] Cushing, Frank Hamilton. (1896). Outlines of Zuni creation myths, *Annual Report Bureau of American Ethnology,* 1891-92, Vol. 13, 325-447. Washington, DC: Government Printing Office.
In this extensive report on the Zuni, names are mentioned on pp. 333-335. [Historically] Zuni adopted Christian baptismal names and kept their Indian names as surnames, example, Felix Pautiatzanilunquia ("Felix Of-the-sacred-dancers-glorious-sun-god-youth").

[9.3.6] de Laguna, Frederica. (1954). Tlingit ideas about the individual. *Southwestern Journal of Anthropology, 10,* 172-191. Refs.
The Tlingit are a sea-going American tribe that live in southern Alaska and northern British Columbia. Naming is related to reincarnation (pp. 181-183). The individual has several names: (1) ordinary, "real name," (2) pet name and/or nickname, and (3) a potlatch name.

[9.3.7] Elmendorf, William W. (1951). Word taboo and lexical change in Coast Salish. *International Journal of American Linguistics, 17,* 205-208. Refs.
In research with the Twana, a Salish-speaking people of the Hood Canal area of Western Washington investigated word and name taboo. Learned that there was a taboo on speaking the name of a dead adult or even a word which bore a phonetic resemblance.

[9.3.8] Fiske, Shirley. (1978). Rules of address: Navaho women in Los Angeles. *Journal of Anthropological Research, 34,* 72-91. Refs. Fig.
Interviews were conducted with small samples of inner city and suburban women. Results indicate: (1) Anglo ethnicity shows use of non-reciprocal title and last name, (2) title and last name used when addressing older Indian people. Figure shows the rules for usage.

[9.3.9] Fletcher, Alice. (1870). The religious ceremony of the four winds or quarters, as observed by the Santee Sioux. *Report of the Peabody Museum, 3(19),* 289-295. Fig.
Pp. 294-295 describe the naming ceremony where the child is given a name. A lengthy note also describes other aspects of naming customs.

[9.3.10] Fletcher, Alice C(unningham)., & La Flesche, Francis. (1911; 1972). *The Omaha tribe.* Lincoln: University of Nebraska Press, 2 v., 660p. Reprint of the 1911 ed., which was issued in the *27th Annual Report of the Bureau of American Ethnology.* Pp. 51-65 give extensive coverage on names. There are also scattered references throughout. Hundreds of names are listed showing Indian spelling (and pronunciation) along with English translation.

[9.3.11] Franciscan Fathers. (1912). *Vocabulary of the Navaho language, vol. 2, Navaho-English.* St. Michaels, AZ: Franciscan Fathers, 212p.
Pp. 207-212 have lists of approx. 200 male Navaho names with meaning and approx. 80 female names. Examples of names are: bi'la na'yiskali ("Shot-away Fingers") and for a female, yi'kazba ("She Went to War"). Clan names (p. 206) are also used as personal names, example, yo'o ("Bead Clan").

[9.3.12] Garvin, Paul L. (1947). Christian names in Kutenai. *International Journal of American Linguistics, 13,* 69-77. Refs.
The data were gathered from bands in British Columbia, Montana, and Idaho. While most Kutenai have tribal names, all but some of the old have Christian names, mostly French. 100+ names are listed with pronunciation in Kutenai, location reported, and phonetic type. Short names also given.

[9.3.13] Gatschet, Albert S. (1895). Tecumseh's name. *American Anthropologist, o. s. 8,* 91-92.
Tecumseh was a Shawnee chief (1768?-1813). He was a member of the miraculous panther totem. His name conveys the meaning of a celestial lion which is a meteor.

[9.3.14] Gifford, Edward Winslow. (1932). The southeastern Yavapai. *University of California Publications in American Archaeology & Ethnology, 29,* [177]-252p. Refs. Illus.
General description of the Yavapai (also called Mohave-Apache and Yuma-Apache) who live in Arizona. Pp. 200-202 list names with meanings. There are approx. 90 male names including Bakotel ("big man") and Del ("quail"); 45 female names including Hokwa ("great blue heron") and Wiyela ("mescal").

[9.3.15] Gifford, Edward Winslow. (1936). The northeastern and western Yavapai. *University of California Publications in American Archaeology & Anthropology, 34(4),* 247-345. Refs.
P. 305 has a brief paragraph mentioning naming boys after slain warriors.

[9.3.16] Gilmore, Melvin R. (1929). Arikara account of the origin of tobacco and the catching of eagles. *Indian Notes, 6,* 26-33.
This tribe formerly lived in the Dakotas. Among their ceremonial uses at the naming of a child "was the making of tobacco-smoke offerings to all the Powers of the Four Quarters, to Mother Earth, and to the Chief Above in the heavens" (p. 32).

[9.3.17] Goff, J. H. (1953). Of warriors and chiefs. Emory University Quarterly, *9,* 95-110.
Focus on the Creeks Indians of Georgia and Alabama. Approx. 100 names and titles are described. Also some information on the Cherokees and other Indians of the Southeast.

[9.3.18] Hilger, M. Inez. (1958). Naming a Chippewa Indian child. *Wisconsin Archaeologist, 39,* 120-126.
Based upon an account of John E. Kingfisher, a Chippewa Indian, describes a Chippewa naming ceremony in which the namer, Old Man Mink, gave the child a name which the old man had as a young man.

[9.3.19] Holway, Hope. (1965). The American Indian and his name. *Chronicles of Oklahoma, 43,* 340-344. Refs.
General description of the types of American Indian names. Some were humorous and given by Indians, some were derogatory and given by whites. Other types also described. Examples.

[9.3.20] Kendall, Martha B. (1980). Exegesis and translation: Northern Yuman names as texts. *Journal of Anthropological Research, 36,* 261-273. Refs.
The Yavapai Indians in central and southern Arizona, the Hualapai and Havasupai in northern Arizona, are culturally and linguistically closely related. Their naming patterns and practices are related to theories of the soul and the person on the cultural level. Social interaction patterns are also described. Topics include: nicknames, forms of address, epithet names, twin names, and ghost names.

[9.3.21] Laird, Carobeth. (1976). *The Chemehuevis.* Banning, CA: Malki Museum Press, 349p. Refs.
The Chemehuevis live in close proximity to where California, Nevada, and Arizona come together. Pp. 70-81 explains 80+ names. Entries give the Chemehuevi name transliterated into English, the English translation, and where possible, the etymology. Examples Wikontotsi = Buzzard Head, was given to George Laird because he was bald at birth; Toopoxi = Has Black Lumps, a woman's name, etymology not known.

[9.3.22] Landar, Herbert J. (1961). A note on the Navaho word for coyote. *International Journal of American Linguistics, 27,* 86-88. Refs.
Background of the word and name in Navaho culture. The word refers to one who stinks.

[9.3.23] Littlefield, D. F., Jr., & Underhill, L. E. (1971). Renaming the American Indian: 1890-1913. *American Studies, 12,* Fall, 33-45. Refs.
Critical history of the attempts of Thomas J. Morgan, John Wesley Powell, Hamlin Garland, and others to change the names of Indians to conform to Western-style naming practices.

[9.3.24] Lowie, Robert. (1909; 1975). *The Assinboine.* New York: AMS Press, 270p. Refs.
The Assinboine at the time of the research were residents of Alberta and Montana. Brief mention of naming customs for children. The child may be named according to a supernatural revelation of a relative or by a brave man who (for a fee) would name the infant after one of his martial exploits.

[9.3.25] Lowie, Robert H. (1909; 1975). *The northern Shoshone.* American Museum of Natural History, New York. *Anthropological Papers, vol. 2, Part 2.* New York: AMS, 306p. Refs. (Reprint of the 1909 ed. published by the American Museum of Natural History).
P. 211 has a brief mention of naming. 17 men's names (To'sa-wu'ra, "White Bear") and 6 women's names are listed (Na'soai, "Not-ashamed").

[9.3.26] Lowie, Robert. (1917). Notes on the social organization and customs of the Mandan, Hidatsa, and Crow Indians. *Anthropological Papers of the American Museum of Natural History,* Vol. 21, Part I, 99p. Refs.
Personal names of these 3 tribes are scattered throughout the book. There is also a table (pp. 22-25) which shows over 100 Hidatsa names. Brief description of Hidatsa naming (pp. 51-52). Examples for Mandan include: Two-chiefs, Calf-woman; for Hidatsa, No-arm (maxo'xati), First-squash-blossom (awaxe ra'wita); and Crow, Gray-bull, Magpie.

[9.3.27] Lowie, Robert. (1924). Notes on Shoshonean ethnography. *Anthropological Papers of the American Museum of Natural History, 20(Part 3),* 185-324. Refs.
Pp. 270-272 give some information on naming customs of 4 tribes of the Shoshoneans, the Moapa and Shivwits Paiute, the Paviotso, the Ute, and the Wind River Shoshani. Some examples. P. 311 notes that a Shoshoni will not pronounce his own name.

[9.3.28] Lowie, Robert H. (1954; 1963). *Indians of the Plains.* Garden City, NY: Natural History Press, 258p. (Originally published by McGraw-Hill in 1954).
Naming customs are described on pp. 87, 90, 101-102. Birth-naming among the Cree, change of name for a sick infant, not mentioning the name of a dead person among the Arapaho, and ordinal birth names of Southern Sioux clans.

[9.3.29] Moore, John H. (1984). Cheyenne names and cosmology. *American Ethnologist, 11,* 291-312. Refs. Tables. Figs. Maps.
Systematic evaluation of Cheyenne names from the 1880 census in relation to the cosmology of the Cheyenne and the relationship to their position on the hierarchy of the cosmology. Many examples.

[9.3.30] Morgan, Lewis Henry. (1851; 1962). *League of the Iroquois.* New York: Corinth Books, 477p. (Originally published in 1851 as *League of the Ho-de-no-saunee, or Iroquois* by Sage & Brother in Rochester, NY)
Pp. 89-90 have passing mention of the birth-naming. Near relatives selected a child's name which also usually identified the tribe. Another practice was to give a man a new name when he became a sachem or chief.

[9.3.31] Murdock, George Peter. (1934). Kinship and social behavior among the Haida. *American Anthropologist, 36,* 355-385. Refs.
The Haida live on the Queen Charlotte Islands of British Columbia and on Prince of Wales Island of Alaska. In this extensive study of kinship relations, there are passing mentions of naming customs. P. 359 describes a nephew assumed his deceased uncle's ceremonial name, a girl is named after a deceased woman of her mother's clan. Forms of address also described.

[9.3.31A] Navaho language. (1991). *NewEncyBrit, 24,* 564.
Brief entry. "The Navaho fourth person is a grammatical category that enables the speaker to address someone who is present or within hearing distance without naming him or her, because names are thought to have power, the polite form avoids speaking another's name."

[9.3.32] Noon, John A. (1949; 1964). *Law and government of the Grand River Iroquois*, Viking Fund Publications in Anthropology No. 12. New York: Johnson Reprint, 186 p. (Originally published in 1949 by the Viking Fund)
The Grand River Iroquois were settled as refugees after the American War for Independence in the area of Brantford, Ontario. Pp. 33-34 have a brief mention of each clan having a Keeper of the Names and a description of his function. Names were transferred after the death of the person on whom originally bestowed.

[9.3.33] Nordenskiöld, Erland. (1938). *An historical and ethnological survey of the Cuna Indians*, Comparative Ethnographical Studies 10. Göteborg, Sweden: Göteborgs Museum, 686p. Refs.
The Cuna Indians live in Panama. Pp. 380-384 describe some of their naming customs. Indians have animal names; a man is reluctant to pronounce his own name; nicknames are used only among good friends.

[9.3.34] Ritzenthaler, Robert. (1945). The acquisition of surnames by the Chippewa Indians. *American Anthropologist, 47*, 175-177.
Description of the transition to surnames of this Wisconsin tribe from 1835 under the influence of (1) intermarriage with whites, and (2) the lumbercamps. Examples of new names include: Cadotte, LaRoche, George Cowen, Charley Mustache, and John Kingfisher.

[9.3.35] Rogers, Edward S., & Rogers, Mary Black. (1978). Method for reconstructing patterns of change: Surname adoption by the Weagamow Ojibwa, 1870-1950. *Ethnohistory, 25*, 319-345. Refs.
The area of these Northern Ontario Indians is from the Hudson Bay coast in the north to Manitoba on the west. Use of archival records and field interviews led to information on the development of 28 family surnames, such as Williams, Kanate, and Sakchekapo.

[9.3.36] Rogers, Mary B., & Rogers, Edward S. (1980). Adoption of patrilineal name system by the bilateral Northern Ojibwa: Mapping the learning of an alien system. In William Cowan (Ed.) *Papers of the 11th Algonkian Conference* (pp. 198-230). Refs. Figs. Map.
Related presentation to that of Edward S. Rogers & Mary Black Rogers above. Shows different ways of selecting surnames when pressure for surnames increased during the period 1870-1950. Examples.

[9.3.37] Schomer, Jacqueline. (1980). The effect of the Anglo-American culture on the naming practices of the Native Americans. *Papers of the North Central Names Institute, What's in a Name*, pp. 22-27. Refs.
Brief description of naming practices of American Indians prior to 1887 when they had no surnames. In that year the General Allotment Act which provided land for the Indians required selection of a surname, often a white man's name. The conclusions regard the policy as robbing the Native Americans of their identity. Some data provided by an Indian informant.

[9.3.38] Shehinski, Shelley. (1988, Jan. 29). Names changed by government. *Windspeaker* [Edmonton, Alberta], p. 6.
Many [most? all?] residents of this Indian community near Fort McMurray, Alberta, have taken the town name (Janvier) as their own surname. Indian people traditionally changed their names. This has caused problems in trying to identify records.

[9.3.39] Skinner, Alanson. (1913). Social life and ceremonial bundles of the Menomini Indians. *Anthropological Papers of the American Museum of Natural History, 13*, 1-165. Refs. Photo.

At the time this was written the Menomini, an Algonkian-speaking tribe (pop. 1500), lived on a reservation in Wisconsin. Pp. 36-40 describe some of their naming customs: some children are really god kings and must be named correctly or trouble will occur; there are special names for ordinal position in the family. P. 117 mentions bestowing honorary names after a victory.

[9.3.40] Skinner, Alanson. (1923). Observations on the ethnology of the Sauk Indians. *Bulletin of the Public Museum of the City of Milwaukee*, *5*, 1-57.
Pp. 16-31 deal with names and naming customs. The Sauk have inherited ordinal names. In the 1st month, the child is given another name. Names are also given of the basis of bravery, supernatural experiences of the parents, or personal characteristics. Listing of 350+ names with meanings by gens. Examples, Bears gens, Wa'bano "dawn"; Deer gens, Oka'kaia, "brisket."

[9.3.41] Skinner, Alanson. (1926). Ethnology of the Ioway Indians. *Bulletin of the Public Museum of the City of Milwaukee*, *5*, 181-354.
Members of the Ioway tribe might have several names. There are ordinal names (1st-born male = Henghro, 2nd-born female = Hatika). About 70 names are listed with meanings. Individual names belong to each gens. Thus, the Buffalo gens has Nuya'tci, "forked-corn-sprout" the Snake gens, Wakato'imi, "blue-snake-woman."

[9.3.42] Spier, Leslie. (1928). Havasupai ethnography. *Anthropological Papers of the American Museum of Natural History*, *29*, 81-392.
The Havasupai live in Arizona. Pp. 306-315 give 120+ male and female names in the Indian lang. and in English, some with stories of origin, example, a girl was called *gisinava* (3 strand braid) because she wore her hair that way.

[9.3.43] Spier, Leslie. (1930). *Klamath ethnography*. Berkeley: University of California Press, 338p. Refs.
The Klamath are an Oregon Indian tribe. Pp. 59-61 give some information on 8 male and 8 female names. Included for boys are Lele'ks ("spotted") and Noteo'oks ("curled"); for girls, Lime'lak ("mule colt") and Ha'ntakloth ("big mouth").

[9.3.44] Steckley, John. (1988). How the Huron became Wyandot: Onomastic evidence. *OnoCan*, *70*, 59-70. Refs.
Uses personal names from the Deer, Turtle, and Wolf phratries to demonstrate the Huron origin of the Wyandot. Among the names cited are: *enons* ("1 who makes peace?"), *Annaothaha* ("1 who caused the fish to come?"), and *S8ndak8a* ("eagle").

[9.3.45] Strong, William Duncan. (1929). Cross-cousin marriage and the culture of the northeastern Algonkian. *American Anthropologist*, *31*, 277-288. Refs.
The Indians referred to are of the Naskapi tribe in Northern Labrador. P. 286 has a brief reference to naming customs. Names are given by elderly paternal or maternal relatives and "...are believed to have much influence...All people seem to have several names of a purely personal nature."

[9.3.46] Swanton, John R. (1910;1960). Names and naming. In Frederick Webb Hodge *Handbook of American Indians north of Mexico* (pp. 16-18). Refs. New York: Pageant. (Originally published in 1910 in Washington by the Government Printing Office).
General description of naming practices in several Indian tribes. Mentions include: the Delaware, Salish, Kwakiutl, and Maidu tribes.

[9.3.47] Tooker, William Wallace. (1904). Derivation of the name Powhatan. *American Anthropologist*, New Series, *6*, 464-468. Refs.

Powhatan, the name of the Indian leader who was the father of Pocahontas, is also the name of a tribe. The root of the name is traced to meaning "hill of divination."

[9.3.48] Verhovek, Sam Howe. (1993, Nov. 4). The name's the most and least of her: At work with Chief Wilma Mankiller. *New York Times*, p. C1, C10.
Description of the activities of this Cherokee also explains the origin of the title and surname. She was elected as chief of the Cherokee Nation of Oklahoma. The surname was inherited and originally was a title of respect.

[9.3.49] Voth, Henry R. (1905). Oraibi natal customs and ceremonies. *Field Columbian Museum Publication*, No. 97, *Anthropology Series*, *6(2)*, 47-61. Photos.
Observation was made of the Oraibi, the largest (then) of the 7 Hopi villages in Arizona. Pp. 55-61 describe the naming ceremony which begins on the child's 20th day.

[9.3.50] Wafer, Lionel. (1934; 1967). *A new voyage and description of the Isthmus of America*. Nendeln, Liechtenstein: Kraus Reprint, 221p. (Originally published by the Hakluyt Society in 1934).
Views of a surgeon who visited the area [now Panama] in 1681. Mention of Cuna Indians seeking baptism to acquire a European name. The Cuna also believe in name magic. Names of the dead can neither be spoken aloud or given to sons.

[9.3.51] Whitman, William. (1937). *The Oto*, Columbia University Contributions to Anthropology, Vol. 28. New York: Columbia University Press, 132p. Refs.
"The Ota are a small group of Chiwere speaking people who have been classified as Southern Sioux." They are originally from Nebraska. Pp. 67-69 describe their naming customs. They have one unusual type of nickname. If a niece or nephew heard an uncomplimentary description by a tribesman of the uncle and reported it back, the niece or nephew was given that name at a dance.

9.4. ETHNIC NAMES: *Ancient Middle East*

[9.4.1] Astour, Michael. C. (1965). Sabttah and Sabteca: Ethiopian Pharaohs names in Genesis 10. *Journal of Biblical Literature*, *84*, 422-425. Refs.
Comment and discussion on these 2 names with ref. to other sources.

[9.4.2] Avi-Yonah, Michael. (1959). Syrian gods at Ptolemais-Accho. *Israel Exploration Journal*, *9*, 1-12. Refs. Fig.
A table found in a village near Accho [Acre], ancient Ptolemais, dating from the 2nd cent. BC has 7 lines with 5 names. The 3 Greek names are: Diadotos, Neoptolemus, and Philistia. The 2 gods named are oriental: Hadad and Atargatis. Exhaustive refs.

[9.4.3] Bonner, Campbell. (1954). Two notes. *Journal of Egyptian Archaeology*, *40*, 15-18. Refs.
The 1st part of the article deals with the names Nonnos and Nonna which were common in Egyptian papyri. Traced to babbling words such as papa and moma. Suggests that Nonnos and Nonna be uncle and aunt respectively and originated in Syria.

[9.4.4] Cooke, G. A. (1903). A text-book of North-Semitic inscriptions: *Moabite, Hebrew, Phoenician, Aramaic, Nabatean, Palmyrene, Jewish*. Oxford: Clarendon Press, 407p. + plates.
Has treatment on 150 inscriptions + coins. Many names are mentioned.

[9.4.5] Ferguson, W. S. (1929). Lachares and Demetrius Poliorcetes. *Classical Philology*, *24*, 1-31. Refs.

Lachares was one of the Athenian tyrants. According to Ferguson in a note on p. 1, "The name seems foreign (Dorian?)..."

[9.4.6] Gelb, I(gnace) J. (1961). The early history of the West Semitic peoples. *Journal of Cuneiform Studies*, *15*, 27-47. Refs.
Responding to the work of Jean-Robert Kupper *Les nomades en Mésopotamie au temps des rois de Mari* (1957), develops a scholarly position on the West Semites who moved into Babylon. Much of the information available is on the names of persons.

[9.4.7] Gershevitch, Ilya. (1970). Island-Bay and the lion. *School of Oriental and African Studies Bulletin*, *33*, 82-91. Refs.
A selection of 80+ Old Persian names from the Elamite Fortification tablets, each with extensive comment. Examples, Piapkarda = Island Bay, i.e., someone probably from the Bay of Hormuz, Irdarima = Rich Through Truth.

[9.4.8] Goetze, Albrecht. (1958). Remarks on some names occurring in the Execration texts. *Bulletin of the American Schools of Oriental Research*, *151*, 28-31. Refs.
Extended comment on 9 names from these ancient Egyptian texts.

[9.4.8A] Goetze, Albrecht. (1959). The roster of women at 298. *Journal of Cuneiform Studies*, *13*, 98-103. Refs.
Listing from a tablet from the ancient city of Alalakh from 1350 BC. In modern Turkey, it is NE of Antioch. Comment on 26 names, most of which are Hurrian.

[9.4.9] Goetze, Albrecht.(1960). Suffixes in Kanashite proper names. *Revue hittite et asianique*, *18*, 45-55. Refs.
Based on the Cappadocian tables mentioned above. Examination to determine whether the Kanishite language is Indo-European or pre-Indo-European.

[9.4.10] Goetze, A. (1962). Cilicians. *Journal of Cuneiform Studies*, *16*, 48-58. Refs.
Cilicia is between Anatolia and Syria in modern Turkey north of Cyprus. Examination of tablets from Ras Shamra (14th/13th cents. BC) with detailed comments on 15 names, decides that most merchants of Ura were Luwian. After further examination of other tablets concludes that "Cilicia must have been a thoroughly Luwian...country."

[9.4.11] Hinz, Walther. (1965). The Elamite god d.Gal. *Journal of Near Eastern Studies*, *24*, 351-354. Refs.
The Elamite king Untash.d.GAL reigned in the 13th cent. BC in what is now Southwest Iran. After examination of the evidence of several authorities, concludes that when "the Elamites wrote DINGIR; that they pronounced it *napirisa*; and they meant by it Humbam, their Great God."

[9.4.12] Hoffner, Harry A., Jr. (1968). Birth and name-giving in Hittite texts. *Journal of Near Eastern Studies*, *27*, 198-203. Refs.
Description of birth and naming in mythological texts. Suggestion of possible relevance for historical parents.

[9.4.13] Horsnell, Malcolm John Albert. (1974). The year-names of the first dynasty of Babylon: With a catalogue of the year-names from Sumuabum to Samsuiluna. *DissAbstrIntl*, *37(12)*, Section A, p. 7897.
Described as "an up-to-date, critically annotated catalogue of...the year-names...of the first seven of the eleven kings of the First Dynasty of Babylon (1894-1595 B. C.)."

[9.4.14] Horsnell, M(alcolm). J(ohn). A(lbert). (1977). Grammar and syntax of the year-names of the First Dynasty of Babylon. *Journal of Near Eastern Studies*, *36*, 277-285.

The First Dynasty was 1894-1595 BC. Years were dated in 2 ways: the regnal year of the king and the year-name designated by an official. After examination of much scholarly material, concludes that the year-name is translated as active-transitive, not passive, example, "the year: RN did such-and-such."

[9.4.15] Huffmon, Herbert Bardwell. (1963). Amorite personal names in the Mari texts. A structural and lexical study. *Dissertation Abstracts, 25(3)*, p. 1867. (University Microfilms No. 64-8177, 369p.)
Collection, analysis, and classification of the Amorite personal names in the Mari texts. Lists of names. Glossary. Thoroughly documented with 100s of citations and refs.

[9.4.16] Kapelrud, Arvid S. (1952). *Baal in the Ras-Shamra texts*. Copenhagen: G. E. C. Gad, 156p. Refs.
Ras Shamra is the modern Arabic name for the ancient city of Ugarit. It is off the Syrian coast on the Mediterranean at the same latitude as Cyprus. Pp. 44-64 (refs. pp. 149-156) discuss various forms of the god Baal. These include: *aliyn b'l,* Hadad, Lord of Sapan, and others.

[9.4.17] Krahmalkov, Charles. (1969). The Amoritic enclitic particle TA/1. *Journal of Semitic Studies, 14,* 201-204. Refs.
Analysis and discussion with examples.

[9.4.18] Littmann, Enno. (1953). Nabatean inscriptions from Egypt, intro. & classical notes by David Meredith. *Bulletin of the School of Oriental & African Studies, 15,* 1-28. Refs. Map. Plates.
The inscriptions appear to be the work of Nabataean caravan people who traded in Egypt and wrote graffiti during the 1st cent. in the eastern desert of Egypt. 54 inscriptions are given and translated, many with more than one name.

[9.4.19] Macqueen, J. G. (1959). Hattian mythology and Hittite monarchy. *Anatolian Studies, 9,* 171-188. Refs.
The Hattians were the original residents of Anatolia (modern Turkey). The Hittites invaded around 1900 BC, and influenced their mythology. Discussion and comment on the gods and goddesses and parallels in other cultures. Extensive comment on the names Tabarna and Tawanannas, names borne by kings and queens.

[9.4.20] Meek, Theophile S. (1935). The iterative names in the Old Akkadian texts from Nuzi. *Revue d'assyriologie et d'archeologie orientale* [Paris], *33,* 51-55. Refs.
500 different personal names were found in texts from Gasur (Nuzi). 90 showed iteration (or reduplication), as A-ba-ba. The names are listed with comments.

[9.4.21] Noth, Martin. (1956). Remarks on the sixth volume of the Mari texts. *Journal of Semitic Studies, 1,* 322-333. Refs.
The Mari 6th vol. contains 75 personal names, many of which are West Semitic. Noth discusses some of them pointing out relationships (among others) to biblical Ishmael, Amasa, and Levi.

[9.4.22] Oxtoby, Willard Gurdon. (1962). Some inscriptions of the Safaitic Beduin. In *Dissertation Abstracts, 23,* 2884-2885.
The 480 inscriptions at 6 sites tell about the life of these pre-Islamic Arabs. Names apparently included in the complete dissertation.

[9.4.23] Sasson, J. M. (1966). Remarks on two "Anatolian" personal names from Mari. *Revue Hittite et Asianique, 24,* 155-159. Refs.
The name Aplahanda from 1800 BC was thought to be Anatolian. Sasson interprets it as the West Semitic "Let me Venerate Adad." Aplahanda's son Yatar-dAmi had an

Amorite name as did 10 others. Concludes that both Aplahanda and his son had Semitic rather than Anatolian names.

[9.4.24] Shevoroskin, V. (1984). Theophoric names in Carian. *Onomata, 9,* 9-15. Refs.
Carian is a late South Anatolian (Hittite-Luwian) language. Detailed analysis of a number of names found in inscriptions from Egypt. None are translated into English.

[9.4.25] Shevoroskin, V. (1988). Carian proper names. *Onomata, 12,* 497-505. Refs. Greek summary.
Detailed examination of approx. 50 inscriptions in this late South Anatolian (Hittite-Luwian) language found in Upper Egypt.

[9.4.26] Tod, Marcus N. (1951). An ephebic inscription from Memphis. *Journal of the Egyptian Archaeological Society,* No. 37, 86-99.
In Ancient Greek society, an ephebus was a youth entering manhood. This inscription from Memphis, Egypt from about 220 AD lists 66 ephebes. Their names have Greek, Egyptian, Semitic, and Roman elements. Examples include Apia, Kasios, and Mikis.

[9.4.27] Tscherikower, V. (1937). Palestine under the Ptolemies: A contribution to the study of the Zenon papyrii. *Mizraim, 4-5,* 9-90. Refs.
The Zenon papyrii date from 259 BC when Zenon was an official of the government in Alexandria. P. 52 mentions the hellenization process where Jews assumed Greek names. Pp. 57-66 show references with comment on 66 names in Greek form.

[9.4.28] Wiseman, Donald J. (1959). Ration lists from Alalakh VII. *Journal of Cuneiform Studies, 13,* 19-33. Refs. Table. Fig.
Alalakh is an ancient city between Aleppo and the Mediterranean (modern Syria). 280 + cuneiform tablets from Level VII, approx. 1750 BC, were transliterated. The figure shows some cuneiform examples

[9.4.29] Wiseman, Donald J. (1959). Ration lists from Alalakh IV. Journal of Cuneiform Studies, *13,* 50-62. Fig.
See: Wiseman above. 318 cuneiform tablets from approx. 1400 BC were transliterated.

[9.4.30] Zgusta, Ladislav. (1961). Overlapping families of names and other difficulties in the anthroponymy of Asia Minor. *Atti e memorie del VII Congresso Internazionale di Scienze Onomastiche, Firenze, Apr. 1961* [7th ICOS], Vol. 3, 327-333. Refs.
About Ancient Greece and parts of the Ancient Middle East that spoke Greek. Identification of 5 types of problem encountered when trying to determine whether a name is indigenous or from either Greek or Latin, example, Diddianus [Zgusta favors Latin on this one].

[9.4.31] Zgusta, Ladislav. (1962). The indigenous names of Lycia and Cilicia Aspera. *Archiv Orientalni, 30,* 624-631. Refs.
Comment on H. J. Houwink ten Cate's *The Luwian population groups of Lycia and Cilicia Aspera during the Hellenistic period* which "correlates one type of indigenous names of Asia Minor with the Luwian language and population."

[9.4.32] Zgusta, Ladislav. (1965). Some principles of work in the field of indigenous anthroponymy of Asia Minor. *Annali del Istituto orientale di Napoli Sezione linguistica, 6,* 89-99. Refs.
Description of the types of errors that can be made in assigning the etymology of names in Ancient Greek inscriptions. Examples, names that sound similar in 2 languages are not necessarily related. Thus the modern name Montgomery vs. the ancient Cilician name Montgomeris are similar by chance.

9.4.1. ETHNIC NAMES: *Ancient Middle East: Akkadian*

[9.4.1.1] Driver, G. R. (1957). Aramaic names in Accadian texts. *Rivista Degli Studi Orientali*, *32*, 41-57. Refs.
Discusses 90+ Aramaic transliterations of foreign names (Assyrian, Babylonian, Persian, and South Arabic). example, the Aramaic *ACHLIKID represents Accadian "Ahi-alik-idiya* meaning 'my (divine) brother is going at my side.'"

[9.4.1.2] Gelb, Ignace J. (1955). Old Akkadian inscriptions in Chicago Natural History Museum: Texts of legal and business interest. *Fieldiana: Anthropology*, *44*, 161-338. Refs. Plates.
Information on over 200 names (including some Sumerian) found on tables from approx. 2000 BC presumably from the Diyala River region, east of the Tigris. Index of names is on pp. 324-333 Examples of names are: Bubu, Ibibi, Admar, and Enana.

[9.4.1.3] Rasmussen, Carl George. (1981). A study of Akkadian personal names from Mari. *DissAbstrIntl*, *42(4)*, 1613-A.
Based upon the Mari texts from the Upper/Middle Euphrates region during the middle of the Old Babylonian period. Approx. 1000 of the 3484 names in the Mari texts are Akkadian. Types of names assessed include: verbal sentence names, nominal sentence names, designating names, substitute names, names referring to master/mistress, and names referring to the king or kingship.

9.4.2. ETHNIC NAMES: *Ancient Middle East: Aramaic*

[9.4.2.1] Fales, Frederick M. (1977). An Aramaic onomastics in the Neo-Assyrian period. *Oriens Antiquus*, (Centro per le Antichita e la Storia dell'arte del vincino Oriente), *16*, 41-68. Refs.
An extended review of Edward Lipinski [87:8.5.12].

[9.4.2.2] Kaufman, Stephen. (1970). "Si' gabbar, Priest of Sahr in Nerab." *Journal of the American Oriental Society*, *90*, 270-271. Refs.
2 Aramaic stellae from the 7th cent. BC found at Nerab (near Aleppo have the inscription *Si'gabbar*, *Priest of Sahr*. The West-Semitic Si' is a form of the Mesopotamian moon god Sin.

[9.4.2.3] Rabinowitz, Isaac. (1956). Aramaic inscriptions of the fifth century B.C.E. from a North-Arab shrine in Egypt. *Journal of Near Eastern Studies*, *25*, 1-9. Refs. Plates.
BCE means before the Common Era, i.e., 5th cent. BC. Comment on inscriptions found on 8 silver vessels found at Tell el-Maskuta, 12 miles west of Ismailia, Egypt. Ref. to a chief named Gesem.

9.4.3. ETHNIC NAMES: *Ancient Middle East: Assyrian*

[9.4.3.1] Fales, F. M. (1979). A list of Assyrian and West Semitic women's names. *Iraq*, *41*, 55-73. Refs. Illus.
Analysis of a Neo-Assyrian fragment from the Kouyunjik collection. 118 names are evaluated, 80 of them complete.

[9.4.3.2] Gelb, Ignace J. (1954). Two Assyrian king lists. *Journal of Near Eastern Studies*, *13*, 209-230. Refs. Photos.

Translation and transliteration of the Khorsabad king list from Dur-Sarru-kin and the SDAS king list showing points of agreement of 100 kings.

[9.4.3.3] Gelb, Ignace J. (1960). The name of the goddess Innin. *Journal of Near Eastern Studies, 19,* 72-79. Refs.
Systematic presentation of evidence to show that the name of the Sumerian goddess was Innin rather than Inanna, Ninni, or some other variation.

[9.4.3.4] Goetze, Albrecht. (1953). The theophorous elements of the Anatolian proper names from Cappadocia. *Language, 29,* 263-277. Refs.
The research was based upon the "Cappadocian" tablets which go back to the 20th cent. BC near the current Kültepe, ancient Kanis, in central Turkey. Detailed examination of a number of Anatolian names leads to the conclusion that the theophorous elements in Cappadocian tablets are Kanishite in nature and the "appearance of these elements leaves no doubt that (Proto-)Indo-Europeans were present in Cappadocia as early as the period of Assyrian colonization, i.e. in the 20th century B. C."

[9.4.3.5] Goetze, Albrecht. (1954). Some groups of ancient Anatolian proper names. *Language, 30,* 349-359. Refs.
Detailed examination of names with 6 characteristic endings, examples, *-man, -iyal* found on Cappadocian tablets (see entry above).

[9.4.3.6] Harper, Richard P. (1967). A dedication to the goddess Anaitis at Ortakoy, north of Akseray, (Nitalis?). *Anatolian Studies, 17,* 193. Refs. + plate 17, not paged.
An inscription found at Cappadocia (northwest Turkey) to the Persian goddess Anaitis contains the epithet "barzochara" which is interpreted as "the great goddess Anaitis, the Delight-in-Victory."

[9.4.3.7] Kaufman, Stephen A. (1978). Enigmatic Adad-Milki. *Journal of Near Eastern Studies, 37,* 101-109. Refs.
Examination of the issue for the "existence of a cult of a god Adad-Milki in late Neo-Assyrian times." The name could mean "Adad-Milki is my god" or "Ad is king of the gods."

[9.4.3.8] Steinkeller, Piotr. (1982). Mesopotamian god Kakka. *Journal of Near Eastern Studies, 41,* 289-284. Refs. Fig.
Analysis of an Ur III tablet from a town in the southernmost part of Assyria shows that Kaka was a lesser god who had a cult following.

9.4.4. ETHNIC NAMES: *Ancient Middle East: Egypt*

[9.4.4.1] Arkell, A. J. (1963). Was King Scorpion Menes? *Antiquity, 37,* 31-35. Refs. Map. Fig.
On the basis of maceheads found at Hierakonpolis, Egypt, concludes that King Scorpion was Menes who united Upper and Lower Egypt.

[9.4.4.2] Budge, E. A. Wallis. (1926). *Dwellers on the Nile.* London: Religious Tract Society, 326p. Illus.
P. 20 mentions that in Ancient Egypt a man honored the name of his mother over that of his father. Also notes that in the large number of funerary telae in the Cairo and British museums "the name of the mother of the deceased person is given, but no mention is made of the father."

[9.4.4.3] Caminos, Ricardo A. (1972). Another hieratic manuscript from the library of PWEREM son of Kiki. *Journal of Egyptian Archaeology, 58,* 205-224. Refs. Illus.

Prob. dates between 310-30 BC. Names of gods mentioned throughout. On p. 210 there is some information on naming and magic to insure protection from the gods.

[9.4.4.4] Deakin, G. B. (1974). A note on two new instances of the rare proper name MRJW-MRJW. *Zeitschrift für ägyptische Sprache und Altertumskunde, 100*, 150. Refs. Reports on finding 2 further examples of a New Kingdom name which is translated as "Beloved, Beloved."

[9.4.4.5] Fischer, Henry G. (1973). *Journal of Egyptian Archaeology, 59*, 44-46. Refs. Illus.
Speculation on an inscription involving names found at Giza.

[9.4.4.6] Fischer, Henry G. (1974). An Eleventh Dynasty couple holding the sign of life. *Zeitschrift für ägyptische Sprache und Alterskunde, 100*, 16-28. Refs. Illus.
Includes some references to names and name-endings.

[9.4.4.7] Gardiner, Alan. (1936). The Egyptian origin of some English personal names. *Journal of the American Oriental Society, 56*, 189-197. Refs.
Responding to a guidebook that said that the name *Humphrey* has Egyptian roots, points out that it does not, that Moses and Miriam have doubtful Egyptian roots but that Phineas and Susan can be accepted as Egyptian.

[9.4.4.8] Gardiner, Alan. (1958). The personal name of the king serpent. *Journal of Egyptian Archaeology, 44*, 38-39. Refs.
Comment on the name of the King Serpent of the 1st dynasty that was found on a tablet at Sakkara. Proposes that the postulated name Iterty refers to his rule over both Lower and Upper Egypt.

[9.4.4.9] Griffiths, J. Gwyn. (1951). Is Chalbes a Greek name? *Annals du services des antiques l'Egypte, 51*, 219-220. Refs.
Although the name Chalbes appears in the Busiris legend of Ancient Egypt, concludes that it may be of Semitic or Greek origin, as others may think.

[9.4.4.10] Hauben, Hans. (1975). The Prosopographia Ptolemica: Progress report. [Reports on the progress of research "Forschungsberichte"]. *Onoma, 19*, 541-554. Refs.
Description of this extensive project to catalog all of the individuals who lived under Ptolemaic rule (323 BC to 30 BC). The geographical area covered is Egypt and its possessions. 8 vols. were published by 1975 with more scheduled.

[9.4.4.11] Hayes, William C. ed. & trans. (1955; 1972). *A papyrus of the Late Middle Kingdom in the Brooklyn Museum* [Papyrus Brooklyn 35.1446]. Brooklyn, NY: Brooklyn Museum, 161p. Refs. Plates. (Originally published in 1955; reprinted in 1972). The texts of the papyrus date from 1833 BC to 1745 BC and are from Thebes. One side lists 76 individuals and their fathers who ran away to avoid performing service for the state, example, " No. 61. The son of Gewa, Inyotef." The other side lists 33 Egyptian servants and approx. 40 servants whose names are North West Semitic. Analyses are made of the names.

[9.4.4.12] Honeyman, A. M. (1960). Two votaries of Han-'Ilat. *Journal of Near Eastern Studies, 19*, 40-41. Refs.
Concludes that the names of both the father and son whose names appear on the 4th inscribed bowl of Han-'Ilat are theophorous.

[9.4.4.13] Kitchen, K. A. (1972). Ramesses [Rameses] VII and the twentieth dynasty. *Journal of Egyptian Archaeology, 58*, 182-194. Refs. Diagram.
Contains some limited information on kings. More information on the names of queens.

[9.4.4.14] Mueller, Dieter. (1973). Three mummy labels in the Swansea Wellcome Collection. *Journal of Egyptian Archaeology*, *59*, 175-180. Refs. Illus.
There are 3 labels listed, one with a message. Several names are given. Comments.

[9.4.4.15] Nicknames are as old as ancient Egypt. [What's on Your Mind]. (1952, Nov.). *Science Digest*, p. 35. Illus.
Reports a lecture by John A. Wilson of the University of Chicago. Lists common nicknames as, Red, Baldy, Lazy, Donkey, Nosy, and the Cat.

[9.4.4.16] Oates, John F. (1963). The status designation: perses tes epigones. *Yale Classical Studies*, *18*, 1-129. Refs.
Systematic analysis of the status designation which has puzzled papyrologists of the Ptolemaic period in Egypt. Many citations of the designation.

[9.4.4.17] Oates, John F. (1964/65). The romanization of the Greek East: The evidence of Egypt. *Bulletin of the American Society of Papyrologists*, *2*, 57-64.
Analysis of the 196 names in Yale papyrus Inv. no. 296 from Philadelphia in the Fayum area of Egypt about 217 AD. While many residents were Roman citizens, the regular Roman praenomen, nomen, cognomen pattern was not regularly followed.

[9.4.4.18] Parker, Richard A. (1966). King Py, a historical problem. *Zeitschrift für ägyptische Sprache und Altertumskunde*, *93*, 111-114. Refs. Illus.
On the basis of 5 bits of data, suggests that *Py* is a hypocoristic form of Pi'ankhy, a brother of Shabaka.

[9.4.4.19] Pritchard, James B(ennett). (1955). *Ancient Near Eastern texts relating to the Old Testament*. Translators & annotators: W. F. Albright [& others], 2nd ed, corrected & enlarged. Princeton, Princeton University Press, 544p. Refs.
Pp. 10-12 tell the story "The god and his unknown name of power" which is taken from 2 mss. of the 19th Dynasty (1350-1200 BC). The story tells how the goddess Isis succeeded in learning the secret name (of many other names) of the supreme god Re which was the source of his power.

[9.4.4.20] Quaegebeur, Jan. (1971). The study of Egyptian proper names in Greek transcription. *Onoma, 18,* 403-420. Refs.
Overall survey of the wealth of material available in Greek translation. Many authors (mostly all non-English) cited.

[9.4.4.21] Ranke, Hermann. (1950). The Egyptian pronunciation of the royal name "Khefren" and its cognates. *Journal of the American Oriental Society, 70*, 65-68. Refs.
Discussion and analysis of the name of the builder of the 2nd pyramid of Giza. After presenting many views, concludes that in ancient times the name was pronounced differently than that of modern interpretations.

[9.4.4.22] Reinmuth, O. W. (1967). A working list of the prefects of Egypt 30 B. C.-299 A. D. *Bulletin of the American Society of Papyrologists, 4*, 75-128. Refs.
Contains a list of, "Their names, terms of office, and references to them which have appeared since A. Stein, *Die Praefekten von Aegypten*, 1950." Lists about 130 prefects in chronological order. Extensive comments on some, such as Julius Ursus.

[9.4.4.23] Sijpesteijn, P. J. (1990). The astrologer Askletarion. *Mnemosyne, 43*, 164-165. Comment on variations of the name of the astrologer (probably of Egyptian origin) who predicted his own death and that of the emperor Diocletian (who ruled 284-305 AD).

[9.4.4.24] Simpson, William Kelly. (1953). New light on the god Reshef. [Brief Communications]. *Journal of the American Oriental Society, 73*, 86-89. Refs.
Suggests that recent evidence associates the god Reshef (Egyptian Ershop) with a stag in Anatolia and a gazelle in Egypt.

[9.4.4.25] Simpson, W. K. (1972). A tomb chapel relief of the reign of Amunemhet and some observations on the length of the reign of Sesostris III. *Chronique d'Egypte, 47*, 45-54. Refs. Illus.
Some names and titles mentioned. One was the king's sister Merestekh, identified with Mr.s.th, "she loves intoxication."

[9.4.4.26] Thompson, Herbert. (1932). Eponymous priests under the Ptolemies. In *Studies presented to F. Ll. Griffith* (pp. 16-37). London: Oxford University Press. Refs.
The Ptolemies had different types of calendar. They had regnal years and fiscal years. There was also dating by the year and month of the priest at Alexandria for some documents. There is a listing by ruler with the name and dates of the priests from 285-181 BC.

[9.4.4.27] Wilson, John A. (1954). A group of sixth dynasty inscriptions. *Journal of Near Eastern Studies, 13*, 242-264. Refs. Photos.
Description of inscribed blocks found near the Step Pyramid and the Pyramid of Unis. Among the names mentioned is that of a noble, Bia, and his wife, Idut. Extensive comments and analysis. Also, ref. to a deified vizier, Mehu.

[9.4.4.28] Yeivin, S. (1954) Ancient Egyptian transcriptions of Canaanite names in the Execration Texts. *Proceedings of the 23rd Congress of Orientalists*, pp. 77-78.
Technical on how the Egyptians transliterated Canaanite names which might not have the same exact sounds in Egyptian, example, guttural, like *ayin*.

9.4.5. ETHNIC NAMES: *Ancient Middle East: Hittite*

[9.4.5.1] Carter, Charles. (1980). Notes on the name written DINGIR IS EL KU US in Hittite texts, *Journal of Near Eastern Studies, 39*, 313-314. Refs.
Interprets the names *Iselku-, Isku-,* and *Milku-* found in Hittite cuneiform tablets as not 3 different divine names but 1 *Milku-*.

[9.4.5.2] Gelb, I(gnace) J. (1951/52). The double names of the Hittite kings. *Rocznik Orientalistyczny* [Poland], *17*, 143-154. Refs.
Develops the position that the "Hittite kings used cuneiform Hittite names whenever writing in Cuneiform Hittite language and hieroglyphic Hittite names whenever writing in Hieroglyphic Hittite language." (p. 153).

[9.4.5.3] Kitchen, K. A. (1965). A late Luvian personal name in Aramaic. *Revue Hittite et Asianique, 23*, 25-28. Refs.
An explanation of how an Aramaic letter from the 5th cent. BC containing the name Knzsrm can have its etymology explained on the basis of Aramaic spelling. The name is *kinda-sirma from Lydian or Late Luvian names from Aramaic.

9.5. ETHNIC NAMES: *Arabic*
(See Also: 9.32. ETHNIC NAMES: *Islamic*)

[9.5.1] Beeston, A(lfred). F(elix). L(andon). (1971). *Arabic nomenclature: A summary guide for beginners*. Oxford: University Press, not paginated. [6 pages].

Differentiates *ism* (personal name), *nasab* (genealogical chain), *nisba* (tribal designation), *laqab* (nickname), and *kunja* (another type of nickname such as Abu Burda, "father of a cloak."

[9.5.2] Donner, Fred M. (1984). Some early Arabic inscriptions from al-Hanakiyya, Saudi Arabia, *Journal of Near Eastern Studies, 43,* 181-208. Refs. Figs.
The site of the inscriptions is about 110 km. ENE of Medina, Saudi Arabia. They date from the 1st-2nd cent. A. H. (year of the Hegira). There are several figures of the inscriptions and also transcriptions. At least 2 names are shown, Asim and Abu. Others have some questions. The graffiti appear to be prayers.

[9.5.3] Ism. (1978). *New encyclopedia of Islam*, Vol. 4, pp. 179-181. Leiden: Brill. Refs.
Classification and description with examples of names in Arabic-Islamic usage; the *kunja*, a name compound with abu (father of) or umma (mother of); the *ism*, the name as Asad Muhammad; *nasab*, pedigree; *nisba*, referring to place of origin or tribe, and *lakab*, nickname.

[9.5.4] Kniffka, Hannes. (1990). Calling names across cultures. *Proceedings of the 17th ICOS, Helsinki, 13-18 Aug. 1990, 2,* 11-21. Refs.
Description of name styles and forms of address in Saudi Arabia. Comparisons with Egypt, Germany and the US.

[9.5.5] Lewitter, F. I., Hurwich, B. J., & Nubani, N. (1983). Tracing kinship through father's first name in Abu Ghosh, an Israeli Arab patrilineal society. *HumBio, 55,* 375-381. Refs. Tables. Figs.
Abu Ghosh is a village near Jerusalem. It is unique in that residents can trace their ancestors back 7 or 8 generations. "Surnames are not used...Rather, a person's given name is followed by father's first name, paternal grandfather's first name, etc." The 9 most common names are: Muhamed, Ahmad, Mahmud, Ali, Yusef, Ibrahim, Said, and Hassan. They constitute 51% of the names in the 8 generations. [Female names were not mentioned].

[9.5.6] Palestine, Government of. (1931). *Transliteration from Arabic and Hebrew into* English, from Arabic into Hebrew, and from Hebrew into Arabic with transliterated lists of personal and geographical names for use in Palestine. Jerusalem: H. M. Stationery Office, 85p.
Description of transliteration procedures as shown in title. List of 260 Arabic names and English transliteration; list of 160 Hebrew names and English transliterations.

[9.5.7] Parkinson, Dilworth B. (1982). Terms of Address in Egyptian Arabic. *DissAbstrIntl, 43,* 437A. (University Microfilms No. DA8215065).
Description of Egyptian (Cairene) terms of address.

[9.5.8] Paxton, Evelyn. (1972). Arabic Names. *Asian Affairs, 59,* 198-200.
Concise intro. to Arabic names. Examples.

[9.5.9] Plancke, M. (1971). The Onomasticum Arabicum Project. *Onoma, 18,* 426-432. Refs. Table. Figs.
Description of a large-scale project on Arabic linguistics. One part is devoted to prosopography (inscriptions), a 2nd to preparation of computer programs for Arabic texts, a 3rd to a computer database for names.

[9.5.10] Qutub, Ishaq Y. (1963, Mar. 16). Arabic names and name giving. *Asian Student, 11,* p. 5.

Concise systematic overview of Arabic name-giving. Several examples including Haddad ("blacksmith"), Samman ("grocer"), and Sakakini ("maker of knives"). Topics also include nicknames and use of titles.

[9.5.11] Schimmel, Annemarie. (1989). *Islamic names*. Edinburgh University Press, 176p. Refs.
View of the world of Islamic personal names. Topics include: the types of name, naming practices, nicknames, changing of name, Turkish surnames. Approx. 2400 names are in the index. Text proper seems to have most if not all of the meanings.

[9.5.12] Tushyeh, Hanna Y., Lawson, Edwin D., & Rishmawi, George. (1989). Palestinian first names: An introduction. *Names, 37*, 245-264. Refs. Tables.
Classification of the names of 768 schoolchildren by frequency, sex, meaning, perceived identification ("Christian," "Muslim," or "Neutral"), and actual usage by Christians and Muslims.

[9.5.13] Tushyeh, Hanna Y., & Hamdallah, Rami W. (1992). Palestinian surnames derived from nicknames. *Names, 40*, 237-252. Refs. Tables.
Analysis of 413 surnames collected from the West Bank that can be classified as nicknames. There were 12 major categories. Among them were names derived from: animals (Abu-Diab, "father of wolves"), personal characteristics (Abu-Karsh, "father of the big belly"), and historical (Saleebi, "crusader"). All names are listed showing spelling in the Roman alphabet, phonetic transcription, meaning, and Arabic form.

[9.5.14] Watt, W. M. (1953). His name is Ahmad. *Muslim World, 43*, 110-117. Refs.
Discussion of the emergence of the name *Ahmad* referring to Muhammad.

[9.5.15] Yassin, M. Aziz F. (1986). The Arabian way with names. *Linguist, 25(2)*, 77-85. Refs.
Sets up system for Arabic personal names as, (1) micronames (SubaaH, saalim) (2) macronames (includes teknonyms, "abu bakr," "umm Aali," and patronyms, "ibn siina," "bint ka9b," and (3) brachynyms, divided into nicknames such as "bu tamba," ("fat one"), and diminutives. Several lists of examples.

9.6. ETHNIC NAMES: *Baltic*
(Includes Lithuanian and Latvian, no Estonian entries)

[9.6.1] Klimas, Antanas. (1969). Some problems in Lithuanian onomastics. A case study of the family names (surnames) of a Lithuanian village. *Lituanus, 15*, 41-50. Refs.
Research in the village of Pelekonys, county of Alytus, on the Nemunas River was done on the surnames of the 45 families living there. Of the 20 surnames represented, 11 have Slavic roots, example, Klimas < Latin Clemens via Slavic; the rest are Baltic (Lithuanian), example, Serys. "the feeder of animals."

[9.6.2] Klimas, Antanas. (1971). Family names in a Lithuanian village. *Proceedings of the 10th ICOS, Vienna, 1969 (Disputationes ad montium vocabula allorumque nominum significationes pertinentes), 2*, 247-254. Refs.
A shorter version of Klimas above.

[9.6.3] Raun, Alo. (1982). Tarapita. In Egle Victoria Zygas & Peter Voorheis (Eds.) *Folklorica: Festschrift for Felix J. Oinas*, Indiana University Uralic & Altaic Series, Vol. 141 (pp. 204-206). Refs.
Speculates that the name of this problematic god (Tarapita) may mean "'guardian (or caretaker) of the holy grove (or enclosure).'"

[9.6.4] Salys, Antanas. (1951). Names and surnames. [Language Lore]. *Marian* [Chicago], June, p. 15; Sept., p. 18.
Concise intro. to Lithuanian naming practices; effects of christianization on naming. Many examples including: Taut(i)ginas ("defender of the people"), Kreivys ("the crooked one"), and Kari-gaila ("one who is concerned over the warriors").

[9.6.5] US. Central Intelligence Agency. (1963). *Latvian personal names.* Washington, DC. 70p.
A guide for those not trained in the Latvian language to identify Latvian names. Intro. to the Latvian language and its names structure. Listing of almost 2000 surnames in Latvian form, Germanized form, and feminine form. Thus, as an example, Saulietis would be the regular masculine form, the Germanized would be Sauleet, and the feminine form, Sauliete. Approx. 700 1st names also listed such as, Asja (fem.), Mara (fem.), Andrejs (Andrew), and Janis (John). English equivalents given for some names. Forms of address and titles also shown. Meaning of names not given.

9.7. ETHNIC NAMES: *Brazilian*

[9.7.1] Azevêdo, Eliane; da Costa, Theomaria Pinto; Silva, Maria Christ B. O.; & Ribeiron, Lucia Regina. (1983). The use of surnames for interpreting gene frequency, distribution, and past racial admixture. *HumBio, 55*, 235-242. Refs(pp. 399-408). Tables.
Surnames were used to study genetic aspects in 2 communities in Brazil. In Manaus, the capital of Amazon state, the subject was gene frequency distribution of alcohol dehydrogenase in Black and American Indian mixtures. In Lencois in Bahia, surnames were used to study the racial proportions of blacks and whites.

[9.7.2] Pollitzer, W(illiam). S. (1983). Introduction: Surnames as population markers. *HumBio, 55*, 211-218. Refs(pp. 399-408).
Intro. to a series of papers edited by Gottlieb [29.6]. Gives meanings of names of authors. Then goes on to report a study (part of a larger investigation) from Jacobina in Bahia, Brazil on the relationship of skin pigmentation to surnames. Results indicate the darker the skin, the higher percentage of devotional (religious) names. Animal and plant names were also higher for darker-skinned people. The trend is greater for females than males.

[9.7.3] Tavares-Neto, José & Azevêdo, Eliane S. (1977). Racial origin and historical aspects of family names in Bahia, Brazil. *HumBio, 49*, 287-290. Refs. Tables. Figs.
Rev. of data from 7 research projects shows that 5 devotional surnames (Jesus, Santos, Santana, Nascimento, and Conçeicao) account for 31% of the population. Only Santos is common in every Portuguese population. Discussion of the linkage of these 4 names to the abolition of slavery. Extensive statistical analysis shows that the frequency of devotional names increases with Negro admixture.

[9.7.4] Tavares-Neto, José & Azevêdo, Eliane D. (1978). Family names and ABO blood group frequencies in a mixed population of Bahia, Brazil. *HumBio, 50*, 361-367. Refs. Tables.
Concludes that in Bahia, Brazil devotional surnames (See: Tavares-Neto et al. above) are more of an indicator of black ancestry than the race classification "Bahia White."

[9.7.5] Thonus, Terese. (1991). The influence of English on female names in Brazil. *Names, 39*, 27-38. Refs. Tables.
22% of the names on birth certificates from the city of Curitiba showed some influence from English. The female names were studied because changes in female fashion in names change more often. 6 categories were studied, from Identical (Elaine) to

Pseudo-English (Sheyla). Suggestions about the influence of American TV and use of English in professional life.

9.8. ETHNIC NAMES: *Bulgarian*

[9.8.1] Danchev, Andrei; Holman, Michael; Dimova, Ekaterina; & Savova, Milena. (1989). *An English dictionary of Bulgarian names spelling and pronunciation* [Angliski pravopis i isgovor na imenata b blgarskua ezik]. Sofia: Naouka i Izkoustvo, 228p. Refs.
Bulgarian is different from other Slavic languages that use Cyrillic script. It has other letters and sounds. After intro. material, in both English and Bulgarian, has listings for 15,000 people, places, and institutions. Each listing has the name in Bulgarian, a transliteration into English, and where warranted, a number keyed to the introductory chapter where special points are explained.

[9.8.2] Menges, K. H. (1951). Altaic elements in the Proto-Bulgarian inscriptions. *Byzantion* [Brussels], *21*, 85-118. Refs.
The inscriptions evaluated go back to the 9th cent. Pp. 91-100, deal with titles; pp. 107-118, with personal names and appellations. Examination of various language linkages between Bulgarian, Turkic, Altaic, Chinese, and other languages.

[9.8.3] Ramirez, Antonio. (1989, June 12). Bulgaria imprisons ethnic Turk because he refuses name change. *New York Teacher*, p. 13.
Bulgaria, as part of an assimilation project, wants ethnic Turks to change their Islamic names to Bulgarian ones. Amnesty International is working for release of this man.

[9.8.4] Turks win right to use the Muslim names they were forced to change. (1989, Dec. 30). *New York Times*, p. 10.
One and one-half million Turkish Muslims have been required to acquire new non-Muslim names. After rallies, the Bulgarian government is now allowing use of Muslim names.

9.9. ETHNIC NAMES: *Canadian*

[9.9.1] Alia, Valerie. (1986, Dec.-1987, Jan.). Naming themselves: Inuit take charge of a fundamental right. *Up Here: Life in Canada's North, 3(1)*, pp. 12-15. Illus.
Discusses problems associated with Inuit naming which has gone through 4 phases: (1) original names used, (2) issuing of numbered metal discs along with retention of original names, (3) Project Surname in which the Inuit were renamed, and (4) calls for the Inuit to have the right to name themselves.

[9.9.2] Alia, Valerie. (1989). Re-identifying the Inuit: Names policies in the Canadian North. *OnoCan, 71,* 1-12. Refs. French summary.
Description of Inuit naming customs and how they vary from the English naming system. Description of the disc numbering system and its shortcomings.

[9.9.3] Ames, Jay. (1988, Spring). More hard-to-swallow names. *Bulletin of the North Central Name Society*, pp. 35-37. Refs.
List approx. 30 unique names from the Toronto telephone directory in several categories, examples, palindrome: Ho S. Oh; warrior: *Verdun* Gordon.

[9.9.4] Basing investigation on 'foreign' name illegal: Immigration Commission ordered to change policy. (1987, Nov.). *Canadian Human Rights Advocate, 3(11)*, pp. 3-4.

The Human Rights Review Tribunal has ruled against the Canadian Employment & Immigration Commission in a situation where persons with "foreign" names were investigated as suspects of being illegally in the country. See Also: [9.9.2.1].

[9.9.5] Chiasson, Anselme. (1986). *Chéticamp: History and Acadian traditions*, 3rd ed. Translated by Jean Doris LeBlanc. St. John's, Newfoundland: Breakwater Books, 316p. Chéticamp is an Acadian French settlement on Cape Breton, Nova Scotia, Canada. P. 198 lists some names used in the early days [end of 18th cent.?]. Some were saints' names such as, Barbe, or Eulalie, others were biblical such as, Abraham, Samuel, Judith, or Esther. 20th cent. names show a switch to names such as, Walter, William, and Tommy. Girls' names are not mentioned.

[9.9.6] Dion, Kenneth L. (1985). Sex differences in desirability of first names: Another nonconscious sexist bias? *Academic Psychology Bulletin, 7,* 287-298. Refs.
Work with Toronto newspaper announcements and university graduation lists confirms that males are given more desirable names than females.

[9.9.7] Dunn, Charles W. (1953). *Highland settler: A portrait of the Scottish Gael in Nova Scotia.* Toronto: University of Toronto Press, 179p.
Pp. 136-138 have information on naming customs in communities on Cape Breton, Nova Scotia where there might be 15 John MacLeods or 20 James MacNeils. The solution was to use an individual's 1st name + his father's 1st name. Thus a man whose 1st name was Neil and whose father's name was Jim would be known as Neil Jim (MacLeod). Other naming customs also described.

[9.9.8] Koertvelyessy, T., Collins, M., & Keeping, D. (1986). Population subdivision in Pogo Island, Newfoundland. *American Journal of Physical Anthropology, 69,* 223. [Abstract].
Using the repeated pairs measurement on same pairs of names [isonymy] shows that Pogo Island has 3 times what would be expected by chance.

[9.9.9] Lapierre, André. (1991). When *Auclair* becomes *O'Clair*: Some remarks on Franco-American surnames. *OnoCan, 73,* 49-56. Refs. French summary.
Description of how French-Canadian surnames were modified in the 2nd half of the 19th cent. when 1000s of Quebecers moved to New England. Topics include: translation of name (Boisvert to Greenwood) and modification (Barrette > Barrett; Deveaux > Devoe).

[9.9.10] MacNeil, Neil. (1948). *The Highland heart in Nova Scotia.* New York: Scribner's, 199p. (Also published in 1971 by Saunders, Toronto)
Autobiographical account of growing up on Cape Breton. Pp. 18-20 describe naming customs where individuals have both a Gaelic and an English name. Nicknames also given such as: Little Rory, Holy Angus, Red Rory the Banker. Others throughout the book.

[9.9.11] Mertz, Elizabeth. (1983). A Cape Breton system of personal names: Pragmatic and semantic change. *Semiotica, 44,* 55-74. Refs.
Systematic description of the naming system of a fishing community of 300 in Nova Scotia, Canada. Topics include: abbreviated or familiar names (i.e, Johnnie, Annie), unique short forms such as Tane which was originally Mary Jane, initials, as DJ standing for Donald John; community position names; differences over time. Many examples.

[9.9.12] Milne, J. D(orothy). (1981). How's that for a monicker! *Canadian Genealogist, 3,* 72. Refs.

Unique names from the family register of Thomas E. and Eleanor Somerville of Belleville, Ontario in the 19th cent. One name is Thomasina Eleanor Vermenia Turrena Xenia Somerville.

[9.9.13] Nau, L. T. (1988). The rise and fall of orthonyms: A revolution in the choice of first names. *OnoCan, 70,* 3-14. Refs. French summary.
10 male 1st names have been among the top 10 (these are termed *orthonyms*) much of the time for the past 600 years. These names are: John, Thomas, William, Richard, Robert, James, Henry, George, Edward, and Charles. However, in Ontario in 1985 none of these were in the top ten. There has been a shift away from orthonyms. Similar results indicate a shift away from the previously popular Mary, Elizabeth, and Margaret. Comparisons with American and Quebec samples show a similar trend.

[9.9.14] Nau, Tim. (1991). First names in Yamachiche as evidence of the distinctiveness of Quebec society. *OnoCan, 73.* 1-8. Refs. French summary.
This sample, based upon data from marriage registers of French-speaking Quebecois shows that in the 19th cent. there was a shift from a small 1st name pool to a broader pool. This was contrary to the pattern of English-speaking Canadians. Women also showed shift patterns although not entirely similar. Papal influences on naming discussed. Examples given of 1st names.

[9.9.15] Ness, M. E. (1949, Jan. 11). Austin's the name for useful. *Saturday Night* [Canada], P. 18.
General on the literal meanings of a few popular names. Canadian orientation.

[9.9.16] Punch, Terrence M. (1985). *In which county? Nova Scotia surnames from birth registers, 1864-1877.* Halifax [Canada]: Genealogical Association of the Royal Nova Scotia Historical Society, 104p.
Lists 150 most common names province-wide. Other tables show the most common names by region and by county. The main table (85p. long) lists all surnames by county. The top names province-wide were: McDonald, Smith, McNeil, McLean, and McLeod.

[9.9.17] Wulfman, David S. (1986). Weihnacht and its variants as personal and place names. *Names, 34,* 340-341. Refs.
Questions the current folk etymology of the name *Wynot*, a town *Weihnacht* meaning "Christmas." In Lunenburg County, Nova Scotia, there is a Whynot's Settlement and a number of surnames with variants on *Weihnacht*.

9.9.1. ETHNIC NAMES: *Canadian: Change of Name*

[9.9.1.1] Brock, D. H. (1950, May 9). Surnames can never hurt me. *Saturday Night,* p. 28.
Comment on a name change challenge. A man wanted to change his surname but holders of that name objected. The judge proposed a slight spelling variant, Cameron > Cameren. Brock yearns for the good old days when a name change was easier.

[9.9.1.2] McGuigan, Peter. (1984). The McGuigan-Goodwin confusion on Prince Edward Island. *Canadian Genealogist, 6,* 91-104. Refs. Maps.
Data from Prince Edward Island show that many Goodwins changed their surnames to McGuigan. One suggestion is that the shift on Prince Edward Island is a deanglicization of the surname, i.e., originally, McGuigan, then Goodwin, finally back to McGuigan. Variants of McGuigan (McGoldrick and others) also included in the interpretation. Analysis includes maps from Ireland.

[9.9.1.3] Speirs, Doug. (1986, Jan. 27). More men take wife's surname, official says. *Winnipeg Free Press*, p. 1.
An official of the vital statistics branch office reports dozens of men taking their wives' names. Some at the time of marriage, some later.

[9.9.1.4] Zeldin, Arthur. (1966, June 4). How success may come under any other name [Maclean's Reviews]. *Maclean's*, p.49.
Review of report [not available] by Nancy Loach for the Canadian Institute of Culture Research and the Department of Citizenship and Immigration on name changes. Most changes are for adoption or illegitimacy. A smaller proportion are for ethnic names.

9.9.2. ETHNIC NAMES: *Canadian: Law and Names*

[9.9.2.1] Immigration accepts 'foreign name' defeat. (1988, Mar.). Canadian Human Rights Advocate, *4(3)*, 4.
A Human Rights Review Tribunal ordered the Canada Employment & Immigration Commission (EIC) to cease picking out for investigation people with "foreign-sounding" names arising out of LeDeuff v CEIC [9.9.4].

[9.9.2.2] Neutering more statutes: Now children can be given Mom's maiden name.(1985, Apr. 22). *Alberta Report*, p. 9.
Description of a proposed Alberta provincial amendment to permit married women to pass their birth name along to their children.

[9.9.2.3] Ontario Law Reform Commission. (1976). *Report on changes of name*. Toronto, ON: Ontario Law Reform Commission, 51p.
Review of current practices, summary of survey, and recommendations for reform. Several recommendations include: giving each spouse a choice of surname on marriage (including a hyphenated name), allowing for freedom of choice for a child's name to permit bestowal of either parent's or a combined surname, and simplification of name change procedures.

See Also: [20.9], [20.2.5] for further articles on this subject.

9.9.3. ETHNIC NAMES: *Canadian: Naming Patterns*

[9.9.3.1] Dranoff, Linda Silver. (1985). Ask a lawyer: I'm keeping my own name when I marry. *Chatelaine* [Toronto], *58(Feb.)*, p. 36.
Regulations vary by province in providing for the surname of a child. Possibilities include: the father's surname, the husband's name (if not the father), the mother's surname, a hyphenated name from both parents' surnames, and making up a surname that has parts of each parent's surname.

[9.9.3.2] Embleton, Sheila M. (1990). "But what will you call the children?" *Proceedings of the 16th ICOS, Laval University, Quebec, 1987*, pp. 245-253. Refs.
Contrary to expectations, children of mothers who retained their birth names at marriage, gave the child the father's surname. "The next most common solution is use the mother's surname as a last middle name, with this solution more common for male children than for female children."

[9.9.3.3] Fist fights, ungodly language, nearly wash out christening. (Jan. 11). *Toronto Star*, p. 1.
An irate maternal grandmother rejected the name selected by the unwed teenaged parents. An ambulance was called.

9.9.4. ETHNIC NAMES: *Canadian: Nicknames*

[9.9.4.1]   Davey, William. (1990).   Informal names for places in Cape Breton:
Nicknames, local usage, and a brief comparison with personal nicknames. *OnoCan, 72,*
69-81. Refs. French summary.
In addition to placename material, also has about 20 personal nicknames including Biscuit
Foot MacKinnon (injured by a falling box of biscuits), Leaky Joe (a plumber), and Jack
Hammer Joe.

[9.9.4.2]   Frank, David. (1988).   A note on Cape Breton nicknames. *Journal of the
Atlantic Provinces Linguistic Association, 10,* 54-63. Refs.
Explanation of the development of father-son nicknames in Cape Breton, Nova Scotia.
Description of the influence of the rural emigration to coal and steel districts on
nicknaming.   Many examples, some with explanation of origin.   Included are: Black
Sandy (for his whiskers), Jack the Face (worked on the face of a coal seam), and Sandy
Big Pay (once only got paid 2 cents because of deductions due the company store).

[9.9.4.3]   Taylor, Frank C., & Climo, Percy L. (1987).   Cobourg's celebrated
sobriquets: Those fanciful appellations of student days. *Canadian Genealogist, 9,*
221-224.
A collection of 500+ nicknames, many colorful, prepared for the Cobourg (Ontario)
Collegiate Institute [high school] reunion of 1976. Names include: *Corky* Kewin,
Gooseneck McDonnell, *Mudcat* Eagan, and *Tanglefoot* Mathews.

9.10. ETHNIC NAMES: *Celtic*

[9.10.1]   Bromwich, Rachel. (1956-1958).   Enit, Enide. *Bulletin of the Board of Celtic
Studies, 17,* 181-182. Refs.
Suggests that the name originally came from a character in a Breton story who
represented the tribal goddess of the Veneti.

[9.10.2]   Davies, Wendy. (1978-80).   The orthography of personal names in the charters
of *Liber Landavensis. Bulletin of the Board of Celtic Studies, 28,* 553-557. Refs.
There are 158 charters in the collection from the 6th to the 11th cents. Included are 850
different Welsh names.   Explanations given for variations in spelling include: scribal
errors, changes in sound, lenition, and vowel sounds.

[9.10.3]   Emanuel, Hywel D. (1966).   A double-name formula in Welsh 'saints' lives.'
Bulletin of the Board of Celtic Studies, 21, 133-135. Refs.
The Vita Codoci of Lifris and the *Vita Sancti David* of Rhygyfarch were compiled during
the late 11th cent.   Emanuel's position that the preface clauses *Codocus qui et Sophias*
and *David qui et Dewi,* respectively, refer to a double form of name for each saint,
Cadog-Sophias and David-Dewi.

[9.10.4]   Evans, D(avid) Ellis. (1964).   Some Celtic personal names in the *Commentaries
on the Gallic War. Bulletin of the Board of Celtic Studies, 21,* 1-17. Refs.
Extensive examination of the backgrounds of 6 names mentioned in Caesar's book:
Mandubracius, Adiatunnus, Andocumborius, Catuvolcus, Correus, and Voccionis.

[9.10.5]   Evans, D(avid) Ellis. (1968-71).   Nomina Celtica I: Catamantaaloedis,
Docnimarus, Satigenus. *Études Celtiques, 12,* 195-200. Refs.
Comment on these names as possibly of Celtic origin.   Suggested meanings,
Catamantaloedis, "he who wears the cloak of battle"; Docnimarus, "he whose lot is
great." The meaning for Satigenus is not clear.

[9.10.6] Fowkes, Robert A. (1988). Features of Welsh and British Celtic onomastics. *Names, 36,* 143-149. Refs.
Discussion of 7 prominent names: Tudur, Llewelyn, Lloyd, Vaughn, Coch, Maredudd, and Rhys in terms of spellings, pronunciation, meaning, and usage.

[9.10.7] Hamp, Eric P. (1954-55). Viviane or Niniane--A comment from the Keltic side. *Romance Philology, 8,* 81. Refs.
Disagrees with Nitze [9.17.6.23] that Niannon < Riannon.

[9.10.8] Jackson, Kenneth (H). (1960). The St. Ninian's Isle inscription, a re-appraisal. *Antiquity, 34,* 38-42. Refs. Figs.
Reaction to T. J. Brown. After extensive analysis concludes that the inscription resadfilispusscio should be interpreted to read: [the property of] Resad son of Spusscio.

[9.10.9] MacAlister, R. A. S. (1922). Notes on some early Welsh inscriptions. *Archaeologia Cambrensis, 2,* 198-219. Refs. Illus.
Examination and comment on 20+ inscriptions in South Wales. Names are involved.

[9.10.10] O'Brien, M. A. (1956). Etymologies and notes--Midir. *Celtica, 3,* 173-174. Refs.
Analysis concludes that names such as Midir, Cathair, Brenainn, Conaing, and Patraic are indeclinable names, probably borrowed from some other language.

[9.10.11] Roberts, Brynley F. (1973). The treatment of personal names in the early Welsh versions of *Historia Regum Britanniae. Bulletin of the Board of Celtic Studies, 25,* 274-289. Refs.
Discussion with 4 lists of names showing how some names were kept in the original form (example, Aaron), but many others were altered, example, Ambrosius (Emreys), Aballac (Avallach), and Malim (Mael).

[9.10.12] Wilson, P. A. (1976-77). St. Ninian--An onomastic note. *Transactions of the Dumfriesshire & Galloway Natural History & Antiquarian Society, 3rd Series, 52,* 167-168.
Comment on various spellings of the saint's name.

9.11. ETHNIC NAMES: *Central American*

[9.11.1] Kelley, David H. (1962). Glyphic evidence for a dynastic sequence at Quirigua, Guatemala. *American Antiquity, 27,* 323-335. Refs. Illus.
Presentation of extensive data (glyphs), discussion, and analysis of names in the Quirigua inscriptions in the Maya script.

[9.11.2] Wipf, Karl A. (1967). MesoAmerican Religions: Contemporary Cultures. In Mircea Eliade (Ed.), *The encyclopedia of religion, Vol.9,* 428-436. Refs. New York: Macmillan; London: Collier Macmillan.
On p. 434 there is a ref. to a custom (now dying out) of the Maya & Chiapas giving the child 2 names, 1 Spanish, the other Indian. The Indian name is the real one and an enemy who knows it can do harm.

9.12. ETHNIC NAMES: *Chinese*

[9.12.1] Arlington, L. C. (1923) The Chinese female names. *Chinese Journal of Science & Arts, 1,* 316-325. Table.
Describes different types of female 1st names with many examples. Attention to Fukien and Canton. Table has approx. 65 names with spelling in English and Chinese meaning, and comments. [The article mentions Part 2 as "forthcoming," but in spite of searches, it was not found].

[9.12.2] Bin, Zhu and Millward, Celia. (1987). Personal names in Chinese. *Names, 35,* 8-21. Refs.
Comprehensive description of Chinese naming practices. Surnames have a very long history in China but there are only 930 surnames in current use. One surname (Zhang) is the most common and is held by 70 million people. First and nicknames also described.

[9.12.3] Chao, Yuen Ren. (1976). Chinese terms of address. In *Aspects of Chinese sociolinguistics--Essays by Yuen Ren Chao*, (Anwar S. Dil, Ed.). Refs. Tables. Figs. Stanford, CA: Stanford University Press, 416p. Refs.
Pp. 309-313 deal with forms of address. Pp. 314 describe the types of Chinese name: surname, milk name [baby-name], school name, formal name, and appellation. Examples given. Titles also discussed.

[9.12.4] Chen, Kuang-Ho, & Cavalli-Sforza, L. L. (1983). Surnames in Taiwan: Interpretations based on geography and history. *HumBio, 55,* 367-374. Refs(pp. 397-407). Figs.
Description and analysis of census surname data on isonomic aspects. Results indicate the effects of colonization and major internal migrations.

[9.12.5] Eberhard, Wolfram. (1970). *Studies in Chinese folklore and related essays. Indiana University Folklore Institute Monograph Series, Vol. 23,* Bloomington: Indiana University Center for the Language Sciences, 329p.
Chap. 18, pp. 217-222, (refs. pp. 278-280) is devoted to modern Chinese nicknames and has many examples. 7 types of nickname were identified referring to: (1) animals (erh kou-tse, "dog number 2"), nature objects, (huo huo-shan, "active volcano"), (3) man-made objects (fan-t'ungm "food-barrel"), (4) anatomy (p'i-pao ku, "leatherbag bone"), (5) prominent figures (Yul Brinner), (6) social roles (shih-mu, "teacher's wife"), and (7) personal traits (lien-huan p'i, "chain farter").

[9.12.6] Grafflin, D. (1983). The onomastics of medieval South China: Patterned naming in the Lang-yeh and T'ai-yuan Wang. *Journal of the American Oriental Society, 103,* 383-398. Refs. Exhibits.
Critical detailed examination of the "names found in the two major Chinese lineages during the early modern middle ages reveals a complexity of patterns." Gives a formal description.

[9.12.7] Kingston, Maxine Hong. (1977). *The woman warrior: Memories of a girlhood among ghosts.* New York: Knopf, 209p.
Pp. 1-16 describe the tragic story of the author's aunt in rural China who had a child by a man not her husband. The local villagers wrecked the house in which the unfortunate woman was living with her family. The aunt committed suicide by drowning with the child in the well. Her name was never mentioned again.

[9.12.8] Kristof, Nicholas D. (1990, Nov. 30). China's babies: Better elegant than 'Red.' *New York Times*, pp. A1;A9.

Shift in names that parents give their children to more cultured or cosmopolitan (Yayun, "Asian Games"; Xiu, "Elegant"). Older names include: Jianguo ("Build-the-Country") and Chaoying ("Surpass England").

[9.12.9] Lip, Evelyn. (1988). *Choosing auspicious Chinese names*. Singapore: Times Books International, 168p. Refs. Tables.
Systematic description and explanation of Chinese names. Topics include: history of Chinese naming, importance of a name, generation names, choice of a name, *yin* and *yang* of names, Chinese equivalents of Western names, and Chinese names. Extensive lists of names in different categories.

[9.12.10] Louie, Emma Woo. (1987). History and sources of Chinese American family names. *Publications of the North Central Name Society,* No. 2, 83-98.
Background on Chinese surnames in the United States and in China. There are about 400 Chinese surnames in the US but with 1000 spelling variants. Regardless of the spelling in English, the spelling of the name in Chinese characters remains the same. A Chinese wife in the US may or may not use her husband's surname. Many examples throughout.

[9.12.11] Louie, Emma Woo. (1991). Name style and structure of Chinese-American personal names. *Names, 39,* 225-237. Refs.
Description of 10 name styles used by Chinese-Americans. These styles involve position of the surname (1st or last), hyphenated names, combinations of American and Chinese names, and use of initials. Examples.

[9.12.12] Lu Zhongti with Millward, Celia. (1989). Chinese given names since the Cultural Revolution. *Names, 37,* 265-280. Refs. Tables.
4 groups of Chinese students born in 1966, 1973, 1979, and 1981 show "great differences between the names of those born early in the Cultural Revolution and those born later. The investigation also reveals differences between names for males and females...and a recent trend toward one-character given names."

[9.12.13] Moore, Robert L. (1993). Nicknames in urban China: A two-tiered model. *Names, 41,* 67-86. Refs.
Suggests 2 levels of nickname. One level includes hypocoristic names like Bill (for William) and the affectionate form Billy. The other level includes those names usually conferred by the peer group, as, Daaih-maau ("Big Cat"). Systematic examination of several types of nickname. Cross-cultural comparisons. Examples.

[9.12.14] Serruys, Henry. (1958). Some types of names adopted by the Mongolians during the Yuan & the early Ming periods. *Monumenta Serica* [Catholic University of Nagoya, Japan], *17,* 353-360. Refs.
Many Mongols adopted Chinese names. Many of the names were Buddhist or had a Buddhist link. The most common ended in *-nu* = "slave." Among other types of names described are animal names and Islamic names. Examples given.

[9.12.15] Sharman, Lyon. (1934;1968). Sun Yat-sen: His life and meaning. Stanford, CA: Stanford University Press, 420p. Refs. (Originally published in 1934 by John Day).
The biography of Sun Yat-sen shows that he was known by several names and aliases. Among these were Tai Chu (p. 12), Sun Tai Tseung (p. 22), Sun Wen (p. 45), Nakayama (p. 66), and Hayoshi.

[9.12.16] Sung, Margaret M. Y. (1981). Chinese personal naming. *Journal of the Chinese Language Teachers Association, 16,* 67-90b. Refs.
Systematic and comprehensive Topics include: surnames, milknames, 1st names (12 types), courtesy names, appellations, aliases and pseudonyms, posthumous names, name

taboos, name changes, and women's names. "The underlying significance of Chinese personal names reveals beliefs in spirits, culture-oriented desires and roles as men and women in a patrilineal society." Many examples.

[9.12.17] Watson, James L. (1976). Chattel slavery in Chinese peasant society: A comparative analysis. *Ethnology, 15,* 361-375. Refs.
Pp. 362-368 describe a village in the New Territories of Hong Kong and practices of naming slaves, including nicknames and surnames.

[9.12.18] Watson, Rubie S. (1986). The named and the nameless: Gender and person in Chinese Society. *American Ethnologist, 13,* 619-631.Refs.
Description of naming practices in Chinese society based upon a rural Hong Kong village. Men can have many names (birth, school name, nickname, marriage name, courtesy name, and posthumous name) to define their identity; women have fewer names and lose these (and their identity). Examples.

[9.12.19] Wong, J. S. (1960, May). How to pick a Chinese name. *Holiday,* pp. 36; 38-39.
Brief general description of Chinese naming practices. The Chinese have several types of name: surname, milk name [baby-name], school name, marriage name, and business name. Names other than the surname are chosen for meaning. Author describes how she chose her daughter's name.

[9.12.20] Wu, Ching-chao. (1927). The Chinese family: Organization, names, and kinship terms. *American Anthropologist, 29,* 316-325. Refs.
Brief description of the 8 possible names that a Chinese may have: (1) milk name, (2) school name or genealogical name, (3) Tze name taken about the age of 20, (4) Hao "style" name, (5) Pieh Hao, another type of style name, (6) official title as name, (7) native district as name, and (8) posthumous title.

[9.12.21] Yang, Martin C. (1945). *A Chinese village: Taitou, Shantung Province.* New York: Columbia University Press, 275p.
Pp. 68-72 give information on forms of address. Pp. 124-125 briefly describe naming of a new-born child. Names show expectations. Examples, for boys: Lo ("happiness"), Kwei ("highness"); for girls: Ch'in ("diligence"), Sheng ("thrift"). Sometimes girls (but not boys) are given derogatory names such as Hsia ("little too-many"). Approx. 30 examples

[9.12.22] Yutang, Lin. (1935). *My country and my people.* New York: Reynal & Hitchcock, 382p.
Appendix II, p. 366, has a brief summary on the spelling and pronunciation of Chinese names.

9.12.1. ETHNIC NAMES: *Chinese: Surnames*

[9.12.1.1] Eberhard, Wolfram. (1955). The origin of the commoners in Ancient Tun-Huang. *Sinologica, 4,* 141-155. Refs.
Tun-huang is in northwest China. Evaluation of the ethnic makeup of the surnames of commoners and soldiers during the period 100 BC-1000 AD. Analysis shows origins to be from different sources: Chinese, Tibetan, & Sogdian. Extensive comment on some Sogdian names including Shih, Wen and others.

[9.12.1.2] Jordan, David K. (1972). *Gods, ghosts, and ancestors:The folk religion of a Taiwanese village.* Berkeley: University of California Press, 197p. Refs. Photo.

Bao-an is the pseudonym of this village near Hiskang,north of Tainan on Taiwan. Pp. 12-26 describe how surnames are important in social groups. A single surname tends to dominate in a village as in this one where the surname Guo was held by 164 out of 227 households (72%).

[9.12.1.3] Kang-hu, Kiang. (1934; 1977). *On Chinese studies*. Shanghai: Commercial Press, 403p.
Pp. 126-144 give a systematic presentation of the various types of Chinese names. Examples in English and Chinese characters. Description of 18 types of surname including: political districts (examples, Hung, Shen); directions (examples, Tung-shiang, Hsi-men); and occupations (examples Wu, "magician'; T'u, "butcher").

[9.12.1.4] Louie, Emma Woo. (1991). Surnames as clues to family history. In *Chinese America: History and perspectives*. San Francisco: Chinese Historical Society of America and Asian American Studies Department, San Francisco State University. Refs.
Description of the characteristics of the Chinese language. Explains that an ideograph may be pronounced differently in different Chinese dialects. Further, the same ideograph transliterated into English in the US may vary considerably according to the dialect, i.e., the name Chen in the Mandarin dialect has the same ideograph as Zung in the Shanghai dialect. Other aspects discussed include: spelling of names, changes of name, new patronymics, and monosyllabic 1st names.

[9.12.1.5] Ruofu, Du. (1986). Surnames in China. *Journal of Chinese Linguistics, 14*, 317-327. Refs. (All in Chinese).
Description of the complexities of Chinese names. Most surnames have their origin in ancient times. Among the factors involved with the formation of surnames are: dynasty, place of residence, occupation, and ethnic origin. Only 30 of 55 national minorities in China have surnames.

[9.12.1.6] Wren, Christopher S. (1984, Dec. 9). A problem for the Chinese: Millions of namesakes. *New York Times*, A20.
China has a limited number of surnames. In Shanghai there are only 408 surnames. Most common are Zhang, Wang, Liu, and Li. There is so much duplication of 1st and surnames that nicknames such as Old, Big, and Long-Haired are used.

9.13. ETHNIC NAMES: *Classical Greek*

[9.13.1] Brunner, Theodore F. (1988). The Nemea Akrotatos graffiti: Once again. *Onomata, 12*, 122-125. Refs. Greek abstract.
After evaluation of interpretations of others regarding graffiti found in 1978, concludes there were actually 3 writers: (1) an athlete who just wrote his name, (2) another athlete who wrote "Akratos is handsome", and (3) a person wrote "sez who?"

[9.13.2] Christidis, Tassos. (1972). Further remarks on A-TE-MI-TO and A-TI-MI-TE. *Kadmos, 11*, 125-128. Refs.
Challenges the view of Sourvinou [13.11] who stated that the Mycenean for *a-te-mite* = Artemitos was not probable.

[9.13.3] Develin, R. (1986). Laispodias Andronymios. *Journal of Hellenic Studies, 106*, 184. Refs.
Discussion of the name of a 5th cent. general.

[9.13.4] Dow, Sterling. (1957). Lakhares: A rare Athenian name. *Classical Philology, 62*, 106-107. Refs.

Comment on rare Ancient Greek names in general and occurrences of the name Lakhares.

[9.13.5] Fraser, P. M. & Mathews, E. (1987). *A lexicon of Greek personal names.* Oxford University Press, Vol. 1, The Aegean Islands, Cyprus, Cyrenica. Oxford: Clarendon Press, 489p. Refs.
1st vol. of a projected 6-vol. series. A collection of Greek names derived from inscriptions, tombstones, papyri, & coins, and even amphora stamps. Each name entry indicates the location(s) observed, date, and reference sources. There are approx. 12,000 names listed. A single name (such as Alexander) may have references to as many as 242 individuals. Scholarly.

[9.13.6] Georgacas, Demetrius J. (1959). Greek terms for "flax,""linen," and their derivatives. *Dumbarton Oaks Papers, 13,* 253-269. Refs.
P. 259 has refs. to the surnames Linaras ("flax grower"), Linares (derived from Linari, "flax"), and Linarites, a nickname (meaning not given). All these are derived from the Greek word *linon* ("linen").

[9.13.7] Grace, Virginia R. (1953). The eponyms named on Rhodian amphora stamps. *Hesperia, 22,* 116-128. Refs.
Work is based upon a number of stamped amphora handles which bear eponyms [presumably the name of the maker of the contents] from approx. 2nd-1st cent. BC. Lists 173 eponyms, many previously known but with some additions as well. Has reference to plates which were not seen.

[9.13.8] Hamp, Eric P. (1968). The name of Demeter. *Minos, 9,* 198-204. Refs.
After examination of the work of several scholars on morphological and syntactic arguments concludes that Demeter was the mother of Poseidon.

[9.13.9] Harris, Edward M. (1986). The names of Aeschines' brothers-in-law. *American Journal of Philology, 107,* 99-102. Refs.
Discusses the use by Demosthenes of nicknames as insults. Other nicknames as insults also explained.

[9.13.10] Harrison, Cynthia M. (1982). Persian names on coins of northern Anatolia. *Journal of Near Eastern Studies, 41,* 181-194. Refs. Figs.
Analysis of 4 coins of the 4th cent. BC from Sinope, a Greek city on the Black Sea, leads to the conjecture that the Persians once ruled this area.

[9.13.11] Jones, C. P. (1988). A monument from Sinope. *Journal of Hellenic Studies, 108,* 193-194. Refs.
Sinope [now spelled Sinop] is in modern Turkey on the Black Sea, 200 miles NE of Ankara. Description and analysis of a Greek funerary inscription "Delphinios, son of Orgialeus."

[9.13.12] Morpugo-Davies, Anna. (1968). Thessalian patronymic adjectives. *Glotta, 46,* 85-106. Refs.
Critical examination of Greek patronymic adjectives in Thessaly between the 5th-2nd cents. BC.

[9.13.13] Ortego Villero, Begona. (1989-1990). Algunos antroponimos griegos de Tarento y Heraclea [Greek personal names of Tarentum and Heraclea]. *Onomata, 13,* 202-205. Refs. Spanish. English summary.
Examination of 16 personal names from these Greek colonies in Italy shows their originality leading to many pet names.

[9.13.14] Palmer, L(eonard). R(obert). (1969). *The interpretation of Mycenean Greek texts,* (2nd impression). Oxford: Clarendon Press, 496p. Refs.
Research based upon tablets found at this ancient city on the Greek Peloponnesus. Has a section on personal names (pp. 77-82). One practice noted is that of fathers giving sons half of their names, example, "Onasilosis of the son of Onasikupros." Shortened names and other practices also discussed.

[9.13.15] Pocock, L. G. (1967). The Odyssey, the Symplegades, and the name of Homer. *Studi Micenei ed Egeo-Anatolici, 4,* 92-104. Refs.
Pp. 103-104 give an explanation of the derivation of Homer's name. It was an appellation for "meeting" but not for any particular individual. It was for those who recited tales such as those from the *Iliad.*

[9.13.16] Reilly, Linda Collins. (1969). Greek slave names. *DissAbstrIntl, 30,* 2508A. (University Microfilms No. 69-21,107).
Collection of 3000+ slave names from Greek manumission inscriptions from 5th cent. BC to the 3rd cent. AD. List of the most common slave names.

[9.13.17] Reilly, Linda Collins. (1978). *Slaves in Ancient Greece: A prosopography from the manumission inscriptions.* Chicago: Ares, 171p. Refs.
Covers the period 5th cent. BC to the 3rd cent. AD. Lists 3000+ freed slaves with information on them including name, epigraphical source, ethnic designation or an indication that the slave was born in the master's house. In some cases there is other information such as profession.

[9.13.18] Robinson, D. M. & Fluck, E. J. (1979). *A study of the Greek love-names: Including a discussion of paederasty and a prosopogryphia.* New York: Arno Press, 204 p. (Reprint of the ed. published by the Johns Hopkins Press, Baltimore, which was issued as *No. 23* of the *Johns Hopkins University Studies in Archaeology.* Originally issued in part as E. J. Fluck's Ph. D. thesis under title: *A study of the Greek love-names)*
Listing with available information of the 283 names found on decorated vases with the names of the youthful lovers of the men of the day.

[9.13.19] Sarikakis, Theodore C. (1976). *The hoplite general in Athens: A prosopography.* Chicago: Ares, 95p. Refs.
The term *hoplite general* was used between the 3rd cent. BC until the 4th cent. AD. Originally a military title later became used for an administrator and the most important official in Athens. Approx. 120 hoplite generals are listed and described from data from inscriptions and other sources.

[9.13.20] Snowden, F. M., Jr. (1970). *Blacks in antiquity: Ethiopians in the Greco-Roman experience.* Cambridge, MA: Belknap Press of Harvard University Press, 364p. Refs.
Pp. 14-21 discuss about 40 names held in antiquity. These names are derived from several sources, physical characteristics; region of residence; Ethiopian, Egyptian, or Hebrew sources; and Greek or Latin.

[9.13.21] Stroud, Ronald S. (1972). Greek inscriptions at Corinth. *Hesperia, 41,* 198-217. Refs. Illus.
Examination of fragments of 19 inscriptions from the period before the destruction of Corinth in 146 BC. Speculation over inscriptions which appear to be names. Some not previously recorded.

[9.13.22] Zuntz, Gunther. (1951). On the etymology of the name Sappho. *Museum Helveticum, 8,* 12-35. Refs.

Uses a great many sources to trace the origin of the name to the god Sapon at Mt. Kasios in North Syria. Some references are as far back as the 14th cent. BC.

9.14. ETHNIC NAMES: *Classical Roman*

[9.14.1] Avery, Catherine B. (Ed.), & Johnson, Jotham (Ed. Consult.). (1962). *The New Century classical handbook*. New York: Appleton-Century-Crofts.
Pp. 755-756 give a description of basic naming practices in the classical period of Greece and Rome. Explains praenomen, nomen, and cognomen. Several examples.

[9.14.2] Bailey, D. R. Shackleton. (1988). *Onomasticon to Cicero's speeches*. Norman, OK: University of Oklahoma Press, 140p. Refs.
Introduced by a chapter on Roman naming, has an index to all the personal names in the speeches of Cicero. Includes persons, deities, cognomina, and miscellaneous names.

[9.14.3] Bloch, Raymond. (1991). Organization. [Greek & Roman Civilization]. *NewEncyBrit, 20,* 284.
Very brief entry. Describes types of name among Etruscan, Roman, and other peoples of ancient Italy. The types were: (1) individual name (praenomen), (2) family name or gentilitial names, and (3) nickname (*cognomen*), which appeared later. For more on Roman names, also in *EncyBrit,* See: Ladislav Zgusta [1.49].

[9.14.4] Broughton, T. Robert S. (1951). With the collaboration of Marcia L. Patterson. *The magistrates of the Roman Republic, Vol. 1, 590 B. C. - 100 B. C.* New York: American Philological Association, 588p. Refs.
Collection of information on individuals by name who held administrative titles during each year of the Roman Empire as drawn from a number of sources. Entries include the position, name, and available biographical information (with citations). Positions include: consuls, praetors, aediles, promagistrates of soldiers, and others.

[9.14.5] Broughton, T. Robert S. (1952). *The magistrates of the Roman Empire, Vol. 2, 99 B. C. - 31 B. C.* New York: American Philological Association, 648p. Refs.
Continues vol. 1 and also has an index. Appendix 1 lists those under whom coins were issued; Appendix 2 lists magistrates for whom dates are uncertain; Appendix 3 has a supplementary list of senators.

[9.14.6] Broughton, T. Robert S. (1960). *Supplement to the magistrates of the Roman Empire*. New York: American Philological Association, 89p. Refs.
Contains additions and corrections and bibliography additions to previous vols.

[9.14.7] Cameron, Alan. (1985). Polyonomy in the late Roman aristocracy: The case of Petronius Probus. *Journal of Roman Studies, 75,* 164-182. Refs.
Exhaustive examination from inscriptions and other evidence concludes that while Romans were known by different names, some identifications of Petronius Probus are 2 persons rather than 1.

[9.14.8] Douglas, A. E. (1958). Roman Cognomina. *Greece & Rome, 2nd Series, 5,* 62-66. Refs.
Disagrees with the notion that all Romans had 3 names, praenomen, nomen, and cognomen, example, Marcus Tullius Cicero. Gives several examples of individuals who did not have cognomens.

[9.14.9] Duff, A(rnold). M(ackay). (1928). *Freedmen in the early Roman empire*, reprinted with addenda. Oxford: Clarendon Press, 252p. Refs.

Information on Roman naming customs for slaves and freedmen as well as other Roman naming customs, passim.

[9.14.10] Garton, Charles. (1964). A republican mime-actress? *Classical Review, 78, New Series, 14,* 238-239. Refs.
At the time of Cicero, a woman named *Emphasis* worded a memorial stone for a functionary. Speculation from her name that she was a Greek slave who had been on the stage where actresses used names like Luxuria or Eros to be more acceptable.

[9.14.11] Georgacas, Demetrius J. (1969). Reviews of three books on Roman names. *Names, 17,* 91-106. Refs.
Extended reviews of Kajanto [87:8.17.1], [87:8.18.6], and [87:8.18.7].

[9.14.12] Gordon, Arthur E., & Gordon, Joyce S. (1951). Roman names and the consuls of AD 13. *American Journal of Philology, 72,* 283-292. Refs.
The name C. Silius, a consul, appears in standard works as C. Cilius A. Caecina Largus. The Gordons suggest that C. Silius was one person and that A. Caecina Largus was another.

[9.14.13] Johnston, Mary. (1957). *Roman Life.* Chicago: Scott, Foresman, 478p.
Pp. 115-125 describe the 3 types of Roman name: praenomen (1st name), nomen (name of the gens), and cognomen (branch of the gens) which could also include a nickname. Other types of name discussed include: names of women, slaves, freedmen, and naturalized citizens. Examples.

[9.14.14] Kajanto, Iiro. (1964). Peculiarities of Latin nomenclature in North Africa. *Philologus, 108,* 310-312. Refs.
Some Latin names such as Felix and Fortunatus were proportionately more popular in Africa than elsewhere. Suggests that the popularity of these and some other names was due to the influence of the underlying Punic substratum. Suffixes also discussed.

[9.14.15] Kajanto, Iiro. (1967). A note on the problem of the substratum. *Beiträge zur Namenforschung, 2,* 3-12. Refs.
Examination of 5 examples of names whose origin is questionable as to Latin or non-Latin concludes that "a cognomen should be judged to be both Latin and non-Latin, whereas only the unequivocal cases--like *Solitus* and *Tritus*--should be dismissed as non-Latin."

[9.14.16] Kajanto, Iiro. (1968). The significance of non-Latin cognomina. *Latomus, 27,* 517-534. Refs. Tables.
Draws on material from the 1st to the 3rd cents. in the Roman Empire to evaluate the non-Latin components of the cognomina of *ingenui, incerti,* and *liberti.* The *praetoriani, urbanicieni,* and *uigiles* also considered.

[9.14.17] Kajanto, Iiro. (1972). Women's praenomina reconsidered. *Arctos, Acta Philologica Fennica,* Nova Series, *7,* 13-30. Refs.
Roman women did not possess praenomina although evidence for praenomina for women outside of Rome is presented. Examples. Concludes that women were treated "more as a class, men more as individuals."

[9.14.18] Kajanto, Iiro. (1975). The emergence of the late single name system. *Colloques internationaux du Central National de la recherche scientifique, No. 564,* 421-430. Refs. German and French summaries.
Single names were not uncommon in early Christian times but the time of Constantine was the turning point for the disappearance of the gentilicium and rise of the single name

system. The success of Christianity was not the only factor. Others were: "(1) the devaluation of the gentilicium as a guarantee of Roman citizenship... (2) the large use of a limited number of gentilicia."

[9.14.19] Kajanto, Iiro. (1986). Notes on Christian names derived from Θεόσ (Theós). *Onomata, Revue Onomastique, 10,* 36-41. Refs. Greek summary.
Comment and discussion chiefly on 2 names Theodulus and Theotecnus during approx. the 4th cent.

[9.14.19A] Must, Gusta. (1957). The problem of the inscription on helmet B of Negau. *Harvard Studies in Classical Philology, 62,* 51-59. Refs.
Helmet B is 1 of 2 inscribed bronze helmets found with 24 others near Negau in Steiermark (Styra), Austria in 1811. The helmet B inscription is written in a North Etruscan alphabet right-to-left. The analysis concludes that the inscription dates from no later than the 3rd cent. BC and is written in Raetic with the name of its owner HariXas Titeiva, suggesting further that the 1st name was of Indo-European origin; the 2nd of Etruscan.

[9.14.20] Oliver, Revilo P. (1977). Praenomen of Tacitus. *American Journal of Philology, 98,* 64-70. Refs.
After examination of various views and evidence concludes that the praenomen of Tacitus was Publius.

[9.14.21] Powell, J. G. F. (1984). A note on the use of the Praenomen. *Classical Quarterly, 34,* 238-239. Refs.
Suggests that Romans who used the praenomen alone wanted to be up to date with the Greek fashion at the time of the 1st cent. AD and after.

[9.14.22] Solin, Heikki. (1987). Three Ciceronia. *Classical Quarterly, 37,* 521-523. Refs.
Comment and discussion of correct possible forms of these names which appear in Cicero: *Mundus istum M. En(nios), P. Tullioni Syro,* and *pupilli Bagienni.*

[9.14.23] Syme, Ronald. (1949). Personal names in *Annals I-VI* [Tacitus]. *Journal of Roman Studies, 39,* 6-18. Refs.
Exhaustive research on the background of 29 names whose spelling may cause problems. In some cases all known instances of the name are reported. Names discussed include: Aleteus, Alia, and Anteius.

[9.14.24] Syme, Ronald. (1958). Imperator Caesar: A study in nomenclature. *Historia* [Wiesbaden], *7,* 172-188. Refs.
Extensive scholarly treatment of how titles were acquired at the time of Caesar. Explanation of how Caesar and others incorporated titles in their names, as Imperator Caesar.

[9.14.25] Syme, Ronald. (1986). Three Ambivii. *Classical Quarterly, 36,* 271-276. Refs.
Comment and discussion on 3 men who bore the name Ambivius. Various spellings of the name and note that a number of women bore the related name Ambeivia.

[9.14.26] Thompson, L. A. (1969). Settler and native in the urban centres of Roman Africa. In L. A. Thompson & J. Ferguson (Eds.) *African classical antiquity* (pp. 132-181). Refs. Tables. Map. Ibadan, Nigeria: Ibadan University Press.
Extensive description with many examples of the naming practices in 18 Roman colonies in North Africa from the late 2nd cent. BC to early 2nd cent. AD. Lists of names based upon 100s of inscriptions. Analyses oriented toward African names.

[9.14.27] Thompson, L. A. (1971). Roman and native in the Tripolitanian cities in the early empire. *Libya in History Historical Conference, 16-23 March 1968,* (pp. 235-251). Benghazi, Libya: Faculty of Arts, University of Libya. Refs. Tables. Arabic summary. Review of names inscriptions from the 1st to the 2nd cent. AD gives a picture of the fusion of Roman settlers with North African natives. Table of data on 44 functionaries shows the majority being of Punico-Libyan stock. Data drawn from cities of Osea, Sabratha, & Lepcis.

[9.14.28] Weaver, P. R. C. (1964). *Cognomina Ingenva*: A note. *Classical Quarterly, 14,* 311-315. Refs.
Comment with explanation of disagreement with Duff [9.14.9] on names held by freedmen in Roman empire.

[9.14.29] Weaver, P. R. C. (1965). Irregular *Nomina of Imperial freedmen. Classical Quarterly, 15,* 323-369. Refs.
Discussion of the status of freedmen and slaves based upon names in 1st cent. inscriptions.

[9.14.30] Weaver, P. R. C. (1968). Family dating criteria, Proximi and "Provincia" in the Familia Caesaris. *Journal of Roman Studies, 58,* 110-123. Refs.
The main measure for dating Imperial freedmen is their full name which included the imperial gentilicium which fixes the date of the manumitting emperor. However, records for some freedmen show only the cognomen and this causes problems for dating. The value of the names of wives and children is evaluated.

[9.14.31] Wilkinson, Beryl Marie. (1961). The names of children in Roman imperial epitaphs: A study of the social conditions in the lower classes. *DissAbstrIntl, 22(11),* 2768. (University Microfilms No.61-6579) 204p.
Examination of 1500 epitaphs which contain the names of 2 parents and their child(ren) to evaluate conditions of social class of the slave, free, and free-born populations of Ancient Rome.

[9.14.32] Wiseman, T. P. (1965). (Ti)Tisienus Gallus. *Classical Review, 79, New Series, 15,* 19-20. Refs.
Reports on the name and variation during the 1st and 2nd cents. in Ancient Rome and North Africa. Speculation on whether Gallus was born Titisienus but shortened it to Tisienus.

9.15. ETHNIC NAMES: *Danish*

[9.15.1] Christensen, Birgit. (1986). Personnavnene i to oeslesvigske afgiftslister fra 1580 og c. 1583 [The personal names in two tax-lists from East Slesvig 1580 and c. 1583]. In Vibeke Dalberg & Gillian Fellows-Jensen (Eds.) *Mange baekke små: Til John Kousgard Sørensen på tresårsdagen,* 23-40. Copenhagen: Reitzels. Refs. Figs. Danish. English summary.
Hans is the most common name on both lists. The most significant difference is that the name *Asmus* (Low German form of Erasmus) occurs only in the Åbenrå district and not in the Haderslev.

[9.15.2] Fredericksen, Britta Olrik. (1992). Emund Slemas navn ogrygte [Emund Slema's name and reputation]. *StudAnthroScan, 10,* 5-24. Refs. Fig. Danish. English summary.
Relates to the subject of the article by Brylla [9.53.4.2] on the meaning of *slema*. After examination of several possibilities and origins, concludes that slema here refers to "one who imposes on hospitality."

[9.15.3] Jørgensen, Bent. (1986). Frit og bundet navnevalg [Free and limited choice of name]. In Vibeke Dalberg & Gillian Fellows-Jensen (Eds.) *Mange baekkesmå: Til John Kousgard Sorensen på tresårsdagen 6,* 12, 1985 (pp. 129-146). Copenhagen: Reitzels. Danish. English summary.
Compares the presumed"standard" naming custom (children after grandparents) with those of foundlings in 18th cent. records. Concludes that considerable variation in naming existed within families, that in the 17th and 18th cents., families did not feel obligated to follow "the laws of naming."

[9.15.4] Jørgensen, Bent. (1988). Et signalement af den danske almanaks navnerække [An account of the names in the Danish almanac]. *StudAnthroScan, 6,* 71-87. Refs. Danish. English summary.
There is a personal name for almost every day of the year in the official Danish almanac. Description of changes which began in 1699.

[9.15.5] Jørgenson, Bent. (1991) Fra Abel til Åse: Om fornavne i det kobenhavnske Vor Frue sogn [From Abel to Åse: On forenames in the Copenhagen parish of Our Lady]. *StudAnthroScan, 9,* 101-118. Refs. Danish. English summary.
Evaluation of the doctoral dissertation of Eva Villarsen Meldgaard which deals with 500 names from boys and 500 names from girls in periods from 1650 to the present. Discussion of naming children after relatives or idols, and the naming of twins.

[9.15.6] Kisbye, Torben. (1983). Oscar, Orla, Ossian, Selma, Malvina, Minona: Spor i dansk navneskik fra Ossiandigtningen og den svenske indvandring [Traces in Danish personal nomenclature from the influence of Ossian and the Swedish immigration]. *StudAnthroScan, 1,* 81-105. Refs. Tables. Danish. English summary.
These names have been attributed to the Gaelic poet Ossian. They appeared in translations by James Mcpherson in the 1760s. Only 2 names came from Macpherson/Ossian, Malvina and Minona. Oscar, Ossian, Selma came from Sweden; Orla from German.

[9.15.7] Kisbye, Torben. (1984). Bonum nomen est bonum omen: On the so-called idol names. *StudAnthroScan, 2,* 55-85. Refs. Danish summary.
Idol names are commemorative and/or inspirational 1st names. 10 types are listed including those taken from: the classical period, from the nobility by the working class, from royalty, statesmen, explorers, and entertainers. Many examples.

[9.15.8] Kisbye, Torben. (1988). John Jamieson > Hans Jacobsen: Helsingørskotternes navne--et eksempel på transponeret personnonmenklatur [John Jamieson > Hans Jacobsen: The names of the Elsinore Scots--an example of transposed personal nomenclature. *StudAnthroScan, 6,* 89-126. Refs. Danish. English summary.
Scottish immigrants came to Elsinore from the Middle Ages down to 18th cent. Most had their names either translated (Brown > Brun) or transposed (Andrew > Anders). Some names (Hans Jacobsen, Peter Willumsen) can be identified as Scottish in Danish name disguise. Comparison with later English immigrants.

[9.15.9] Kisbye, Torben. (1990). *Benny, Brian, Johnny* og *Dennis:* Om de engelske drengenavnes historie i Danmark som klassespecifkt faenomen [*Benny, Brian, Johnny* and *Dennis:* On the history of English boys' names in Denmark as a class specific phenomenon]. *StudAnthroScan, 8,* 73-117. Refs. Tables. Figs. Photo. Danish. English summary.
Comprehensive examination of the rise and fall of the status of English names in Denmark. Topics include: definition of English names, assumed influence of Shakespeare, and the availability of English literature in the 19th cent. and English pulp literature in cheap editions.

[9.15.10] Lisse, Christine. (1986). Ønslev, Ulslev og Egelev [Oenslev, Ulslev and Egelev]. In Vibeke Dalberg and Gillian Fellows-Jensen (Eds.) *Mange bække små* (pp. Refs.161-172). Copenhagen: Reitzels. Danish. English summary. Refs.
Background on these 3 13th cent. personal names ending in *-lev* from the Danish island of Falster.

[9.15.11] Meldgaard, Eva Villarsen. (1983). Modern dansk personnavneskik: Fornavne, mellemnavne, slægtsnavne [Modern Danish personal names: Forenames, middle names, surnames]. *StudAnthroScan, 1,* 107-122. Refs. Tables. Danish. English summary.
Data based in part on lists from the 1970s shows there were 19,000 different boys' names; 20,000 different girls' names. Tables show the top 25 for boys and for girls. There are 85,000 different surnames in Denmark but 64% of the population is included in the 50 most common. Middle names are increasing in popularity.

[9.15.12] Meldgaard, Eva Villarsen. (1984). De danske slægtsnavnes historie i nyere tid [The history of Danish surnames since 1526]. *StudAnthroScan, 2,* 39-53. Refs. Fig.
1970 data show that 2/3 of the population have the 50 most common surnames. This is the result of laws which people misunderstood or were unaware of. Surveys history of surnames among the nobility, middle classes, and peasants, with special attention on the peasants.

[9.15.13] Meldgaard, Eva Villarsen. (1989). På sporet af Erasmus [On the track of Erasmus]. *In Studia Onomastica: Festschrift till Thorsten Andersson den 23 Februari 1989,pp.* 223-230. Refs. Swedish. English summary. Stockholm: Almqvist & Wiksell.
Attempts to explain the great popularity of the name *Rasmus* on the island of Funen, Denmark while it was not that popular elsewhere.

[9.15.14] Meldgaard, Eva Villarsen. (1992). Dobbeltnavnets terminologi [Double-name terminology]. *StudAnthroScan, 10,* 151-160. Refs. Danish. English summary.
There is difficulty with proper terms for individuals having more than 1 forename. A pair-name is 2 or more names more or less haphazardly combined; a double name has been defined as a combination of 2 given names where the whole combination is used when addressing the bearer and where the whole combination has a single word stress (Inga Lisa,Karl-Erik). "Multiple name combination" is clumsy. Conclusion: *double name* is the best term for all.

[9.15.15] Nielsen, Karl Martin. (1987). Patronymer og selvros [Patronymics and self-commendation]. *StudAnthroScan, 5,* 5-17. Refs.Photo. Danish. English summary.
Extended evaluation of John Kousgård Sørensen's *Patronymer i Danmark 1. Runetid of middelalder* [Patronymics in Denmark 1. The runic period and the Middle Ages], 1984. Sørenson's interpretation of 430 runic inscriptions that have patronymics is that they are expressions of favorable evaluation either for the deceased or the man erecting the stone. Nielsen disagrees with this.

[9.15.16] Nielsen, Karl Martin. (1988). Runedansk akk. aumata [Runic Danish acc. *aumata]. StudAnthroScan, 6,* 5-10. Refs. Danish. English summary.
Discussion on the derivation of this name found on a runic inscription. Various possibilities considered.

[9.15.17] Söndergaard, Georg. (1986). Egnskarakteristiske slægtsnavne i Danmark [Danish names with local associations]. *StudAnthroScan, 4,* 103-123. Refs. Tables. Danish. English summary.
"The problem concerned has to do with surnames that are associated with particular parts of a country....A corpus of old bynames used by country people on the islands of Lolland and Falster" shows that a group of these names has survived to the current day.

[9.15.18] Søndergaard, Georg. (1990). Computer data bank of Danish names. *Names, 38*, 21-30. Refs. Table. Maps.
Description of the Danish Central Civil Register which has data on 6.5 million people who have lived there since 1968. Data include names, years of birth, and places of residence and makes it possible to show geographical distribution of names. Maps show the distributions for Knud, a 1st name, and Hansen, a surname.

[9.15.19] Vogt, Susanne. (1991). Mødrene slægtsnavn brugt som førstefornavn i dansk adel [The employment of a mother's surname as first forename among the Danish nobility]. *StudAnthroScan, 9*, 61-99. Refs. Tables. Fig. Photo. Danish. English summary.
The mother's surname as a 1st forename can be traced to 1450 and ceased in 1671. "The present survey is based on all the genealogical trees recorded in all hitherto published volumes of *Danmarks Adels Aarbog* [The Yearbook of the Danish Nobility]. Most of these names have not survived. The exception is *Flemming*. Others are Hak and Manderup.

[9.15.20] Weise, Lis. (1989). Mine, *Dine* og *Sine* Kvindenavne på *-ine* [Mine, Dine and Sine: Girls' names in *-ine*. In *Studia Onomastica: Festschrift till Thorsten Andersson den 23 Februari 1989*, pp. 415-425. Refs. Swedish. English summary. Stockholm: Almqvist & Wiksell.
Female 1st names with these suffixes were derived from male names and were popular in Denmark from 1835 to 1910. "The only names to survive in Denmark are the secondary suffixes functioning as girls' names which have been popular since the 1960s." Extensive data presented from government records.

9.16. ETHNIC NAMES: *Dutch*

[9.16.1] Droege, Geart Brueckner. (1964). Personal names contained in place names: German personal names in Middle Dutch place names of Bergen (French Flanders), 1389-1400. *Dissertation Abstracts, 26*, 2198.
19 of 24 Middle Dutch placenames contain Germanic personal names. Included are: Arembouds Capple, Bambeike, and Bullizele.

[9.16.2] Meertens, P. J. (1971). The repertory of Dutch family names. *Onoma, 16*, 149-153. Refs.
Description of the inventory of Dutch surnames based upon the census of 1947 in 15 vols. There is a vol. for each province and the 3 largest cities + a final vol. of a general nature. 8 vols completed at time of article.

[9.16.3] Schoonheim, Tanneke. (1990). Authochthonous names in the *Dictionary of Early Middle Dutch. Proceedings of the 17th ICOS, Helsinki, 13-18 Aug. 1990, 2*, 332-339. Refs. Map.
The *Dictionary* records 13th cent. Early Middle Dutch and includes 1st names and surnames. Nicholas is an example of a 1st name that occurs 1378 times in mss. in the Dictionary with 12 different entries including: clai, claikin, colin, niclais with the main entry being nicholaus.

9.17. ETHNIC NAMES: *English*

[9.17.1] Anscombe, Alfred. (1912-13). The name of Sir Lancelot du Lake. *Celtic Review, 8*, 365-366.

Discusses various conjectures regarding the source of the name. Concludes that Lancelot is a dithematic name of Germanic origin *Lance-loth* < *Wlanci-loth* and means "cloak-pride."

[9.17.2] Arngart, O. (1947-1948). Some aspects of the relation between the English & the Danish elements in the Danelaw. *Studia Neophilologica, 20,* 73-87.
Lists 11 names from the Old English period which are of hybrid formation, example, Gunnsige < Old Norse *Gunne-* + Old English *-sige*. Other names are also mentioned which suggest the existence of a custom of mixed naming. Attention also to names ending in *-thorp* and *-by*.

[9.17.3] Bodkin, E. H. (1960). Names and arms clauses. [Conveyancing]. *Solicitor* [London], *27,* 196-197. Refs.
A names and arms clause is usually interpreted as meaning that a beneficiary in a will is required to assume the name (arms) of the testator. Discussion of the difficulties of enforcing such provisions today.

[9.17.4] Bracey, Gerald W. (1985, Jan.). What's in a name? [Research]. *Phi Delta Kappan, 66,* pp. 374-375. Refs. Drawing.
Report on Erwin & Calev [87:41.15] which indicates that children with desirable names had higher grades.

[9.17.5] Buckatzsch, E. J. (1951). The constancy of local populations and migration in England before 1800. *Population Studies, 5,* 62-69. Refs. Tables.
Reports studies showing how names from tax assessment lists, parish registers, and other sources can be used to study population constancy. Concludes that there was "considerable mobility in local populations in the south and east of England" mainly in rural areas in the 16th-17th cents.

[9.17.6] Chadwick, Hector Munro. (1959). Vortigern. In Hector M.Chadwick, Nora K. Chadwick et al., *Studies in Early British history* (pp. 21-33). Cambridge, England: University Press.
Brief mention of the meaning of the name, "overlord" (p. 27) of this early figure who ruled England c. 425.

[9.17.7] Chadwick, Nora K. (1959). A note on the name Vortigern. In Hector M. Chadwick, Nora K. Chadwick et al., *Studies in Early British history* (pp. 34-46). Cambridge, England: University Press.
Concerned with the role of this ruler. P. 45 has a passing comment on his name.

[9.17.8] Coleman, D. A. (1984). Marital choice and geographical mobility. *Symposia of the Society for the Study of Human Biology, 23,* 19-55. Refs. Tables. Figs.
Pp. 29-34 give evidence from surname analysis from parish registers from Suffolk as early as 1600 and other later registers from other places shows that previous scholars have underestimated the amount of English geographic mobility.

[9.17.9] Dudley, Donald Reynolds & Webster, Graham. (1962). *The rebellion of Boudicca.* London: Routledge & Kegan Paul, 165p.
Appendix II (p. 143) is on the name Boudicca and incorporates a note by K.H. Jackson. He states that the name should only have 1 'c' and that it comes from the Welsh *bouda* and the adjectival *-ico* ending.

[9.17.10] Fellows Jensen, Gillian. (1962). Some observations on Scandinavian personal names in English placenames. *Saga-Book, 16,* 67-71. Refs.
Discussion of the contribution of Scandinavian personal names to English placenames. Names cited include: *Astenabi, Astinole/Astin,* and *Asford.*

[9.17.11] Fellows-Jensen, Gillian. (1983). Anthroponymical specifics in place-names in *-bý* in the British Isles. *StudAnthroScan, 1,* 45-60. Refs. Map. Photo. Danish summary.
While directed to placenames, contains substantial coverage of by-names in the period 1086-1500 from Scandinavian, Norman, English, and possibly German sources.

[9.17.12] Gibson, Jeremy (Sumner Wycherley). (1989). *Unpublished personal name indexes in Record Offices and libraries in Great Britain,* 2nd ed. Baltimore: Genealogical Publishing, 40p.
Records the availability at 50 locations in Great Britain of approx. 800 collections involving names. Includes marriage records, apprentice records, freemason lists, groom lists, etc.

[9.17.13] Hair, P. E. H. (1976). Family and locality: An encouraging exercise in Herefordshire records. *Local Historian, 12,* 3-6. Refs.
Used the Lugger family, originally of Kingsland, near Leominster, Herefordshire to demonstrate place stability over time in the period 1380-1886.

[9.17.14] Johnston, R. J. (1971). Resistance to migration and the mover/stayer dichotomy: Aspects of kinship and population stability in an English rural area. *Geografiska Annaler, 53,* 16-27. Refs. Tables.
The site for the research was Nidderdale in the West Riding of Yorkshire. Concludes that people with more common surnames are less likely to move. 22 common surname groups (such as Ashby, Hullan, and Verity) in 21 districts were studied in the 1951-1961 period.

[9.17.15] Jones, Gwilym Peredur. (1973). Continuity and change in surnames in four northern parishes. *Cumberland & Westmorland Antiquarian & Archaeological Society Transactions, 73,* 143-147. Refs. Tables.
4 parishes (2 in Cumberland, 2 in Westmorland) were examined for population stability by surname analysis of parish registers at 3 periods in the 18th cent. Contrary to some priorheld beliefs, the results from surname analysis suggest there was considerable inflow and outflow of population at this time.

[9.17.16] Joslin, J(ohn) F(rancis). (1980). *Change of name,* (12th ed.), London: Oyez Publishing, 77p. Refs.
Description and discussion of English laws pertaining to change of name. In general, rules are similar to the US. One technical exception is that the change of the 1st name by a Christian is not possible except by an Act of Parliament, the bishop at confirmation, or at adoption (p. 5).

[9.17.17] Kellett-Smith, S. K. (1984). Early bailiwick names. In L. James Marr (Ed.) *Guernsey people* (pp. 219-245). Chichester, Sussex: Phillimore. Refs. Illus.
Marr's vol. is basically a biographical dictionary of 200 Guernsey people from the 16th cent. to recent times. The Kellett-Smith contribution based upon 5 13th-14th cent. sources in the Priaulx Library(Guernsey) lists 550 individuals for whom mention was made in legal records, examples, "Gaydon, John; killed by a fall of stones while working in a quarry." Another, "Oar, Peter; murdered by his wife Benedicta Choffyn.

[9.17.18] Light, John. (1983). Foundling names. *Genealogists' Magazine, 21,* 112-117. Refs. Tables.
Examination of the possible origins of 180+ foundling names of London parishes, 1740-1750. Some children were apparently named for the church or parish in which they were found; for example, Margarets were found at St. Margaret New Fish Street.

[9.17.19] Mastoris, S. N. (1985). A tax assessment of 1504 and the topography of early Tudor Nottingham. *Transactions of the Thoroton Society of Nottinghamshire, 89,* 37-56. Refs.
Lists approx. 90 individuals (only a few women included). Those listed: John Mapurley, Agnes Taverner, Agnes Caunt, and John Carre.

[9.17.20] Newman, David J. M., & Forrester, Colin D. I. G. (1986). The identification of social class by analysis of names. Genealogists' Magazine, 22, 9-11. Refs. Tables.
Response to Nash [9.17.3.13]. Description of a social index [in England] based upon the number of names an individual has. The more the number of names, the higher the social class.

[9.17.21] Patels are coming, The. (1976, Aug. 7). *Economist* [England], p. 56.
Lists the top 20 surnames in England and Wales in 1975. While 18 out of 20 of the 1853 names are on the same list, examination of the top 50 suggest that changes are coming.

[9.17.22] Patterson, Joan. (1980, Aug. 20). Name dropping. *Guardian* [England], p. 11.
Raises the question of why most English women continue to give up their birth names at marriage whereas a substantial proportion of American and German women do not.

[9.17.23] Pearce, Edward. (1979, Aug. 22). By George, the world's turned upside down. *Daily Telegraph* [London], p. 14.
Disagrees with trends in naming children Gary, Lee, Brent, Kirk, or Jimmy. Prefers old standbys such as George, William, Mary, or Margaret.

[9.17.24] Pelteret, David A. E. (1986). Two Old English lists of serfs. *Mediaeval Studies, 48,* 470-513. Refs. Table. Map.
The 1st list is from a 10th cent. ms. from the Ely Abbey estate of Hatfield in Herefordshire. The 2nd is from the 11th cent. from the Rochester Cathedral estate of Wouldham in Kent. Both lists give information on names of serfs at that time.

[9.17.25] Rhodes, Michael. (1987). Inscriptions on leather waste from Roman London. *Britannia, 18,* 173-181. Refs. Fig.
12 pieces of leather waste of unknown date but probably not later than mid-2nd cent. were found. 6 have legible names, 4 Latin, 2 Celtic. Examples of names are: Liber (Latin, "free") and Samia (Celtic) [meaning not given].

[9.17.26] Rowe, M. M., & Jackson, A. M. (Eds.). (1973). Exeter freemen: 1266-1967. *Devon & Cornwall Record Society, Extra Series, 1,* 462p. Refs. Index.
In medieval England, men had to be admitted to membership in society as freemen. Listing of 12,000 men by date of admission. Listings indicate date, 1st name and surname, and occupation. Example, in the Mayor's Court Book of 1703-1727 on Feb. 7, George Bennison, apprentice of Robert Daw, pewterer was admitted.

[9.17.27] Stone, Lawrence. (1977). *The family, sex and marriage in England 1500-1800.* New York: Harper & Row, 800p. Refs.
Pp. 329-330 show how spouses addressed one another in the 18th cent. (very formal by today's standards). P. 409 shows the tendency to name all children "even if it lived for a few hours or days." Children were also named for dead siblings. P. 668 shows the revival in the 1830s of wives referring to husbands as "Mr."

[9.17.28] Stone, O. M. (1963). Name worship and statutory interpretation in the law of wills. *Modern Law Review* [London], *26,* 652-659. Refs.

Deals with English decisions with regard to names and arms clauses (those clauses in wills which require the heir to change the original surname to a new surname, presumably so the name of that family would not die out). Comment on several fine points in some cases.

[9.17.29] Strathern, Marilyn. (1982). The place of kinship: Kin, class and village status in Elmdon, Essex. In Anthony P. Cohen (Ed.) *Belonging: Identity and social organisation in British rural cultures*. (pp. 72-100). St. John's Newfoundland: Institute of Social and Economic Research Papers No. 11. Refs. Fig.
Elmsdon is a North Essex village (pop. 320) whose people are all related. It is south of Cambridge toward London. Some description of their naming practices (pp. 80-81; pp. 86-87; 93-95) closely tied in with close relationships.

[9.17.30] W., M. M. (1960). Names and arms clauses. *Law Journal* [London], *110,* 599-600. Refs.
Recent legal history of names and arms clauses in England (wills requiring a beneficiary to change his/her surname or forfeit the right to an inheritance). While previously thought to be no longer valid, such clauses may appear to be legally sustainable if worded correctly.

[9.17.31] Waggoner, Walter H. (1960, Sept. 25). How's that again? Take an old English name of 12 letters and chances are half will be silent. *New York Times Magazine*, p. 41.
Comment on several British surnames such as, Holmes Sandys, and Marlborough which are pronounced as *homes, sands,* and *mawl-bra.*

[9.17.32] Williams, William Morgan. (1964). *The sociology of an English village: Gosforth*. London: Routledge & Kegan Paul, 246p. Refs.
Gosforth is a small village in Cumberland, Northwest England. Included in this sociological analysis dealing with class and kinship is information on the naming patterns and practices. Patterns of naming are similar from the 16th cent. to today. Forms of address also described.

[9.17.33] Wright, R. P., & Jackson, K. H. (1968). A late inscription from Wroxeter. *Antiquaries Journal, 48,* 296-300. Refs. Plate.
A tombstone in this ancient location in Shropshire appears to commemorate Cunorix. He is presumed to be one of the Irishmen who was settled in Wales by the Romans about 460-475.

[9.17.34] Yule, Valerie. (1979). Party names. *British Psychological Society Bulletin, 32,* 455-456. Refs.
Comment on the surname mix of Parliament in 1964 and 1979; also the political candidates in the elections of 1979, the use of titles, hyphenated names, and "non-English" names.

9.17.1. ETHNIC NAMES: *English: Address, Forms of*

[9.17.1.1] Brewer, W., & 7 others. (1953, Jan. 10). Christian names. [Correspondence]. *New Statesman & Nation, 45,* p. 41.
Brief statement in support of Raine [9.17.1.9].

[9.17.1.2] Brooke, Jocelyn. (1953, Jan. 10). Christian names. [Correspondence]. *New Statesman & Nation, 45,* p. 41.

Expression of agreement with Raine [9.17.1.9] in not accepting widespread use of 1st names. Also decries American practice in correspondence of using Dear John Smith as a salutation instead of Dear Mr. Smith.

[9.17.1.3] Fowler, Roger & Kress, Gunther. (1979). Critical linguistics. In Roger Fowler, Bob Hodge, Gunther Kress, & Tony Trew *Language and control* (pp. 185-213). Refs(pp. 220-222). London:Routledge & Kegan Paul.
Pp. 200-201 describe various naming conventions possible, such as, Gunther Kress, G. R. Kress, G. R. Kress, Esq.

[9.17.1.4] Fraser, G. S. (1953, Jan. 17). Christian names.[Correspondence]. *New Statesman & Nation, 45,* p. 67.
Response to Raine (1953) [9.17.1.9]. Willing to accept use of 1st names in some situations.

[9.17.1.5] Hale, Leslie. (1953, Jan. 24). Christian names. [Correspondence]. *New Statesman & Nation, 45,* p. 95.
Brief response to Raine [9.17.1.9].

[9.17.1.6] Hodge, Bob; Kress, Gunther; & Jones, Gareth. (1979). The ideology of middle management. In Roger Fowler, Bob Hodge, Gunther Kress, & Tony Trew *Language and Control* (pp. 81-93). Refs(pp. 81-93). London: Routledge & Kegan Paul.
Description of a case history of middle management ideology shows how people are addressed.

[9.17.1.7] Parkinson, C. Northcote. (1975, Christmas). Tom, Dick and Harry. *Illustrated London News*, pp. 59-60.
Traces the increasing practice of 1st-naming people in Britain (in 1975) to American influence before WW2 and specifically to Edward VIII who moved in American circles.

[9.17.1.8] Pollock, F. (1919). [Indian names]. *Law Quarterly Review* [London], *35,* 289.
Explains that in the English Law List "Khan" is not a surname but is equivalent to the title "Esquire" used in English-speaking countries.

[9.17.1.9] Raine, K. (1953). Christian names. [Correspondence]. *New Statesman & Nation, 45,* p. 14.
Objection to increasing use of 1st names by individuals not on close terms with the addressee. Does accept use of 1st name and last name as style of address in correspondence.

[9.17.1.10] Struggling young poet, A. (1953, Jan. 31). Christian names. [Correspondence]. *New Statesman & Nation, 45,* p. 122.
A light poetic response to Raine above.

[9.17.1.11] Swan, Michael. (1953, Jan. 24). Christian names. [Correspondence]. *New Statesman & Nation, 45,* p. 95.
Light response to Raine [9.17.1.9].

[9.17.1.12] Wallace, Madeleine L. (1953, Jan. 10). Christian names. [Correspondence] *New Statesman & Nation, 45,* p. 41.
Response to Raine [9.17.1.9]. Defends use of 1st names in address with strangers. Dislikes use of 1st name *and* surname.

[9.17.1.13] Woolf, Leonard. (1953, Jan. 31). Christian names. [Correspondence] New Statesman & Nation, 45, p. 122.

Defends Raine [9.17.1.9]. Explains that the trend of 1st-naming people came from entertainers and politicians.

9.17.2. ETHNIC NAMES: *English: Alias Names*

[9.17.2.1] Dawe, Philip N. (1961). Alias surnames. *Somerset & Dorset Notes & Queries, 28,* 13-15. Refs.
Explains that in England from the 16th cent., alias surnames were a way of preserving the birth name of the wife. Two examples.

[9.17.2.2] H., A. C. (1956). Alias. [Query]. *Scottish Genealogist, 3,* 22.
Queries on 3 aliases found in parish records between 1782 and 1809. One is "Fraser alias Tailor." For reply, See: D. W. [9.49.6].

[9.17.2.3] Leeson, Francis. (1968). Aliases. *Genealogists' Magazine, 15,* 594-599. Refs.
Description of several types of alias (female, adoptive, illegitimacy, distinguishing, status, disguising, and unknown) with examples from records of the 16th-19th cents. Queries about some names of unknown origin. See below.

[9.17.2.4] Oxer, O. E. (1973). A 16th century alias explained. *Genealogists' Magazine, 17,* 330. Refs.
Replying to one of the queries from Leeson above about the name *Oxer* explains that the name goes back to the 1580s where a man took the alias in anticipation of an inheritance (which did not materialize).

9.17.3. ETHNIC NAMES: *English: First Names*

[9.17.3.1] Caplan, N. (1965). Puritan names and the roots of nonconformity. *Congregational Historical Society Transactions* [England], *20,* 19-21. Refs.
Presents evidence that Puritan names such as Fly-fornication Richardson, The-peace-of-God Knight and Small-hope Biggs were bestowed by Nonconformists around the beginning of the 17th cent. demonstrating a link between Puritan sentiment and Nonconformism.

[9.17.3.2] Dawe, P(hilip) N. (1962). Christian name Izzot. *Somerset & Dorset Notes & Queries, 28,* 97-98. Refs.
Replying to a query on the origin of the name *Izzot* or *Izzat* quotes Weekley from *Jack and Jill* [Smith:552] on Isolda, that Izod is one of the variants. Suggests that Izzot/Izzat are from the same source.

[9.17.3.3] Dunn, F. I., & Deterding, Diana. (1978). "Diana", An early occurrence of the name. *Notes & Queries, 223(Dec.),* 552-553. Refs.
Gives sources for 3 13th cent. occurrences of the name in Lancashire.

[9.17.3.4] Franklin, Peter. (1986). Normans, saints, and politics: Forename-choice among fourteenth century Gloucestershire peasants. *Local Population Studies, No. 36(Spring),* 19-28. Refs.
The investigator used a manorial extent, tax assessment, and court rolls to sample 1st names at the Thornbury Manor. In the sampling, 6 1st names accounted for 85% of the males (John, William, Robert, Walter, Richard, and Thomas; 5 names accounted for 80% of the females (Agnes, Edith, Matilda, Alice, and Joan). Comparisons with other studies.

[9.17.3.5] Haden, H. Jack. (1972). Name this child...*Blackcountryman* [England], *5*, 59-60.
Analysis of children baptized at Oldswinford in 1753 and 1756. John, William, Thomas, and Joseph were among the top 5 for boys; Mary, Ann, and Elizabeth were among the top 4 for girls. Other names also listed and commented upon.

[9.17.3.6] Harris, Anne. (1977). Christian names in Solihull, Warwickshire, and Yardley, Worcestershire, 1540-1729. *Local Population Studies, No. 19 (Autumn)*, 28-33.
Analysis of 10,000+ baptismal names for boys and girls along with smaller samples from Rempstone, Nottinghamshire (East Midlands) and Pattingham, Staffordshire (East Midlands). Tabulation of the top frequencies. Comment on "rustic" or "vulgar" names, surnames as 1st names, regional names, and local variations.

[9.17.3.7] Jarvis, S(tanley) M(elville). (1979). *Discovering Christian names*. Aylesbury, Buckinghamshire: Shire, 64p. Refs.
Gives the meaning and background of about 1200 first names. Also lists the names of some prominent people bearing those names. Examples, Ada, "probably a shortened form of Adela, Byron's daughter."

[9.17.3.8] Layng, T. P. R. (1972). Matthew and Martha. *Genealogists' Magazine, 17*, 88.
Points out that in the 17th cent., "Many Cambridgeshire registers contain Matthew as a girl's name; several have Mathy or Mathie for people of either sex." Explanation offered that the "r" in Martha may have been dropped similar to the shift from Partridge to Patridge.

[9.17.3.9] Maidbury, Laurence. (1954). English Christian names in Latin. *Amateur Historian, 1*, 312-314. Refs.
Lists 200+ Latin equivalents for English names found in records before 1700. Thus, Drago = Drew, Aloysius = Lewis, Milo = Myles.

[9.17.3.10] Marshall, Arthur. (1978, Feb. 3). Name this child. [First Person]. *New Statesman* [London], p. 151.
Light approach to naming baby girls. Spoofs names of characters used by writers of youth novels.

[9.17.3.11] Moore, G. A. (1972). Biblical names in the Black Country. *Blackcountryman* [England], *5(1)*, 16.
Recounts approx. 40 Bible names encountered in the Black Country [England] including a Shadrach, Meshech, and an Abednego.

[9.17.3.12] Moyser, P. J. (1985). The choice of a Christian name: Commentary. *Genealogists' Magazine. 21*, 326-327. Refs.
Reacting to Nash [9.17.3.14] reports on frequencies of 1st names in the Moyser/Moiser family between 1883 and 1913. He found 14 Marys and 2 Mays in contrast to the proportions of Nash. Suggests that Nash's Mays were originally named Marys and later changed their names.

[9.17.3.13] Nash, Michael L. (1984). The choice of a Christian name. *Genealogists' Magazine, 21*, 275-280. Refs. Table.
Brief background history of popular names from the 12th cent. Mention of historical styles and influences on naming, especially that of royalty, authors, and more recently, entertainment figures.

[9.17.3.14] Nash, Michael L. (1985). Reply to Moyser. *Genealogists' Magazine, 21*, 327. Refs.

Appears to agree somewhat with comment of Moyser [9.17.3.12] on the explanation of the frequencies of Mary vs. May.

[9.17.3.15] Perring, Douglas. (1985). The choice of a Christian name: Commentary. *Genealogists' Magazine, 21*, 325-327. Refs. Table.
Reply to Nash [9.17.3.13]. Reports on the 5 most common names of boys and girls in the parish register of Rickling, Essex between 1600 and 1859.

[9.17.3.16] Reaney, P(ercy) H(ide). (1951). Notes on Christian names. *Notes & Queries, 196,* 199-200. Refs.
Reacting to Elizabeth Withycombe's Oxford dictionary of English Christian names, 2nd ed., (1949) (1st ed. [Smith:565], makes corrections and cites earlier examples for about 20 names including Sacheverell (traced to 1197).

[9.17.3.17] Rust, L. D. (1982). Re: James. [Note]. *Names, 30,* 56. Refs.
Suggests that the name *James* could have arrived in England through the work of E. W. B. Nicolson (*Pedigree of Jack and allied names* (1892) [Smith:649]), as a form of Jaime, Giammo, etc. as well as from the French form of Jacques.

[9.17.3.18] White, David. (1980, Apr. 3). Naming names in our social no-man's land. *New Society*, pp. 7-8. Illus.
Raises questions about the widespread use of 1st names in business and industry.

[9.17.3.19] Wood, Michael J. (1985). The choice of a Christian name: Commentary. *Genealogists' Magazine. 21,* 325-326. Refs. Table.
Comment in response to Nash [9.17.3.13]. Shows frequencies of 1st names of 480 residents of Dedham, Essex between 1601 and 1720. Among results he shows that several men and women had surnames as 1st names. Examples include Darby, Gibson, and Weston.

[9.17.3.20] Wulcko, Laurance M. (1948). Some Christian names from two country parish registers. *Essex Review, 58,* 96-98. Refs.
Response to a review by Rev. F. W. Austen (citation not given, apparently a review of Elizabeth Gidley Withycombe's *Oxford dictionary of English christian names*). Gives further information on a number of older names including Raynolde < Reginald, Arter (Arthur), Olimpa (Olympia), Jesabell (Jezabel). Some are in the *Oxford dictionary*, some are not.

9.17.4. ETHNIC NAMES: *English: Middle English Names*

[9.17.4.1] Bridgeman, C. G. O. (1919). Notes on the contents of the volume for 1916, 4. The five-hide unit in Staffordshire. *Staffordshire Record Society, Collections for a History of Staffordshire*, pp.134-144. Refs.
Listing of 100+ tenants of 5-hide units [a hide is a measure of land, enough for a family] at the time of Edward the Confessor and at Domesday, with the name of the community and its modern name. Example, In Nortone (now Norton-in-the-Moors), Godric et Elviet was the tenant at the time of Edward; Robert de Stafford at the time of Domesday.

[9.17.4.2] Clark, Cecily. (1987). A witness to post-Conquest English cultural patterns: The *liber vitae* of Thorney Abbey. In A. M. Simon-Vandenbergen *Studies in honour of René Derolez* (pp. 73-85). Ghent: Uitgever. Refs.
Thorney Abbey was in the northwest corner of Cambridgeshire. Analysis of the names shows influences of Old English, Latin, French, and Scandinavian.

[9.17.4.3] Clark, Cecily. (1987). *Willelmus Rex? vel alius Willelmus?. Nomina, 11,* 7-33. Refs.
Detailed examination of the trends in naming based upon 12th cent. records at Bury St. Edmonds. Extensive document citations. Extensive references. Many examples.

[9.17.4.4] Clark, Cecily & Owen, Dorothy. (1978). Lexicographical notes from King's Lynn. *Norfolk Archaeology, 37,* 56-69. Refs.
Draws on burgesses' names in the Pipe Roll for 1166 and 2 unpublished sources, the Trinity Gild of Lynn list (about the same time), and the confraternity list of the Hospital of St. Mary Magdalen at Gaywood (c.1300). Comments on 26 early medieval bynames. Names mentioned include Agnes le Candilwif ("female candle-merchant"), Simon Milnemus ("mouse in a mill"). The backgrounds of an additional 35 listed names are less clear.

[9.17.4.5] Ekwall, Eilert. (1956). *Studies on the population of medieval London.* Stockholm: Almqvist & Wiksell, 333p. Refs.
Focuses on Middle English between 1250 and 1350. 71p. of intro. material. Ekwall's thesis is that London during this period showed a Midland dialect. Extensive analysis of 1000s of individuals by name from documents of the period. Many entries give information on surname.

[9.17.4.6] Fellows Jensen, Gillian. (1973). The names of the Lincolnshire tenants of the Bishop of Lincoln, c. 1225. In *Acta Bibliothecae Regiae Stockholmiensis, 16,* 86-95. Refs. Systematic analysis of the tenants' names by origin (English or Scandinavian), by occupation, by byname, and by patronym. Many examples.

[9.17.4.7] Hjertstedt, Ingrid. (1987). *Middle English nicknames in the lay subsidy rolls for Warwickshire. Studia Anglistica Upsaliensis,* No. 63, 247p. Refs. Maps. Distributed by Almqvist & Wiksell, Stockholm.
Extensive systematic analysis of 43 medieval rolls shows 610 nicknames of various types [these "nicknames" are one source of modern surnames]. Entries for each name include dates, roll, various spellings, possible origin(s), and comments. Nicknames not previously recorded by other researchers are identified. Names newly identified include: Dapyr("dapper"), Chast ("chaste, virtuous"), and Longgeters ("long gaiters").

[9.17.4.8] Hunnisett, R. F. (1980). Problems of medieval English surnames. *Family History, 11,* 69-88. Refs.
Systematic explanation of how to make the best choice for standardization of a medieval name, nickname, name from a place, local feature, occupation, or patronym. Many examples.

[9.17.4.9] Insley, John. (1987). Some aspects of regional variation in Early Middle English personal nomenclature. *Leeds Studies in English, New Series, 18,* 183-199. Refs.
Deals with regional variations during the period between the 11th and 13th cents. along the northern border of Anglo-Saxon England. In this area, there were names of Anglian, Scandinavian, Gaelic, Britonic, and French origin. Many examples. Many documents referred to.

[9.17.4.10] Kristensson, Gillis. (1965). Another approach to Middle English dialectology. *English Studies, 46,* 138-166. Refs.
To investigate Middle English dialects in the regions of Lindsey, Kesteven, and Holland, Lincolnshire, the Lay Subsidy Roll of 1327 was studied. About 150 surnames cited with derivations and variations show shifts in pronunciation.

[9.17.4.11] Kristensson, Gillis. (1967). *A survey of Middle English dialects 1290-1350: The six northern counties and Lincolnshire.* Lund Studies in English. Lund: C. W. K. Gleerup, 299p. Refs. Maps.
"The purpose of this investigation has been to examine all place-names and surnames whose etymology can be determined beyond reasonable doubt." P. xiii. Data are based upon Lay Subsidy Rolls. Comprehensive analysis of many types of vowel and consonant formation in the names through various languages, all with citations.

[9.17.4.12] McClure, Peter. (1973). Lay subsidy rolls and dialect phonology. In *Otium et negotium: Studies in onomatology and library science presented to Olof von Feilitzen, Acta Bibliothecae Regiae Stockholmiensis, 16,* 188-194. Refs.
Reaction to Kristensson (1965, 1967) above who argued that early scribes were accurate and that spelling on the lay subsidy roles represented the local dialect. McClure's examination of Nottinghamshire subsidies of 1327 and 1332 and other records raises questions about scribal accuracy and inferences on the local dialect.

[9.17.4.13] McKinley, R(ichard) (Alexander). (1990/91). Medieval Latin translations of English personal bynames: Their value for surname history. *Nomina, 14,* 1-6. Refs.
Explanation of the types of Latin forms and their value in understanding the people involved. Many examples.

[9.17.4.14] Mills, A. D. (1963). Some Middle English occupational terms. *Notes & Queries, New Series, 10,* 249-257. Refs.
Gives a number of refs. on occupational terms perhaps not usually seen. Lists with comment approx. 75 terms that were used as surnames. Most are not in the *Oxford English Dictionary.* Included are: Calver, one who tends calves; Crockere, potter; and Mustarder, one who makes or sells mustard. Citations for 1st usages.

[9.17.4.15] Mills, A. D. (1966). Names of women in fourteenth century Dorset. *Dorset Natural History Proceedings, 88,* 203-206. Refs.
Names of 536 women property holders from the Dorset Lay Subsidy Roll of 1332. Has 45 different names. Most common names are Alice, Maud, Agnes, Christi(a)na, and Joan which account for more than half the women. Comment on all names.

[9.17.4.16] Reaney, P(ercy) H(ide). (1961). Onomasticon Essexiense: A proposal for the systematic collection of personal-names and surnames of Essex. *Essex Review, 61,* 133-142; 202-215. Refs.
Extensive background on the development of names in England with special reference to Essex. Tables of names frequencies from the 14th cent. 2nd part of review goes back to the 13th cent. and gives outline of types of surviving names from the 14th and 15th cents.

[9.17.4.17] Rumble, Alexander R. (1984). The status of written sources in English onomastics. *Nomina, 8,* 41-56.
Evaluation of the sources for names in documents before 1300. Consideration of variations due to errors, later copies, edited copies, and other factors. Many documents evaluated including the Great Domesday Book, Little Domesday Book, Exon Domesday Book, coins, and charters.

[9.17.4.18] Sundby, Bertil. (1952). Some Middle English occupational terms. *English Studies, 33,* 18-20. Refs.
Reports 12 Middle English terms (surnames) to be added to the work of Fransson [Smith:3204] and Thuresson [9.17.9.52]. Examples include: Baggesemer = "bagmaker," Fuyrbeter = "firebeater," i.e., one who stokes fires.

[9.17.4.19] Tait, James. (1916). The Domesday survey of Cheshire, Remains Historical & Literary Connected with the Palatine Counties of Lancaster & Chester, *Chatham Society, 75, New Series,* 1-258. Refs. Map.
Following a lengthy intro. shows the land holdings at the time of Domesday in Cheshire. Text of Domesday is in Latin and English. Names appear in Latin, English and sometimes, French. Thus Wulfric can appear as Uluric in Latin or Norman. Apparently, the French could not pronounce the initial "Wu." 340 names are listed, those of Scandinavian origin such as Segrid or Ulf are so indicated.

9.17.5. ETHNIC NAMES: *English: Nicknames*

[9.17.5.1] Ames, Jay. (1982). A Rose could be a Ruse or a Rouse. *Verbatim, 8(3),* 14-15.
Based upon experience with the British Armed Forces, shows how about 50 surnames give rise to widely used nicknames, examples, Millers are called"Dusty;" Woods, "Timber;" and Murphys, "Spud." Other nicknames are applied to bald men: "Shino" and "Helio-head." Ames himself (apparently red-headed) was called 40 more nicknames including: Ginger, Flame'ead, Krasny, and Beachball.

[9.17.5.2] Ames, Jay. (1985). British Armed Forces nicknames. *Bulletin of the Illinois Name Society, 3(4),* 14-16.
Describes about 30 surnames that gave rise to regular nicknames, i.e., Murphys called Spud (potatoes); Grays or Greys, Dolly (from a popular Boer War song); Bells, Dinger or Ding-Dong; and Carpenters, Chips or Chippy.

[9.17.5.3] Harré, Rom. (1975). The origins of social competence in a pluralist society. *Oxford Review of Education, 1,* 151-158. Refs.
Analysis of the role of nicknames in the social world of the child between 5 and 12. Maintains that in a social group such as a school class there is room (or slot) for only one "Piggy." Other types of nickname also discussed.

[9.17.5.4] Till, W. G. (1979). Black Country nicknames. *Blackcountryman* [England], *12(2),* 16-18.
The Black Country is the area west and northwest of Birmingham, England. Surnames are so common that nicknames are widely used. Approx. 40 nicknames are given including: Wicked Will Partridge, Brick End Wilkes, and Soft Water Jack Wilkes.

[9.17.5.5] Vines, Maxwell L. (1979). The theological struggle of Woodbine Willie. *Foundations, 22,* 261-272. Refs.
The Reverend Geoffrey Anketell Studdert-Kennedy was a British chaplain in WWI who later became well-known. The suggestion was that he got the name of Woodbine Billie from his service in France where he distributed Woodbine cigarettes to the troops with one haversack and copies of the New Testament with another.

9.17.6. ETHNIC NAMES: *English: Old English*

[9.17.6.1] Anscombe, Alfred. (1920). The name of Penda. *Notes & Queries, 12th Series, 6,* 246.
Penda was the name of a king of Mercia who ruled from 626-655. Concludes that Penda represents an Alemannic shift of B to P. Other evidence cited on Bardney, Partney, & Boothby.

[9.17.6.2] Astley, John. (1886). Anglo-Saxon names. *Notes & Queries, 7th Series, 1,* 209.

Raises question on the meaning of the prefix Os, whether < Anglo-Saxon Hus (house). [See replies by Buckley [9.17.6.6], Charnock [9.17.6.7], Krebs [9.17.6.16], Stevenson [9.17.6.30], and Taylor [9.17.6.33].

[9.17.6.3] Beeaff, Dianne Ebertt, (1978). Aelfraed and Haranfot: Anglo-Saxon personal names. *History Today, 28,* 688-690. Illus.
Concise description of English names from the 4th-13th cents. Many examples.

[9.17.6.4] Birch, Walter de Gray. (1899; 1964). *Index Saxonicus: An index to all the names of persons in Cartularium Saxonicum: A collection of charters relating to Anglo-Saxon history.* New York: Johnson Reprint, 140p. (Originally published by Phillimore in London in 1899).
An index of at least 10,000 entries from over 1350 charters and documents to 975 AD. Thus, for St. Dunstan of Canterbury, there are 60+ citations.

[9.17.6.5] Bolton, W. F. (1962). Background and meaning of Guthlac. *Journal of English & Germanic Philology, 61,* 595-603. Refs.
Discussion of the possible meaning of this saint's name. The 8th cent. monk Felix gave 2 connotations, the tribe of Guthlacingas and spiritual warfare.

[9.17.6.6] Buckley, W. E. (1886). Anglo-Saxon names. [Reply to Astley]. *Notes & Queries, 7th Series, 1,* 329-330. Refs.
Replying to Astley [9.17.6.2], traces the *Os* root (as in Oswald) to Old Norse as the general title prefixed to all the principal gods.

[9.17.6.7] Charnock, R(ichard) S(teven). (1886). Anglo-Saxon names (reply to Astley) [9.17.6.2]). *News & Queries, 7th Series, 1,* 331. Refs.
Reply to Astley [9.17.6.2]. Refers Astley to Wachter or Meidinger.

[9.17.6.8] Clark, C. (1987). English personal names ca. 650-1300: Some prosopographical bearings. *Medieval Prosopography, 8,* 31-60. Refs.
Scholarly, detailed analysis focusing on the language and cultural trends in English naming patterns during this period. Influences discussed include: Old English, Scandinavian, Continental German, and Norman.

[9.17.6.9] Cook, Albert S. (1891). The name Caedmon. *PMLA, 6,* 11-28. Refs.
Caedmon was a 7th cent. English poet described by Bede. Extensive collection of comment by various authorities including Palgrave on the possible Semitic origin of the name.

[9.17.6.10] Derolez, René. (1987). Anglo-Saxons in Rome. *Old English Newsletter, 21,* 36-37. Refs. Figs.
Description of 5 graffiti Runic inscriptions from the 7th Cent. thought to be possibly English. Figures show the graffiti.

[9.17.6.11] Dodgson, J(ohn). McN(eal). (1987). Domesday Book: Place-names and personal names. In J. C. Holt (Ed.), *Domesday Studies: Papers read at the Novocentenary Conference of the Royal Historical Society and the Institute of British Geographers, Winchester, 1986* (pp. 121-137). Woodbridge, Suffolk [England]: Boydell Press. Refs. Table. Map.
Discussion of 30-40 typical paleographical, literal confusions "due to miscopying and the clash of alternative alphabets."

[9.17.6.12] Dodgson, John McNeal. (1990). Notes on some bynames in Domesday Book. *Proceedings of the 16th ICOS, Laval University, Quebec, 1987, pp. 221-228. Refs.*

Tengvik's Old English Bynames [Smith:3195] is the standard work but needs to be updated by the work of von Feilitzen [Smith:1664], Reaney [9.17.9.40], and others.

[9.17.6.13] Ekwall, Eilert. (1951). *Two early London subsidy rolls: Edited with an introduction, commentaries, and indices of taxpayers.* Lund, Sweden: C. W. K. Gleerup, 402p. Refs. Plates.
The lay subsidies of 1292 and 1319 were occasional taxes on personal property. Chapter 4 (pp. 34-42) lists and analyzes font names and surnames, example, Perkin < Petrekyn, Maikin < Matthew. French influence is evident. Other information is found throughout the book.

[9.17.6.14] Gordon, E. V. (1935). Wealhpeow and related names. *Medium Aevum, 4,* 169-175. Refs.
Discussion concludes that Wealhpeow ("chosen" + "servant") is an old common Germanic name.

[9.17.6.15] Hughes, John P. (1954). On *H* for *R* in English proper names. Journal of English & Germanic Philology, 53, 601-612. Refs.
Hypothesizes that the "alternation of *H* and *R* between the 13th and the 16th cents. accounts for the modification and variations in names such as Rogers > Hodge and Hobson; Richard > Hick, Hicks, and Hixon. Many examples.

[9.17.6.16] Krebs, H. (1886). Anglo-Saxon names (reply to Astley [9.17.6.2]). *Notes & Queries, 7th Series, 1,* 331. Refs.
Relates *Os* root to gods such as Odin, Loki, and Thor, demi-gods, and deified heroes.

[9.17.6.17] Kristensson, Gillis. (1975). Databehandling av personnamnsmaterial [Computer-processed and stored Old and Middle English) personal names]. *SydOrtÅrss,* pp. 34-42. Refs. Swedish. English summary.
Description of computer data-base for 3 investigations: *Survey of Middle English Christian names and by-names, Survey of Middle English topographical terms,* and *A survey of Middle English dialects 1200-1350.*

[9.17.6.18] Kristensson, Gillis. (1975). Personal names or topographical terms in place-names? *Onoma, 19,* 459-467. Refs.
Asserts that to know about the origin of Old English place-names, more is needed to be known about topological terms and personal names of that period.

[9.17.6.19] Lehiste, Ilse. (1958). Names of Scandinavians in the *Anglo-Saxon Chronicle. PMLA, 73,* 6-22. Refs.
The Anglo-Saxon Chronicle (the main source of Anglo-Saxon history from the 7th to the 12th cent.) contains a number of Scandinavian names. Extensive comment and analysis made of about 50 of these names with special attention to spelling variations as reflective of the pronunciation at different periods.

[9.17.6.20] Lund, Niels. (1975). Personal names and place names: The persons and the places. *Onoma, 19,* 468-485. Refs.
Raises questions about whether personal names compounded with placename elements (*-thorp, -by*) in the Danelaw (Danish settlements in pre-Conquest Britain) represent those who originally founded the settlement. Concludes that it is more likely that they represent the names of others who at some stage might have owned the settlement.

[9.17.6.21] Murray, M. A. (1942). The divine king in Northumbria. *Folklore, 53,* 214-215.
Analysis of the deaths of 13 royal personages from Saxon Northumberland who had names beginning with Os ("God" or "Divine") including Osbald (Bold God), Osred

(Divine Word), and Oswy (Divine War). Concludes that the deaths of most of these can be explained by the theory of the sacrifice of the divine king.

[9.17.6.22] Myrc, John. (1902; 1969). Instructions for a parish priest. In Edward Peacock (Ed.), *Old English Text Society, Old Series, No. 209.* Reprinted by Greenwood in 1969.
Pp. 4-5 describe the normal baptism and naming ritual and also the procedure a midwife should follow in an emergency during delivery. Intro. to book refers to Mirk as author.

[9.17.6.23] Nitze, William A. (1953/54). An Arthurian crux: Viviane or Niniane? *Romance Philology, 7,* 326-333. Refs.
Evaluation of explanations of the origin of this name from the story of Merlin. One related interpretation is that Viviane is a scribal error of substituting U or V for N. Explores the possibility the name < Riannon or from Befind.

[9.17.6.24] Okasha, Elizabeth. (1971). *Hand-list of Anglo-Saxon non-runic inscriptions.* Cambridge [England]:Cambridge Univ. Press, 159p. Refs. Maps. Photos.
Reports on 158 inscriptions. The majority are from 700-1000 AD. 80% of the stones are from the North of England. There are also non-stone items such as brooches, rings, and coins but these appear to have been moved from place of origin. Entries include where the inscription was found, present location, inscription, translation, comment, and reference citations. Many names shown.

[9.17.6.25] Picton, J. A. (1886). Anglo-Saxon names. [Reply to Astley]. *Notes & Queries, 7th Series, 1,* 331. Refs.
Reply to Astley [9.17.6.2] on the origin of the prefix *-Os.* Cites several refs. and relates to Sanskrit "to shine, be radiant."

[9.17.6.26] Reaney, P(ercy) H(ide). (1952). Three unrecorded O. E. personal names of a late type (Feldwine, Pyttwine and Springwine). *Modern Language Review, 374.* Refs.
The 1st element of these names is that of a place.

[9.17.6.27] Reaney, P(ercy) H(ide). (1953). Notes on the survival of Old English personal names in Middle English. *Studier i Modern Spraktenskap, 18, 84-112. Refs.*
Listing of 300+ names with meaning and sources which appear to have died out in Old English and are recorded independently in Middle English. Included are Beowulf, Godmund, and Tidwine.

[9.17.6.28] Sisam, Kenneth. (1953). Anglo-Saxon royal genealogies. *Proceedings of the British Academy, 39,* 287-348. Refs.
Extensive historical review of documents and other materials. Shows names of rulers during the Old English period. Refs. to Beowulf.

[9.17.6.29] Skeat, Walter W. (1891, May 9). Anglo-Saxon names: The 'Liber Vitae.' *Notes & Queries, 7th Series, 11,* 376-377. Refs.
Replying to Taylor [9.17.6.33], points out that the *Liber Vitae* is included in The oldest English texts, edited by Dr. Sweet, published in 1885 by the Early English Text Society.

[9.17.6.30] Stevenson, W. H. (1886). Anglo-Saxon names (reply to Astley [9.17.6.2]). *Notes & Queries, 7th Series, 1,* 331. Refs.
Traces the *Os* root to Gothic anzeis (half-gods) and relates to Greek Theos and Sanskrit Deva.

[9.17.6.31] Strachan, L. R. M. (1935). Flaed in feminine Anglo-Saxon names. *Notes & Queries, 168,* 247. Refs.

Examination of Searle's *Onomasticon Anglo-Saxonicum* [Smith:1657] shows 26 names + variations ending in -flaed (beauty). Examples include: Aelfflaed, Hunflaed, and Wilflaed.

[9.17.6.32] Sundby, Bertil. (1972). Middle English example of alliteration as a principle of name-giving. *Neuphilologische Mitteilungen, 73,* 437-447. Refs.
4 types of alliteration have been identified in Old English naming patterns. The practice had tended to die out after the Conquest. However, a 15th cent. family document relating to the Crofts family of the North-West Midlands does show 3 types of alliteration. More research is needed to determine whether this example is unusual or "reflects a more wide-spread tendency."

[9.17.6.32A] Taylor, Isaac. (1886). Anglo-Saxon names. [Reply to Astley] [9.17.6.2]. *Notes & Queries, 7th Series, 1,* 331. Refs.
Relates the *Os* in proper names to the Old Norse *as* and the Gothic *ainsi* "god."

[9.17.6.33] Taylor, Isaac. (1891, May 2). Anglo-Saxon personal names. *Notes & Queries, 7th Series, 11,* 352-353. Refs.
Calls for republication of the *Liber Vitae.*

[9.17.6.34] Thomas, Charles. (1985). St. Euny's church, Redruth: A note on the inscription. *Cornish Archaeology, 24,* 173-174. Refs.
Speculation on an inscription MAVOVIH/VITO from the post-Roman period which is interpreted as possibly being MAVORI(I) FILI/VITORI, "(the stone) of Mavorius, of the son of Victor."

[9.17.6.34A] Turville-Petre, J. E. (1956-57). Hengest and Horsa. *Saga Book of the Viking Society, 14,* 273-290. Refs.
Discussion and analysis of stories and legends of the brothers Hengest and Horsa who were assumed to be the progenitors of the 8th cent. royal house of Kent. Both names are associated with horses and horse deities.

[9.17.6.35] Wainwright, F. T. (1942). North-west Mercia, AD. 871-924. *Transactions of the Lancashire & Cheshire Antiquarian Society, 94,* 3-55. Refs.
Devoted to the Cheshire area. Pp. 32-38 draw attention to the Scandinavian elements in personal names. A list of about 50 names from Cheshire Domesday shows the powerful Scandinavian element.

[9.17.6.36] Whitelock, Dorothy. (1937-1945). Scandinavian personal names in the Liber Vitae of Thorney Abbey. *Saga-Book of the Viking Society, 12,* 127-153. Refs.
The *Liber Vitae* contains a list of individuals identified with the abbey from the 11th to the 13th cents. Of these there are 123 entries of clear Scandinavian origin. These and those of partial Scandinavian origin listed and/or discussed.

[9.17.6.37] Woolf, Henry Bosley. (1937/38). The name of Beowulf. *Englische Studien, 72,* 7-9. Refs.

Offers the possibility that Beowulf is really a nickname for Aelfhere. Discussion of the role of alliteration in presenting the evidence.

9.17.6.1. ETHNIC NAMES: *English: Old English: Coins*

[9.17.6.1.1] Archibald, Marion M., & Blunt, C. E. (1986). *Sylloge of coins of the British Isles, 34,* British Museum: *Anglo-Saxon coins, V: Athelstan to the reform of Edgar, 924-* c. 973. London: British Museum Publications, 151p. Refs. 66 Plates.

Coins of English and Viking rulers of this period. Also categorized by mints and moneyers. Hundreds of coins described and shown in plates with inscriptions of names of rulers and moneyers.

[9.17.6.1.2] Biddle, Mark. (1987). Early Norman Winchester. In J. C. Holt (Ed.), *Domesday Studies: Papers read at the Novocentenary Conference of the Royal Historical Society and the Institute of British Geographers, Winchester, 1986* (pp. 311-331). Woodbridge, Suffolk [England]: Boydell Press. Refs. Table. Map.
Uses surnames, especially those of moneyers to show the composition of the population at the time of the Conquest and shortly after.

[9.17.6.1.2A] Blunt, C. E. (1973). The origins of the Stafford mint. In *Otium et negotium: Studies in onomatology and library science presented to Olof von Feilitzen. Acta Bibliothecae Regiae Stockholmiensis, 16,* 13-22. Refs.
Covers the period from the reign of Athelstan (c. 930) to Henry II (c. 1165. Discusses the origins of the mint and also records "an important and long lost variety of the reign of Edgar." Includes aspects of moneyers' names.

[9.17.6.1.3] Mossop, H(enry). R(ichard). (1970). Ed. by Veronica Smart, intro. by Michael Dolley and an analytical note by C. S. S. Lyon. *The Lincoln mint c. 890-1279.* Newcastle upon Tyne: Corbitt & Hunter, 32p. Plates. Illus. Folding Chart.
Extensive description and analysis of coins of this period with the names of kings (Aethelraed to Edward the Confessor). Coins also include names of the moneyers (those that made the coins). See Also: Smart below.

[9.17.6.1.4] Smart, Veronica. (1970). A note on the moneyers of the mint of Lincoln. In H. R. Mossop The Lincoln mint: c. 890-1279 (pp. 20-27).
Analysis of the names of the 140+ moneyers during the Old English period. There is a progression from Scandinavian, Celtic, Continental, through Old English elements.

[9.17.6.1.5] Smart, Veronica. (1973). Cnut's York moneyers. In *Otium et negotium: Studies in onomatology and library science presented to Olof von Feilitzen, Acta Bibliothecae Regiae Stockholmiensis, 16,* 221-231. Refs.
Systematic analysis of the epigraphy of a number of coins. 3/4 of the names are derived from Norse. 28 of the moneyers' names appeared only at York; 16 York names also appeared elsewhere.

[9.17.6.1.6] Smart, Veronica. (1986). Scandinavians, Celts, and Germans in Anglo-Saxon England: The evidence of moneyers' names. In M. A. S. Blackburn *Anglo-Saxon monetary history: Essays in memory of Michael Dolley* (pp. 171-184). Refs. Tables. Leicester [England]: Leicester University Press.
Relationship to Germanic languages. Information on 10th-11th cent. Old English, Continental, Germanic, and Scandinavian moneyers in England. Interpretation of different ethnic influences.

9.17.7. ETHNIC NAMES: *English: Population Structure and Names*

[9.17.7.1] Boldsen, J. L., Mascie-Taylor, C. G. N., & Lasker, Gabriel. (1986). An analysis of the geographical distribution of selected British surnames. *HumBio, 58,* 85-96. Refs. Tables.
Statistical methods show the geographical distribution of 8 common surnames (Smith, Jones, Wright, White, Johnson, Taylor, Wilson, and Williams) in England and Wales.

[9.17.7.2] Darwin, George H. (1875). Marriage between first cousins in England and their effects. *Journal of the Statistical Society, 38,* 153-184. Refs.

This early investigation used surnames to evaluate the effect of 1st-cousin marriages on insanity and infant-mortality. Results were not conclusive and were cautiously interpreted. Some data from Wales included.

[9.17.7.3] Dobson, T., & Roberts, D. F. (1971). Historical population movement and gene flow in Northumberland parishes. *Journal of Biosocial Science, 3,* 193-208. Refs. Tables. Figs.
Used surname analysis to measure constancy of population in Northumberland [England] in the 18th cent.

[9.17.7.4] Fraser Roberts, J(ohn). A(lexander). (1947). The frequencies of the ABO blood groups in south-western England. *Annals of Human Genetics, 14,* 109-116. Refs. Tables.
Among other analyses, used surnames to determine the blood type percentages of ethnic groups. Surnames for those in 2 Welsh categories are listed. Summary concludes "Donors with names having the prefixes Mac and O' are much lower in A than the remainder."

[9.17.7.5] Kuchemann, Christine F., Lasker, Gabriel W., & Smith, Douglas I. (1979). Historical changes in the coefficient of relationship by isonymy among the populations of the Otmoor villages. *HumBio, 51,* 63-77. Refs. Tables.
Analysis of marriage entries in church registers for 6142 individuals from 8 parishes from 1773-1950 + data from 1976 was completed. A 2nd analysis combined those with the same surname but different spellings, example Goff and Gough. Isonymy "between parishes tended to increase from 1800 to about 1900 and to decrease by 1976."

[9.17.7.6] Lasker, Gabriel W. (1982). Genetic structure of the human population of Britain as revealed in the distribution of surnames. In Melvyn Firestone *Anthropological studies in Great Britain and Ireland* (pp. 19-26). Refs. Tempe: Arizona State University.
Explanation of isonymy and its role in genetics and population structure. Summary of several British studies which have surnames and isonymy to study population dynamics. Gives advantages of surname analysis.

[9.17.7.7] Lasker, Gabriel W. (1983). The frequencies of surnames in England and Wales. *HumBio, 55,* 311-340. Refs(pp. 399-408). Table.
All marriages in England and Wales for 3 mos. in 1975 were the sample. Results show, "The rarer the surname, the more frequently,...it occurs in the same district. Rare surnames (those occurring 1 to 6 per 100,000) account for 93% of different surnames but for only 0.5% of the coefficient of relationship [isonymy]."

[9.17.7.8] Lasker, Gabriel W. (1988). Repeated surnames in those marrying into British one-surname "lineages": An approach to the evaluation of population structure through the analysis of the surname in marriages. *HumBio, 60,* 1-9. Refs. Tables.
Used 1st quarter 1975 marriage records for all of England to evaluate repeated pairs of surnames. Results with 6 common surnames were above random expectations. Results also reported with some Irish, Welsh, and Scottish surnames.

[9.17.7.9] Lasker, Gabriel W.; Coleman, David A.; Aldridge, Nicholas; Fox, Wendy R. (1979). Ancestral relationships within and between districts in the region of Reading, England as measured by isonymy. *HumBio, 51,* 445-460. Refs. Tables. Map.
Isonymy data were obtained on 4794 persons married in districts of Reading, Berkshire in 1972-73. "In Reading and its environs there is relatively little differentiation in the pattern of biological interrelationships as seen in the distribution of surnames."

[9.17.7.10] Lasker, G(abriel) W., Kaplan B(ernice) A., & Mascie-Taylor C. G. N. (1985). And who is thy neighbor? Biological relationship in the English village. *HumBio* [Budapest], *16,* 97-103. Table. Refs.
Using Ri (Coefficient of Relationship by Isonymy) with 10 villages in Cambridgeshire in terms of isonymy and location of residence determined that residents of adjoining houses are 3 times as closely related as are residents of other pairs of houses. Refs.

[9.17.7.11] Lasker, Gabriel W., & Mascie-Taylor, C. G. N. (1983). Surnames in five English villages: Relationship to each other, to surrounding areas, and to England and Wales. *Journal of Biosocial Science, 15,* 25-34. Refs. Tables. Map.
Evaluation and comparison of the pattern of surname distribution of 5 Cambridgeshire villages with patterns of England and Wales using isonymy to measure inbreeding.

[9.17.7.12] Lasker, G(abriel) W., Mascie, C. G. N., & Coleman, D(avid). A. (1986). Repeating pairs of surnames in marriages in Reading (England) and their significance for population structure. *HumBio, 58,* 421-425. Refs.
Used the method of repeating pairs of surnames to study marriages. "Repetitions of pairs of surnames were significantly more frequent... than expected at random."

[9.17.7.13] Pollitzer, William S., Smith, Malcolm T., & Williams. W. Robert. (1988). A study of isonymic relationships in Fylingdales Parish from marriage records from 1654 through 1916. *HumBio, 60,* 363-382. Refs. Tables. Figs.
The parish is on the coast of North Yorkshire, England. Records of 2600 marriages were analyzed by isonymy and the repeated pairs technique. Ethnic origin by identifiable surnames shows: Old English, 56%; French, 21%; German, 9%; Celtic, 8%, and 7%, Scandinavian.

[9.17.7.14] Roberts, D. F. (1980). Inbreeding and ecological change: An isonymic analysis of secular trends in a Tyneside parish over three centuries. *Social Biology, 27,* 230-240. Refs. Tables. Figs. Map.
Whickham is a community near Newcastle, England. Marriage records were studied by isonymy from 1566-1866 and show a general relationship "of inbreeding level with demographic change and particularly with socioeconomic pattern."

[9.17.7.15] Roberts, D. F., & Rawling, C. P. (1974). Secular trends in genetic structure: An isonymic analysis of Northumberland parish records. *Annals of Human Biology, 1,* 303-410. Refs. Tables. Figs. Map.
Marriage records from 4 parishes from 1656 to 1812 demonstrate secular trends in inbreeding and also differences between parishes.

[9.17.7.16] Souden, David & Lasker, Gabriel W. (1978). Biological interrelationships between parishes in East Kent: An analysis of Marriage Duty Act returns for 1705. *Local Population Studies, 15,* 30-39. Refs. Figs. Maps.
Investigated 35 parishes in East Kent. Using name listings of 1705, correlated male surnames of each parish with one another for isonymy. Explains how problems of different spellings of a name (example, Hamon and Hammond, Knight, Night, and Nite) were resolved. Demonstrates how isonymy in historical records can show migration.

[9.17.7.17] Sturges, Christopher M., & Haggett, Brian C. (1987). *Inheritance of English surnames.* London: Hawgood Computing, 35p. Refs.
Assumptions based upon 1000 hypothetical couples living in England in 1350 led to the development of mathematical models to predict the survival rate of surnames. Depending upon the mathematical model selected, it appears that the survival rate would be 19%-35%.

9.17.8. ETHNIC NAMES: *English: Scandinavian Names in England*

[9.17.8.1] Fellows Jensen, G(illian). (1969). Scandinavian personal names in Lincolnshire and Yorkshire. *Onoma, 14,* 23-24.
Summarizes a study reported in vol. 7 of the Copenhagen University Institut for navneforskning.

[9.17.8.2] Insley, John. (1985). Some Scandinavian personal names in South-West England from post-Conquest records. *StudAnthroScan, 3,* 23-58. Refs.
Extensive examination of Pipe Rolls and other sources provides names and citations, example, Asmoth is an Old Danish feminine name found in several records. Information is shown in 38 main entries along with variants and forms from different languages. Concludes that "it is probable that the bulk of the present material...is a reflection of the influx of Scand[inavian] landowners in that area during the reigns of Canut and his sons."

[9.17.8.3] von Feilitzen, Olof. (1965). Notes on some Scandinavian personal names in English 12th-Century records. *Anthroponymica Suecana, 6,* 52-68. Refs.
Lists 60+ personal names and bynames not previously recorded nor "adequately listed." Entries show language origin (Old Danish, Old Norse, or Old Swedish) and documents where found. Names include: Baldi, Gimp, and Gisla.

9.17.9. ETHNIC NAMES: *English: Surnames*

[9.17.9.1] Ammon, Linda. (1976). Smith and Jones. *Population Trends, 4,* 9-11. Refs. Tables.
Listing of the most common 50 surnames in the birth, death, and marriage registers + a combined category from the Registrar General (England and Wales) for 1853 and the 1st quarter of 1975. The 10 most common names are still the same. Most names that were in the top 50 in 1853 are still there although the order has shifted somewhat. Some new names have been introduced.

[9.17.9.2] B., A. (1887). Midland names in the so-called Roll of Battle Abbey. *Midland Antiquary, 4,* 129-131.
Comment on about 30 Midland surnames that were in the Roll and still appeared at the time of the article. Names include Baskerville, Devile, and Mountford.

[9.17.9.3] Battye, Kathleen M. (1982). Norah who? *Yorkshire Life, 36(11),* 21. Illus.
Possessing an unusual surname has some advantages when another person with the same surname (such as Nora and Compo) becomes famous.

[9.17.9.4] Brett, Donald. (1985). The use of telephone directories in surname studies. *Local Historian, 16,* 392-404. Refs.
Extensive analysis of occupational surname patterns (Smith, Wheeler, Fuller, Tucker, and Walker) shows that the centers of frequency are still evident after centuries of population movement.

[9.17.9.5] Camsell, Margaret. (1986). Devon locative surnames in the fourteenth century. *Nomina, 10,* 137-147. Refs.
Evaluation based upon the 1332 Subsidy Roll which listed 10,600 names. Analysis of surnames by district indicates that people in Devon at that time had not moved far from their place of origin. Examples. Statistics provided for districts.

[9.17.9.6] Charnock, Richard Steven. (1868; 1968). *Ludus patronymicus; or, The etymology of curious surnames.* Detroit: Gale Research, 166p. Refs. (Originally published in London in 1868 by Turner).

Gives background information on about 1700 names such as Badman (root is from a bathman or a baptizer) and Heaven (derived from Evan or Evans. Listing of approx. 3500 additional "peculiar" surnames.

[9.17.9.7] Dodgson, John Mc(Neal). (1973). Two coals to Newcastle. *In Otium et negotium: Studies in onomatology and library science presented to Olof von Feilitzen, Acta Bibliothecae Regiae Stockholmiensis, 16,* 46-48. Refs.
1 "coal" is a discussion of the derivation of the name Jubbins, originally a nickname for a pot-man (1 who carried beer), < ME *jubbe* a 4-gallon tub.

[9.17.9.8] Emmison, F. G. (1986). Surnames derived from placenames. *Genealogists' Magazine, 22,* 13-15. Refs.
Explanation of how a placename surname may indicate where an ancestor was from, example, Ardley, Coxall, Utting, etc. Also indicates that the present surname may perpetuate an older spelling, example, Aunger for Unger.

[9.17.9.9] Foster, Irene. (1980). By any other name. *North Cheshire Family Historian, 7,* 101-106. Refs. Table.
Table shows the top 50 surnames of England and Wales (combined) for 1853 and 1975. Top 5 in 1853: Smith, Jones, Williams, Taylor, and Davies; for 1975, Smith, Jones, Williams, Brown, and Taylor. Also, some explanation of spelling variations.

[9.17.9.10] Franklyn, Julian. (1963). English surnames. *Armorial* [Scotland], *4,* 37-39.
Comment on British authorities Bardsley and Reaney.

[9.17.9.10A] Freeman, J(ohn) W(illiam). (1968;1986). *Discovering surnames: Their origins and meanings,* 2nd ed. Aylesbury, Buckinghamshire [England]: Shire, 72 p.
Sections cover surnames developed from nicknames, occupations, locations, and patronyms. Additional sections devoted to Saxon, French, Scandinavian, Irish, Scottish, and Welsh surnames. Approx. 1000 names appear.

[9.17.9.11] Harcourt-Bath, William. (1934). Suppression of the particle 'de' in English surnames. *Notes & Queries, 167,* 285-286.
Richard de Harcourt in 1347 was the last member of the family to use the 'de.' The 1st recorded member not to use it was Thomas in 1417. Explanation offered.

[9.17.9.12] Harden, A. (1957). Rainbow as a surname. *Notes & Queries, New Series, 4,* 316.
The name has 2 roots. One is the OE Regenbeald which became the ME Regnebaud and then the Modern English Rainbow. The 2nd root is from the French Rimbaud < ragin = conseil and bald = audacieux.

[9.17.9.13] Hoskins, W(illiam) G(eorge). (1984). *Local history in England,* 3rd ed. London: Longman, 301p. Refs(pp. 281-290). Maps. Illus.
Pp. 211-234 deal with surnames. Evaluates older conclusions that people in England remained fairly close to their ancient place of origin. Describes research of McKinley and Redmonds. Presents 3 cases of the dispersal of surnames from Suffolk and Devon. Gives suggestions for further research on surnames.

[9.17.9.14] Hughes, Pennethorne. (1967). *Your book of surnames.* London: Faber & Faber, 59p. Refs. Illus.
A popular presentation on English surnames drawn from many sources, 1st names, places, nicknames, occupations, et al. Systematic. Many examples.

[9.17.9.15] Jacobs, Nicolas. (1978). Clanvowe. *Notes & Queries, 223,* 292-295. Refs. Suggests that the Herefordshire name of Clanvowe is derived from Llanfocha, the Welsh name of St. Maughans, Monmouthshire.

[9.17.9.16] Jones, Malcolm & Dillon, Patrick. (1987). *Dialect in Wiltshire and its historical, topographical and natural science contexts.* Trowbridge, Wiltshire [England]: Wiltshire County Council, 206p. Refs.
Wiltshire is a county in Southwest England. Pp. 97-98 deal with some surnames (and variations) developed from placenames. Examples of surnames discussed are: Wells, Ridge, and Feny. An occupational name discussed is Fuller. Attention paid to regional pronunciation.

[9.17.9.17] Kaplan, Bernice A. & Lasker, Gabriel W. (1983). The present distribution of some English surnames derived from place names. *HumBio, 55,* 243-250. Refs. Table. Using telephone directories, established that surnames derived from placenames are closer to original site at levels well above chance. Among the 97 surnames used are: Boston, Gloucester, and Halifax.

[9.17.9.18] Kristensson, Gillis. (1969). Studies on Middle English surnames containing elements of French origin, *English Studies, 50,* 465-498. Refs.
Middle English topographical surnames of French origin from 14 counties. Included are: Pantry, Plank, and River. Entries also show sources and earliest recorded use.

[9.17.9.19] Kristensson, Gillis. (1977). Studies on the early 14th century population of Lindsey (Lincolnshire). *Scripta Minora, Publications of the Royal Society of Letters at Lund, 2,* 39p. Refs. Maps. Lund: C. W. K. Gleerup, 39p.
To examine dialect differences concerning the relationship of Lindsey with its neighbors, the Subsidy Rolls from 1327 and 1332 were studied for the names of immigrants from other parts of the county and other parts of England. The names of these immigrants are listed along with other information.

[9.17.9.20] Kruck, William E. (1986). The name of the comet. *Names, 34,* 245-254. Refs.
Edmond Halley (1656-1742) is commemorated by the comet named after him. There is controversy about how the name was pronounced in his day whether "hay-ley," "hal-ley" or "haw-ley." However, rightly or wrongly, the pronunciation "hal-ley" has come to be the accepted one.

[9.17.9.21] Lanahan, William F. (1974). What's in a name? Family surnames and social upheaval in Medieval England. *Social Studies, 65,* 218-222.
General on English, Welsh, and Irish surnames. Many examples including: Ames (a maternal uncle), May (a distant relative), Napier (1 who looked after the lord's fine linens), and Latimer (a Latin expert who interpreted at court for foreign diplomats).

[9.17.9.22] Lasker, Gabriel W., & Roberts, D. F. (1982). Secular trends in relationship as estimated by surnames: A study of a Tyneside parish. *Annals of HumBio, 9,* 299-307. Refs. Tables. Figs. German and French abstracts.
Used baptismal surname records of the Tyneside parish of Whickham in 7 time periods between 1577 and 1758. Correlated names of each sex of 1 time period with the other periods and with the other sex over all periods. Fluctuations in results related to historical factors.

[9.17.9.23] Leeson, Francis. (1964). The study of single surnames and their distribution. *Genealogists' Magazine, 14,* 405-412. Refs. Tables. Map.

Gathering of statistics of frequencies of the surname-sound Lee (includes Lea, Legh, Leigh, Ley, and others + Leeson) from the 16th to the 20th cent. and a map showing the various locations of the names. Serves as a model.

[9.17.9.24] Leeson, Francis. (1965, May). The history and technique of surname distribution studies. *Family History, 3 (Nos. 14/15)*, pp. 35-37; 45. Refs. Tables.
Reports that single name studies exist for surnames such as, Boddington, Kitchener, Lee, Mann, and Scattergood. Gives specific suggestions on how to do a single name study.

[9.17.9.25] Leeson, Francis. (1970). The development of surnames: I, Occupational surnames in West Sussex. *Genealogists' Magazine, 16*, 404-425. Refs. Tables. Map.
Lists 152 different surnames from Poling, Loxfield. A table shows location of names and also number of entries in the recent London telephone directory. Among the names included are: Cottle (cutler), Carter, and Hopper (dancer).

[9.17.9.26] Leeson, Francis. (1971). The development of surnames: II, Locative names in West Sussex. *Genealogists' Magazine, 16*, 536-549. Refs. Maps.
Continued research of Leeson above with 208 locative names surviving. Extensive mapping of name locations. Sample names included are: Cobden (Coppa's Valley), Coltstaple (Coll's boundary-mark), and Trollope (troll-valley).

[9.17.9.27] Loyd, Lewis Christopher. (1951;1975). *The origins of some Anglo-Norman families*. Baltimore, MD: Genealogical Publishing, 140p. Refs. Map. (Originally published in Leeds, England as Vol. 103 of the Harleian Society in 1951).
Extensive background information on 315 Anglo-Norman families who came to Britain between 1066 and 1205. Shows how the family names (surnames) were derived from places in Normandy and other nearby areas. Names seen today include: Haig, Harcourt, Mortimer, and Quincy.

[9.17.9.28] Maidbury, Laurence. (1954). English surnames in Latin. *Amateur Historian, 1*, 368-371.
Translations of 200+ English surnames into Latin. "It is...not wise to draw any etymological conclusions from the l[L]atin form without research into each individual case." Examples include: Bacchus = Backhouse, de Blanco Pane = Whitbread, Talliator = Taylor.

[9.17.9.29] Maidbury, Laurence, (1954-56). Family history in surnames. *Amateur Historian, 2*, 114-117.
Brief history of the development of surnames from Eric Aesc, King of Kent, in 512 to Norman hereditary names, and coverage of the Fitz element. Suggestions for researchers on surnames.

[9.17.9.30] Martin, Charles Trice. (Ed.). (1910; 1982). *The record interpreter: A collection of aberrations, Latin words, and names used in English historical manuscripts and records*. Chichester, Sussex: Phillimore, 464p. (Originally published in 1910).
Approx. 1200 Latin forms of English surnames (Castor = Bever, de Casa Dei = Godshall) are on pp. 429-450. Approx. 960 Latin Christian names (Dionysius = Denis) are on pp. 451-464.

[9.17.9.31] Martin, Edward A. (1972). The evolution of a surname [in West Cornwall]. *Devon & Cornwall Notes & Queries, 32*, 113-119. Refs.
Demonstrates the evolution of a placename surname to a 1st name-derived surname by tracing members of the Drew Martin family from 1522-1591.

[9.17.9.32] Martin, Edward A. (1974). The name Coswarth and surname-derived first-names. *Devon & Cornwall Notes & Queries, 33*, 25-26. Refs.

In 1553, Guildford Dudley was one of the 1st examples of the use of a surname as a 1st name. In Cornwall, there were others, example, Colan Bluett, son of Frances Bluett and Elizabeth Colan. The Colan name was also used by others as a 1st name. Other examples.

[9.17.9.33] Matthews, C. M. (1963). Surnames of occupation. *History Today, 13,* 449-458. Illus.
According to Matthews, "the London telephone directory of today gives as good a cross-section of people of the Middle Ages as we are likely to get." (p. 51). Comment and discussion of the meaning and origin of occupation names including: Slater, Thatcher, Milner, and Baxter.

[9.17.9.34] McKinley, R(ichard) A(lexander. (1969). The survey of English surnames. *Local Historian, 8(7),* 299-302. Refs.
Description of the survey of English surnames being carried out by McKinley at Leicester University. Focuses on population mobility, surnames < placenames, and tracing one surname from a particular place and noting its spread.

[9.17.9.35] McKinley, R(ichard) A(lexander. (1969). Norfolk surnames in the sixteenth century, *Occasional Papers, No. 2, Second Series,* Department of English Local History. Leicester: Leicester University Press, pp. 1-60. Refs. Tables. Maps.
Extensive examination of the surnames of this area of eastern England in the 16th cent. One major tabulation of the 18,500 names checked shows the following types: Locative, 19%; Topological 11%; Patronymic and Metronymic, 26%; Occupational, 19%; Physical Characteristics, 3%; Others and Doubtful, 24%. Concludes there was a great deal of local movement. Many examples.

[9.17.9.36] McKinley, R(ichard) A(lexander). (1981). Hereditary names and the chronology of their evolution. *Family History, 11,* 275-283. Refs.
Uses evidence chiefly from Oxfordshire to show the shift from bye-names (or no bye-name) to hereditary surnames.

[9.17.9.37] McKinley, Richard (Alexander). (1988). *The surnames of Sussex, Vol. 5, English Surnames Series.* Oxford, England: Leopard's Head Press, 483p. Refs. Maps.
Scholarly detailed examination of the surnames in this area of southern England. One important factor was the isolation of Sussex from much of the rest of England. Topics include: Introduction, History, Locative and Topographical Surnames, and Surnames derived from Occupation, Personal Names, and Nicknames. Extensive index.

[9.17.9.37A] McKinley, Richard (Alexander). (1990). *A history of British surname.* London: Longman, 230p. Refs. Tables.
The author's purpose is to provide the non-specialist, amateur historian and genealogist with a history of British surnames. Topics included are: hereditary surnames, locative surnames, topographical surnames, surnames from personal names, occupational surnames, and from nicknames. Shows the contributions made by local historians.

[9.17.9.38] *Penguin dictionary of surnames, The.* (1978). 2nd ed. London: Allen Lane, 444p. Refs.
Extensive collection of approx. 12,000 items. Surnames derived from 1st names (Jackson), location (Shaw), occupation (Fuller), and nicknames (Moneypenny).

[9.17.9.39] Reaney, P(ercy) H(ide). (1965). Archbishop Harsnett: His surname and its origin. *Essex Archaeological Society Transactions,* 1, 259.
Traces the name originally to de Halsnode in a Kent Assize Roll of 1240 meaning, "the private wood in the corner or nook of land."

[9.17.9.40] Reaney, Percy Hide. (1976; 1977). *A dictionary of British surnames*. 2nd ed. with corrections and additions by R. M. Wilson. London: Routledge & Kegan Paul, 366p. Refs. (Originally published in 1958) 1st edition described in [87:8.23.2.31]. Standard reference on English surnames.

[9.17.9.41] Redmonds, G(eorge). (1972). Surnames and place-names. *Local Historian, 1,* 3-7. Refs.
Surname research sometimes helps placename research. Gives several example of surnames preceding placenames. Special attention to *Beecroft* and *Grymmoth*.

[9.17.9.42] Redmonds, G(eorge). (1972). Surname heredity in Yorkshire. *Local Historian, 10,* 171-177. Refs.
Surnames began to be hereditary in the 12th cent. Describes types of surname and when each became a surname. Examples.

[9.17.9.43] Redmonds, G(eorge). (1972). Problems in the identification of some Yorkshire filial names. Genealogists' Magazine, 17, 205-212. Refs. Maps.
Analysis of 20+ names ending in *-son* indicates that some are derived from placenames and have undergone modification over the years (Kettleson/Kittleson, Grimson, Gummerson/ Gomerson). Among others including (Tolleson, Coulson, Silson), the evidence is not strong for filial derivation.

[9.17.9.44] Redmonds, G(eorge). (1975). Lancashire surnames in Yorkshire: The distribution and development of Aspinall and Ridehalgh in the West Riding. *Genealogists' Magazine, 18,* 13-18. Refs. Map.
Points out that (1) families (and surnames) have moved from one locality to another, (2) spelling of names has evolved. Traces Aspenewell to Aspinwall to Aspinald, Asman, and Assman; Ridehalgh to Redyall and Riddick. 40+ variants of these 2 names traced.

[9.17.9.44A] Redmonds, George. (1985). Surnames and settlement. *Old West Riding, 4,* 7-10. Refs. Table.
Demonstration of the relationship of the modern names of 14 settlements in Huddersfield (England) to the surnames of the 1st residents (some going back as far as the 13th cent). An example is Ebson House which was traced back to Richard Hebbesen in 1325.

[9.17.9.45] Robson, John M. (1988). Surnames and status in Victorian England. *Queen's Quarterly* [Canada], *95,* 642-661. Refs.
Shows that the social atmosphere was conducive to change of surname (methods being by deed-poll, Royal Licence, and private Act of Parliament). Review of controversies involving some name changes. List of some names (p. 650) that may have caused difficulty including: Asse, Honeybum, and Quicklove.

[9.17.9.46] Rose, Arthur. (1951). Surnames are nicknames. *Chambers's Journal, Ninth Series, 5,* 19-20.
Concise description of surname naming; includes example of patronyms (Wilson, Johnson), names derived from place (Attwater, Hill), occupation (Miller, Lambert), and nicknames (Lovejoy, Keepguest).

[9.17.9.47] Rylance, T. (1980). Canting arms or canting names. *Coat of Arms, New Series, 4(114),* 257-258.
Refers to the period around the 12th cent. Suggests that the shields of knights might have preceded their names. With the advent of canting around 1300, some families changed their shields to correspond to an acquired surname. The Montague family shifted from the griffin segreant Or to *argent three fusils in fess gules*.

[9.17.9.48] Senior, A. (1951, 6 Feb.). Local place-names and surnames. *Transactions of the Halifax Antiquarian Society* [England], 15-35. Refs.
Based upon 506 paid returns on the 1379 Poll Tax in the 20 townships of Halifax. Explanation of types of surname and entries for individual names. There were 278 placenames (Holgate, Bradshaw); 132 patronyms (Judson, Gibson); 76 occupational names (Naylor, Fletcher); 12 nicknames (Fox, Peacock); and 10 not classified.

[9.17.9.49] Shaw, David H. (1978, Winter). Surnames in Bedfordshire: Parts I-VII. *Bedfordshire Magazine, 16,* 296-297; *16,* 342-347; *17,* 35-37; *17,* 73-79; *17,* 108, 113-117; *17,* 165-170; *17,* 250-255; *17,* 297-302.
These 7 installments provide a systematic survey of the surname situation in Bedfordshire. There are explanations with full examples of patronyms, toponyms, occupational names, and nicknames.

[9.17.9.50] Spiegelhalter, Cecil. (1940). Surnames of Devon, V, Descriptive names: Nicknames. *Devonshire Association for the Advancement of Science, Literature, and Art, Reports & Transactions, 72,* 273-281. Refs.
Extensive review of Middle English surnames in Devon from several sources including Norman-French (Burgoyne, Power), morality plays (Bishop, Abbot), Shakespeare names (Benbow, Breakhead), bird names (Crane, Hawke), and color nicknames (Gray, Rudd). Jewish names include Deulesalt (French form of the translation of Isaiah, "God save him"), Deulecresse = Gadalya ("God prosper him"), and Deulegard = Shemaria ("God guard him"). *Note:* The previous 4 parts are listed in Smith [87:6.16].

[9.17.9.51] Spiegelhalter, Cecil. (1947). Surnames of Devon, VI, French place-names and Devon family-names. *Devonshire Association for the Advancement of Science, Literature, & Art: Reports & Transactions, 79,* 197-209. Refs.
Some French placenames appeared as surnames in Devon and elsewhere in England. Some surnames have died out but remain as placenames or parts of placenames. 150 surnames are listed with background material, example "Kain--From Caen (Cadomum). C[alvados region]. Maurice de Cadomo, 1083; Rog. Kayn, 1351; Cane, Dartmouth, 1648."

[9.17.9.52] Thuresson, Bertil. (1950). *Middle English occupational terms* [Lund Studies in English, XIX]. Lund: C. W. K. Gleerup, 295p. Refs.
Systematic and extensive classification and listing of over 900 occupational "terms." Many of these terms can also be identified as surnames. Example, Honeyman, "A man who sells honey or has charge of bees;" Spenser, "one who dispenses...provisions in a household."

[9.17.9.53] Turner, E. A. (1956). The Welsh element in Shropshire surnames. *Transactions of the Caradoc & Severn Valley Field Club* [Shropshire], *1947-1950, 13,* 89-96. Refs.
Goes back to the 14th cent. to describe the increase in the percentage of Welsh surnames in Shropshire. Description of Welsh naming practices including nicknames such as Gwyn ("white"), Gough ("red"), and Penwyn ("white head"). Origin of names like Bowles, Iago, and Tudor explained.

[9.17.9.54] Tynan, Kenneth. (1975, Oct. 2). No place for Higgins. *The Listener,* p. 444.
Names such as Higgins, Jones, and Wilkinson were acceptable in Engl. literature until the beginning of the 19th cent. At that time poets became class-conscious and looked down on "proletarian" names of this type.

[9.17.9.55] Watson, Rex. (1975). A study of surname distribution in a group of Cambridgeshire parishes, 1538-1840. *Local Population Studies, No. 15,* 23-32. Refs. Tables. Figs. Map.
Sophisticated analyses of the 8 parishes concludes that the most common surnames of a parish tend to persist; comparisons shown between parishes; listing of most common names in 4 or more parishes.

[9.17.9.56] Your family name. (1965, Oct.). *Modern Maturity,* pp. 28-29. Illus.
Brief. On surnames. Includes 9 coats-of-arms including Stanford, Lockhart, and Snooks (derived from Seven Oaks).

9.17.9.1 ETHNIC NAMES: *English: Surnames: Specific*

[9.17.9.1.1] Collins, R. G. (1983, July). The Brontë name and its classical association. *Ariel, 14,* 51-57. Refs.
Patrick Brunty, father of the Brontë sisters, was born of a poor Irish family and was self-educated. He changed his name to that of Bronté, the city of classical associations which had surrendered to Nelson (a hero of Brontë's). Analysis of the possible reasons for the selection.

[9.17.9.1.2] Dodgson. J(ohn) M(cNeal). (1967). Hodge and Podge. *Notes & Queries, 212, Feb.,* 49-50. Refs.
Suggests that a possible explanation of the name Hodge is from a dialect form of "hog." Dodge as having a similar origin from dog.

[9.17.9.1.3] Edwards, Gillian M. (1953, Nov. 12). As good as a king's. *Country Life,* p. 1565.
Gives meanings for 40+ English surnames derived from agricultural occupations. Included are Goddard (goat-herd), Runciman (horsekeeper and dealer), Chivers/Cheevers (goat-keeper).

[9.17.9.1.4] Johnson, William Redpath. (1971). The family of Redpath. *History of the Berwickshire Naturalist's Club, 39,* 44-47. Refs.
Traces the family to 1333 to the hamlet of Redpath in Berwickshire. Some members of the family changed the surname to Ridpath.

[9.17.9.1.5] Pascoe, W. H. (1972). The origin of the name "Pascoe." *Devon & Cornwall Notes & Queries, 32,* 173-175. Refs.
The name *Pascoe* can be traced back to 4th cent. Cornwall. It has 40+ different spellings. The origin of the name is from the time of the year that children were born. Pask < Heb. pesakh (Passover).

[9.17.9.1.6] Pinsent, R. F. J. H. (1975). A surname and a source? *Devon Historian, 10,* 32-35. Refs.
Traces the Pinsent name to 1121 through various documents in England. Exploration of other origin possibilities in Normandy and the Danelaw. There is some geographical evidence in that Mont Pincon is the highest point in Normandy. The word Pincon means "finch" in French. Other language possible origins considered.

[9.17.9.1.7] Porteous, J. Douglas. (1982). Surname geography: A study of the Mell family name c. 1538-1980. *Transactions of the Institute of British Geographers, New Series, 7,* 395-418. Refs. Figs. Maps.
Extensive systematic national and regional analysis of records of the Mell family in England. Clusters of the family were indentified in Yorkshire-Lincolnshire and the Greater London area. The name is probably of Scandinavian origin.

[9.17.9.1.8] Porteous. J. Douglas. (1985). Place loyalty. *Local Historian, 16*, 343-345. Refs.
Uses surname analysis of the Mell family as an illustration of how an extended family has lived in a locality for an extended period. The Mell family was traced to 1279 and was clustered in 2 locations, Humberhead and Greater London.

[9.17.9.1.9] Porteous, J. Douglas. (1987). Locating the place of origin of a surname. *Local Historian, 17*, 391-395. Refs. Maps.
Uses the surname *Mell*, a family of the Humberhead region of England, as a case study of how to locate the place of origin of a surname.

[9.17.9.1.10] Porteous, J. Douglas. (1988). *The Mells: Surname geography, family history*. Saturna Island, BC, Canada: Saturna Island Thinktank Press, 93p. Refs. Maps.
Evaluation of several possible origins and meanings of the Mell name. Coverage of material on surname geography in articles by Porteous above.

[9.17.9.1.11] Rigg, A. G. (1987). Nigel of Canterbury: What was his name? *Medium Aevum, 56*, 304-307. Refs.
Nigel was a prominent 12th cent. Canterbury monk. After evaluating the available evidence, concludes that Nigel was entitled to 3 surnames: de Sarneis, of Whiteacre, or Canterbury but that he was known as Whiteacre.

[9.17.9.1.12] Sill, Geoffrey M. (1978, Feb.). A brief digression on Daniel "De" Foe. *Notes & Queries, 223*, 39-40. Refs.
Suggests that Daniel Foe's change of his surname to DeFoe was not a pretension of nobility but rather identification with a Norman family origin around the beginning of the 16th cent.

[9.17.9.1.13] Stanes, Robin. (1975). Retter: The making of a surname. *Devon & Cornwall Notes & Queries*, 124-125.
Suggests that Retter is an occupational name referring to "retting" (processing flax). The name arose in Devon after 1642.

[9.17.9.1.14] Steer, Barbara D. G. (1954, Sept.). Lerwill: A rare surname. *Notes & Queries, New Series, Vol. 1*, 370-372. Refs.
Traces this rare name to 1219 through various documents (with varied spellings such as, Lerywell, Luriewell, Lurewill, and others.

[9.17.9.1.15] Western, W. G. (1987). The origin of the family name *Western* in Devon. *Devon Historian, 34*, 16-17. Refs.
Disagreement with Reaney [87:8.23.2.31] on the origin of the name *Western* meaning "the man from the West." Suggests that the origin can be traced back to the 13th cent. in Devon as Westhorne or Wasthorne.

9.18. ETHNIC NAMES: *Ethiopian*

[9.18.1] Giorgis, Kabreab W. (1973). The entry-word in Ethiopian names. *Ethiopian Library Association Bulletin, 2*, 11-20. Refs. Tables.
Explanation of how Ethiopian names vary from Western names in how they are entered correctly in catologing. Ethiopian names are listed in order by: (1) 1st name, (2) name of father, and (3) attributes or titles. There is no punctuation. Tables give numerous example

[9.18.2] Messing, Simon D. (1974). Individualistic patterns in Amhara onomastics. *Ethos, 2*, 77-91. Refs.

Name-bestowal patterns of Amharic and Tigre-Tigrinya groups in Ethiopia. Categories include: Circumstances of Birth, Descriptive, Relationship, and Transformation. The appendix shows 144 names each with translation and implications, example, "Dagitu F[emale], 'the kind one,' the parents hope she will be kind to them when grown up."

[9.18.3] US. Central Intelligence Agency. (1965). *Amharic personal names.* Washington, 53p. Microfilm by Library of Congress, 1970.
Description of Amharic, the principle language of Ethiopia. Main table shows approx. 1500 names. Each name is shown in Amharic followed by 2 transcriptions, lang. origin and meaning.

9.19. ETHNIC NAMES: *Faroese*

[9.19.1] Johansen, Anfinnur. (1993). Hin fyrsta føroyska fólkanavnalógin [The Faeroes' first Personal Names Act]. *StudAnthroScan, 11,* 97-110. Refs.
In 1992, Denmark gave the Faroese power to regulate their own names. Among the new rules: a child must be named within 6 mos. of birth, a child may only have 2 forenames, only 1 surname (non-hyphenated) may be used as a middle name, and patronyms and metronyms have been reintroduced.

[9.19.2] Poulsen, Jóhan Hendrik W. (1985). Fólkanøvn í Føroyum [Personal names in the Faroe Islands]. *StudAnthroScan, 3,* 59-71. Refs. Faroese. English summary.
Extensive coverage of naming influences from the 16th cent. on. These include: Christianity, Old Norse, civil servants, and English influence. 2 unique naming customs described: (1) naming both boys and girls after lost ship crews, (2) "Friday" and "Sunday" names where children born on those days have names beginning with F and S.

9.20. ETHNIC NAMES: *Finnish*

[9.20.1] Blomqvist, Marianne. (1989). Anderssons i Finland [Andersson in Finland]. *StudAnthroScan, 7,* 101-110. Refs. Table. Swedish. English summary.
Andersson, originally a Swedish name, is the 3rd most common surname of the *-son* type (preceded by Johanson and Karlsson), it is the 7th overall. It is found at all social levels. The distribution of Andersson varies regionally. In some areas, the Anderssons are Finnish-speaking.

[9.20.2] Blomqvist, Marianne. (1989). 1985 års släktnamnslag i Finland: innehåll och tillämpning [Finland's Family Names Act 1985: Its provisions and application]. *StudAnthroScan, 7,* 133-143. Refs. Swedish. English summary.
Results of the law are shown in a sample of 26,002 couples in 1986. 92.1% of the women took the surname of the husband, 7.5% retained their birth name, 7% took hyphenated names, less than 1% of the men took the wife's surname. [Percentages do not appear to add correctly].

[9.20.3] Blomqvist, Marianne. (1990). Swedish family names in Finland. *Studia Fennica, 34,* 130-140. Refs. Tables.
Brief history of the Swedish language and Swedish naming practices in Finland. Tables show the most common Swedish names in Finland in 1970 and aspects of them. Because of historical factors, many Finns took Swedish names but in 2 periods 1906-1907 and 1935-1937, many Finns changed their names.

[9.20.4] Blomqvist, Marianne. (1992). Reviderad personnamnslag i Finland 1991 [Revised personal names legislation passed in Finland in 1991]. *StudAnthroScan, 10,* 91-98. Refs. Swedish. English summary.
New provisions broaden protection for surnames. There are also changes in the laws so that individuals may change their forenames at an earlier age. Some revisions in the law are planned.

[9.20.5] Kepsu, Saulo. (1991). Forna finska förnamn [Early Finnish forenames]. *StudAnthroScan, 9,* 33-59. Refs. Fig. Swedish. English summary.
Examination of "forename usage among the Finnish-speaking population of Finland--as distinct from the normalized forms recorded by Swedish-speaking officials--from the Middle Ages down to the end of the 18th century, and to suggest ways of tracing these names." Also emphasizes the roles of placenames and unofficial forms of forenames.

[9.20.6] Lehikoinen, Laila. (1990). The appellations of inhabitants and their usage as farmstead and village names. *Studia Fennica, 34,* 84-90. Refs. Maps.
Farmsteads in Finland, particularly in the Karelia area are derived from 1st names. However, "In West Finland farmstead names are usually primary in relation to surnames."

[9.20.7] Lindqvist, Tor-Erik. (1990). A tale of three towns: A presentation of a project and the problems involved. *Proceedings of the 17th ICOS, Helsinki, 13-18 Aug. 1990,* 2, 111-117. Refs.
Description of a project involving 1st names used for christening from the 17th cent. to the 1930s in 3 types of Finnish linguistic community: (1) Swedish-speaking, (2) Swedish- and Finnish-speaking; and (3) Finnish-speaking.

[9.20.8] Mikkonen, Pirjo. (1986). De finländska rotesoldaternas tillnamn [The surnames of locally maintained regular soldiers in Finland]. *StudAnthroScan, 4,* 59-72. Refs. Tables. Figs. Swedish. English summary.
Description of types of Finnish and of Swedish names used for soldiers. "By the early 1780s at the latest 'typical' soldiers' names accounted for 60-100 per cent of surnames in all the companies studied." Examples of soldiers' names include: Onni ("happiness, luck"), Sota ("war"), and Toivo ("hope").

[9.20.9] Närhi, Eeva Maria. (1987). The changing of surnames in Finland during the twentieth century, particularly in 1906 and 1935. *StudAnthroScan, 5,* 109-121. Refs. Tables.
200,000 Finns changed their surnames (mostly from Swedish) to Finnish at these times. The 1935 data show that changes took place at all levels of society and all regions. Tables show the most common names changed. These include: Johansson, Helenius, Karlsson. The most popular new surnames are: Nurmi, Laine, and Lehta.

[9.20.10] Närhi, Eeva Maria. (1989). *Anderssons* attlingar i Finland [The heirs to *Andersson* in Finland]. *StudAnthroScan, 7,* 111-120. Refs. Swedish. English summary.
Description of mass movements in the 1st half of the 20th cent. to replace non-Finnish surnames with Finnish. Andersson was selected as representative of the non-Finnish names which had Finnish replacements.

[9.20.11] Närhi, Eeva Maria. (1990). The Onomastic Central Archives: The foundation of Finnish onomastics. *Studia Fennica, 34,* 11-25. Refs. Figs. Maps. Photo.
Pp. 21-24 are devoted to personal names. There are collections of surnames and personal names. A figure shows various Finnish forms of Johannes [John].

[9.20.12] Selenius, Ebba. (1985). Husbonde- och husmorsnamn i Snappertuna [The names of farmers and their wives in Snappertuna]. *StudAnthroScan, 3,* 103-120. Refs. Swedish. English summary.
Snappertuna is a Swedish-speaking parish in western Finland. "Farmer names are those names used when referring to the master on a farm, and are derived from the farm's name." Farmer names locate the farmer geographically. Wives also derive their names from the farm.

[9.20.13] Thors, Carl-Eric. (1971). On personal names among the nobility and professional classes in Finland in the 17th and 18th centuries. *Proceedings of the 10th ICOS, Vienna, 1969 (Disputationes ad montium vocabula allorumque nominum significationes pertinentes), 2,* 359-364.
On the development of Finnish surnames. Description of Swedish and German on the surnames of the nobility with names such as Adlercreutz ("eagle-cross") and Sabelhjerta ("sabre-heart"). The clergy and other learned families showed Old Testament influence on naming patterns with names such as David and Essias (Isaiah). Other sources for names also described. Examples.

[9.20.14] Valtavuo-Pfeifer, Ritva. (1983). Namnbruk i Kristinestad 1724-1855: Populära flicknamn [Name usage in Kristinestad, Finland, from 1724 to 1855: Popular girls' names]. *StudAnthroScan, 1,* 62-80. Refs. Tables. Swedish. English summary.
Extensive tables and figures show the trends of the most popular names such as Maria, Anna, Katarina, Elisabet, and Margareta.

9.21. ETHNIC NAMES: *French*

[9.21.1] Blayo, Yves. (1973). Name variations in a village in Brie, 1750-1860. In E. A. Wrigley (Ed.), *Identifying people in the past* (pp. 57-63; 151-154). Refs. Tables.
In a family reconstitution study of a village near Paris used a variation of the Russell Soundex code for French names.

[9.21.2] Bradbury, Jim. (1989). Fulk le Réchin and the origin of the Plantagenets. In Christopher Harper-Bill, Christopher J. Holdsworth, & Janet L. Nelson (Eds). *Studies in medieval history presented to R. Allen Brown* (pp. 27-41). Refs. Woodbridge, Suffolk [England]: Boydell Press.
Pp. 38-39 list 20+ nicknames of the Counts of Anjou beginning in the 12th cent. Among these are: Ralph, the Badly-Tonsured; Robert, the Devil; Theobald, the Tricky; and Ralph, Ass's Head.

[9.21.3] Layton, Robert. (1971). Patterns of informal interaction in Pellaport. In Frederick George Bailey (Ed.), *Gifts and poisons.* Oxford: Basil Blackwell. 318p.
Pellaport (pop. 250) is a small village in the northern French Jura. Brief passing description (pp. 106-107) of how ungracious people were mocked by being called nicknames such as, "the Customs Official," "the Seigneur," and "the Pasha."

[9.21.4] Meigs, P. (1941). An ethno-telephonic survey of French Louisiana. *Annals Association of American Geographers, 31,* 243-250. Refs. Maps.
Used 115 Louisiana and 6 Texas telephone directories to identify the 10 most common names in each district and used these as samples to locate the French area. The top 12 French names (including LeBlanc, Landry, Hebert, and Broussard) are listed and categorized as Creole, Acadian, or Latinized German.

[9.21.5] Nitze, William A. (1956). On the derivation of Old French Enygeus (Welsh Innogen, Shakespeare Imogen). *Zeitschrift für französische Sprache und Literatur, 66,* 40-42. Refs.

Examination of several possibilities lead to conclusion that Innogen is traced to the Irish *Ingen* ("maiden"), Welsh *Innogen,* and Breton *Enog(u)en,* rather than directly from the Greek *Eugenos.*

[9.21.6] Pelan, Margaret. (1954). The nominal suffix *'-tine(e)'. Modern Language Review, 49,* 13-22. Refs.
A collection of French words ending in *-tin(e)* shows at least 15 personal names. Examples are: Albertin, Catin, Margotin. Discussion of the implications of this kind of ending.

[9.21.7] West, Robert C. (1986). *An atlas of Louisiana surnames of French and Spanish origin.* Baton Rouge, LA: Geoscience Publications, Louisian State University, 217p. Refs. Maps.
Background on the surnames of early settlers in Louisiana who were mostly French. 100 names are each described with separate entries. Maps show areas where households with the name presently exist. Pronunciation of each name is given along with early history and current information. Among the most common names are: Hébert, Landry, Broussard, LeBlanc, and Guidry. 7 of the names are of Spanish origin.

9.22. ETHNIC NAMES: *German*

[9.22.1] Bellingham, Mary; Brandt, Edward R.; Cutkomp, Kent; Frye, Kermit, & Whitmer, Karen. (1991). *Research guide to German-American genealogy.* St. Paul, MN: German-Interest Group, 215p. Refs.
Ch. 4, Personal Names, (pp. 21-27), is a general description of types of surname and 1st names. Also shows examples of German name changes in America, examples Schneider to Snyder, then to Taylor or Tailor; translations of 1st names, Friedrich to Fred; Gertraud to Gertrude. Examples throughout.

[9.22.2] Diament, Henri. (1989). La métononmasie des noms de personnes germaniques sous la Renaissance et de nos jours [Metonomasia of Germanic personal names in the Renaissance and modern periods]. *OnoCan, 71,* 13-23. Refs. French. English summary.
Discussion with examples of types of name translation. During the Renaissance, names were translated from the vernacular into Latin, example, Kramer to Mercator; sometimes into Greek, Schwarzerd to Malanchthon. In the modern era, names have been from German to English, examples, Battenberg to Mountbatten; German/Yiddish to English, example, Steinberg to Stonehill; German/Yiddish to French, example, Rosenberg to Montrose; and German/Yiddish to Portuguese, example, Wolfsohn to Lobofilho.

[9.22.3] Hartmann, Torsten. (1985). A concept-specific semantic differential for the rating of German 1st and 2nd names. *Journal of Social Psychology, 125,* 787-788. Refs.
Used a German version of the semantic differential at the University of Kiel [Germany] to rate 104 1st names and 2ndary names (surnames). 12 of the names showed stereotyping. A negatively perceived surname rated along with a 1st name can affect the rating of the 1st name. No examples given.

[9.22.4] Hassebrauck, Manfred. (1988). Beauty is more than name deep: The effect of women's first names on ratings of physical attractiveness and personality attributes. *Journal of Applied Social Psychology, 18,* 721-726. Refs. Table.
In a follow-up to S. Gary Garwood et al. [87:41.20], set up more refined procedures which were carried out in Germany. Results indicate that contrary to Garwood, there was no relationship between the assigned 1st name and rating of beauty.

[9.22.5] Hilbig, Frederick Walter. (1968). *Americanization of German surnames and the related process of changes in Europe.* Unpublished master's thesis. University of Utah, Salt Lake City, 83p. Refs.
Develops basic ideas about the transition of German surnames in Europe and America; spelling changes. Extensive work with directories shows presumed variations of 12 names, example, Teufelbeiss (Devil bite) has 18 variants including Devilbiss and Divelbliss.

[9.22.6] Jones, George F. (1990). *German-American names.* Genealogical Publishing, 268p. Illus.
A 5 chapter intro. gives information on onomastics, surnames, 1st names, German sound shifts, German dithematic names, and High Germans vs. Low German. The dictionary has a large collection of 12,700 surnames. Examples include: Teich "pond"; Schlesinger "from Silesia"; and Kaufdasbier "buy the beer."

[9.22.7] Leighly, John. (1983). *German family names in Kentucky place names.* American Name Society, *Monograph No. 2,* 84p. Refs. Tables.
Based upon 1719 current and former placenames brought by immigrants from the colonial period. Names are placed in several categories. The largest (340) is Authentic German Family Names (examples, Hildebrand, Kaiser). A 2nd is Pronunciation Preserved but Spelling Changed (example, Clybur from Keliber). A 3rd is Translations (example, Pepper from Peffer or Pfeffer). Other categories also. Extensive tables.

[9.22.8] Löffler, Heinrich. (1989). Onomastic research in German speaking countries. *NomAfr, 3(1),* 7-16. Refs.
Survey of onomastics in the German-speaking countries: Austria, East and West Germany, and Switzerland. The article includes personal names and nicknames. Among the contributors to onomastics who are mentioned are: Ernst Förstemann, Adolf Bach, and Friedhelm Debus.

[9.22.9] Maenchen-Helfen. O. (1955). Pseudo-Huns. *Central Asiatic Journal, 1,* 101-106. Refs.
After examining the literature, concludes that *hun* in such names as Hunirix, Hunila, and Huna is not from the same origin as the Huns that Attila led.

[9.22.10] Nelson, Lowry, Jr. (1981). Heidegger, or harrower of the earth. [The State of Letters]. *Sewanee Review, 89,* 153-156.
Speculation on the possible meaning(s) of the surname (German) of the famous theologian.

[9.22.11] Nicolaisen, Wilhelm F. H. (1986). Fun and games. *Grazer Linguische Studien* [Germany], *25,* 215-221. Refs.
Description of approx. 70 nicknames that became surnames. Many have negative connotations (Dick, "thick"; Zornig, "angry"; Billig, "cheap"). Others relate to animals or intimate parts of the anatomy. [The article is in English but a German slang dictionary would be helpful]

[9.22.12] Penzl, Herbert. (1987). *hlewagastiz:* Names and early Germanic morphology. *Names, 35,* 22-27. Refs.
Comment and discussion on the onomastic implications of a runic text from 400 AD for the study of early Germanic names as part of Germanic.

[9.22.13] Smith, Kenneth L. (1989). *German church books: Beyond the basics.* Camden, ME: Picton Press, 223p. Refs.
Ch. 2 (pp. 33-64) on names (German) has sections on spelling variations, dialectic variants, farm names, and patronyms which may be helpful to researchers. Examples.

[9.22.14] Spiegl, Fritz. (1979, May 3). What's in a name? *The Listener*, p. 615.
Comments on the meaning in German of the names of some musicians. Examples
include: Musikant ("musician"), Geiger ("orchestra conductor"), and a viola player
named Kuschemaul ("shut your mouth"). Others mentioned are Erlichman ("honest
man"), and Holzenbein ("wooden leg").

[9.22.15] Thode, Ernest. (1988). *Atlas for Germanic genealogy*, 2nd ed. Marietta, OH:
Heritage House, 74p. Maps.
Pp. 16-19 have maps showing regions of name frequency. Nis is a common male 1st
name in the north; Frauke, a female name. For surnames, maps show suffixes identified
with a region.

[9.22.16] Tvedt, Kevin. (1990). Using surnames to trace German origin. *GGSA
Bulletin* (German Genealogical Society of America), *4(1)*, pp. 1, 3-6. Maps.
Discussion of Low German and High German dialects. Maps and description of surname
differences in: (1) forms of patronymics and dipthongs, (2) indications of place of origin,
(3) regional sounds and word geography, and (4) regional varieties of some surnames.

[9.22.17] Weiss, Volkmar. (1980). Inbreeding and genetic distance between
hierarchically structured populations. *Mankind Quarterly, 21*, 135-149. Refs. Tables.
Summary of author's papers in German based upon studies in East Germany using
surnames.

For another article on German surnames, See: [23.2].

9.23. ETHNIC NAMES: *Greek (Modern)*

[9.23.1] Aschenbrenner, Stanley E. (1975). Folk model vs. actual practice: The
distribution of spiritual kin in a Greek village. *Anthropological Quarterly, 48*, 65-86.
The village of Karpofora (pop. 350) is in Messenia, the southwestern province of the
Peloponnesus. Pp. 68-69 describe the Orthodox Christian baptism customs. A preferred
form is to ask the parents' wedding sponsor to baptize the 1st child. The godparent
chooses the child's name. The custom is that the 1st 2 children of each sex are named
after the grandparents.

[9.23.2] Bogiatzoglou, Basos E. (1988). Tourkika kai Tourkogene eponyma sten
Hellada [Turkish influence on Greek surnames]. *Onomata, 12*, 96-107. Refs. Greek.
English summary.
Centuries of Greek rule and the arrival of refugees from the Middle East from 1922 on
have influenced Greek surnames.

[9.23.3] Campbell, J(ohn). Kennedy). (1964). *Honour, family, and patronage: A study
of institutions and moral values in a Greek mountain community*. Oxford: Clarendon,
393p. Refs. Illus.
The Sarakatsani shepherds and their families (about 4000 people) live during the summer
in Zagori, a mountainous district northeast of Jannina in the Epirus province. In winter
they move down from the mountains. Among their naming customs: after marriage a
woman is called by the feminine form of her husband's 1st name (p. 186); godfather
names the child (p. 220) although usually after one of the grandparents or a saint whose
day is on the day the baptism occurs; the community may stop using a man's surname
if it is felt he has married beneath him, or has lost his wealth (pp. 300-301); and
nicknames may be either flattering or ridiculing (p. 315).

[9.23.4] Du Boulay, Juliet. (1974). *Portrait of a Greek mountain village*. Oxford:
Clarendon, 296p. Refs. Illus. Plates.

Based upon a small village (pop. 144 in 1966), p. 138 has a passing mention of the role of the male child to keep the name alive.

[9.23.5] Hardie, M. M. (1923). The significance of Greek personal names. *Folk-Lore, 34,* 149-154.
Naming customs in a rural isolated area, Kastoria in western Macedonia. Description of naming customs including: belief in reincarnation, naming after grandparents, posthumous sons, and dead siblings.

[9.23.6] Herzfeld, Michael. (1982). When exceptions define the rules: Greek baptismal names and the negotiation of identity. *Journal of Anthropological Research, 38,* 288-302. Refs.
The rural communities of Pefko, Rhodes and Glendi, Crete were investigated in regard to naming practices. Description of variations from usual rules of naming (1st male child for paternal grandfather, 1st female child for maternal grandmother) such as when a child was "promised" to a saint for cure of infertility. Extended comment on types of naming.

[9.23.7] Hoffman, Susannah M. (1976). The ethnography of the islands: Thera. In M. Dinen and E. Friedl (Eds.) *Regional variation in Modern Greece and Cyprus: Toward a perspective on the ethnography of Greece. Annals of the New York Academy of Sciences, 268,* 328-340.
Thera is at the southernmost tip of the Cyclades islands, 125 miles south of Athens. Pp. 333-334 describe naming patterns: 1st 2 children of each sex are named for the grandparents, with the 1st child being named for the same-sexed parent's parent. Further children named for uncles, aunts, or patron saints.

[9.23.8] Katranides, Aristotle. (1970). Some rules for modern Greek nicknames. *Word, 26,* 402-409.
Extensive systematic description of various types of nickname mostly of hypocoristic form. They follow 3 rules: (1) reduction (aristotélis > áris or télis, (2) reduplication (sofia > fifi), (3) affixation (katsaróla ("saucepan") + > katsarol*lítsa* ("little saucepan"). Many examples.

[9.23.9] Kenna, Margaret E. (1976). Houses, fields, and graves: Property and ritual obligation on a Greek island. *Ethnology, 15,* 21-34.
This fictitiously named island is 20 hours by ship from Piraeus. Naming patterns for children described: 1st son after paternal grandfather, 2nd for maternal, 1st daughter for maternal grandmother, 2nd for paternal grandmother. Other children are named according to a system after other relatives. Exceptions explained. Names are also associated with property.

[9.23.9A] Kyrris, P. (1967). The noble family of Logaras of Lapethos, Cyprus: Some new information about their careers, activities, and landed properties. *Rivista di Studi Bizantini e Neoellenici, 4,* 107-149. Refs.
Pp. 134-135 list (in Greek script) 22 1st names (Dora, Helene) and 17 surnames (Fantos, Kittos) from the village of Livera in Cyprus [time period not specified].

[9.23.10] Loizos, Peter. (1975). *The Greek gift: Politics in a Greek village.* New York: St. Martin's Press; Oxford: Basil Blackwell, 326p. Refs.
Pp. 96-97 show that many villagers have the same 1st name; some have identical 1st and surname. Nicknames serve to differentiate. They are used to the owner's face [unlike some other cultures]. Examples include: the Bat, the Cheese-eater, and the Fat Man.

[9.23.11] Philippides, Marios. (1989-90). The name Sphrantzes in Ubertino Puscolo. *Onomata, 13,* 208-211. Refs.

After evaluation concludes that George Sphrantzes (1401-1477) was the author of *Chronicon Minos* and that the *Chronicon Maius* is by a forger Makarios Melissourgos-Melissenos who used the name Phrantzes.

9.24. ETHNIC NAMES: *Hawaiian*

[9.24.1] Ka'ano'i, Patrick & Snakenberg, Robert Lokomaika'iokalani. (1988). *The Hawaiian name book: Hawaiian translation.* Honolulu: Bess, 43p. Refs.
Description of how names from English and other languages are Hawaiianized, examples, Jim > Kimo, Dorothy and Theodore (both) > Makannaakua [apparently there are no sex markers in Hawaiian]. 500 male and female names listed.

[9.24.2] Root, Eileen M. (1987). *Hawaiian names--English names.* Kailua, HI: Press Pacifica, 163p. Refs.
Very brief description of Hawaiian language and naming. Listing of 800 Hawaiian names with meaning (Hawaian names are unisex), examples, Kumu = "base, foundation, beginning, source"), Pu'ukani = "sweet voiced." A 2nd section lists 400+ English names and meaning along with transliteration into Hawaiian and an equivalent name in Hawaian, examples, the same meaning is Hiwahiwa.

9.25. ETHNIC NAMES: *Hispanic*

[9.25.1] Lavender, Abraham D. (1992). The distinctive Hispanic names (DHN) technique: A method for selecting a sample or estimating population size. *Names, 40,* 1-16. Refs. Tables.
Explains the development of a procedure for using a selected small number of names to estimate the size of an ethnic population. In this report it is Hispanic voters in Miami Beach who are a mix of those from Cuba, Puerto Rico, and other places. Most practical list included: Rodriguez, Gonzalez, Garcia, Perez, Hernandez, Lopez, Sanchez, Martinez, Diaz, and Ramos.

[9.25.2] Shaw, Richard F. (1960). An index of consanguinity based on the use of the surname in Spanish-speaking countries. *Journal of Heredity, 51,* pp. 221 and 230.
Proposes an index of consanguinity which takes into consideration the full names of both parents for those from Spanish-speaking countries.

9.26. ETHNIC NAMES: *Huguenot*

[9.26.1] Roche, Owen I. A. (1965). *The days of the upright.* New York: Clarkson N. Potter, 340p. Refs.
Pp. 322-328 are devoted to a brief intro. and listing of 550+ Huguenot names drawn from early records. Examples include: Cabot, Crommelin, Foucoult, and Vidal.

[9.26.2] Tsushima, Jean. (1987). What *Is* a 'Huguenot name'? *Huguenot & Walloon Gazette, 1,* 43-47.
Points out that there is no such thing as a Huguenot name. In France, many families were split into Catholic and Huguenot categories. In England, the problem is similar plus the question of whether they were of English or French/Anglo-Norman descent. Examples.

[9.26.3] Tsushima, Jean. (1990-91). Impact--Some reactions to foreign surnames: Or, the art of getting it wrong. *Nomina, 14,* 25-40. Refs. Maps.

In a light vein. Shows how French Huguenot names in England became distorted in spelling. These distortions in written records make tracing ancestry difficult. Author uses her own name to illustrate how distortions in foreign names still goes on.

9.27. ETHNIC NAMES: *Hungarian*

[9.27.1] Antal, Laszlo. (1988). Remarks on Hungarian nicknames [affectionate names]. *Ural-Altaische Jahrbücher/Ural-Altaic Yearbook, 60,* 7-11. Ref.
Lists 26 1st names and their affectionate forms [called nicknames in the article], examples, Ferenc, Feri; Katalin, Kati. Uses vowel and consonant analysis to predict an affectionate name form, examples, Mihály should yield Mihi but gives Misi. Concludes that speakers must learn many exceptions to rules.

[9.27.2] Forgács, Krisztina. (1990). Hungarianization of Jewish surnames. *Proceedings of the 17th ICOS, Helsinki, 13-18 Aug. 1990, 1,* 322-328. Refs.
Evaluation of previously restricted archives from 1869-1945 regarding petitions by Hungarian Jews for change of name. Most (85%) had German names. The most common names for those who changed were professions (Kovács, "smith," Molnár, "miller," etc.) and adjectives (Kis, "small", Nagy, "big", etc.). Many names had links or connections to the original (initials, sound, translation). Many examples.

[9.27.3] Hajdú, M. (1972). A survey of the most frequent Hungarian Christian names of the 18th-20th centuries. *Annales Universitatis Scientiarum Budapestinensis de Rolando Eotvos nominatae, Sectio linguistica, 3,* 37-51. Refs. Map.
Analysis of the 10 most common male and female names from 8 periods from 1770-1967. Men's names were more resistant to change; women's names showed greater change. Further extensive tables by period and geographic area show regional differences. Further differences are also noted.

[9.27.4] Hajdú, Mihály. (1983). *Magyar-angol, angol-magyar keresztnévszót* [Hungarian-English, English-Hungarian dictionary of Christian names]. Budapest: ELTE: Magyar Nyelvészeti Tanszékcsoport Névkutatö Munkaközössége, 117p. Refs.
Approx. 1800 names listed with pronunciation, derivation, and frequency. Names not used in Hungary are marked. Examples of entries include: Arvid < Norwegian means "eagle" + "man." The name Arvid is not found in Hungary. Imre shows 20 variations. A 2nd shorter section lists common English 1st names with their Hungarian equivalents, examples Benedict = Benedek.

[9.27.5] Mephisto. (1952). Those Hungarians. [Mephisto Musings]. *Musical America, 72,* 11.
Comment that Hungarians reverse the order of their names so that the name we know as Béla Bartók becomes Bartók Béla in Hungary.

[9.27.6] Nogrady, Michael. (1990). Treatment of Hungarian names in Canada. *Proceedings of the 16th ICOS, Laval University, Quebec, 1987,* 433-440. Refs.
Problems of Hungarian immigrants in adapting their names to languages which have differences in alphabets. Some names in Hungarian have diacritical marks, some do not. Some 1st names have English equivalents, some do not.

[9.27.7] Paetzke, H. H., & Rajk, L. (1986). A man with many names: From Hungary's buried past. [Editorial]. *Dissent, 33,* 320-326.
Interview with Rajk, son of a Hungarian communist leader. After the father was executed in 1949, the son, beginning at the age of 4 months, was given 4 different changes of name by the age of 16. At that time, he regained his birth name. The changes took place under different political regimes.

9.28. ETHNIC NAMES: *Icelandic*

[9.28.1] Foote, Peter. (1973). A note on some personal names in *Faereyinga saga*. In *Otium et negotium: Studies in onomatology and library science presented to Olof von Feilitzen, Acta Bibliothecae Regiae Stockholmiensis, 16,* 96-108. Refs.
The saga was written in Iceland. Events took place in the Faeroe Islands and other places. Analysis of many names in the saga by country of origin.

[9.28.2] Hollander, Lee M. (1952). Two unrecognized Celtic names: Vagn Ákason and Thórvald Tíntein. *Studies in Honor of Albert Morey Sturtevant, University of Kansas Publications, No. 29,* pp. 71-75. Refs.
Suggests that the Vagn of Vagn Ákason in the Icelandic *Jómsvíkinga Saga* is from Welsh meaning "little" (modern Vaughn). The name Tíntein refers to "stronghold on the hill."

[9.28.3] Sigmundsson, Svavar. (1992). Ný lög um íslensk mannanöfn [New Icelandic Personal Names Act]. *StudAnthroScan, 10,* 81-90. Refs. Icelandic. English summary.
A new law passed in 1991 deals with 1st (given) names and surnames. Among the provisions for 1st names: a child may receive 3 given names but the names must be Icelandic or assimilated into Icelandic forms, a boy may not have a girl's name and vice versa. There is a list of permitted names. Rules on surnames as well.

[9.28.4] Stemshaug, Ola. (1983). Landnáma som personnamnkjelde [The Landnáma as a source for personal names]. *StudAnthroScan, 1,* 7-20. Refs. Map. Norwegian. English summary.
The Landnáma is the "original document about the settlement of Iceland (ca 870-930)." Evaluation of this work as a source for personal names. Suggests that caution must be used.

9.29. ETHNIC NAMES: *Indo-Pakistani Sub-Continent*

[9.29.1] Balagangadhara Rao, Yarlagadda. (1990). Surnames of Telugu people. *Proceedings of the 17th ICOS, Helsinki, 13-18 Aug. 1990, 1,* 157-166.
Telugu is a language group and a people in Andra Pradesh, near Madras in southern India. Discussion of surnames among the different societal groupings in that cultural group. Presentation of arguments against the position of the women's movement to keep birth names at marriage. Examples of surnames.

[9.29.2] Bhalla, V. & Bhatia, K. (1976). Isonymy in a Bhatia leut. *Annals of Human Genetics, 39,* 497-500. Refs. Table.
The *leut* here is apparently a small community with ethnic and religious ties. The investigation was done on this community in North India which migrated to Delhi from Pakistan in 1947. The most common names were: Tanang, Rilla, Neelu, and Dhagga. 63 of 345 couples (18.26%) showed isonymy between husband's father and spouse's mother.

[9.29.3] Britto, Francis. (1986). Personal names in Tamil society. *Anthropological Linguistics, 28,* 349-365. Refs.
Report on the Tamils of Tamil Nadu [formerly Madras state] in South India. The Tamils have a name structure radically different from that of Western society. The Tamils have 1 or 2 given names but no family name (a caste name is optional). Name categories are explained with examples. Difficulties of cataloging Tamil names described.

[9.29.4] Chekki, D. A. (1967). Naming patterns and kinship cohesiveness. *Quarterly Journal of Indian Studies in Social Sciences, 1,* 179-181. Refs. Tables.

Genealogies of 115 Brahman families in a suburb of Dharwar, northern Mysore, India, were studied for naming patterns. The traditional pattern of naming children after dead relatives is not as common now as it once was. Modern names are increasing. The traditional pattern is to name the 1st son after the paternal grandfather, 1st dau. after the paternal grandmother (this is in contrast to many Western practices).

[9.29.5] Dil, Afia. (1975). A comparative study of the personal names and nicknames of the Bengali-speaking Hindus and Muslims. *Studies on Bengal, Papers Presented at the 7th Annual Bengal Studies Conference,* University of Minnesota, Minneapolis, pp. 51-71. Refs. Tables.
Systematic description of key aspects of Bengali Hindu and Muslim names. Includes surnames used by each group and by both groups, examples, Mojumdar (keeper of accounts), Poddar (examiner of coins). Extensive tables show various types of names including title and title suffix. Nickname patterns also described.

[9.29.6] Gokhale, Shobhana. (1957). Cultural significance of the personal and placenames from Vākāṭaka inscriptions. *Bulletin of the Deccan College Research Institute* (BDCRI) [India], *18,* 173-185. Refs.
The inscriptions are from Madhya Pradesh in central India. Discussion of names from inscriptions from 300-1300 AD. Description of sources of names, gods, animals, spirits, etc. Approx. 85 names explained.

[9.29.7] Henley, Alix. (1979). *Asian patients in hospital and at home.* London: King Edward's Hospital Fund for Children, 188p. Figs.
Ch. 8 (pp. 87-104) describes Indian, Sikh, and Moslem naming systems in contrast with the British. Listing of 260+ names in appropriate categories. Text exercises on names.

[9.29.8] Loewenthal, Isidore. (1911). Intro. by S. M. Z. The name 'I'sa. *Muslim World* [Hartford], *1,* 265-282.
This article was originally published in Calcutta in 1861. After extended comments on the controversy on whether Jesus should be referred to as 'I'sa or Yushua, suggests that 'I'sa be retained for work with Muslims but that Yushua be used with Hindus.

[9.29.9] Mehrotra, R. R. (1979). Name change in Hindi: Some sociocultural dimensions. *Anthropological Linguistics, 21,* 205-210. Refs. Tables.
In India, name changes take place for the following reasons: (1) dissatisfaction with name, (2) becoming a monk, (3) change of religion, (4), change in social values, (5), change of caste names, and (6) change of 1st name by in-laws (for a woman). Those in some occupations also change their names: entertainers, writers, criminals, and prostitutes.

[9.29.10] Nikhilanda, Swami. (1957). Aum: The word of words. In Ruth Nanda Anshen (Ed.) *Language: An inquiry into its meaning and functions.* (pp. 80-85). New York: Harper.
"The most sacred word in the Vedas...is Aum." It is the mother or source of all names and forms according to the Hindu religion.

[9.29.11] Patil, Vimla. (1990). *Baby names: Over 4000 beautiful Indian names for your child.* Calcutta, India: Rupa & Co., 72p.
Listing of names with meanings, examples, Vimla is a female name and means "pure"; Moti, a male name means "pearl." Most names appear to be Hindu from Sanskrit but there are several names from Arabic.

[9.29.12] Schimmel, Annemarie. (1987). Some remarks about Muslim names in Indo-Pakistan. In Shaul Skaked, David Dean Shulman, & Gedaliahu A. G. Strousma

Gilgul: Essays on transformation, revolution, and permanence in the history of religions (pp. 217-222). Leiden, Holland: E. J. Brill.
Names in this area showed more variety than those from the Maghrib. The pattern showed "a whole string of names to men and women combining *kunya, ism,* several *alqāb* into one grand name." One category is *gratitude,* example, Hibat Allāh ("God's gift") showing appreciation for the birth of a son. Patterns of the Sufis and Shii described.

[9.29.13] Wilson, Susan R. (1981). The analysis of g-isonymy data. *Annals of Human Biology, 8,* 341-350. Refs. Tables.
Further analysis of the data of K. Bhatia to determine the random and non-random components of generalized isonymy (when 2 individuals who have the same surname are related through marriage although not necessarily to each other).

9.30. ETHNIC NAMES: *Iranian*

[9.30.1] Frye, R. N. (1962). Some early Iranian titles. *Oriens, 15,* 352-359. Refs.
Sources in pre-Islamic Iranian contain titles which have 3 categories: (1) actual offices with titles, (2) honorifics, and (3) personal or family names. Comment and conjecture on various aspects, the name Varaz.

[9.30.2] Memar-Sadeghi, Abdomaljid. (1980). Changing personal names and titles in written Farsi (1921-1978): A sociolinguistic study with pedagogical implications. *DissAbstrIntl, 41,* 3617A. (Order No. 8026560, 254p.)
The persianization and simplification of 1st names, surnames, and titles. Definition of the relationship between sociolinguistic change in names and titles to sociocultural events in Iran and the influence of Westernization and modernization.

[9.30.3] Nader, Habibi. (1992). Popularity of Islamic and Persian names in Iran before and after the Islamic revolution. *International Journal of Middle East Studies, 24,* 253-260. Refs. Tables. Figs.
From data collected at 5 intervals between 1963 and 1968 analyzed the types of name (Persian, Islamic, and Arabic) given to children in the city of Hamadan (pop. 300,000) in midwestern Iran. Name types were analyzed by sex, urban/rural background of father, and father's occupation. Changes noted and interpreted in light of the political changes in Iran.

9.31. ETHNIC NAMES: *Irish*

[9.31.1] Breen, Richard. (1982). Naming practices in western Ireland. *Man, 17,* 701-713. Refs. Tables.
First names and middle names of the parish registers of Tuogh from 1925-1950 were tallied. The regular naming pattern is to name the 1st 2 children of each sex after the grandparents; later children after relatives. Middle names were chosen because they were saints' names. Nicknames have been more short-lived in Tuogh compared with the report of Fox on the Tory Islanders [87:8.37.6].

[9.31.2] Browne, Charles R. (1895). The ethnography of the Mullet, Inishkea Islands, and Portacloy, County Mayo. *Proceedings of the Royal Irish Academy, 3,* 587ff. Refs. Tables. Plates.
An extensive ethnological investigation of this district in Northwest Ireland. Pp. 602-605 give the complete names of 62 men plus other information on them. Pp. 616-617 list approx. 130 surnames by frequency of families that hold that name. Those with the largest number are: Lavelle, 31; Barrett, 27; Reilly, 27; Gaughn, 23; and Monoghan,

20. P. 618 lists 29 names with their modern and ancient forms. Examples, Boland <
O'Beollain, Earley < O'Mailfomhair, Loftus < O'Lachtna.

[9.31.3] Browne, Charles R. (1896). The ethnography of Ballycroy, County Mayo.
Proceedings of the Royal Irish Academy, 4, 74-111. Refs.
An extensive anthropological investigation was done on this district in Northwest Ireland.
Pp. 86-88 give the full names of the 50 men in the sample. P. 97 lists the 47 surnames
with frequencies of the district. Most common are: Conway, 31; Cafferky, 25; Lenahan,
20; Kane/Keane, 16; and M'Manamon, 16.

[9.31.4] Browne, Charles R. (1898). The ethnography of Graumna and Lettermullen,
in the County Galway. *Proceedings of the Royal Irish Academy, 5,* 223-268. Refs. Illus.
These 2 treeless (apparently relatively barren) islands are about 30 miles west of Galway.
An extensive anthropological report gives extensive measures on 60 males with their 1st
names and surnames. Also given are the 60 surnames with frequency of families.
Included are: M'Donogh, 69; Flaherty, 60; and Conneely, 24.

[9.31.5] Browne, Charles R. (1900). The ethnography of Carna and Mweenish, in the
parish of Moyruss, Connemara. *Proceedings of the Royal Irish Academy, 6,* 503-538.
Refs. Illus.
Detailed anthropological measurements on 38 men by name in these communities in
western Ireland. Frequency of surname by family is also given for 95 families. Most
common surnames are: Conneely, 51; Mulkerrin, 35; and M'Donogh, 30.

[9.31.6] Butler, Hubert. (1972). *Ten thousand saints: A study in Irish and European
origins.* Kilkenny, Ireland: Wellbrook Press, 334p. Refs. Glossary.
Butler believes that the Irish inherited their saints from their pre-Celtic past. The saints
were taken from the mythologies of other cultures. Description of many, many saints.
A few are: Mael ("bald"), Dub ("black"), and Glunsalach ("dirty kneed").

[9.31.7] Cargill, D. C. (1972). Irishmen in Scottish census records. *Irish Ancestor, 4,*
8-12.
The 1851 census returns of the Royal Artillery regiment at Leith Fort and the 13th Light
Dragoons at Edinburgh list approx. 120 soldiers from Ireland and members of their
families. Each listing shows name, marital status, age, rank, and previous occupation.
The records are unusual in that they also show the specific places in Ireland.

[9.31.8] Connolly, Frank. (1973). The Hearth Money Rolls for the parishes of Ramoan
and Culfeightrin. *The Glynns* [Ireland], *1,* 10-15.
The Hearth Money tax was for Charles II. The Rolls from 1669 list approx. 200 people.
All except the very poor had to pay the tax. Some of those on the lists were: Hugh
Muloony, Alexander McGee, Brice Dunlapp, and Roger Horseman.

[9.31.9] de Brun, P. (1975). A census of the parishes of Prior and Killemlagh, Dec.
1834. *Journal of the Kerry Archaeological & Historical Society, 8,* 114-135.
Daniel O'Connell, the Irish Liberator, instigated surveys in 1834-35. This one is a listing
of heads of household by name, number of people in household, sex, and religion by
parish in Prior (3375 Catholics, 10 Protestants) and Killemlagh (2546 Catholics, 20
Protestants).

[9.31.10] Dispossessed landowners of Ireland, 1664. (1971). *Irish Genealogist, 4,*
275-302; 429-444.
Listing of 1630 entries from Leinster, Munster, Ulster, and Connaught of heads of
families who lost their lands through the Cromwellian Settlement. Virtually all were
Catholic. The period of difficulty was 1641-52.

[9.31.11] Dolley, Michael. (1967). OE *Christ-thegn: An unsuspected instance of early Middle Irish influence on English name-giving. *British Numismatic Journal, 36,* 40-45. Refs. Illus.
After extensive examination of coins of the 10th cent. suggests that "Christ-thegn was in fact a Hiberno-Norseman who had borne the name Gilla Crist since his baptism."

[9.31.12] Dolley, Michael. (1973). The forms of the proper names appearing in the earliest coins struck in Ireland. In *Otium et negotium: Studies in onomatology and library science presented to Olof von Feilitzen, Acta Bibliothecae Regiae Stockholmiensis, 16,* 49-65. Refs.
Detailed description of 60 coins, c. 997, includes names of moneyers.

[9.31.13] English and its varieties: Family names, Christian names. *Encyclopedia of Ireland.* Dublin: A. Figgis; New York: McGraw-Hill, 463p. Map.
Pp. 119-122 has a brief concise history of hereditary surnames. Map showing original location of many surnames. Information on 1st names has lists of 45 male and 25 female names. These lists show origins of names and also substitute forms and equivalents. Thus Eoin is the Gaelic form of John "gift of God" and is the equivalent of John; Aisling in Gaelic ("an epiphany") is substituted for Esther.

[9.31.14] Jennings, Brendan (1951). Irish names in the Malines ordination registers, 1602-1749. *Irish Ecclesiastical Record* [Dublin], *75,* 149-162. Refs.
The Malines seminary is in Belgium. The list of names of 857 candidates for orders includes: "529 Franciscans, 205 Dominicans, 107 members of the regular clergy, 11 Jesuits, 2 Augustinians, 1 Cistercian, 1 Discalced Carmelite, and 1 Capuchin."

[9.31.15] Kane, Eileen. (1968). Man and kin in Donegal: A study of kinship function in a rural Irish and an Irish American community. *Ethnology, 7,* 245-258. Refs.
The Cashel (pseudonym) is an isolated village (pop. 300). P. 238 briefly describes "string names" (nicknames) used for identification. Examples include: Pat the Clock, Black John, and Blue Mold.

[9.31.16] Messenger, J. C. (1967). *Inis Beag: Isle of Ireland.* New York: Holt, Rinehart & Winston, 136p; p. 75.
General study of a small island which has only 13 surnames. Most 1st names are saints' names. Each person has a reference name which is never used in direct address. For men this is the 1st name or nickname followed by that of his father, as Sean Michael.

[9.31.17] Ó Cuív, Brian. (1986). Aspects of Irish personal names. *Celtica, 18,* 151-184. Refs.
Wide-ranging survey of Irish names, mainly from the 5th cent. to the 13th cent. Topics include: Ogamic sources, ms. sources, criteria for analysis of names, women's names, ghost-names, and surnames.

[9.31.18] Ó Muraile, Nollaíg. (1987). The Gaelic personal name *(An) Dubhaltach. Ainm, 2,* 1-28. Refs. Table.
(An) Dubhaltach is a rare Gaelic name. Examination of 12+ sources from the 16th and 17th cents. (the Annals, Fiants, Hearth Money Rolls, etc.) document occurrences.

[9.31.19] O'Brien, M(ichael). A. (1971). Notes on Irish proper names. *Celtica, 9,* 212.
Posthumous publication. Lists 12 Irish personal names which "though found in Welsh, do not occur elsewhere in Irish." Included are: Baccán ("small"), Coccán ("red"), and Techán ("fair").

[9.31.20] Popish inhabitants of the half barony of Ikerrin in 1750. *Irish Genealogist, 4,* 578-583.

Listing of Catholic inhabitants of this area who were assessed for damage to property and robbery "due to activities of the Whiteboys and similar organizations." Approx. 450 individuals listed.

[9.31.21] Stokes, Whitley. (1890, Sept 20). *Old Norse names in the Irish Annals. Academy, No. 959,* 248-249. Refs.
Identification of approx. 150 Old Norse names from the Irish Annals.

[9.31.22] Turner, Brian S. (1974). The Methodist baptismal registers of County Louth, 1829-1865. *County Louth Archaeological & Historical Journal, 18,* 132-139. Refs.
Listing of the Drogheda register 1829-1865 (about 220 names) and the register of Dundalk 1837-1865 (about 40 names). Most entries have the names of both parents.

9.31.1. ETHNIC NAMES: *Irish: First Names*

[9.31.1.1] Coghlan, Ronan; Grehan, Ida, & Joyce, P. W. (1989). *Book of Irish names: First, family & place names.* New York: Sterling Publishing, 387 Park Ave., South, 128p.
Part I by Coghlan has entries for about 1000 1st names. These entries show etymology, meaning, &, where relevant, the Irish form. Part II, by Grehan, has information on about 80 surnames. Part III is on placenames.

[9.31.1.2] de Breffny, Brian. (1969). Christian names in Ireland. *Irish Ancestor, 1,* 34-40.
Some variations of Irish 1st names cause confusion. There are 5 categories, (1) names that can be used for both sexes (Sydney), (2) names usually applied to one sex but occasionally used with the other (Edie, Kit), (3) diminutives which differ greatly from the original (Toby < Theobald, (4) different names that are used interchangeable (Peter = Patrick), and (5) Irish-English equivalents (Siobhan = Joanna). Many examples.

[9.31.1.3] MacLysaght, E(dward A. (1970). Christian names in Ireland. *North Munster Antiquarian Journal, 13,* 53-56. Refs.
Listing of most common names for men and women from the medieval period on.

9.31.2. ETHNIC NAMES: *Irish: Gaelic*

[9.31.2.1] Dobbs, Margaret E. (1948). The prefix 'Mess' in Irish personal names. *Journal of the Royal Society of Antiquaries of Ireland, 77,* 147-149. Refs.
Traces names with Mess (meaning, "a blade") as a prefix to the period 100 BC-100 AD. One example is Mesdelmond and his 4 sons, Messgegra, Mesroida, Mesdana, and Mesdomnand. Suggests that there is a link between the Gaelic and Sumerian roots of Mess.

[9.31.2.2] Fox, Robin. (1978). The Tory Islanders: A people of the Celtic fringe. Cambridge, England: Cambridge University Press, 210p. Refs. Figs. Illus.
Tory Island is off the North coast of Ireland. Ch. 4 (pp. 66-81) is devoted to kinship and naming. Using Synge [87:8.37.20] as a basis for comparison, describes the somewhat complex system of English-Gaelic naming.

[9.31.2.3] Fox, Robin. (1982). Principles and pragmatics on Tory Island. In Anthony P. Cohen (Ed.) *Belonging: Identity and social organisation in British rural cultures.* (pp. 50-71). St. John's Newfoundland: Institute of Social & Economic Research Papers No. 11. Refs. Figs. Photo.
Pp. 54-60 have a briefer presentation than Fox above.

[9.31.2.4] Ó Corráin, Donnchadh & Maguire, Fidelma. (1981). *Gaelic personal names.* Dublin, Ireland: Academy Press, 188p. Refs.
Intro. to Irish personal names followed by entries for approx. 1000 names. Index also includes English forms so that Irish forms can be located, i.e., Hannah can be found under A'ine, Ono'ra, and Siba'n. Each entry gives pronunciation, sex, meaning, information on etymology, and prominent bearers of the name.

9.31.3. ETHNIC NAMES: *Irish: Population Structure and Names*

[9.31.3.1] Relethford, John H. (1982). Isonymy and population structure of Irish isolates during the 1890s. *Journal of Biosocial Science, 14,* 241-247. Refs. Tables.
Data were derived from 7, small, isolated Irish communities (4 are on small islands). Used surname frequencies to estimate kinship and geographic distances to study population structure.

[9.31.3.2] Relethford, John H., & Lees, Francis C. (1983). Correlation analysis of distance measures based on geography, anthropometry, and isonymy. *HumBio, 55,* 653-665. Refs. Tables.
12 towns in western rural Ireland were studied. Isonymy was one measure used.

[9.31.3.3] Relethford, John H.; Lees, Francis C., & Crawford, Michael. Population structure and anthropometric variation in rural western Ireland: Isolation by distance and analysis of the residuals. *American Journal of Physical Anthropology, 55,* 233-245. Refs.
Isonymy was one of several measures used to study population structure.

9.31.4. ETHNIC NAMES: *Irish: Stereotypes and Names*

[9.31.4.1] Cairns, Ed. (1980). The development of ethnic discrimination in children in Northern Ireland In Jeremy & Joan Harbison (Eds.) *A society under stress: Children and young people in Northern Ireland* (pp. 115-127 (includes tables); refs pp. 177-189).
Reviews a series of unpublished studies with Catholic and Protestant boys and girls to conclude that there is a difference between ethnic discrimination based upon stereotype cues (names) and racial discrimination based upon perceptual cues such as skin color.

[9.31.4.2] Cairns, Ed. (1987). *Caught in crossfire: Children and the Northern Ireland conflict.* Belfast: Appletree Press; Syracuse, NY: Syracuse University Press, 176p. Refs(pp. 166-176).
Pp. 100-101 describe the disguised study of Cairns above of social categorization in which children (Catholic and Protestant) "remembered" 1st names previously defined as Catholic, Protestant, and Foreign. Examples include: Catholic, Patrick, Mary; Protestant, William, Elisabeth.

[9.31.4.3] Cairns, S. E. (1975). Investigation of salience for young children in Northern Ireland of adult-generated stereotypic Protestant and Catholic first names. *Bulletin of the British Psychological Society, 31,* 64. (Abstract).
Catholic and Protestant children 5-6 yrs old heard lists of names. Results conclude that "while the children were more familiar with names associated with their own group they had not yet learned to categorize the names associated with the other denomination."

[9.31.4.4] Stringer, Maurice & Lavery, Collette. (1987). The acquisition of ethnic categorization by British university students in Northern Ireland. *Social Behaviour, 2,* 157-164. Refs. Tables.

In a follow-up to Stringer and McLaughlin-Cook below, used non-Irish university students to identify Protestants and Catholics by name and location. Results indicate the non-Irish students quickly learned the cues.

[9.31.4.5] Stringer, Maurice & McLaughlin-Cook, Neil. (1985). The effects of limited and conflicting stereotypic information on group categorization in Northern Ireland. *Journal of Applied Social Psychology, 15,* 399-407. Refs. Tables.
Used 3 types of cues (name, location, and school) to see how female undergraduates (Protestants and Catholics) distinguished themselves from others. Examples of cue names are: George Thompson (Protestant), Patrick Murphy (Catholic), & Boris Lansky (neutral). Concludes that ability to identify accurately is not necessarily an indication of prejudice.

9.31.5. ETHNIC NAMES: *Irish: Surnames*

[9.31.5.1] Alwill, Gerard. (1976). The 1841 census of Killeshandra parish. *Breifne, 5,* 7-19. Map.
This parish is in County Cavan, Ireland. The census counted 12,539 individuals. P. 11 lists the most common surnames: Reilly, Brady, Smith, Sheridan, Masterson, and Johnston.

[9.31.5.2] Bell, Robert. (1988). *The book of Ulster surnames.* Belfast: Blackstaff Press, 285p. Refs.
Major entries for 500+ surnames. These entries give meaning, prominent bearers of the name, and where in Ulster holders of the name are to be found. Refs. also to the name in the Republic and Scotland.

[9.31.5.3] de Breffny, Brian. (1982). *Irish family names: Arms, origins, and locations.* Dublin: Gill & Macmillan; New York: Norton, 192p. Refs. Color photos.
Background on 200 of the most common names plus several hundred more. Names included are Rourke, Buckley, Collins, and Murphy.

[9.31.5.4] Hume, A. (1858). Surnames in the County of Down. *Ulster Journal of Archaeology, 1st Series, 6,* 211-234. Refs. Tables. Map.
Extensive analysis and listing of surnames from the census of 1851 and the voters list of 1852. There were 252 surnames represented in the county. The 10 most common surnames were: Smith, Martin, McKee, Moore, Brown, Thompson, Patterson, Johnson, Stewart, and Wilson. Comparisons were made with County Antrim [Smith:3226].

[9.31.5.5] Mac Giolla Domhnaigh, Padraig. (1975). *Some Ulster surnames,* New ed. with a foreward by Edward McLysaght. Clódóiri [Ireland]: Circle Press, 69p. (Originally published in 1923 as *Some anglicized surnames in Ireland* by the Gael Co-operative Society).
Has entries for 400+ surnames. Shows that many "English" surnames are anglicizations of Gaelic names, example, Stone in West Mayo and in West Galway is an anglicized form of Clogherty (O'Clochartaigh), and of O'Mailehluiche in Sligo, North Mayo, North Leitrim and North Roscommon.

[9.31.5.6] MacLysaght, E(dward A. (1969). Surnames of County Clare. *North Munster Antiquarian Journal, 12,* 85-89. Refs.
Comment by a well-known onomastician on a number of aspects of Irish surnames including: Mc vs. Mac, use of the "O," mispronunciation, translation, and change of name.

[9.31.5.7] MacLysacht, E(dward) A. (1976). The Irish-Norman names. *Ireland of the Welcomes, 25(4),* 13-14.
Explanation of how Norman names came to Ireland. Listing of the 30 most common surnames of Norman origin. These include: Barrett, Costello, Prendergast, and Purcell.

[9.31.5.8] MacLysaght, Edward. (1980). *The surnames of Ireland,* 5th ed. Dublin: Irish Academic Press, 313p. Refs. Maps. (Originally published as *Guide to Irish surnames* in 1964).
Intro. and listing of approx. 4000 names. Locations given where the name originated.

[9.31.5.9] McCarville, Evelyn. (1952). What's in an Irish name. *Extension* [Chicago], *46,* 10ff.
Concise systematic presentation of the background and meaning of Irish surnames. Historical effects on Irish naming. Many examples throughout.

[9.31.5.10] McGuigan, Peter. (1985). The development and distortion of Irish surnames. *Canadian Genealogist, 7,* 11-20. Refs.
Brief history of Irish surnames from 795 AD; distortion of Irish surnames; and revival of Irish surnames. Explanation of how surnames could have Irish, semi-Irish, and English forms, examples. MagUigann, McGuigan, and Goodwin (or Goodman or Goodfellow), respectively. Many examples.

[9.31.5.11] Ó Danachair, Cáoimhín. (1975). Auxiliary family names. In Bo Alqvist, Breandán Mac Aodha, & Gearóid Mac Eoin (Eds.) *Hereditas* (pp. 228-232). Dublin: Folklore of Ireland Society.
In rural areas of Ireland, surnames such as O'Sullivan are so common that auxiliary names are used. Some combine a father and son's name, "The Sean Thaidhgs," "The Paddy Jimeens." Others come from occupations, "The Troopers," "The Piss Gatherers." Several types described with examples. Influence of nicknames mentioned.

[9.31.5.12] Ó Murchadha, Diarmid. (1985). *Family names of County Cork.* Dun Laoghaire, Dublin [Ireland]: Glendale Press, 332p. Refs.
Has separate articles on about 50 of the best-known surnames such as Sullivan ("dark-eyed") and Leahy ("heroic"). Also has index of places.

[9.31.5.13] O'Laughlin, Michael C. (1993). *The master book of Irish surnames: Locations, ethnic origins, variant spellings & sources.* Kansas City: Irish Genealogical Foundation, 304p. Indexes.
Has 60,000 Irish surnames shown in 3 indexes. The 1st is a variant index which lists 3134 names with more than one spelling. The 2nd index shows the places in Ireland where the name has been found. The 3rd index lists written sources which have referred to the name.

[9.31.5.14] Pender, Seamus (Ed.). (1939). *A census of Ireland, circa 1659: With supplementary material from the Poll Money Ordinances.* Dublin: Stationery Office, 946p. Refs. Tables.
The returns are by barony (district) and list the principal Irish names and their frequency in each. Thus, in the barony of Balrothery (Dublin) the 4 most common names were: Kelly, 16; Harford, 17; White, 17; and Russell, 15 (p. 387).

[9.31.5.15] Perceval-Maxwell, M. (1973). *The Scottish migration to Ulster in the reign of James I.* London: Routledge & Kegan Paul; New York: Humanities Press, 411p. Refs.
Pp. 286-289 demonstrate how surnames were used to identify those regions of Scotland from which those settlers came who settled in Fermanagh, Ulster. Muster lists of 1622 and 1630 were used. Among the most common names are Elliott, Armstrong, Scot, and

Stewart. Analysis of the 14,000 surnames suggests that most who settled in Ulster came from the counties bordering England or from up the west coast to Argyllshire.

[9.31.5.16] Turner, Brian S. (1968). Family names in the baronies of Upper and Lower Massereene. *Ulster Folklife, 14,* 76-78. Refs.
The area concerned is west of Belfast. Descriptions of the origins of the families. Listing of the 20 most common surnames with their frequencies in 1962. Includes: Lavery/Lowery, 179; Campbell, 153; Wilson, 152; and Thompson, 142.

[9.31.5.17] Turner, Brian S. (1975). An observation on settler names in Fermanagh. *Clogher Record, 8,* 285-289. Refs.
Fermanagh is a county in the southwest of Northern Ireland. The 5 most common names are: Maguire, Johnston, Armstrong, McManus, and Elliott. Turner traces these names to the western and middle Marches of 17th cent. England and Scotland where there were "troubles."

9.31.5.1. ETHNIC NAMES: *Irish: Surnames: Specific*

[9.31.5.1.1] Mathews, Anthony. (1968). *Origin of the surname McGuiness with a short history of the sept.* Compiled by Anthony Mathews. Dublin: Anthony Mathews, 35p. Refs.
Meaning, variations of the name, prominent bearers in various parts of Ireland and overseas.

[9.31.5.1.2] Mathews, Anthony. (1968). *Origin of the surname O'Flaherty with a short history of the sept.* Compiled by Anthony Mathews. Dublin: Anthony Mathews, 43p. Refs. Illus.
Meaning, variations of the name, prominent bearers in various parts of Ireland and overseas.

[9.31.5.1.3] Mathews, Anthony. (1968). *Origin of the surname O'Kelly with a short history of the sept.* Compiled by Anthony Mathews. Dublin: Anthony Mathews, 50p. Refs. Illus.
Meaning, variations of the name, prominent bearers in various parts of Ireland and overseas. Variations of O'Kelly include: Kelly, Kealy, Quealy, and Coakley.

[9.31.5.1.4] Mathews, Anthony. (1971). *Origin of the O'Neills with a short history of the sept.* Compiled by Anthony Mathews. Dublin: Anthony Mathews, 79p. Refs.
Meaning, variations of the name, prominent bearers in various parts of Ireland and overseas. Variations include: Neal, Neil, O'Neil, McNeel et al. O'Neil means "champion."

[9.31.5.1.5] Mathews, Anthony. (1972). *Origin of the McKennas with a history of the sept.* Dublin: Anthony Mathews. not paginated, 26p.
Variations of the name (MacKinney, Kenny etc.), prominent bearers of the name in Ireland and overseas.

[9.31.5.1.6] Mathews, Anthony. (1973). *Origin of the McCanns with a short history of the sept.* Compiled by Anthony Mathews. Drogheda, Ireland: Anthony Mathews, approx. 32p. Maps. Refs.
Meaning, variations of the name, prominent bearers in various parts of Ireland and overseas. Variations include Can, Canny, and Caney.

[9.31.5.1.7] Williams, J(ames). D. (1977). *History of the name 'Murphy'.* Ennis, Clare [Ireland]: History House, 60p. Refs. Illus.

Background on name.   Information on prominent bearers in Ireland and abroad. Variations of Murphy include Murchoe, Murpy, Morphy, and Morrin.

[9.31.5.1.8] Williams, J(ames). D. (1977).   *History of the name 'O'Brien'*. Dublin: Mercier Press, 48p. Refs. Illus.
Background on name.   Information on prominent bearers in Ireland and abroad.

[9.31.5.1.9] Williams, J(ames). D. (1977).   *History of the name 'O'Kelly'*. Dublin: Mercier Press, 64p. Refs. Illus.
Background on name.   Information on prominent bearers in Ireland and abroad.

[9.31.5.1.10] Williams, J(ames). D. (1978).   *History of the name 'O'Neill'*. Dublin: Mercier Press, 62p. Refs. Illus.
Background on name.   Information on prominent bearers in Ireland and abroad.

[9.31.5.1.11] Williams, J(ames). D. (1978).   *History of the name 'O'Sullivan'*. Dublin: Mercier Press, 62p. Refs. Illus.
Background on name.   Information on prominent bearers in Ireland and abroad.

9.32. ETHNIC NAMES: *Islamic*
(See Also: 9.5. ETHNIC NAMES: *Arabic*

[9.32.1] Eickelman, Dale. (1967).   Rites of passage: Muslim rites.   In Mircea Eliade (Ed.), *The encyclopedia of religion*, Vol. 12, pp. 398-403. Refs.
New York: Macmillan; London: Collier Macmillan. P. 400 has a description of naming customs in the Islamic world.   The emphasis is on Morocco.

[9.32.2] Erder, Yoram. (1990).   The origin of the name Idris in the Qur'an: A study of the influence of Qumran literature on early Islam. *Journal of Near Eastern Studies, 49,* 339-350. Refs.
After examination of a number of materials, concludes that Idris is a mixture of Enoch, Nabu, Hermes Trimegistros, and Hermes-Mercury with Doresh ha-Torah.   Two channels the Enoch literature could have entered Islam from are Harran and Yemen.

[9.32.3] Nadvi, S. Salman. (1987).   Names of Islam. *NomAfr, 1(2),* 22-31. Refs.
Intro. to Muslim names followed by topics which include: corrupted names (Ibn Rushd > Averroes), names derived from professions, names of Allah, combinations of Arabic and Persian names, and biblical names.   Examples given for each category.

[9.32.4] Nu'Man, Muhammad Armiya. (1981).   *Muslim names and their meanings*. Jersey City, NJ: New Mind Productions, 20p.
Listings of Islamic names in English with their meanings.   Has names of Allah, Muhammad, and prophets along with approx. 175 male and 175 female names.

[9.32.5] Rights of the Turks protested. [Bulgaria]. (1990, Jan. 3). *New York Times*, p. A12.
Demonstrations against ethnic Turks in Bulgaria who have recently been given religious rights and permission to use their Muslim names which had been forbidden.

[9.32.6] Smith, Antar Ibn-Stanford Ibn-Edward Ibn-George. (1985). *Muslim names and birth-rites*. Jackson, MI: Qur'anic Civilization Association, 108p. Refs.
Directed to those converts to Islam who wish to name their children in accordance with the guidelines of the religion.   Topics include child-naming rites, the Muslim naming system, permissible names, and non-permissible names.   Legal proofs for statements provided throughout.

9.33. ETHNIC NAMES: *Italian*

[9.33.1] Bailey, Frederick George. (1971). What are the signori? In Frederick George Bailey (Ed.), *Gifts and poisons*. Oxford: Basil Blackwell, 318p.
Pp. 238-239 describe forms of address and reference (Signor, Cavaliere, Signor, etc.) surname, 1st name, or nickname, also *tu* or *voi* in the small community of Losa (pop. 800) in the Maritime Alps of Italy.

[9.33.2] Cole, John W., & Wolf, Eric R. (1974). *The hidden frontier: Ecology and ethnicity in an Alpine Valley*. New York: Academic Press, 348p.
Reports on 2 villages in northern Italy, German-speaking St. Felix and Romance-speaking Tret. Description of how family members take on their identity from the name of the homestead in both communities (pp. 239-241).

[9.33.3] Fight for freedom on Italian names. (1965, Apr. 9). *Times* [London], p. 13.
Points out restrictions on naming in Italy originally passed by decree in 1919. Among them: (1) no child can have the same name as a living father, (2) surnames cannot be used as 1st names, and (3) children of Italian citizenship cannot be given foreign names such as Oscar. A private bill is before the Chamber of Deputies to overcome the restrictions.

[9.33.4] Grant, W. Leonard. (1953). On Giovanni Aurispa's name. *Philological Quarterly, 32,* 219-223. Refs.
After examination of evidence, concludes that for 15th cent. Sicilian-born Italian writer Aurispa is not an honorific but a real name that belonged to the Pichunerio family.

[9.33.5] Herlihy, David. (1973). Problems of record linkages in Tuscan fiscal records of the 15th cent. In E. A. Wrigley (Ed.), *Identifying people in the past* (pp. 41-56, 151-154). Refs. Table. London: Edward Arnold.
Describes the 16 vol. survey *Castato of 1427* and other surveys. These surveys tell much about life in that period. Among many other observations, the surveys show that parents would give the same name to more than one child, that there was name variation, and there were scribal errors.

[9.33.6] Herlihy, David. (1988). Tuscan names, 1200-1530. *Renaissance Quarterly, 41,* 561-582. Refs.
Extensive systematic description of the evolution of Tuscan names based partially upon computer analysis of 60,000 entries for heads of household. Among many findings, the majority of names in Pistoia in 1219 did not honor a saint but by 1427, 13 of the top 15 names accounted for 70% of the population and were saints' names.

[9.33.7] Lasker, Gabriel W., Chiarelli, B; Marsali, M.; Fedele, F.; & Kaplan, Bernice. (1972). Degree of human genetic isolation measured by isonymy and marital distances in two communities in an Italian Alpine valley. *HumBio, 44,* 351-360. Refs. Tables.
The 2 small, isolated Alpine communities of Bellino and Casteldelfino of Val Varaita were studied over periods from 1771-1970. Results "show that high rates of isonymy (and high inbreeding) are marked by small population size as well as by low migration rates."

[9.33.8] Lopez, Robert Sabatino. (1954). Concerning surnames and places of origin. *Medievalia et Humanistica, 8,* 6-16. Refs.
Reply to Emery [44.9] who criticized toponymic surnames as evidence for the area of origin of the bearer. Uses Genoa, Italy from the 13th to the 15th cents. to make a case for toponyms relating to surnames.

[9.33.9] Zei, G., Guglielmo, C. R., Siri, E., Moroni, A., & Cavalli-Sforza, L. L. (1983). Surnames as neutral alleles: Observations in Sardinia. *HumBio, 55,* 357-365. Refs(pp. 399-408). Figs. Map.
11 dicoceses on the island of Sardinia were analyzed using surnames as biological markers.

9.33.1. ETHNIC NAMES: *Italian: Nicknames*

[9.33.1.1] Brogger, Jan. (1970). *Montaverese.* Bergen [Norway], Universitestsforlaget, 160p. Refs.
Pp. 87-92 (refs on p. 158) describe research in this Calabrian village in southern Italy on nicknames. A nickname can be acquired by a man and transmitted to his children. The table shows 42 nicknames with the meanings for 28 of them. Examples include: Pilato (Pilate) for a man who refused to take a stand, Cazicalati ("trousers down"), and Fattogiorno ("already daytime") for a farm worker who regularly slept late in the morning.

[9.33.1.2] Chapman, Charlotte Gower. (1971). *Milocca: A Sicilian village.* Cambridge, MA: Schenkman, 263p.
In 1928 Chapman studied this village (then with a pop. of 2500) in the southwest corner of Sicily. Pp. 236-238 list about 60 nicknames of 3 main types: personal (unique to that individual), location, and personal (applicable to more than one individual). Examples include: Vapuretto ("little steamboat" for a fat priest who huffed and puffed), Navisi ("from Navo") and Mangia Lasagni ("eats noodles").

[9.33.1.3] Cohen, Eugene N. (1977). Nicknames, social boundaries, and community in an Italian village. *International Journal of Contemporary Sociology, 14,* 102-113. Refs.
Description of nicknaming patterns in Collefiore (pop. 750), a community in Southern Tuscany about 150 km.north of Rome. Concludes that, "Nicknames operate as boundary- defining and boundary-maintaining mechanisms for groups to whom separateness, difference, and distinctions are of particular value and importance."

[9.33.1.4] Italian nicknames. [Contributors' Club]. (1889, Feb.). *Atlantic Monthly, 63,* pp. 282-283.
Comment on the Italian use of nicknames or *sopranomi.* Several references to artists. Examples include: Verocchio ("blue-eyed"), Lorenzo del Sarto ("the tailor's Lawrence"), and Il Zucco ("the squash").

[9.33.1.5] Jacquemet, Marco. (1992). Namechasers: How belonging to a community became a crime. *American Ethnologist, 19,* 733-748. Refs.
Description of how the justice department of the city of Naples uses nicknames to identify and prosecute those involved in criminal gang activities. Types of nickname are: (1) physical qualities ('o Nasecano, "dog nose"), (2) personality ('o Ciaccheré, "the chatterbox"), (3) based on relatives or past experience ('o Cocchieriello, "the coachman"), and (4) honorific ('o Mitre, "the machine gun"). At least 50 examples.

[9.33.1.6] Severi, Carlo. (1980). Le nom de lignée: Les soubriquets dans un village d'Émilie [Lineage names: Nicknames in a village of Émilie]. *L'Homme, 20(4),* 105-118. Refs. Tables. French. English summary.
Frassinora is a rural village (pop. 987) in the Northern Italy province of Modene. Nicknames become 2nd family names. Examples include Le Chat, Le Coq, and Maître d'École. Many examples.

[9.33.1.7] Wallman, Sandra. (1973). Preliminary notes on 'Soprannomi' in a part of the Piedmont. *Studi Piedmontesi, 2,* 126-132. Refs.
Soprannomi are nicknames. Discussions of a 2nd system of surnames based on soprannomi. No examples.

9.34. ETHNIC NAMES: *Japanese*

[9.34.1] Batchelor, John. (1894). Items of Ainu folk-lore. *Journal of American Folk-Lore, 7,* 15-44. Refs.
The Ainu are an aboriginal Caucasian people who live in the northern islands of Japan. Pp. 36-40 describe their naming customs [in 1894]. Among these: names of dead persons may not be used, names can be either lucky or unlucky, and names must have a good sound or meaning. The naming ceremony is also described. The Ainus are [in 1894] in the process of acquiring additional Japanese names.

[9.34.2] Befu, Harumi & Norbeck, Edward. (1958). Japanese usages of terms of relationship. *Southwestern Journal of Anthropology, 14,* 66-86.
Description of kin terms of reference and address in Japanese culture. There is greater use of relationship in address than in North America. There is, however, a shift toward greater use of 1st names and patronyms.

[9.34.3] Chira, Susan. (1989, Jan. 3). What's in a Japanese name? For many women, obscurity. *New York Times*, pp. A1, A9.
Opposition to a Japanese law requiring women to use only their married names after marriage.

[9.34.4] Haberman, Clyde. (1984, Mar. 29). What's in a name? To the Japanese, everything. *New York Times*, p. A2. Photo.
To acquire citizenship in Japan, a person has had to take a Japanese name. New legislation will remove this requirement.

[9.34.5] Lee, Motoko Y. (1976). The married woman's status and role as reflected in Japanese: An exploratory sociolinguistic study. *Signs, 1,* 991-999. Refs.
Forms of address for men and women reflect the subordinate linguistic status of women. Lee cautions whether this reflects social inferiority.

[9.34.6] Sibata, Takesi. (1978). Lexical system of personal names in an idiolect. [12th ICOS, Bern, 1975]. *Onoma, 22,* 333-339.
Description of naming practices in Okinawa, Japan and a new law for family registration of surnames "the ex-*samurai* class men registered their surnames, and the ex-samurai class women and the common people registered their childhood names. From then on, it became customary to register a name which was equivalent to a surname, however, the tradition of childhood names has still continued."

[9.34.7] Yasuda, Norikazu. (1983). Studies of isonymy and inbreeding in Japan. HumBio, 55, 263-276. Refs(pp. 399-408). Tables.
History of Japanese surnames; extensive tables of most common surnames. Works in isonymy shows decrease in consanguineous marriages in Japan. One table shows the 60 most common surnames in each of 3 studies.

[9.34.8] Yasuda. Norikazu & Furosho, Toshiyuki. (1971). Random and non-random breeding from isonymy study. I. Small cities of Japan. *American Journal of Human Genetics, 23,* 303-316. Refs. Tables.
Data from Ohdate (pop. 60,000) in northeastern Japan, a farming and commercial city and Mine (pop. 35,000) a mining city were studied for isonymy analysis for the last cent.

Results indicate an increase in changes of surname and a decrease in frequency of consanguineous marriage. Most common surnames in Ohdate were: Sato, Hatakeyama, Sasaki, Ito, and Sugahara; in Mine: Yamamoto, Tanaka, Ito, Yamada, and Nakamura.

[9.34.9] Yasuda, Norikazu & Furusho, Toshiyuki. (1971). Random and nonrandom inbreeding revealed from isonymy study. II. A group of farm-villages in Japan. *Japanese Journal of Human Genetics, 15,* 231-240. Refs. Tables. Figs.
Study of 11 farm-villages of the Uto district used isonymy to evaluate high pedigree inbreeding due to random genetic drift shows preference for marrying relatives. Most frequent surnames include: Sato, Nakajima, Tanaka, and Nakayama.

9.35. ETHNIC NAMES: *Jewish*
(Includes Jewish names from all periods)
(See Also: 9.37. ETHNIC NAMES: *Maltese)*

[9.35.1] Amir, Yehoshua. (1988). The interpretation of Hebrew names according to Philo. In Lester L. Grabbe *Etymology in early Jewish interpretation* (pp. 233-235). Atlanta, GA: Scholars Press. Originally published in Hebrew in *Tarbiz, 31,* (1961), p. 297ff.
Discussion of the Hebrew language ability of the philosopher Philo.

[9.35.2] Angel, Marc D. (1973). The Sephardim in the United States: An exploratory study. In *American Jewish Yearbook, 74,* 77-137. Refs. Tables. New York: American Jewish Congress, Philadelphia: Jewish Publication Society.
P. 125 explains that the custom for American Sefardic Jews is to name the child after living grandparents. The current trend is to give the child an English equivalent for a Spanish or Turkish name, but the Hebrew name (for religious purposes) is retained. Almost 80% of Askenazic spouses go along with the custom.

[9.35.3] Angel, Marc D. (1984). Sephardic-Ashkenazic intermarriage. *Sh'ma: A Journal of Jewish Responsibility, 14,* 44-46.
Refers to Angel above.

[9.35.4] Arad, Miriam. (1984, Oct. 10). The name game. [Randomalia]. *Jerusalem Post* (Intl Ed.), p. 18.
Current fashions in Israel. Explains that Abrahams are called Avi or Rami; Rivkas, Riki or Rivi. Other names also discussed.

[9.35.5] Beider, Alexander. (1991). Jewish patronymic and metronymic surnames in Russia. *Avotaynu, 7(4),* 3-15. Refs. Tables. Maps.
Systematic detailed description of the types of patronymic and metronymic surnames based upon parliamentary lists from the 1900s . Classification of name by source: (1) sacred names (*shemot ha-kadashim*) or vernacular (*kinnuim).* Female names also addressed. Tables show distribution of name types in different parts of Russia. Table 5 shows approx. 200 male and 100 female 1st names.

[9.35.6] Beider, Alexander. (1992). Jewish surnames in the Russian Empire. Avotaynu, 8(3), 3-7.
Description of the rationale of his *Dictionary of Jewish surnames from the Russian Empire* [9.35.6.1].

[9.35.7] Beit-Arieh, Itzhaq. (1983). A First Temple period census document. *Palestine Exploration Quarterly, 115,* 105-108. Refs. Photos.
Based upon an ostracon found at Tel'Ira in the Beer-Sheva Valley. English translation reads: "Roll call: Berechiah, Gibbea, Mokir, Shelemiah." Comment on the names.

[9.35.8] Cleveland, Ray L. (1973). A comment on the "floral nicknames" in the Geniza documents. *Journal of the American Oriental Society, 93,* 200-202.
Responding to Goitein's (1970) [87:8.40.10] statement about "floral nicknames," which were difficult to explain, points out that contemporary Arabic uses these words as collectives, i.e., qamha = stalk of wheat, not a kernel of wheat; fula [fool-a] = bean plant, not a single bean.

[9.35.9] Emery, Richard W. (1959). *The Jews of Perpignan in the thirteenth century.* New York: Columbia University Press, 202p. Refs. Tables. Map.
Sources were 17 notarial registers at Perpignan written during 1261-1287 which provide a wealth of material on life at that time. Records of business transactions (mostly moneylending) of the 228 Jews of Perpignan (Jews in other cities mentioned also). Half had names that indicated geographical origin. Examples., Cresques de *Marsilia,* Vitalis Mosse de *Narbona,* Davinus Bonifilii de *Carcassona.* Other names include: Aron Astruc, Cresques Bendit, and Samiel Salamon Natan. Individuals referred to throughout. Complete listing of all mentioned on pp. 200-202.

[9.35.10] Fowler, Jeanane D. (1987). *Theophoric personal names in Ancient Hebrew: A comparative study. Journal for the Study of the Old Testament, Supplement Series 49.* Sheffield, England: Sheffield Academic Press, 410p. Refs.
Theophoric names are names which incorporate God (in some form) as part of the name, examples., Raphael ("God heals"), Eliel ("My God is El"), Abimelek ("the (Divine) Brother is King"). Author states "the main purpose of this work is to discover what concepts of the deity are revealed in Hebrew personal names, and to find out to what extent Hebrew ideas concerning the deity are distinct from those of other Semitic religions,..." 100s of Biblical and extra-biblical names are categorized and analyzed. [Some knowledge of Hebrew would be helpful].

[9.35.11] Friedman, Lee Max. (1948). *Pilgrims in a new land.* Philadelphia: Jewish Publication Society of America, 471p. Refs. Figs.
Ch. 15, pp. 196-218 (notes pp. 417-424), is on American Jewish names. Systematic intro. to names in general and special focus on Jewish names. Description of the *shem hakodesh* (sacred) name used for religious purposes and the *kinnui* (vernacular name) used in the vernacular; assumption of surnames in Europe; and change of name by immigrants.

[9.35.11A] Glazier, Jack. (1987). Nicknames and the transformation of an American Jewish community: Notes on the anthropology of emotion in the urban Midwest. *Ethnology, 26,* 73-85. Refs.
The report is based upon the Jewish community (Sefardic and Ashkenzic) of Indianapolis. Contrasts the role of nicknaming in an urban setting with practices in rural Europe.

[9.35.12] Gorr, Shmuel. (1992). *Jewish personal names: Their origin, derivation and diminutive forms.* Edited by Chaim Freedman. Teaneck, NJ: Avotaynu, 112p. Refs.
Encompasses 1400 names and variants developed from 80 root male and 80 root female names. Thus, Aharon is the root name for Aron, Oren, Arke, Arushke, and others. There is also a list of 300 surnames developed from 1st names. These include Heschel < Yehoshua; Jesselson < Yosef; and Tumarkin < Tamar.

[9.35.13] Hillaby, Joe. (1982-84). Hereford gold: Irish, Welsh and English land: The Jewish community at Hereford and its clients, 1179-1253. Part I. *Transactions of the Woolhope Naturalists' Field Club, Herefordshire, 44,* 358-419. Refs. Tables. Illus.
Description of the Jewish community of this area of England. Most Jews were in the money-lending business. While the focus of the article is on financial transactions, at least 25 different names are mentioned. These include: Abigail, Contessa, Elias, Manasser, Melin, Samar, and Serfdeu. Naming patterns show: toponyms (Isaac of

Bristol), patronyms (Aaron, son of Josce [Joshua]; Genta, daughter of Isaac); a grandson relationship (Abraham, grandson of Abigail); and an in-law relationship (Manasser, son-in-law of Hamo).

[9.35.14] Hirschson, Niel. (1974). Marrano names among the Portuguese explorers of Southern Africa. *Jewish Affairs, 29(8)*, 51-57. Refs. Illus.
Description of the role of Marrano Jews (those Jews forcibly converted to Christianity but who often secretly maintained their Jewish identity). Several explorers described including: Bartholomeu Diaz, Silva Porto, Serpa Pinto, and Paiva Andreda.

[9.35.15] Isenberg, Shirley Berry. (1988). *India's Bene Israel: A comprehensive inquire and sourcebook*. Berkeley, CA: Judah L. Magnes Museum, 443p. Refs.
Extensive research on the Jews of India. Ch. 13 (pp. 154-159) is devoted to names. Appendix 9 has a listing of names and village links. About 150 listed altogether.

[9.35.16] Jewish family names. (1955, 1956; 1957; 1958). *Rhode Island Jewish Historical Notes* (Providence). *1*, 239-243; *2*, 86-91; 238-240; *3*, 118-146; *4*, 238-240; 254-281. Intro. List of 24 Rhode Island Jews who did change their names, mostly surnames. Extensive additional lists of Jews (who did not change their names) by surname in Providence, Pawtucket, Woonsocket, and other Rhode Island communities between 1850 and 1902. Lists name of head of household for families and also individuals boarding or living alone. Indicates address and occupation. Comment on p. 118 of vol. 3.

[9.35.17] Kormos, Charles. (1987). Why names matter. *Jewish Spectator*, pp. 46-48.
Intro. to Jewish names. Description of the work on Jewish names at the Museum of the Diaspora, Tel Aviv, Israel.

[9.35.18] Kurzweil, Arthur. (1980). *From generation to generation: How to trace your Jewish genealogy and personal history*. New York: William Morrow, 353p.
Ch. 1 (pp. 105-127) is devoted to names. Gives historical background and types of names. Gives 120 examples. of surnames derived from nicknames, occupations, and physical characteristics.

[9.35.19] Lawson, Edwin D. (1991). Most common Jewish first names in Israel. *Names, 39*, 103-124. Refs. Tables.
The approx. 100 most frequent Jewish 1st names for men and for women based upon samples of 10,000 were identified and analyzed. Names were categorized as Biblical, Traditional, Modern Hebrew, and non-Hebrew. For both groups, 90% of the names came from Hebrew, for males 70% came from the Bible; for women, 40%. Entries for each name show pronunciation, meaning, and Bible citation where relevant.

[9.35.20] Marcus, Ralph. (1953). The name *Makkabaios*. In *The Joshua Starr Memorial Volume: Studies in History & Philology, Jewish Social Studies, Publication No. 5*, pp. 59-65. Refs. New York: Conference on Jewish Relations.
After reviewing various theories, suggests that the root for Maccabee is "(source of) of hope" rather than the commonly accepted "hammer."

[9.35.21] Naveh, J(oseph). (1970). The ossuary inscriptions from Giv'at ha-Mivtar. *Israel Exploration Journal, 20*, 33-37 + Plates 9-17.
Inscriptions from a location in North Jerusalem c. Hasmoneans to 70 AD. One inscription in Aramaic refers to "Simon, builder of the sanctuary." Others refer to Jehonathan, the potter; Martha, Jehochanan, Saul, and Salome, daughter of Saul (none of these are the biblical figures).

[9.35.22] Porten, Bezalel. (1968). *Archives from Elephantine: The life of an ancient Jewish military colony.* Berkeley: University of California Press, 421p. Refs.
The community dates from the 5th cent. BCE (Before the Common Era) and was located near the present Aswan dam in Egypt. Many types of names are mentioned throughout the book: Akkadian, Aramaean, Egyptian, and others but the section (pp. 133-150) deals with Jewish names. 160 names are listed. Most are theophoric and are listed in various type categories with meaning, &, in many cases, Bible citations. Non-theophoric names also described.

[9.35.23] Rodrigue-Schwarzwald, Ora. (1988). Hebrew proper names in Judeo-Spanish. In Tamar Alexander & Galit Hasan-Rokem (Eds.), *Jerusalem Studies in Jewish Folklore, Vol. 10,* (pp. ix-x, 94-109. Refs. Hebrew. English summary.
The Hebrew names chosen for children in Judeo-Spanish (Ladino) are in 2 categories: (1) heroes from the Bible and post-Bible sources, and (2) positive vales such as success, luck, and blessings. The onomasticon for males is larger than for females. Hebrew names "were used extensively in Judeo-Spanish idioms and proverbs."

[9.35.24] Rosenwaike, Ira. (1990). Leading surnames among American Jews. *Names, 38,* 31-38. Refs. Tables.
Used data from a large national sample of the American Cancer Society to identify the 25 most common Jewish surnames. The top 5 are: Cohen, Miller, Schwartz, Friedman, and Levine. One analysis shows the percentage of those with the surname who are Jewish, i.e, 92.5% of the Bernsteins are Jewish, but only 5.4% of the Millers are. Comparisons with data from Israel.

[9.35.25] Roth, Cecil. (1962). The membership of the Great Synagogue, London, to 1791. *The Jewish Historical Society of England, Miscellanies, 6,* 175-185.
Has list of 307 members going back to 1708. Notes on many.

[9.35.26] Samra, Myer. (1989). Naming patterns among Jews of Iraqi origin in Sydney. *Jewish Journal of Sociology, 31,* 25-37. Refs.
Research was based upon 50 interviews done during the 1970s with Iraqi Jews who had immigrated to Australia after WWII. Description of various patterns of naming children including naming children after grandparents, anglicization of names, and taking of a 2nd name.

[9.35.27] Stahl, Abraham. (1992). Children's names as a reflection of ideological differences among Israeli parents. *Names, 40,* 283-294. Refs. Tables.
In evaluation of two groups of Israeli parents, Orthodox and Modern, differences in the naming patterns emerge. Both sexes of the Modern group show fewer traditional names (Abraham, Sarah) and more of the new names (Amir, Adi). Both sexes of the Orthodox show more renewed Hebrew names (names which historically were rarely used (Gideon, Thamar).

[9.35.28] Strizower, Schifra. (1971). *The Bene Israel of Bombay.* New York: Schocken, 176 p.
Pp. 56-58 (refs. on p. 169) give a brief description of naming patterns among the Bene Israel (Jews of the Bombay, India area). Most, but not all, use biblical 1st names and surnames.

[9.35.29] van Son, Sol. (1990). Holland. [From Our Contributing Editors]. *Avotaynu, 6(2)* 27.
Report of an 18th cent. Dutch-Jewish family where 1st names of girls were changed in documents from Yiddish to Dutch forms, 1 was Gitele to Judith, a 2nd was Kendele to Keetje. Other changes also mentioned.

[9.35.30] Voet, Joop. (1987). Origin of Dutch surnames. *Avotaynu, 3(2),* 30-31.
Report of documents showing surname adoption in Holland by Napoleonic decree by members [assumed to be] of the Jewish community. Voet's paternal ancestor was a porter, hence the name Voet ("foot"). On the maternal side, the ancestors were unusually tall. The name Boom ("tree") may have been a factor in its selection.

[9.35.31] Wagaw, Teshome G. (1987-88). The emigration and settlement of Ethiopian Jews in Israel. *Middle East Review, 20(2),* 41-48.
Ethiopian Jews migrating to Israel take Hebrew 1st names and are encouraged to use their father's name as surname. In Ethiopian tradition, a male uses his 1st name and father's 1st name. Females keep their birth names after marriage.

9.35.1 ETHNIC NAMES: *Jewish: Ancient Israel*

[9.35.1.1] Cohen, Naomi G. (1976). Jewish names as cultural indicators in antiquity. *Journal for the Study of Judaism, 7,* 97-128. Refs.
Scholarly systematic investigation showing that "Jewish" names in antiquity (Greek and Roman periods) demonstrated identification of the bestower and also to the non-Jewish cultural milieu. The names Abraham, Shime'on, and Reuben and their variations are used as extended examples. Extensive refs.

[9.35.1.2] Hachlili, Rachel. (1979). The Goliath family in Jericho: Funerary inscriptions from a 1st cent. AD Jewish monumental tomb. *Bulletin of the American Schools of Oriental Research, 235,* 31-65. Refs. Tables. Figs. Photos.
Extensive scholarly analysis. Includes an onomasticon of 13 personal names, in Hebrew script, some also in Greek. Among the names are: Akabia, Eleazar, Ishmael, and Mariah. The family name Goliath appears to be a nickname derived from members of the family who were tall (as seen from their bones). The family also showed recurrences of names.

[9.35.1.3] Ilan, Tal. (1989). Notes on the distribution of Jewish women's names in Palestine in the Second Temple and Mishnaic periods. *Journal of Jewish Studies, 40,* 186-200. Refs. Tables.
Using a variety of sources from the period (330 BCE-200 CE) locates names of 247 women, 2040 men. The women's names were derived from Hebrew, Greek, Aramaic, Latin, Persian, and Nabatean but 58.2% had Hebrew names. The most popular were: Salome and Mariamme (or its shorter version, Maria). Concludes that women were discriminated against since they were only 10% of the sample.

[9.35.1.4] Lawton, Robert Brooks, Jr. (1977). *Israelite personal names on Hebrew inscriptions antedating 500 BC.* Unpublished doctoral dissertation, Harvard University, 120p. Refs.
Comprehensive scholarly examination of the structure, form, and meaning of approx. 175 names from inscriptions. Most names occurred more than once. Meanings are given. Example, *'byw* found in Samaria Ostraca 52.2 (& other places) is an illustration of a predicate subject name. It means "Yahweh is my Father" and is found in the Old Testament as Abijah. Extensive bibliography.

[9.35.1.5] Leon, Harry Joshua. (1960). *The Jews of ancient Rome.* Philadelphia: Jewish Publication Society of America, 378p. Refs. Tables. Illus.
An earlier article by this author on this subject is cited in [Smith:1268]. Chap. 5, pp. 93-121, has analyses by language and sex of the 517 names found on Roman inscriptions dating from the beginning of the 2nd cent. Latin names include: Donatus, Margarita, and Vitalis; Greek, Alexander, Daphne, and Irene; Semitic, Eli, Maria, and Rebecca.

[9.35.1.6]   Levine, Baruch A. (1967).   Levites.   In Mircea Eliade (Ed.), *The encyclopedia of religion*, Vol. 8, pp. 523-532. Refs. New York: Macmillan; London: Collier Macmillan.
P. 525 points out that in Ancient Israel, there was a practice of papponymy among the Levites in which sons were named after their grandfathers.

[9.35.1.7]   Porten, B(ezalel). (1971).   Domla'el and related names. *Israel Exploration Journal, 21*, 47-49. Refs.
Identification of 8 Israelite names from the Bible and other sources that can be classified as "Names of encouragement." Included are: Domla'el' ("Be silent before God"), De'u'el ("Acknowledge God"), and Penuliah ("Turn to the Lord").

[9.35.1.8]   Rokeah, David. (1968), A new onomasticon fragment from Oxyrhynchus and Philo's etymologies. *Journal of Theological Studies, 19,* 70-82. Refs.
Evaluation of a papyrus fragment from Egypt from the 2nd or 3rd cent. AD.   The fragment lists 35 Hebrew names. Linguistic examination of several of these with relation to Philo and his knowledge of Hebrew.

[9.35.1.9]   Rokeah, David. (1970).   2745.   Onomasticon of Hebrew names. In R. A. Coles, Daniele Foraboschi, Abdulla Hassan Soliman el-Mosallamy, J(ohn) R. Rea, & Ursula Schlag (Eds.) *Oxyrhynchus papyri* (pp. 1-6; 96 + Plate 1), *Vol. 36, Graeco-Roman Memoirs, No. 51*. Refs. Photo.
Described by Rokeah above.   However, does include comments by the editors and a photo of the actual papyrus.

[9.35.1.10]   Silverman, M. H. (1969).   Aramaean name-types in the Elephantine documents. *Journal of the American Oriental Society, 89,* 691-709. Refs.
The Elephantine documents are from the Jewish military colony in Egypt around the 1st half of the 5th cent. BCE. This was a period of Aramaization of the colony. Analysis of theophorous/divine elements of this Aramaic influence show that they are part of the Aramaization.

[9.35.1.11]   Yadin, Yigael. (1973).   Epigraphy and crucifixion. *Israel Exploration Journal, 23,* 18-22. Refs.
Description of a crucifixion where an inscription and skeletal remains of a man named Yohochanan were found in a burial cave in Israel. He was nicknamed posthumously "the one hanged knees apart."

[9.35.1.12]   Zeitlin, Solomon. (1952).   Bar Kokba and Bar Kozeba. *Jewish Quarterly Review, 63,* 77-80. Refs.
Argues that the leader of the Jewish rebellion against Rome was called Bar Kokba ("son of the star" or "man of the star" and not Bar Kozeba ("son of a liar").

9.35.2. ETHNIC NAMES: *Jewish: Change of Name*

[9.35.2.1]   Bering, Dietz. (1992).   *The stigma of names*: *Antisemitism in German daily life, 1812-1933*. Trans. by Neville Plaice.   Ann Arbor, MI: University of Michigan Press, 345p. Refs. Tables. Illus.
Detailed systematic analysis of Jewish names in Germany. Demonstrates that, far from being a recent innovation at the time of the Nazis, anti-Semitism as shown in the stigma attached to Jewish names had occurred from 1815 on. Many tables and refs. Extensive biblio.

[9.35.2.2]   Frank, Margit. (1993).   Från *Kohn* till *Baron von Karony:* Judiska namnförändringar i dikt och verklighet [From *Kohn* to *Baron von Korony:* Jewish name

changes in fiction and reality]. *StudAnthroScan, 11,* 47-61. Refs. Swedish. English summary.
Gives background on the historical reasons for Jewish name-changing. Describes how this is reflected in literature.

[9.35.2.3] Kugelmass, J. Alvin. (1952). Name-changing--and what it gets you. *Commentary, 14,* 145-150.
Reports 2 surveys with Jews who changed their names. The 1st by mail brought no returns. In the 2nd by telephone, all reported they were sorry they had changed their names.

9.35.3. ETHNIC NAMES: *Jewish: Chinese*

[9.35.3.1] Leslie, D(aniel). (1962). Some notes on the Jewish inscriptions of K'aifeng. *Journal of the American Oriental Society, 82,* 346-361. Refs.
Based upon 4 Jewish stone inscriptions from the 15th-17th cents. Show at least 15 Hebrew male names (examples., Adam, Moses, Joshua, and Ezra) which are listed along with Mandarin transcription and suggested K'aifeng pronunciation.

[9.35.3.2] Leslie, Daniel. (1963-64). The Chinese-Hebrew memorial book of the Jewish community of K'aifeng, I. *Abr-Nahrain* [Australia], *4,* 19-49. Refs. Tables. Plates.
Based upon a ms. reported in 1851 but apparently much older. After evaluating the evidence, concludes that the register was a memorial book and not a register of the congregation as previous scholars thought. Contains lists of clans in Chinese and Hebrew. While Hebrew male names such as Aaron, Ezra, and Jeremiah are listed, no Hebrew names for women are shown.

[9.35.3.3] Leslie, Daniel. (1964-65). The Chinese-Hebrew memorial book of the Jewish community of K'aifeng, II. *Abr-Nahrain* [Australia], *5,* 1-28. Refs. Figs. Genealogical diagrams.
Extension of article above. Scholarly analysis of 17 family trees beginning in the 15th cent.

[9.35.3.4] White, William Charles. (1966). *A compilation of matters relating to the Jews of K'ai-feng Fu,* 2nd ed. New York: Paragon Book Reprint, 228p. Refs. Illus. (Originally published by University of Toronto Press in 1966).
Description of a colony of Jews living in China. Listing of names in English and Chinese developed from various records going back to the 13th cent.

9.35.4. ETHNIC NAMES: *Jewish: First Names*

[9.35.4.1] Colodner, Solomon. (Compiler). (1981). *What's your name? A dictionary of names.* New York City: Cole Publications, 63p.
There are 4 listings, 2 for boys, 2 for girls, giving English names and Hebrew equivalents. Each listing contains between 200 and 300 entries to help the Jewish parent select a name from the Hebrew or a suitable English equivalent; also to locate a suitable equivalent for the opposite sex.

[9.35.4.2] Kaganoff, Benzion C. (1955). Jewish first names through the ages. *Commentary, 20,* 447-452.
Brief history of Jewish naming with attention to the intro. of non-Jewish names. Discussion of the *kinnui* (non-Jewish) name used for business purposes and the *shem hakodesh,* the name used for religious purposes. Since women did not participate in religious activities, there was less pressure on them to have a Jewish name.

[9.35.4.3] Lawson, Edwin D., & Glushkovskaya, Irina. (1994). Naming patterns of recent immigrants from the former Soviet Union to Israel. *Names, 42,* 157-180. Refs. Tables.
To identify patterns of 1st names over 3 generations, 2 samples of 100 Jewish families were interviewed. Sample 1 came mainly from European Russia; Sample 2 from Central Asia. Both samples show that the traditional pattern of naming a child after a deceased relative is still strong although declining somewhat. The European Russia sample shows a tendency to use a Russian name identified by the family and/or the Jewish community with a Hebrew name while the sample from Central Asia tends to use a Russian (or Farsi) name but one not identified with a Jewish name or deceased relative.

[9.35.4.4] Newman, Louis Israel. (1965). *The Jewish people, faith and life.* New York: Bloch, 277p. Refs.
Pp. 239-249 give listing of Hebrew names with English "equivalents." There are approx. 150 male and 150 female names. Examples include Schmuel [Samuel] > Sheldon [sound], Nathaniel > Theodore meaning, "gift of God"], Dinah > Diana [sound], and Orah > Claire [meaning, "light"]. Refs. on p. 274.

[9.35.4.5] Sidi, Smadar Shir. (1989). *The complete book of Hebrew baby names.* San Francisco: Harper & Row, 176p.
Entries for 5000 names showing, origin, current popularity, and pronunciations. Nicknames given for some names. Orientation is toward modern Israeli names.

9.35.5. ETHNIC NAMES: *Jewish: Naming Patterns*

[9.35.5.1] Frieman, D. G. (1965). *Milestones in the life of the Jew.* New York: Bloch, 116p.
Chap. 2 (pp. 10-13) has a very brief description of Jewish naming practices. Among other comments points out that in Talmudic times that one rabbi, Rabbi Gamaliel while he was still alive had a grandson with the same name.

[9.35.5.2] Trepp, Leo. (1962). *Eternal faith, eternal people.* Englewood Cliffs, NJ: Prentice-Hall, 455p.
Pp. 218-221 give a general intro. to Jewish naming. Some description of kinnui or link names, here called civic names as differentiated from religious names. Examples., Leo is substituted for Judah since Leo means "lion" and Judah was compared to a lion by his father Jacob.

[9.35.5.3] Zborowski, Mark & Herzog, Elizabeth. (1952). *Life is with people: The Jewish little-town of Eastern Europe.* New York: International Universities Press, 456p. Refs.
Pp. 320-323 have a description of naming customs. Anecdotal.

9.35.6. ETHNIC NAMES: *Jewish: Surnames*

[9.35.6.1] Beider, Alexander. (1993). *A dictionary of Jewish names from the Russian Empire.* Teaneck, NJ: Ktav, 760p. Refs. Tables. Map.
Intro. has 100+ pp. dealing with history and types of Jewish surname. Main section includes over 50,000 names showing the geographical district they are from. Additionally, the Daitch-Mokotoff Soundex system is shown. This numerical system makes it easier to locate a name when the exact spelling is not known.

[9.35.6.2] Brasch, R. (1969). *The Judaic heritage: Its teachings, philosophy, and symbols.* New York: David McKay, 437p.

Pp. 388-403 describe the development of Jewish surnames beginning with the edicts of Emperor Joseph of Austria in 1797. Pp. 424-428 is a general section on names. Also describes how the name Jehovah mistakenly came about.

[9.35.6.3] Gold, David L. (1986). How not to etymologize a Jewish family name: The case of *Themal*. *Names, 34,* 342-345. Refs.
Reporting that the etymology of a name is unknown is preferable to an imaginative or suppositional explanation that is not scientifically suppportable.

[9.35.6.4] Gold, David L. (1986). Jewish aspects of Shoumatoff's *The mountain of names: A history of the human family*. *Names, 34,* 408-415.
Reactions to the several points described by Shoumatoff with comments and explanations.

[9.35.6.5] Gold, David L. (1987). The Jewish family names in the *Oxford Dictionary of Surnames*. *Jewish Language Review, 7,* 139-179. Refs.
Gives the rationale for categorizing names as Jewish in the *Oxford dictionary of surnames* [1.17]. Explanation of the term *ornamental* as a category of names, meaning a "nice-sounding name in the culture." Other general comments on Jewish names.

[9.35.6.6] Gold, David L. (1987). More on Jewish family names and more letters from the Jewish Family Name File. *Jewish Language Review, 7,* 147-179. Refs.
Comment on work of various writers on Jewish surnames. Answers to questions on Jewish names.

[9.35.6.7] Guggenheimer, Heinrich W., & Guggenheimer, Eva H. (1992). *Jewish family names & their origins*. Hoboken, NJ: Ktav, 882p. Refs.
Involves 65,000 + names although some are variants. Types of name include: Ashkenazi, Sefardi, traditional, modern Israeli, and others. Entries show language of origin, meaning, and in some cases, Bible ref.

[9.35.6.8] Hirsch, Claus W. (1992, Spring). Comparing most common German-Jewish surnames with their American counterparts. *Avotaynu, 8(1),* p. 30. Refs. Table.
Comparison of the frequencies and ranks from a WWI memorial book of German-Jewish fatalities with a 1990-91 Manhattan telephone directory. Table shows the top 20 surnames are the same from both sources although the order is not the same.

[9.35.6.9] Jewish family name file. (1987-89). *Onoma, 29,* 50.
Notice on the maintenance of a file by the Association for the Study of Jewish Languages at the University of Haifa, Israel.

[9.35.6.10] Kaganoff, Benzion C. (1956). Jewish surnames through the ages: An etymological history. *Commentary, 22,* 249-259.
Comprehensive examination of the development of surnames among Ashkenazi and Sephardic Jews. Names were developed from patronymics and matronymics as well as occupation, location, and acronyms, translations, and nicknames. New names were developed with the formation of the State of Israel. Many examples.

[9.35.6.11] Kormos, Charles; Lawson, Edwin D., & Ben Brit, Joseph. (1992). Most common surnames in Israel: Arabic and Jewish, Part I, *OnoCan, 74,* 23-38. Refs. Tables; Part II, *74,* 75-92. Refs.
Evaluation of the 200 most common surnames in Israel. These 200 and their variants "account for 50% to 70% of the surnames in the country." Language origins of the names categorized and show that 53% are concerned with religion. Additional tables show types of surname and language of origin. Part II has entries for each name showing

its rank in the top 200, language of origin, meanings, and where appropriate, Bible citation.

[9.35.6.12] Kraemer, Ross. (1989). On the meaning of the term "Jew" in Greco-Roman inscriptions. *Harvard Theological Review, 82,* 35-53. Refs.
Evaluation of several meanings of the term from inscriptions in the ancient world from the Ptolemaic to the Byzantine periods. The term Jew is interpreted to indicate being Jewish by ethnicity, religion, or geographic region. However, the term was given as a surname for children.

[9.35.6.13] Markreich, Max. (1961). Notes on transformation of place names by European Jews. *Jewish Social Studies, 23,* 265-284. Refs.
While most of this study is devoted to placenames, pp. 278-284 deal with placenames assumed by Jews as surnames. Hundreds of localities are listed with region or country and the Jewish surnames derived from them, example, Bacharach (Rhineland) > Bach, Backer.

[9.35.6.14] Markrich, Max. (1958). Faubus. [Names in Brief]. *Names, 6,* 125. Refs.
Disagrees with anonymous author [42.1.3] on Faubus as a name taken by Jews as equivalent in meaning to Phoebus. Faubus is not a Jewish surname but a peasant name for "bean-man."

[9.35.6.15] Massarik, Fred. (1966). New approaches to the study of the American Jew. *Jewish Journal of Sociology, 8,* 175-191. Refs.
Description of the obstacles to the study of the American Jewish community. However, one method of identifying Jewish households is the use of distinctive Jewish names such as Cohen or Berman. A 1964-65 study of Los Angeles based upon a 1958 study is reported. The 35 names on the list are not listed except for Cohen and Berman.

[9.35.6.16] Neumann, Joshua H. (1965). Some acronymic surnames. *Revue internationale d'Onomastique* [Paris], *17,* 267-274. Appendix.
Description of 70+ Jewish acronymic surnames. Examples include Katz = Kohen TZedek ("Priest of Righteousness") and Shalit = SHeyichye Leorech Yamim Tovim ("May he live a long life"), literally ("May he live the length of many good days").

[9.35.6.17] Rosenwaike, Ira. (1990). Mortality patterns among elderly American Jews. *Journal of Aging & Judaism, 4,* 289-303. Refs.
Used 22 distinctive surnames developed from an American Cancer Society survey to evaluate the mortality patterns of a sample of 100,000+ individuals with those surnames. The sample is to predict the mortality patterns of the total population of American Jews. The 22 surnames are listed (p. 301) and include: Cohen, Friedman, Goldberg, Levine, and Goldstein.

[9.35.6.18] Stern, William. (1974). On the fascination of Jewish surnames. *Leo Baeck Institute Year Book XIX.* London: Secker & Warburg, pp. 219-235. Refs.
Introduction to Jewish surnames. Comments on the contributions of Gerhard Kessler (*Die familiennamen der Juden in Deutschland,* 1935) and others. Explanations and comment on 20+ names whose origins are puzzling. Included are: Gomperz, Lamm, and Falk.

[9.35.6.19] Tolédano, Joseph. (1986). An analysis of Moroccan-Jewish surnames. *Avotaynu, 2(2),* 10-12. Refs.
Explains that at the end of the 15th cent. there were lists of Jewish surnames in Morocco. These names were derived from: Hebrew, Aramaic, Berber, Arabic, Spanish, and Portuguese. Types of names described include: patronyms, placenames, descriptive names, occupational, and personal qualities. At least 50 examples.

[9.35.6.20] Tura, Perez. (1956). Names, fine and otherwise. [Letters from Readers]. *Commentary, 22,* 577.
Response to Kaganoff [9.35.4.2].

9.36. ETHNIC NAMES: *Lappish*

[9.36.1] Anderson, Myrdene. (1984). Proper names, naming, and labeling in Saami. *Anthropological Linguistics, 26,* 186-201. Refs. Table.
The Saami are also known as Lapps and live mostly in Norway, Sweden, and Finland. This investigation was done in the Finnmark county of Norway. Pp. 190-193 are devoted to personal names. A table shows 19 female and 20 male 1st names with Norwegian equivalents. Also, surnames. Examples, (Norwegian followed by Saami), Kristine, Ristiina; Nils, Niilas. For surnames, Hetta, Sara, and Gaup. Names in table are listed by frequency. Another section describes name symbols used to show ownership of reindeer. P. 196 mentions nickname usage.

[9.36.2] Pehrson, Robert N(iel). (1957). *The bilateral network of social relations in Konkama Lapp district, Publication 3,* Indiana University Research Center in Anthropology, Folklore, & Linguistics, 128p. Refs.
Konkama is the farthest north of the 36 Swedish Mountain Lapp districts. Pp. 32-33 describe the importance of kinship terms vs. personal names in personal address or a combination, as, "Will Lars Johan-Male Cousin eat fish?"

[9.36.3] Pehrson, Robert N., & Whitaker, Ian R. (1952). Naming among the Karesuando Lapps. *Journal de la Société Fino-Ougrienne, 56,* 1-4. Refs.
Basic patterns of Lappish naming. Several examples., especially of nicknames.

[9.36.4] Whitaker, Ian. (1955). *Social relations in a nomadic Lappish community.* Oslo: Utgitt av Norsk Folkemuseum, 178p. Refs.
The Lainiovuoma Lapps live in the northernmost area of Sweden. Quotes a source (p. 53) that the Lapp only addresses his own children by their Christian names. If there is a kin relationship; the kinship term and the 1st name. There is also a special type of namesake relationship (p. 91) in which individuals having the same 1st name or a related one (Johannes, Jonas, Ian, etc.) are assumed to have some reciprocal obligation for assistance.

[9.36.5] Whitaker, Ian. (1977). Colloquial naming among the Lainiovuoma Lapps (Sámi). *Journal de la Société Finno-ougrienne, 75,* 45-54. Refs. Table.
Description of their naming practices and changes between 1952 and 1977. "The commonest pattern of colloquial naming is for an individual's Christian name (in its Lappish form) to be appended to the genitive Lappish version of that of one of his/her parents." Thus Heikka-Biettar (Heikka's son) would be recorded in church registers in Swedish as Per Henriksson.

9.37. ETHNIC NAMES: *Maltese*

[9.37.1] Aquilina, Joseph. (1961; 1981). *Papers in Maltese linguistics.* Valletta: University of Malta, 240p. Refs.
Also published in 1945 in *Scientia, 11,* pages not specified. The article "Race and language in Malta" discusses the origin of surnames in Malta (pp. 181-188) to show the mixed ethnic background in Malta of Semitic, Indo-European, and Jewish roots. At least 20 examples. from each group. Among these are: from Semitic, Fenech ("rabbit") and Said ("happy"); from Indo-European, Jones and Bianchi; and from Jewish, Abela ("mourner") and Bondi ("Good Day").

[9.37.2] Herndon, Marcia Alice. (1971). *Singing and politics: Maltese folk music and musicians. DissAbstrIntl, 32(5),* 2496-B, Order No. 71-27,284, 370p.
Analysis of the song duel of Maltese folk music shows the role of the nickname, surname, and 1st name in determining the status of members of singing groups. About 15 specific nicknames listed such as Bambinu ("Christ child"), Qamar ("moon"), and Mortudell ("luncheon meat") are listed. Pp.193, 198, 237-244, 311-314. 89 refs.

[9.37.3] Mangion, Giovanni. (1978). A bibliographical note on Maltese onomastic studies. *Onoma, 22,* 39-46. Refs.
Nothing *per se* specifically on names. Biblio. however, is annotated and does contain 8-9 items.

[9.37.4] Wettinger, Godfrey. (1968). The distribution of surnames in Malta in 1419 and the 1480s. *Journal of Maltese Studies, 5,* 25-48. Refs.
General discussion of the listing of the surnames of 1518 individuals along with their community of residence on the *angara* (public unpaid work roster). The list (included) shows 1466 Christians and 52 Jews. Some names are Semitic (Abdilla, Agius, Buhagiar, et al.); others are not (Abela, Gini, Apap, et al.).

[9.37.5] Wettinger, Godfrey, (1969). The Militia List of 1419-20: A new starting point for the study of Malta's population. *Melita Historica* [Malta], *5,* 80-106. Refs.
Intro. and discussion followed by listing of 1667 members of the militia by surname and 1st name with district. All members of the population, except priests, served Christians as well as Jews. Examples. of names include (from Civitas also known as Mdina): Johanni de Biglera, Niculinu Nuara, Josef Levi, and Brahim Biglemin.

[9.37.6] Wettinger, Godfrey. (1973). Arabo-Berber influences in Malta: Onomastic evidence. *Proceedings of the 1st Congress on Mediterranean Studies of Arabo-Berber Influence,* 484-495. [Algiers]. 300 surnames, 200 nicknames, and placenames were collected, most documented before 1530. Attention paid to Arab influence on the names and those of Jews showing Arabo-Berber influence. Examples of Arabo-Berber names include: Abdilla, Axisa, Muhammed, and Zurki; Jewish names, Capo, Fenech, and Hakim.

9.37.1. ETHNIC NAMES: *Maltese: Nicknames*

[9.37.1.1] Aquilina, Joseph. (1964; 1976). A comparative study in lexical material relating to nicknames & surnames. *Journal of Maltese Studies, 2,* 147-176. Refs.
Reprinted in Joseph Aquilina *Maltese linguistic surveys* (pp. 185-214). Valletta: University of Malta, 1976. Scholarly presentation of the evolution of earlier Maltese surnames from Semitic (Hebrew and Arabic) stock and later Maltese names from Romance stock. Listings of names in several categories. Many examples.

[9.37.1.2] Boissevain, Jeremy. (1965). *Saints and fireworks: Religion and politics in rural Malta.* London: Athlone Press; New York: Humanities Press, 154p. Refs.
Brief mention (p. 37) that when a man moves to his wife's village, he usually does not acquire a village nickname but is either known as the husband of his wife or by his native village's name [apparently, the children do receive nicknames].

[9.37.1.3] Boissevain, Jeremy. (1969). *Hal-Farrug: A village in Malta.* New York: Holt, Rinehart & Winston, 104p. Refs.
Pp. 43-44 deal with nicknames. Families have their own nicknames. There are also individual nicknames. In this village nicknames are extensively used since there is a limited number of surnames. Nickname examples. include: Gardill (greenfinch), Hahaj (from a deep laugh), and Tal-Marokk (of Morocco),

[9.37.1.4] Buxton, L. H. Dudley. (1921). Personal and place names in Malta. *Man,*
21, 146-147.
Brief note on Maltese personal names.   Villagers are normally known by their
"sur-nickname" rather than the name registered for official purposes, example, Tal Duda
(a maggot). The practice is that "if a man marries, his wife adopts the family nickname.
For example, if he is called Tal Naxaro, she will become Naxaro also.   In Gozo,
however, the husband, when he marries, adopts the nickname of his wife's family, in
other words the sur-nickname of his mother-in-law."

[9.37.1.5] Herndon, Marcia & McLeod, Norma. (1972). *The use of nicknames as*
evaluators of personal competence in Malta: Sociolinguistic working paper. Austin, TX:
Southwest Educational Development Lab., 18p. (ERIC Document Reproduction Service
No. ED 252 075).
Pp. 9-15 deal with nicknames. In communities where surnames are common, nicknames
of 4 types are used. Examples include: Tat-Taxi (of taxi), Il Qamar (the moon), Bocci
(marbles), and Fredu Taz-Zabbar (Fred from Zabar).

[9.37.1.6] Pullicino, Joseph Cassar. (1956).   Social aspects of Maltese nicknames.
Scientia, 22, 66-94. Refs.
Extensive systematic description of Maltese nicknames with examples.   Among the
several types of names described are (examples are shown only in English): Personal
("Baby"); Geographical ("the German"); Physical ("the Long-Chinned'); Animal ("the
Wolf"); Bird ("the Goldfinch"); and Occupational ("the Horseman"). Nicknames can be
inherited.

[9.37.1.7] Wettinger, Godfrey. (1971). Late medieval Maltese nicknames. *Journal of*
Maltese Studies, 6, 34-46. Refs.
Discussion of Maltese nicknames.   Most nicknames of the medieval period were of
Semitic origin. Examples of nicknames include: Barri (bull), Fgejlu (tiny horse-radish),
and Raddiena (spinning wheel). List of approx. 100 nicknames.

9.38. ETHNIC NAMES: *Manx*

[9.38.1] Farrant, E. J. P. (1979). Identifying Manx surnames. *Genealogists Magazine,*
19, 322-324. Refs.
Among other general observations, explains that C, K, or Q as an initial letter of a
surname replaced an original Maq which meant "son of" and was part of a patronym.

[9.38.2] Megaw, Basil. (1976).   Norseman and native in the Kingdom of the Isles.
Scottish Studies, 20, 1-44. Refs. Tables. Maps. Illus. Photo. facing p. 1.
While concerned mostly with placenames, pp. 16-18 have some information on epithets
and patronymics showing Gaelic influence during the 11th-13th cents. Some information
on precursors of Manx Gaelic surnames with *Mac-*.

9.39. ETHNIC NAMES: *Mexican*

[9.39.1] Berlin, Brent. (1962). A Tzeltal surname origin myth. *Folklore, 73*, 230-232.
In Tenejapa, a Tzeltal Indian village in the highland state of Chiapas (in Southern Mexico
bordering Guatemala), there are 104 Tzeltal surnames, 14 Spanish. The name Mendez
(vulture) is supposedly derived from the story of a lazy man who exchanged places with
a vulture.

[9.39.2] Collier, George A., & Bricker, Victoria R. (1970).   Nicknames and social
structure in Zinacantan. *American Anthropologist, 72*, 289-302. Refs. Tables.

Zinacantan (pop. 7,650) is a Tzotzil-speaking township in Chaiapas, the southernmost province bordering Guatemala. Systematic evaluation of naming practices, including nicknames. The conclusion is that nicknames are becoming formal names by replacing Indian surnames. Comparisons with 18th cent. data. Many examples, some humorous.

[9.39.3] Foster, George M. (1964). Speech forms and the perception of social distance in a Spanish-speaking Mexican village. *Southwestern Journal of Anthropology, 20,* 107-122. Refs.
The village investigated was Tzintzuntzan (pop. 2000), a peasant community 230 miles west of Mexico City on Lake Patzcuaro. Description of forms of address with name. Attention paid to nicknaming and appropriate use, example, Chaparro ("Shorty") for a man who is short would only be called this to his face by an intimate friend. Some nicknames are inherited.

[9.39.4] Guiteras-Holmes, C(alixta). (1961). *Perils of the soul: The world view of the Tzotzil Indians.* New York: Free Press of Glencoe, 371p. state.
Pp. 68-69 describe their use of surnames. Individuals have 2 surnames, 1 Spanish, the other Indian.

[9.39.5] Lasker, Gabriel & Kaplan, Bernice. (1974). Anthropometric variables in the offspring of isonymous matings. *HumBio, 46,* 713-717. Refs. Tables.
Inbreeding is hypothesized as being related to shorter height and to other measurements. Theoretically, children of isonymous marriages should be more inbred. Samples were taken of Mexicans and Peruvians. 7 of 26 anthropometric measurements of the Mexican sample were depressed at a significant level. The Peruvian sample was not depressed, nor was the combined sample.

[9.39.6] Lasker, Gabriel W., & Kaplan, Bernice. (1985). Surnames and genetic structure: Repetition of the same pairs of names of married couples, a measure of subdivision of the population. *HumBio, 57,* 431-440. Refs. Tables.
Studied married couples in Paracho, Mexico to develop the repeated measurements technique involving surnames to demonstrate class-like behavior in a Mexican town.

[9.39.7] McCullough, John M.; Giles, Eugene; & Thompson, Richard A. (1985). Evidence for assortative mating and selection in surnames: A case from Yucatan, Mexico. *HumBio, 57,* 375-386. Refs. Tables. Fig.
A sample of 1276 individuals was examined for surname data in Ticul, a small city on the North Yucatan plain. The Maya there use surnames of both Maya and Spanish origin. Results indicate that: (1) persons tend to marry those with like surname origins, (2) there is a reduction in the proportion of Maya surnames.

[9.39.8] Roys, Ralph L(oveland). (1940). Personal names of the Maya of Yucatan. *Contributions to American Anthropology and History, No. 31,* 31-48. Refs. Tables.
Systematic report on names of the Maya. Includes patronyms, *naal* names (mother names), titles, slave names, boy names, and unclassified names. Extensive tables.

[9.39.9] Tierney, Robert W. (1979). Verbal aggression in Mexico City. *Maledicta, 3,* 277-278.
Usage of irreverent nicknames, *apodos,* in Mexico City. A few examples.

[9.39.10] Tozzer, Alfred M. (1907). *A comparative study of the Mayas and the Lancandones.* New York: Macmillan, 195p. Refs. Plates.
The Lancandones of Chiapas, Mexico belong to the Maya-Quiche stock. Pp. 40-42 use 5 different types of name: (1) address (terms of relationship, (2) family animal names, (3), clan (?) animal names, (4) names for order of birth, and (5) animal names based on order of birth.

[9.39.11] Villa Rojas, Alfonso. (1947). Kinship and nagualism in a Tzeltal community. *American Anthropologist, 49,* 578-587. Refs.
[Nagualism refers to belief in supernational beings that control human behavior. It is not related to names or naming]. Description of the Tzeltal Indian community of Oxchuc (pop. 3000) in Chiapas State. Clans have Spanish surnames (Lopez, Mendez, Gomez) but no aboriginal names. "Each clan is divided into...lineages, to be recognized by their aboriginal names, such as: Nich, Ichilok, Kulub, Cojton, etc." [1st names are not explained but appear to be Spanish].

[9.39.12] Vogt, Evon Z. (1969). *Zinacantan: A Maya community in the highlands of Chiapas.* Cambridge, MA: Belknap Press of Harvard University Press, 733p. Refs.
Tzotzil, a Mayan language is spoken in this community. Pp. 144-145, 154 describe naming. Each person has 3 names, a 1st name borrowed from Spanish, a Spanish surname, and an Indian surname. Nicknames are used extensively. Pp. 621-624 list Spanish and Tzotzil surnames and 1st names along with translations.

[9.39.13] Waterhouse, Viola. (1981). Mexican Spanish nicknames. In Andrew Gonzalez & David Thomas (Eds.) *Linguistics across continents* (pp. 19-23). Manila: Summer Institute of Linguistics.
Short (hypocoristic) and affectionate forms of 1st names used by the Chontal Indians of Mexico described. From 1st part of name: Flor from Florinda; from medial part: Feli from Ofelia; from final part: Tolo from Bartolo. Many examples.

9.40. ETHNIC NAMES: *Miscellaneous*

[9.40.1] Bice, Christopher. (1970). *Names for the Cornish: Three hundred Cornish Christian names.* Padstow: Lodenek Press, 32p. Illus.
Background and comment, pronunciation guide. Selevan is pronounced se-LEV-un and is the Cornish form of Solomon. Delen means "petal' in Cornish.

[9.40.2] Birket-Smith, Kaj. (1965). *The paths of culture.* Madison: University of Wisconsin Press, 537p.
Pp. 298-300 describe naming customs among primitives in different parts of the world, Eskimo Greenlanders, North American Indians, Melanesians, and Polynesians. In China, individuals change their names, progressing from "milk name" to "book name" to "title name."

[9.40.3] Bredart, Serge. (1989). Categorization of familiar persons from their names: A case of interference. *British Journal of Psychology, 80,* 273-283. Refs. Tables.
Report done in Belgium in 3 somewhat complex experiments in which French-speaking respondents had to categorize (1) famous people and (2) less-famous people on the basis of their surname as to whether they were either Flemish or Walloon. Results show an interaction between degree of familiarity and an interference effect; the less-familiar names had more interference.

[9.40.4] Charles, Prince of Schwartzenberg. (1960). Names and arms in Old Bohemia. *Armorial* [Scotland], *2,* 3-6.
Explains that in the 13th cent. a noble's surname or title was taken from his coat of arms. Examples include Rose, Ronn ("log" from German).

[9.40.5] Constantinescu, Ilinca. (1991). Subsystems of foreign names. *Revue Romaine de Linguistique, 36,* 237-241. Refs.
Description of how some non-Rumanian names came into Rumanian with changes, some without.

[9.40.6] Ferreira, Valentina. (1990). The system of patronymic names in the Iberian peninsula. *Proceedings of the 17th ICOS, Helsinki, 13-18 Aug. 1990, 1,* 314-321. Refs. Historical overview of patronymics on the Iberian peninsula going back to pre-Roman times and including the Moorish period. Examination of several theories of the *-ez* suffix (*-es* in Portugal; *-is* in Valencia) as patronymic indicators.

[9.40.7] Gellner, E. (1969). *Saints of the Atlas.* Chicago: University of Chicago Press, 317p. Refs.
Pp. 35-38 describe naming patterns of the Berbers of the High Atlas region of Morocco. A man's name consists of his 1st, his father's 1st, and a 3rd name indicating a larger group, possibly associated with his grandfather. A woman's name even after marriage has her 1st name, her father's 1st name, and the group name. Examples.

[9.40.8] Gonda, J. (1952). *Sanskrit in Indonesia.* Nagpur [India]: International Academy of Indian Culture, 456p. Refs.
Pp. 212-216 give an estimated 250+ names of people in Indonesia whose names are derived from Sanskrit or Sanskrit elements. Many of the names are those of royalty or nobles.

[9.40.9] Hemon, Roparz. (1976). Diminutive suffixes in Breton. *Celtica, 17,* 85-93. Refs.
Extensive discussion with examples. Thus, *Corrigan* < Old Breton *corr* + suffixes *-ic* and *-an*. Other examples include Alanic, and Budican. 30+ names cited.

[9.40.10] Hooker, J. T. (1989-90). Names in Linear A and Linear B. *Onomata, 13,* 123-130. Refs. Table.
Comparison of 30+ names for similarities and differences in Linear A and Linear B from Ancient Crete leads to the conclusion that "we may have to reckon with the presence of Greek-speakers among the population of Crete before the period of Knossian hegemony on the fifteenth century B. C."

[9.40.11] Humphrey, Caroline. (1978). Women, taboo, and the suppression of attention. In Shirley Ardener (Ed.) *Defining females: The nature of women in society* (pp. 89-108). New York: Wiley. Refs.
In Mongolia, even today within kin groups, juniors do not use personal names for seniors although seniors can address juniors freely. There is a taboo on the wife's use of names for male members of her husband's family (or even their wives), pp. 91-92.

[9.40.12] Just, Peter. (1987). Bimanese personal names: The view from Bima Town and Donggo. *Ethnology, 26,* 313-328. Refs.
Following up the work of Brewer [87:8.34.1], on the Bimanese of the Indonesian island of Sumbawa, compares two cultures there on naming practices. One is the majority Dou Mbojo in the lowlands; the other, the minority Dou Donggo, in the highlands.

[9.40.13] Kajanto, Iiro. (1962). On the problem of names of humility in early Christian epigraphy. *Arctos, Acta Philologica Fennica, New Series, 3,* 45-53. Refs.
Discussion and analysis of available data leads to the conclusion that names such as Proictus and Stercorius are not names of humility.

[9.40.14] Khera, Sigrid. (1972). An Austrian peasant village under rural industrialization. *Behavioral Science Notes, 1,* 29-36. Refs.
Berg (pop. 800) near St. Georgen in Attergau was studied. People are identified not by family name but by housename, the name of the farm holding where the person lives (p. 30).

[9.40.15] Lorchirachoonkul, Vichit. (1982). A Thai Soundex system. *Information-Processing & Management, 18,* 243-255. Refs. Tables.
Development of a Soundex system for Thai.

[9.40.16] Miran, M. Alam. (1975). *Naming and address in Afghan society.* (ERIC Document Reproduction Service No. ED 109 915).
Description of Afghani (Afghan Persian, or Dari) naming patterns and practices; 1st and 2nd names, differences between girls' and boys' names; kinship names; ox-names, nicknames, technonyms, honoritic titles, surnames, and patterns of address. Examples.

[9.40.17] Morrow, Robert D. (1989, Sept.). What's in a name? In particular, a Southeast Asian name? *Young Children,* pp. 20-23. Refs. Photos.
Description of naming styles of Vietnamese, Cambodian, Laotian, and Hmong cultures. Some examples.

[9.40.18] Name dropping. (1976, 13 Mar.). [International Report]. *Economist,* [England], p. 56.
Hoxha, the leader of Albania, has issued a decree to have people whose surnames do not please the government rename themselves or the government will do it. The purpose is to wipe out traces of religion.

[9.40.19] Ott, Sandra. (1981). The circle of mountains: A Basque shepherding community. Oxford: Clarendon, 238p. Refs.
Field study of a small community in the French Basque province of Soule. Pp. 42-43 describe house names. A person can be known by the house name rather than by 1st name

[9.40.20] Peter, Prince of Greece and Denmark. (1954). *The aristocracy of Central Tibet: A provisional list of the noble houses of Ü-Tsang.* Kalimpong, Tibet, 43p. Illus.
Has 205 name entries. Each shows the name transliterated into English, in translation, and the name in Tibetan characters. Example Lha-lu = "Serpent God."

[9.40.21] Skeat, Walter William & Brogden, Charles Otto. (1906; 1966). *Pagan races of the Malay Peninsula.* New York: Barnes & Noble, Vol. 1, 724p; Vol. 2, 855p. Refs. (Originally published by Macmillan in 1906).
Vol. 1 (pp. 717-723) has lists of 200+ personal names by tribe. Some meanings are given. Vol. 2 has several items on names: children are named on the basis of a dream by parents; the pattern painted on the headband is the name of the person; expulsion from the tribe is conducted by the magician who burns the headband (p. 12).

[9.40.22] Tay, J. S. H., & Yip, W. C. L. (1984). The estimation of inbreeding from isonymy: Relationship to the average inbreeding coefficient. *Annals of Human Genetics, 48,* 185-194. Refs. Tables.
After using extensive statistical procedures concludes that remote consanguinity has little impact on the inbreeding coefficient and questions the isonomy method of measuring inbreeding. The authors provide data based upon a Singapore study.

[9.40.23] US. Central Intelligence Agency. (1965). *Armenian personal names.* Washington, DC. 50p.
Background information on Armenian names. Table showing equivalents of Armenian letters in European languages. Main table has approx. 1700 Armenian 1st names in Armenian, English transliteration, Russian, English transliteration from Russian. Meanings of names not included.

[9.40.24]   Van Langendonck, Willy. (1990).   On the combination of forename and surname, with special reference to Flemish dialects. *Proceedings of the 17th ICOS, Helsinki, 13-18 Aug. 1990*, *2*, 436-443. Refs. Map.
Description of various types of 1st name and surname and combinations in Flanders, Belgium.   Concludes that in the 20th cent. "there has been an evolution from the personal name pattern /surname + forename/ to the reverse pattern /forename + surname/."

[9.40.25]   Vašek, Antonin. (1988).   On one case of language maintenance in the immigrant. *Onomata*, *12*, 586-599. Refs. Greek summary.
Studied 154 Czech immigrant families in the town of Larkin, North Dakota to see what changes, if any, had been made to their surnames and 1st names in the process of acculturation.   Some dropped the diacritical marks, others made other changes. Explanation of why so many Vojtěchs/Vojtas changed their names to Albert. Organized, detailed. Many examples.

[9.40.26]   Warmington, Brian H. (1991).   Religion and culture. [North Africa]. *NewEncyBrit*, *24*, 907.
Brief statement: "The great majority of Carthaginian personal names, unlike those of Greece and Rome, were of religious significance; e.g., Hannibal, 'Favoured by Baal,' or Hamilcar, 'Favoured by Melkart.'"

9.41. ETHNIC NAMES: *Norwegian*

[9.41.1]   Alhaug, Gulbrand. (1992).   Lemmatisering av namnevariantar: ein nivåmodell basert på norsk materiale [Lemmatization of name variants: A level model based on Norwegian material]. *StudAnthroScan*, *10*, 115-150. Refs. Tables. Figs. Norwegian. English summary.
Lemmatization here refers to grouping of 1st name variants at 3 levels: (1) graphemically different,(2) graphemically different but same pronunciation, and (3) archi-level, phonemic variants. There is also an etymological level. This analysis applied to 45,000 Norwegian female names. Many examples.

[9.41.2]   Flom, George T. (1920).   Semantic notes on characterizing surnames in Old Norse. *Journal of English & Germanic Philology*, *19*, 350-364. Refs.
Background on Old Norse surnames and nicknames.   Discussion of the work of other scholars.   Detailed analysis of about 15 names found in Eystein's *Jordebug* or in the Norwegian charters.   Names discussed include: Flik, Olfuss, and Gubba.

[9.41.3]   Hagland, Jan Ragnar. (1988).   Nokre onomastiske sider ved runematerialet frå bygrunnen i Trondheim og Bryggen i Bergen [Onomastic aspects of the runic inscriptions found in the city foundations in Trondheim and at Bryggen, Bergen]. *StudAnthroScan*, *6*, 13-25. Refs. Norwegian. English summary.
700-800 medieval runic inscriptions have been found, some on wooden sticks.

[9.41.4]   Haugen, Einar. (1969).   *The Norwegian language in America: A study in bilingual behavior*, (2nd ed.). Bloomington: Indiana University Press, 699p.
Describes the Norwegian adaptation to the United States.   Chap. 9 (pp. 191-218) is on naming and explains: the problems of transition to a single patronym, farm names, surnames from places, modifications of surnames in English, English name substitutes, and 1st names. Many examples. Refs(pp. 310-313. Tables. Sample genealogies.

[9.41.5]   Kimmerle, Marjorie M. (1945).   A study in connotation. In *Elizabethan studies and other essays in honor of George F. Reynolds. University of Colorado Studies, Series B, Studies in the Humanities*, *2*, 337-343. Refs.

The research was based on records of communities in Dane County, Wisconsin from 1860 on. Explains that Norwegians on immigrating to the US had the choice for surnames of either using patronymics (example, Olsen) or farm names (example, Hodnefjeld, "peaked mountain"). Farm names had rankings and connotations. Patronymics became more popular. Examples.

[9.41.6] Kruken, Kristoffer. (1989). Norske namnedagar [Norwegian name days]. *StudAnthroScan, 7,* 121-131. Refs. Table. Norwegian. English summary.
Description of the new (1989) Norwegian name calendar which has 770 names based upon names frequencies between 1900 and 1982. 2/3 of the names are new. Equal proportions of men and women in the new calendar.

[9.41.7] Mundal, Else. (1990). Forholdet mellom gudar og jotnar i norrøn mytologi i lys av det mytologiske namnematerialet [The relationship between gods and giants in Old Norse mythology in the light of mythological name evidence]. *StudAnthroScan, 8,* 5-18. Refs. Norwegian. English summary.
Evaluation of the relationship between gods and giants. Using Snorri's *Edda,* examines the names evidence to show the 2 groups are: (1) kin, (2) not separated by sharp borderlines, and (3) indivisible parts of the Old Norse universe. Also, the giants represent a store of qualities for gods and men.

[9.41.8] Mundal, Else. (1992). Å snu namnet [Switching names]. *StudAnthroScan, 10,* 77-79. Refs. Norwegian. English summary.
Describes the custom of changing the name of a sick child [apotropaism or fortune and remedy name] to another name with which the child had been christened. The practice continued until the 19th cent. in the Sunnmore area just north of Bergen.

[9.41.9] Schmidt, Tom. (1992). Jetmund. *StudAnthroScan, 10,* 25-47. Refs. Tables. Maps. Norwegian. English summary.
Traces the name to the 15th cent. In the 16th cent., 13 out of 15 name-bearers came from Nordfjord and Sunnmøre. The name spread in the 17th cent. By the 19th, it was less frequent. The concentration "in these areas is explained by an early English influence." There was also a local cult of St. Edmund.

[9.41.10] Seim, Karin Fjellhammer. (1991). Flere onomastiske sider ved runematerialet fra bygrunnen i Trondheim og Bryggen i Bergen [Further onomastic aspects of the runic material found in the Trondheim and Bryggen excavations]. *StudAnthroScan, 9,* 21-32. Refs. Norwegian. English summary.
Cites evidence critical of Hagland [9.41.3] that there is a high proportion of Icelandic runic ownership tags found in the Trondheim and Bryggen inscriptions.

[9.41.11] Svanevik, Anne. (1990). Some reflections on official name procedures in Norway. *Proceedings of the 17th ICOS, Helsinki, 13-18 Aug. 1990, 2,* 408-415. Refs. Table.
Since 1980, Norwegian law on personal names has been liberalized. People can change 1st names easily. Other changes have also been made. Some difficulties and contradictions might have been resolved if the government had consulted onomastic scholars.

[9.41.12] Svanevik, Anne. (1991). Norges nyeste personnavnlogivning sammenliknet med de nye personnavnlovene i Danmark, Sverige og Finland [Norway's most recent legislation on personal names compared with the new laws in Denmark, Sweden and Finland]. *StudAnthroScan, 9,* 119-132. Refs. Norwegian. English summary.
The 1979 legislation requires couples to "keep their own surnames or to take the name of either partner as their mutual surname." For children, it does not matter if the parents

are not married. The child can be given either surname, but will be given the mother's if no preference is expressed. Comparisons with other countries.

9.42. ETHNIC NAMES: *Oceania*

[9.42.1] Crocombe, R. G., & Rere, Vaine. (1959). Naming in Atiu. *Journal of the Polynesian Society, 68,* 180-187.
Description of naming customs in one of the Cook Islands (in the Pacific near New Zealand). Includes death names (to commemorate the death of a relative), and nicknames. Older naming customs dying out.

[9.42.2] Flint, E. H. (1964). The language of Norfolk Island. In Alan Strode C. Ross & A. W. Moverley *The Pitcairnese language* (pp. 189-269). New York: Oxford University Press.
The extensive glossary for the language has at least 7 words that came from names. Frederick, Hannah, Hattie's gown, Henry, and Sandford are all fish. George is a sea-shell; tom is a male animal. Possible sources for these are given.

[9.42.3] Stokes, J. F. G. (1930). An evaluation of early genealogies for Polynesian history. *Journal of Polynesian Studies, 39,* 1-42. Refs. Tables.
Contrasts genealogies of New Zealand, Rorotonga, Tahiti, and Hawaii beginning with the mythologies of creation and the naming process. 13 island groups compared. List of names (some with meaning) in genealogical lists.

9.42.1. ETHNIC NAMES: *Oceania: Australian*

[9.42.1.1] Baker, Sidney J(ohn). (1966). *The Australian language*, 2nd ed. Sydney: Currawong; San Francisco: Tri-Ocean, 517p. Refs.
Ch. 12, People and Places, pp. 268-274, has a section on approx. 85 slang nicknames which became words, example, game as Ned Kelly, refers to an extremely courageous person; to give someone a Charlie, is to run someone out. Pp. 274-276 briefly cover 1st names, unusual names, and changed names.

[9.42.1.2] Cantor, M. E. L. (1956). Change of name in Western Australia. *Australian Law Journal, 30,* 289-290. Refs.
A 1923 law in Western Australia departs from usual common law practice by not allowing individuals to use assumed names even without fraudulent intent.

[9.42.1.3] Gore, Stuart. (1968). *Holy smoke: From the scriptures according to Saltbush Bill.* Sydney Australia: Ure Smith. 112p.
Included are: to play Larry Dooley (to cause trouble), Lizardy Bill (whom people treated as a doormat), and Buckley's choice (no chance at all).

[9.42.1.4] Hart, C. W. M., & Pilling, Arnold R. (1966). *The Tiwi of North Australia.* New York: Holt, Rinehart & Winston, 118p.
The Tiwi are an aboriginal people who live on Bathurst and Melville Islands which are off the northwest coast of Australia. Pp. 20-21 describe naming practices in a culture which is unique in that all females are always married. Children are named by the man currently living with the mother. Theoretically, a child can be renamed several times although in practice this does not quite follow.

[9.42.1.5] Hatt, D. & Parsons, P. A. (1965). Association between surnames and blood groups in Australian populations. *Acta Genetica et Statistica Genetica, 15,* 309-318. Refs. Tables. Figs. French summary. German summary.

Surnames were used to identify the regions of the British Isles that blood donors were from. "The regional variations found in the British Isles were found to be largely preserved in the Australian population."

[9.42.1.6] Mallows, R. J. (1980, Spring). Who owns a pen name? *Author* [England], *91*, 14-15.
Description of an Australian legal case in which author Trevor Sykes wrote under the name of Pierpont for some time. Subsequently Sykes left his employer. Since Sykes was publicly associated with Pierpont, the court ruled that Sykes could take the name with him.

[9.42.1.7] Ryan, J. S. (1966). Isolation and generation with a conservative framework: A unique dialectical situation for English. *Orbis, 15*, 35-50. Refs.
Pp. 40-41 give the background of 4 terms involving names that have come into Australian English. Examples are Buckley's chance (little likelihood) and blind Freddie (< an incompetent police commissioner).

[9.42.1.8] Tylor, Edward Burnett (1903?; 1958). *The origins of culture*. New York: Harper (Torchbooks), 416p. Refs. (Originally published as Chs. 1-9 of *Primitive culture* by John Murray of London).
Gives information on primitive cultures. Pp. 254-255 describe naming of children with numbers by Australian aborigines; Pp. 396-397 have some comments on false eponyms, examples, chic and cant.

[9.42.1.9] Warren, B. H. (1958). Tormenter Harslett. *Names, 6*, 125.
A daughter in Australia was given this name by her jockey father to fulfill a vow made for winning a race.

9.42.2. ETHNIC NAMES: *Oceania: New Zealand*

[9.42.2.1] B., E. R. (1945, Apr. 6). What's your name; fun with a directory. *New Zealand Listener, 12(302)*, 8.
Examination of a Post Office Directory showed interesting surnames in a number of categories including: financial, colors, birds, and religious. In the religious group were: 269 Bishops, 11 Parsons, 86 Priests, 9 Friars, and 101 Churches.

[9.42.2.2] Kuschel, Rolf. (1988). Cultural reflections in Bellonese personal names. *Journal of the Polynesian Society, 97*, 49-70. Refs.
Naming customs on this small island in the Solomon Islands. Describes primary, 2ndary, honorific, and insulting names. Examples.

[9.42.2.3] Scott, Forrest S. (1986). Personal names of students, and other Auckland onomastics. *Te Reo, 29*, 257-300. Refs. Tables. Figs.
Intro. material. Basis for popularity of names with studies drawn from *The Times*, influence of reading and viewing, and phonological factors. Main material is a comprehensive, systematic report of New Zealand names 1973-1985 with extensive tables and figs. and comparisons with the US, Canada, England, and Australia. More recent birth-names also described.

9.42.2.1. ETHNIC NAMES: *Oceania: New Zealand: Maori*

[9.42.2.1.1] Best, Elsdon. (1902). Maori nomenclature. *Journal of the Royal Anthropological Institute of Great Britain & Ireland, 32*, 182-201.

Extensive coverage of nomenclature. Includes forms of address for relatives and others. Personal names described, examples, Horo-mata, ("eye-swallower"), Kaka, ("the parrot"). Changing of names is common.

[9.42.2.1.2] Best, Elsdon. (1906). The lore of the Whare-Kohanga, Part III. *Journal of the Polynesian Society, 15,* 147-162. Refs.
The Whare-Kohanga are a Maori tribe. Pp. 154-157 describe child-naming customs and the types of name a person has. A few examples are given.

[9.42.2.1.3] Mead, A. D. (1958). Personal Maori names recorded by Richard Taylor. *Journal of the Polynesian Society* (New Zealand), *67,* 58-69.
Listing of unbaptized 1037 men (941 names) and 1004 women (879 names) from records of the Wanganui district of New Zealand in 1843. 77 of the names are used by both sexes.

[9.42.2.1.4] Smith, T. H. (1892). *Transactions of the New Zealand Institute, 25,* 395-412. Mostly on placenames. However, pp. 395-398 give information on personal naming and forms of address. Among the customs: most names can be used by either sex, there are no surnames.

[9.42.2.1.5] Walker, R. J. (1969). Proper names in Maori myth and tradition. *Journal of the Polynesian Society, 78,* 405-416. Refs.
Describes the close relationship of personal names to placenames in New Zealand. Relates the custom of visiting Maori chiefs having an overnight liaison as a guest prerogative. If a pregnancy resulted, the chief named the child. Names used to show such as this were used to show links between groups. Mythology had strong influence on naming. Names also used to commemorate battles.

9.42.3. ETHNIC NAMES: *Oceania: Papua New Guinea*

[9.42.3.1] Glasse, R. M. (1987). Huli names and naming. *Ethnology, 26,* 201-208. Refs.
The Huli number about 60,000 and live in the Tagari River basin of Papua-New Guinea. The study collected 82 1st names, 50 male, 26 female. Examples include: Timu (male) = "arrow," Tugu (female) "to cry." Not all names have meaning. Surnames appear to be identified with a founding ancestor. Listing of the 1st names and 73 surnames.

[9.42.3.2] Harrison, Simon. (1985). Names, ghosts, and alliance in two Sepil River societies. *Oceania, 56,* 138-146. Refs.
The Sepik River is in Papua New Guinea. Naming systems of 2 societies, the Manambu and the Iatmul are compared. Both are complicated and share many features but do have differences.

[9.42.3.3] Hogbin, H. Ian. (1943). A New Guinea infancy: From conception to weaning in Wogeo. *Oceania, 13,* 285-309. Refs.
Wogeo, the largest of the Schouten islands, is 30 miles off the North coast of New Guinea. "The father's and the mother's kinfolk have the right of choosing one each [child's name], but the final selection rests with the grandfathers or the father's and the mother's eldest brother." (p. 293).

[9.42.3.4] Poole, FitzJohn Porter. (1981). Transforming "natural" woman: Female ritual leaders and gender ideology among Bimin-Kuskusmin. In Sherry Ortner & Harriet Whitehead (Eds.). *Sexual meanings: The cultural construction of gender and sexuality* (pp. 116-165). Refs. Cambridge, England: Cambridge University Press.

This primitive tribe of about 1000 live in West Sepik Province of Papua New Guinea. They are unique in that they have a *waneng aiyem ser*, a sacred leader, a woman who possesses a female name, a male name, and a sacred name. She also bestows female names.

9.43. ETHNIC NAMES: *Peruvian*

[9.43.1] Lasker, Gabriel W. (1968). The occurrences of identical isonymous surnames in various relationships in pedigrees: A preliminary analysis of the relation of surname combinations to inbreeding. *Journal of Human Genetics, 20,* 250-257. Refs. Tables. Fig. 204 adults in San José, Peru were interviewed to identify isonymy in different types of relationships such as, individual's father and spouse's father, spouse's father and spouse's mother, and individual's mother and spouse's mother.

[9.43.2] Lasker, Gabriel W. (1969). Isonymy (recurrence of the same surnames in affinal relatives): A comparison of rates calculated from pedigrees, grave markers, and death and birth registers. *HumBio, 41,* 309-321. Refs. Tables.
In San Jose, Peru, isonymous pairs were studied by the 4 indexes in the title. Cemetery records show lower than expected isonymy. Differences over the past 3 generations were not important.

[9.43.3] Lasker, Gabriel W. (1977). A coefficient of relationship by isonymy: A method for estimating the genetic relationship between populations. *HumBio, 49,* 489-493. Refs. Table.
Used isonymy to evaluate 1148 individuals in 5 communities on the North coast of Peru.

[9.43.4] Lasker, Gabriel W. (1978). Increments through migration to the coefficient of relationship between communities estimated by isonymy. *HumBio, 50,* 235-240. Refs. Table.
Further analysis of the Lasker 1977 study above [9.43.3], in Peru concludes that not including the effects of outmigration has tended to overstate the isonymy relationship.

[9.43.5] Salomon, Frank. (1986). Names and peoples in Incaic Quito, Retrieving undocumented historic processes through anthroponymy and statistics. *American Anthropologist, 88,* 387-399. Refs.
Sophisticated computer techniques were used to study the names of culturally non-Inca aborigines. Studies were based upon records for 6 villages from 1559.

9.44. ETHNIC NAMES: *Philippine*

[9.44.1] Estolas, Josefina Villanueva. (1965). Relationship of nicknames to Filipino children's self-perception. *DissAbstrIntl, 25,* 5732-5733.
Data were gathered on 800 children in the Philippines. Among results there was confirmation of the importance of the nickname in the child's self-image. Children who disliked their nicknames showed more problems on the self-perception scale.

[9.44.2] Lohr, Steve. (1985, Feb. 5). Filipinos take nicknames, but not seriously. *New York Times,* p. A10.
Nicknames of prominent people include Joker Rroyo, a lawyer; Bong Bong Marcos, son of the former president; Ding Dong Teehankee, a Supreme Court judge, and Butz Aquino, brother of Benigno Aquino, Jr.

9.45. ETHNIC NAMES: *Polish*

[9.45.1] Nalibow, Kenneth L. (1973). *Genus versus sexus. Professional titles, working titles and surnames for women in contemporary standard Polish.* Bern: Herbert Lang, 139p. Refs.
In the Polish language, surnames and titles have feminine forms. However, with the increase in the number of working women, there are patterns of women using the masculine forms. Many examples of various forms cited from newspapers.

[9.45.2] Pauls, John P. (1969). Type, structure and usage of surnames in the Brest-Litovsk region. *Onoma, 14,* 102-108. Refs.
Also in *Proceedings of the 9th ICOS, London, July 3-8, 1966.*
Typical surnames were collected from this region prior to WW2 where the language was West-Polessian, a North-Ukrainian dialect. Origins of the names are: patronyms, location, occupation, and descriptive nicknames. Approx. 100 surnames listed, many showing origin and meaning.

[9.45.3] Rzetelska-Felezko, Ewa. (1978). A system of family names in North Polish dialects. *Onoma, 22,* 282-287. Refs.
Explanation with example of how members of a family, husband, wife, son, and daughter can have different forms of the surname.

9.46. ETHNIC NAMES: *Portuguese*

[9.46.1] Bentley, Jeffery Westwood. (1987). Ethnographic study of a rural parish in Northwest Portugal. *DissAbstrIntl, 47,* 2633A.
1 chapter is devoted to nicknames. Suggests that they express an ideal of equality in a community were there are material differences.

[9.46.2] Cutileiro, Jose. (1971). *A Portuguese rural society.* Oxford: Clarendon, 314p.
There is a passing mention (p. 135) on how nicknames function as a form of social control in a small village in southeast Portugal near the Spanish border. Thus, a man perceived as bad is called (ironically), "the Jesuit."

9.47. ETHNIC NAMES: *Russian*

[9.47.1] Benson, Morton. (1964). The compilation of a dictionary of Russian personal names. *Names, 12,* 15-22. Refs.
Description of the problems in compiling a dictionary, especially with varying forms of 1st names and stress and morphology of surnames.

[9.47.2] Davidson, R. M. (1975). The translation of surnames in Dostoevsky. *Journal of Russian Studies, No. 30,* 28-31. Refs.
Most of the time, Russian surnames are transliterated into English. However, this results in losing the possible meaning of the name. Examples given showing how meanings of the name can be translated from the Russian of Dostoevsky to enhance the meaning of the literature, examples, Lebezyatnikov = "to fawn," Svidrigaylov = Attila, Smerdyakov = "Smellie."

[9.47.3] Gunnemark, Erik. (1988). Gorbachóv and other Russian family names. *Modern Språk* [Sweden], *82,* 48-49.
Explains that Gorbachóv means "hunchback"; Zjúkov and Krushchóv, "beetle-men." Information on about 12 other Russian surnames.

[9.47.4] Iivanen, Leevi. (1960). The rendering of English proper names in Russian. *Slavonic & East European Review, 39,* 137-147. Refs. (mostly Russian).
History and discussion on the problems of transcribing English names into Russian. Suggests that a uniform style would be desirable.

[9.47.5] Lambert, Tom. (1960, Apr.). A little boy named Differential. *Catholic Digest,* pp. 94-96. [Condensed from *New York Herald Tribune,* Nov. 24, 1959].
Russians in the period around the 40s gave their children patriotic names, such as, Great Worker, Differential, or Ninel (Lenin spelled backwards). Trend now (1959) shifting toward Russian names.

[9.47.6] Mydans, Seth. (1985, Feb. 16). In Russia, traditional names are popular again. *New York Times,* p. 48.
Survey results published in Izvestia shows that most popular names for boys are Alexander, Dmitri, and Sergei; and Yekaterina, Anna, and Maria for girls. Post-Revolution type names that are no longer in style include Himalaya, Birch, Granite, Diesel, and Ninel (Lenin spelled backwards).

[9.47.7] Nakhimovsky, A. D. (1976). Social distribution of forms of address in contemporary Russian. *International Review of Slavic Linguistics, 1,* 79-118. Refs. Table.
Description of various current practices; examples from literature. Table (p. 115) shows 10 variations of style with examples of use of the name in address.

[9.47.8] Nikonov, V. A. (1971). The personal name as a social symbol. *Soviet Anthropology & Archeology, 10,* 168-195. Refs. Tables.
General on Russian names. Many cross-cultural references. Theme is the shift of class differences in the selection of 1st names to a more common selection at all levels. All refs. are non-English.

[9.47.9] Pauls, John P. (1963). Soviet pseudonym-surnames. *Atti e Memorie del Congresso dello Sezione Antroponimica, VII Congresso Internazionale di Scienze Onomastiche, Firenze, Apr. 1961 [7th ICOS], Vol. 3,* pp. 257-260. Refs.
The original names of 13 leaders of the Soviet Union. Lenin had 99 pseudonyms. The name Lenin has 3 possible origins. His birth name Iljanov < Lat. Julianus. Stalin = "steel." His birth name was Dzugashvili and he had 16 pseudonyms. Others were: Molotov = "hammer" and Skriabin = "ship's scraper."

[9.47.10] Schmemann, Serge. (1982, June 10). Soviet history and kids' names. *New York Times,* p. 14.
Description of changing fashions in Russian names from the post-1917 era Industriyas and Oktyabrinas to the current "old" names such as Nikolai and Dimitri.

[9.47.11] Unbegaun, B. O. (1967). Russian surnames derived from aphetic baptismal names. *Melbourne Slavonic Studies, 1,* 49-51.
An aphetic name is one derived from a non-initial syllable of a name, example, Koljagin < Nikolaj. The source for common names can be identified fairly easily, but less common names cause problems. 35+ unusual names are traced including: Dronov < Andron; Lenin < Aleksandr; and Politov < Ippolit.

9.48. ETHNIC NAMES: *Scandinavian*
(See Also: 9.15 ETHNIC NAMES: *Danish;* 9.19 ETHNIC NAMES: *Faroese;* 9.20.
ETHNIC NAMES: *Finnish;* 9.28. ETHNIC NAMES: *Icelandic;* 9.41. ETHNIC
NAMES: *Norwegian,* and 9.53. ETHNIC NAMES: *Swedish)*

[9.48.1] Brylla, Eva. (1992). De nordiska personnamnslagarna: En jamforande oversikt
over nu gallande namnratt [The Nordic personal names acts: A comparative survey of
current name law]. *StudAnthroScan, 10,* 99-113. Refs. Swedish. English summary.
Survey of 1970s legislation in Denmark, Finland, Sweden, and Norway with some
attention to the Faeroes and Iceland. Among the differences: (1) Norway and Sweden
allow full siblings to have different surnames, (2) In Denmark people are encouraged to
have middle names, and (3) Norway is the most liberal on surname change; Finland the
most conservative.

[9.48.2] Hagland, Jan Ragnar. (1990). Kva tid vart *thorgíl* til *thorgils* i nordiske språk
[When did thorgisl become *thorgils* in the Scandinavian languages?]. *StudAnthroScan,
8,* 35-46. Refs. Norwegian. English summary.
"The name *thorgisl,* attested in Viking Age runic inscriptions, eventually developed into
thorgils in all the Scandinavian languages." Shows the chronological development and
geographical spread of the name.

[9.48.3] Mercer, A. C. B. (1954). Scandinavian surnames in Britain. *Norseman, 12,*
304-308.
General description and discussion of Scandinavian names in Great Britain and how they
have survived with modification as surnames. Examples include: Thorfinn as Turpin,
Sigurd as Seward, Ragnvold as Reynold, and Hamund as Hammond.

[9.48.4] Salberger, Evert. (1985). Två mansnamn i urnordiskan [Two masculine names
in Proto-Scandinavian]. In *Nordiska namnstudier: Festskrift till Harry Stahl 22 september
1985* (pp. 354-371). Uppsala: Lundesquistska. Swedish. English summary.
New interpretations of two Runic names, *hadulaikaR* from Ryfylk county, Norway, and
ssigaduR from Bohuslan province in Sweden.

[9.48.5] Sturtevant, Albert Morey. (1952). Regarding the Old Norse name Gefjon.
Scandinavian Studies, 24, 166-167. Refs.
The origin and meaning of Gefjon, a goddess, has been controversial. Examination of
various possibilities including those based upon verbs meaning "to give" and "to
arrange."

[9.48.6] Sturtevant, Albert Morey. (1953). Regarding the name Asa-Thor.
Scandinavian Studies, 25, 15-16. Refs.
Explanation of how Odin's son Thor received the epithet *Asa-*.

[9.48.7] Sturtevant, Albert Morey. (1958). The Old Norse proper name *SVIPDAGR*.
Scandinavian Studies, 30, 30-34. Refs.
Extensive analysis of the name of the hero in the *Svipdagsmól.* Concludes that the name
Svipdagr refers to a mythical person who received magic power from his mother. It
"may be appropriately translated by 'The Magical Dagr.'"

9.49. ETHNIC NAMES: *Scottish*

[9.49.1] Cohen, Anthony P. (1982). A sense of time, a sense of place: The meaning
of close social association in Whalsay, Shetland. In Anthony P. Cohen (Ed.) *Belonging:
Identity and social organisation in British rural cultures* (pp. 21-49). St. John's

Newfoundland: Institute of Social & Economic Research Papers No. 11. Refs. Figs. Photos.

Whalsay (pop. 1,076) is an island 2 miles NE of the largest Shetland island (N of Scotland). It is a fishing community. P. 41 has a brief reference to the naming pattern in one family where a grandfather, John Jamieson Irvine is known as "Aald Glybie' because he lived in a cottage on glebe land. His children were known as Glybie's Magnie, Glbyie's Will, etc.

[9.49.2] Editor (Robert Gayre). (1961). Law of name and title in Scotland. *Armorial* [Scotland], *2,* 236-237.
Indicates that a 1961 Scottish court ruling requires that a person who holds a territorial title (MacSporran of Glensporran) must either use the title regularly or not at all (John MacSporran). A person cannot have a title but just use it for social occasions such as a St. Andrew's Night dinner.

[9.49.3] Jackson, Kenneth (H). (1965). The Ogam inscription at Dunadd. *Antiquity, 39,* 300-302. Refs. Fig.
An 8th cent. Ogam (an early Irish alphabet) inscription found in Argyll, Scotland was evaluated. The inscription is thought to be in Pictish. One speculation is that it may mean something like "Kilroy was here," or "Irish go home."

[9.49.3A] Sandison, Alexander. (1959). Shetland surnames. *Genealogists' Magazine, 13,* 44-45; 76-77.
Discussion with examples of the Norse influence on naming in the Shetlands. As late as the early 1800s, patronymics were used. Women used the suffix *daughter* as in Donaldsdaughter. Rules of 1st-naming practices given.

[9.49.4] Taylor, A. B. (1966). Personal names in Orkney. In John Shearer, William Groundwater, & John Mackay (Eds.), *The new Orkney book* (pp. 58-62). London: Nelson.
Most 1st names in this island north of Scotland follow the common stock of Scotland. Some names of Norse origin survive. Among these are Magnus, Ivor, and Thora. Surnames include: Flett ("flayer"), Turfus < Old Norse Thorfinsson, Kirkness, and Sinclair.

[9.49.5] Travers, James. (1980). Analysing personal names. *Management Services in Government, 35,* 149-154. Tables.
Results of 4 surveys in Scotland between 1858 and 1976 from the General Registrar Office, Scotland of the 10 most common surnames and 1st names for men and women. One table also shows the distribution of surnames by initial letter.

[9.49.6] W., D. (1961). Aliases. [Reply]. *Scottish Genealogist, 8(4),* 13-14. Refs.
Reply to A. C. H. on aliases. Shows citations indicating that sometimes sept names were used as aliases as were occupational names, examples "Nicol Loure 'alias' Sadler." Loure < Latin *lorum,* "thong." and would thus pertain to a saddle-maker. Citations to the 16th and 18th cents.

9.49.1. ETHNIC NAMES: *Scottish: First Names*

[9.49.1.1] Mackay, R. L. (1974). Male christian names among the clan Mackay: An analysis of 2131 names. *Armorial* [Scotland], *6,* 203-211. Tables.
Using data from the 18th to the 20th cents. shows in 12 tables various name distributions. In 1794 the 5 most popular names for Mackays and non-Mackays were: John, William, Donald, Hugh, and Alexander. While there are some variations, data from the 20th cent. do show a consistency with earlier results.

[9.49.1.2] MacKay, Robert L. (1978). Christian name patterns of the men of the principal clans in Sutherland, 1678-1834. *Scottish Genealogist, 5,* 73-76. Refs.
11 clans including Mackay, Sutherland, and Ross were studied. Results indicate that 9 1st names (John, William, Donald, Alexander, George, James, Robert, Angus, and Hugh) accounted for 82.85% of the 1st names.

[9.49.1.3] McCracken, Alex. (1972). Lieutenancy minutes for the subdivision of Eskdale. *Transactions of the Dumfriesshire & Galloway Natural History & Antiquarian Society, 49,* 84-97. Refs. Table.
The "Lieutenancy" notebook is a "complete list of the men aged 19 to 23 living in the parish." The list has 868 names (indicating also the parish) in 1801. Most common names (in order) are: Armstrong, Little, Beattie, Scott, and Murray.

9.49.2. ETHNIC NAMES: *Scottish: Nicknames*

[9.49.2.1] Ennew, Judith. (1980). *The Western Isles today.* Cambridge: Cambridge University Press, 128p.
The Western Isles are to the west of Scotland and include Lewis, the Uists, and Barra. Pp. 77-79 describe naming customs. Nicknames are very commonly used and one community (Ness on Lewis) has a telephone directory listing people by nickname. Gaelic names are also used.

[9.49.2.2] Henderson, Hamish. (1962). Bynames among the tinkers. *Scottish Studies, 6,* 95-96.
Scots tinkers use nicknames widely. Some individuals have 2 nicknames, 1 used to the man's face, the other when he is not around. 24 nicknames are listed including: Scrappin' John, Love-in-a-Close, and Vinegar Bottle.

[9.49.2.3] MacColl, Ewan & Seeger, Peggy. (1986). *Till doomsday in the afternoon: The folklore of a family of Scots Travellers, the Stewarts of Blairgowrie.* Manchester, England: Manchester University Press, 325p. Refs.
The Travellers are apparently itinerant workers and entertainers. Pp. 21-23 describe family nicknames, example (p. 22), " . . . the Higginses are sometimes called the *Slavvery Higgins,* because the're aye dreepin' at the mooth." Several other examples as well.

[9.49.2.4] MacLeay, John. (1980). Adam's ale and the forky-tail. *Scots Magazine, 112,* 530-534. Illus.
Light approach to all kinds of nicknames. Includes some for people including: Bonnie Charlie, Kate Bar Lass, and Wizard of the North.

[9.49.2.5] Mewett, Peter G. (1982). Exiles, nicknames, social identities and the production of local consciousness in a Lewis crofting community. In Anthony P. Cohen (Ed.) *Belonging: Identity and social organisation in British rural cultures* (pp. 222-246). St. John's Newfoundland: Institute of Social & Economic Research Papers No. 11. Refs. Fig.
Clachan is the pseudonym for a small community (128 households) on the island of Lewis off the northwest coast of Scotland. 90 of the 141 men share both a 1st name and a surname with at least one other person. One table shows the frequency of same 1st and surname. Most common surnames are: MacLeod, MacDonald, and Munro; most common 1st names, John, Donald, and Murdo. Nicknames help to differentiate. Most common nicknames are epithets after 1st name. Other types as well. No examples.

[9.49.2.6] Parman, Susan. (1976). General properties of naming, and a specific case of nicknaming in the Scottish Outer Hebrides. *Ethnos, 41,* 99-115. Refs.

The investigation was conducted in the village of Shawbost, 18 miles from Stornoway on the Isle of Lewis. Description of naming and nicknaming practices. Types of nickname include: place (Iain Fhibhig, "John from Fibhig"), occupation (Inis Gobha, "Inis the Blacksmith"), and Gaelic (Tasag, "Ghost"). Many examples.

[9.49.2.7] Russell, J. M. (1980). The Doodies and the Daurna-mentions. *Scots Magazine, New Series, 113,* 38-45. Photos.
Anecdotes from Cockenzie and Port Seton, near Edinburgh. Since so many people have the same surname in these fishing villages, additional names are used, example, Doodie is used as an additional unofficial family name for Tommy Thomson since there are so many Tom Thomsons. Simple nicknames are also used: Dagwood (from the comic strip), Flae, Flit, and Dockers.

9.49.3. ETHNIC NAMES: *Scottish: Population Structure*

[9.49.3.1] Clegg, E. J. (1986). The use of parental isonymy in inbreeding in two Outer Hebridean populations. *Annals of Human Biology, 13,* 211-224. Refs. Tables. Map. German summary. French summary.
2 small islands, Scalpay and Berneray, of the Outer Hebrides of Scotland, were studied using 4 kinds of parental isonymy for the years 1861-1971 to study inbreeding. Females showed greater lability in migration. Most common names on Scalpay were Morrison and McLeod; on Berneray, Macaskill and McLeod.

[9.49.3.2] Mascie-Taylor, C. G. N., Lasker, G(abriel) W., & Boyce, A. (1987). Repetition of the same surnames in different marriages as an indicator of the structure of the population of Sanday Island, Orkney Islands. *HumBio, 59,* 97-108. Refs. Tables.
The Orkneys are off the north coast of Scotland. Marriage records over a 111 year period were evaluated for name repetition in (1) groom's father vs. bride's father, (2) groom's father vs. bride's mother, (3) birth name of groom's mother vs. bride's mother, and (4) groom's mother vs. bride's mother. Comparisons with other studies.

[9.49.3.3] Roberts, D. F., & Roberts, M. J. (1983). Surnames and relationships: An Orkney study. *HumBio, 55,* 341-347. Refs(pp. 399-408). Table.
Isonymy techniques overestimate kinship by 7 times in comparison with pedigree analysis. This is explained by the earlier patronymic system of naming in the Orkneys.

[9.49.3.4] Robinson, A. P. (1983). Inbreeding as measured by dispensations and isonymy on a small Hebridean Island, Eriskay. *HumBio, 55,* 289-295. Refs(pp. 399-408). Tables.
Research from this Scottish Catholic island based upon data from 1855 to 1979 on births and marriages and dispensations given by the Church shows that isonymy gives higher estimates of inbreeding than dispensations do.

9.49.4. ETHNIC NAMES: *Scottish: Surnames*

[9.49.4.1] Blake, John L. (1966). Distribution of surnames in the Isle of Lewis, *Scottish Studies, 10,* 154-160. Refs. Table.
Focuses somewhat on the population stability as reflected in surnames. Table of the top 23 surnames from the 1961 Electoral Register for different districts of Lewis is compared with 1890-91.

[9.49.4.2] Clouston, J. Storer. (1924). The people and surnames of Orkney. *Proceedings of the Orkney Antiquarian Society, 2,* 31-36. Refs.

History of the influences on Orkney surnames from the Norse period. Many accounts from the 17th cent. Influence of the Scots described. Many examples.

[9.49.4.3] Donaldson, Gordon. (1984). Surnames and ancestry in Scotland. *Highlander, 22(1),* 29-32.
Gives advice based upon experience for those interested in Scottish surnames.

[9.49.4.4] Dorward, D(avid). (1970). Some interesting Mac names. *Scotland's Magazine, 66(Feb.),* 42-43. Illus.
Mac as a prefix can mean: (1) son of, as in MacDonald, (2) son of, in a figurative sense, example, MacLung, son of the sea (sailor), (3) son of in a combination form, example, MacLean means son of the servant of St. John. In this case formed by the combination of Mac + gille + Eoin (John). The gille (servant) reduced to simply the letter l.

[9.49.4.5] Griest, Terry L. (1986). *Scottish tartans and family names.* Annapolis, MD: Harp & Lion Press, 133p. Refs.
Introductory information on Scottish names including spelling. Listing of approx. 3000 names with clan.

[9.49.4.6] Hughes, Charles P. (1963). Scottish surnames. *Scotland's Magazine, 59,* 44-45. Illus.
Intro. to the 4 major categories of Scottish surnames: patronym, location, occupation, and nickname.

[9.49.4.7] Kirkpatrick, Harold. (1973). The origin of the Kirkpatricks. *Scottish Genealogist, 20,* 33-36. Refs.
Speculation on the background of the name in Dumfriesshire. Sometimes the name was spelled Kilpatrick. Possibility that the Gaelic "G" is like the English "K." Concludes that tradition points to a Celtic origin of the name.

[9.49.4.8] MacDonald, Donald F. (1965, Sept.). Good morning Mr. Mackerel! *Scots Magazine,* pp. 538-542. Illus.
Rails against the English influence where Scottish names prefixed by *Mac* are not capitalized, example, *Macdonald.* Explanation of the Irish *Mc.* Listing of about 38 Scottish surnames in English and Gaelic with their meaning.

[9.49.4.9] MacGregor, Alasdair Alpin (Douglas). (1949). *The Western Isles.* London: Hale, 366p.
Pp, 40 describes the most prominent surnames on the Western Isles. A footnote (no specific source but dated 1750) states, "The common inhabitants of Lewis are the Morisons, McAulays, and MacKivers, but when they go from home, all who live under Seaforth [Lord Seaforth's domain] call themselves Mackenzies."

[9.49.4.10] Mackenzie, W(illiam) C(arl). (1903). *History of the Outer Hebrides: Lewis, Harris, North and South Uist Benbecula, and Bara.* Paisley, Scotland: Gardner, 623p. Refs.
Pp. 64-65 give some 1890-1891 surname data for schoolchildren in 3 parishes of Lewis. The top 5 (of 9) surname frequencies were: Macleod, 585; Macdonald, 364; Morison, 239; Mackenzie, 184; and Mackay, 166.

[9.49.4.10A] MacMillan, Somerled. (1970). Some Gaelic surnames and their English adaptations. *Scottish Genealogist, 17,* 109-115.
Gives origin of 35+ Scottish surnames, example, MacLean (servant of St. John), Gilles (servant of Jesus), and MacPhail (servant of St. Paul).

[9.49.4.11] Sandison, Alexander. (1968). Surnames found in Shetland in 1804 and 1954 *Genealogists' Magazine, 15,* 500-504 Refs.
The data from 1804 were lists totaling 3000 names of heads of families eligible for a charity meal. The 1954 list was 13,600 electors. Surnames were ranked for each listing. Variant spellings considered. Concluded that over half of Shetlanders are descendants of Scottish immigrants.

[9.49.4.12] Stewart, A. I. B. (1986). The evolution of Gaelic surnames in Kintyre. *Scottish Genealogist, 33,* 188-191.
Evaluation of lists of Kintyre tenants from 1505 to 1653. Shows evolution of the spelling of the name. Discussion of some of the names on the lists, including: McCallum, McAchern, and McVicar.

[9.49.4.13] Whyte, Donald. (1981). What's in your name? *Scots Magazine, 115,* 161-166. Illus.
Concise general intro. to Scottish surnames.

9.49.4.1. ETHNIC NAMES: *Scottish: Surnames: Specific*

[9.49.4.1.1] MacAndrew, Robert. (1963). The name *MacAndrew* in Scotland: A brief outline. *Scottish Genealogist, 10,* 17-19. Refs.
Traces the name to Donald Makandro in 1502. Other old records described.

[9.49.4.1.2] McMurtrie, Douglas. (1982). The McMurtries in Scotland. *Scottish Genealogist, 29,* 96-101. Refs.
Information on the McMurtrie family world-wide. Various records show variations in the spelling of this name, including: McMurtre, Makmuryte, McKirdy, and Makwrerdy.

[9.49.4.1.3] McNaughton, D. (1981). The origins of an unusual surname [McLew]. *Scottish Genealogist, 28,* 35-36. Refs.
Comments on different theories on the origin of the name.

[9.49.4.1.4] McRobert, William. (1976). Variations in the spelling of the name McRobert, mainly from the parish registers of Kirkcudbrightshire. *Scottish Genealogist, 23,* 4-5.
Research in the history of this family from 1684 demonstrates several variations in spelling including: McRobin, Crobin, McRobinen, and McCrabbie.

[9.49.4.1.5] Slorance, Andrew J. (1978). The psychology of names. *Scottish Genealogist, 25,* 84-85.
Autobiographical account of the original spelling of the name *Storach* was recorded as *Storance* (probably by a clerk) at the registration of a birth in 1806. The family decided they liked the change and kept it.

[9.49.4.1.6] Watson, Harry D. (1982). The Swankies of Arbroath and Auchmithie: An unusual local surname. *Scottish Genealogist, 24,* 18-24. Refs. Tables.
Goes back to 1490 to the trace the development of *swanky* from a word to a personal name, then, to a surname.

9.50. ETHNIC NAMES: *Slavic*
(See Also: 9.8. ETHNIC NAMES: *Bulgarian,* 9.45. ETHNIC NAMES: *Polish,* 9.47.
ETHNIC NAMES: Russian, and 9.56 ETHNIC NAMES: Ukrainian)

[9.50.1] Kaleta, Zofia. (1987-89). The evolutionary stages of Slavic surnames in the
context of European name-giving. *Onoma, 29,* 11-25. Refs.
Develops a system for understanding the evolution of Slavic surnames from
protosurnames of the 11th cent. to newer ones. Data from Czech, Polish, Croatian,
Serbian, Bulgarian/Macedonian, and Russian from historical administrative texts from
each area and cent. There are 5 stages.

[9.50.2] Kaleta, Zofia. (1990). On the stabilization of Slavic surnames. *Proceedings
of the 17th ICOS, Helsinki, 13-18 Aug. 1990, 1,* 53-68. Refs.
Addressed to 6 Slavic areas: Czech, Polish, Croatian, Serbian/Bosnian, Bulgarian/
Macedonian, and Russian. There are 5 stages in the development of surnames. Stage
3 is the period of stabilization. Examination of documents from the 10th to the 17th
cents. in each of the language areas traces the developments of surnames. Many
examples.

[9.50.3] Klymasz, Robert. (1959). Bilingualism in Slavic surnames. *Proceedings of the
Linguistic Circle of Manitoba & North Dakota* [Winnipeg], *1,* 29-31. Refs.
The study was based upon data from Manitoba. Presentation with examples of
bilingualism (change of original name): (1), full assimilation, Bygarski Robert, (2),
partial assimilation, Ozarow > Arrow, and (3), surname retained but in a hybrid form,
Ilkow > Hillcoff.

[9.50.4] Pasterczyk, Catherine E. (1985, Feb.). Russian transliteration variations for
searchers. *Database, 8(1),* 68-75.
Shows how Slavic surnames can be transliterated in different ways. This can cause
retrieval problems. Explanation of how to search a name using different approaches.
Examples.

[9.50.5] Slavutych, Yar. (1963). Typical surnames in the East Slavic languages. *Atti
e Memorie del Congresso dello Sezione Antroponimica, VII Congresso Internazionale di
Scienze Onomastiche, Firenze, April 1961 [7th ICOS], Vol. 3,* pp. 295-307. Refs.
Systematic classification & description (with many examples of the types of surname in
3 separate, but related, language groups: show translations into English.

9.51. ETHNIC NAMES: *South American*

[9.51.1] Butinov, N. A. (1960). Ličhnye imena na dočhnečhkach ostrova paski [Personal
names in the Easter Islands Tablets]. *Journal of Austronesian Studies, 2,* 3-7. Refs. Illus.
Examination of several Easter Island tablets leads to the conclusion that recurrent names
are those of important chiefs. Russian. English summary.

[9.51.2] Massolo, Maria Laura. (1990). Teenage granny: Portrayals of women in the
Falkland Islands. *Names, 38,* 283-294. Refs.
Describes nicknames of women in the Falklands. Categories include: physical characteristics, (Sweaty Betty); events, (Fifty Kilos, her panties were made of 50 kg. sacks);
childhood names (Bunny); negative names (Flash Al, a woman who flirted; Teenage
Granny, a 50-year-old who dressed as a teenager and was sexually active with young
men). There is a continuum of nicknames from ideal to hate, revealing ambivalence
toward males. A few examples of each type.

[9.51.3] Pinto-Cisternas, J.; Castelli, M. C.; & Pineda, L. (1955). Use of surnames in the study of population structure. *HumBio, 57,* 353-363. Refs. Tables.
Surname frequencies were used to study their value as an indicator of inbreeding, endogamy, and population structure in the parish of Los Teques, Miranda State, Venezuela from 1790-1869.

9.51.1 ETHNIC NAMES: *South American: Indians*

[9.51.1.1] Chakraborty, Rnajit., Barton, Sarah H., Farrell, Robert E. Schull, William J. (1989). Ethnicity determination by names among the Aymara of Chile and Bolivia. *HumBio, 61,* 159-177. Refs. Tables.
The Aymara, a people living in northern Chile and western Bolivia are a genetic mixture of Aymara Indians and Spanish Caucasoids. A coding system allowed classification of surnames into Aymara or Spanish. Samples of names given.

[9.51.1.2] Lave, J(ean Elizabeth) C(arter). (1967). *Social taxonomy among the Krikati (Ge) of Central Brazil.* Unpublished doctoral dissertation. Harvard University, Cambridge, 385p. Refs.
Ch. 5 (pp. 133-191) reviews literature on naming in primitive societies. Then, goes on to describe the Krikati procedure in which sisters and brothers exchange names for their cross-sexed children. The tribe also has complex "name sets" (several people having the same name). Nicknames also described. Refs. are on pp. 324-331.

[9.51.1.3] McDowell, John H. (1981). Towards a semiotics of nicknaming: The Kamsa example. *Journal of American Folklore, 94,* 1-18. Refs.
Kamsa example. The Kamsa tribe of Indians (pop. 3000) live in the Sibundoy Valley of Southwestern Colombia. They have 4 names: (1) legal, including 1st name and surname, (2) kinship terms used for address, (3) garden names, and (4) "ugly" names, derogatory names not used in the person's presence. Few examples.

[9.51.1.4] Nimuendaju, Curt. (1939; 1967). *The Apinaye'* (Robert H. Lowie. Trans.), Anthropological Publications. Osterhout N. B.: Netherlands, 189p. Refs. (Originally published in 1939 by Catholic University of America Press)
The tribe is located in Maranhao State in Northern Brazil [apparently along one of the tributaries of the Tocantins River]. Pp. 22-24 describe the naming customs, one of which is that names are "transferred" from one person to another in a ceremony.

[9.51.1.5] Nimuendaju, Curt & Lowie, Robert H. (1939). The associations of the Serente. *American Anthropologist, 41,* 408-415.
The Serente are from the Akwe branch of the Central Ge of the Rio Tocantins area of Brazil. P. 411 has a brief mention of the naming of boys and girls.

[9.51.1.6] Priest, Anne. (1964). Methods of naming among the Siriono Indians. [Brief Communications]. *American Anthropologist, 66,* 1149-1151. Refs.
The Siriono of NE Bolivia came out of the jungles around 1940 to work on ranches and plantations, their naming practices changed. Several types of name with illustrative examples are shown: hunting, descriptive, occasion, proper, and kinship.

[9.51.1.7] Scheffler, H. W. (1976). On Krikati and Siriono: A reply to Lave. [Discussion and Debate]. *American Anthropologist, 78,* 338-341. Refs.
Reply to criticism by Lave [9.51.1.2] dealing with name bestowal among the Krikati.

[9.51.1.8] Viertler, Renate B. (1976). *Greeting, hospitality, and naming among the Bororo of Central Brazil. Working papers in Sociolinguistics No. 37.* Austin, TX:

Southwest Educational Development Lab., 10p. (ERIC Document Reproduction Service No. ED 252 076).
The Bororo are an Indian tribe. Description of the importance of names in social etiquette, especially in social visits.

9.52. ETHNIC NAMES: *Spanish*

[9.52.1] Iszaevich, Abraham. (1980). Household renown: The traditional naming system in Catalonia. *Ethnology, 19,* 315-325. Refs.
The research was done in Barbará, a Catalonian village in Tarragona, Spain. Discussion of the custom in this community of using the *renom,* the household name. The renom can be used as either a term of reference or address and can be applied to any member of the household. Differentiation between renom and nickname.

[9.52.2] Pitt-Rivers, Julian Alfred. (1977). *The fate of Shechem or the politics of sex*: *Essays in the Anthropology of the Mediterranean.* Cambridge: Cambridge University Press, 193p. Refs.
Based on Andalusia, Spain. In various places, touches on naming customs for infants, use of 1st names, surnames, nicknames and forms of address.

[9.52.3] Scott, Reid. (1969). *Cultural understanding: Spanish Level 1.* Hayward, CA: Alameda County School Department, 50p. Refs. (ERIC Document Reproduction Service No. 046 292).
Units included general treatment of names, nicknames (1st names, affectionate names, short names), forms of address, surnames, and Spanish style of naming.

[9.52.4] Scott, Reid. (1972). *Understanding Spanish-speaking cultures. Selected concepts that may be developed at Spanish Level 1.* Hayward, CA: Alameda County Superintendent of Schools, 68p. Refs. (ERIC Document Reproduction Service No. 111 199).
Similar to above except that the topic of nicknames is given more treatment. Examples include: El Gordo ("fat man"), Quince Unas ("15 digits," for someone missing a finger), + 12 others.

9.52.1. ETHNIC NAMES: *Spanish: First Names*

[9.52.1.1] Fernandez-Suarez, Yolanda. (1989-90). Spanish personal names of Greek origin. *Onomata, 13,* 107-114. Refs. Tables.
Using an electoral roll of the province of Leon, Spain, identified 11.6% of the 1st names as being of Greek origin. Examples include: Angel, Pedro, and Felipe. Among university students, 14% had names of Greek origin. Many examples.

[9.52.1.2] Garcia, Nasario. (1989). Teaching Hispanic culture using Spanish first-names. Paper presented at the Annual Meeting of the American Association of Teachers of Spanish and Portuguese (San Antonio, TX, Aug. 10-14, 1989). 19p. (ERIC Document Reproduction Service No. ED 314 938).
Description of the naming patterns and practices of Guadalupe (pop. 161), New Mexico in the 1880s. Types of name include: religious, virtuous, warlike, physical characteristics, animal, nature, and miscellaneous. Nicknames or short forms were not common. Suggests that the study of Spanish 1st names is useful for the study of Spanish culture.

9.52.2. ETHNIC NAMES: *Spanish: Nicknames*

[9.52.2.1] Barrett, Richard A. (1978). Village modernization and changing nickname practices in Northern Spain. *Journal of Anthropological Research, 34,* 92-108. Refs.
Benabarre (pop. 1,000) is a village in the pre-Pyrenees area of Huesca Province. Nicknames are more widely used than surnames in everyday interaction. A sample shows that 83% of nicknames are inherited, example, Corvet ("Little Crow"), 17% are personal, example, La Puncha ("The Thorn"), given to a woman who nags her husband. With modernization, surnames may be used more.

[9.52.2.2] Brandes, Stanley H. (1975). *Migration, kinship, and community: Tradition and transition in a Spanish village.* New York: Academic Press, 220p. R(p. 199-206). The research on depopulation of a small village, Besedas, in sw Castile. P. 28 points out the influence of occupation on surnames, examples, Trapero ("cloth dealer"); Ovejero ("sheep worker"). Pp. 141-145 deal with use of nicknames, about 15+ examples including: Pinocho ("big nose"), Carpanta ("lazy"), and Huevona ("eggs").

[9.52.2.3] Christian, William A. (1972). *Person and God in a Spanish valley.* New York: Seminar Press, 215p.
Christian stayed in several villages in the Namsa Valley of northern Spain. Pp. 22-27 describe types of nickname (physical, personality characteristic, event, inherited) and their function. A few examples. Points out (pp. 26-27), "Women and men like to be called by their given name, not their nickname, and I sense here partly a fear of losing control."

[9.52.2.4] Freeman, Susan Tax. (1970). *Neighbors: The social contract in a Castilian hamlet.* Chicago: University of Chicago Press, 233p.
Valdemora is a small community in Castile 150 km. NE of Madrid. Pp. 118-119 indicate that the inhabitants do not use nicknames for each other but as boundaries for insiders and outsiders (the town was too small). Nicknames were used when real names were not known. Nicknames were applied to people from neighboring towns.

[9.52.2.5] Gilmore, David D. (1982). Some notes on community nicknaming in Spain. *Man, 17,* New Series, 686-700. Refs.
The research was done in a farming town of about 8000 in Southwest Andalusia. After describing several types of nickname explains that, "there is a powerful psychic link between the personal name, the way it is used by others and the concept of self."

[9.52.2.6] Hoyer, Eva. (1976). Nicknames in northern Spain. *Folk* [Copenhagen], *18,* 103-111. Refs. Fig.
Description of the nicknaming practices in a village of 600 in Old Castile, Spain. Every adult has a good-tempered nickname and "many have one or more spiteful ones" (p. 107). Nicknames serve 2 functions: (1) to distinguish a person from others with the same name and (2) to serve as outlets for aggression. About 15 examples given including: El Catalan ("from Cataluna"), El Carpintero ("The Carpenter"), Orejas ("Ears", has big ears), and Horma ("Ant", she is small).

[9.52.2.7] Kenny, Michael. (1961). *A Spanish tapestry: Town and country in Castile.* London: Cohen & West, 243p.
Pp. 86-87 describe type and function of nicknames, including their inheritance by males and females. Several examples including: El Corcho (the Cork), Santiago el Tumbas (James the Death), a grave digger; and El Matasanos (the Killer of the Healthy), used for a male nurse and the doctor.

[9.52.2.8] Limon, José. (1979). *The folk performance of Chicano and the cultural limits of political ideology.* Austin, TX: Southwest Educational Development Laboratory, 22p. Refs. (ERIC Document Reproduction Service No. ED 198 695).
While mostly directed at the usage of the term *chicano,* there are references to individual nicknames and their usage (pp. 15, 19). Examples include: El Chueco ("the bent one"), La Ardilla ("the squirrel") and El Profe ("the professor").

[9.52.2.9] Pitt-Rivers, J(ulian). A(lfred). (1961;1971). *The people of the Sierra,* 2nd ed. Chicago: University of Chicago Press, 232p. Refs. 2nd ed., 1971.
Focus of the study is on the social life and customs of the people of cities and town of Andalusia, Spain. Major consideration to names is that to nicknames (pp. 160-169). Many types of nickname with examples are discussed. Types include: occupational, regional, personality, metronyms, patronyms. Nicknames can be inherited as well.

9.52.3. ETHNIC NAMES: *Spanish: Surnames*

[9.52.3.1] Alvarez, Grace D. (1971). Categories of Spanish toponymical surnames. Proceedings of the 10th ICOS, Vienna, *1969 [Disputationes ad montium vocabula allorumque nominum significationes pertinentes],* 2, 177-184. Refs.
7 types of Spanish topological surnames described with examples drawn from the Madrid telephone directory. Examples include: Negrete ("black"), Gallego (river in Huesca, village in Murcia, patrial of Galicia), and Contreras (town in Burgos, village in Cuenca). [*patrial* here refers to "place"].

[9.52.3.2] Buechley, Robert W. (1961). A reproducible method of counting persons of Spanish surname. *Journal of the American Statistical Association, 56,* 88-97. Refs. Tables.
Demonstration of the development of a list of 306 surnames which are "typical of the 86% in-marrying Ladino population of California." The list is given.

[9.52.3.3] Giesecke, G. Lee. (1973). *A comparison of computerized techniques for recognizing Spanish names.* Alexandria, VA: Human Resources Research Organization, 20p. Refs. Tables.
To identify the relationship between those with Spanish surnames and those who identify themselves as Spanish or Mexican, data were secured on over 20,000 Air Force enlisted men. Results show correlations but caution is suggested in using the surname technique outside of the Southwest.

[9.52.3.4] Rosenwaike, Ira. (1991). The most common Spanish surnames in the United States: Some new data sources. *Names,* 39, 325-331. Refs. Tables.
2 new sources of data, the National Death Index and Medicare enrollment files allow examination of regional differences in rankings of the 15 top frequency ranks of Spanish surnames. Rankings in Puerto Rico differ from those in the US. Reflecting place of origin (Cuba, Mexico or Puerto Rico) data show different rank frequencies for surnames in California, Texas, Florida, and New York.

[9.52.3.5] Steiner, Mary Florence. (1953). The etymological study of Old Spanish personal names. *Dissertation Abstracts, 13,* 1205. (University Microfilms No. 6245).
Investigation of the names found in the *Primera chronica general* after the election of Pelayo as king of Leon and before the rule of Ferdinand. Attention to etymology and meaning of Spanish names of Latin, Greek, German, Arabic, Hebrew, and other origins.

[9.52.3.6] Talbert, Robert H. (1955). Spanish-name people in the Southwest and West: *Socio-economic characteristics of white persons of Spanish surname in Texas, California,*

Colorado, and New Mexico. Fort Worth, TX: Leo Patishman Foundation, Texas Christian University, 90p. Refs.
Explanation of why the term *Spanish-name people* is used. Description of demographic, educational, marital, and economic factors associated with Spanish-name people. No specific names are listed.

[9.52.3.7] US. Department of Commerce. Bureau of the Census. (1980). *Census list of Spanish surnames*. Washington, DC: Department of Commerce, 56p. + Instruction Sheet. Lists approx. 15,000 Spanish surnames. This list by government agencies to assist in certain programs where classification of a person is needed.

9.53. ETHNIC NAMES: *Swedish*

[9.53.1] Benson, Sven. (1989). Några personnnamn i svenska ortnamn: En namnstrukturell studie [Some personal names in Swedish place-names: A structural study in names]. In *Studia Onomastica: Festschrift till Thorsten Andersson den 23 Februari 1989*, pp. 9-17. Refs. Maps. Swedish. English summary. Stockholm: Almqvist & Wiksell International.
Evaluation of Sven, Karl, Erik, Knut, Per, Anders, Jon, and Bengt as placename elements. Examination of their geographic distribution.

[9.53.2] Benson, Sven. (1990). Variations in the Swedish forename system. *Proceedings of the 17th ICOS, Helsinki, 13-18 Aug. 1990, 1*, 194-201. Refs.
In 1500 in Sweden, there was only 1 forename (1st name). Toward the end of the 16th cent., children of the nobility and royal families began to get 2 forenames (1st name + middle name). Traces the pattern of development to the clergy and the lower classes. Currently, about 50% of the population has 2 forenames, 1/3 have 3 or more, < 10% have 1 forename.

[9.53.3] Bernander, Inga. (1980). Dopnamnet som fornamn, hemmans- och gardsnamn i Varo: En undersokning med hjalp av 1600-talsmaterial [Christian names as elements of personal names and farm-names in Varo: An investigation based upon 17th cent. sources]. *SydOrtÅrss*, pp. 5-22. Refs.
Description of farm names brought into use after the Danish-Swedish treaty of 1645 when records were brought back to Denmark. Secondary names also developed using the farmer's name.

[9.53.4] Blixt, Sam; Ekstrans, Magnus; & Kallenius, Gunnar. (1989). Databaser som hjalp i ortnamns- och personnamnsforskning: Personoch lokalhistoriska databasen i Oskarshamn (PLF) [Data bases as a help to research into place-names and personal names: The data base for personal history and local history at Oskarshamn (PLF)]. *SydOrtÅrss*, pp. 53-72.
Reports on data bases for 110 parishes of Kalmar in Eastern Småland.

[9.53.5] Blomgren, Sven. (1987). Lårda släktnamn hos praster i Skara och Karlstads stift [Erudite surnames adopted by clergymen in the dioceses of Skara and Karlstad]. *StudAnthroScan, 5*, 43-55. Refs. Swedish. English summary.
In the 17-18th cents., Church of Sweden clergy commonly adopted Latin surnames. Most of these came from local placenames, some from nature.

[9.53.6] Cronberg, Olof. (1988). Personnamn i Skytts harad 1664-1815 [Personal names in the hundred of Skytt, 1664-1815]. *SydOrtÅrss*, pp. 11-18. Refs. Swedish. English summary.
The 100 of Skytt is in SouthWwest Scania in the South of Sweden. The name index has 8700 recorded marriages. 75% used some of the 10 most common names. The 4 most

common male names were: Jöns, Nils, Anders, and Per; the 5 most common female names were Kirstina, Elna, Karna, Hanna, and Anna. Statistics also reported on patronymics by sex.

[9.53.7] Ejder, Bertil. (1988). Om rikskanslern Arild Huitfeldts dopnamn och om namnet på fiskeläget och sommarorten Arild i Kullen [On the Christian name of the Danish nobleman *Arild Huitfeldt* and on the name of the summer resort *Arild*]. *SydOrtÅrss*, pp. 5-10. Refs. Swedish. English summary.
Description of the transition about 1580 of Arvid to Arild. The community Arild corresponds to the original "Arvid's village."

[9.53.8] Furtenbach, Börje. (1987). De svenska soldatnamnen och deras betydelse för släktnamnsbildningen [Swedish soldiers' names and their significance in the development of surnames]. *StudAnthroScan, 5,* 57-90. Refs. Tables. Swedish. English summary.
Soldiers' names were the majority in the 17th and 19th cents.; local names in the 18th. Some soldiers' names have survived. Extensive tables show the frequencies of various categories of soldiers' names.

[9.53.9] Gillingstam, Hans. (1990). Elgensstiernas *Ättartavlor* som källa vid studiet av äldre adligt namnskick [Elgenstierna's Genealogies as evidence of early naming practices among the nobility]. *StudAnthroScan, 8,* 69-72. Refs. Swedish. English summary.
Critical of the source material of this work which makes the results unsuitable.

[9.53.10] Hallberg, Göran. (1988). Personnamnen i Västra Karups vigsellangder 1689-1860 [Personal names in the marriage records of the northwest Scanian parish of Västra Karup]. *SydOrtÅrss*, pp. 19-28. Refs.
Description of several projects transferring data from parish registers to data-bases.

[9.53.11] Hedblom, Folke. (1985). *Swedish personal names in America. Swedish American Genealogist, 5,* 17-35. Refs.
Data are based upon interviews with Americans of Swedish descent (mostly in Minnesota) conducted in the 1960s. Description of the types of name change involving, surnames, 1st names, farm names, by-names, and nicknames. At least 50 examples of different types.

[9.53.12] Henningsson, Per. (1993). Den svenska almanackans namnlängd 1901-1993 [The Swedish name-day calendar, 1901-93]. *StudAnthroScan, 11,* 71-96. Refs. Swedish. English summary.
The 1901 calendar was revised in 1986 and again in 1993. The new calendar has 2 names for each day, there are no hyphenated names, or pet forms. There are 369 men's names and 350 women's. Background given on the changes.

[9.53.13] Linde, Gunnar. (1985). Den heliga Helenas grav och källa och Sancta Elinae kyrka [The tomb and spring of St. Helena and the church of St. Elin]. In *Nordiska namnstudier: Festskrift till Harry Stahl 22 september 1985* (pp. 324-343). Uppsala: Lundesquistska. Swedish. English summary.
While directed at the placenames St. Helena and St. Elin also has information on the saint herself who had both these names. Helena became the usual form in the 15th century.

[9.53.14] Lindquist, E. (1967). Swedish American pseudonyms: One aspect of the Swedish immigrant literary tradition. *Swedish Pioneer Historical Quarterly, 18,* 148-156. Refs.
During the period approx. 1880-1940, a large number of Swedish American writers used one or more pseudonyms. Oliver A. Linder used 13. Examples of pseudonyms used by the writers include: Bror John, Morbror Marten, Cornelius Corncob, and Pepin Telefonson.

[9.53.15] Peterson, Lena. (1980). "Thruvo"--ett felläst personnamn ["Thruvo", a misread personal name]. *Ortnamnssållskapets I Uppsala Årsskrift*, 21-23. Refs. Swedish. English summary.
Concludes that the woman's name *Thruvo* found in the *Liber daticus Lundensis* and in *Danmarks gamle Personnavne* must be a misreading of the Danish *Thruun*.

[9.53.15A] Peterson, Lena. (1980). Till frägan om den gamla genitivformen av nordiska mansnamn på -*marr* [On the question of the old genitive form of Scandinavian men's names in -*marr*]. *Namn och Bygd, 68,* 86-92. Refs. Swedish. English summary.
Supports the position "that the Scandinavian personal-name element -*marr* originally had the genitive form -*aR.*"

[9.53.16] Peterson, Lena. (1981). Personnamnselementet -modh: Ett bidrag till dess harledning [The personal name element -modh: A contribution to its etmymology]. *Namn och Bygd, 69,* 15-41. Refs. Swedish. English summary.
Explains that there are 2 ways of explaining the name element. 1, a Scandinavian adjective meaning "courageous" and 2, bahuvrihi-compounds.

[9.53.17] Peterson, Lena. (1984). Harald och andra namn på -*(v)ald* [Harald and other names in -*(v)ald*]. *StudAnthroScan, 2,* 5-25. Refs. Swedish. English summary.
Evaluation of this name element in terms of strong and weak forms and in Swedish, Old Norwegian, and Modern Icelandic.

[9.53.18] Peterson, Lena. (1986). Personnamnstypologi och ortnamnsdatering [The typology of personal names and the dating of placenames]. *NORNA-rapporter, 33,* 37-48. Refs. Tables. Figure. Swedish. English summary.
Comparison of the distribution of dithematic, monothematic, and hypocoristic names in viking-age runes and in some placenames in Denmark and Sweden shows differences.

[9.53.19] Peterson, Lena. (1988). Mono- and dithematic personal names in Old Germanic. In *Probleme der Namenbildung: Rekonstruktion von Eigennamen und der ihnen zugrundeliegenden Appelative: Akten eines internationalen Symposiums in Uppsala 1-4 Sept. 1986,* Edited by Thorsten Andersson. Uppsala: Uppsala University, pp. 121-130. Refs.
Contrast between views of mono- and dithematic names between Scandinavian and German scholars. Discussion of the variation system of naming in which "you could indicate membership of a tribe or family by naming the child after another member of the family by using one element of that member's name."

[9.53.20] Sandström, Raija. (1984). Civilståndets inverkan på anteckningar av kvinnors tillnamn I 1800-talets kyrkböcker på Nedertoneå landsbygd I Norra Sverige. [The influence of civil status on women's bynames on the parish registers of Nedertonea countryside in Northern Sweden in the nineteenth century]. *Fenno-Ugrica Suecana* [Uppsala]), *7,* 149-156.
Procedure for registering women: single, married, widowed, and remarried with reference to inclusion or not of bynames.

[9.53.21] Strandberg, Svante. (1989). Mansnamnet **Tolke.* In *Studia Onomastica: Festschrift till Thorsten Andersson den 23 Februari 1989,* pp. 375-382. Refs. Swedish. English summary. Stockholm: Almqvist & Wiksell.
On the derivation of the male name **Tolke* from either of 2 placenames.

[9.53.22] Strandberg, Svante. (1993). Personnamn i ortnamn: Kritisk översikt [Personal names in place-names]. *StudAnthroScan, 11,* 5-24. Refs. Swedish. English summary.

Placenames open up possibilities for reconstruction of personal names for which there are no other records. "There is no record of the OSw man's name *Sighvald*,...but place-names show that it was used way back in pre-Viking times."

[9.53.23] Wahlberg, Mats. (1987). En östgötsk skattelängd från 1300-talet [A fourteenth-century tax roll from Östergötland]. *StudAnthroScan, 5,* 31-42. Refs. Tables. Photos. Swedish. English summary.
"The personal names found in the roll include a previously unknown man's name, *A(r)nthorn*. Of the 88 people whose names can be made out, 54 had old native names, 33 Christian names, and 1 the German man's name *Gozvin*. The commonest names are to be found in the Christian category."

[9.53.24] Wahlberg, Mats. (1990). Swedish soldiers' names: Official surnames given in the Swedish army 1682-1901. *Proceedings of the 17th ICOS, Helsinki, 13-18 Aug. 1990, 2,* 460-467. Refs.
The Swedish standing army and navy system which began in 1682 developed a category of surname known as *soldiers' names*. These names can be classified in different ways. Many are quite distinctive and are still used. Examples are given which include: Modig ("brave"), Ros ("rose"), and Pinkrus ("slightly intoxicated").

[9.53.25] Wahlberg, Mats. (1990). Svenska soldatnamn: En forskiningssöversikt [Swedish soldiers' names: A research review]. *StudAnthroScan, 8,* 47-68. Refs. Swedish. English summary.
Examines 4 aspects of soldiers' names: (1) origins, (2) types, (3) name givers and name giving, (4) influence of soldiers' names on Swedish surnames. Soldiers' names show 3 main features: (1) an older pattern of bynames, (2) influence of placenames, and (3) the fixed, numbered system of *rotar*.

9.53.1 ETHNIC NAMES: *Swedish: Change of Name*

[9.53.1.1] Hedblom, Folke. (1984). Svenska personnamn i Amerika: En aktuell forskningsuppgift [Swedish personal names in the United States: A proposed field of research]. *StudAnthroScan, 2,* 87-105. Refs. Swedish. English summary.
Swedish 1st names and surnames went through a great deal of transformation when immigrants arrived in the US, examples, Anders Eriksson > Andrew Erickson; his wife Johanna Persdotter > Joan Erickson. 1000s of lists of Swedish-Americans have been microfilmed which represent an opportunity for scholars to investigate this transformation.

[9.53.1.2] Kvillerud, Reinert. (1993). Personbinamn som motsvarar förnamn och efternamn i det allmänna namnförrådet [Personal bynames corresponding to forenames and surnames in the general name stock]. *StudAnthroScan, 11,* 63-70. Refs. Swedish. English summary.
Newspaper analysis shows that people substitute other names for their original names. "The reasons may be changes in style and taste, fashion and attitudes." Some changes have similar structure (Agneta to Annette). Others are more convenient (Ernfrid to Sven). The types of changes that men make are different from those of women.

[9.53.1.3] Name-droppers. (1963, July 8). *Newsweek*, p. 55.
Description of a Swedish plan to introduce new surnames to overcome the surplus of Anderssons, Karlssons, Petterssons, et al.

9.53.2. ETHNIC NAMES: *Swedish: First Names*

[9.53.2.1] Benson, Sven. (1986). Svenska förnamnsgrupper [Combinations of forenames in Swedish]. *StudAnthroScan, 4*, 125-154. Refs. Tables. Swedish. English summary.
Examination of various types of forenames (US 1st names and middle names) used by members of the 1980 Swedish parliament. Most had 2 forenames. Statistics on number of syllables. 3-syllable names more common in southern Sweden and among farmer's sons and of the upper classes.

[9.53.2.2] Benson, Sven. (1989). Studier i adlig namngivning [Studies in name-giving among the nobility]. *StudAnthroScan, 7*, 71-99. Refs. Tables. Swedish. English summary.
Study of forenames in 5 large families of the nobility in the 20th cent. These names are compared with those of commoners in the Swedish parliament of 1980. The nobility, while differing among themselves, differ from commoners in having more forenames.

[9.53.2.3] Dahlstedt, Karl-Hampus. (1986). Personnamnet *Hampus* [The personal name *Hampus*]. StudAnthroScan, 4, 13-55. Refs. Tables. Figs. Swedish. English summary.
Found occurrences of the name as early as 1549-1550 in Finland but not as a baptismal name. In the 17th and 18th cents. it was an appellation meaning "fool, idiot." Hampus was also found in the Morner family who alternated *Hampus* and *Hans* "either as names for the same person or when a child was baptized Hampus after an older relative called Hans." Further information on the spread of the name.

[9.53.2.4] Gillingstam, Hans. (1988). Några nyfynd belysande namnet *Hampus* som hypokorism för *Hans* [New finds shedding light on the name *Hampus* as a hypocorism for *Hans*]. *StudAnthroScan, 6*, 127-130. Refs. Swedish. English summary.
Supplements work of Karl-Hampus Dahlstedt above. Shows an even earlier example of *Hampus* (1704-1705) from *Hans* and also a feminine form *Hampina*.

[9.53.2.5] Kvillerud, Reinert. (1983). Vanligare skrift- och uttalsenliga förnamn i svenskan: Ett försök till lexialisering [The most usual Swedish Christian names in standardised written and spoken form: An attempt at lexicalization]. *StudAnthroScan, 1*, 124-132. Refs. Tables. Swedish. English summary.
Based upon data from the 1970s, lists the top 100 male 1st names and the top female 1st names and their frequencies. "By taking pronunciation into account, ...attempts to transfer the name vocabulary from a merely graphic level to a graphic-phonetic one."

[9.53.2.6] Peterson, Lena. (1992). Gölin. *StudAnthroScan, 10*, 43-53. Refs. Swedish. English summary.
Detailed analysis of the vowel and other changes of this female name which came from Old Swedish and is now found in the province of Jämtland.

9.53.3. ETHNIC NAMES: *Swedish: Law and Names*

[9.53.3.1] Andersson, Thorsten. (1984). Efternamn och jämställdhet: Jamstalldhets-principen i 1982 års svenska personnamnslag [Surnames and equality: The principle of equality in the Swedish Personal Name Act of 1982]. *StudAnthroScan, 2*, 107-122. Refs, Swedish. English summary.
The law provides equality between the sexes and for children born inside or outside of marriage. Couples, at marriage, can return to their birth surnames or choose either partner's surname. Either parent's surname can be given to children. The law also provides that surnames ending in *-dotter* can be inherited by males.

[9.53.3.2] Ekdahl, Bertil. (1984, Nov.). Child custody rules in the context of Swedish family law. Social Change in Sweden, No. 31, 1-10. (Available from Swedish Information Service, Swedish Consulate General, New York, 10012).
In addition to other issues, describes legislation for surname choice at time of marriage and for children.

[9.53.3.3] Ericsson, Brit-Marie. (1986). The Names Act 1982: The first five years of its application and criticism. *StudAnthroScan, 4,* 155-165. Refs. Swedish. English Summary.
A survey of parish offices indicates no great change in surname patterns. "It is more usual than before for a married woman to combine her maiden name and the name she acquired by marriage, using one of the names as a middle name....There are so far no examples of a married man combining his name with that of his wife."

[9.53.3.4] Peterson, Lena. (1987). Något om verkningarna av 1982 års svenska personnamnslag: "Jämställdhetslagen" [Some notes on the effect of the Swedish names act 1982: "The act of equality"]. *NORNA-rapporter, 35,* 135-144. Refs. Swedish. English summary.
Description of the changes in the law allowing a husband and wife several choices of a surname at marriage. One alternative for a woman is to change her surname into a name formed from her mother's or father's 1st name plus the ending *-dotter.*

9.53.4. ETHNIC NAMES: *Swedish: Nicknames*

[9.53.4.1] Brylla, Eva. (1990). Morphological types of Old Swedish personal by-names. *Proceedings of the 17th ICOS, Helsinki, 13-18 Aug. 1990, 1,* 224-231. Refs.
Description with examples of various types of by-name. Concludes that "secondary by-names seem to have been formed from nouns and adjectives, but word-groups are also common. Likewise, there are primary by-name formations."

[9.53.4.2] Brylla, Eva. (1993). Fortsatt diskussion om binamnet *Slema* [Further discussion of the byname *Slema*]. *StudAnthroScan, 11,* 41-46. Refs. Swedish. English summary.
Disagrees with the interpretation of Fredericksen [9.15.2] because the evidence she used was written 275 years after Emund Slema lived. Also discounts an interpretation of Knut-Olaf and Dagmar Falk but doesn't rule out that the name is of Slavonic origin.

[9.53.4.3] Vide, Sten-Bertil. (1973). Namn, benämning, egenskap [Names, designations, qualities]. *SydOrtÅrss,* pp. 18-24. Refs. Swedish. English summary.
Some names can be associated with qualities, e.g, *Ludendorff-luden* ("hairy") and can be used as an appellative, referring to a person with this characteristic.

9.53.5. ETHNIC NAMES: *Swedish: Runic Names*

[9.53.5.1] Jansson, Sven B. F. (1963). A newly-discovered rune-stone in Törnevalla church, Östergötland. In Arthur Brown & Peter Foote (Eds.) *Early English and Norse Studies: Presented to Hugh Smith in honour of his sixtieth birthday* (pp. 110-119). London: Methuen. Refs. Photos.
After examination, comments "We know then who commissioned the stone. It was the members of the guild fraternity who (...'raised this stone in memory of Dräng, Öger's son, their guild brother).'" Comparisons with other rune stones.

[9.53.5.2] Otterbjörk, Roland. (1983). *faruki, kurR* and *ublubR:* Namnproblem i sörmländska runinskrifter [Problematic names in the runic inscriptions of Södermanland, Sweden]. *StudAnthroScan, 1,* 21-44. Refs. Swedish. English summary.
Consideration of several problems in the interpretation of a runic inscription. These are: (1) the inadequacy of runic spelling, (2) confusion between similar-looking runes, (3) damaged runes, and (4) "unexpected" names, a byname used without the 1st name.

[9.53.5.3] Peterson, Lena. (1981). *Kvinnonamnens böjning i forsvenskan: De ursprungenligen starkt böjda namnen* [The inflection of women's names in Old Swedish]. Ph. D. Dissertation. *Anthroponymica Suecana, 8,* 1-212. Refs. Swedish. English summary, pp. 194-197.
Based upon 5000 name forms in runic inscriptions and medieval documents. The major topic considered is "developments in case-inflections from the runic inscriptions of the 11th century to manuscripts written as late as 1500." Shows that by 1500 Modern Swedish had begun.

[9.53.5.4] Peterson, Lena. (1993). Namnformen uifin på Oklundahällen--nominativ eller ackusativ [The name *uifin* on the Oklunda rock--nominative or accusative?]. *StudAnthroScan, 11,* 33-40. Refs. Figure. Swedish. English summary.
Discussion of the meaning and interpretation of this runic inscription.

[9.53.5.5] Salberger, Evert. (1979). Ett personnamn på Skaftarp-stenen [A personal name of the Skaftarp-stone]. *SydOrtÅrss,* pp. 36-49. Refs.
Concludes that runic inscription *sen-uku-starki* of the Skaftarp-stone in the province of Smaland is to be separated into *uk and u [the sen has been interpreted as Sven or Sten], so that u-starke* is interpreted as "'Ostarke' ('un-strong')...originally a surname."

[9.53.5.6] Salberger, Evert. (1979). Tillnamnet på Simri-stenen 2 [The surname of the Simris-stone 2]. *SydOrtÅrss,* pp. 21-35. Refs. Swedish. English summary.
There are other interpretations of this rune-stone in the province of Skane. This interpretation of the text is "after Forkun, after the father of Asulf."

[9.53.5.7] Salberger, Evert. (1985). Kasusfrågor i runsvenska namnfraser [Problems of case in Runic Swedish name phrases]. *StudAnthroScan, 3,* 11-21. Refs. Swedish. English summary.
Presents a different interpretation of the phrase in U 357, a rune stone in Skepptuna parish. Also gives another interpretation of Vs 14, an inscription from a church in Västmanland.

[9.53.5.8] Salberger, Evert. (1986). *rolkn-:* En rungutnisk ägarformel [An ownership phrase in runic Gutnish]. *StudAnthroScan, 4,* 5-12. Refs. Swedish. English summary.
The 6 runes on a brooch found on the island of Gotland can be interpreted as "Ro(d)likn owns (this brooch)."

[9.53.5.9] Salberger, Evert. (1987). Namnet runsv. *ehuith* samt en attribuering [The runic Swedish name ehuith and an attribution]. *Ortnamnssällskapets i Uppsala Årsskrift,* pp. 18-34. Refs. Swedish. English summary.
Gives an additional interpretation of a rune stone at Kista farm in Spånga, Uppland (U 75).

[9.53.5.10] Salberger, Evert. (1987). Mansnamn på Östra Dalby-stenarna i Veckholm [Men's names on the Östra Dalby stones in Veckholm]. *StudAnthroScan, 5,* 19-30. Photo. Swedish. English summary.
Gives an interpretation of runic stone U 706 which is different from that of Sven B. F. Jansson [In Swedish, complete citation not given].

[9.53.5.11] Salberger, Evert. (1989). Binamnet i Kareby-funtens bindruna [The byname in the bind-rune on the Kareby font]. *StudAnthroScan, 7*, 63-69. Refs. Figs. Swedish. English summary.
Detailed examination of a font inscription in a church in Bohuslän. Concludes this is a pair of half lines translated as: Let him who can decipher: the name Torbjörn (the) Raven.

[9.53.5.12] Salberger, Evert. (1990). Fathur /askiarth /: En namnfras på Hässelby-stenen i Harbo [A name phrase on the Hässelby stone in Harbo]. *Ortnamnssällskapets i Uppsala Årsskrift*, pp. 53-62. Refs. Swedish. English summary.
Reports on a rune stone in Uppland in Harbo, Uppland (U 1177). Reinterprets Sven B. F. Jansson's interpretation "Åsger and Mäginbjörn and Litle had this stone raised after Tobbe, Åsgerd's father. Oper cut [the runes]." Changes conclusion to "after Tobbe, [their] father, Åsgerd [after her husband]."

[9.53.5.13] Salberger, Evert. (1990). Mansnamn på Mellbystenar [Male names on Melby stones]. *SydOrtÅrss*, pp. 17-33. Refs. Swedish. English summary.
Comments on names found on a rune-stone at Mellby church in Småland. Also, comment on Sm 142, another rune-stone on Värneslätt in the parish of Mellby.

[9.53.5.14] Salberger, Evert. (1991). *sih*thor:* Ett runsvenskt mansnamn [A Runic Swedish man's name]. *StudAnthroScan, 9*, 5-11. Refs. Swedish. English summary.
Discussion and comment on a rune-stone from Uppland (U 440). Thinks that the name previously translated as *Tord* should be translated as *Torn*. Related inscriptions described.

[9.53.5.15] Salberger, Evert. (1991). Tre runskanska mansnamn [Three Scanian runic male names]. SydOrtÅrss, pp. 107-126. Refs. Swedish. English summary.
Believes that rune-stone Skivarp (DR 270), erected in memory of a man should be read as Gaeira. Thinks that the stone of Stora Herrestad (DR 293) might have referred to *Gunnar, Gunne,* or some name in *Gud* or *Gunn.* The rune-stone of Hastad (DR 318) has male names *brant(r)* ("Brand") and *kuba* ("Gubbe's).

[9.53.5.16] Salberger, Evert. (1993). Froderyd-stenens brodranamn [The names of two brothers on the Froderyd stone]. SydOrtÅrss, pp. 36-44. Refs. Photo. Swedish. English summary.
Comments on the interpretation of the names *khiRbiarn* and *sull* on stone (Sm 69).

[9.53.5.17] Sikström, Tomas. (1990). Knikis: Ett personnamn på ett västgötskt runstensfragment [The personal name on the fragment of rune stone in Västergötland]. *Ortnamnssällskapets i Uppsala Årsskrift*, pp. 70-74. Refs. Swedish. English summary.
Suggests that the name, while rare, means "walks with bent knees."

[9.53.5.18] Strid, Jan Paul. (1989). *Ludvig, Auðon* och *Othbiorn*: Om ett personnamnselement och den runsvenska utvecklingen av diftongen *au* [A personal name element and the development of the *au* diphthong in Runic Swedish]. *StudAnthroScan, 7*, 5-24. Refs. Swedish. English summary.
Detailed examination of how $au > ou > o > \bar{o}$. Thus, Auðun and other names shifted, Auðun > Oðun.

[9.53.5.19] Westlund, Börje. (1989). Kvinneby--en runinskrift med hittills okända gudanamn? [Kvinneby: A runic inscription containing hitherto unknown names of gods?]. *StudAnthroScan, 7*, 25-52. Refs. Figs. Photos. Swedish. English summary.
Detailed interpretation (differing from that of Ivar Lindquist) of an 11th cent. copper amulet found in Oland. Interpretation of inscription is "keep evil from Bofi. May Thor protect him with that hammer...will get nothing from Bofi. Gods are below him and above him." Names mentioned are Böfi and Thörr.

[9.53.5.20] Wiktorsson, Per-Axel. (1993). Ett personnamn på U 940 [A personal name on the stone U 940]. *StudAnthroScan, 11,* 25-31. Refs. Photo. Swedish. English summary.
E. Salberger interpreted "hont" as a byname "hand" to the female name Gillog. This interpretation considers it as a separate man's name.

[9.53.5.21] Williams, Henrik. (1991). Runsvenska namnproblem 1: Om *Erik* på Vaksalastenen (U 96) [Runic Swedish name problems 1: On Erik in the Vaksala inscription (U 960)]. *StudAnthroScan, 9,* 13-19. Refs. Figs. Swedish. English summary. Gives a different interpretation of this name from that of Elizabeth Svärdström (1970).

9.53.6. ETHNIC NAMES: *Swedish: Surnames*

[9.53.6.1] Blomgren, Sven. (1984). Lärda släktnamn bland västgötastudenter i Uppsala [Erudite family-name forms adopted by Uppsala University students from Västergötland]. *StudAnthroScan, 2,* 27-38. Refs. Swedish. English summary.
Data from the 17th and 18th cents. show that these students had 2 major types of surname: "either a Latin suffix was added to a Swedish place-name (or part thereof), or the Swedish place-name (or a significant part thereof) was translated into Latin or Greek AND then given a Latin suffix. Other students created family names from a Latinized version of their father's 1st name or occasionally from his occupation."

[9.53.6.2] Brown, Andrew. (22 Jan. 1983). By any other name, *Spectator* [London], pp. 11-12. Description of Swedish naming practices which allow several possibilities in bestowing a surname on a child. The child may have either parent's surname or birth name. More possibilities are available if either parent or both parents have been divorced.

[9.53.6.3] Panelius, Olav. (1987). Uppkomsten av tillnamn bland allmogen i Borgå socken i Finland [The adoption of surnames among the peasantry in the parish of Porvoo (Borgå), Finland]. *StudAnthroScan, 5,* 91-107. Refs. Tables. Swedish. English summary.
The research is based on a parish in a predominantly Swedish-speaking area of Uusimaa (Nyland) province in the mid-18th cent. At that time, surnames began replacing farm names. The most common type of surname was *Bergman, Lindberg,* and *Nyström.* "The use of these new surnames first spread among servants, especially those in service at country houses."

9.53.7. ETHNIC NAMES: *Swedish: Theoretical Aspects*

[9.53.7.1] Peterson, Lena. (1983). Ett mansnamn i runinskriften på det gotländska Timansbrynet [A man's name in the Runic inscription on a Gotland whetstone]. *Namn och Bygd, 71,* 115-124. Refs. Swedish. English summary.
Concludes that the correct reading of an 11th cent. inscription *ulfvair* is *Ulfhvatr.*

[9.53.7.2] Peterson, Lena. (1985). *Jularbo,* mansnamnet **Hiule* och något om ortnamn på (H)jul- [*Jularbo,* the masculine name **Hiule and notes about place-names in (H)jul.* In *Nordiska namnstudier: Festskrift till Harry Stahl 22 september 1985* (pp. 344-353). Uppsala: Lundesquistska. Swedish. English summary.
Presents evidence that the name Jularbo from Dalecarlia is not from the Old Swedish **Hiulaarve* "Hjule's heir" and related to the 14th cent. Hiulbiorn and Hiulfast. Rather, the 1st element hiul refers to a round element of the landscape or means "water-wheel."

[9.53.7.3] Peterson, Lena. (1989). Comments on two papers on the semantics of proper names. [Names Forum]. *Names, 37,* 83-92. Refs.

Comment on the paper of Pamp [87:22.13]. Disagrees with several of his points dealing with appellations and names. [The 2nd paper by Dalberg deals with placenames].

9.54. ETHNIC NAMES: *Swiss*

[9.54.1] Ellis, Walter & Friedl, John. (1976). Inbreeding as measured by isonymy and by pedigree in Kippel, Switzerland. *Social Biology, 23,* 158-161. Refs. Tables. Figs.
Kippel is an isolate Alpine village (pop. 470 in 1970). The relationship between inbreeding & isonymy & between inbreeding & pedigree was evaluated. Results indicate that isonymy gives a number 2.5 times that of pedigree analysis.

[9.54.2] Ellis, W. S., & Starmer, W. T. (1978). Inbreeding as measured by isonymy, pedigrees, and population size in Törbel, Switzerland. *American Journal of Human Genetics, 30,* 366-376. Refs. Tables. Figs.
Törbel (pop. 600) is an isolated community in the German-speaking canton of Valais. Extensive statistical analyses were made relating the measurement of inbreeding by pedigree and isonymy methods.

[9.54.3] Friedl, J., & Ellis, W. S. (1974). Inbreeding, isonymy, and isolation in a Swiss community. *HumBio, 46,* 699-714. Refs. Tables.
Results from the isolated Swiss alpine village of Kippel (pop. 462) in Canton Valais in Switzerland. Genealogies for 4-6 generations back were used to study factors associated with isonymy and inbreeding.

[9.54.4] Hussels, Irene (1969). Genetic structure of Saas, a Swiss isolate. *HumBio, 41,* 469-479. Refs. Tables.
The Saas valley is in southern Switzerland south of the Rhone. Parish registers dating from the 16th cent. were used to measure inbreeding using isonymy and pedigree. The 10 most common surnames (Andenmatten, Ruppen, Supersaxo, etc.) are listed along with the 10 least common (Zender, Zermili, Furrer, etc.).

[9.54.5] Löffler, Heinrich. (1988). Names and regional respectively national identity in a polylingual country such as Switzerland. *NomAfr, 2,* 159-170. Refs.
Although Switzerland has 4 or 5 cultures there is still a Swiss identity. This is reflected in naming practices. Surnames are locally bound; 1st names are generally associated with a language area but the rules are changing.

[9.54.6] Morton, N(ewton).E., & Hussels, Irene. (1970). Demography of inbreeding in Switzerland. *HumBio, 42,* 65-78. Refs. Tables. Fig.
Isonymy was one of the measures used in this investigation of inbreeding in Switzerland.

[9.54.7] Senn, Alfred. (1948). Swiss names. *Swiss Record, 1,* 71-82. Refs.
Systematic description of aspects of Swiss 1st names and surnames. Focus is on those in German. Examples.

9.55. ETHNIC NAMES: *Turkish*

[9.55.1] Clauson, Gerard. (1956). A note on the name Qapqan. *Journal of the Royal Asiatic Society of Great Britain & Ireland,* 73-77. Comment on the personal name Qapqan which goes back to an 8th cent. Turkish ruler.

[9.55.2] Kamm, Henry. (1985, Feb. 8). Toll in Bulgaria's Turkish unrest put at 100. *New York Times,* A11.

Disorders in Bulgaria have occurred as a result of governmental force to require ethnic Turks to change their names to Bulgarian ones.

[9.55.3] Lewis, Geoffrey L. (1957). *Turkey*. London: Benn, 222p. Refs.
Description of language reform in the 30s mentions a preference in switching to old Turkish names such as Ertuḥrul, Attilâ, and Oḥuz from Islamic Mehmed, Ahmed, and Ismail (p. 99). Surnames were made compulsory in 1935 (p. 108).

[9.55.4] Mansuroglu, Mecdut. (1954). On some titles and names in Old Anatolian Turkish. *Proceedings of the 23rd International Congress of Orientalists, Cambridge, 21st-28th August 1954*, pp. 194-195.
Comment on 8 titles and names. Included are Paša ("sovereign") and ābdẠl ("gypsy", "stupid").

[9.55.5] Mansuroglu, Mecdut. (1955). On some titles and names in old Anatolian Turkish. *Ural-Altaische Jahrbucher, 27,* 94-102. Refs.
Several titles analyzed systematically for meaning and origin in Arabic and Persian. Included are: Pasha, Aptal, and Yazi.

[9.55.6] Spencer, Robert F. (1961). The social context of modern Turkish names. *Southwestern Journal of Anthropology, 17,* 205-217. Refs.
Historical intro. to modern Turkish surnames and other names. Reference to Ataturk and the Name Law of 1930. Description of 6 categories of surname: occupational, place, heroic and tribal eponym, object, *lakap* (lineal), and attractive or euphonic.

9.56. ETHNIC NAMES: *Ukrainian*

[9.56.1] Buyniak, Victor O. (1987). Some problems regarding the rendition of Latin baptismal names into Ukrainian. *OnoCan, 69,* 18-21.
There are problems relating the names which appear on baptismal certificates with Ukrainian or Polish variant names (i.e., the everyday names by which immigrants to Canada may have been known). Some conversions are simple (Iannus = Ivan, Philippis = Pylyp), others are more complicated (Georgius = Jurij, Alexandra = Les'ko). Many examples

[9.56.2] Gauk, Roma Z. (compiler) & Slavutch, Yar. (Ed.). (1961). *Ukrainian christian names: A dictionary*. Edmonton, Alta, Canada: Orma Publications, 31p.
Following an intro., lists approx. 450 male and female Ukrainian 1st names in Cyrillic and English. Each entry shows the name of the patron saint according to the Gregorian calendar along with the appropriate date. Examples include Irene, Apr. 29th, and David, January 14th.

[9.56.3] Hursky, Jacob P. (1957). The patronymic surnames in Ukrainian. *Dissertation Abstracts. 17,* 1331. University of Pennsylvania.
Systematic analysis of surnames. Includes surnames derived from 1st name, occupation, social status, ethnic origin, and nicknames.

[9.56.4] Vlasenko-Bojcun, Anna. (1984). *Onomastic works*. Translated by Ania Bojcun-Savage. Ukrainian Free University, Series Monographs No. 37. Munich-Denver-Miami Beach, 144p. Refs.
One chapter deals with changes in Ukrainian surnames in the United States (pp. 67-75), giving types of change, transliteration, suffix changes, etc. There are numerous examples A 2nd chapter is devoted to the surname Kovshevych, its meaning, origin, and prominent family members (pp. 76-80).

9.57. ETHNIC NAMES: *Welsh*

[9.57.1] Anscombe, Alfred. (1919). The name of *Cerdic*. *Y Cymmrodor, 29,* 151-202. P. 201 concludes "...(1) that the O(ld) English] name of Cerdic presents the Suevic-Mercian g > c shift and (2) like the Alemannic *Cart-*, represents an older form GARD-."

[9.57.2] Davies, Phillips G. (1987, Fall). Names in the Welsh enclave in Jackson, Ohio (1880-1908). *Journal of the North Central Name Society, Fall,* 28-35. Refs. Tables.
The Welsh church of this community had about 200 members. The membership spanned 3 generations. Many of the 1st generation were from Wales. Most common surnames are listed. Among them: Jones, Davis, Morgan, and Evans. Among the most common 1st names are: Mary, Margaret, Elizabeth, and Jane for women; David, Thomas, John, and William for men.

[9.57.3] Fisher, R. A., & Vaughan, Janet. (1939). Surnames and blood groups. *Nature, 144,* 1047-1048. Table.
Used Welsh surnames Davis, Edwards, Harris, Jones, Lewis, Morgan, Phillips, and Roberts to identify a Welsh sample for a study of blood types in Britain.

[9.57.4] Gruffydd, W. J. (1912). Bledhericus, Bleddri, Bréri. *Revue Celtique, 33,* 180-183. Refs.
Identification of the 3 names in 12th cent. Wales as Bleheric the Welshman.

[9.57.5] Hamp, Eric P. (1978). Gwion and Fer Fi [Fi/'/]. In Varia II. Ériu, *29,* 29-30. Refs.
Background and comment on the youthful name of Taliesin.

[9.57.6] Jackson, Kenneth (H). (1961). The Idnert inscription: Date, and significance of *Id-*. *Bulletin of the Board of Celtic Studies, 19,* 232-234. Refs.
Analysis of a name inscribed on what is known as the Llanddewibreti stone in Wales. Concludes that the carving is from the 7th cent. and the *Id-* part means "lord."

[9.57.7] Jarman, A. O. H. (1969). A note on the possible Welsh derivation of Viviane. In *Gallica: Essays presented to J. Heywood Thomas by colleagues, pupils and friends* (pp. 1-12). Cardiff: University of Wales Press. Refs.
Suggests that Vivian or Niniane may have come from the Welsh *chwyfleiam*. Relevance of Merlin discussed.

[9.57.8] Jones, Gwilym Peredur. (1926-1927). The Scandinavian element in Welsh. *Zeitschrift für Celtische Philologie, 16,* 162-166. Refs.
Comment on 40+ personal and placenames which have or may have Old Norse elements. Examples include Cristin, Grufffydd, and Osbwrn.

[9.57.9] Lewis, Henry. (1933-36). The honorific prefixes *To- and Mo-*. *Zeitschrift für Celtische Philologie, 20,* 138-143. Refs.
Extended discussion of examples where these prefixes occur in Old Welsh materials.

[9.57.10] Morgan, T. J. (1987). Philip Knarry. *Bulletin of the Board of Celtic Studies, 34,* 125-126. Refs.
After evaluating evidence, explains that the name *Knarry* found in the Black Book of St. David's could come from Cynarwy.

[9.57.11] Morris, T(homas) E(vans). (1938). Welsh personal and place names. Broadcast in the program for Wales, 4th July, 1938. London: British Broadcasting Corporation, 12p.

Background material on personal names and surnames of Wales. Examples of 1st names include: Arthur, Griffith, and Idris; surnames, Bevan, Parry, and Bowen.

[9.57.12] Parry-Williams, T. H. (1921-23). Balchnoe. *Bulletin of the Board of Celtic Studies, 1,* 110. Refs.
The name *Balchnoe* appears in 2 Welsh works. Wonders whether Balchnoe was a Hebrew and whether Noe has anything to do with Noah.

[9.57.13] Paterson, D. R. (1920). Scandinavian influence in the place names and early personal names of Glamorgan. *Archaeologia Cambrensis, Series 6, 20,* 31-89. Refs. Pp. 74-89 are devoted to 60+ Old Norse personal names collected from 12th and 13th cent. sources (refs are on pp. 34-35). Sample names traced include Alger, Cole, and Northman.

[9.57.14] Pokorny, J. (1956). Middle-Welsh *Owein. Celtica, 3,* 306-308. Refs. Traces the name to mean "shepherd."

[9.57.15] Richards, G. Melville. (1966). Mechyll, Mechell, Llanfechell. [Miscellanea] *Archaeologia Cambrensis, 115,* 168-170. Refs.
Discussion of the saint's name with citation back to 1254. Unable to relate the Latin form *Machutus* to the Welsh *Mechyll.*

[9.57.16] Richards, G. Melville. (1969). Arthurian Onomastics. Transactions of the Honourable Society of Cymmrodorion, 250-264. Refs.
Discussion and analysis of names associated with Arthurian legends. Mention of bearers of names associated with Arthur, e.g., Guinevere, and placenames with Arthur as an element.

[9.57.17] Richards, G. Melville. (1970-71), Places and persons of the early Welsh Church. *Welsh History Review, 5,* 333-349. Refs.
Comment and discussion of figures in the Welsh Church during the 4th-7th cents. Pp. 342-343 categorizes (with examples) and comment Welsh saints as biblical, Latin or Roman, or pure Celtic.

[9.57.18] Richards, G. Melville. (1972). Mailoc. *Habis* [Seville, Spain], *3,* 159. Comment on the name of this bishop (572 AD) as possibly from Welsh *Mael* (prince, chief, leader).

[9.57.19] Taylor, A. J. (1981-82). Scorched earth at Flint in 1294. *Journal of the Flintshire Historical Society, 30,* 89-105.
Flint is a county in North Wales (not far from Liverpool). Listing of 75 individuals who lost property there due to the war in 1294 and money awarded to them for damages. Names shown include Thomas, (the limeburner); Geofrey Dawber (the plasterer), and Godfrey Carpenter.

[9.57.20] Williams, A. R. (1949). Welsh names. *Folk-Lore, 60,* 392-393.
General on Welsh names, 1st names and surnames.

[9.57.21] Williams, Ifor. (1935). Names on the Llanddetty stone. *Archaeologia Cambrensis, 90,* 87-94. Refs. Plates.
Discussion based upon name inscriptions on a cross found at Llanddetty, Wales. Interpretation that the name Gwaddan means "the mole" and that Gurhi means "bold one."

9.57.1. ETHNIC NAMES: *Welsh: First Names*

[9.57.1.1] Gruffudd, Heini. (1982). Enwau Cymraeg i blant: Welsh names for children, 2nd ed. Talybont, Dyfed [Wales]: Y Lolfa, 94p. Refs.
Lists over 1000 names all with translation, explanation, background, meaning, and prominent bearers. Examples, Ioan < Latin *Johannes* < Hebrew. "Equivalent of "John", = "Jehovah has favored." Garth a form of Gareth "ridge"); Ffiona a form of Ffion ("foxglove"); Nona, a var. of Non ("fair," "white") or the Lat. "9th", 5th-6th cent. saint, mother of Dewi (St. David).

[9.57.1.2] Hourahane, Peter. (1964). (Compiler). *Names for the Welsh: 500 Welsh Christian names*. Merthyr Tydfil, Wales: Triskel Press, 32p.
Listing of male and female names with etymology. Some with meaning, some with prominent bearers. Examples, Ceidio (male) was an early Welsh saint; Gwenfron (female) means fair-breasted.

[9.57.1.3] *Welsh first names for children: Their meanings explained*. (1978). Cardiff [Wales]: Emeralda, 48 p.
Alphabetical listing of approx. 700 names, most with meanings. Examples, Siarl is the Welsh form of Charles; Gwen, "As an adjective it means 'beautiful, fair, holy'. Used alone it is often a diminutive of such names as 'Gwenhwyfar' 'Gwenllian' and 'Gwenfron'."

9.57.2. ETHNIC NAMES: *Welsh: Surnames*

[9.57.2.1] Ashley, David J. B., & Davies, H. Duncan. (1966). The use of the surname as a genetic marker in Wales. *Journal of Medical Genetics, 3*, 203-211. Refs. Tables.
Responses by 558 men in the Swansea area show a relationship between a Welsh surname and ability to speak Welsh. Those with Welsh surnames vs. those with non-Welsh surnames show differences in blood measures and in hair color (the Welsh had darker hair color). List of 66 Welsh surnames including identification of the 35 most common.

[9.57.2.2] Benjamin, E. Alwyn. (1980-1983). A statistical comparison of the principal surnames in use in Penarth, 1881, with those in use in Aberystwyth, 1871. *Ceredigion, 9,* 257-259. Table.
These 2 communities of approx. equal population (6,000) were compared in terms of the percentage of the population included in the 12 most frequent surnames. For Aberystwyth, the top 12 includes 58.9%; for Penarth, 16.9%. These percentages are interpreted to mean that Penarth was a more dynamic community drawing people from a greater distance.

[9.57.2.3] Benjamin, E. Alwyn. (1987). The Welsh patronymic custom. *Local Historian, 17,* 405-407.
Comment on the problems of naming in Wales where there are relatively few surnames.

[9.57.2.4] Fowkes, Robert A. (1994). Welsh surnames of occupational origin. *Names, 41,* 288-297. Refs.
While occupational surnames are quantitatively fewer than patronyms in Welsh, they are important. "About a score of them have significance in the production and development of surnames. Half of them are treated here." Included are Coedwr, Goyder "woodsman, forester", Meddyg "doctor, physician", and Towr "roofer, thatcher."

[9.57.2.5] Jones, P. M. S. (1984). Don't envy the Joneses. *Family History, 13,* 152-156. Refs.

A Welsh investigator's description of the difficulties in tracing ancestors when they have common names such as William Jones.

[9.57.2.6] Lloyd, J. E. (1929). The Scudamore family. *Bulletin of the Board of Celtic Studies, 4,* 166-168.
Concludes that the Scudamores 1st appeared in Welsh Herefordshire. The 1st element of the name indicates a Norse influence, the 2nd refers to watery, marshy, ground.

[9.57.2.7] Morgan, Prys. (1968). *Background to Wales: A course of studies in modern Welsh life.* Llandybie, Wales: Christopher Davies.
Chapter 2 (Pp. 16-22) is devoted to Welsh surnames. Includes a concise description of Welsh naming practices. Table 1 shows 41 Welsh names with anglicized forms, example, Rhys > Rice, Reece, Preece (ap Rhys); Table 2 shows 18 adjectival names anglicized, examples, Bychan (fychan) ("little," "younger") > Vaughan, Baughan; and Table 3 gives 9 Welsh surnames from places, example, Powys.

[9.57.2.8] Morgan, Prys. (1986). The rise of Welsh hereditary surnames. *Nomina, 10,* 121-135. Refs.
Detailed history of the development of surnames in Wales. Begins with a description of the pre-surname period at 1100. Many examples.

[9.57.2.9] Morgan, Prys. (1990-91). Locative surnames in Wales: A preliminary list. *Nomina, 14,* 7-23. Refs.
While most Welsh surnames are patronymics, there are 100s that are derived from placenames. Some of these may come from more than one source, i.e., Kyffin, Coydmore, et al.; still others may also come from England, examples, Britton, Flint, et al. There are approx. 250 entries by district with citations and earliest date. Example, Magor, same spelling with a geographical equivalent in Monmouthshire. An early example is in the *Bulletin of the Board of Celtic Studies, 24,* 186. Richard Magor was a monk 1395-1400. The name is currently found in telephone directories in Newport, Cardiff, and other cities.

[9.57.2.9A] Morgan, T. J., & Morgan, Prys. (1985). *Welsh surnames.* Cardiff: University of Wales Press, 211p. Refs.
"The primary aim of this work is not to explain the 'meanings' of Welsh names: rather it tries to provide a historical survey of how the distinctive Welsh surnames came about." Traces the evolution, changes, modifications of surnames from early texts to modern directories. Many surnames are traced as far back as the 13th cent. Detailed, scholarly, many citations.

[9.57.2.10] Thomas. David. (1978). The Welsh connection. *Geographical Magazine* [London], *50,* 489. Map. Photos.
Explanation of why Welsh surnames are so distinctive. Discussion of the Welsh influence on naming in the US, especially in the Southeast, using data from the 1st Census.

[9.57.2.11] Thomas, David. (1979). Welsh emigration to the United States: A note on surname evidence. *Cambria, 6,* 1-9. Refs.
Expansion of Thomas above.

[9.57.2.12] Thomas, David. (1987). Early Welsh settlement in the USA: The surname evidence. *Transactions of the Honourable Society of Cymmrodorion,* 53-63.
Similar to Thomas above.

[9.57.2.13]   Thomas, Peter Wynn. (1987-89).   A quantitative analysis of the geographical distribution of *AP* surnames in Wales. *Onoma, 29,* 26-38. Refs. Tables. Figs. Map.
Evaluation of Welsh surnames based upon a sample of "the farming community in Wales as listed in...British Telecom Yellow Pages directories." Used cluster analysis and maps to demonstrate regional differences. Among the top 10 names used were Bellis < Ab Elis (Ellis); Bowen < Ab Owain (Owen); and Powell < Ap Hywel.

[9.57.2.14]   Williams, D. Elwyn. (1961).   A short inquiry into the surnames in Glamorgan from the thirteenth to the eighteenth centuries. *Transactions of the Honourable Society of Cymmrodorion, 2,* 45-87. Refs. Diagrams. Lists.
Glamorgan is a county in Southeast Wales. Extensive, scholarly examination into many aspects of Welsh surnames including nicknames. Hundreds of examples.

9.58. ETHNIC NAMES: *West Indian*

[9.58.1] Crowley, Daniel J. (1956). Naming customs in St. Lucia, *Social & Economic Studies, 5,* 87-92. Refs.
St. Lucia, West Indies, has a population of 85,000, mostly Roman Catholic. 70% of the children, born at the time of the study, were illegitimate. This, plus the types of loose marriage requirements and taking on of a surname, complicates the naming process.

[9.58.2] James, Alice V. (1983). Isonymy and mate choice on St. Bart, French West Indies: Computer simulations of random and total isonymy. *Humbio, 55,* 297-303. Refs(pp. 399-408). Tables.
Concludes that "the Crowe-Mange method of estimating random isonymy is not accurate for an isolate...because demographic aspects...are not taken into account."

10. EDUCATION

[10.1] Bourque, Paul; Dupuis, Norbert; & Van Houten, Ron. (1986). Public posting in the classroom: Comparison of posting names and coded numbers of individual students. *Psychological Reports, 59,,* 295-298. Refs. Tables.
Research with 3rd-graders shows improvement in weekly spelling scores when results are posted by name or coded numbers.

[10.2] Clark, Thomas L. (1972).   The environment of names in the classroom. *Elementary English, 49,* 1061-1063.
Classroom exercises for an elementary school teacher to use to demonstrate aspects of onomastics. Personal names included.

[10.3] Clark, Thomas L. (1973, Mar.). Environment of names in the classroom. *Education Digest, 38,* pp. 56-57.
Shorter version of Thomas above.

[10.4] Cunningham, Patricia. (1988). Names: A natural for early reading and writing. *Reading Horizons, 28,* 114-122. Refs.
Suggestions for those working with kindergartners and 1st graders to stimulate reading and writing.

[10.5] Davies, Anne. (1988, June). Children's names: Landmarks for literacy? *Resources in Education, 23,* p. 37. Summary. (ERIC Document Reproduction Service ED 290 171).

Investigated how 12 children, ages 3-5, developed understanding of the written form of their own 1st names while learning other words. Concludes that "learning the written form of one's own name is a unique case of written language learning." ERIC Document has Refs. Tables. Figs.

[10.6] Gitter, Lena L. (1968). Hey, you. *Marriage* [Indiana], *50,* 21-25.
Popular. General on 1st names. Does have suggestions for teaching young children their names and how to write them.

[10.7] Kostka, Gail. (1988, Aug.). The name's the game. *Instructor, 98,* p. 34.
Several ideas for the classroom instructor [probably elementary school] to stimulate interest in names. Activities suggested include work on: pseudonyms, stage names, popular names, nicknames, juniors, and others.

[10.8] Kuehne, Oswald R. (1951). Family names as motivation for the study of foreign languages. *Modern Language Journal, 35,* 552-561.
To interest students in foreign languages, language students were asked to give the meanings of non-English names from telephone or city directories. Listing of 500+ names by language (some with sub-categories). Languages included were: Greek, Latin, French, German, Italian, and Spanish. Included among the names are: Cerf < French ("hart"), Essig < German ("vinegar"), Alfieri < Italian ("flag bearers"), and Ortega < Spanish ("blackberry bush").

[10.9] Lieberman, Evelyn. (1985). *Name writing and preschool child.* (ERIC Document Reproduction Service No. 269759). 33p.
"The results support the conclusion that name writing is ideographic and not based on knowledge of letter names or on understanding letter/sound correspondence."

[10.10] Seefeldt, Carol. (1984, July). What's in a name? Lots to learn. *Young Children, 39(5),* 24-30. Refs.
Suggestions for teachers of younger children on ways of learning personal names that can enhance education.

[10.11] Simons, Elizabeth Radin. (1984, Nov.-Dec.). The folklore of naming: Using oral tradition to teach writing. *Teachers & Writers, 16(2),* 1-3. Refs.
A teacher of folklore, mostly at the high school level, explains how she has used personal names (1st, nicknames, and surnames) in the classroom as a teaching device in the teaching of writing. Class work touches on tradition, religion, family, and popularity as a factor in the naming process.

[10.12] Simons, Elizabeth Radin. (1985, May). The folklore of naming. Educational Digest, 50, 28-29.
Condensed version of Simons above.

[10.13] Thomas, Jacqueline. (1985, Apr.). *Language awareness for multicultural populations: Building positive attitudes.* Paper presented at the annual meeting of the Teachers of English to Speakers of Other Languages. New York. (ERIC Document Reproduction Service No. ED 259 555).
One teaching unit is devoted to names and nicknames and includes 3 class activities to make pupils more aware of names. [Class level not stated but appears to be middle school or below].

[10.14] Vellender, Anne. (1989). What's in a name? Literacy events in an infant classroom. [Teacher inquiry in the classroom]. *Language Arts, 66,* 552-557. Refs.
Describes how focusing on the name can promote reading and language skills.

[10.15] Villaume, Susan K., & Wilson, Louisa Cam. (1989). Preschool children's explorations of letters in their own names. *Applied Psycholinguistics, 10,* 283-300. Refs. 38 children, ages 25 months to 65 months participated in various tasks to determine their ability to use their names. The children's names were established as a source for testing hypotheses about the development of language.

[10.16] Wood, Florence. (1966, Aug./Sept.). What's in a name? *Instructor, 76,* 37. Ideas for teaching personal names to kindergartners.

11. FIRST NAMES

[11.1] Barry, Herbert, III., & Harper, Aylene S. (1993). Sex differences in linguistic origins of personal names. In E. Wallace McMullen (Ed.) *Names new and old: Papers of the Names Institute* (pp. 243-260). Refs. Tables. Madison, NJ: Privately published. Comparison of 100 male & 100 female names listed by Elsdon C. Smith in 1950 [87:1.13] in terms of linguistic origins. More of the male names come from Germanic or Celtic sources and designate hero status; female names are more from Latin and Greek and typically identify animate or inanimate objects. A table lists all names by frequency rank, root, trait category, and meaning. A 1991 report affirms that male names tend to be more forceful and traditional.

[11.1A] Beadle, Muriel. (1973, Oct. 21). The game of the name. *New York Times Magazine,* pp. 38ff.
Touches on many aspects of 1st names drawing from well-known sources such as, McDavid & Harary, Elsdon C. Smith, and Alice Rossi.

[11.2] First names. (1966). *Reader's Digest great encyclopedic dictionary,* pp. 2067-2076. Pleasantville, NY: Reader's Digest Association, 2094p.
Pp. 2067-2076 list approx. 500 male and 500 female names + variations. Entries give pronunciation and origin. Some meanings are included.

[11.3] Horn, Jack. (1975, Feb.). A Rose is a Rose is a Rosie. [Newsline]. *Psychology Today,* pp. 22; 24.
Review of Van Buren [87:26.1.36] on 1st names, short names, and affectionate names.

[11.4] Kopelman, Richard E. (1985). Alliteration in mate selection: Does Barbara marry Barry? *Psychological Reports, 56,* 791-796. Refs.
Alliteration here refers to husband and wife having 1st names beginning with the same 1st letter, examples, Alice and Al, Barbara and Bob. The hypothesis was that same initial letter of 1st name would be a positive factor in mate selection. 9 samples show that this alliteration occurs but only 1 is at a significant level. With nicknames [really, short names and affectionate names], 8 of the 9 samples show results in the predicted direction.

[11.5] McWilliam, Roy. (1942, Sept 26). War influences Christian names. [World of Women]. *Saturday Night,* p. 22.
General on naming practices. Comment on topical names. Points out that Prime Minister Gladstone had a number of boys named after him.

[11.6] Murphy, Francis Xavier. (1967). Names, Christian. *New Catholic Encyclopedia, 10,* 201-203. Refs. New York: McGraw-Hill.
Description of Christian (1st) names from earliest times to the 11th century.

[11.7] Rose, Christine. (1987). *Nicknames: Past and present: A list of nicknames for given names used in the past and present time.* San Jose, CA: Rose Family Association, 29p.
Approx. 1100 entries show affectionate and short forms of 1st names (referred to by some as nicknames). Thus, Adelaide may appear as Addy, Adele, Dell, Della, or Heidi; Belinda as Bella, Belle, or Linda; Barnabas as Barney or Berney; Aaron as Erin, Ron, or Ronnie.

[11.8] Waitt, Robert W. (1985). The choice of a Christian name [Commentary]. *Genealogists' Magazine, 21,* 369. In a reply to Nash [9.17.3.13], questions the use of the term *Christian* for 1st name as appropriate for Jews, Muslims, or Buddhists.

11.1. FIRST NAMES: *Baby-Names*

[11.1.1] Baptismal names. [Reply to J. C.]. (1952). Sign [Union City, NJ], *31(1),* 52.
Points out that Catholic Canon 761 requires a saint's name at baptism. Comment on failure to do so.

[11.1.2] Cole, William. (1981, July 1). Uninspired name is just too much. *New York Times,* p. C20.
A writer solves the problem of naming his son by giving the wife's birth name, Williams.

[11.1.3] Dunkling, Leslie Alan. (1987). *You name it! All you need to name your baby.* London: Faber & Faber, 269p.
Lists 4000 names with meanings. Intro. has "101 interesting ideas" for parents. These ideas range from giving Automobile Names (Aston, Ferrari) to Risky Names (Pleasant, Charity), to Wanted Names (Desirée, "wanted") [the child was wanted]. The idea suggestions are keyed to the main listing.

[11.1.4] Evans, Cleveland Kent. (1991). *Unusual and most popular baby names.* Chicago: Signet, 192p.
Entries for the 500 most popular names (and their variants) for boys and for girls in 1989. Listings also of unusual names.

[11.1.5] Ferguson, Rosalind. (1987). *Choose your baby's name: A dictionary of first names.* Penguin: Hammondsworth, Middlesex, 253p.
Has a pronunciation guide. Derivations and meanings of names more complete than most baby books.

[11.1.6] Foderaro, Lisa W. (1987, Nov. 13). Whose surname(s) for baby? *New York Times,* p. A22.
Baby-naming patterns have been changing. Examples show families where the child has been given the wife's birth surname, a hyphenated name representing both parents, and alternation patterns where one child has been given one parent's surname and a 2nd child the other parent's surname.

[11.1.7] Glickman, Bob. (1990). *The worst baby name book.* Kansas City, MO: Andrews & McMeel, not paged.
Humorous approach to parents so that they would not give a name which would cause the child anguish. 250 entries for male names, 200 for female. Examples, Elmer, Horace, Ida, and Bebe.

[11.1.8] Hoag, Joy Marie. (1969, Mar.). What's in your name? *Family Digest* [Huntington, IN], *24*, 65-70.
Popular presentation with suggestions for parents on naming children.

[11.1.9] Johnson, Charles & Sleigh, Linwood. (1973). *The Harrap book of boys' and girls' names*, rev. London: Harrap. 273p. Refs.
Appears to be a republishing of Sleigh & Johnson (1962), [87:10.3.10-10.3.11]. However, it is a single vol. and the formerly separate sex entries are combined into a single main section.

[11.1.10] Maynard, Rona. (1990, Aug.). What's in a name? It may influence a child's identity. *Chatelaine*, p. 94.
General on naming, mostly referring to girls. Suggests that if parents wish to give a child an unusual name, to give it as a middle name where it may be used or not as decided by the child.

[11.1.11] Rennick, Robert M. (1968). The Brooklyn Public Library baby-naming service. *New York Folklore Quarterly, 24*, 212-220. Refs.
Around 1938, the library developed an extensive baby-naming service which lasted at least until the time the article was written. The New York Public Library was continuing also to provide service for people interested in names.

[11.1.12] Richman, Daniel Avram. (1993). *From Aaron to Zoe: 15,000 great baby names*. Boston: Little, Brown, 285p. Refs.
Has main entries for 15,000 names. These entries give information on origin, meaning, famous namesakes, level of popularity, and unusual spellings. Additionally, there are lists by ethnic group, meanings, and occupations.

[11.1.13] Richman, Daniel A(vram)., Marosi, Stephen B., Staniec, Fran, & Arnold, Cheryl L. (1991). *Baby-Namer: Over 14,000 names to choose from.* San Diego: StudyWare. 4 diskettes (3 1/2") IBM-compatible, also available for Macintosh.
A computer program to help in selecting, or finding out more about, a name. User can select names to fit criteria (1st letter, language or ethnic group, sex, meaning, popularity, etc.). Computer will produce names that fit the criteria. Entries appear to be identical with Richman listing above.

[11.1.14] Rosenkrantz, Linda & Satran, Pamela. (1988). *Beyond Jennifer and Jason: An enlightened guide for naming your baby*. New York: St. Martin's Press, 300p.
General on baby-naming; consideration of many aspects. Many quotes on names from popular sources.

[11.1.15] Schwegel, Janet. (1988;1990). *The baby name countdown: Meaning and popularity for over 50,000 names*. Edmonton, Alberta [Canada]: Personal Publishing, 224p. Refs. (Also published in the United States in 1990 by Paragon Press, New York. [The American edition is somewhat rearranged but appears to be essentially the same] Lists the 100 most popular names in Canada and the US by region. Another section has an index of popularity for each of 1400 male and 1900 female names along with the meaning for each. Unusual names (those occurring less than once in 1000) are also listed but without meaning. There are approx. 18,000 male and 27,000 female names in this listing.

[11.1.16] Streshinsky, Shirley. (1967, Oct.). How to choose the right name for your baby. *Parents Magazine*, pp. 62ff.
General suggestions.

[11.1.17] *3500 names for baby: Boys' and girls' names plus every name's meaning and origin.* (1969). New York: Dell, 64p.
Gives basic information on origin and meaning. Related names cross-indexed.

[11.1.18] *3000 uncommon names for baby: For special baby girls and boys. Special names with their origins and meanings.* New York: Dell, 64p.
Similar to above but contains unique names, such as Melita (Greek, "little honey flower"), Prunella (Latin, "plum-colored"), and Rory (Gaelic, "red").

[11.1.19] Turner, Barbara Kay. (1991). *Baby names for the '90s.* New York: Berkeley Books, 263p. Refs.
Based upon registration lists and a survey gives information on 10,000 names, also trends in naming, and most popular names. Entries include: rank (among most common 500), pronunciation, language derivation, meaning, and variant spellings.

[11.1.20] Ward, Andrew. (1979, Mar. 3). Naming the baby: 'Encratis' won't do. *New York Times,* pp. C1, C18.
Reactions of an editor of *Atlantic* on reading *3,000 uncommon names for baby,* Dell, 1976.

[11.1.21] Wyatt, Katherine & Burrow, Lesley. (1980). *Children's names and horoscopes.* With horoscopes by Roger Elliot. London: Ebury Press, 152p. Illus.
Popular. Contains entries for approx. 480 girls' names; 460 boys' names + general zodiac signs.

11.2. FIRST NAMES: *Specific*

[11.2.1] Borgmann, Dmitri A. (1986). "X" as in Xerxes. In A. Ross Eckler (Ed.) *Names and games: Onomastics and recreational linguistics* (pp. 51-54). Lanham, MD: University Press of America. Refs.
Lists 100 male and 50 female names beginning with X. The names are taken from Charles Johnson & Linwood Sleigh *The Harrap book of boys' and girls' names,* revised, 1973. Examples include: Xander, Xavier, Xeron for men; Xara, Xenia, Xylota for women.

[11.2.2] Don't tread on Harvey. [Life and Leisure]. (1965, Aug. 30). *Newsweek.* pp. 75-76.
Description of an organization formed to protest the negative portrayal of Harvey in the media.

[11.2.3] Evans, Cleveland Kent. (1993). How Vanessa became a butterfly: A psychologist's adventure into entomological etymology. *Names,* 41, 276-281. Refs.
Many baby-name books give the origin of Vanessa as being from Greek and meaning "butterfly." This investigation traced the name to the literary invention of Jonathan Swift who honored his friend Esther Vanhomrigh by taking the first syllable of her surname and combining it with the affectionate form of her 1st name, Essa. Concludes that..."the entomologist Johan Fabricius probably named a genus of butterfly *Vanessa* after the character in Swift's poem."

[11.2.4] Hawes, J. (1974, Nov. 14). Oscar. *Notes & Queries, 5th Series, 2,* p. 388.
Raises question of the derivation of this name.

[11.2.5] Jerram, C. S. (1875). Oscar. *Notes & Queries, 5th Series, 3,* 10-11. Refs.
Reply to Hawes above that the name *Oscar* is derived from the Gaelic *oscarra* ("fierce").

[11.2.6] Koenig, V. Frederick. (1956). The etymology of Fierabras. *Modern Language Notes, 71,* 356-357. Refs.
The name *Fierabras* originates from a 16th cent. French farce involving a Saracen giant. Fierabras means, "flailing arms." This is different from Fierabrace, a nickname of William of Orange.

[11.2.7] Orgel, Irene. (1958, Nov. 16). John, Jean, Juan, Jan. *New York Times Magazine,* pp. 28-29.
General on the name *John.* Mention of historical figures with the name. Forms of the name in other languages.

[11.2.8] Riley, Morgan T. (1956). Yes, we called her Rose. *American Rose Annual,* pp. 74-84. Refs.
Variations with comment on the name Rose in many countries at different times from Ancient Greece on. Included are: Rhoda, Rosina, Rosalia, Roseta, Rhodope, Rosaclara, Rosalu, Rose Anne, Rosamond, & many others.

[11.2.9] Tibon, Gutierre. (1954). Celia. [Names in Brief]. *Names, 2,* 134.
Celia was assumed to be derived from the Latin *coelum* ("heaven"). It is actually from Etruscan and means *September.*

11.3. FIRST NAMES: *Unisex*

[11.3.1] Barry, Herbert, III, & Harper, Aylene S. (1994). Feminization of unisex names from 1960 to 1990. *Names, 41,* 228-238. Refs. Tables.
33 unisex names which appeared in both 1960 and 1990 were identified from Pennsylvania Department of Health records. Analysis of data concludes that "names tend to evolve from masculine to unisex to feminine. Popularity of unisex names is usually brief. Most names given to a substantial number of boys and girls in 1 of the 2 years, 1960 or 1990, had low frequencies of one sex or both sexes in the other year.

[11.3.2] Chamberlin, Jo Hubbard (Mr.). (1960, Feb.). I'm tender about gender. *Coronet,* pp. 55-57.
Anecdotal description of the difficulties a person has with a name that can be used by both sexes. Examples of 13 names in this category include: Gene Tierney and Gene Tunney, Dana Wynter and Dana Andrews.

12. GOD

[12.1] Barr, James. (1963). God. In James Hastings (Ed.) *Dictionary of the Bible* (pp. 333-338), rev. ed., by Frederick C. Grant & H. H. Rowley. New York: Scribner.
Systematic coverage. Includes: prehistory concepts, names of God, changes in concept of God, anthropomorphism, and Christology.

[12.2] Bourke, Myles M. (1958). Yahweh, the Divine name. *Bridge, A Yearbook of Judaeo-Christian Studies, 3,* 271-287. Refs.
Discussion of various interpretations of Ex. 3:14, "I AM THAT I AM."

[12.3] Broadie, Alexander. (1987). Maimonides and Aquinas on the names of God. *Religious Studies, 23,* 157-170.
Concludes "as regards the traditional names of God, Maimonides holds that they fail entirely to signify God's nature whereas Aquinas holds that they do so signify though inadequately [p. 165]. Concludes that, "...even while denying that proposition he [St. Thomas] accepts it [p. 170]."

[12.4] Burrell, David. (1990, Apr.). Naming the names of God: Muslims, Jews, Christians. *Theology Today, 47,* 22-29. Refs.
Uses the positions of al-Ghazali, Maimonides, and Aquinas to demonstrate Islamic, Jewish, and Christian various views of God.

[12.5] Chopra, Y. N. (1975). Worshipping the right God. *Philosophy, 50,* 94-96. Refs.
Takes issue with the definition of P. T. Geach that the word God is not a proper name but a descriptive term.

[12.6] Denny, Frederick Mathewson. (1987). Names and naming. In Mircea Eliade (Ed.), *The encyclopedia of religion, Vol. 10,* pp. 300-307. New York: Macmillan; London: Collier Macmillan.
Describes the role of naming in different cultures followed by the names of deity in: Ancient Israel and Judaism, Christianity, Islam, Sikhism, Hinduism, Mahayana Buddhism, and nonliterate and ancient traditions. These include: Australia, Africa, Ancient Egypt, and Ancient Rome. Human naming traditions described in Judaism, Christianity, Islam, Hinduism, China, and some nonliterate societies. Concise, scholarly.

[12.7] Gleason, R. W. (1964). *Yaweh: The God of the Old Testament.* Englewood Cliffs, NJ: Prentice-Hall, 124p. Refs.
Appendix (p. 113-124) has the names of God including: Elohim, El Elyon, Baal, and Ab.

[12.8] Gómez, L. M. (1965). From the names of God to the name of God: Nicholas of Cusa. *International Philosophical Quarterly, 5,* 80-102. Refs.
Explanation of Catholic theologian Nicholas of Cusa [Nicholaus Cüsanus, 1401-1464] and his views on the names of God.

[12.9] Gordon, Cyrus H. (1970). His name is "One." *Journal of Near Eastern Studies, 29,* 198-199. Refs.
Comment on Zechariah 14:9 that the name of God is "One."

[12.10] Gray, John. (1953). The god YW in the religion of Canaan. *Journal of Near Eastern Studies, 12,* 278-283. Refs.
Evaluation from ancient inscriptions of theories on the origin of YW.

[12.11] Hartman, Louis F. (1963). *Encyclopedic dictionary of the Bible,* trans. & adaptation of A. Van den Born's *Bibjbels Woordenboek,* 2nd rev. ed. New York: McGraw- Hill, 2634 columns.
Entries on cols. 1604-1608 are under Names & Name of God; cols. 1810-1812 cover personal names.

[12.12] Hill, Thomas. D. (1983). *VIII genitus homo* as a nomen sacrum in a twelfth-century Anglo-Latin fever charm. *Notes & Queries, 30,* 487-488. Refs.
The term *VIII genitus homo* is found in G. Storms' *Anglo-Saxon Magic* and is found in a prayer against fever. Hill traces the term meaning "eight-born man" to the *Secrets of Enoch* as a secret name for God which is thought to be more magical than religious.

[12.13] Katz, P. (1954). Jeja, Jaja. *Vetus Testamentum, 4,* 428-429. Refs.
Disagreement with Walker [12.23] on interpretation of spellings and interpretations of Yahweh in various forms.

[12.14] Kimbrough, S. T., Jr. (1989). Bible translation and the gender of God. *Theology Today, 46,* 195-202.

Discussions of different translations into English of YHWH, Adonai, and Elohim against considerations of gender in the preparation of the text of psalms for a new Methodist hymnal.

[12.15] King, William. (1965). *An historical account of the heathen gods and heroes: Necessary for the understanding of the ancient poets.* Carbondale: Southern Illinois University Press, 256p. Plates.
Stories and descriptions of approx. 380 Greek and Roman gods and goddesses from Classical Antiquity. Examples include Calliope, Daedalus. and Jupiter.

[12.16] Leishman, Thomas L., & Lewis, Arthur T. (1965). *The Bible handbook,* (2nd ed.). New York: Nelson, 283p.
Ch. 10 (pp. 185-192) discusses 12 names of God found in the Old and New Testaments. Examples, The Most High, Elohim, and The Lord of Hosts.

[12.17] Manley, G. T. (1962). Names of God. In J. D. Douglas (Ed.), *The new Bible dictionary* (pp. 477-480). Grand Rapids, MI: Eerdmans. Refs.
Systematic scholarly approach to biblical references. 18 different names are shown. Some not usually reported are: The Lord is my banner, The Lord is our righteousness, and Ancient of days.

[12.18] Moeller, Henry R. (1962). Four Old Testament problem terms. *Bible Translator* [Amsterdam], *13,* 219-222. Refs.
Pp. 21-22 have material on the divine epithet *Shaddai* (Gen. 17:1). Suggestion that Shaddai is from Akkadian and means "heart-knower."

[12.19] Murphy, R(ichard). T(homas). A(quinas). (1967). Yahweh. *New Catholic encyclopedia, 14,* 1065-1066. Refs.
Concise description of the name of God. Biblical refs.

[12.20] Rolnick, Philip A. (1992). Fatherhood and names of God. *Names, 40, 271-282. Refs.*
Discussion of criticism by feminists of the name "Father" in referring to God as legitimizing male dominance in church and society. Goes on to discuss arguments that all names of God are metaphorical. Concepts of God are evolving. "Divergent ethical ramifications will result from our names of God."

[12.21] Translating the divine name. (1952). *Bible Translator* [London], *3,* 171-204. Refs.
The article is devoted to the linguistic and theological problems of devoting divine names into Indonesian such as Elohim, YHWH, and Adonai.

[12.22] Walker, Norman. (1951). The writing of the divine name in the Mishna. *Vetus Testamentum, 1,* 309-316. Refs.
Goes back to the Mishna (190 AD.) to comment on the appearance of the name of God as Jah-Jah, then Jeh-Jah.

[12.23] Walker, Norman. (1953). The writing of the divine name in Aquila and the Ben Asher Text. *Vetus Testamentum, 3,* 103-104. Refs.
Aquila, a disciple of Rabbi Akiva, translated the Old Testament into Greek about 130 AD. For the Hebrew Jaweh, he wrote Jah-Jah so that Greek-speaking Hebrew readers would not pronounce the Divine Name.

12.1. GOD: *Bible*

[12.1.1] Goitein, S. D. (1956). *YHWH* the Passionate: The monotheistic meaning and origin of the name *YHWH*. *Vetus Testamentum, 6,* 1-9. Refs.
Develops the position that *yahwa* is "the imperfect form of *hwy* which means: the One who loves passionately."

[12.1.2] McKenzie, John L. (1965). *Dictionary of the Bible.* Milwaukee, WI: Bruce, 954p. Pp. 315-318 define the concept and discuss the names of God. Pp. 603-605 discuss the concept of name in the Old and New Testaments.

[12.1.3] Murphy, R(ichard). T(homas). A(quinas). (1967). Name of God. *New Catholic Encyclopedia, 10,* 200-201. Refs. New York: McGraw-Hill.
Comment on the meaning of the use of God's name by the Israelites. Other entries for God are under: El, Elohim, Elyon, Jehovah, Adonai, Shaddai, and Yawweh.

[12.1.4] Schild, E. (1954). On Exodus iii 14--"I AM THAT I AM." *Vetus Testamentum, 4,* 296-302. Refs.
Scholarly critical discussion of this passage. Concludes that, "the 'existential' interpretation of this passage is the only natural and syntactically correct exegesis."

[12.1.5] van Imschoot, P., & Louis F. Hartman. (1963). God. In Louis F. Hartman *Encyclopedic dictionary of the Bible*: *A translation and adaptation of A. van den Born's Bijbels Woordenboek,* 2nd. rev. ed, 1954-1957. New York: McGraw-Hill, columns 878-883. Refs.
Description of the various meanings of God in the Old and New Testaments. Bible citations.

[12.1.6] Walker, Norman. (1956). Elohim and Eloah. *Vetus Testamentum, 6,* 214-215. Refs.
Questions whether "elohim where it signifies "God" as distinct from "gods," is really a mimated singular."

12.2. GOD: *YHWH*
(See Also: 13. GODS)

[12.2.1] Cross, Frank Moore, Jr. (1962). Yahweh and the God of the Patriarchs. *Harvard Theological Review, 55,* 225-259. Refs. Fig.
Exhaustive description and analysis of the various positions held by theologians on the various names of God. Concludes that Yahweh was originally a cultic name for 'El "if we suppose that the god Yahweh split off from 'El in the radical differentiation of his cultus, ultimately ousting El from his place in the divine council...." (pp. 256-257).

[12.2.2] Driver, G. R. (1954). The interpretation of Yhwh as a participial form from a causative theme of the verb. [Reflections on recent articles]. *Journal of Biblical Literature, 73,* 125-131. Refs.
Disputes the position of Oberman [12.2.7] on Yhwh that proper names cannot stand in a construct state. Driver gives examples of proper names with prenominal suffixes from Accadian, Ugaritic, Arabic, Hebrew, and other languages which imply a construct state.

[12.2.3] Freedman, David Noel. (1960). The name of the God of Moses. *Journal of Biblical Literature, 79,* 151-156. Refs.
Scholarly discussion of various meanings of YHWH. One point concluded is that in Ex. 34:6 and 14, the proper subject of the verb *yahweh* is *el* as in El Shaddai.

[12.2.4] Gardner, W. R. W. (1908-09). The name 'Yahweh.' *Expository Times, 20,* 91-92.
According to Gardner, the usual roots for the name have been either from *HAYA* (to be) or *HAVA* (to breathe). Gardner gives another alternative *HAVA* (to love) which would translate as *the Loving God.*

[12.2.5] Hyatt, J. Philip. (1955). Yahweh as "the God of my father." *Vetus Testamentum, 5,* 130-136. Refs.
Speculates that Yahweh was a patron deity of one of Moses' ancestors, that the family of Moses came from Midian, and that Yahweh means "to be, to exist."

[12.2.6] Niles, Daniel Premaseelan. (1975). The name of God in Israel's worship: The logical importance of the name Yahweh. *DissAbstrIntl, 36,* 5365A-5366A. (University Microfilms No. 75-23,162, 267 pages).
"The intention of the study is to show the theological importance that the name Yahweh received in Israel's faith."

[12.2.7] Obermann, Julian. (1949). The divine name *YHWH* in the light of recent discoveries. *Journal of Biblical Literature, 68,* 301-323. Refs.
Scholarly critical examination of the name *YHWH*. At least 15 other names for God are also mentioned. Among them: "Doer of wonder," and "Maker of peace and Creator of Evil." Topics included are: YHWH as a proper name, as a nomen agentis, theophanous formations, the epithet.

[12.2.8] Walker, Norman. (1958). Yahwism and the divine name "Yhwh." *Zeitschrift für Alttestamentische Wissenschaft, 70,* 262-265. Refs.
Concludes that Yah-weh is a combination of the Kenite moon god Yah + the Egyptian *w-*'. The suffix means "one." Ikhnaton called his new deity "God-One." Thus Yah-weh means "Yah-One."

13. GODS

[13.1] Best, Elsdon. (1920). Maori genius for personification with illustrations of Maori mentality. *Transactions of the New Zealand Institute, 53,* 1-12.
Description of myths of the deities of the Maori. Rangi is the Sky Parent; Papa, the Earth Mother. Other gods explained also.

[13.2] Chandler, Tertius. (1962). Ikhnaton and Moses. *American Imago, 19,* 127-139. Refs.
Supports Freud's position linking Moses to Ikhnaton. Points out that, "Adonai, the main Jewish name for God, must be Aton, the god of Ikhnaton" (p. 128).

[13.3] Clader, Linda L. (1976). *Helen: The evolution from divine to heroic in Greek epic tradition.* Leiden, Holland: Brill, 90p. Refs. (Mnemosyne: Bibliotheca Classica Batava, Supplementum Quadrigesimum Secundum).
After exhaustive analysis of the name in and outside Homeric poetry concludes (p. 80) "the Spartan Helen is a nature divinity, associated with growing things, and she is closely related to other manifestations of the fertility goddess of the Mediterranean, who is elsewhere celebrated by the carrying of baskets."

[13.4] Herskovits, Melville Jean. (1966). *New World Negro, The: Selected papers in Afroamerican studies.* Ed. by Frances S. Herskovits. Bloomington: Indiana University Press, 370p. Refs.
P. 269 has a brief mention of day-names and their relationship to marital compatibility. Pp. 321-329 (which also appeared in *American Anthropologist,* 1937, *new series 39,*

635-643) deal with the correspondence between African gods and Catholic saints in Brazil, Cuba, and Haiti. Example, the Dahomean serpent-deity is indentified with St. Patrick and with Moses.

[13.5] Montalbano, Frank J. (1951). Canaanite Dagon, origin, nature. *Catholic Bible Quarterly* [Washington], *13,* 318-397. Refs.
Traces the cult of Dagan from the upper Euphrates at the time of Sargon I (2400-2300 BC) through other periods and places to Canaan. Concludes that the original meaning was "cloudy" or "rainy" that Dagon (different spelling) was derived from the word for grain but the Philistines connected it with the root *dag* meaning "fish."

[13.6] Murtonen, A. (1951). The appearance of the name Yhwh outside Israel. *Studia Orientalia* [Helsinki], *16,* 3-11. Refs.
Presents over 18 names of the Kassite period of Babylonia (approx. 13th-14th cents. BC) in cuneiform which include the Yhwh component. Other evidence also presented showing similar names in West Semitic and Ugaritic.

[13.7] Palmer, L. R. (1958). New religious texts from Pylos. *Transactions of the Philological Society*, pp. 1-35. Refs.
Analysis of a new set of Linear B tablets in terms of linguistic characteristics. Much of the material deals with religious figures. These include the deities: Wa-na-kat-te, Poseidon, and Dipsioi among others, with some information on their names.

[13.8] Partow, Shin. (1960). *Prashina.* Teheran: Teheran University Press, 228p. Refs.
Wide-ranging analysis of the names of the gods of the ancients. Shows similarities, parallels, and variations in the pantheons of cultures such as, Ancient Egypt, China, Greece, Babylon, Iran, and others. Hundreds of of gods mentioned. Among the gods mentioned are Ra, Apas, and Afra.

[13.9] Skutsch, Otto. (1987). Helen, her name and nature. *Journal of Hellenic Studies, 107,* 188-193. Refs.
After examination of scholarly material concludes "two mythological figures are fused in Helen; that Helen in the story of Troy is a calque on her abduction by Theseus, and that commentators on Aeschylus' Agamemnon should give some thought to Helen as the threatening corposant [electrical phenomenon, i.e., St. Elmo's fire]."

[13.10] Sotiroff, George. (1978). The names of pagan divinities. *Onomastica, No. 53,* pp. 10-16. Refs.
Appears to be substantially the same as [87:12.12].

[13.11] Sourvinou, Christiane. (1970). *A-TE-MI-TO* and *A-TI-MI-TE. Kadmos, 9,* 42-47.
After examination of tables and evaluation of comments of others, concludes that *a-te-mi-to* and *a-ti-mi-te* thought possibly to be identified with Artemis, are not. Further "that the name of Artemis does not occur in the Linear B tablets. The words interpreted as forms of this theonym may designate a cult person."

[13.12] Tsevat, Matitiahu. (1954). The Canaanite god Salah. *Vetus Testamentum, 4,* 41-49; 322. Refs.
Analysis of the name Salah which is also an element in the name Methusaleh. For the Canaanites Salah was the god of the infernal river who judged those who went to the netherworld.

[13.13] Wagner, Heinrich. (1979). Origins of pagan Irish religion and the study of names. *Bulletin of the Ulster Place-Name Society, 2nd series, 2,* 24-38. Refs.

Attempts to show the relationship of ancient Irish gods and goddesses to those of other languages and cultures, especially Indo-European and Greek. Many examples brought in including Tara who is an aspect of the Earth-goddess and the goddess Arduinna who is semantically similar to the Irish goddess Brighid. Wide-ranging, documented.

[13.14] Wyllie, Robert W. (1966). Some notes on the Effutu deities. *Anthropos, 61,* 477-480. Refs.
The Effutu, a tribe of Ghana, have a chief god Nyimpo and a pantheon of 77 lesser gods who are listed. The 21 of these gods for whom there is information are described, "Kwesi Budi is the receptionist for the gods."

[13.15] Youtie, H. G. (1944). Sambathis. *Harvard Theological Review, 37,* 209-218.
Fragments of an ostracon (potsherd) from the 3rd or 4th cent. AD found at Karanis, Egypt written in Greek lists Greek and Egyptian deities along with an oriental 1--Sambathis.

14. GRAFFITI

[14.1] Even ancients put their names on trees, walls. (1992, Mar. 29) *Buffalo News*, p. F12. [Syndicated from the *Washington Post*].
German scientist Werner Eck has reported on tourists writing on trees and walls. 4829 graffiti have been found at religious shrines in Egypt dated from the 3rd cent. BC to the late Roman era. Graffiti also at Mt. Sinai.

[14.2] Feiner, Joel & Klein, Stephan Marc. (1982). Graffiti talks. *Social Policy, 12(3),* 47-53. Refs. Illus.
Based upon graffiti in New York City subways. Attempts to explain the motivation/s of the graffiti writer who wants his/her name or nickname to go out into the world.

[14.3] O'Donnell, Richard. (1994, July/Aug.) There really was a Kilroy. [Did You Know?]. *Reminisce*, p. 19.
The popular graffito "Kilroy Was Here" is traced to James J. Kilroy who during WWII was an inspector at the Fore River Shipyard in Quincy, Massachusetts. He put this phrase on ships being built there in large letters to prevent some worker fraud. The phrase went out on the ships which were sent out before being painted over.

15. HUMOR AND NAMES

[15.1] Armour, Richard. (1971, Aug. 28). My backward youth. *Saturday Review, 54,* pp. 4-5.
Anecdotal about high school days when there was a fad to spell names backward as Noxin for Nixon whose Vice President was Orips Wenga.

[15.2] Duckert, Audrey R. (1962). Notes and queries. *Names,* 10, 145-147.
Description of some situations where hoax names were used. One case was where a man signed a bad check *Trine Gettit*.

[15.3] Forsey, Eugene. (1938, Sept.). What's in a name? *Canadian Forum, 18,* p. 180.
Calls attention to approx. 35 individuals whose occupation seems appropriate to the their names. Included are: Sir George Penny, Treasurer of the King's Household; Kandel Brothers, electrical supplies; and Turner, Parker, & Weaver, auto supplies.

[15.3A] Frumkes, Lewis Burke. (1987). *Name crazy: What your name really means.* New York: Simon & Schuster (Fireside), 127p. Illus.

An alphabetical listing of approx. 350 1st names each with a purported analysis, example, "Dennis, spell it backward and find out what Dennis did." All names are done with a light satiric touch.

[15.4] Gasque, Thomas J. (1991). Names as humor in the thirty-nine years of the journal *Names*. *Names, 39,* 217-224. Refs.
While covering the whole area of onomastics, does include research dealing with humor in personal names. The work of 8 scholars is described. These include: Pyles [Smith:579], Lu Zhongti [15.4], and Rennick [87:28.1], [87:46.15].

[15.5] Gilbreth, F. B. (1958). *How to be a father.* New York: Crowell, 133p.
Pp. 12-20 contain 2 short selections on naming a child, written with a light touch. Mention of overused names, such as Linda and Shirley. Short lists of non-recommended names.

[15.6] Hexter, J. H. (1983). Call me Ishmael; Or a rose by any other name. *American Scholar, 52,* 339-353.
Autobiographical (and humorous) account by a man who was originally named Milton K. Hexter but went by the name of Jack Hexter. Later, under pressure, he took a middle initial of H. Hexter's adventures with his names are amusingly described.

[15.7] Hunt, George W. (1987, Jan. 17). Of many things. *America,* cover ii.
Editor who doesn't think that the current [1987] "sound" of the names of football players (Dexter Manley, Douglas Flutie) compares with names from previous days such as Bronco Nagurski and Johnny Blood.

[15.8] Loomis, C. Grant. (1956). Surnames in American wordplay. *Names,* 4, 86-95. Refs.
Draws 88 examples (edited) from G. D. Prentice's *Prenticeana, or wit and humor in paragraphs,* (1860). Example No.10, "Mr. and Mrs. Brewer of Wayne Co. have 22 children. Theirs is, perhaps, the most extensive brewery in the West."

[15.9] Marcus, Leonard. (1973). Game of the name: Musical personages. *High Fidelity & Musical America, 23,* 4.
Listing of 41 fictitious punning names for musicians. Includes: Mischa Solemnis, director of the chorus; Tim Penny and Roland E. Drumm, percussion; and Drummond Phyfe, bagpipe bandmaster.

[15.10] Prentice, George G. (1860). *Prenticeana; or, Wit and humor in paragraphs.* New York: Derby & Jackson, 306p.
Consists of approx. 1800 humorous short paragraphs, including many puns. A number involve names, example, "a Newbern paper says that Mrs. Alice Day of that city was lately delivered of four sturdy boys. We know not what a Day may bring forth."

[15.11] Price, Roger; Stern, Leonard; & Sloan, Lawrence. (1985). *The baby boomer book of names.* Los Angeles: Price/Stern/Sloan, 334p. Refs. Cartoons.
A lighthearted book with various supposed associations of names, example "Lena eats chicken soup for breakfast and thinks gravy is a beverage." Also has a section on brief meanings of names and one on diminutives.

[15.12] What's in a name? (1988, Aug.). *National Lampoon,* p. 74.
Listing of 21 unusual names with stories from newspapers. Examples include Sydbet M. Swindler arrested for evading taxes, Dr. George G. Innocent accused of grand theft, and Dr. A. Cockburn, a urologist.

[15.13] Wright, Sylvia. (1954, June). Who the hell is holy, fair, and wise? *Harper's Magazine, 208,* 29-31. Illus.
On the difficulties of being named Sylvia. Light touch.

[15.14] Yapp, Wilfred. (1974, Nov. 29). Two's company, three's a cacophony. *Daily Telegraph Magazine* [London], p. 16.
Comment on names mostly associated with business, as Marks & Spencer, Massey-Ferguson, and Coca Cola, even poking fun at his own.

16. INDEXING AND NAMES
(See Also: 6. CATALOGING AND NAMES)

[16.1] Blom, Eric. (1957). Lexicographer's dilemma. *Musical Times* [London]: *98,* 546-547.
Using the 19th cent. musician Michel-Richard Delalande as an example, describes the problems of indexing surnames with *de, van,* and *von.* Suggests cross-listing.

[16.2] Hunnisett, R. F. (1972). *Indexing for editors, Archives & the User, No. 2.* British Records Association, 145p. Refs.
Chapter IV, Persons (pp. 38-72), gives rules for indexing of individuals including the periods before 1750; cross-referencing also covered. Many illustrations. Thus, Van Gogh should be under "G", but Van Dyck under "V", and Lloyd George under "G".

17. INFLUENCE OF NAMES
(Includes DESTINY, MAGIC, and SUPERSTITION

[17.1] Beirne, Eric. (1972). *What do you say after you say Hello? The psychology of human destiny.* New York: Grove Press, 457p. Refs.
Pp. 77-82 describe the influence the name may have on the personality. Brief mention of Ikhnaton, Egyptian religious leader.

[17.2] Bouisson, Maurice. (1961). *Magic: Its history and principal rites.* New York: E. P. Dutton, 319p. Refs.
Pp. 101-109 deal with magical aspects of names from China, Egypt, and Israel, the Qabalah, Gnosticism, and Islam.

[17.3] Cavendish, Richard. (1983). Names. In Richard Cavendish (Ed.) *Man myth, & magic: The illustrated encyclopedia of mythology religion, and the unknown* (pp. 1940-1944). New ed., Yvonne Deutch, (Ed.). New York: Marshall Cavendish, 12 vol. Illus.
Review article on magic and superstition associated with the naming process and the power of the invocation of the name of God in Judaism and Christianity, and also gods in other religions.

[17.4] Clodd, Edward. (1920; 1968). *Magic in names and in other things.* Detroit: Singing Tree Press, 238p. Refs. (Originally published by Chapman & Hall in London in 1920).
Ch. 3 (pp. 27-156) is a wide-ranging survey of primitive naming prohibitions associated with magic. Included are the customs of some tribes in pronouncing the names of self, spouses, and relatives.

[17.5] Dienstfrey, Harris. (1983, Jun). Name calling. *Psychology Today*, p. 13.
Report on a survey of 165 individuals who had surnames consonant with their occupations to determine whether the surname had an effect on their choice of

occupation. None reported that it did. Respondents included: Hugh Law, an attorney; Joe Barber, a barber; etc.

[17.6] Hilarion. (1987). Channeled by M. B. Cooke. *Childlight: Parenting for the new age.* Queenville, Ont: Marcus Books, 156p.
Develops a system of showing that the sound of the name (1st) influences the personality of the individual. Letters of the alphabet described and analyzed for influence and meaning for 1000 names.

[17.7] Lipsitt, Lewis P. (1990). Name calling: The calling in a name. *Connecticut Onomastic Review, No. 3,* pp. 72-76.
Theorizes there may be some destiny in the names of some individuals. Examples C. C. Woodhull, a yacht broker, in Essex, CT; Allan J. Lightman, a laser specialist.

[17.8] Magic. (1991). *NewEncyBrit, 7,* 671-672.
P. 672 has a very brief mention of magic and names. Names were used by magicians to bring harm or good to people. In some societies, people bear 2 names, a real one and a secret one. Further, that "gods and spirits are commonly believed to have special magic names, known only to a chosen few."

[17.9] Model of civil rights memorial unveiled. (1988, July 30). *New York Times* (Nat), p. 7. Photo.
Maya Lin, who also designed the Vietnam War memorial said, "The name is one of the most magical ways to bring back a person."

[17.10] Noah, Timothy. (1986, Dec. 15). The other me. [Washington Diarist]. *New Republic, 195,* p. 42.
How sound and meaning of one's name affects others and self. Examples include: Winston Lord (ambassador to China), Sally Ride (astronaut), and the author himself.

[17.11] Power, Michael & Weinberg, Eugene. (1991). Cognomen syndrome: A pilot study. *Journal of Irreproducible Results, 36,* 24-25. Refs.
Light approach to individuals whose surnames relate to their occupation (Cognomen Syndrome). Among the 5 types suggested are: Direct, Lord Brain, a neurologist; Indirect, M. J. Mountain, a consulting geologist; and Contrary, Frank G. Butcher, a surgeon. 35+ Examples.

[17.12] Rubenstein, Carin. (1983, Jan.). Name calling. *Psychology Today, 17,* p. 13.
Related to the article by Dienstfrey [17.5], identifies 6 social scientists whose surnames are related to their occupation. Examples include Lawrence Wrightsman who teaches about psychology and the law and Peter Steinglass who deals with the married alcoholic.

[17.13] Ruthven, K. K. (1986). The disclosures of inscription: Ezra (Loomis) (West) Pound. *AUMLA, Journal of the Australasian Universities Modern Language Association, No. 66,* 159-178. Refs.
Systematic analysis of how each of the names influenced Pound and his writing.

[17.14] Sobel, Dava. (1982, Aug.). Fateful names. [Column]. *Omni,* p. 39.
Lewis Lipsitt, a psychologist at Brown University, believes that a surname is destiny. Examples include Harry Smiley, an orthodontist, and Mr. Post, a mailman.

[17.15] Wray, Herbert. (1982, Feb. 6). Names that work. *Science News,* p. 89.
Reaction to the research of Lipsitt [17.7] who has observed the effect of surname on occupation, example, Dr. Harry Smiley, Columbia University orthodontist.

18. JUNIOR and NAMES

[18.1] Cameron, Catherine. (1987). The trouble with junior: Father-naming, child abuse, and delinquency. *Sociology & Social Research, 71,* 200-203. Refs. Tables.
Father-named adolescents (whites, blacks, and Hispanics) in a home for delinquent minors were compared with a local high school sample. Results indicate that those in the home showed: (1) a higher percentage of those father-named and (2) a higher percentage of those abused named for fathers.

[18.2] D., T. R. (1976). What's in a name? *Coat of Arms, New Series, 2,* No. 97, 24.
Description of some difficulties of a genealogist. The princely house of Reuss named all males Heinrich. When one line totaled 100 Heinrichs, the numbering began again.

[18.3] Van Buren, Abigail. (1988, Dec. 31). Mistaken Identity. [Dear Abby]. *Evening Observer* [Dunkirk-Fredonia, NY], p. 14.
Comes down against the practice of a father naming a son after himself. A reader describes a "Junior" who was also a forger and made a great deal of legal trouble for the father.

[18.4] Yao, Blake. (1990). *Is being a junior a help or handicap?* State University of New York, College at Fredonia, 14p. Refs. Tables. (ERIC Documentation Reproduction Service No. ED 328 846).
Investigated mental illness and naming a child after the father. Birth records in Western New York showed that 19% of males were named after the father. However, "results from a Western New York psychiatric hospital failed to support Plank's hypothesis [87:18.7] that Jrs. have a higher rate of mental illness than the average population. However, there is a difference for affective disorders, i.e., the rate of affective disorders is higher for Jrs. than expected in the general population."

19. JUVENILE LEVEL: BOOKS and ARTICLES ON NAMES

[19.1] Bethers, Ray. (1966). *How did we get our names?* London: Macmillian, 46p. Illus.
For grade school children. Explains the origin of patronyms, influence of occupation, place, nickname, and miracle plays on surname. Also shows how foreign names were changed into English.

[19.2] Lee, Mary Price & Lee, Richard S. (1985). Illus. by Debora Weber. *Last names first: And some first names too.* Philadelphia: Westminster Press, 119p. Refs. Illus.
Systematic overview of the world of surnames. Includes nicknames, unusual names, and the names of spies.

[19.3] Pitt, Valerie. (1971). *Let's find out about names.* Illus. by Pat Grant Porter. New York: Franklin Watts, 48p.
Intro. to personal names and naming. For children in the lower grades.

[19.4] Rothman, Anne & Hicks, Kenneth. (1984). *Amy's book.* Wayne, PA: Banbury Books, [42] p. Illus.
Uses the name Amy to explain the naming process. Directed to the elementary school level. Gives different forms of the name. Describes some of those who bore the name or a variation.

[19.5] Rothman, Anne & Hicks, Kenneth. (1984). *Jason's book.* Wayne, PA: Banbury Books, [44] p. Illus.

Similar in style to *Amy's book* above. Gives historical background. Gives the story of Jason's Golden Fleece. Description of famous Jasons.

[19.6] Williams, Jay & Lubell, Winifred. (1962). *I wish I had another name*. New York: Atheneum, not paged, about 34p. Illus.
Rhymed text for imagined names for boys and girls from A to Z.

20. LAW AND NAMES

[20.1] Bugliari, Joseph B. (1958). Domestic relations: Change of minor's surname: Parental rights in a minor's surname. *Cornell Law Quarterly, 46,* 144-150. Refs.
Court decisions indicate that, "the father's *right* is predominant over the mother's *wishes,* but with the child's interest overriding both."

[20.2] Carlsson, Kathleen A. (1971). Surnames of married women and legitimate children. *New York Law Forum, 23,* 552-569. Refs.
Review of cases where a married woman had used her husband's 1st name. Points out there is no law for a woman to legally change her name at marriage. Discussion of cases where the husband has the right to choose the surname of a child; mothers of an illegitimate child.

[20.3] Cohen, Roger. (1991, July 19). Suit over novel's use of real name is dismissed. [Law]. *New York Times*, B7.
In Federal District Court, Judge Thomas C. Platt dismissed a suit by a professional musician who claimed that she had been defamed in a novel.

[20.4] Confronting jailed suspect with perpetrators's nickname was interrogation. *Criminal Law Reporter: Court Decisions, 40,* 2132-2133. Refs.
Report of a decision from the New Hampshire Supreme Court. A policeman used a nickname said to be that of a man who had committed a crime. The suspect was not warned but did answer to the nickname. Since there was no coercion, this admission was harmless error.

[20.5] Everts, Palmer W. (1953). When names are important. *Title News, 32,* 25-27.
Explanation of the legal term *idem sonans* "that the law excuses the bad spelling of a name if the word so spelled, sounds right." Examples, Jetta and Jetter. Another point is that the middle initial is important [in titles].

[20.6] Gregg, John M. (1957). The fictitious names act: Effective legislation or a nullity? *University of Pittsburgh Law Review, 19,* 132-144. Refs.
After reviewing legislation and court decisions in Pennsylvania from 1917 to 1957 concludes that the procedures are effective.

[20.7] Margolick, David. (1991, May 10). Don't be surprised if the next landmark ruling is 'Day v. Knight' or 'Dog v. Katz.' [At the Bar]. *New York Times*, p. B18.
Describes shift in fictitious names in lawsuits initiated by women from names such as Jane Roe to Emma G. (for Emma Goldman), Jane Liberty and Hope. Most of these names appear to be used in suits involving women's issues.

[20.8] Morris, Percy S. (1960). The middle initial. *Dicta* [Denver], 37, 361-367. Refs.
Discussion of problems of the Colorado law with regard to middle initial and middle name. Recommendation for legislative remedy.

[20.9] New appointee rules: OK to discriminate against people with 'non-Canadian' names. (1986, Nov.). *Canadian Human Rights Advocate, 2(11),* pp. 1, 8.

Nicolas Cliche of the Human Rights Tribunal ruled in a case brought by Jacques LeDeuff. LeDeuff was charged with a driving offense and was then checked out as an illegal immigrant since his name sounded "foreign." See Also: [9.9.4] and [9.9.2.1].

[20.10] Padrnos, Dennis. (1960). Fictitious names statute. *South Dakota Law Review*, 5, 133-139. Refs.
This type of statute requires a person or copartnership doing business under an assumed or fictitious name to file that information with a local official. Comment on the shortcomings of such a statute.

[20.11] Parents give child different surname. (1979, Feb. 23), *Evening Observer* [Dunkirk-Fredonia, NY], p. 13. (UPI).
Judge Samuel P. King, a federal district judge in Hawaii, ruled that Adolf Befurt and Alena Jech had the right to name their child Adrian Jebef, a name neither held.

[20.12] Parisi, Albert J. (1987, Oct. 11). State baby-naming proposal goes awry. *New York Times*, Sect 11, 1.
New Jersey proposed a law to allow unwed mothers to give the child their own surname, or with children born of artificial insemination, the husband's surname. Other liberalizations also suggested. Passage of the new law has been delayed.

[20.13] Probable cause: Nickname known to police. (1985, Apr.). *Arrest Law Bulletin*, 4, 3-4.
In a legal case, it was ruled that a known nickname is sufficient identification to arrest a suspect.

[20.14] Treece, James M. (1968). Some qualifications on everyman's absolute right to use his own name in business. *Texas Law Review, 46*, 436-452. Refs.
Discusses legal aspects of situations where an individual sells a business that bears his/her name then sets up a new business with a similar name.

20.1. LAW AND NAMES: *Name Change*
(See Also: 7. CHANGE OF NAME, 46.2. WOMEN AND NAMES: *Law and Legal Aspects*)

[20.1.1] Fight for a name. (1990, Nov. 5). *Newsweek*, pp. 71, 73.
Legal problems over a child's name when the parents divorce. Various arguments made.

[20.1.2] LawPak. (1989). *Ohio name change*. Clifton Heights, OH: LawPak, 50p. Illus.
Suggestions on how to change the name of an adult or a minor through court procedure in Ohio. A court procedure is advised over common law change. Tells when one is better off with a lawyer. Forms included.

[20.1.3] Scott, Timothy. (1989). *Changing your name legally in Massachusetts*. Springfield, MA: Tim Scott Publishing, 7p. (unnumbered).
Brief description of how to change the name of an adult or minor in Massachusetts. Forms included.

[20.1.4] Warda, Mark. (1988). *How to change your name in Florida*. Clearwater, FL: Sphinx Publishing, 36p. Refs.
Suggestions on how to change the name of an adult or a minor through court procedure in Florida. A court procedure is advised over common law change. Forms included.

[20.1.5] Weisenthal, Lee. (1956). Injunction against informal name change. *Wayne Law Review, 2,* 228-230. Refs.
Review of the legal status of mothers who, after divorce, change the surname of the child without agreement of the father.

[20.1.6] What's in a name. [Torts]. (1966, May 13). *Time,* pp. 81-82.
Courts are testing whether a person with the same or similar name to that of a prominent person can use the name in business. Some courts rules yes, some no. Example of a change to avoid difficulty was that of English actor Jimmy Stewart changed his name to Stewart Granger to avoid similarity with the American actor.

20.2. LAW AND NAMES: *Women and Surnames*
(See Also: 46.2 WOMEN AND NAMES)

[20.2.1] Contempt in court. (1988, Oct.). *Harper's Magazine,* p. 21.
Court transcript from the case in Pittsburgh where the judge did not like lawyers using the Ms. title. See Also [46.2.2].

[20.2.2] Daum, Roslyn Goodman. (1974). The right of married women to assert their own surnames. *University of Michigan Journal of Law Reform, 8,* 3-102. Refs.
Exhaustive systematic review of the law of name change, problems involved, legal avenues open, and the consequences of providing women with a choice of name. Special attention to Massachusetts.

[20.2.3] Lamber, Julia C. (1973). A married woman's surname: Is custom law? *Washington University Law Quarterly, Vol. 1973,* 779-819. Refs.
Careful analysis and comment on a number of cases dealing with a married woman's choice of surname. Many legal citations. Extensive state-by-state table showing applicable laws applying to different name situations such as, marriage, voting, and driver's license.

[20.2.4] Spencer, Margaret Eve. (1973). A woman's right to her name. *UCLA Law Review, 21,* 665-690. Refs.
Presents a number of arguments to support change in the common law rule that requires a woman to take her husband's name at marriage. This change would allow the woman to retain her maiden name at marriage.

[20.2.5] Tummon, Katherine. (1986). Re Paul and Wright: Children's surnames and the equality of married women. *Canadian Journal of Women & the Law, 1,* 547-551. Refs.
Involves the case of a couple in Ontario who were initially turned down when they wanted to give their son the wife's birth surname. On appeal, they were successful in demonstrating that the Vital Statistics Act violated the Canadian Charter of Rights & Freedom.

21. MIDDLE NAMES

[21.1] Barry, Herbert, III. (1987). Maternal identification and male bonding of some recent presidents of the United States. *Psychohistory News, 6,* 2.
Six of the 10 most recent presidents had middle names which were their mother's premarital surname. This may have expressed bisexual conflict as opposed to presidents who did not take their mother's surname and were more closely bonded to wife and children.

[21.2] Donovan, Mary. (1965, May 13). What's in a name. [Letter to the Editor]. *Senior Scholastic,* pp. 28.
An inquiry on Spanish and Chinese middle names is answered by the editor.

[21.3] Joubert, Charles E. (1985). Factors related to individuals' attitudes toward their names. *Psychological Reports, 57,* 983-986. Refs.
University students rated their 1st, middle, and last names on scales and also answered other questions on names. Among other results, they reported liking middle names less.

22. MISCELLANEOUS ASPECTS OF NAMES

[22.1] Behrendt, R. (1973, Apr.). Who's who in international chaos. *Esquire,* pp. 118-119.
Lists about 200 names of prominent people. These names, mostly in pairs, can often be confused with one another due to similarity of either 1st or surname or occupation, examples, John Huston, John Ford; Patti Page, Janis Page, Ann Page.

[22.2] Bernard, Thomas L. (1993). Names, nationality, and the incongruity factor. In E. Wallace McMullen (Ed.) *Names new and old: Papers of the Names Institute* (pp. 319-322). Refs. Table. Madison, NJ: Privately published.
It is expected that surnames in the US will show ethnic diversity. Surprising as it might seem to some, other countries also show ethnic diversity in surnames. Examples: Mitterand, the French leader has a name with German roots; Fujimori, the Peruvian leader has a Japanese surname. Other names given.

[22.3] Boom town. (1983, Apr. 11). *Time,* p. 21.
The mayor of San Francisco signed a bill requiring candidates for public office to use their legal names after a transvestite ran under the name *Sister Boom Boom.* Other candidates were James Bond Zero and Crown Prince Arcadia.

[22.4] Bracey, Gerald W. (1985, May). More on the naming of offspring [Research]. *Phi Delta Kappan, 66,* p. 653. Drawing.
Report on Ford, Masters, & Miura [87:41.17] which reported no correlations between children's academic and social performance and grades.

[22.5] Brown, W. P. (1978). A cross-national comparison of English-language category norms. *Language & Speech, 21,* 50-67. Refs.
12 categories of speech norms in Britain and the US were compared. One category was female names; a 2nd, male names. In the British norms, Margaret, Elizabeth, and Ian occurred significantly more often. In the US, it was Sue, Bob, and Bill.

[22.6] Burnham, David. (1984, Apr. 17). When an ethnic name makes a voter fair game. *New York Times,* p. A18. Photo.
How Frank L. Tobe of Washington, DC develops lists of ethnic voters for political campaigns.

[22.7] Clay, Grady. (1992). Names on the wall: The public impact of the Vietnam veterans memorial. *Names,* 40, 321-324. Photo.
Description of the selection process which was "no-name" (the designer's name was not mentioned). Reactions of some viewers at the memorial.

[22.8] Cornog, Martha. (1987). Names for sexual and body parts: Regularities in "Personal" naming behavior. *Publications of the North Central Name Society,* No. 2, 133-151. Refs.

Based upon a collection of names from men and women. Explains and gives examples of various types of name, examples, teknonymic, a penis is called Hank Junior by a man whose name is Hank; human-type, a woman calls her vulva Sophia after Sophia Loren. These names serve functions for: (1) jokes, (2) a secret language for lovers, and (3) make it easier for the public at large to talk about sexual behavior.

[22.9] Davidian, H., & Naraghi, M. M. (1978). Assessment of difficulties encountered in psychiatric follow-up studies. *Acta Psychiatrica Scandinavica, 57,* 290-298. Refs. Tables.
Reports a follow-up study on 107 depressed patients. Only 45 were found and interviewed. Among the reasons for untraceability were: use of several names and nicknames. Recommendation for having complete and correct names.

[22.10] Diament, Henri. (1986). Dangerous christenings: The case of code names of French secret agents in the Second World War. *Names, 34,* 30-47. Refs.
The codenames (cryptonyms) used by French secret agents made errors that could lead to detection. Discussion of several types of error with illus. Examples include: Lieutenant Lheureux, codename Joie (obvious connection) and André Rossignol, codename Pigeon (rossignol *bird* in French).

[22.11] Eckler, A. Ross. (1986, May 19). Gary Gray, meet Edna Dean. *Word Ways, No. 2,* 109-110.
Used telephone directories to measure predicted vs. actual occurrence of 8 male transposable names such as GARY GRAY and 8 female names. Also lists approx. 50 other transposable names including: Ruby Bury, Elsa Sale, and Claus Lucas.

[22.12] Eutychus. (1986, Nov. 7). [Initial Impressions]. *Christianity Today, 30,* p. 7.
Comment in a light vein on having the "right" initials.

[22.13] Flaumenhaft, A. S. (1970, June). Men of letters. *Harvest Years,* 22-23.
Story of an encounter of the author with a lady and the discussion of the distinction of longer names.

[22.14] Freeman, William M. (1957). *The big name.* New York: Printers' Ink Books, 213p.
Describes the advantages of testimonials using names of prominent figures in the promotion of products and services. Many names referred to including Humphrey Bogart for cigarette lighters, Mitch Miller for Thom McAn shoes, and President Eisenhower for homburg hats.

[22.15] Gross, John. (1974, June 7). Naming names. *Times Literary Supplement,* p. 610.
Explanation of why the *Times Literary Supplement* was abandoning anonymous reviews. One major reason: personal accountability.

[22.16] Holloway, David. (1978, Apr. 22). Reading all about yourself. *Daily Telegraph* [London], p. 13.
Comment on the interest that people have in looking up their own entries or those of acquaintances in directories.

[22.17] Meadow, Kathryn P. (1977). Name signs as identity symbols in the deaf community. *Sign Language Studies, 16,* 237-245. Refs.
"A *name sign* is a formalized gesture referring to an individual"s proper name." Data from 371 deaf people showed by whom their names were assigned: peers, 43%; parents, 30%; teachers, 13%. This pattern is in contrast to that of the hearing population. 45%

of the peer-conferred names were negative. Suggestions made for improving the situation.

[22.18] Meeter, Glenn. (1986). Names and naming in fiction and life: A personal onomastics odyssey. *Publications of the North Central Name Society, No. 1,* 117-139.
A novelist describes the similarities and differences between naming characters in a novel and naming his own daughters.

[22.19] Mors, Otto. (1951). Bahaya twin ceremonies. *Anthropos, 46,* 442-452.
The Bahaya, a tribe of about 350,000, live on the west coast of Lake Victoria in Tanzania. P. 444 describes naming ceremonies associated with twins. Parents get special names as do the twins, and subsequent siblings.

[22.20] *PhoneDisc USA.* (1992). Marblehead, MA: Digital Directory Assistance, 3 CD-ROM discs, 2 residential, 1 business.
Contains lists of millions of telephone subscribers. Lists can be searched (and downloaded) by surname and by location.

[22.21] Rennick, Robert M. (1969). Successive name-changing: A popular theme in onomastic folklore and literature. *New York Folklore Quarterly, 25,* 119-228. Refs.
Discussion and comment on several folklore stories of successive name-changing. All more-or-less similar to the one about a man named *Levy* who changed his name to *Sullivan,* then a 2nd change to *Kilpatrick* with the explanation that he could say that his previous name was *Sullivan.*

[22.22] Room, Adrian. (1986). *Dictionary of translated names and titles.* London: Routledge & Kegan Paul, 460p.
Has about 4000 entries of English names or title followed by equivalents in French, German, Italian, Spanish, and Russian. Entries include personal names along with placenames. Personal names include: Michelangelo, Elijah, Cicero, and William the Silent. Although most items are literary or place, there is a listing of about 75 1st names, thus Stephen is Etienne in French, Stefan in German, Stefano in Italian, and Estaban in Spanish.

[22.23] Room, Adrian. (1987). *Dictionary of coin names.* London & New York: Routledge & Kegan Paul, 250p. Refs.
Contains about 1500 entries for coin names, a number of which refer to individuals. Examples include: an *antonianus,* a Roman silver coin named after Marcus Aurelius Antoninus; a *giulio,* an Italian silver coin named after Pope Julius II; and a *maria,* a Spanish silver coin named after the wife of Charles II of Spain.

[22.24] Sanford, A. J., Moar, K., & Garrod, S. (1988). Proper names as controllers of discourse focus. *Language & Speech, 31,* 43-56. Refs.
Three experiments at the University of Glasgow indicate that named characters are a major factor in focus control. Specifically, named characters are more likely to be used in continuation stories and references to named characters are read more rapidly.

[22.25] Stuart, Jesse. (1962, July 28-Aug. 4). Are we a nation of digits? It won't be long before we have numbers instead of names. [Speaking Out]. *Saturday Evening Post,* pp. 8, 11.
Autobiographical. Describes frustrating experiences in daily life where one's assigned numbers seem more important than one's name. Mentions the army, Social Security, bank, and others.

[22.25A] Sunners, William. (1951). *How to coin winning names.* New York: ARCO, 156p.

Directed at those entering commercial naming contests for products, etc. One table has approx. 900 male & 800 female 1st names with meanings. Another table has 1600 and 1800 meanings with names, i.e., Wind Place = Keith; Ancient = Priscilla. Table of reversible names; list of gods & goddesses.

[22.26] Swift, Jonathan Z., & Buxton, Richard G. A. (1991). Relationships of similarity. [Myth & Mythology]. *NewEncyBrit, 24,* 726. Refs.
Brief general remarks on human names coming from animals and animal names from humans. Caution urged, however, in interpretations.

[22.27] Tabori, Paul. (1961). *The art of folly.* Philadelphia: Chilton, 259p.
Pp. 151-160 are devoted to the chapter, "What's in a Name?" The focus is fashions in names from several countries, especially France, examples, *Victoire Constitution Robert, Plein d'amour pour la patrie Machol.* Also, some names apparently related to destiny, example, "Mrs. Rum of Chicago divorced her husband for drunkenness and recovered her maiden name which was Miss Cork." (p. 158).

[22.28] Walls, R. M. (1969, Oct.). The Bible has a name for it. *Harvest Years, Vol. 9,* p. 45.
Story of how a family gave a "help" to the Bible as a way of selecting the proper name for a son.

[22.29] Weissenburger, Fred D., & Loney, Jan. (1975). More on the "alphabetic neurosis." *Psychology in the Schools, 12,* 215-218. Refs.
Using sample of 1st and 6th graders in Iowa found no relationship between alphabetic position of surname and age, sex, achievement, intelligence, general adjustment, self-esteem, or impulse control.

[22.30] Westermann, Claus. (1991). Sacred kingship. *NewEncyBrit, 26,* 988-993. Refs.
Brief entry on p. 991 describes throne names where in ancient Africa, Mesopotamia, and Egypt, the king received a throne name on coronation.

23. NAMING PROCESS: *Historical Patterns*

[23.1] Akenson, Donald H. (1984). Why the accepted estimates of the ethnicity of the American people, 1790, are unacceptable. *William & Mary Quarterly, 41,* 102-119. Refs. Tables.
Critical evaluation of the ACLS- (American Council of Learned Societies) AHS (American Historical Society Report) by Howard Frederick Barker [Smith:3048]. Used name analysis to identify ethnicity. Reference to work of the McDonalds [23.12]. Seriously questions the methodology of the ACLS report which extrapolated from what was thought to be representative names to estimates of ethnic population.

[23.2] Akenson, Donald H. (1984). Reply. *William & Mary Quarterly, 41,* 125-129. Refs.
Reply to Purvis [23.17]. Specifically criticizes the estimates of the German population of Pennsylvania using surnames.

[23.3] Akenson, Donald H. (1984). Communications. *William & Mary Quarterly, 41,* 681-682. Refs.
Reply to Landsman [23.8]. Accepts some of his views on ethnicity.

[23.4] Deas, Anne Simons. (1978). *Recollections of the Ball family of South Carolina and the Comingtee plantation.* Charleston, SC: South Carolina Historical Society, 195p. (Copyright 1909, no publisher listed).
Analysis of family records (pp. 184-189) shows that a small number of names were often used. For men, these were John, William, Elias, or Isaac; for women, Elizabeth, Anne, Eleanor, and Mary.

[23.5] Eichler, Ernst. (1990). Onomastics in the German Democratic Republic: Results and present state. *Proceedings of the 16th ICOS, Laval University, Quebec, 1987,* pp. 239-244. Refs.
Onomastics in the GDR developed as an independent branch of linguistics. Description of the roles of proper names in various functions.

[23.6] Kolb, Avery E. (1974). *The grand-families of America, 1776-1976.* Baltimore: Gateway Press, 103p. Refs. Maps.
Traces with maps 30+ selected surnames to England, France, Germany, and other countries and shows where they tended to settle in the US at the time of the Revolution. These surnames include: Clark, Lee, Anderson, Nelson, and Campbell. Tables show the ranks of the top 50 names in 1776 and 1976; most common names in regions.

[23.7] Kolb, Avery E. (1974). The mystery of the "unassigned" New Englanders. *National Genealogical Society Quarterly, 62,* 265-269. Refs.
The First Census of 1790 shows that a 5th to a 4th of the New England respondents did not identify their ancestry. Using surname analysis, these people were traced to the lower West Country and the Yorkshire Ridings of England.

[23.8] Landsman, Ted. (1984). Communications. *William & Mary Quarterly, 41,* 680-681. Refs.
Responding to Akenson [23.2], the McDonalds [23.12], and Purvis [23.17], criticizes surname projections and ports of departure for the US as measures of ethnicity. Asks for definition of ethnicity.

[23.9] Lavender, A. D. (1988). Hispanic given names in five United States cities: Onomastics as a research tool in ethnic-identity. *Hispanic Journal of Behavioral Sciences, 10,* 105-125. Refs. Tables.
Examination of the naming patterns in 5 Hispanic communities (Miami, Tampa, San Antonio, Denver, and Albuquerque). Tables show the top 20 male and top 20 female names in each community. Name forms are classified as bicultural, Spanish, or English. Results support the bicultural theory of adjustment.

[23.10] Lavender, Abraham D. (1989). United States ethnic groups in 1790: Given names as suggestions of ethnic identity. *Journal of American Ethnic History, 9,* 36-66. Refs. Tables.
Uses an index *TEN* based upon 8 traditional English Names, John, William, Thomas, Richard, Robert, James, Henry, and George to place ethnic groups on a continuum of distance from traditional English culture. Groups were: English, Scots, Welsh, French, German, etc. While supportive of previous general conclusions on ethnic identity, the study of 1st names suggests some reexamination of the current literature.

[23.11] Logue, Larry M. (1987). Modernization arrested: Child naming and the family in a Utah town. *Journal of American History, 74,* 131-138. Refs. Table.
Used records of St. George, a small settlement in southwest Utah to examine Mormon naming practices in the 19th cent. vs. general American. Results show increase in naming sons after fathers by Mormons. This is interpreted as helping to provide for more family continuity in the face of severe pressures.

[23.12] McDonald, Forrest, & McDonald, Ellen Shapiro. (1980). The ethnic origins of the American people, 1790. *William & Mary Quarterly, 37,* 179-199. Refs. Tables.
Extensive discussion of the methodological flaws in the work of Barker & Hansen (1931) Annual Report of the American Historical Association [Smith:3048] where surnames were used to estimate ethnic origin. Reexamination of the data shows that the estimates were distorted. Revised figures show a stronger Celtic influence in the South. Many surnames listed and commented on.

[23.13] McDonald, Forrest, & McDonald, Ellen Shapiro. (1984). Commentary. *William & Mary Quarterly, 41,* 129-135. Refs.
Responses to Purvis [23.17] and Akenson [23.1].

[23.14] McDonald, Forrest & McDonald, Ellen Shapiro. (1984). Reply. *William & Mary Quarterly, 41,* 682-683. Refs.
Reply to Landsman [23.8]. Defends name analysis as only one tool of historical analysis.

[23.15] Merritt, Jesse. (1956). Long Island family names. *New York Folklore Quarterly, 12,* 125-126.
Gives a rhymed muster roll of approx. 75 surnames of men recruited for sea duty from Long Island villages in 1814 for the crew of a ship in operations against the British. Includes: Griffin, Snedecor, Halsey, Penny, and Payne.

[23.16] Otto, Julie Helen. (1994). Stratford-area examples of some personal names. *Nexus* [Boston], *11,* 28-50. Refs.
Data from the Stratford, CT area prior to 1800. Listing of individuals with citations of individuals with these 1st names: Abel, Asahel, Beulah, Diantha, Huldah, Jehiel, and Zadok.

[23.17] Purvis, Thomas L. (1984). The European ancestry of the United States population, 1790. *William & Mary Quarterly, 41,* 85-101. Refs.
Historical approach. Contains evaluations of a number of studies dealing with European ancestry which relied on surname analysis to measure ethnicity. Surname lists are given.

[23.18] Purvis, Thomas L. (1984). Commentary. *William & Mary Quarterly, 41,* 119-125. Refs. Tables.
Disagrees with conclusions of Akenson [23.1]. Defends his own methodology.

[23.19] Rennick, Robert M. (1985). Percy Scholes and W. Fraser Mitchell as critics of Bardsley's *Curiosities of Puritan nomenclature. Bulletin of the Illinois Name Society, 3(Spring-Summer),* 11-26. Refs.
From scholarly evidence concludes that the so-called Puritan names were never as common on either side of the Atlantic as Bardsley [Smith:725] seems to have indicated.

[23.20] Stewart, George R. (1954). *American ways of life.* New York: Doubleday, 312p.
Chap. 10 (pp. 204-227, Personal Names, provides an introductory historical view of American names from Jamestown to recent times. Fig. shows popular 1st names of Harvard and Princeton grads from 1780-1840.

24. NAMING PROCESS: *Patterns and Practices*

[24.1] Alia, Valerie. (1984). Would a rose by any other name smell at all? *Canadian Woman Studies/Les Cahiers de la Femme, 5(3),* 86-88. Refs.
Wide-ranging discussion of the importance of naming practices, especially for women.

[24.2] Bloch, Marc (Leopold) (Benjamin). (1961). *Feudal society*. Chicago: University of Chicago Press; London: Routledge Kegan Paul, 499p. Refs.
Pp. 45-46 describe Scandinavian influence on names before 1066 lasting in Lincolnshire and Yorkshire until the 14th cent. and in Lancashire until the end of the Middle Ages. Pp. 137-141 give some information on Germanic naming processes showing influence of mother's name for males as well as father's. Two modes of transmission shown by Joan of Arc who was known as both Jeanne d'Arc and Jeanne Romée. D'Arc was the father's surname; Romée, the mother's.

[24.3] Bouchard, Constance B. (1988). Patterns of women's names in royal lineages, ninth-eleventh centuries. *Medieval Prosopography, 9(Spring)*, 1-32. Refs. Figs.
A survey of naming patterns of the Carolingians, the Ottonians, the Capetians, and the Rudolphians shows that the "kings named their daughters for their own rather than their wives' relatives until the end of the tenth century." However, there was no general rule for naming.

[24.4] Bouchard, Constance B. (1988). The migration of women's names in the upper nobility, ninth-twelfth centuries. *Medieval Prosopogrophy, 9(Autumn)*, 1-19. Refs. Figs.
Follows from Bouchard above. Uses the names Beatrix, Hadwidis, Mathilda, Gerberge, Constance, Gisela, and Judith to show that men of the 11th-12th cents. accepted a pattern of naming their daughters after their wives' relatives.

[24.5] Brown, Richard D. (1976). *Modernization: The transformation of American life, 1600-1865*. New York: Hill & Wang, 229p.
Describes shift in traditional family naming patterns to more individualistic patterns around 1800 (p. 102) in Northern states.

[24.6] Charles, Lucille Hoerr. (1951). Drama in first-naming ceremonies. *Journal of American Folklore, 64*, 11-35.
Comprehensive, systematic presentation of 1st-naming ceremonies in 100s of primitive societies all over the world.

[24.7] Duckert, Audrey. (1963). Notes and queries. *Names, 11*, 196-198.
General on naming, dissatisfaction with one's name, change of name.

[24.8] Duncan, R. M. (1963). A note on the naming of infants. *Names, 11*, 134-135.
Reaction to Myron Brender [87:25.2.3]. Suggests that reference should be made to the use of mother's birth name for middle name of 1st-born child. Other comments.

[24.9] Furstenberg, Frank F. Jr., & Talvitie, Kathy Gordon. (1980). Children's names and paternal claims. *Journal of Family Issues, 1*, 31-57. Refs. Tables.
404 pregnant teen-agers, mostly African American, and unmarried at time of conception, were interviewed beginning in 1966-67 over a 5 year period. one hypothesis was that naming a child after a family member represents a commitment. "Half the boys inherited either their father's 1st name, middle name, or both given names." Some children bore the father's surname even though the parents did not marry.

[24.10] Harder, Kelsie B. (1993). Literary names mainstreamed as given names. In E. Wallace McMullen (Ed.) *Names new and old: Papers of the Names Institute* (pp. Refs. 231-242). Madison, NJ: Privately published.
Comment and discussion on names from literature that influenced selection of 1st names. Approx. 70 listed with sources. Examples Diana < Diana Vernon in Scott's *Rob Roy*; Belinda < Pope's *Rape of the Lock*.

[24.11] Lebell, Sharon. (1988). *Naming ourselves, naming our children*. Freedom, CA: Crossing Press, 102p. Refs.

After a review of current naming practices suggests that children of Sharon Lebell and John Loudon be given names following the pattern for girls of a 1st name, an optional 2nd name, father's surname, and mother's surname; boys, 1st name, optional 2nd name, mother's surname, and father's surname; as, Kyle Dylan Loudon Lebell and Joshua Lebell Loudon.

[24.12] Lieberson, Stanley & Bell, Eleanor O. (1992). Children's first names: An empirical study of social taste. *American Journal of Sociology, 98,* 511-554. Refs. Tables.
Analysis of birth records in New York State 1973-1985 suggests that the power of cultural themes in naming patterns shows "that long-standing stereotyped role assignments still have a subtle but major effect on the naming process." Education and race modify these patterns. Focus on differences in the educational level of the mothers as a factor. Sex differences in name phonemes discussed. Among the extensive tables are listings of the most popular names by sex and race.

[24.13] Lurie, Alison. (1983, Feb. 20). My name or yours. *Observer* [London], p. 27
Reacting to feminist solutions for naming practices, suggests that sons be given fathers' surnames; daughters, mothers'.

[24.14] Marty, Martin E. (1985, Feb. 5-13). Heritage in names [M. E. M. O.]. *Christian Century*, p. 167.
A famous writer describes his pleasure at his 1st granddaughter being 1st-named in memory of her grandmother and being middle-named with her mother's family surname.

[24.15] Mothers explain choice of babies' names. (1962, July). *Today's Health, 40,* p. 55.
Responses to a nation-wide survey of mothers by diaper services show, among other findings, that: 38% named a child after a relative, usually the father for boys, no "Juniors" were used; 24% used names that were modern, different, and unusual; 80% were given middle names. Of these, only 4% were family names.

[24.16] Newman, Michael. (1975, Mar. 16). What's in a name. [The Guest Word]. *New York Times Book Review*, p. 39.
Comment on the author's names, others in his family, writers, and others.

[24.17] Powell, Mary. (1990). More about Southeast Asia names (and humility). [Letters]. *Young Children, 45,* 80.
Reply in response to Morrow [9.40.17]. Agrees with his point "Respect the child's choice of name."

[24.18] Rack, Philip. (1982). *Race, culture, and mental disorder.* London: Tavistock, 305p. Refs.
Description of the effect of hospital interaction in England on people from Asia. One aspect being differences in naming patterns (pp. 202-203). Appendix 2 (pp. 262-263) contains brief descriptions of Muslim, Sikh, and Hindu naming patterns.

[24.19] Sommerville, C. John. (1982). *The rise and fall of childhood.* Beverly Hills, CA: Sage, 254p. Refs.
Puritanism (p. 109) brought in recognition of people as individuals. This meant expansion of the repertoire of 1st names (Ebenezer, Ichabod) and intro. of phrase names (Praise-God, Sin-Deny).

[24.20] Trippett, Frank. (1978, Aug. 14). The game of the name. [Time Essay]. *Time,* pp. 66-67.
General comment on naming.

[24.21] Tylor, E(dward B(urnett). (1889). On a method of investigating the development of institutions: Applied to laws of marriage and descent. *Journal of the Anthropological Institute of Great Britain & Ireland, 18,* 245-273. Refs. Fig.
Pp. 248-250 give some information on teknonymy as practiced by the Bechuana in Africa and people in India.

[24.22] Tylor, Edward Burnett (1903?; 1958). *Religion in primitive cultures.* New York: Harper (Torchbooks), vol.1, 416p; vol. 2, 539p. Refs. (Originally published as Chs. 11-19 of *Primitive culture* by John Murray of London).
Vol. 1, pp. 254-255 describe naming of children with numbers by Australian aborigines. Vol. 2 has a description of naming customs in New Zealand and among the Cheremiss in Russia (p. 91). Pp. 516-518 also describe various naming ceremonies including those of the Jakun [now Malaysia] and the Maori of New Zealand.

[24.22A] van Gennep, Arnold. (1960). *The rites of passage.* Trans. by Monika B. Visedom & Gabrielle L. Caffee. Chicago: University of Chicago Press, 198p. Refs.
Pp. 62-63 have some general comments on the function of naming including this statement, "When a child is named, he is both individualized and incorporated in society." (p. 62).

[24.23] Walton, Eliza Charles. (1987, Feb. 1). Naming the living to honor the dead. *New York Times,* Sec. 23, p. 30.
The satisfaction of naming a child after a dead brother.

[24.24] Werner, M. A. (1967). Names, Baptismal. *New Catholic Encyclopedia, 10,* 200. Refs.
Canon law establishes the "right of parents to select the name, but the obligation of giving the name is the pastor's."

25. NAMING PROCESS: *Theoretical and Linguistic Aspects*

[25.1] Carruthers, Peter. (1983). Understanding names. *Philosophical Quarterly, 33,* 19-36. Refs.
Argues that proper names do not have sense, that there is a difference between opaque and transparent names.

[25.2] Christoph, Ernst-Michael. (1987). *Studien zur Semantik von Eigennamen: Ein Beitrag zur allgemeinen und deutschen* [Studies on the semantics of proper names: A contribution to general and German onomastics]. *Namenkundliche Informationen, Beiheft 10.* Leipzig: Karl Marx University, 131p. Refs. German. English summary (pp. 123-126).
Sets up a system of 45 *semes* (classifications) for proper names. Thus, the name Maria Therese Margarethe Henkel, née Wiegand involves several semes in a hierarchy. Hundreds of refs., mostly in German.

[25.3] Christoph, Ernst-Michael. (1991). *Eigennamen als Bestandteile des Lexikons? Ein Diskussionsbeitrag zur Semantikforschung in der Onomasktik.* [Proper names as special items of the lexicon: A discussion of the semantic contribution of semantic research to onomastics]. *Zeitschrift für Phonetik, Sprachwissenschaft, und Kommunikationsforschung, 44,* 357-371. Refs. Figs. German. English abstract.
Presentation of a hierarchical system involving several types of names including personal.

[25.4] Hahn, E. Adelaide. (1969). Naming constructions in some Indo-European languages. *Philological Monographs of the American Philological Association,* No. 27. Cleveland OH: Case-Western Reserve Press, 222p. Refs.

Scholarly approach to the similarities of the word for name and its usage in Indo-European languages. Covers Hittite, Indo-Iranian (Indic, Iranian), Greek, Latin, Germanic (Gothic and Old English), Celtic (Gaelic and Britannic), and Tocharian.

[25.5] Leys, O. (1971). Sociolinguistic aspects of namegiving patterns. *Onoma,* 18, 448-455. Refs.
Discussion of sociolinguistic factors in naming. They are: masculine v. feminine, familiar v. non-familiar, urban v. rural, higher v. lower economic class, age, education, and ideological.

[25.6] McClure, Edmund. (1883). Some notes on personal names, chiefly those of the British Isles. *Notes & Queries, 6th series, 7,* 241-242; 381-383. [Mentions that a further note was to be forthcoming. No additional note was found after searching].
Explanation of how Western names came originally from the Indo-European language to Greek, Welsh, Germanic, Slavonic, and other langs. Many examples.

[25.7] Nicolaisen, W(ilhelm) F. H. (1976), Words as names. *Onoma,* 20, 142-163. Refs.
Uses personal and placenames to distinguish 3 levels of meaning of names: (1) lexical, (2), associative, and (3) onomastic.

[25.8] Nicolaisen, W(ilhelm) F. H. (1986). Naming and abstraction. In Edward Callary (Ed.), *From Oz to the Onion Patch* (pp. 11-26), *Publications of the North Central Name Society, Number 1.*
Critique of the views of 4 philosophers on names: Socrates, Hobbes, John Stuart Mill, and Russell. Calls for an independent *onomastic philosophy* or an *onomastic theory of names.*

[25.9] Pulgram, Ernst. (1959). Name, class name, noun. *Die Sprache, 5,* 165-171. Refs.
Distinguishes between a name, a class name, and a noun.

[25.10] Sanneh, L. O. (1989, Oct. 4). Naming and the act of faith. *Christian Century, 106,* p. 875.
Uses a quote from St. Paul (II Tim. 1:5) to emphasize the religious aspects of naming.

[25.11] Wescott, Roger W. (1984; 1993). The phonology of proper names. *Geolinguistics, 10,* 37-43. Refs. Also in E. Wallace McMullen (Ed.) *Names new and old: Papers of the Names Institute* (pp. 301-310). Refs. Madison, NJ: Privately published. [The article was 1st published in *Geolinguistics* in 1984 and reprinted in 1993].
Description and explanation of the types of phonic changes that take place with names. Examples, *regressive additive* (Ann < Ann or Anna), *word-medial* insertions (Thompson < Tom's son), *consonant deletion* (Watt < Walter), and others.

26. NICKNAMES

[26.1] Anderson, Chester. (1978). The Banana Slug or Charlie the Slug. [Miscellany]. *Maledicta, 2,* p. 278.
A man in California has these terms for a nickname.

[26.2] Becker, C. M. (1989). "Tardy George" and "Extra Billy": Nicknames in the Civil War. *Civil War History, 35,* 302-310. Refs.
Intro. and comments on nicknames of at least 150 Civil War figures. Many of these are probably not seen in other lists. Nicknames include: King of Spades for Robert E. Lee

(since he made the troops dig so many trenches), Gentle Anna for Ann Etheridge, a Michigan nurse, and Father Nepture for Gideon Welles, Secretary of the Navy.

[26.3] Bell, Robert A., Buerkel-Rothfuss, Nancy L., & Gore, Kevin E. (1987). "Did you bring the yarmulke for the cabbage patch kid?": The idiomatic communication of young lovers. *Human Communication Research, 14,* 47-67. Refs.
100 couples were tested on various measures. Among the aspects of communication were nicknames invented for each other and for others. Included are: Pookers, Special K, and Long Duck Dong.

[26.4] Bertrand, Gary L. (1985). Cajun nicknames and other words. In Gerald L. Cohen (Ed.) *Studies in slang, Part I* (pp. 68-70). Frankfurt am Main: Peter Lang. Refs.
Previously appeared in *Comments on Etymology,* 1984, *13*(7-8), 9-10. Cajun nicknames from the Lake Charles area of Louisiana in the early part of the cent. About 10 examples including Teedon ("small don"), TiCrotte ("small excrement"), and Croppo ("little frog").

[26.5] Birnbach, Lisa. (1980). *The official preppy handbook.* New York: Workman, 224p.
P. 12 shows the 12 most popular nicknames (with origins) for boys, and for girls. Included are Skip, Chip, and Kip for males; Muffy, Buffy, and Bootsy for females.

[26.6] Blakely, Mike. (1983, July). Western nicknames. [Western Camp Tales]. *American West, 26,* 24-25.
Description of about 30 characters out of the Old West and how they got their nicknames. Included are: "Flat Nose" Curry, "Black Face" Bryant, and "Deacon Jim" Miller.

[26.7] Christiansen, Norman Henrik. (1986). A preliminary contribution to an understanding of the use of playfulness in family therapy. *DissAbstrIntl, 46,* 1517A.
Nicknames were one aspect of playfulness studied.

[26.8] Christodoulou, G. N., Gargoulas, A., Papaloukas, A., Marinopouluo, A., & Rabavilas A. D. (1979). Peptic ulcer in childhood: Psychological disorders. *Psychotherapy & Psychosomatics, 32,* 279-301. Refs.
In a study of children with peptic ulcers, it was reported that 7 of the 30 had nicknames. None of the controls did. No mention of examples or type of nickname.

[26.9] Clark, Thomas L. (1986). Noms de felt: Names in gambling. *Names, 34,* 11-29. Refs.
Differentiates between nicknames (derived childhood or background, Chip, Pub, Chicago Mike) and monickers (from professional activity, gambling, Wizard, Suitcase Murphy, Door Card Charlie). Categorized 58 names from a tournament. Pen names also described as well as types of players (C-Note Charlie, one who uses $100 bills; Jonah, one who brings bad luck).

[26.10] Connolly, Michael Coleman. (1988). The Irish longshoremen of Portland, Maine, 1880-1923. *DissAbstrIntl, 49,* 3116A. Includes extensive list of nicknames.

[26.11] De Sola, Ralph. (1982). *Crime dictionary.* New York: Facts on File, 219p. Refs.
Contains approx. 7500 items, possibly 100+ onomastic items, including: Abu Ammar, Yasir Arafat's pseudonym; Acid King, ex-Harvard professor Timothy Leary; and "marihuana-filled brownies," Alice B. Toklas.

[26.12] Dickison, Roland. (1990). Naming procedures for outlaws. *Proceedings of the 17th ICOS, Helsinki, 13-18 Aug. 1990, 1,* 273-275. Refs.
Charles Boles known as Black Bart was a famous California stage coach robber who was active in the 1870s and 1880s. People have been puzzled about how he got the name. After checking numerous possibilites (named after the famous Welsh pirate of the same name, dress, appearance, or habits), concludes that the name came from a science fiction story (now lost) of that period.

[26.13] Dignowity, Hartman. (1927). Nicknames in Texas oil fields. *Texas and Southwestern Lore, 6,* 98-101.
Nicknames of oil men of Borger in the Panhandle and McCamey in the Big Lake district. Listing of approx. 60 nicknames, many with stories behind them. Some are ironic: "Mercury" was slow; "Little Bill, a man over 6 ft. tall. Some other names are: "Tattoo Pete," "Pay Day Slim," and "Midnight Pete."

[26.14] Duckert, Audrey R. (1963). Nicknames. [Notes and Queries]. *Names, 11,* 74-76. General on nicknames. Examples from history, crime, sports, academe, the military, and music.

[26.15] Franzwa, Gregory M. (1967). *The story of Old Ste. Genevieve.* St. Louis: Patrice Press, 169p.
Ste. Genevieve is an old Mississippi River town (pop. 4450) 65 miles south of St. Louis. Pp. 32-33 give about 20 nicknames of residents including: Boob, Dizzy, and Toothpick. Nicknames are used to the face.

[26.16] Freestone, Basil. (1990). *Harrap's book of nicknames and their origins: A comprehensive guide to personal nicknames in the English-speaking World.* London: Harrap, 371p.
Intro. Approx. 5000 entries. Nicknames given and explained. Index of true names. Examples include: Wrong-Way Corrigan, Yogi, and the Yorkshire Ripper.

[26.17] Garraty, John A. (1986, Dec.). 101 things every college graduate should know about American history. *American Heritage,* p. 24ff. Illus.
Items 35-54 give the nicknames of men prominent in American history. These include: His Rotundity (John Adams), The Pathfinder (John C. Fremont), and The Little Giant (Stephen A. Douglas).

[26.18] Gasque, Thomas J. (1990). Some other words for nicknames. *Names, 38,* 304.
Lists the word for *nickname* in 26 languages. Examples in French, *sobriquet;* in Thai, *cheu len;* in Arabic, *sho'hrah.*

[26.19] Gasque, Thomas J. (1994). Looking back to Beaver and the Head: Male college nicknames in the 1950s. *Names, 42,* 121-131. Refs.
The main purpose of the study was to evaluate how alumni from the classes of 1956-1962 from a small college in South Carolina felt about the nicknames they had at the time of college attendance and at the present time. They were also asked about those names of fellow alums that they remembered. The most remembered names were Sonny, Shot, Head, Speck, Bear, Groceries, and Beaver. Concludes "Nicknames were found to be either endearing or critical, functioning as social controls."

[26.20] Graybill, Guy. (1984-85). Dippy, son of Puddin.' *Pennsylvania Folklife, 34(2),* 85-89. Refs. Photos.
Anecdotal on about 30 nicknames from Paxtonville, PA. Included are: Flicker, Moon, Rip, and Muzzy. A few women's names are shown including: Ment, Lib, Punch, and Judy.

[26.21] Harris, Ron. (1979, July). What's in a nickname? *Ebony,* pp. 76-78; 80, 82. Information on about 35 nicknames. Included are Judge William Thompson (Turkey), McKinley Morganfield (Muddy Waters), Martin Luther King, Jr. (Little Mike), and Dr. Benjamin Mays (Buck Benny).

[26.22] Heider, Karl G. (1980). The Gamecock, the Swamp Fox, and the Wizard Owl: The development of good form in the American totemic set. *Journal of American Folklore, 93,* 1-22. Refs.
Extensive analysis of the nicknames and legends surrounding 3 generals of the American War for Independence who came from 3 areas of South Carolina, Thomas Sumpter known as the Gamecock; Francis Marion, the Swamp Fox; and Andrew Pickens, the Wizard Owl.

[26.23] Holland, Theodore J., Jr. (1990). The many faces of nicknames. *Names, 38,* 255-272. Refs.
Analyzes the approach and methodology of 60+ studies dealing with nicknames. Topics include: cross-cultural studies, children, and the work of Skipper on sociological aspects of deviants, athletes, blues singers, and others.

[26.24] Holland, Theodore J., Jr. (1990). Code-mediated adaptation: "Cold-Water Mike" and other steam-era railroaders' nicknames. *Connecticut Onomastic Review, No. 3,* pp. 53-59. Refs.
Railroaders' nicknames occur as instances of restricted linguistic coding. Discussion of various categories of nicknames. One type involving interpersonal relations, another with man-machine relations. An example of a man-machine nickname is Cold Water Mike (a fireman who could not maintain a proper fire). This type of nickname has a regulatory effect.

[26.25] Holland, Theodore J., Jr. (1990). The nicknames of steam-era railroaders: A code-mediated adaptation. *Names, 38,* 295-304. Refs. Figs.
Similar to above but has statistics and figures.

[26.26] Jacobs, Leland B. (1953). Helping children understand name-calling. *Elementary English, 30,* 337-340. Intro. to naming for children.
Differentiates between some types of name-calling (nicknames) which is positive, examples, Screwball, Mutt, and other types which are harmful, examples, Double Crosser, Road Hog.

[26.27] Kalcik, Susan J. (1985). Women's handles and the performance of identity in the CB community. In Susan J. Kalcik and Rosan A. Jordan (Eds.) *Women's folklore, women's culture* (pp. 99-108). Refs(pp. 234-245). Philadelphia: University of Pennsylvania Press.
Research was based on the northern region of Virginia near Washington. Psycho-social analysis of CB handles used by couples and by women. Demonstrates how handles are related to public, private, real, and fantasy identities. Names given for each member of 25+ couples, examples, Cinderella and Country Squirrel; also names for 40+ women, examples, China Doll, Foxy Fraulein.

[26.28] Kealey, Robert J. (1984). *Everyday issues related to justice and other gospel values.* Washington, DC: National Catholic Educational Association, 82p. (ERIC Document Reproduction Service No. ED 259 981).
There is one lesson on unkind nicknames among the lessons for children dealing with daily situations such as stealing, cheating in school, and waste of food.

[26.29] Kingsbury, Stewart & Kingsbury, Millie. (1986). Jazz Babies and Flying Sheiks: Cultural reflections in USNA nicknames of the Roaring Twenties. *Publications of the North Central Name Society, No. 1,* 161-172.
1st author's experience with being nicknamed at the Naval Academy. 75+ nicknames taken from Annapolis yearbooks of the 20s are listed, many with origin. Included are: Jazz Baby, Stud, Flaming Youth, and Shimmy.

[26.30] Leslie, Paul L., & Skipper, James K., Jr. (1990). Toward a theory of nicknames: A case for socio-onomastics. *Names, 38,* 273-282. Refs.
Calls for a theory of nicknames. Asks researchers to: (1) document nicknames and their origins in specific samples, (2) analyze nickname data by positing nickname categories, and (3) analyze conditions under which nicknames are used.

[26.31] Lewis, Margaret Jane. (1970). Some nicknames and their derivations. *Mississippi Folklore Register, 4,* 52-57,
Reports a campus study of 300 nicknames. Categories include: physical characteristics, 30%, (Porky, Ears); 1st name derivatives, (Flo < Florence), 15%; and baby talk derivatives, 17%, (Booth < younger sibling's pronunciation of Ruth). Many examples.

[26.32] Lloyd, Gregory. (1988, Spring). Name that swab. *Bulletin of the North Central Name Society,* pp. 65-69.
Anecdotal report of the names a sailor was called at various stages in the Navy. Examples in training: "Dixie Cup," "Blue Jacket." Specialist medics were called: "Saw Bones;" radiomen, "Sparks." 35+ names given.

[26.33] Lutz, George Winston. (1983). Play, intimacy and conflict resolution: Interpersonal determinants of marital adaptation. *DissAbstrIntl, 43,* 1991B.
Nicknames were one aspect of the informal play behavior of couples that was studied in relation to marital adaptation. No examples.

[26.34] Maurer, David W., & Futrell, Allan W. (1982). Criminal monickers. *American Speech, 57,* 243-255. Refs.
Differentiates monickers as a special category of nicknames used in the criminal world by those who do not wish to have their real names known. Main section lists 80+ monickers, most with some explanation of their origin. Examples include: Charley Blade, Chops Broyles, Grave-Yard Jim.

[26.35] McGeachy, John, III, (1978). Student nicknames for college faculty [Topics & Comments]. *Western Folklore, 37,* 281-296. Refs. Tables.
Reports from two higher education institutions, Setrales (a pseudonym?) and State University. Questionnaires were circulated and students were asked to supply surnames for nicknames and to make comments. Extensive listing of nicknames, examples, Groucho Marx (glasses and cigar), Bashful (1 of the 7 dwarfs).

[26.36] Michaels, Ken (1968, May 12). The good old nicknames: Where are they now? *Chicago Tribune Magazine,* Pp. 72-73.
Nostalgic description of about 50 nicknames from the old neighborhood. Included are: Marty Meter-Reader, Frog-Jaws, The Atheist, and The Toilet-Flusher.

[26.37] Monagan, Charles. (1986, May/June). Sweet nothings: "Honey" may be a bit sticky, but as a term of endearment it beats the pants off the tender whisperings off "poopeedoodle" and "snugglepups." *Saturday Evening Post,* p. 14.
Monagan's reactions to his wife's calling him "Honey."

[26.38] Nemy, Enid. (1987, Aug. 23). What's in a nickname? Don't ask. [New Yorkers, etc.]. *New York Times,* Section I, p. 58.

How several people acquired their nicknames including: Lenny (Nails) Dykstra of the New York Mets, Frances (Shang) Ferguson Paterson, and Calvin (King) Tompkins.

[26.39] Newman, Edwin. (1982, Oct. 27). Real election issue: Do nicknames work? *New York Times*, p. A-27.
Description of shift to "nicknames" (short names and affectionate names) from original given names, James > Jimmy (Carter), Robert to Bob (Dole), Anthony Wedgwood Benn > Tony Benn.

[26.40] No more a nickname nation. (1985, Feb. 6). *New York Times*, p. A22.
Editorial comment on the decline of nicknames in the US although sports still has some.

[26.41] Noble, (Wilfred) Vernon. (1976). *Nicknames: Past and present*. London: Hamish Hamilton, 183p.
Contains approx. 775 nicknames for people, place, and events. A large percentage are for people (Last of the Red Hot Mommas = Sophie Tucker). Some have become words (havelock = a covering for a soldier's cap used to protect the neck in warm climates, after Sir Henry Havelock, an officer in India; Jacobites, those who supported James II of the Stuarts after he fled to France in 1688 (James is derived from the Hebrew Jacob).

[26.42] Pacanowsky, Michael & Anderson, James A. (1981, May). *Cop talk and media use*. Paper presented at the annual meeting of the International Communication Association, Minneapolis, 22p. (ERIC Document Reproduction Service No. ED 207 110).
Investigation of the radio talk of 25 peace officers in a community of 10,000. One of the major aspects of the paper is the use of nicknames, especially those drawn from the media. Some of the job-related nicknames mentioned are: Bogart, Mr. Bill, and Kojak.

[26.43] Pilcher, William W. (1972). *The Portland longshoremen: A dispersed community*. New York: Holt, Rinehart & Winston, 128p. Refs. Photo.
Description of the use of nicknames (Mule-Shoes, Longdong, Bignose, Preacher) which are used in the ingroup context only and away from the presence of women and children (pp. 104-113). 17 names listed.

[26.44] Pina-Cabral, João de. (1984). Nicknames and the experience of community. [Correspondence]. *Man, 19,* 148-150. Refs.
After evaluating the work of Breen [9.31.1], Gilmore [9.52.2.5], and Pitt-Rivers [9.52.2.9], proposes a definition that "nicknames are unwritten and unsystematically derived names which are given by the community to the individual, the household or the family, usually independent of their stated choice."

[26.45] Rees, Nigel & Noble, Vernon. (1985). *A who's who of nicknames*. London: George Allen & Unwin, 194p. Refs.
Listing and explanation of 840 examples of several types of nickname as John Tyler known as *The Accidental President* as a result of W. H. Harrison's death a month after taking office; a boy named Cockcroft who boasted of his sexcapades known as *Cockaloft*; and names like *Dusty* Miller because of their linkage with the surname.

[26.46] Rogers, James. (1970). The folklore of faculty names at the Academy. Keystone *Folklore Quarterly, 15,* 74-80. Refs.
Nicknames bestowed on 10 teachers [apparently at a private boys' school]. Some teachers had more than one nickname. Origins of the nicknames given with a poll showing percentages of pupils aware of the name.

[26.47] Skipper, James K. (1986). Nicknames, coal miners and group solidarity. *Names, 34,* 134-145. Refs. Table.

Interviewed 45 male and female miners in Virginia and West Virginia to understand the dynamics of solidarity in a dangerous occupation. Most miners' nicknames have significance as social acceptance. The names are used *only* in the mines. Extensive table shows each nickname, source, and other information. Examples include: Preacher Woman, Bubble Eye, and Cock Man.

[26.48] Skipper, James K. (1986). Nicknames, folk heroes and jazz musicians. Popular *Music & Society, 10(4),* 51-62. Refs. Table.
Analysis of data on nicknames of 2599 jazz musicians parallels the rise and fall of the popularity of nicknames of baseball players and criminals. Names mentioned include Ferdinand (Jelly Roll) Morton, John (Dizzy) Gillespie, and Bill (Count) Basie.

[26.49] Skipper, James K., Jr., & Leslie, Paul. (1990). The systematic study of personal nicknames: A small step forward. *Names, 38,* 253-254.
Intro. to a special issue of *Names* devoted to nicknames featuring articles by Theodore J. Holland, Jr. [26.23], Paul Leslie & James K. Skipper, Jr. [26.30], Maria Laura Massolo [9.51.2], Brenda S. Wilson & James K. Skipper, Jr. [26.3.11] and Edwin D. Lawson [2.8].

[26.50] Smith, J. Jerome. (1981). Gender marking on citizens band radio: Self-identity in a limited-channel speech community. *Sex Roles, 7,* 599-601. Refs.
Users of CB radios assign themselves nicknames known as handles. Analysis shows that male CBers are clearly identified by their handles; females are not. Semantic differential analysis shows that male handles project virility; female handles do not show gender marking. 10 male handles are listed including Snowman and Spanky; the 10 female handles include Love Bug and Baby Holstein.

[26.51] Solomon, Jolie. (1989, June 12). The boss's nickname can speak volumes: Office workers relieve stress by giving boss a nickname. [Managing]. *Wall Street Journal,* B1, Col 1.
Report of nicknames given administrators by subordinates in industry and business. Nicknames can show both hostility and humor. Among the nicknames given bosses are: Little Lord Fauntleroy, Prince of Darkness, and Neutron Jack.

[26.52] Thomas, Rosemary Hyde. (1980). Traditional types of nicknames in a Missouri French Creole community. *Missouri Folklore Society Journal, 2,* 15-25. Refs.
Description of a type of nickname "dit" (called names) in the Old Mines area which is south of St. Louis in the Ozark foothills. Currently, the greatest number of nicknames are considered anecdotal "prankish." Mercy My Beads got his name from schoolmates when he dropped his rosary down a privy. 30+ examples of nicknames including some of French origin (examples, Carbine, Biche).

[26.53] Vannah, Thomas. (1990, Mar.). The kids at work. [Nicknames]. *New England Business,* pp. 81-85. Photos.
Describes business executives who prefer to be known in business by their nicknames. These include Richard ("Bink") Garrison, Adolf F. ("Sonny") Monosson, Eileen ("Ginger") More, and others.

26.1. NICKNAMES: *Blues Singers*

[26.1.1] Skipper. James K., & Leslie, Paul L. (1988). Nicknames and blues singers, Part I: Frequency of use 1890-1977. *Popular Music & Society, 12(1),* 37-47. Refs. Table.
Statistics based upon 570 blues singers indicate a higher percentage of nicknames than of comparison groups, baseball players, criminals, and jazz musicians. The pattern of

nicknames for blues singers does follow the other groups. Analysis of blues nickname usage.

[26.1.2] Skipper, James J., Jr., & Leslie, Paul L. (1988). Women, nicknames, and blues singers. *Names, 36,* 193-202. Refs. Table.
Evaluation of the nicknames of 571 blues singers from 1890 to 1977. Results indicate a lower percentage of nicknames for females; blacks more likely to have nicknames. Few of the nicknames were associated with blues singing. Largest category of nicknames was for physical characteristics. Table shows 28 female blues singers including Bessie Smith (Empress of the Blues), Josephine Miles (Evangelist Mary), and Joanne Horton (Pub). Implications discussed.

[26.1.3] Skipper, James K., Jr., & Leslie, Paul. (1989). Nicknames and blues singers 1890-1977, Part II: Classification and analysis. *Popular Music & Society, 13(3),* 29-43. Refs. Tables.
Classified nicknames of 464 male and 105 female blues singers into 7 categories related to blues, 9 categories not-related to blues. Appendix lists all names and categories. Examples include Jelly Jaw (J. D. Short), Bacon Fat (Andre Williams) and Aunt Jemima (Edith Wilson).

26.2. NICKNAMES: *Presidents*

[26.2.1] Anderson, Jack & Binstein, Michael. (1992, Apr. 13). Nicknames simple for Secret Service. *Evening Observer* [Dunkirk-Fredonia, NY], p. A4. [Nationally syndicated column].
Describes 15 codenames for presidents & their families. These nicknames had to be short and easily pronounced. Examples, Reagan = Rawhide, Amy Carter = Dynamo, Pat Nixon = Starlight.

[26.2.2] Berger, Josef. (1961, Apr 16). And why nicknames? *New York Times Magazine*, pp. 64, 66, 70.
Taboo on President Kennedy's nickname. General on nicknames of prominent individuals including: Dorothea (Dolley) Madison, James (Ten-Cent Jimmy) Buchanan, and Jerome (Dizzy) Dean.

[26.2.3] Rosenblatt, Roger. (1980, Dec 24). Is Reagan Dutch or O & W? [Essay]. *Time,* p. 68.
General on presidential nicknames.

26.3. NICKNAMES: *Sports*

[26.3.1] Grosshandler, Stan (1978). Where have all those grand old nicknames gone? *Baseball Research Journal, 7,* 60-63.
Describes a number of baseball nicknames in loose categories. These include: home state (*Bama* Rowell), *Jersey* Joe Stripp), rural (*Cy* Young, *Rube* Walberg), and talkative (*Gabby* Street, *Lippy* Leo Durocher).

[26.3.2] Horn, Jack C. (1985, June). Jolting Joe has left and gone away. [Play]. *Psychology Today*, pp. 70-71. Photos.
Summary and comment on the work of Skipper [87:26.1.29] on the decline of nicknames for baseball players.

[26.3.3] Jackson, Donald D. (1989, Apr.). He welted the sphere a prodigious biff. *Smithsonian, 20,* 184.

On colorful baseball nicknames of years ago. 30+ examples include Hank (Bow Wow) Arft, William (Pickles) Dillhoefer, Hugh (Losing Pitcher) Mulcahy; Buck (Leaky) Fausett, and Emil (Hilly Billy) Bildilli.

[26.3.4] Jenkins, Dan. (1986, Mar.). Everything but the kitchen sink. [Sports]. *Playboy, 33,* p. 2.
Reacting to Chicago Bear football player William "The Refrigerator" Perry, suggests that other teams might come up with names, such as Bob "Barcalounger" Bates and Vinny "Vacuum Cleaner" Gambino.

[26.3.5] Skipper, James K., Jr. (1987). Nineteen twenty-seven Yankees: Great team, great nicknames. *Baseball Research Journal, 16,* 24-27.
The many colorful nicknames of this team. Included are: Miller (Rabbit, Hug) Huggins, George Herman (Babe, Nigger, Sultan of Swat) Ruth, and Tony (Poosh'Em Up) Lazzeri.

[26.3.6] Skipper, James K., Jr. (1989, Spring). Baseball nicknames: Are they still with us? *Bulletin of the North Central Name Society,* pp. 1-5. Refs.
There are fewer public nicknames than years ago. There are, nevertheless, many colorful ones. 50+ examples including: Dave "Cobra" Jackson and Orel "Choir Boy" Hershiser. Names used outside the US include "Rusty" Staub as "Le Grand Orange" in Montreal; Bob Horner (no nickname in the US) as "Red Devil" in Japan.

[26.3.7] Skipper, James K., Jr. (1990). Placenames used as nicknames: A study of major league baseball players. *Names, 38,* 1-20. Refs. Tables. Appendix.
Analysis of the types of place nicknames of 122 players. Most were used in the early part of the 20th cent. Extensive appendix gives entries for each player by nickname type. Examples, Lou Gehrig who played 1933-1939 is listed from the Eastern US. He was known as "Columbia Lou" since he had attended Columbia University.

[26.3.8] Skipper, James K., Jr. (1992). *Baseball nicknames: A dictionary of origins and meanings.* Part on All American Girls Baseball League players compiled by Brenda Wilson. Jefferson, NC: McFarland, 374p. Refs.
Sociological implications of the decline of baseball nicknames. Main section has over 4100 entries where those associated with baseball are described and the origin of their nicknames explained. Covers player, umpires, managers, and others. One section is on the All American Girls Baseball League. There are appendices for: (1) Negro League Players, (2) umpires, and (3) personalities associated with baseball. Example of a player's name: "Mookie" Wilson who got his nickname from a childhood mispronunciation of "milk." The family gave the name.

[26.3.9] Sullivan, Robert. (1987, Jan. 5). What's in a name? [Scorecard]. *Sports Illustrated, 66,* p. 7.
Names in sports include a Memphis State basketball player named Vincent Askew who is known as Vincent Van Go. No other names of individuals given.

[26.3.10] Wheeler, Timothy J. (1987). Basketball names. *Word Ways, 20,* 122-124.
Directs attention to names of 25+ basketball players with unusual names. These include Barry ("Go-In") Goheen, Bo Cocuz, and Pooh Richardson.

[26.3.11] Wilson, Brenda S., & Skipper, James K., Jr. (1990). Nicknames and women professional baseball players. *Names, 38,* 305-322. Refs. Tables.
While women generally have fewer nicknames than men, women baseball players were as likely as male players to have public nicknames. "Public nicknames may be a reflection of the power differential between men and women in given environment." Appendix gives systematic classification and listing of 126 nicknames.

[26.3.12] Yeutter, Frank. (1960, July 27). Current nicknames lack sparkle of old monickers. *Sporting News,* P. 14.
Mention of about 50 old-time baseball nicknames including: Topsy (Tullus Frederic) Hartsel, The Crab (Johnny) Evers, and Reindeer (Bill) Killefer.

27. NUMEROLOGY AND NAMES

[27.1] Billigmeier, Jon-Christian. (1967). Alphabets. In Mircea Eliade (Ed.), *The encyclopedia of religion, Vol. 1,* pp. 216-222. Refs. New York: Macmillan; London: Collier Macmillan.
Pp. 220-222 deal with *gematria,* the numerical significance of letters. Each letter was assigned a numerical value. Gematria was practiced in Greece and was also involved with Egyptian, Jewish, Christian, and Islamic practices. One belief was that if 2 or more words had the same numerical value, those words or names must have a similar significance, examples, Theos ("God") = Agathos ("Good") = Agios ("Holy") = 284.

[27.2] Dodge, Ellin. (1985). *You are your first name.* New York: Simon & Schuster (Fireside), 435p. Refs.
Uses numerology to give brief personality descriptions of approx. 1500 names. Each description has 3 parts, Major Talent, Personality Ingredients, and Personality Extremes.

[27.3] Locks, Gutman G. (1985). *The spice of Torah-Gematria.* New York: Judaica Press, 318p. Refs.
Extensive mathematic analysis of words and names from the Pentateuch for meanings and relationships.

28. POPULAR NAMES

[28.1] Baker, R. J. (1972). Natural selection, onomastics, and population control: The Shufflebottom hypothesis. *Dalhousie Review, 51,* 332-336. Refs.
Examination of the reasons by names such as Addlehead, Backoff, Ramsbottom, and Shufflebottom appear to be dying out. After consideration of 4 hypotheses, concludes that girls with such a name marry out to get rid of it; males cannot get a girl to marry them.

[28.2] Callary, Edward. (1987, Fall). John and Mary, meet Michael and Sarah. *Journal of the North Central Name Society,* Pp. 40-47. Tables.
Describes the 1st names of approx. 600 babies born at the DeKalb and Sycamore (Illinois) hospitals in 1986. Tables show the most common names of boys, girls, and parents. An additional table shows the frequencies of all names. Unique names also shown. These include: Bonnie Boddy, Mary Cherry, Ruble Farmer, and Terry Twitty.

[28.3] Callary, Edward. (1988/89, Winter). Given names in Dekalb/Sycamore, 1987. *Bulletin of the North Central Name Society,* pp. 21-28.
Listing of frequencies of 1st names by sex in this Northern Illinois area. Apparently these are birth names.

[28.4] Callary, Edward. (1992). Names in DeKalb. *Bulletin of the North Central Name Society, Summer,* 31-35.
Lists names of approx. 600 children born at a rural hospital in northern Illinois in 1991. The 5 most popular names for boys were: Jacob, Zachary, Cody, Andrew, and Christopher; for girls: Brittany, Ashley, Kaitlyn, Sarah, and Amanda (some had variant spellings).

[28.5] Carlson, Katherine. (1989/90, Winter). Current infant names in Northern Illinois, 1989. *Bulletin of the North Central Name Society*, pp. 21-27. Refs.
Lists names from the *Chicago Tribune* of boys and of girls who were born in DuPage County and which had a frequency of 15 or more. Separate listings for middle names. All lists compared to a 1983 study by Betty Kay Koulos [87:29.15].

[28.6] Chaput, Donald C. (1963). What were they called? Name changes since the Civil War. *Michigan History, 47*, 335-337.
Comparison of frequencies of 1st names from a Civil War list of Michigan officers with a 1961 sample in Pontiac, MI. Top names show a continuity. Low frequency names of the 2 lists are quite different. Greater variety of names in 1961.

[28.7] Doherty, Jack. (1959, Feb. 22). Sibylline syllables. *New York Times Magazine*, pp. 56, 58.
Concludes that presidential hopefuls with the most syllables in their surname would be most likely to be president. Among those most eligible in the 1960 election were Kennedy and Symington.

[28.8] Downey, Mike. (1985, July 7). Boris bounces back; *Sporting News*, p. 7.
A famous person can restore the popularity of a name that has fallen into disfavor, examples, *Boris* Becker, *Arnold* Palmer.

[28.9] Duckert, Audrey. (1965). Notes and queries. *Names, 13,* 136-138.
Passing mention of the fading of some 1st names such as, Thankful, Hopestill, Gideon, and Ezekiel.

[28.10] Eckler, A. Ross. (1986). President Smith, where are you? In A. Ross Eckler (Ed.) *Names and games: Onomastics and recreational linguistics* (pp. 64-66). Lanham, MD: University Press of America.
Shows frequencies of presidential surnames to demonstrate that 28 of 37 presidents had surnames which were statistically more common.

[28.11] Evans, Cleveland Kent. (1986). Most popular names in Missouri, 1986. *Bulletin of the North Central Name Society*, pp. 37. Table.
List of the 40 most popular names for boys and for girls for whites and non-whites.

[28.12] Evans, Cleveland Kent. (1989, Spring). Adam and Andre, Lindsay and Lakeisha: Racial differences in first names, 1987. *Bulletin of the North Central Name Society*, pp. 43-65. Refs. Tables.
Contrasts names used by blacks and whites in 4 areas of the US. Data from Florida show that blacks use more uncommon names. Other data show that there are differences in the top choices by whites and blacks. Discussion of the *La-* prefix and other prefixes used in black names. Extensive tables.

[28.13] Greene, Bob. (1988, Jan.). The Linda Hop. *Esquire, 109,* 27ff.
Describes the organization of Lindas who held a national convention.

[28.14] Henley, Arthur. (1970, June). Your child's name could mark him for failure. *Ladies Home Journal, 87*, pp. 137, 139.
Popular article based upon the work of psychologists such as Nicolay, Hartman, and Bruning & Buchanan, and others. Examples of poor choices of names include: Clarence, Horace, and Egbert.

[28.15] Joubert, Charles E. (1985). Sex differences in given name preferences. *Psychological Reports, 57,* 49-50. Refs.

Male college students prefer common names from the current time period or a previous one, whereas females did not.

[28.16] Latham, Joe. (1975, Dec. 11). What's in a name? Or why Macs are rife. *New Society*, 591-593. Tables.
Analysis of key surnames can give information on the ethnicity of the population in an area. Tabulations include data from telephone directories in 18 British Isles areas.

[28.17] Michael and Jessica, you have company. (1987, Apr. 23). *New York Times*, p. B4.
Top male names for New York City for 1986 were: Michael, Christopher, Jonathan, Anthony, David, Daniel, Joseph, John, Jason, and Andrew. Top female names were: Jessica, Jennifer, Stephanie, Nicole, Amanda, Melissa, and tied for 9th place, Danielle and Elizabeth.

[28.18] Naming names. (1985, Jan. 21). *People Weekly*, pp. 16-17. Table. Photos.
Reactions to Leslie Dunkling [87:10.1.3] and Cleveland Kent Evans (no ref. cited) on trend-setting names.

[28.19] Picking infant's name influenced by geography (Associated Press). (1987, Apr. 26). *Buffalo News*, p. E2.
Gerber Products Co. (baby food) surveyed 2544 parents and reported most popular names. In the East, Lauren, Gregory; Northern states, Jennifer, Michael; Midwest, Katherine, Ryan; Northeast, Haley, Matthew.

[28.20] Smith, Jack. (1986, July 12). Girls swing back to traditional names for their dolls, Mattel survey finds. *Toronto Star*, p. L9 [*Los Angeles Times* story].
Survey of doll names confirms Dunkling [87:10.1.3] with leading choices of Jennifer, Susan, Jessica, Mary, and Jane.

[28.21] Suffer the little children. [Fads]. (1962, Sept. 21). *Time*, p. 69.
On fashions in naming children. Trends indicate: Celtic names for boys (Kevin, Sean, etc.); variant spellings for girls (Lori, Billye); decline of juniors; and hyphenated names for girls (Jo-Anne, Mary-Lee) spreading throughout the US.

[28.22] US. Social Security Administration. Office of Operational Policy and Procedures. (1985). *Report of distribution of surnames in the social security number file, Sept. 1, 1984*. Baltimore, MD: Dept. of Health & Human Services, Social Security Administration, Office of Operational Policy & Procedures, 106p. Tables.
Listing of the 5000 most frequent surnames (using the 1st 6 letters). There are 2 main tables, 1 by frequency, 1 in alpha order. Additional tables show frequencies by initial letter, overall frequency, and by length of name. Most common names are: Smith, Johnso, Willia, Brown, Jones, Martin, Miller, Davis, Anders, and Wilson. [Only the 1st 6 letters of names are counted].

[28.23] Warren, Virginia Lee. (1972, May 13). Naming the baby: Jennifer and Jason are the vogue. *New York Times*, p. C16. Table.
Top 10 names for boys and girls for 1898, 1948, and 1964. Also, most popular names in New York City, Dallas (showing French influence), and Berkeley, California. [the article does say *French* influence].

29. POPULATION STRUCTURE AND NAMES
(See Also: 34. PUBLIC HEALTH AND NAMES)

[29.1] Cavalli-Sforza, L(uigi) L(uca)., & Bodmer, W(alter) F(red). (1971). *The genetics of human populations*. San Francisco: Freeman, 965p. Refs. Table. Fig.
Explains isonymy (when couples of the same surname but with different parents marry) and its advantages and limitations as a measure of the inbreeding coefficient.

[29.2] Crow, James F. (1983). Surnames as markers of inbreeding and isolation--Discussion. *HumBio, 55*, 383-397. Refs(pp. 399-408).
General on the history of the isonymic contribution to the study of inbreeding. Apparently the 1st to use the term *isonymic* although he credits a colleague, Charles Cotterman, with the suggestion.

[29.3] Crow, James F., & Mange, Arthur P. (1965). Measurement of inbreeding from the frequency of marriages between persons of the same name. *Eugenics Quarterly, 12*, 199-203. Refs.
Application of genetics theory to a sample of 12 surnames from a Hutterite population using isonymy as a measure of inbreeding.

[29.4] Devor, Eric J. (1983). Matrix methods of analysis of isonymous and nonisonymous surname pairs. *HumBio, 55*, 277-268. Refs(pp. 399-408). Tables. Figs.
Surname data were collected from the Church marriage register of Abiquiu, a village in northern New Mexico founded in 1754 by a mixed Spanish-Indian population. Two time periods were examined, 1882-1910 and 1947-1977. Analysis used surname-pair matrices as well as traditional isonymy and concludes that surnames can also be used to study marital structure.

[29.5] Goode, Erica E. (1988, Jan. 11). More than just entries on the family tree. [Behavior: To scientists, surnames plot the movement of cultures]. *U. S. News & World Report*, p. 53.
Describes the relevance of surnames to the work of Cavalli-Sforza [29.1] on genetics and Swedlund [29.19] on economic history. Other work also mentioned.

[29.6] Gottlieb, Karen. (Ed.). (1983). Surnames as markers of inbreeding and migration. *HumBio, 55*, 209-408. Refs.
A collection of papers presented at a conference and meetings held in Eugene, Oregon involving isonymic aspects of population structure and genetics. Preface is on pp. 209-210. Papers are in 4 areas: Surnames as population markers, Marital isonymy as a measure of population structure, Communality of surnames between groups as a measure of population structure, and Use of 1st names in tracing descent. Extensive refs. and biblio. are on pp. 399-408. Individual papers listed by author in this bibliography.

[29.7] Gottlieb, Karen. (1983). Genetic demography of Denver, Colorado. Spanish surname as a marker of Mexican ancestry. *HumBio, 55*, 227-234. Refs(pp. 399-408). Tables.
In an analysis of 496 newborns and their 982 parents in Denver, a Spanish surname as a predictor of partial or total Mexican ancestry was accurate about 95% of the time.

[29.8] Holgate, P. (1971). Drift in the random component of isonymy. *Biometrics, 27*, 448-451. Refs.
Shows that isonymy increases in a population with time. Also describes results with a branching model.

[29.9] Hurd, James P. (1983). Comparison of isonymy and pedigree analysis measures in estimating relationships between three "Nebraska" Amish churches in Central Pennsylvania. *HumBio, 55,* 349-355. Refs(pp. 399-408). Tables. Fig.
Data on 380 married adults in northern Pennsylvania were evaluated by surname analysis and pedigree. Cautions to be observed in data interpretation with so few surnames suggested.

[29.10] Kashyap, Lalit K. (1980). Trends of isonymy and inbreeding among the Ahmadiyyas of Kashmir. *Journal of Biosocial Science, 12,* 219-225. Refs.
The Ahmadyyas of Kashmir, a small religious sect, are an offshoot of the Sunni Moslems. Isonymic analysis works well in this group which had 984 marriages in 4 generations.

[29.11] Kashyap, Lalit K., & Tiwari, S. C. (1980). Kinetics of genetic kinship as inferred by isonymy among the Ahmadiyyas of Kashmir Valley. *HumBio, 52,* 311-324. Refs. Tables. Map.
Based upon same population as that of Kashyap above. More sociological background material. Isonymic analysis by village and generation.

[29.12] Lasker, Gabriel W., & Steegman, Theodore, Jr. (1985). Relationships among companies of militia in the Colony of New York in 1760 estimated by an analysis of their surnames. *Social Biology, 32,* 136-140. Refs. Table. Figs.
In 1760, in the New York Colony, membership in the militia was required. Surname analysis of 8 companies shows that within-company relatedness was as high as in genetic isolate communities.

[29.13] Morton, Newton E. (1973). Kinship bioassay. In Newton E. Morton (Ed.). *Genetic structure of population* (pp. 158-163). *Vol. 3, Population Genetics Monographs. Hawaii Conference on Population Structure,* University of Hawaii, 1973.
Mathematically oriented demonstration that kinship can be estimated in different ways, among them isonymy.

[29.14] Rogers, L. A. (1987). Concordance in isonymy and pedigree measures of inbreeding: The effects of sample compositions. *HumBio, 59,* 753-767. Refs. Tables. Figs.
To estimate inbreeding, isonymy and pedigree techniques were used on the Mennonite congregation of Harvey, McPherson, and Marion Counties, Kansas. With control in sampling differences, concordance may improve.

[29.15] Shin, Eui-Hang & Yu, Eui-Young. (1984). Use of surnames in ethnic research: The case of Kims in the Korean-American population. *Demography, 21,* 347-359. Refs. Tables.
22% of the Korean American population has Kim as a surname. Research using the Los Angeles-Orange County area, Chicago, Atlanta, and Columbia, SC communities demonstrates that a predictive equation can be developed for the size of the Korean population in a community based upon the frequency of Kims.

[29.16] Smith, Daniel Scott. (1989). All in some degree related to each other. *American Historical Review, 94,* 44-75. Refs. Tables.
Used isonymy to determine the level of kinship propinquity in communities of New England and many other areas of the US in 1790. These data were used to support a theory for the eminence of New England in the 2nd half of the 19th cent., that the level of kinship propinquity was a factor in the development of the character for this eminence.

[29.17] Sorg, Marcella H. (1983). Isonymy and diabetes prevalence in the island population of Vinalhaven, Maine. *HumBio, 55,* 305-311. Refs(pp. 399-408). Tables.

Results indicate that isonymy overestimates inbreeding "but to be of some use when applied cautiously to specific problems." (p. 305).

[29.18] Stevenson, J. C., Brown, R. J., & Schanfield, M. S. (1983). Surname analysis as a sampling method for recovery of genetic information. *HumBio, 55,* 219-225. Refs(pp. 399-408). Tables.
Used surnames as one approach in identification of the ethnic background of Germans, Italians, Irish, and Polish in a Milwaukee sample. The other approach was to ask directly. Results show no difference in blood types between the 2 approaches. Ethnic neighborhoods discussed.

[29.19] Swedlund, Alan C. (1971). The genetic structure of an historical population: A study of marriage and fertility in Old Deerfield, Massachusetts. *Research Reports,* No. 7, Department of Anthropology, University of Massachusetts, Amherst, 78p. Refs. Tables. Figs. Map.
Used isonymy to study the amount of inbreeding in this Northwest Massachusetts community in samples, 1700-1809, 1820-1839.

[29.20] Swedlund, Alan C. (1975). Isonymy: Estimating inbreeding from social data. *Eugenics Society Bulletin, 7,* 67-73. Refs.
Description of studies of population structure which used the isonymy method for making inferences about the level of genetic inbreeding. Summarizes over 20 studies including those of Roberts & Rawling [9.17.7.15], Hussels [9.54.4], and Lasker et al. [9.33.7].

[29.20A] Swedlund, Alan C. (1980). Historical demography. *Current developments in anthropological genetics, 1,* 17-42. Refs. Tables.
Overview of historical demography and its application to the study of longevity. Surname analyses based upon residents of Deerfield, Massachusetts, 1850-1910.

[29.21] Swedlund, A. C., & Boyce, A. J. (1983). Mating structure in historical populations: Estimation by analysis of surnames. *HumBio, 55,* 251-262. Refs(pp. 299-408). Tables. Fig.
Used isonymy to investigate inbreeding in the population structure in and around Deerfield, MA over 5 periods from before 1790 to 1849. Also used isonymy to show that the elites tended to marry elites.

[29.22] Weiss, Kenneth M., Chakraborty, Renajit, Buchanan, Anne V., & Schwartz, Robert J. (1983). Mutations in names: Implications for assessing identity by descent from historical records. *HumBio, 55,* 313-322. Refs(pp. 309-408). Tables.
The research was based upon Spanish names in Laredo, TX. Focused on variations (mutations) in names in relation to studies of isonymy. Expression of concern for use of isonymy as a research tool with large populations.

30. PRONUNCIATION AND NAMES

[30.1] Bender, James F. (1943). *NBC handbook of pronunciation.* New York: Crowell, 287p.
Shows the pronunciation of approx. 12,000 entries using 2 forms of spelling, a version of the International Phonetic Alphabet and an English respelling. Approx. 15% of the entries are personal names.

[30.2] Bender, James F. (1955). *NBC handbook of pronunciation,* 2nd ed. with supplement. New York: Crowell, 289p.
Similar to 1st ed. but deletes 2000 names and adds 5000 more.

[30.3] Bender, James F. Revised by Thomas L. Crowell, Jr. (1964). *NBC handbook of pronunciation*, 3rd ed. New York: Crowell, 418p.
Has 20,000+ entries. Some entries deleted from previous edition. There is a "30% increase over 2nd edition." There is a "Names in the News" section with approx. 600 entries.

[30.4] British Broadcasting Corporation. Pronunciation Unit. (1980). *Recommendations to announcers regarding the pronunciation of some composers' names*, 10th ed. [London]: British Broadcasting Corporation, 161p.
Shows the pronunciation for 1st and surnames of approx. 1700 composers from all over the world from Nils Henrik Aasheim [Åsheim] (néelss hénrick áwss-haym) <-aw as in 'law'> of Norway to Bernard Zweers (báirnaart zváirz) of Holland.

[30.5] British Broadcasting Corporation. Pronunciation Unit. (1980). *Recommendations to announcers regarding the pronunciation of some conductors' names*, 12th ed. [London]: British Broadcasting Corporation, 101p.
Shows the pronunciation for 1st and surnames of approx. 1400 orchestral conductors from all over the world from Claudio Abbado (klówdi-ō Ābáadō <-ow as in 'now'> to Ronald Zollman (rónnald zólmĀn <-ol as in 'olive'>, 1st name is anglicized).

[30.6] British Broadcasting Corporation. Pronunciation Unit. (1983). *Recommendations to announcers regarding the pronunciation of some instrumentalists' names*, 2nd ed. 139p. Similar to above. Contains approx. 3300 entries. Also includes names of quartets, ensembles such as Amadeus, Amici.

[30.7] Dunlap, A. R. (1974). The replacement of *schwa* & /i/ in the English pronunciation of names. *Names, 22,* 85-92. Refs.
Explanation of how stress patterns have changed in a number of personal and place names. Examples cited include Adelbert, Cromwell, and Augustine.

[30.8] Greet, W(illiam). Cabell. (1944). *World words: Recommended pronunciations.* New York: Columbia University Press, 402p. Refs.
Intro. to pronunciation in many languages. There are 10,000 names included. Most are placenames but there may be 15-20% that are personal names. Entries usually show country and two types of pronunciation, one with diacriticals, the 2nd without. Charles De Gaulle would be "sharl' duh gohl'" (without diacritics).

[30.9] Greet, W(illiam). Cabell. (1948). *World words: Recommended pronunciations,* 2nd ed., rev. & enlarged. New York: Columbia University Press, 608p. Refs.
Similar to above but contains 25,000 entries.

[30.10] Herzfeld, John. (1987). Call him Vincent [Van Gogh]. *Art News, 86(Summer),* 15.
Comments on different ways of pronouncing Van Gogh.

[30.11] Infante, G(uillermo) Cabrera. (1987, Aug.). To kill a foreign name. *World Literature Today, 61,* 531-534.
Humorous description of how "foreign" names are mispronounced, including Infante's.

[30.12] Lipski, John M. (1976). Prejudice and pronunciation. *American Speech, 51,* 109-118. Refs.
Presents the view that mispronunciation of ethnic names is often reflective of underlying prejudice. Difficulties with Polish surnames described.

[30.13] MacClintock, Lander. (1965). Once more on the pronunciation of Dufay. *Acta Musicologica, 37,* 75-78. Refs.

There has been some controversy over the proper pronunciation of the name of this 15th cent. Flemish composer. After examination of evidence (including signatures with musical notes), disagrees with Stainer (1898) who wrote, "There is little doubt that Dufay's name should be pronounced as of three syllables with the 'a' broad and open, as in French." Concludes that the long accepted version is correct.

[30.14] McDavid, Raven & O'Lain, Raymond K. (1976). The name researcher and the Linguistic Atlas. *Names in South Carolina, 23,* 23-28. Refs.
Description of the work on the Linguistic Atlas including the type of interview conducted. 1600+ individuals were interviewed along the East Coast. Among the tasks was checking and comparing the pronunciation of 1st names and surnames in different regions. Forms of address also investigated.

[30.15] Name that general. (1991, May 13). *Maclean's,* p. 9.
On Gen. Colin Powell who pronounces his name *Coe-lin* the same way as WWII hero Colin Kelly.

[30.16] Noory, Samuel. (1965). *Dictionary of pronunciation.* New York: A. S. Barnes; London, Thomas Yoseloff, 519p.
Pp. 385-506 give the pronunciation of approx. 14,000 names. Approx. 1/3 of these are personal names.

[30.17] Powell sets British straight. (1991, Apr. 27). *New York Times,* A4.
Gen. Colin Powell pronounces his 1st name KOH-lin, not KAH-lin. However his parents did pronounce it KAH-lin. KOH-lin was more popular since it was the name of Pearl Harbor hero Capt. Colin Kelly.

[30.18] Safire, William. (1989, July 23). Marry-O? Mahr-yo? *New York Times Magazine,* p. 10.
Light approach to the correct pronunciation of the 1st name of the governor of New York, Mario Cuomo. Conclusion appears to be that the governor prefers Mahr-ee-oh.

[30.19] Steuart, Bradley. (Ed.). (1990). *The Soundex reference guide.* Bountiful, UT: Precision Indexing, 253p.
Listing of 125,000 surnames which are keyed to the Soundex system where all names pronounced the same way are given the same index number, example, R3000 includes Reade, Reedie, Ready, Reed, and Reede. The Soundex numbers are useful when seeking further information on the name from the National Archives or the American Genealogical Lending Library in Bountiful, Utah.

[30.20] Urdang, Laurence. (1985). Obiter dicta: The (proper?) pronunciation of proper names. *Verbatim, 11(3),* 23.
Some comments on personal names also. Contrast of differences between spelling and pronunciation in names such as Bach, Lech (Walesa), and Saint-Saens.

[30.21] Ware, John N. (1956, Feb.). Enroughty, Darby, and General McClellan. [A Communication]. *American Heritage, 7(2),* 120.
Account of how a family had its surname pronounced Darby (due to a clause in a will) and how this fact figured in a Civil War battle.

31. PROVERBS AND NAMES

[31.1] Kingsbury, Stewart A. (1987). Names in proverbs and proverbial sayings. *Publications of the North Central Name Society, No. 2,* 116-132.

Analysis of the names in a proverb collection. While most refer to places and things, God, the Devil, or the Church, 8 refer to personal names, e.g., "every Jack must have his Jill", "a bad Jack may have a good Jill." A few others cite a specific name: "as crazy as Wes Ford's cat" or "Hobson's choice."

[31.2] Richmond, W. Edson. (1974). Names in proverbs and proverbial expressions: A tentative statement. *Indiana Names, 5,* 5-18.
Names appear in a number of proverbs. Knowledge of the original meaning and context of these names enhances understanding of proverbs. Approx. 135 proverbs listed including some dealing with personal names; for example, Lafayette, we are here!

32. PSEUDONYMS

[32.1] Force, Helen H. (Ed.). (1967). *Who is who.* Santa Ana, CA: Professional Library Service, 109p.
Approx. 3000 entries for locating authors and their pseudonyms. Example, Shalom Aleichem is the pseudonym for Solomon J. Rabinowitz. Authors apparently were contemporary at publication.

[32.2] Nosnikrap, A. J. (1985, Apr.). Pseudonimity. *Musical Times, 126,* 202-203.
Report from the British Library music catalog on approx. 40 composers who wrote under names other than their original. Among them: C. E. Crawley > Corelli, Helen Rhodes > Guy d'Hardelot, and Philip Heseltine > Peter Warlock.

[32.3] Pall, Ellen. (1989, Apr. 30). In the grasp of romance. *New York Times Book Review,* pp. 1, 37.
Autobiographical. Tells how a writer chose a pseudonym and how her writing was typed for a number of years. Now she writes a different type of novel under her birth name.

[32.4] Room, Adrian. (1989). *A dictionary of pseudonyms and their origins: With stories of name changes.* Revised edition of *Naming names: Stories of pseudonyms and name changes with a Who's Who.* Jefferson, NC & London: McFarland & Co, 349p. Refs.
The format has been changed for this edition. Instead of 40 names lists for different categories, there is a single main section with between 5 and 6 thousand entries with the stories (where applicable) included. The Voltaire, Defoe, and Real Names appendices have been retained.

[32.5] Williams, Franklin B., Jr. (1954). Renaissance names in masquerade. *Publications of the Modern Language Association [PMLA], 69,* 314-323. Refs.
Examination of books printed before 1675 shows many variations of the author's normal name. Types and examples discussed show: (1) transformations in Latin (Adamson to Adamides), (2) Hebraizations (Johnson to Bariona), (3) Greek versions (Struther to Strutheros), (4) modern language versions (Hall to De la Salle), and (5) scrambled names (Pooly to Yloop). Many examples.

33. PSYCHOLOGY AND NAMES

[33.1] Goodman, Mary Ellen. (1970). *The culture of childhood: Child's eye views of society and culture.* New York: Teachers College Press, 167p. Refs.
View on pp. 26-27, 29 that the most important linguistic aid to a child's development is the child's own name, example, where are Johnny's eyes?"

[33.2]   Horne, Marcia D. (1986).   Potential significance of first names: A review. *Psychological Reports, 59,* 839-845. Refs.
Reviews about 30 psychological investigations relating 1st name concerning self-image, interpersonal relations, and achievement.   Almost all are included in Lawson (1987) *Personal Names and Naming.*

[33.3]   Mai-Dalton, Renate R., & Sullivan, Jeremiah J. (1981).   The effects of manager's sex on the assignment to a challenging or a dull task and reasons for the choice. *Academy of Management Journal, 24,* 603-612. Refs. Tables.
Used fictitious names Paul Sandman and Jane Adamson to show that each sex preferred its own sex for the challenging task, the opposite sex for the dull.

33.1. PSYCHOLOGY AND NAMES: *Clinical Psychology*

[33.1.1]   Reilly, Dennis M. (1975).   Family factors in the etiology and treatment of youthful drug abuse. *Family Therapy, 2,* 149-171. Refs.
One of the approaches in family therapy is to explore its naming patterns (pp. 166-167). This can explore the dynamics with a family, the possible effects of a girl being named Eve or Virginia, a boy being named Victor or being a junior.

[33.1.2]   Reilly, Dennis M. (1978).   Death propensity, dying, and bereavement: A family systems perspective. *Family Therapy, 5,* 35-55. Refs.
Suggests that in research into family mourning and its dynamics that the naming patterns and processes be carefully evaluated as a clue to understanding the problems of a specific family (p. 46).

[33.1.3]   Reilly, Dennis. (1979).   Drug abusing families: Intrafamilial dynamics and brief triphasic treatment.   In Edward Kaufman & Pauline Kaufman (Eds.) *Family therapy of drug and alcohol abuse* (pp. 115-130). New York: Gardner Press. Refs.
Pp. 123-128 describe the clinical exploration of the family naming process. Case history of a married 21-year-old drug abuser, Bill, who was a "junior" and his wife Dierdre who was named after "Dierdre of the Sorrows."

[33.1.4]   Reilly, Dennis M. (1984).   Family therapy with adolescent drug abusers and their friends: Defying gravity and achieving escape velocity. *Journal of Drug Issues, 14,* 381-391. Refs.
In a clinical situation, exorcizing "ghosts" haunting a family, analyses of names and naming patterns are used to understand the dynamics of grieving for lost loved ones (p. 388).

33.2. PSYCHOLOGY AND NAMES: *Learning and Names*
(Includes Memory)

[33.2.1]   Blount, Roy, Jr. (1985, June).   As well as I do my own. *Atlantic, 255,* pp. 40-41. Illus.
Comment on problems of remembering names as one gets older.

[33.2.2]   Bornstein, Arthur. (1964).   *Bornstein's miracle memory course.* Englewood Cliffs, NJ: Prentice-Hall, 239p.
Development of a system for remembering. Pp. 93-138 focus on names.

[33.2.3]   Fury, Kathleen. (1986, Oct.).   Names dropping (The working life). *Working Woman,* p. 200. Illus.

Experiences of the difficulties in remembering names. Finds name tags helpful. Solution is to have names woven into the fabric on garments as with Gloria Vanderbilt clothes.

[33.2.4] Hanley, J. Richard, & Cowell, Elaine S. (1988). The effects of different types of retrieval cues on the recall of names of famous faces. *Memory & Cognition, 16*, 545-555. Refs. Tables.
Reports 2 experiments in the psychology of memory. Respondents were given 3 types of cue, a 2nd photograph, initials, or biographical information when they were unable to remember the names. Different cues gave different results. Authors conclude that there are successive distinct stages in face recognition.

[33.2.5] Hanley-Dunn, Patricia, & McIntosh, John L. (1984). Meaningfulness and recall of names by young and old adults. *Journal of Gerontology, 39*, 583-585. Refs.
Young and old adults were tested on recall of 4 lists of names, young-relevant, old-relevant, both relevant, and nonmeaningful. Contrary to other studies, the older sample remembered as many names as the young and were superior on the old-relevant and both relevant lists. There were no differences on the nonmeaningful list. However, older adults perceived their performance as lower than that of the young adults.

[33.2.6] Hersey, William D. (1963). *How to cash in on your hidden memory power.* Englewood Cliffs, NJ: Prentice-Hall, 252p.
Chs. 9-10 (pp. 90-122) concern remembering the names of people. Sets up a system. One major idea is to associate some important image with the person, as a physical feature. Example, "Adam--see a picture of 'Adam' polishing the apple on the pudgy nose."

[33.2.7] Karma, Inez. (1956, Mar. 18). Cocktail party namesmanship. *New York Times Magazine*, p. 78.
Light approach to the problems of recalling names at cocktail parties.

[33.2.8] Lorayne, Harry. (1975). *Remembering people: The key to success.* Chelsea, MI: Scarborough House, 220p.
Develops the premise that remembering people's names is essential for success. Gives a number of suggestions for developing an association between the person and the name which will help recall the name. Most involve mental images. Examples for 1st names: Douglas = dug glass, Babette = bad bet; surnames: Fletcher = fetch her, Otis = elevator. Lists of names.

[33.2.9] Lorayne, Harry. (1975, Sept.). How to remember names and faces. *Ladies Home Journal*, pp. 84ff.
High points from above.

[33.2.10] Mason, Susan E. (1986). Age and gender as factors in facial recognition and identification. *Experimental Aging Research, 12*, 151-154. Refs.
A sample of 20-year-old women and a sample of 75-year-old women were measured on name-face association tasks. The younger sample did better; other results indicate that both old and young participants remembered best pictures of their cohorts and of their sex.

[33.2.11] McWeeny, Kathryn H., Young, Andrew W., Hay, Dennis C., & Ellis, Andrew W. (1987). Putting names to faces. *British Journal of Psychology, 78*, 143-149. Refs. Tables.
Male and female respondents were asked to learn the occupations and surnames of photographs of 16 middle-aged men. Results indicate that names are much harder to recall than occupations. Suggests that for people "personal identity nodes" are created.

[33.2.12] Merrill, Arthur A. (1967). *Remembering names: Improvement is easy.* Chappaqua, NY: Analysis Press, 57p. Refs.
Suggestions for improving memory of names. Topics include: motivation, mnemonic devices, and practice. Extensive biblio. Derivations of 400 names.

[33.2.13] Nilsson, Lars-Göran; Law, Janine; & Tulving, Endel. (1988). Recognition failure of recallable unique names: Evidence for an empirical-law of memory and learning. *Journal of Experimental Psychology: Learning, Memory, & Cognition 14,* 266-277. Refs. Tables. Figs.
Used names to study laws of memory. Concludes that unique names do not follow special rules for memory.

[33.2.14] Nuttin, Jozef M., Jr., (1985). Narcissism beyond Gestalt and awareness: The name letter effect. *European Journal of Social Psychology, 15,* 353-361. Refs. Tables. Figs.
Carefully controlled experiments (in Flemish) with grade school and university respondents at Louvain conclude that "letters belonging to own first and/or family name are preferred above not-own name letters."

[33.2.15] Smith, Steven M. (1985). A method for teaching name mnemonics. *Teaching of Psychology, 12,* 156-158. Refs.
A class exercise showing how to develop associations which assist in the memorization of names.

[33.2.16] Winograd, Eugene, & Church, Vaughan E. (1988). Role of spatial location in learning face-name associations. *Memory & Cognition, 16,* 1-7. Refs.
Results from 9 experiments conclude that a constant location facilitates learning. This constant location is an additional cue. An example is learning names in a classroom where students are assigned seats.

33.3. PSYCHOLOGY AND NAMES: *Perception and Names*

[33.3.1] De Haan, E. H. F., Mehta, Z. M., Young, A. W., & Newcombe, F. (1987). Deciding whether faces and names are familiar: A study on patients with localized brain-lesions. *Journal of Clinical & Experimental Neuropsychology, 9,* 278. [Abstract].
Laboratory results support the superiority of the right brain hemisphere in *face* processing; the left brain hemisphere at recognition of people's names.

[33.3.2] Frazier, Robert; McDonald, David G., & Edwards, David. (1968). Discrimination between signal and non-signal stimuli during sleep. *Psychophysiology, 4,* 369.
A polygraph measured autonomic responses of sleeping subjects (Ss) to tape recordings of (1) their own name, (2) another name, and (3) a tone. Results show that all autonomic responses were consistently larger to the Ss own names. Responses to the tone were the least.

[33.3.3] Van Lancker, D., & Klein, K. K. (1990). Preserved comprehension of personal names in global aphasia. [Meeting Abstract]. *Journal of Clinical & Experimental Neuropsychology, 12,* 82.
Four aphasic patients did worse on auditory-verbal tests using single words but about the same on tests of personal names of famous people.

[33.3.4] Young, Andrew W., McWeeny, Kathryn H., Ellis, Andrew W., & Hay, Dennis C. (1986). Naming and categorizing faces and written names. *Quarterly Journal of Experimental Psychology, 38A,* 297-318. Refs. Tables.

5 experiments, each under various conditions, conclude that "faces can only access name (phonological) codes via an intervening semantic representation, whereas written names can access semantic and name codes in parallel."

33.4. PSYCHOLOGY AND NAMES: *Physiological Psychology and Names*

[33.4.1] Flude, Brenda M., Ellis, Andrew W., & Kay, Janice. (1989). Face processing and name retrieval in an anomic asphasic: Names are stored separately from semantic information about familiar people. *Brain & Cognition, 11,* 60-72. Refs. Tables. Fig.
Work with a patient who had a brain tumor demonstrates that a patient has "full access to semantic information about people while being unable to name them...."

[33.4.2] O'Boyle, Michael W., & Murray, James. (1988). Hemispheric-assymmetry in the identification of four-letter names traced in the right and left palms. *Brain & Language, 34,* 294-301. Refs. Fig.
In an investigation of name recognition in right-handed males names such as Mike, Mark, Bill were traced with a stylus on the palms of blindfolded males. The results indicate a left palm/right hemisphere superiority.

34. PUBLIC HEALTH AND NAMES
(See Also: 29. POPULATION STRUCTURE AND NAMES)

[34.1] Devor, Eric J., & Buechley, Robert W. (1979). Population history and cancer incidence in Hispanic New Mexicans. *American Journal of Physical Anthropology, 50,* 432. [Abstract].
Used surnames to identify "native New Mexicans" vs. other groups to conclude that the cancer pattern of Hispanics is more like that of American Indians than that of Anglos.

[34.2] Duncan, Burris; Smith, Ann N., & Briese, Franklin W. (1979). A comparison of growth: Spanish-surnamed with non-Spanish surnamed children. *American Journal of Public Health, 69,* 903-907. Refs. Figs.
Surnames were used to separate schoolchildren in Denver neighborhoods. Results indicate that Spanish-surnamed children tended to be shorter in height, of lower weight, and smaller head circumference.

[34.3] Enstrom, James E., & Operskalski, Eva A. (1978). Multiple sclerosis among Spanish-surnamed Californians. *Neurology, 28,* 434-438. Refs. Tables.
Surnames were used in a study of Spanish-surnamed whites with multiple sclerosis. Results indicate that foreign-born white Spanish-surnamed Californians have a multiple sclerosis death rate of .07; those born in California, .42; the rate for white Californians is .83. The data suggest that Spanish-Americans have a lower death rate and that local environmental factors are also important.

[34.4] Gottlieb, K(aren) & Kimberling, W. J. (1979). Admixture estimates for the gene pool of Mexican-Americans in Colorado. *American Journal of Physical Anthropology, 50,* 444. Refs.
Used Spanish surnames to identify the percentage of Spanish contribution in disputed paternity blood samples.

[34.5] Samet, Jonathan M., Key, Charles R., Kutvirt, Daniel M., & Wiggins. Charles L. (1980). Respiratory disease mortality in New Mexico's Indians and Hispanics. *American Journal of Public Health, 70,* 492-297. Refs. Figs.

Spanish surnames were used. Pueblo Indians were separated. Lung cancer rates were lower in American Indians and Hispanic males. Lower cigarette usage is given as a factor. Other health factors also considered.

35. RECREATIONAL ASPECTS OF NAMES

[35.1] Bergmann, Dmitri A. (1986). "X" as in Xerxes. In A. Ross Eckler (Ed.) *Names and games: Onomastics and recreational linguistics* (pp. 51-54). Refs.
Lanham, MD: University Press of America. Lists 100 masculine and 50 feminine names beginning with X. Included are: Xander, Xeres, and Xenia.

[35.2] Cohen, Philip M. (1986). Well-endowed chairs. In A. Ross Eckler (Ed.) *Names and games: Onomastics and recreational linguistics* (pp. 31-34). Lanham, MD: University Press of America.
Approx. 90 imaginary names of endowed chairs at universities. Includes: the Hunt N. Peckham Chair of Secretarial Studies; the Les Carew Chair of Sexology, and the Rick Shaw Chair of Transportation.

[35.3] Douglass, Richard E. (1986). The name is the game. In A. Ross Eckler (Ed.) *Names and games: Onomastics and recreational linguistics* (pp. 28-29). Lanham, MD: University Press of America.
Listing of fitting names for 12 occupations. Examples for medicine, Mona Nucleosis, Lance Boyle; for banking, Irving Trust, Otto Loan; and for wives of men in professions, chiropractor, Ophelia; chair manufacturer, Fanny.

[35.4] Eckler, A. Ross. (1986). Carmilla Karstein. *Names and games: Onomastics and recreational linguistics* (pp. 9-10). Lanham, MD: University Press of America.
Replies to a query by Michael J. Murphy whether Carmilla Karstein, a name used by the Irish novelist J. S. LeFanu, is an anagram. Replies from readers include: Allistair R. McKenna and Karin N. MacAllister.

[35.5] Eckler, A. Ross. (1986). The Francis Xavier O'Brien problem. In A. Ross Eckler (Ed.) *Names and games: Onomastics and recreational linguistics* (pp. 42-43). Lanham, MD: University Press of America.
Suggests that the initials F. X. O'B. predict Francis Xavier O'Brien. A rejoinder points out F. X. O'Byrne as well.

[35.6] Eckler, A. Ross. (1986). Name play. In A. Ross Eckler (Ed.) *Names and games: Onomastics and recreational linguistics* (pp. 10-12). Lanham, MD: University Press of America.
Examples of wordplay in signing a wedding book, retirement book, etc. Examples for the JOHNSON-PIOTROWSKI wedding, some wedding advice: HOW KISS? JOIN PRONTO!

[35.7] Eckler, A. Ross. (1986). Presidential anagrams. In A. Ross Eckler (Ed.) *Names and games: Onomastics and recreational linguistics* (pp. 55-61). Lanham, MD: University Press of America.
50+ anagrams from the presidents. Includes DWIGHT DAVID EISENHOWER (HE DID VIEW THE WAR DOINGS), HARRY S. TRUMAN (RASH ARMY RUNT), and JAMES A. GARFIELD (LEAD FAR, SAGE JIM).

[35.8] Eckler, A. Ross. (1986). Telephomnemonics. In A. Ross Eckler (Ed.) *Names and games: Onomastics and recreational linguistics* (pp. 18-24). Lanham, MD: University Press of America.

Speculation and discussion of the relationship of 7-digit telephone numbers to names, example, 564-6766 spells Johnson.

[35.9] Eckler, A. Ross. (Ed.). (1986). *Names and games: Onomastics and recreational linguistics*. Lanham, MD: University Press of America, 281p.
An anthology of 99 articles published in *Word Ways, The Journal of Recreational Linguistics* from Feb. 1968 to Aug. 1985. dealing with aspects of wordplay with names. Sections dealing with personal names include: (1) anagramming personal names, (2) palindromes, (3) names of imaginary people, (4) strange names, (5) presidential names, and (6), names that made the dictionary. Most are listed under author in the recreation section of this vol.

[35.10] Eckler, Faith W. (1986). Last will and testament. In A. Ross Eckler (Ed.) *Names and games: Onomastics and recreational linguistics* (pp. 15-16). Lanham, MD: University Press of America.
Word puzzle based upon biblical pairs.

[35.11] Francis, Darryl. (1986). Caroline. In A. Ross Eckler (Ed.) *Names and games: Onomastics and recreational linguistics* (pp. 3-9). Refs. Lanham, MD: University Press of America.
Exploration of words that can be developed from CAROLINE. Examples. include COLERAIN, COLINEAR. Then, various additional words that can be obtained by juggling letters.

[35.11A] Grant, Jeff. (1986). Nim aid, Idi Amin. In A. Ross Eckler (Ed.) *Names and games: Onomastics and recreational linguistics* (pp. 13-15). Lanham, MD: University Press of America.
Transposals of AMIN (IMAN); transdeletions, AMIDIN, and other variations of IDI AMIN.

[35.12] Hager, Virginia R. (1986). Saints and doctors. In A. Ross Eckler (Ed.) *Names and games: Onomastics and recreational linguistics* (pp. 29-30). Lanham, MD: University Press of America.
Many words begin with DR. If lay people wanted assistance for particular specialties they could choose Dr. Ivel if they were persistent talkers, Dr. Ibble for kidney problems, or Dr. Izzle for runny noses. About 20 others also given. About 35 saints also listed including: St. Amp for postal workers, St. Agger for alcoholics, and St. Accato for musicians.

[35.13] Harlan, Sam. (1986). A presidential rectangle. In A. Ross Eckler (Ed.) *Names and games: Onomastics and recreational linguistics* (pp. 79-80). Lanham, MD: University Press of America.
Development of a 17 by 31 rectangle of letters composed of the 33 different surnames of the presidents.

[35.14] Morton, Mike & Eckler, A. Ross. (1986). Reaganagrams. In A. Ross Eckler (Ed.) *Names and games: Onomastics and recreational linguistics* (pp. 68-84). Lanham, MD: University Press of America.
A number of anagrams based upon RONALD WILSON REAGAN such as NO DARLINGS, NO ERA LAW and A DOLLAR GROWN INSANE.

[35.15] Oberlander, Frank & Oberlander, Mary. (1986). More well-endowed chairs. In A. Ross Eckler (Ed.) *Names and games: Onomastics and recreational linguistics* (pp. 34-36). Lanham, MD: University Press of America.
Continues Cohen [35.2] with about 70 more endowed chairs including the Windsor Calm Chair of Meteorology.

[35.16] Partridge, Harry B. (1986). Ronald Reagan and the fateful L. In A. Ross Eckler (Ed.) *Names and games: Onomastics and recreational linguistics* (pp. 66-68). Lanham, MD: University Press of America.
On the letters in the surnames of presidents and their supposed meaning.

[35.17] Randolph, Boris. (1986). Scottish occupations. In A. Ross Eckler (Ed.) *Names and games: Onomastics and recreational linguistics* (p. 36). Lanham, MD: University Press of America.
Using the prefix *Mac-* comes up with 30 imaginary occupational names. Included are: MacArbre (mortician), MacAroon (baker), and MacKerel (fisherman).

[35.18] Silverman, David L. (1986). Lady Moll Boon. In A. Ross Eckler (Ed.) Names and games: Onomastics and recreational linguistics (pp. 1-3). Lanham, MD: University Press of America.
Pokes fun at anagramming personal names.

[35.19] Silverman, David L. (1986). Names that match their owners. In A. Ross Eckler (Ed.) *Names and games: Onomastics and recreational linguistics* (pp. 27-28). Lanham, MD: University Press of America.
Listing of humorous names (imaginary). Examples include: an Israeli lush, Bar-Fligh; a lavish Italian, Extrava Ganza; and a Japanese steno, Takaleta.

[35.20] Silverman, David L. (1986). Palindromic people. In A. Ross Eckler (Ed.) *Names and games: Onomastics and recreational linguistics* (p. 54). Lanham, MD: University Press of America.
Discussion of palindromic names. Includes: U Nu, Lon Nol, Mary Byram, and Leon Noel.

[35.21] Silverman, David L. (1986). Robert Abplanalp, bat reborn. In A. Ross Eckler (Ed.) *Names and games: Onomastics and recreational linguistics* (pp. 13). Lanham, MD: University Press of America.
On palindromes of Abplanalp.

36. RELIGIOUS FIGURES AND NAMES

[36.1] Attwater, Donald. (1958). *A dictionary of saints: Based upon Butler's "Lives of the saints"*. New York: P. J. Kenedy, 280p. Lists the 2500 saints which are in Alban Butler's *Lives of the saints* (1956).
Entries give the name of the saint and brief description, date of commemoration and page references to Butler's *Lives*.

[36.2] Benedictine monks of St. Augustine's Abbey, Ramsgate. (1947). *The book of saints,* 4th ed. New York: Macmillan, 708p. Refs.
Approx 8500 entries, 5000 of them from the Roman Martyrology. Entries include the present state of the saint's cult. A calendar of saints given.

[36.3] Black, M. (1951). The origins of the name Metatron. *Vetus Testamentum, 1,* 217-219. Refs.
Metatron is a figure from Jewish religious writings who is a mediator between God and man. Black traces the name to Philo.

[36.4] Davidson, Gustav. (1967). *A dictionary of angels including the fallen angels.* New York: Free Press, 387p. Refs. Illus.
Alphabetic listing of approx. 2300 angels, fallen angels, and demons derived from a number of Jewish, Christian, and Muslim sources. Angels include: Metatron, Michael,

and Gabriel; demons/devils Beelzebub, Belial, and Mephistopheles. The appendix shows angels of the zodiac, the angels of punishment, the names of Lilith, and others. Many illus. Extensive biblio.

[36.5] Hamilton, Mary. (1906-07). The pagan element in the names of saints. *Annals of the British School of Athens, 13,* 348-358. Refs.
Discusses 4 modern Greek saints, St. Dionysios, St. Artemidos, St. Eleutherios, and St. Elias and the pagan elements surrounding them.

[36.6] Meimaris, Yiannis E. (1986). *Sacred names, saints, martyrs and church officials in the Greek inscriptions and papyri pertaining to the Christian Church of Palestine.* Athens: Research Center for Greek & Roman Antiquity, 292p. Refs. Map.
Scholarly systematic presentation of 1300 inscriptions from the beginning of the Church until the 7th cent. Inscriptions are categorized by person named; indication of location and the background of the person named. Example, Mary has 43 inscriptions at places like Nazareth and Rihab.

[36.7] Nau, Tim. (1993). The names of the popes. *OnoCan, 75,* 59-66. Refs.
Before the year 1000, almost all popes used their birth names. After that, almost none did. Description of the reasons why. Discussion of Angelo Roncalli's selection of John XXIII for his name.

[36.8] O'Connell, J. P. (1952, Feb.). Is Vernon a saint's name? *Extension* [Chicago], *46,* 28.
There is no Saint Vernon but Vernon is often considered a variation of Berno. There was a Saint Berno whose feast day is Jan. 13.

[36.9] Olson, B. Lynette, & Padel, O. J. (1986). A tenth-century list of Cornish parochial saints. *Cambridge Medieval Celtic Studies, 12,* 33-71. Refs. Maps. Plates.
Extensive documentation and comment on 46 saints. Maps show locations of churches or chapels dedicated to these saints. Saints included are: Salamun, Entonin, and Erbec.

37. SAME NAME
(Individuals having the same or similar name to another's)

[37.1] Bauer, Harry C. (1960). Confused authorships. *Library Review* [Glasgow], *136,* 560-565.
How libraries cope with authors with the same surname or identical entire names. Mentioned are 2 Stephen Vincent Benets (a general and his grandson), Oliver Wendell Holmes and his son, the 2 Winston Churchills and others.

[37.2] Moss, Robert F. (1990, Oct. 22). Of Moss and men. *New York*, p. 42. Illus.
On the problems of having the same name as others.

[37.3] No, David Charles Heyman doesn't have a split personality. (19 Sept. 2). *People Weekly*, p. 58.
Two babies with the same name were born on the same day at the same Chicago hospital.

[37.4] Steinbreder, John. (1989, Apr. 3). Think you've got it bad? Just try going through life as a Steinbrenner soundalike. [Point After]. *Sports Illustrated*, p. 114.
Autobiographical. Describes the ups and downs of having a surname similar to that of sports celebrity George Steinbrenner.

[37.5] Vetter, Craig. (1985, Feb.). The other Craig Vetter. *Playboy, 32,* p. 33.
Difficulties encountered on discovering someone else has the identical name.

[37.6] West, Richard. (1977, Aug. 8). Jones the pen...Jones the post...Jones a spy?
Daily Telegraph [London], p. 8.
On the confusion that people suffer when others have the same name.

[37.7] What's in a middle name? Ask Donald Cram, carpet cleaner, and Donald Cram,
Nobel laureate. (1987, Nov. 2). *People Weekly, 28,* p. 61. Photo.
Confusion of two men with the same 1st name but different middle names. As students
both had the same nickname, Cramberry.

38. SOCIOLOGICAL ASPECTS OF NAMES

[38.1] Harris, Huntington. (1950). The theory of personal names. *Dissertation
Abstracts International, 11(01),* 191-192. (University Microfilms No. 2111, 164p.).
Uses formulations of Peirce, Dewey, Mead, and others to develop five general rules of
personal names and personal name usage.

[38.2] Lutterer, Ivan. (1967). Sociolinguistics and the study of personal names.
Proceedings of the International Congress of Linguistics, Bucharest, 1967, 581-587. Refs.
Tables.
Relates the choices for 1st names to aspects of change in the social structure (religion,
government, fashion, and education). Special attention to Czechoslovakia.

[38.3] Skipper, James K., Jr. (1968). Family names and social class as a teaching
technique. *American Sociologist, 3,* 37-38.
Shows that when students were randomly given 6 ethnically specific surnames to assign
to a social class, the majority assigned Hawthorne to Class I; Goldberg, Class II;
O'Brien, III; Stevenson, IV; Walczewski, V; and Stantospirito, VI.

[38.4] Skipper, James K., Jr. (1989). Public nicknames of famous football players and
coaches: A socio-historical analysis and comparison. *Sociological Spectrum, 9,* 103-123.
Refs. Tables.
Uses nicknames to show "the general shift in American society from a *Gemeinschaft* to
a *Gesellschaft* type. Classification of 169 nicknames into major categories. Many
examples including "Red" Grange, "Buddy" Young, and "Crazylegs" Hirsch.

[38.5] Waters, Mary C. (1989). The everyday use of surname to determine ethnic
ancestry. *Qualitative Sociology, 12,* 303-324. Refs.
Based upon 60 interviews conducted with Catholic respondents in suburbs of Philadelphia
and San Jose who were descendants of European immigrants concludes that surnames are
used to fill gaps in the assumption of ancestry. Among other findings reports that there
is more of a tendency to identify ethnicity with father's side where the surname is.

39. SOUND AND NAMES

[39.1] Collinge, N. E. (1966). Names and resistance to sound shifts. *Proceedings of
the 8th ICOS, Amsterdam,* pp. 94-95.
"It would seem that names are characterized by a strong tendency to independence and
nonconformity, in relation to shift patterns, to particular shifts, and even to 'organized
resistance' to shifts."

[39.2] Cutler, Anne; McQueen, James; & Robinson, Ken. (1990). Elizabeth and John: Sound patterns of men's and women's names. *Journal of Linguistics, 26,* 471-482. Refs. Table. Figs.
Analysis shows, among other results, that male names have more strong initial syllables and less syllables than female names. Differences in the male/female structure of names may be accounted for by semantic or sociological principles. A more sociological view is that when names are given in pairs, that of the male is given a harder sound, and is given 1st.

[39.3] Slater, Anne Saxon & Feinman, Saul. (1985). Gender and the phonology of North American first names. *Sex Roles, 13,* 429-440. Refs.
Investigated sex-associated features in the structural characteristics of 1st names. Concludes that female names: (1) had more sounds and syllables, (2) varied the position of the stressed syllable more, and (3) are more likely to end with a vowel or a sonorant sound. No examples.

40. SPELLING AND NAMES

[40.1] Hughes, (James) Pennethorne. (1965). We spell it with a 'y.' *The Listener*, p. 154.
Comment on how names came to be spelled differently. Among the explanations: in the Late Middle Ages people prided themselves on spelling their names differently, dialect, bad copying, and ignorance. Not only did the 'i' become a 'y' as in Smith to Smyth, but the 'h' moved in and out as in Hosegood to Osgood.

[40.2] Papp, A. H. R. E. (1959). *Nomina sacra in the Greek papyri in the first five centuries A. D.: The sources and some deductions.* Leiden:Brill, 127p. Refs.
Continues the work of L. Traube on nomina sacra concerning certain sacred words which were contracted in Greek, example, *theos,* originally 4 letters, contracted to theta sigma with a stroke over. Marshals evidence from many sources. Concludes (p. 124) that the practice originated from Jewish members of early Christian congregations (who would not write the tetragrammaton).

[40.3] Schwartzenberg, Charles. (Prince). (1981). Names of noble families. Family History, 11, 265-274.
Discusses the difficulties of including or not including the *von* in Germanic families, as von Schwartzenberg. Discussion continued of the of in titles as in the Duke of Wellington. Some comments on the hyphenated names of nobles.

41. STATISTICS AND NAMES

[41.1] Dewdney, A. K. (1986, May). Computer recreations: Branching phylogenies of the Paleozoic and the fortunes of English family names. *Scientific American,* pp. 16-18, 21-22. Figs.
Explains the contributions of computer simulations by David M. Raup and by Christopher M. Sturges & Brian C. Haggett to the understanding of how some species die out and others proliferate. Sturges & Haggett have explained how 3/4 of the surnames [English] have now died out.

[41.2] Watson, H. W., & Galton, Francis. (1875). On the probability of the extinction of families. Intro. by Francis Galton. *Journal of the Anthropological Institute of Great Britain & Ireland, 4,* 138-144. Refs.
Develops mathematical treatment following principles of genetics that with time the number of surnames will decrease.

[41.3] Watson, H. W. (1889). Probable extinction of families. In Francis Galton, *Natural Inheritance* (pp. 241-248). New York: Macmillan.
Reprint of Watson above.

[41.4] Yasuda, N(urikazu), Cavalli-Sforza, L(uigi), Skolnick, M., & Mornoni, A. (1974). The evolution of surnames: An analysis of their distribution and extinction. *Theoretical Population Biology, 5,* 123-142. Refs. Tables.
Used surname distribution and evolution from 40 parishes in the Upper Parma Valley of northern Italy from 1600 to 1960 to test theories of Karlin and McGregor.

42. STEREOTYPES AND NAMES

[42.1] Andersen, Christopher P. (1987). *The baby boomer's name game.* New York: Putnam (Perigee Books), 255p. Refs. Tables.
A revision and update of *The name game* (1977) [87:41.2].

[42.2] Friedrich, Otto. (1986, Aug. 18). What's in a name? *Time,* p. 76.
General on stereotypes and popularity.

[42.3] Frommer, Myrna. (1982). Names. *Et cetera (ETC), 39,* 106-108.
General on names and stereotypes of 1st names. Some mention also of Jewish *kinnui* [vernacular name in English] names in addition to names in Hebrew.

[42.4] Infante, Dominic A., Pierce, Linda L., Rancer, Andrew S., & Osborne, W. J. (1980). Effects of physical attractiveness and likeableness of first name on impressions formed of journalists. *Journal of Applied Communication Research, 8,* 1-9. Refs.
To study stereotypes of women journalists, variables of attractiveness and name were manipulated. Results indicate that a liked name is a powerful asset and may overcome the effects of unattractiveness.

[42.5] Johnson, Dirk. (1990, Oct. 12). Where an Irish name can be ticket to office. [Illinois Journal]. *New York Times,* A12. National Ed.
Report on the election situation in Illinois. Voters prefer candidates with Irish names even though the Irish are outnumbered by German, Poles, African Americans, and others. One explanation is that voters know that the Irish get along with other groups. Another is that there is less prejudice against the Irish.

[42.5A] Kasof, Joseph. (1993). Sex bias in the naming of stimulus persons. *Psychological Bulletin, 113,* 140-163. Refs. Tables.
Investigation of 230 published reports on sexism indicates that the research is confounded by favoring males over females in the selection of names which were used as stimuli. These biases were positively correlated with outcome measures. Suggestions made for the improvement of research in this area.

[42.6] Leak, Gary, K., & Ware, Mark E. (1989). The role of name desirability in person perception. *Journal of Psychology, 123,* 43-49. Refs.
3 studies were done relating name desirability to person perception. The target names, Gertrude and Christy, failed to produce significantly different results.

[42.7] Linville, Deborah R. (1982). *Prejudice toward women applicants based on their first names.* Unpublished master's thesis. Rensselaer Polytechnic Institute, Troy, NY. 42p. Refs. Tables.
Women's 1st names were rated as either "sexy" or "nonsexy." Sexy names include: Dawn, Jennifer, and Cheryl; nonsexy, Ethel, Mildred, and Esther. These names were

then attached to credentials which were evaluated for clerical or management positions. Results indicate that nonsexy names had a better chance for management positions.

[42.8] London, Robb. (1990, Oct. 19). What is in a familiar name could well be a judgeship. *New York Times*, B20.
Reports results in Texas and Washington State where candidates with more familiar names have a better change of winning elections. Specifically, refers to well-qualified Fred Biery losing to Gene Kelly. Another was Charles Johnson winning over Keith Callow in Washington State.

[42.9] Meer, Jeff. (1983, May). Call me James. [States of Mind]. *Psychology Today, 17*, 18.
Refers to article by Von O. Leirer et al. [42.1.7].

[42.10] Noel, Richard C., & Allen, Mary J. (1976). Sex and ethnic bias in the evaluation of student editorials. *Journal of Psychology, 94*, 53-58. Refs.
Used fictitious names James Robinson, Joan Robinson, Juan Rodriquez, and Juanita Rodriquez as attributed authors to show sexist and white bias.

[42.11] O'Sullivan, Chris S.; Chen, Audrey; Mohapatra, Simani; Sigelm Lee; & Lewis, Erik. (1988). Voting in ignorance: The politics of smooth-sounding names. Journal of *Applied Social Psychology, 18*, 1094-1106.
Stimulated by the Illinois Democratic gubernatorial primary in which LaRouche candidate Mark Fairchild won over party-backed George Sangmeister, tested the effect of name preference under 2 conditions: (1) where name only was known, and (2) where name and position on issues were known. Results show that name effect was strong under name-only condition; insignificant where issues were known.

[42.12] Price, Roger & Stern, Leonard. (1960). *What not to name the baby*. Los Angeles: Price, Stern, Sloan, 127p. Cartoons. Also published in 1966 as *How dare you call me that* in London.
Has a light approach that people fit stereotypes of their names. Spoofs on about 45 male and 45 female names.

[42.13] Robinson, Cardew. (1975, Dec. 25 & 1976, Jan. 1). You name it. *The Listener*, p. 882.
Discussion of sound and association of names, Edward Pratt not sounding as formidable as Boris Karloff. Other names mentioned include: Englebert Humperdinck, Machiavelli, and Borgia.

[42.14] Sumser, John. (1992). Not just any Tom, Dick or Harry: The grammar of names in television drama. *Media, Culture & Society, 14*, 605-622. Refs.
Study of how the content of mass media messages is received. Analysis of how names (both 1st names and surnames) are used and perceived. The assumption was that there were certain kinds of "type" names, a jealous husband, policeman gone bad, a gambler, etc. Regular characters such as Ironside were not used. Rather, it was "type names." Names were taken from 106 television programs which had been broadcast earlier and which it was thought the respondents would not have seen. Results indicate that respondents were able to match descriptions such as "most educated" or "preppie, young, blonde high school girl who was the only daughter of well-to-do parents." with the correct name (from the original broadcast) out of 4 choices. Whites were more accurate than non-whites. Women were slightly more accurate than men. Women were slightly better overall than men.

[42.15] White, Diana. (1981, Apr.). What's in a name? *Glamour,* pp. 127-128, 130. Discussion of implications of studies by John W. McDavid, Edwin D. Lawson, Christopher P. Andersen, Sue Browder, Rom Harré and others.

42.1. STEREOTYPES AND NAMES: *First Names*

[42.1.1] Andrews, Lori B. (1982, Aug.). The X factors. *Parents Magazine, 57(8),* p. 32, 34, 40.
Among the factors that might affect a woman's success in business might be a 1st name that projects a negative image. Interpretations based on the work of Ashley and Garwood are discussed.

[42.1.2] Elkin, Stanley. (1988, May). Elkin on Stanleyness. *Harper's,* p. 36.
On the stereotype of a Stanley.

[42.1.3] Ingram, Marsha Jill. (1978). *First name stereotypes in sex-role attribution.* Unpublished bachelor's thesis. Newcomb College, Tulane University, New Orleans, 67p.
Extensive research in 2 parts. In Part 1, sex-role androgeny scores were developed for individuals and correlated with various categories of name (1st name, nickname, etc.). Part 2 (which was not supported) hypothesized that people with less sex-typed names would be perceived as more androgenous.

[42.1.4] Lacey, Marj Frazier. (1974, Feb.). Names can hurt. *McCall's,* p. 55.
Unconventional names such as Hubert or Bertha can hurt a child. Ref. to work of Herbert Harari and John W. McDavid [87:41.25].

[42.1.5] Lawson, Edwin D. (1992). Psychological dimensions of women's names: A semantic differential analysis. *Namenkundliche Informationen, 61/62,* 35-71. Refs. Tables.
Also: ERIC Document Reproduction Service No. ED 343 409. Summary in *Research in Education,* 1992, *27(7),* 87.
In a follow-up to Lawson [87:41.33] evaluated stereotypes of over 500 different women's names on 6 dimensions using the Osgood semantic differential. The dimensions used were: Good-Bad, Strong-Weak, Active-Passive, Sincere-Insincere, Intelligent-Dumb, and Calm-Weak.

[42.1.6] Lawson, Edwin D., & Roeder, Lynn M. (1986). Women's full first names, short names, and affectionate names: A semantic differential analysis. *Names, 34,* 175-184. Refs. Tables. Figs.
Sampling of nine triads such as Barbara, Barb, and Barbie indicates that on semantic differential dimensions women clearly dislike the affectionate (Barbie) form, but men do not.

[42.1.7] Leirer, Von O., Hamilton, David L., & Carpenter, Sandra. (1982). Common first names as cues for inferences about personality. *Personality & Social Psychology Bulletin, 8,* 712-718. Refs.
Results from 2 studies of 3 forms of 1st names: full (as Edward), hypocoristic (as Ed), and affectionate (as Eddie) were used to evaluate stereotypes based on form. Experiment 1 employed a free-sorting procedure to show the 3 name forms indicate different personality types. Experiment 2 demonstrated that different personality patterns were identified by the different name forms.

[42.1.8] Mehrabian, Albert. (1990). *The name game.* Bethesda, MD: National Press Books, 160p.

Popular presentation. Research based upon factor analysis of approx. 900 male names and 700 female names on 6 dimensions: success, morality, health, warmth, cheerful, and male-female. Raters used 38 subscales for each name. Example show that Abner is rated very low on success; Abraham, high on morality.

[42.1.9] Royko, Mike. (1989, Nov.). What's in a name? *Readers Digest*, pp. 195-196. [Condensation from *Chicago Tribune*, June 4, 1987].
Anecdotal and humorous on naming children.

[42.1.10] Steele, Kenneth M., & Southwick, Laura E. (1989). First names and first impressions: A fragile relationship. *Sex Roles, 21,* 517-52Refs.
Measured judgments using the semantic differential on 4 "good" and 4 "bad" male 1st names under 2 conditions: (1) without photographs, (2) with photographs. Results without photographs confirm the work of Lawson [87:41.29 and others] but results with photographs do not show the effect of 1st name on 1st impressions.

43. STYLE AND NAMES
(See Also: 3. ADDRESS; 9.17.1. ETHNIC NAMES: *English: Address*

[43.1] Baker, Russell. (1987, June 7). First-name fixation. *New York Times Magazine*, p. 14.
Uses the observation that Washingtonians referred to Col. Oliver North (Iran scandal) as Ollie to spoof 1st-naming of people like Mayor Ed Koch, Henry Kissinger, and others.

[43.2] Bauer, Harry C. (1958). "Bonum nomen, bonum omen." [Seasoned to Taste]. *Wilson Library Bulletin, 33,* 4.
Explanation of why people are listed under surname rather than font-name (1st name). There are more individuals with the same 1st name than the same last name, example, John vs. Smith.

[43.3] Burke, W. (1962, Sept.). First things first. *Atlantic, 210,* p. 97.
Points out that mainland China puts the surname 1st, orientals in Japan and Hawaii put it last, and Koreans do it both ways.

[43.4] Dion, Kenneth L. (1987). What's in a title? The Ms. stereotype and images of women's titles of address. *Psychology of Women Quarterly, 11,* 21-36.
Two studies indicate that women who prefer the Ms. title give the impression of being more-achievement oriented, socially assertive, and dynamic but lacking in interpersonal warmth as compared to other titles. 20 refs.

[43.5] Kilpatrick, James J. (1985, June). Good night, Sam-Bob. *Nation's Business*, p. 6.
Bemoans the rise of short forms (Al, Jim) and affectionate forms (Jimmy, Bobby) in everyday life (politics, hospitals, license plates). Compares these forms in Congress today (117 out of 435) with 16 in a list 50 years ago.

[43.6] Minton, A(rthur). (1958). Some aspects of the form of personal names. *American Speech, 33,* 35-45. Refs.
Examination of a number of styles of 1st name, middle name(s), surname, and use of initials. Many examples.

[43.7] Rovere, Richard H. (1958, Aug. 16). John Knox rides again. *New Yorker*, Pp. 74, 76, 78-79.
Notes that since previous article [Smith:1561A] was completed, he has noted that the use of 3 names of prominent New York City clergyman, example, John Haynes Holmes,

there has been a decided shift to 2 names and an initial, as, the Reverend Robert J. McCracken.

44. SURNAMES
(Includes Family Names, Last Names, and Patronyms)
(See Also: 9. ETHNIC NAMES for surnames of various ethnic groups)

[44.1] Ashley, Leonard R. N. (1991). Nicknames and surnames: Neglected origins of family names, especially surnames derived from inn signs. *Names,* 39, 167-179. Refs. Calls for the expansion for categories of surnames derived from nicknames to include women's occupations (Baxter, Webster), matronymics (Babson, Gittleson), pet names (Bard < Bartholemew), and names derived from inn signs (Cheever, Lamb).

[44.2] Baker, Ross K. (1987, Nov.). Hyphen-ated Americans. *American Demographics, 9,* p. 64.
Hyphenated in this article refers to emerging practice of couples combining their surnames at marriage so that the wife does not lose her identity. Anecdotal.

[44.3] Baum, S. V. (1958). Legend-makers on the campus. [Miscellany]. *American Speech, 33,* 292-293. Refs.
Describes how the surnames Rinehart and Rowbottom became the rallying cries for spring carousing on the campuses at Harvard and the University of Pennsylvania, respectively.

[44.4] Chavez, Angelico (Fray). (1957). New Names in New Mexico, 1820-1850. *El Palacio* [Santa Fe], *64,* 291-318; 367-380. Refs.
Information on 300+ surnames of new arrivals shows that French-Canadian, US American, and North European names exceeded Spanish and Mexican. Data were obtained from baptismal and marriage records and other sources. Entries include name of the individual and when available names of parents and children as well as geographical background information.

[44.5] Chua-Eoan, Howard G. (1989, Apr.). It hyphened one night. [Behavior]. *Time* (Can and US eds), p. 60. Illus.
The problems of coping with a hyphenated surname.

[44.6] Eckler, A. Ross. (1986). Single-letter surnames. In A. Ross Eckler (Ed.) *Names and games: Onomastics and recreational linguistics* (pp. 37-40). Lanham, MD: University Press of America.
Lists 52 surnames found in telephone directories composed of only the single letter O. Included are Su O of Trenton, NJ and Ook Whon O of Urbana, IL. Also, 11 names are listed composed of only I or U. Other single-letter names are listed in directories but may be in error.

[44.7] Eckler, A. Ross. (1986). The terminal man. In A. Ross Eckler (Ed.) *Names and games: Onomastics and recreational linguistics* (pp. 45-51). Lanham, MD: University Press of America.
List of 35+ terminal names (last names in a directory) from US telephone directories, examples. Hero Zzyzzx, B. Zzyzzk. 20 names from other countries also listed.

[44.8] Eckler, A. Ross. (1993). Single-letter surnames. In E. Wallace McMullen (Ed.) *Names new and old: Papers of the Names Institute* (pp. 261-264). Madison, NJ: Privately published.
Similar to Eckler [44.6].

[44.9] Emery, Richard W. (1952). The use of the surname in the study of medieval economic history. *Medievalia Humanistica, 7,* 43-50. Refs.
Criticizes Lopez [9.33.8] and other writers who assume that surnames of the 13th cent. such as *Gualterius englesius* ("the Englishman, Walter") mentioned in a Genoese [legal] act indicate that the person is really from England. Emery lists surnames and gives reasons to question whether the persons were actually from those places. Among the explanations, an ancestor might have come from the place, it might have been a nickname.

[44.10] Eno, Joel N. (1988/89). The nomenclature of Connecticut families: Parts 1- *Connecticut Nutmegger, 21,* 215-216 (Part 1); 416-421 (Part 2); 609-612 (Part 3).
Lists over 250 colonial individuals and gives meaning of their 1st and surnames, examples, Barnes, < OE, "at the barn,"; Hide, < OE, "hid (120 acres of land." The purpose is to show that: (1) the list represents CT families today, and (2) that 1st names were only unusual or canting religious names. Lists are from Hartford, New Haven Colony, and Saybrook.

[44.11] Francis, Darryl. (1986). A color ado. In A. Ross Eckler (Ed.) *Names and games: Onomastics and recreational linguistics* (pp. 41-42). Refs. Lanham, MD: University Press of America.
Responding to Smith's *Treasury of name lore* [87:1.15] on color names, provides a list of 100+ colors that are also surnames. Included are: Amber, Claret, Shell, and Sherry.

[44.12] Haugaard, Kay. (1986). The daughter of the farrier. *Word Ways, 19,* 118-119.
107 surnames derived from occupations. Included are: Carver, Fletcher, Thatcher, and Warner.

[44.13] Hector, Leonard Charles. (1967). Names, Medieval. In *New Catholic Encyclopedia, 10,* 203-24. New York: McGraw-Hill.
Description of the rise of surnames beginning with the end of the 10th cent. Also mentions that 2 or more living children of the same parents could have the same baptismal names.

[44.14] Jaffe, A. J., Cullen, Ruth M., & Boswell, Thomas D. (1980). *The changing demography of Spanish Americans.* New York: Academic Press, 426p. Refs. Table.
Pp. 335-341 are concerned with statistics on the Spanish-origin populations in the US based upon Census Bureau reports. The table on p. 340 identifies 5 groups of Spanish Americans, Mexican, Cuban, Puerto Rican, Central and South America, and Other Spanish and gives the percentages of those with and without Spanish surnames.

[44.15] Lardner, Rex. (1974, Oct.). What your name means to you. *Pageant,* 83-88.
Popular presentation on surnames.

[44.16] Paffard, Michael. (1980). The fascination of a name. *Use of English, 32,* 33-40. Refs.
Apparently directed at 2ndary school teachers. Explains how surnames can develop into an interesting class project. General discussion of types of surname. Many examples.

[44.17] Roberts, Warren E. (1981). Hoosier, Yankee, and Yoho: Some comments on family names in Indiana. *Kansas Quarterly, 13,* 73-83. Refs.
General. On the importance of surnames in the study of folklore with special reference to Indiana. Attention to Hoosier, Yankee, and Yoho as surnames.

[44.18] Sabine, William H. W. (1957). Surnames of the American presidents. *Manuscripts, 9,* 252-257; 260.

Gives origins, example, Cleveland is the name of a hamlet in Yorkshire. "*Cleve* was the Middle English spelling of cliff. The 'cleveland' was the land abutting the cliff.'"

[44.19] Smith, Elsdon C. (1971). Surnames from landscape feature. *Proceedings of the 10th ICOS, Vienna, 1969 (Disputationes ad montium vocabula allorumque nominum significationes pertinentes), 3,* 399-409.
Background on how topological features came into use as surnames to supplement the small number of 1st names. Many examples including: Atwell, Underwood, Brugger, Serrano, and Meadows.

[44.20] Stein, Lou. (1986). *Clues to our family names.* Bowie, MD: Heritage, 196p. Refs.
Surnames evaluated along 5 themes: early development, nicknames, occupations, patronyms, and placenames. Index refers to 2000+ names covered in the text where their meanings are discussed.

[44.21] Surname. (1991). *NewEncyBrit, 24,* 411.
Brief entry. Gives basic information on surnames. For extended entry also in *NewEncyBrit,* See: Zgusta [1.49].

44.1. SURNAMES: *Specific*

[44.1.1] Cummins, W. A. (1973). Telephone directories and summaries, *Genealogists' Magazine, 17,* 266-269. Refs.
Explains how telephone directories can be used to estimate the percentage of Cummins/Cummings or variations in England that came from Ireland or Scotland. The same technique can be applied to other surnames such as Murphy.

[44.1.2] Emerson, O. B. & Hermann, John P. (1986). William Faulkner and the Falkner family name. *Names, 34,* 255-265. Refs.
Extensive examination of various views on why Faulkner changed the spelling of his name from the original *Falkner* to *Faulkner* which was the spelling before his great-grandfather changed it.

[44.1.3] Faubus. [Note]. (1957). *Names, 5,* 225.
Points out that the name Faubus is a German form of Phoebus (according to Elsdon Smith in the *Dictionary of American family names* (1956). It is a name used by Jews with the meaning equivalent to that of Me'ir and Uri. An abstract of the Smith 1973 edition is [87:43.1.18]).

[44.1.4] Packer, J. I. (1986, May 16). The unspectacular Packers. *Christianity Today,* p. 12.
Reactions to an advertising circular *The amazing book of the Packers in America.* Finally, decides not to order.

45. UNIQUE NAMES
(Includes Low Frequency, Peculiar, Uncommon, and Unusual Names)

[45.1] Anderson, Timothy. (1985). Unique and common first names of males and females. *Psychological Reports, 57,* 204-206.
Responding to studies reporting that males with unique names are more likely to be disturbed than females, evaluated the birth names of 6125 boys and girls, concluding that it is "more an anomaly...for a male to receive a unique first name."

[45.2] Armour, Richard. (1970). East is East but West is best. *Saturday Review, 53,*
Oct. 3 1970, p. 4.
Observes that there are proportionately more people named West than North, East, and
South.

[45.3] Bell, Robert A. (1984). Relationship of loneliness to desirability and uniqueness
of first names. *Psychological Reports, 55,* 950. Refs.
Students completed the UCLA Loneliness Scale. Judges rated their names on desirability
and uniqueness. Results indicate that loneliness is more related to desirability than
uniqueness.

[45.4] Carlova, John. (1959, Oct.). What's in a name? Plenty! *Coronet,* p. 107.
The two drivers in an auto accident were named Mr. Crash and Miss Collision. An
Oklahoma tippler was named Daniel Drunkard. Other unique names also mentioned.

[45.5] Clancy, Daniel Francis. (1954). Names that made news. *American Mercury, 79,*
115-116.
35+ unique names from the news include: Please Wright, a postmaster; Joseph Drunk,
arrested for drunken driving in New York City; and John St. Peter, a morgue worker.

[45.6] Exotic taste, An. (1890, Mar.). [Contributors Club]. Atlantic Monthly, 65,
430-431.
Comment on a few unique Southern names and anecdotal report of a Louisiana girl
named *Ettolie* which really turned out to be *Etoile* [French, "star"]. Another girl was
named *Alone* Jones. *Alone* was the name of a novel.

[45.7] Fotheringham, Allan. (1991, Apr. 29). A name! A name! Anything for a name!
Maclean's, p. 64. Cartoon.
Description of the Society for the Verification and Enjoyment of Fascinating Names of
Actual Persons (SVEFNAP). Lists at least 40 unique names including: I. M. Digger,
an undertaker; Sam Driller, a dentist; and Procter R. Hugg, Jr., a judge.

[45.8] Gardner, Martin. (1986). Major Minor. In A. Ross Eckler (Ed.) *Names and
games: Onomastics and recreational linguistics* (pp. 43-45). Refs. Lanham, MD:
University Press of America.
Reports a man named Minor W. Major. Comments section additionally reports a
sergeant (military rank) Major and a Major Floyd E. Minor.

[45.9] God, according to a court decree, lives in Fresno, California. (1981,Nov. 20).
Christianity Today, p. 76.
About a man who changed his name [apparently his surname] to God.

[45.10] Gross, John. (1986, Feb. 20). What's in a name? Count the ways. *New York
Times,* C19.
Reactions to John Train's *Most remarkable names* and Sloan's *Baby boomer book of
names.*

[45.11] Harris, M. C. (1960). What's in a name. *Daughters of the American
Revolution, 94(June-July),* 446.
Lists 50 women and 40 men with unusual names. Most are 1st names. Examples for
women are: Barbara Goose, Freelove Tuttle, and Experience Sanders; for men, Wanton
Corey, Consider Hills, and Welcome Picksley.

[45.12] Helfer, H. (1954, Dec. 5). Something in a name. *New York Times Magazine,*
p. 274.

Lists a few unusual names, O. W. Fillerup of the Wine Institute, Shirley Long marrying Michael Short.

[45.13] Lambdin, William G. (1973). Wild and woolly names. *College Composition & Communication, 24,* 275-276.
General on unique names. Several are mentioned including: Mary Lou Wham, Julia C. Barefoot, States Rights Gist, and E Pluribus Unum Husted.

[45.14] Liguori, Irene. (1989, Dec. 16). Original Donald Duck isn't a Disney quack. *Buffalo News,* p. C1.
The problems of a man whose real name is Donald Duck.

[45.15] Lindskoog, Kathryn. (1984, Mar. 2). Did you hear the one about Cardinal Sin? *Christianity Today,* p. 27.
Has about 13 unique names, some not seen elsewhere. Included are: J. Dwight Pentecost of Dallas Theological Seminary, a surgeon name Corpus and a nurse named Basin.

[45.16] Lorenz, Brenna. (1989). Origins of unusual personal names from the Southern United States. *Names, 37,* 201-230. Refs. Tables.
The South is noted for its unique 1st names. Description of several types including: names derived from states (Arkansas, Okla), from blends (Bernestine < Bernice and Ernestine), and phonetic selling of foreign names (Waneta < Juanita). 26 tables show the different types along with documentation.

[45.17] Lowry, Lillian. (1953). Christian names in Western Kentucky. *Midwest Folklore, 3,* 131-136.
Responding to Arthur Palmer Hudson [Smith:1636], points out that there are a number of unusual and original white 1st names. Among these are people named after celebrities, movie stars, and circumstances at birth. Some families have only used initials. Many examples.

[45.18] Marshall, Arthur. (1978, Mar. 31). Names please. [First Person]. *New Statesman* [London], p. 432.
Reacting to Train's book *Remarkable names of real people* [87:46.20], selects some odd names to mention, Tunis Wind, Sharon Willfahrt, Cinderella Hardcock, and Noble Teat, then adds a few of his own.

[45.19] Melting the pot. [Egos]. (1982, Mar. 23). *Time,* p. 7
Deals with name changes among entertainers. One exception is Rip Torn, which is really his name.

[45.20] Name of the game is names. (1969, Apr. 30).
Christian Century, 86, 63
Lists 15+ religious books which have unusual combinations of title and author, examples, *Breakfast with the risen Lord* by Frye and *The sin no one talk about* by Parrott.

[45.21] Nilsen, Don L. F. (1987). Names: Some subsidiary functions. *Publications of the North Central Name Society, No. 2,* 108-115. Refs.
Wide-ranging survey of 100+ unique names with background material. Examples include Warren Peace, Iva Reason, and Jack Knife. The Coolidge effect also described.

[45.22] O'Shaughnessy, Marjorie. (1962). It sounded as though you said, "Plonia Hoogenboozem." [ANS Notes]. *Names, 10,* 79-80.

Listing of approx. 60 unusual names in various categories. Among them: Oveta Culp Hobby, public figures; Mischa Violin (violinist), occupations; and a girl named Mountain marrying a man named Pond (couples).

[45.23] Sears, Albert D. (1952, Nov. 16). What's in a name? *New York Times Magazine*, p. 42.
Listing of a number of individuals associated with events in contrast to their names. Examples include Minnie Penman who retired after teaching penmanship, "A motorist...crashed through Mr. St. Peter's gate."

[45.24] Sidney, John. (1956). Names that aren't. *American Mercury, 83,* 29-31.
Comment on about 30 1st name/surname combinations that might cause ridicule. Included are: Katz Meow, Pearl Tooth, and Meek Beaver.

[45.25] Sign of the goat [Law]. (1953, Mar. 16). *Time,* p. 27.
Column devoted to unusual names stimulated by a Philadelphia man who changed his name from Henry Green to Peaceful Heart. Listing of about 10 unusual 1st names and 10 unusual surnames.

[45.26] Stohlman, Martha Lou. (1971, Jan. 23). Appellations. *Saturday Review,* pp. 4,6.
Looking at the Springfield, Missouri telephone directory helps recall characteristic Ozark 1st names. Examples include Irl, Burl, Murl, Warrie, and Rillis.

[45.27] Sullivan, Robert. (1985. Oct. 14). Maafala in for Maafala. *Sports Illustrated, 63,* p. 19.
Notes that the University of Hawaii has 4 sets of brothers on the football team, the Kafentzises, the Nogas, the Goeases, and the Maafalas.

[45.28] Train, John. (1985) *Most remarkable names*. New York: Clarkson N. Potter, 132p. Illus.
Foreward by George Plimpton. Continues Train's work on unusual names. See: [87 46:20-21]. This listing of approx. 500 names (Train claims verification of all of these) includes: Muffy Virgin, Oscar Asparagus, and Salome Casanova.

[45.29] What's in a name (UPI). (1984, Nov. 30). *Evening Observer* [Dunkirk-Fredonia, NY], p. 12.
Parents (formerly Claudia and Cecil McGirt) gave their son the name Dr. Semaj Al-anubiaimhotepokorohamz with 34 single-spaced typed pages between Semaj and the last part.

[45.30] What's in a name? (1982, July 19). *New York Times*, p. A12.
Enten Eller, indicted for failing to register for the draft, explained that Eller is Danish for "either/or," and Enten Eller is the title of a book by Kirkegaard.

[45.31] Wulf, Steve. (1987, Dec. 21). *Sports Illustrated*, p. 9.
Arkansas Razorback fans wear plastic snouts and shout "Sooie, pig." A couple named their son Ray Zorback Ford, their choice for a girl, Sue E. Ford.

[45.32] Young, Dariel A. (1980, Dec.). What's not in a name. [Newsline]. *Psychology Today, 14,* pp. 23-24.
Summary of research of Richard L. Zweigenhaft [87:46.27]. Men and women with unique 1st names score no lower than others on personality tests. Juniors scored lower than those with numerical suffixes.

[45.33] Zero for 1069. (1980, Jun 2). *U. S. News and World Report*, p. 8.
Story of Michael Herbert Dengler who tried to legally change his name to 1069. The courts did agree to allow him to switch to One-Zero-Six-Nine.

[45.34] Zuckerman, Diana. (1985, Mar.). Call me Ishmael. [Children]. *Psychology Today*, p. 12. Ref.
Discussion of Ford, Masters, & Miura [87:41.17] who reported no correlations between children's academic and social performance in school and their names.

46. WOMEN AND NAMES

[46.1] Alia, Valerie. (1984). Women, names, and power. *Women & Language, 8*, 34-35. Refs.
Uses numerous cross-cultural examples to illustrate the relationships between naming practices and power (usually male-domination).

[46.2] Dion, Kenneth L. & Schuller, Regina A. (1990). Ms. and the manager: A tale of two stereotypes. *Sex Roles, 22*, 569-577. Refs. Table.
Concludes that "a woman preferring Ms. as her title of address was seen...as possessing the 'requisite' personality characteristics of a successful, middle manager; whereas a traditionally titled woman was not."

[46.3] Duggan, Deborah A., Cota, Albert A., & Dion, Kenneth L. (1993). Taking thy husband's name: What it might mean. *Names, 41*, 87-102. Refs.
Review of 9 empirical studies about identity and marital names of women. Included are studies of Holt [87:34.1.4], Intons-Peterson [46.3.2], and Kupper [46.3.3].

[46.4] Rudnyckyj, J. B. (1969). Brief submitted to the Royal Commission on the Status of Women on behalf of the Canadian Institute of Onomastic Sciences. *OnoCan, No. 40*, pp. 5-9.
Recommends that married women should: (1) be required to assume their husbands' surnames, (2) should be allowed to use their birth 1st names, and (3) show the feminine form of their husbands' surname if from a language with feminine suffixes.

[46.5] Rudnyckyj, J. B. (1991). Socio-onomastic status of women. *Rudnyckiana, No. 7*, pp. 12-20. Refs.
Supports the position that a married woman should use her own 1st name (not that of her husband) but should adopt her husband's surname. (Paper read at the 16th ICOS but not included in the *Proceedings*).

46.1. WOMEN AND NAMES: *Birth Names*

[46.1.1] Center for a Woman's Own Name. (1974). *Booklet for women who wish to determine their names after marriage*. Barrington, IL: Center for a Woman's Own Name, 56p. Refs.
Description of procedures to follow for women who want to keep their surname after marriage. Section on children's names. List of experienced attorneys.

[46.1.2] Embleton, Sheila & Atkinson, Donna L. (1985). Maiden name retention. *Ontario Genealogical Society Seminar Annual, 7*, 37-47. Refs.
Brief review of the history of women assuming husband's name at marriage in England. Anecdotal reports to maiden name retention. Results of a survey.

[46.1.3] Hughes, Marija Matich. (1971). And then there were two. *Hastings Law Journal, 23,* 233-247.
Overview of the law (1971) with regard to a married woman using her birth name or any name other than her husband's; proposed legislation, names of children; other issues; and solutions. Many legal citations.

[46.1.4] Kohout, Joan S. (1973). The right of women to use their maiden names. *Albany Law Review, 38,* 105-124. Refs.
Review of the legal literature. Presentation of arguments in favor of a woman's right to retain her maiden (birth) name at marriage.

[46.1.5] Linden, Myra J. (1986). The use of married women's maiden names on Illinois gravestones: A preliminary report. *Publications of the North Central Name Society, No. 1,* 173-186. Refs. Fig.
3345 married women's names were obtained from Illinois cemetery markers. Reports among other findings that the use of maiden [birth] names was 40% in 1890; in the 1920s, 30%; in the 1930s, 17%; and 26% in the 1940s.

[46.1.6] Lublin, Joann S. (1975). Ms.--Taken identity. *Seventeen, 34,* 47-48.
Suggestions for women who wish to keep their birth names after marriage, example, having both wife's and husband's names for checking accounts.

[46.1.7] MacDougall, Priscilla Ruth. (1972/73). Married women's common law rights to their own surnames. *Women's Rights Law Reporter, 1,* 2-14. Refs.
Review of important court decisions in Alabama and Maryland on a woman's right to retain her birth name at marriage; the early feminist crusade; American case law, and statutory abrogation. Concludes that the US follows English common law which allows but does not compel women to assume their husband's name at marriage. Looks forward to passage of the Equal Rights Amendment.

[46.1.8] Name of the dame. (1973, Aug. 20). *Newsweek,* pp. 49-50.
Concise description of the legal status of a woman' right to keep her own name at marriage.

[46.1.9] Quindlen, Anna. (1987, Mar. 4). The name is mine: This is why I have never changed it. [Life in the 30s]. *New York Times, Section C,* P. 12.
Autobiographical. Kept her birth name after marriage. Kept her identity but there are also some difficulties.

[46.1.10] Slade, Margot. (1984, Dec. 17). The last-name game: A balancing act. *New York Times,* p. B14. Illus.
Aspects of problems of identification involved with name change at marriage and after.

[46.1.11] Walterscheid, Ellen. (1989, July-Aug.). The name game: Keeping your surname after marriage. *Women in Business,* pp. 18-19, 14. Illus.
On the choices available for a woman with regard to retaining her birth name at marriage. Some information on legal rights and hyphenation.

[46.1.12] Whitehorne, Katharine. (1978, Mar. 5). Naming the game. *Observer* [London], p. 27. Portrait.
Anecdotal of the author who kept her birth name.

[46.1.13] Williamson, Jane. (1982, Apr.). The name game. *Working Woman,* p. 118.
General on women retaining their birth names. Recommends working women retain theirs at marriage. Information on how to regain a birth name.

46.2. WOMEN AND NAMES: *Law and Legal Aspects*

[46.2.1] Byciewicz, Shirley Raissi & MacDonnell, Gloria Jeanne Stillson. (1993). Married women's surnames. *Connecticut Law Review, 5,* 598-621. Refs.
Review of the legal status of married women's names. Attention to rules for voting, use of motor vehicles, social security, passport, etc. Advice for women who wish to retain their birth names.

[46.2.2] Call him foolish. (1988, July 25). *Time,* p. 37.
Report of a Federal judge in Pittsburgh who threatened a lawyer with jail when she insisted on being referred to as Ms. Wolvovitz, rather than Mrs. Lobel, after her husband. The judge later apologized.

[46.2.3] Gordon, Lois B. (1974). Pre-marriage name change, resumption and reregistration statutes. *Columbia Law Review, 74,* 1508-1527. Refs.
Review of name change procedures in several types of situation, state-by-state. Extensive documentation.

46.3. WOMEN AND NAMES: *Surnames*

[46.3.1] Foss, Karen A., & Edson, Belle A. (1989). What's in a name? Accounts of married women's name choices. *Western Journal of Speech Communication, 53,* 356-373. Refs. Fig.
Questionnaire results from 3 groups of married women (those who adopted their husband's surname, those who retained their birth name, and those who chose a hyphenated name) lead to a formulation of how each group perceives the self, the relationship, and the culture.

[46.3.2] Intons-Peterson, Margaret Jean, & Crawford, Jill. (1985). The meanings of marital surnames. *Sex Roles, 12,* 1163-1171. Refs.
Questionnaires completed by 2 adult groups (1 younger and unmarried, the other older with some married) indicate that for both sexes names are an important source of identity. Both sexes underestimate how much women identify with premarital names.

[46.3.3] Kupper, Susan J. (1990). *Surnames for women: A decision-making guide.* Jefferson, NC: McFarland, 147p. Refs.
Interviews of 362 women and 70 husbands are used to explore the various types of surname choice. The sample was select and mostly urban/suburban and well-educated. Choices for surname for women today include: keeping birth name, when marrying taking a hyphenated name, taking the husband's surname, and creating a new surname for self and husband. Other possibilities and alternatives for children also covered. Also attention to legal aspects of name change.

47. WORDS FROM NAMES

[47.1] Alia, Valerie. (1991). The politics of eponymy: Power, protection, classification, commemoration. *OnoCan, 73,* 57-66. Refs.
Defines 2 types of eponym: protective and commemorative. *"Protective eponymy* is a kind of collective alias. It shelters the political 'criminal' and collectivizes individual action." Example, Ned Ludd [for followers of Ned Ludd]. Commemorative eponymy attributes responsibility to an individual (pasteurization, Victorian Age).

[47.2] Auger, C. P. (1975). *Engineering eponyms,* (2nd ed. rev.). London: The Library Association, 122p. Refs.

Entries for approx. 750 engineering eponyms (from the US, Britain, and Europe). Most entries give dates of original inventor/developer, name of the invention, and often 2 references. Among the eponyms are: the Davy Safety Lamp for miners and the De Laval Steam Turbine.

[47.3] Beecher, Carla. (1994, May/June). Crowd control: When sports fanatics turn violent. *Illinois Quarterly*, pp. 22-25.
Side entry on p. 23 attributes the term *hooligan* to "Patrick Hooligan, an Irishman living in the Southwark section of London... around the turn of the century." He was the leader of a gang of ruffians who came to the attention of the police. See Also: [47.17].

[47.4] Beeching, Cyril Leslie. (1982). A dictionary of eponyms, (2nd ed.). London: Clive Bingley, 214p.
Information on 400 words derived from people's names. Includes Pinkerton (detective), pompadour (hair style), and Rastafarian (from Ras Tafari, Haile Selassie, Emperor of Ethiopia).

[47.5] Burchfield, R. W. (Ed.). (1972). *A supplement to the Oxford English dictionary, 4 Vols*. Oxford: Clarendon.
Contains many words derived from names, examples, boysenberry from Rudolph Boysen, an American horticulturalist; Croesus, referring to a rich man, goes back to the 6th cent. BC king of Lydia.

[47.6] Chapman, Diane. (1982, Autumn). Eponymous anonymous. *Verbatim, 9(2)*, 1-2.
General on eponyms (words derived from people). Approx. 75 mentioned including: derby, bowler (hat), and graham cracker.

[47.7] Clark, Thomas L. (1987). *The dictionary of gambling and gaming*. Cold Spring, NY: Lexik House, 263p. Refs.
In this dictionary of approx. 4800 items, there are approx. 50 terms that were derived from personal names. These include: a Dolly Parton (a single pip on each die, snake eyes), a Jack Benny (a 3 and a 9 card, because Benny claimed to be 39), and Jackson five (5 $20 bills, from the portrait of Jackson).

[47.8] Espy, Willard R. (1978). *Thou improper, thou uncommon noun*. New York: Clarkson N. Potter, 366p. Refs.
Has name origins of over 2000 words, at least a third seem to be eponyms. Includes words such as pants (Pantaleone, patron saint of Venice), jock strap (from Jock, Scottish short form of John), and merkin, a type of mop (from Mabel, once a common name for scullery maids.

[47.9] Fichtner, E. G. (1967). The etymology of 'goliard.' *Neophilologus, 51*, 230-237. Refs.
Explains that in the limited Church sense *sensus tropologicus*, goliard (a term applied to wandering clerics and then to the kind of poetry associated with them) can be connected to the biblical Golias (Goliath).

[47.10] Francis, Darryl. (1986). McGovern words. In A. Ross Eckler (Ed.) *Names and games: Onomastics and recreational linguistics* (pp. 61-64). Lanham, MD: University Press of America.
Development of such words as anti-McGovern, anti-McGovernite, McGovernism, McGovernize, etc. at the time of the 1972 presidential election when Senator George McGovern was running as a candidate.

[47.11] Garfield, Eugene. (1977). The mystery of the transposed journal lists: Wherein Bradford's law of scattering is generalized according to Garfield's law of concentration. *Essays of an Information Scientist, 1,* 222-22Refs.
Relates to eponyms (Bradford's law and Garfield's law) which related to a small number of journals accounting for most of the significant literature on a specific topic.

[47.12] George, K. E. M. (1986). Forenames as common nouns in English and French. *Neophilologica, 58,* 39-45. Refs.
Many names, both in English and in French, have become words. Systematic classification of these names into Animate and Inanimate categories with sub-categories as well. There are 200-300 examples including *adonis* which is a handsome young man in both languages and Tom, Dick, and Harry = Pierre, Paul, et Jacques.

[47.13] Gold, David L. (1986). How did biblical personal names come to designate wine bottles in English? *Names, 34,* 351-35. Refs.
Comment and discussion on wine bottles named *jorum, jeroboam, rehoboam, methusaleh, salmanazar, balthazar,* and *nebuchadnezer.*

[47.14] Greenway, John. (1961). The growth of John Henry. [Notes & Queries]. *Western Folklore, 20,* 275.
Points out that the phrase "I put my John Hancock on it" meaning to sign one's name has now become confused with the legend of John Henry so that now people say "I put my John Henry on it."

[47.15] Hengst, Karlheinz. (1990). LSP onomastics in the German Democratic Republic. *Proceedings of the 16th ICOS, Laval University, Quebec, 1987,* 317-326. Refs.
Describes how personal names can be used in LSP (language specific situation) in specific areas of science (terms such as ampere, volt), industry (bikini names such as Andrea, Dagmar) and other areas.

[47.16] It's safer to name men for roses than to name roses for men. (1953, Oct. 24). Saturday Evening Post, p. 12.
Naming roses after living people (or even streets or city squares) may be a risky business since the popularity of the person commemorated may go down. A few examples given.

[47.17] Jarv, Harry. (1973). Hooliganism: The origin of the word and its implications. In *Otium et negotium: Studies in onomatology and library science presented to Olof von Feilitzen, Acta Bibliothecae Regiae Stockholmiensis, 16,* 170-180. Refs.
Traces the Russian and Finnish use of this word to London in the 1880s or early 1890s. There is special reference to Clarence Rook's *The Hooligan nights* published in London in 1899. See Also: [47.3].

[47.18] Lapierre, André. (1988). French eponyms revisited. *OnoCan, 70,* 15-22. Refs. Tables.
Analysis of 1429 opaque eponyms from the *Petit Robert* dictionary concluding that "a distinction ought to be made between eponyms which have evolved within a linguistic tradition and others which came into the language as loanwords."

[47.19] Manser, Martin H. (1988). *Melba toast, Bowie's knife & Caesar's wife: A dictionary of eponyms.* New York: Avon, 244p.
Has entries for approx. 750 names or expressions that have entered the language. Many are derived from personal names of real people although there are many from literature. Examples of eponyms from real people are: quisling < Vidkun Quisling (Norwegian collaborator with the Nazis); pasteurize < Louis Pasteur, French chemist.

[47.20] Merton, Robert King. (1973). *The sociology of science: Theoretical and empirical investigations* Chicago: University of Chicago Press, 605p. Refs.
Ch. 14, Priorities in Scientific Discovery (pp. 286-324) deals with eponyms in science, such as, Halley's comet, Hooke's law, etc. Ch. 20, The Mathew Effect in Science (pp. 439-459) reports on the Mathew effect, that the already famous scientist gets more credit for a discovery than a discovery of the same calibre by an unknown. Reports how this influences memory of names of co-authored article. Pp. 550-551 discuss order of names in co-authored contributions.

[47.21] Stigler, Stephen M. (1980). Stigler's law of eponymy. In *Science and social structure: A festschrift for Robert K. Merton, Transactions of the New York Academy of Sciences, 2nd series, 39,* 147-157. Refs. Table.
Stigler's law is, "No scientific discovery is named after its original discoverer." Marshals evidence to support this view. Evaluation of 80 books published 1816-1970 on use of eponyms. Gauss and Laplace cited as examples of eponymic discoveries that were not original.

[47.22] Symons, W. M. (1975). Three "technical" terms. *Old Cornwall, 8,* 177-178.
One of the terms is *Jan Luke.* It is/was used to refer to work done by an employee for himself or a friend and not entered on the time sheet. The work was done for Jan Luke.

[47.23] Thrush, Paul W. (Compiler & Ed.) & Staff of the Bureau of Mines. (1968). A dictionary of mining, mineral, and related terms. Washington, DC: US Department of the Interior, 1269p. Refs.
Has about 55,000 entries. Many of them eponyms from people, Beethoven exploder, Colbourn process, and Marsaut lamp are examples.

[47.24] Trillin, Calvin. (1987, May 2). Uncivil liberties. Nation, p. 566.
Humorous comment on naming service areas on turnpikes after people.

[47.25] Tuleja, Tad. (1987). *Namesakes.* New York: McGraw-Hill (Stonestrong Press), 226p. Refs.
An entertaining guide to the origin of more than 300 words derived from people. Includes Big Ben at the House of Parliament (Sir Benjamin Hall), bloomers (Amelia Jenks Bloomer, feminist and reformer), and Rubik's cube (Erno Rubik, Hungarian teacher). Has special section of 14 items on false leads, i.e., cesarian section is not from Caesar.

[47.26] Tuleja, Tad. (1990). *Marvelous monikers.* New York: Harmony, 206p.
Reprinting of above.

[47.27] Zusne, Leonard. (1987). *Eponyms in psychology: A dictionary and biographical sourcebook.* Westport, CT: Greenwood Press, 339p. Refs.
Entries for 800+ eponyms. Description of with biographical information on the person from whom the term takes it origin. Hundreds of refs. support the entries. Among the entries: Antigone Complex, Braille, Coolidge Effect, and Occam's Razor.

47.1. WORDS FROM NAMES: *Medical*

[47.1.1] Alsop, Stewart. (1971, Sept. 6). Taming the beast. *Newsweek,* p. 76.
Well-known Washington columnist with a possibly new disease is discomfited on learning that if the disease is confirmed, it will be named after the physician, i.e., Glick's disease, not Alsopitis.

[47.1.2] Anderson, Robert H. (1985). Editor's note. [Editorial Review]. International Journal of Cardiology, 8, 229. Refs.
Intro. to Burchell [47.1.6] on medical eponyms.

[47.1.3] Anderson, Robert H., & Becker, A. E. (1979). Accessory atrioventricular connections. [Letter to the Editor]. *Journal of Thoracic & Cardiovascular Surgery, 78,* 310-311. Refs. Illus.
Considers that the term bundle of Kent is inappropriate. Raises questions on eponyms.

[47.1.4] Anderson, Robert H.; Becker, Anton E.: Brechenmacher, Claude; Davies, Michael J.; & Rossi, Lino. (1975). Ventricular preexcitation: A proposed nomenclature for its substrates. *European Journal of Cardiology, 3,* 27-36. Refs.
States that eponyms such as Kent bundle, James fiber, or Mahaim fiber are no longer adequate and should be replaced by new (non-eponymic) terms.

[47.1.5] Archer, John. (1975). Epitomes. *Journal of the American Medical Association, 234,* 152.
The current style of the above journal does not use the possessive for an eponym, as, Cushing disease, not Cushing's disease.

[47.1.6] Burchell, Howard B. (1985). Thoughts on eponyms. [Editorial Review]. *International Journal of Cardiology, 8,* 229-234. Refs.
On the pros and cons of medical eponyms.

[47.1.7] Cogan, David. G. (1978). The rise and fall of eponyms. *Archives of Ophthalmology, 96,* 2202-220
Points out that while eponyms in medicine have their place, they can become obsolete. Mentions several eponyms including: Tay-Sachs disease, Schilder's disease, and Menke's syndrome.

[47.1.8] Cohen, M. Michael., Jr. (1979). Craniosynostitis and syndromes with craniosyntosis: Incidence, genetics, penetrance, variability, and new syndrome updating. *Birth Defects: Original Article Series, 15(5B),* 13-6Refs. Tables. Figs.
Description of a number of skull disorders having eponyms. Examples include the Apert, Couzon, and Carpenter syndromes. Background to the name bestowal not given. First mention of the Antley-Bixler syndrome.

[47.1.9] Cross, Harold E. (1973). The use and abuse of eponyms. *American Journal of Opthalmology, 76,* 598-601. Refs.
On the pros and cons of eponyms in ophthalmology. Suggests rules is the usage of eponyms.

[47.1.10] Dirckx, John H. (1983). *The language of medicine: Its evolution, structure, and dynamics,* (2nd ed.). New York: Praeger, 193p. Refs.
Pp. 78-84 systematically review various types of medical eponym. Also mention errors of common usage or understanding. Many eponyms listed.

[47.1.11] Editor. Associate. (1971). Comments. *Pediatrics, 48,* 330-331.
Reply to H. E. Thelander [47.1.36]. Agrees that there is criticism of eponyms but quotes O. W. Holmes in supporting them.

[47.1.12] Edwards, Robert M. (1970). Eponymic nomenclature: A step backward. [Letter to the Editor]. *American Journal of Psychiatry, 126,* 1329-1330.
Reacting to a psychiatric glossary which called the term "mongolism" and which recommended "Down's syndrome," agrees with DSM II (*Diagnostic and statistical*

manual of mental disorders) that "Autosomal trisomy of Group G" or "Trisomy 21" is a better term than Down's syndrome.

[47.1.13] Eponyms. [Editorials]. (1969). *Journal of the American Medical Association, 207,* 1142-114
Both eponyms and non-eponyms have useful places in medicine. Medical language is in constant flux. Terms come and go. Those that survive of both types will fill a need.

[47.1.13A] Garfield, Eugene. (1983). What's in a name? The eponymic route to immortality. Current Comments. *Essays of an information scientist, 6,* 384-395. Refs. Overall survey of medical eponyms. Many examples with citations.

[47.1.14] Ghosh, Jata S. (1975). Occurrence of disease and syndrome eponyms in the titles of medical literature. *Methods of Information in Medicine, 14,* 34-38. Refs. Table. German abstract.
Evaluated 2435 papers in the 1973 *Index Medicus*. Found that 72.2% of the papers had a disease and syndrome eponym in their title. There were 91 candidates used including: Adams-Stokes syndrome, Addison's disease, and Adie's syndrome. The ratio of the eponym to the descriptive title is 9:1.

[47.1.15] Half life of eponyms. (1970). [Letter to Editor]. *Journal of the American Medical Association, 213,* 456. Refs.
While some eponyms in medicine endure, others fade away. People like eponyms because many hope to be remembered.

[47.1.16] Hatcher, John. (1972). Fame is a name. *Nursing Times, 68,* 1298-1299.
Several names perpetuated in medicine and stories connected with them. Included are: Bunsen burner, Dover's powder, and Glauber's salt.

[47.1.17] Hecht, Frederick. (1983). Limiting eponyms. [Editorial Correspondence]. *Journal of Pediatrics, 102,* 485-486.
Complains there should be a limit on the creation of new eponyms.

[47.1.18] Henri-Louis Roger: Roger's disease. (1970). [Editorials]. *Journal of the American Medical Association, 213,* 496-497.
Brief description of the man for whom Roger's disease (asymptomatic interventricular septal defect) was named.

[47.1.19] Hutchinson, J. (1898). Cases of Mortimer's malady. *Archives of Surgery* [London], *9,* 307-314.
Original report of the disorder named after a patient.

[47.1.20] Jablonski, Stanley. (1991). *Jablonski's dictionary of syndromes & eponymic diseases.* Malabar, FL: Krieger Publishing, 665p. Refs. Illus.
Comprehensive encyclopedia lists approx. 17,600 entries by name of scientist or disease. Example Moritz Kaposi, Hungarian dermatologist, is associated with 15 different skin diseases and disorders. Entries are cross-listed so that Kaposi is the primary association for only 8 of the entries. Sometimes a disease will have 3 names associated with it. In the case of the Sensenbrenner-Dorst-Owens syndrome (cranio-ectodermal dysplasia syndrome), there are links to 3 scientists who are mentioned just the once.

[47.1.21] K., A. D. (1966). Doctor, your eponyms are showing. [Aequanimitas]. *Canadian Medical Association Journal, 95,* 1215-1216. Refs.
General on eponyms. Expresses approval of them.

[47.1.22] Kay, H. E. M. (1973). In praise of eponyms. *Lancet, 2,* 1256.
A view for eponyms. Many fields have eponyms.

[47.1.23] Lennox, Bernard. (Ed.). (1980). *Ffrangeon Roberts' medical terms: Their origin and construction.* (6th ed.). London: Heinemann, 132p.
Pp. 100-102 briefly mention medical eponyms. Some eponyms use capitals, as Bright's disease, some have no capitals as, parkinsonism. Favors eponyms where no exact name can be applied or where the scientific name would be too long.

[47.1.24] Magalini, Sergio I. & Scrascia, Euclide. (1981). *Dictionary of medical syndromes,* 2nd ed. Philadelphia: Lippincott, 944p. Refs.
Gives (p. viii) the advantages of using eponyms to describe medical syndromes. Coverage of medical eponyms.

[47.1.25] Newmark, Peter. (1983). Names not to be forgotten. *Nature, 303,* 749. Refs.
Some scientific phenomena are named after their discoverers such as, Hardy-Zuckerman virus, Baird's sandpiper, and the IRAS-Araki-Alcock comet. Newmark considers the current system somewhat confusing.

[47.1.26] Quick, Armand J. (1970). Eponyms. [Letter to the Editor]. *Journal of the American Medical Association, 214,* 761-762. Refs.
As someone who has been eponymized, denies seeking immortality. Says that an eponym is a shorthand. Also states that the eponym capitalized indicates following the exact procedure; non-capitalized, following the general procedure.

[47.1.27] Ravitch Mark M. (1968). Eponyms. *Medical Times, 96,* 1149-1151.
Points out that eponyms may: (1) commemorate someone who was not the 1st to describe a medical condition, structure, or operation, (2) may not have understood the condition, (3) may refer to a condition which is different than the one originally thought, or (4) is a historically perpetuated error. Refs. to specific eponyms.

[47.1.28] Ravitch Mark M. (1977). Poland's syndrome: A study of an eponym. *Plastic & Reconstructive Surgery, 59,* 508-512. Refs.
Points out that eponyms may commemorate: (1) someone who was not the 1st to describe a medical condition, structure, or operation, (2) may not have understood the condition, (3) may have been misunderstood, or (4) all of the above may be true. Poland's syndrome is an example.

[47.1.29] Ravitch Mark M. (1979). Dupuytren's invention of the Mikulicz enterotome with a note on eponyms. *Perspectives of Biological Medicine, 22,* 170-184.
General on eponyms which are seen as fallible. Description of a practical joke with eponyms played by students in the journal of the Cardiff Medical Students' Club. Account of the Duputren invention as a case history on the fallibility of eponyms.

[47.1.30] Robertson, M. G. (1972). Fame is the spur the eponym doth raise. [Letters]. *Journal of the American Medical Association, 221,* 1278. Refs.
Facetious reaction to naming diseases after physicians.

[47.1.31] Rolleston, Humphry. (1937). Medical eponyms. *Annals of Medical History, 9,* 1-12. Refs. Illus.
Extensive review of medical eponyms with the pros and cons of using them. Many examples to illustrate points.

[47.1.32] Schmickel, Roy D. (1983). Limiting eponyms. [Letter to Editor]. *Journal of Pediatrics, 102,* 485-486.
Reply to Hecht [47.1.17]. Defends the use of eponyms but accepts some limitations.

[47.1.33]   Skinner, Henry Alan. (1970).   *The origin of medical terms,* 2nd ed. Baltimore: Williams & Wilkins, 438p. Refs. Illus.
Contains 4000 terms, some of them are eponyms such as Purkinje's cells, sheath of Schwann, and Froelich's syndrome.

[47.1.34]   Tashima, Charles K. (1957).   Given names in medical nomenclature. *Gastroenterology, 33,* 129-130. Refs.
Listing of 9 medical eponyms which include a "given" name before the surname. Included are the Argyll Robinson pupil and the Graham Steell murmur.

[47.1.35]   Tashima, C. K. (1965).   Tashima's syndrome. [Letters]. *Journal of the American Medical Association, 194,* 208.
Reactions to different types of medical eponyms; whether an eponym is after the patient or the physician. Also points out other eponymic difficulties. Suggests a new eponym, Tashima's syndrome, for physicians who look for a disease to attach their name to.

[47.1.36]   Thelander, H. E. (1971).   Eponyms and other inane titles for diseases. [Letters to the Editor & Reply]. *Pediatrics, 48,* 230-231.
Questions 13 medical eponyms such as Reye's, Downs', and Bartter's syndromes.

[47.1.37]   V., S. (1971).   Discrimination in eponymdom. *Journal of the American Medical Association, 218,* 104
Response to Alsop [47.1.1] who complained that when a new disease is discovered, it is the physician rather than the patient who is commemorated.

[47.1.38]   Vee, Samuel. (1970).   Keeping eponyms in the family. *Journal of the American Medical Association, 214,* 762.
Favors keeping medical eponyms. Suggests that where an eponymic disease turns out to have 2 or more varieties that additional eponyms be coined.

47.2. WORDS FROM NAMES: *Recreational Aspects*
(See Also: 35. RECREATIONAL ASPECTS OF NAMES)

[47.2.1]   Ashley, Leonard R. N. (1986).   Floral eponyms. In A. Ross Eckler (Ed.) *Names and games: Onomastics and recreational linguistics* (p. 87). Lanham, MD: University Press of America.
A 20-item quiz seeking personal names that become floral words, e.g., a German botanist, fuchsia; an English botanist, forsythia.

[47.2.2]   Ashley, Leonard R. N. (1986).   Proper dress. In A. Ross Eckler (Ed.) *Names and games: Onomastics and recreational linguistics* (pp. 87-89). Lanham, MD: University Press of America.
A 25-item questionnaire (with answers) of names, several of them persons dealing with aspects of clothing. Examples include tattersall, a cloth design from (Richard) Tattersall, an English horseman and mercerize, from John Mercer, who invented the process.

[47.2.3]   Ashley, Leonard R. N. (1986).   What's in a name? In A. Ross Eckler (Ed.) *Names and games: Onomastics and recreational linguistics* (pp. 81-86). Lanham, MD: University Press of America.
A 50-item questionnaire (with answers at the end) on words that developed from names, many of them personal. Examples include: Hoyle, mackintosh, and martinet.

47.3. WORDS FROM NAMES: *Science*

[47.3.1] Bagnall, Bob. (1989, June 10). The importance of not being Smith. *New Scientist* [England], p. 64-64.
Humorous. Notes that with scientific eponyms there only seems to be one person involved, i.e., Boyle's law, Einstein's law of relativity. There is an advantage of not having a common name.

[47.3.2] Ballentyne, D(enis) W(illiam) G(eorge); & Walker, L. E. Q. (1961). *A dictionary of named effects and laws in chemistry, physics, and mathematics,* 2nd rev. & enl. ed. New York: Macmillan, 234p. Illus.
Has approx. 1170 terms identified with the name of the discoverer or someone associated with the phenomenon or process. Includes: Knudsen Flow, Sullivan's Test, Coulomb, and Farad.

47.4. WORDS FROM NAMES: *Slang*

[47.4.1] Cohen, Gerald Leonard. (1985). My name is Hanes. In Gerald L. Cohen (Ed.) *Studies in slang, Part I* (pp. 66-67). Frankfurt am Main: Peter Lang. Refs. Also in *Comments on Etymology*, 1978, *8(6),* 6-7 and *Verbatim*, 1979, *6(1),* 10-11.
Traces this expression meaning that one has to leave in a hurry to a man who had criticized President Jefferson's policies without knowing to whom he was speaking. Then, learning to whom he was talking (Jefferson himself), departed quickly.

[47.4.2] Cohen, Gerald Leonard. (1985). *Jim-Dandy* 'super, peachy.' In Gerald L. Cohen (Ed.) *Studies in slang, Part I* (pp. 134-137). Frankfurt am Main: Peter Lang. Refs.
Traces the expression *Jim-Dandy* to an American black song about Dandy Jim.

[47.4.3] Cohen, Gerald Leonard. (1985). Origin of *smart Aleck.* In Gerald L. Cohen (Ed.) *Studies in slang, Part I* (pp. 85-105). Frankfurt am Main: Peter Lang. Refs.
Extensive exploration of leads points to Alexander Hoag, a criminal of the 1840s in New York City who attempted to cheat the police out of their cut in his operation.

[47.4.4] Cohen, Gerald Leonard. (Ed.). (1985). *Studies in slang, Part I.* (*Forum Anglicum, 14(1)*). Frankfurt am Main: Peter Lang, 164p. Refs.
Includes articles on names by Cohen on the origin of expressions, *My name is Hanes* [47.4.1], *smart Aleck* [47.4.3], and *Jim-Dandy* [47.4.2]; by Pogue [47.4.6] on *Jim-Dandy*; by Tamony [47.4.8] on *real McCoy, Rileyed,* and *Kelsey's nuts*; and by Süsskind & Cohen [47.4.7] on the term *shlemiel.*

[47.4.5] Olesen, Virginia & Whittaker, Elvi. (1968). Conditions under which college students borrow, use, and alter slang. *American Speech, 43,* 222-228. Refs.
Development of slang at the University of California School of Nursing at San Francisco. One term was "a Florence Nightingale" describing an overeager student.

[47.4.6] Pogue, Marilyn. (1985). *Jim* in *jim-dandy* < *gim/jim/jimp* 'spruce' or *jimmy* 'exactly.' In Gerald L. Cohen (Ed.) Studies in slang, Part I (pp. 139-155). Frankfurt am Main: Peter Lang. Refs.
Extensive detailed investigation of the origin of the expression *jim-dandy* fails to lead to a personal name but rather other explanations.

[47.4.7] Süsskind, Nathan & Cohen, Gerald Leonard. (1985). Origin of *shlemiel* 'simpleton, unlikely bungler.' In Gerald L. Cohen (Ed.) *Studies in slang, Part I* (pp. 71-84). Frankfurt am Main: Peter Lang. Refs.

Exploration of the possible origins of the term going to the Bible, a poem by Heinrich Heine, and a 13th cent. Jewish story. Definitive conclusion not given.

[47.4.8] Tamony, Peter. (1985). Names and slang: A few etymological contributions. In Gerald L. Cohen (Ed.) *Studies in slang, Part I* (pp. 106-123). Frankfurt am Main: Peter Lang. Refs. Part 1 on the real McCoy appeared in *Comments on Etymology*, 1979, *8(15)*, 3-13; Part 3 on Kelsey's nuts appeared in *Comments on Etymology*, 1982, *11*(9-10), pages not shown.
Exploration of several possible origins of the term *real McCoy* (1 refers to Kid McCoy, the boxer); *Rileyed* (being drunk); and *Kelsey's nuts*, as in "tight as Kelsey's nuts," which took its origin from John Kelsey who manufactured nuts and bolts for autos in their early days.

AUTHOR INDEX

Akenson, Donald H., (1984) [23.1]; [1984] [23.2]; (1984) [23.3]

Alhaug, Gulbrand, (1992) [9.41.1]

Alia, Valerie, (1984) [24.1]; [46.1]; (1986) [9.9.1]; (1989) [9.9.2]; (1991) [47.1]

Alsop, Stewart, (1971) [47.1.1]

Alston, R. C., (1977) [2.1]

Alvarez, Grace D., (1971) [9.52.3.1]

Alwill, Gerard, (1976) [9.31.5.1]

Ames, Jay, (1982) [9.17.5.1]; (1985) [9.17.5.2]; (1988) [9.9.3]

Amir, Yehoshua, (1988) [9.35.1]

Ammon, Linda, (1976) [9.17.9.1]

Anderson, Chester, (1978) [26.1]

Andersen, Christopher P., (1987) [42.1]

Anderson, Jack & Binstein, Michael, (1992) [26.2.1]

Anderson, Lynn R.; Finn, Martha; & Leider, Sandra, (1981) [3.1]

Anderson, Myrdene, (1984) [9.36.1]

Anderson, Robert H., (1985) [47.1.2]

Anderson, Robert H., & Becker, A. E., (1979) [47.1.3]

Anderson, Robert H.; Becker, Anton E., Brechenmacher, Claude, et al., (1975) [47.1.4]

Anderson, Timothy, (1985) [45.1]

Andersson, Thorsten, (1984) [9.53.3.1]

Andrews, Lori B., (1982) [42.1.1]

Angel, Marc D., (1973) [9.35.2]; (1984) [9.35.3]

Anscombe, Alfred, (1912-13) [9.17.1]; (1919) [9.57.1]; (1920) [9.17.6.1]

Antal, Laszlo, (1988) [9.27.1]

Antubam, Kofi, (1963) [9.1.3.1]

Aquilina, Joseph, (1961; 1981) [9.37.1]; (1964; 1976) [9.37.1.1]

Arad, Miriam, (1984) [9.35.4]

Archer, John, (1975) [47.1.5]

Archibald, Marion M., & Blunt, C. E., (1986) [9.17.6.1]

Aristides, Nikolai, (1977-1978) [3.2]; (1980-1981) [1.1]

Arkell, A. J., (1963) [9.4.4.1]

Arlington, L. C., (1923) [9.12.1]

Armour, Richard, (1970) [45.2]; (1971) [15.1]

Armstrong, Orland K., (1931) [9.2.1]

Arney, Roberta, (1993) [2.2]

Arngart, O., (1947-1948) [9.17.2]

Aron, Michael, (1976) [1.2]

Asante, Molefi Kete, (1991) [9.1.1]

Aschenbrenner, Stanley E., (1975) [9.23.1]

Ashley, David J. B., & Davies, H. Duncan, (1966) [9.57.2.1]

Ashley, Leonard R. N., (1986) [47.2.1]; (1986) [47.2.2]-[47.2.3]; (1989) [1.3], (1991) [44.1]

Astley, John, (1886) [9.17.6.2]

Astour, Michael C., (1965) [9.4.1]

Atkinson, Donna L., (1987) [3.3]

Attwater, Donald, (1958) [36.1]

Auger, C. P., (1975) [47.2]

Avery, Catherine B., (Ed.), & Johnson, Jotham, (Ed. Consult.), (1962) [9.14.1]

Avi-Yonah, Michael, (1959) [9.4.2]

Azevêdo, Eliane; da Costa, Theomaria
    Pinto; Silva, Maria Christ B. O., et
    al. [9.7.1]

B., A., (1887) [9.17.9.2]
B., E. R., (1945) [9.42.2.1]
Bagnall, Bob, (1989) [47.3.1]
Bailey, D. R. Shackleton, (1988)
    [9.14.2]
Bailey, Frederick George, (1971)
    [9.33.1]
Baker, Mona, (1990) [1.18]
Baker, R. J., (1972) [28.1]
Baker, Ross K., (1987) [44.2]
Baker, Russell, (1987) [43.1]
Baker, Sidney J(ohn), (1966)
    [9.42.1.1]
Balagangadhara Rao,
    Yarlagadda, (1990) [9.29.1]
Ballentyne, D(enis) W(illiam)
    G(eorge), & Walker, L. E. Q.,
    (1961) [47.3.2]
Barnes, Clive, (1989) [7.1.1]
Barnes, Robert B., (1982) [9.3.1];
    (1980) [9.3.2]
Barnhart, Clarence L., (1954) [1.4]
Barnhart, Clarence L., (Ed.), (1975)
    [1.5]
Barr, James, (1963) [12.1];
    (1969-70) [5.1]
Barrett, Richard A., (1978) [9.52.2.1]
Barry, Herbert, III, (1987) [21.1]
Barry, Herbert, III, & Harper, Aylene
    S., (1993) [11.1]; (1994) [11.3.1]
Batchelor, John, (1894) [9.34.1]
Bates, D., (1986) [2.3]
Battye, Kathleen M., (1982) [9.17.9.3]
Bauer, Harry C., (1958) [43.2]; (1960)
    [37.1]
Baum, S. V., (1958) [44.3]
Beadle, Muriel, (1973) [11.1A]
Becker, C. M., (1989) [26.2]
Beeaff, Dianne Ebertt, (1978)
    [9.17.6.3]
Beecher, Carla, (1994) [47.3]
Beeching, Cyril Leslie, (1982) [47.4]
Beegle, D. M., (1953) [5.2]
Beeston, A(lfred) F(elix) L(andon),
    (1971) [9.5.1]
Befu, Harumi & Norbeck, Edward,

(1958) [9.34.2]
Behrendt, R., (1973) [22.1]
Beider, Alexander, (1991) [9.35.5];
    (1992) [9.35.6]; (1993) [9.35.6.1]
Beirne, Eric, (1972) [17.1]
Beit-Arieh, Itzhaq, (1983) [9.35.7]
Bell, Robert A., (1984) [45.3]
Bell, Robert A., Buerkel-Rothfuss,
    Nancy L., & Gore, Kevin E., et al.,
    (1987) [26.3]
Bell, Robert, (1988) [9.31.5.2]
Bellingham, Mary; Brandt, Edward R.;
    Cutkomp, Kent, et al., (1991)
    [9.22.1]
Bender, James F., (1943) [30.1];
    (1955) [30.2]
Bender, James F. Revised by Thomas
    L. Crowell, Jr., (1964) [30.3]
Benedictine monks of St. Augustine's
    Abbey, Ramsgate, (1947) [36.2]
Benjamin, E. Alwyn, (1980-1983)
    [9.57.2.2]; (1987) [9.57.2.3]
Benson, Morton, (1964) [9.47.1]
Benson, Sven, (1986) [9.53.2.1];
    (1989) [9.53.1]; [9.53.2.2]; (1990)
    [9.53.2]
Bentley, Jeffery Westwood, (1987)
    [9.46.1]
Berger, Josef, (1961) [26.2.2]
Bergmann, Dmitri A., (1986) [35.1]
Bering, Dietz, (1992) [9.35.2.1]
Berlin, Brent, (1962) [9.39.1]
Berlyn, Phillippa, (1965) [9.1.7.1]
Bernander, Inga, (1980) [9.53.3]
Bernard, Thomas L., (1993) [22.2]
Berry, J., (1960) [9.1.1.1]
Bertrand, Gary L., (1985) [26.4]
Best, Elsdon, (1902) [9.42.2.1.1];
    (1906) [9.42.2.1.2]; (1920) [13.1]
Bethers, Ray, (1966) [19.1]
Bhalla, V. & Bhatia, K., (1976)
    [9.29.2]
Bice, Christopher, (1970) [9.40.1]
Biddle, Mark, (1987) [9.17.6.1.2]
Billigmeier, Jon-Christian, (1967)
    [27.1]
Bin, Zhu & Millward,Celia, (1987)
    [9.12.2]
Birch, Walter de Gray, (1899; 1964)
    [9.17.6.4]
Birket-Smith, Kaj, (1965) [9.40.2]

Birnbach, Lisa, (1980) [26.5]

Black, M., (1951) [36.3]

Blake, John L., (1966) [9.49.4.1]

Blakely, Mike, (1983) [26.6]

Blayo, Yves, (1973) [9.21.1]

Blixt, Sam; Ekstrans, Magnus; & Kallenius, Gunnar, (1989) [9.53.4]

Bloch, Marc (Leopold) (Benjamin), (1961) [24.2]

Bloch, Raymond, (1991) [9.14.3]

Blom, Eric, (1957) [16.1]

Blomgren, Sven, (1984) [9.53.6.1]; (1987) [9.53.5]

Blomqvist, Marianne, (1989) [9.20.1]; [9.20.2]; (1990) [9.20.3]; (1992) [9.20.4]

Blount, Roy, Jr., (1985) [33.2.1]

Blunt, C. E., (1973) [9.17.6.1.2A]

Boahen, A. Adu, (1964) [9.1.1.2]

Bodkin, E. H., (1960) [9.17.3]

Boas, Franz, (1932) [9.3.2A]

Bogiatzoglou, Basos E., (1988) [9.23.2]

Boissevain, Jeremy, (1965) [9.37.1.2]; (1969) [9.37.1.3]

Boldsen, J. L., Mascie-Taylor, C. G. N., & Lasker, Gabriel, (1986) [9.17.7.1]

Bolton, W. F., (1962) [9.17.6.5]

Bonner, Campbell, (1954) [9.4.3]

Boot, M., Lourens, P., & Lucassen, J., (1983) [8.1]

Borgmann, Dmitri A., (1986) [11.2.1]

Borkowski, Casimir, (1977) [8.2]

Bornstein, Arthur, (1964) [33.2.2]

Bouchard, Constance B., (1988) [24.3]; (1988) [24.4]

Bouchard, Gérard & Pouyez, Christian, (1980) [8.1.1]

Bouisson, Maurice, (1961) [17.2]

Boulanger, Jean-Claude, (Ed.), (1990) [1.6]

Bourke, Myles M., (1958) [12.2]

Bourque, Paul; Dupuis, Norbert; & Van Houten, Ron, (1986) [10.1]

Bracey, Gerald W., (1985) [9.17.4]; [22.4]

Bradbury, Jim, (1989) [9.21.2]

Brandes, Stanley H., (1975) [9.52.2.2]

Braroe, Niels Winther, & Braroe, Eva Ejerhed, (1977) [9.3.3]

Brasch, R., (1969) [9.35.6.2]

Braun, Frederike, (1988) [3.4]

Bredart, Serge, (1989) [9.40.3]

Breen, Richard, (1982) [9.31.1]

Brett, Donald, (1985) [9.17.9.4]

Brewer, W., & 7 others, (1953) [9.17.1.1]

Brickell, John, (1737; 1911; 1968) [9.2.2]

Bridgeman, C. G. O., (1919) [9.17.4.1]

British Broadcasting Corporation. Pronunciation Unit, (1980) [30.4]; [30.5]; (1983) [30.6]

British Library, (1984) [2.4]

Britto, Francis, (1986) [9.29.3]

Broadie, Alexander, (1987) [12.3]

Brock, D. H., (1950) [9.9.1.1]

Brogger, Jan, (1970) [9.33.1.1]

Bromwich, Rachel, (1956-1958) [9.10.1]

Brooke, Jocelyn, (1953) [9.17.1.2]

Broughton, T. Robert S., (1951) [9.14.4]; (1952) [9.14.5]; (1960) [9.14.6]

Brown, Andrew, (1983) [9.53.6.2]

Brown, Richard D, (1976) [24.5]

Brown, Roger & Gilman, Albert, (1960) [3.5]

Brown, Rusty, (1983) [7.1]

Brown, W. P., (1978) [22.5]

Browne, Charles R., (1895) [9.31.2]; (1896) [9.31.3]; (1898) [9.31.4]; (1900) [9.31.5]

Brunner, Theodore F., (1988) [9.13.1]

Bryant, Margaret F., (1976) [1.7]

Brylla, Eva, (1990) [9.53.4.1]; (1992) [9.48.1]; (1993) [9.53.4.2]

Buckatzsch, E. J., (1951) [9.17.5]

Buckley, W. E., (1886) [9.17.6.6]

Budge, E. A. Wallis, (1926) [9.4.4.2]

Buechley, Robert W., (1961) [9.52.3.2]

Bugliari, Joseph B., (1958) [20.1]

Buhlmann, Walbert, (1953) [9.1.6.1]

Bumppo, Natty, (1975) [7.2]

Burchell, Howard B., (1985) [47.1.6]

Burchfield, R. W., (Ed.), (1972) [47.5]

Burgesse, J. Allan, (1943) [9.3.4]

Burke, W., (1962) [43.3]

Burnham, David, (1984) [22.6]

Burrell, David, (1990) [12.4]

Burton, Orville Vernon, (1985) [9.2.3]

Butinov, N. A., (1960) [9.51.1]

Butler, Hubert, (1972) [9.31.6]
Buxton, L. H. Dudley, (1921)
  [9.37.1.4]
Buyniak, Victor O., (1987) [9.56.1]
Byciewicz, Shirley Raissi &
  MacDonnell, Gloria Jeanne Stillson,
  (1993) [46.2.1]

Cadbury, Henry J., (1962) [5.3]
Cairns, Ed, (1980) [9.31.4.1]; (1987)
  [9.31.4.2]
Cairns, S. E., (1975) [9.31.4.3]
Callary, Edward, (1987) [28.2];
  (1988/89) [28.3]; (1992) [28.4]
Cameron, Alan, (1985) [9.14.7]
Cameron, Catherine, (1987) [18.1]
Caminos, Ricardo A., (1972) [9.4.4.3]
Campbell, J(ohn) Kennedy), (1964)
  [9.23.3]
Camsell, Margaret, (1986) [9.17.9.5]
Cantor, M. E. L., (1956) [9.42.1.2]
Cantwell, Mary, (1983) [3.6]
Caplan, N., (1965) [9.17.3.1]
Cargill, D. C., (1972) [9.31.7]
Carlinsky, D., (1973) [7.1.2]
Carlova, John, (1959) [45.4]
Carlson, Katherine, (1989/90) [28.5]
Carlsson, Kathleen A., (1971) [20.2]
Carruthers, Peter, (1983) [25.1]
Carter, Charles, (1980) [9.4.5.1]
Cavalli-Sforza, L(uigi) L(uca), &
  Bodmer, W(alter) F(red), (1971)
  [29.1]
Cavendish, Richard, (1983) [17.3]
Center for a Woman's Own Name,
  (1974) [46.1.1]
Chadwick, Hector Munro, (1959)
  [9.17.6]
Chadwick, Nora K., (1959) [9.17.7];
  (1961) [3.7]
Chakraborty, Rnajit., Barton, Sarah H.,
  et al., (1989) [9.51.1.1]
Chamberlin, Jo Hubbard (Mr.), (1960)
  [11.3.2]
Chandler, Tertius, (1962) [13.2]
Chao, Yuen Ren, (1976) [9.12.3]
Chaplais, Pierre, (1987) [5.3.1]
Chaplin, J. H., (1959) [9.1.1.3]
Chapman, Charlotte Gower, (1971)
  [9.33.1.2]
Chapman, Diane, (1982) [47.6]

Chaput, Donald C., (1963) [28.6]
Charles, Lucille Hoerr, (1951) [24.6]
Charles, Prince of Schwartzenberg,
  (1960) [9.40.4]
Charnock, Richard Steven, (1868; 1968)
  [9.17.9.6]; (1886) [9.17.6.7]
Chavez, Angelico (Fray), (1957) [44.4]
Che-Mponda, Aleck H., (1973) [9.1.2]
Chekki, D. A., (1967) [9.29.4]
Chen, Kuang-Ho, & Cavalli-Sforza, L.,
  (1983) [9.12.4]
Chiasson, Anselme, (1986) [9.9.5]
Chira, Susan, (1989) [9.34.3]
Chopra, Y. N., (1975) [12.5]
Christensen, Birgit, (1986) [9.15.1]
Christian, William A., (1972)
  [9.52.2.3]
Christiansen, Norman Henrik, (1986)
  [26.7]
Christidis, Tassos, (1972) [9.13.2]
Christodoulou, G. N., A. Gargoulas, et
  al., (1979) [26.8]
Christoph, Ernst-Michael, (1987)
  [25.2]; (1991) [25.3]
Chua-Eoan, Howard G., (1989) [44.5]
Clader, Linda L., (1976) [13.3]
Clancy, Daniel Francis, (1954) [45.5]
Clark, Cecily, (1987) [9.17.4.2]-
  [9.17.4.3]; [9.17.6.8]; (1991/1992)
  [1.8]
Clark, Cecily & Owen, Dorothy,
  (1978) [9.17.4.4]
Clark, Thomas L., (1972) [10.2];
  (1973) [10.3]; (1986) [26.9]; (1987)
  [47.7]
Clarke, David, (1984) [8.1.2]
Clarke, Tom C. (1977) [6.1]
Clauson, Gerard, (1956) [9.55.1]
Clay, Grady, (1992) [22.7]
Clegg, E. J., (1986) [9.49.3.1]
Cleveland, Ray L., (1973) [9.35.8]
Clodd, Edward, (1920; 1968) [17.4]
Clouston, J. Storer, (1924) [9.49.4.2]
Cobb, Joseph B., (1851) [9.2.2.1]
Cody, Cheryll Ann, (1987) [9.2.2.1A]
Cogan, David G., (1978) [47.1.7]
Coghlan, Ronan; Grehan, Ida, & Joyce,
  P. W., (1989) [9.31.1.1]
Cohen, Anthony P., (1982) [9.49.1]
Cohen, Eugene N., (1977) [9.33.1.3]
Cohen, Gerald Leonard, (1985)
  [47.4.1]; (1985) [47.4.2]; (1985)

[47.4.3]
Cohen, Gerald Leonard, (Ed.), (1985)
    [47.4.4]
Cohen, M. Michael, Jr., (1979)
    [47.1.8]
Cohen, Naomi G., (1976) [9.35.1.1]
Cohen, Philip M., (1986) [35.2]
Cohen, Roger., (1991) [20.3]
Cole, John W., & Wolf, Eric R., (1974)
    [9.33.2]
Cole, William, (1981) [11.1.2]
Coleman, D. A., (1984) [9.17.8]
Collier, George A., & Bricker, Victoria
    R., (1970) [9.39.2]
Collinge, N. E., (1966) [39.1]
Collins, R. G., (1983) [9.17.9.1]
Colodner, Solomon, (Compiler), (1981)
    [9.35.4.1]
Combrink, Johan, (1990) [9.1.5.1]
Connolly, Frank, (1973) [9.31.8]
Connolly, Michael Coleman, (1988)
    [26.10]
Connor, Jane; Byrne, Fiona; Mindell,
    et al., (1986) [3.8]
Constantinescu, Ilinca, (1991) [9.40.5]
Cook, Albert S., (1891) [9.17.6.9]
Cooke, G. A., (1903) [9.4.4]
Cornevin, R., (1954) [9.1.1.4]
Cornog, Martha, (1987) [22.8]
Crammer, Marjorie, (Compiler), (1975)
    [2.5]
Crocombe, R. G., & Rere, Vaine.
    (1959) [9.42.1]
Croft, Bernard, (1976) [3.9]
Cronberg, Olof, (1988) [9.53.6]
Cross, Frank Moore, Jr., (1962)
    [12.2.1]
Cross, Harold E., (1973) [47.1.9]
Crow, James F., (1983) [29.2]
Crow, James F., & Mange, Arthur P.
    (1965) [29.3]
Crowley, Daniel J., (1956) [9.58.1]
Cummins, W. A., (1973) [44.1.1]
Cunningham, Patricia, (1988) [10.4]
Cushing, Frank Hamilton, (1896)
    [9.3.5]
Cutileiro, José, (1971) [9.46.2]
Cutler, Anne; McQueen, James; &
    Robinson, Ken, (1990) [39.2]

D., T. R., (1976) [18.2]

Dabbs, Jack A., (1971) [3.10]
Dahlstedt, Karl-Hampus, (1986)
    [9.53.2.3]
Dammann, Ernst, (1954) [9.1.6.2]
Danchev, Andrei; Holman, Michael;
    Dimova, Ekaterina, et al. (1989)
    [9.8.1]
Daniel-Rops, Henri, (1962) [5.4]
Darwin, George H., (1875) [9.17.7.2]
Daum, Roslyn Goodman, (1974)
    [20.2.2]
Davey, William, (1990) [9.9.4.1]
Davidian, H., & Naraghi, M. M.,
    (1978) [22.9]
Davidson, Gustav, (1967) [36.4]
Davidson, Leon, (1962) [8.3]
Davidson, R. M., (1975) [9.47.2]
Davies, Anne, (1988) [10.5]
Davies, Phillips G., (1987) [9.57.2]
Davies, Wendy, (1978-80) [9.10.2]
Dawe, Philip N., (1961) [9.17.2.1];
    (1962) [9.17.3.2]
de Breffny, Brian, (1969) [9.31.1.2];
    (1982) [9.31.5.3
de Brun, P., (1975) [9.31.9]
de Fraine, J. & Hartman, Louis, (1963)
    [5.5]
De Haan, E. H. F., Mehta, Z. M., et
    al., (1987) [33.3.1]
de Laguna, Frederica, (1954) [9.3.6]
De Sola, Ralph, (1982) [26.11]
Deakin, G. B., (1974) [9.4.4.4]
Deas, Anne Simons, (1978) [23.4]
DelaBarre, D. M., (1961) [7.3]
Denny, Frederick Mathewson, (1987)
    [12.6]
Derolez, René, (1987) [9.17.6.10]
Develin, R., (1986) [9.13.3]
Devor, Eric J., (1983) [29.4]
Devor, Eric J., & Buechley, Robert W.,
    (1979) [34.1]
Dewdney, A. K., (1986) [41.1]
Diament, Henri, (1986) [22.10];
    (1989) [9.22.2]
Dickison, Roland, (1990) [26.12]
Dickson, Paul, (1986) [1.9]
Dienstfrey, Harris, (1983) [17.5]
Dignowity, Hartman, (1927) [26.13]
Dil, Afia, (1975) [9.29.5]
Dion, Kenneth L., (1985) [9.9.6];
    (1987) [43.4]
Dion, Kenneth L. & Schuller, Regina

Dion, Kenneth L. & Schuller, Regina A., (1990) [46.2]
Dirckx, John H., (1983) [47.1.10]
Dobbs, Margaret E., (1948) [9.31.2.1]
Dobson, T., & Roberts, D. F., (1971) [9.17.7.3]
Dodge, Ellin, (1985) [27.2]
Dodgson, J(ohn) M(cNeal), (1967) [9.17.9.1.2]; (1973) [9.17.9.7]; (1987) [9.17.6.11]; (1990) [9.17.6.12]
Doherty, Jack, (1959) [28.7]
Doke, Clement M(artyn), (1931) [9.1.7.2]
Dolley, Michael, (1967) [9.31.11]; (1973) [9.31.12]
Donaldson, Gordon, (1984) [9.49.4.3]
Donner, Fred M., (1984) [9.5.2]
Donovan, Mary, (1965) [21.2]
Dorff, Daniel, (1984) [1.10]
Dorward, D(avid), (1970) [9.49.4.4]
Douglas, A. E., (1958) [9.14.8]
Douglass, Richard E., (1986) [35.3]
Dow, Sterling, (1957) [9.13.4]
Downey, Mike, (1985) [28.8]
Dralle, Penelope Wasson, & Mackiewicz, Kathelynne, (1981) [7.4]
Dranoff, Linda Silver, (1985) [9.9.3.1]
Driver, G. R., (1954) [12.2.2]; (1957) [9.4.1.1]
Droege, Geart Brueckner, (1964) [9.16.1]
Du Boulay, Juliet, (1974) [9.23.4]
Duckert,Audrey R., (1962) [15.2]; (1963) [24.7]; [26.14]; (1964) [7.5]; (1965) [28.9]
Dudley, Donald Reynolds & Webster, Graham, (1962) [9.17.9]
Duff, A(rnold) M(ackay), (1928) [9.14.9]
Duggan, Deborah A., Cota, Albert A., & Dion, Kenneth L., (1993) [46.3]
Duncan, Burris; Smith, Ann N., & Briese, Franklin W., (1979) [34.2]
Duncan, R. M., (1963) [24.8]
Dunkling, Leslie Alan, (1987) [11.1.3]; (1990) [3.11]; (1993) [1.11]
Dunlap, A. R., (1974) [30.7]
Dunn, Charles W., (1953) [9.9.7]
Dunn, F. I., & Deterding, Diana, (1978) [9.17.3.3]

Dunn, R(obert) D., (Ed.), (1984) [1.12]

Eberhard, Wolfram, (1955) [9.12.1.1]; (1970) [9.12.5]
Eckler, A. Ross, (1986) [22.11]; [28.10]; [35.4]-[35.9]; [44.6]-[44.8]
Eckler, Faith W., (1986) [35.10]
Editor (Robert Gayre), (1961) [9.49.2]
Editor, Associate, (1971) [47.1.11]
Edwards, Gillian M., (1953) [9.17.9.1.3]
Edwards, Robert M., (1970) [47.1.12]
Eichler, Ernst, (1990) [23.5]
Eickelman, Dale, (1967) [9.32.1]
Ejder, Bertil, (1988) [9.53.7]
Ekdahl, Bertil, (1984) [9.53.3.2]
Ekwall, Eilert, (1951) [9.17.6.13]; (1956) [9.17.4.5]
Elkin, Stanley, (1988) [42.1.2]
Ellis, W. S., & Starmer, W. T., (1978) [9.54.2]
Ellis, Walter & Friedl, John, (1976) [9.54.1]
Ellwand, Geoff, (1986) [7.6]
Elmendorf, William W., (1951) [9.3.7]
Emanuel, Hywel D., (1966) [9.10.3]
Embleton, Sheila M., (1990) [9.9.3.2]
Embleton, Sheila, & Atkinson, Donna L., (1985) [46.1.2]
Emerson, O. B. & Hermann, John P. (1986) [44.1.2]
Emery, Richard W., (1952) [44.9]; (1959) [9.35.9]
Emmison, F. G., (1986) [9.17.9.8]
Ennew, Judith, (1980) [9.49.2.1]
Eno, Joel N., (1988/89) [44.10]
Enstrom, James E., & Operskalski, Eva A., (1978) [34.3]
Erder, Yoram, (1990) [9.32.2]
Ericsson, Brit-Marie, (1986) [9.53.3.3]
Ervin-Tripp, Susan, (1969) [3.12]; (1972) [3.13]-[3.14]
Escott, Paul D., (1979) [9.2.2.2]
Espy, Willard R., (1978) [47.8]
Estolas, Josefina Villanueva, (1965) [9.44.1]
Eutychus, (1986) [22.12]
Evans-Pritchard, E. E., (1948) [9.1.1.5]
Evans, Cleveland Kent, (1986) [28.11]

Evans, D(avid) Ellis, (1964) [9.10.4];
    (1968-71) [9.10.5]
Everett, David & Pilachowski, David H.
    (1986) [8.4]
Everts, Palmer W., (1953) [20.5]
Eybers, I. H., (1971) [5.6]
Ezeanya. S. N., (1967) [9.1.4.1]

Fales, F. M., (1977) [9.4.2.1];
    (1979) [9.4.3.1]
Farrant, E. J. P., (1979) [9.38.1]
Fayer, Joan M., (1988) [7.7]
Fee, Gordon D., (1971) [5.7]
Feiner, Joel, & Klein, Stephan Marc,
    (1982) [14.2]
Feinsilver, Lillian Mermin, (1983)
    [3.15]
Fellows Jensen, Gillian, (1962)
    [9.17.10]; (1969) [9.17.8.1];
    (1973) [9.17.4.6]; (1983) [9.17.11]
Ferguson, Rosalind, (1987) [11.1.5]
Ferguson, W. S., (1929) [9.4.5]
Fernandez-Suarez, Yolanda, (1989-90)
    [9.52.1.1]
Ferreira, Valentina, (1990) [9.40.6]
Fichtner, E. G., (1967) [47.9]
Finnegan, Ruth H., (1970) [9.1.1.6]
Fischer, Henry G., (1973) [9.4.4.5];
    (1974) [9.4.4.6]
Fisher, R. A., & Vaughan, Janet, (1939)
    [9.57.3]
Fiske, Shirley, (1978) [9.3.8]
Flaumenhaft, A. S., (1970) [22.13]
Fletcher, Alice, (1870) [9.3.9]
Fletcher, Alice C(unningham), & La
    Flesche, Francis, ([9.3.10]
Flint, E. H., (1964) [9.42.2]
Flom, George T., (1920) [9.41.2]
Fluck, E. J. See: Robinson, D. M., &
    Fluck, E. J.
Flude, Brenda M., Ellis, Andrew W., &
    Kay, Janice, (1989) [33.4.1]
Foderaro, Lisa W., (1987) [11.1.6]
Foote, Peter, (1973) [9.28.1]
Force, Helen H., (Ed.), (1967) [32.1]
Forgács, Krisztina, (1990) [9.27.2]
Forsey, Eugene., (1938) [15.3]
Fortes, M. Meyer, (1955) [9.1.1.7]
Foss, Karen A., & Edson, Belle A.,
    (1989) [46.3.1]
Foster, George M., (1964) [9.39.3]

Foster, Irene, (1980) [9.17.9.9]
Fotheringham, Allan, (1991) [45.7]
Fowkes, Robert A., (1988) [9.10.6];
    (1994) [9.57.2.4]
Fowler, Jeanane D., (1987) [9.35.10]
Fowler, Roger & Kress, Gunther, (1979)
    [9.17.1.3]
Fox, Robin, (1978) [9.31.2.2]; (1982)
    [9.31.2.3]
Francis, Darryl, (1986) [35.11];
    [44.11]; [47.10]
Franciscan Fathers, (1912) [9.3.11]
Frank, David., (1988) [9.9.4.2]
Frank, Margit, (1993) [9.35.2.2]
Franklin, Peter, (1986) [9.17.3.4]
Franklyn, Julian, (1963) [9.17.9.10]
Franzwa, Gregory M., (1967) [26.15]
Fraser Roberts, J(ohn) A(lexander),
    (1947) [9.17.7.4]
Fraser, G. S., (1953) [9.17.1.4]
Fraser, P. M. & Mathews, E., (1987)
    [9.13.5]
Frazier, Robert; McDonald, David G.,
    & Edwards, David, [33.3.2]
Fredericksen, Britta Olrik, (1992)
    [9.15.2]
Freedman, David Noel, (1960)
    [12.2.3]; (1963) [5.1.1]
Freeman, John William, (1968;1986)
    [9.17.9.10A]
Freeman, Susan Tax, (1970) [9.52.2.4]
Freeman, William M., (1957) [22.14]
Freestone, Basil, (1990) [26.16]
Friedl, J., & Ellis, W. S., (1974)
    [9.54.3]
Friedman, Lee Max, (1948) [9.35.11]
Friedrich, Otto, (1986) [42.2]
Frieman, D. G., (1965) [9.35.5.1]
Friend, J(ohn Albert) Newton, (1957)
    [1.13]
Frommer, Myrna, (1982) [42.3]
Frumkes, Lewis Burke, (1987) [15.4A]
Frye, R. N., (1962) [9.30.1]
Fuller, J. William, (1983) [5.8]
Furstenberg, Frank F. Jr., & Talvitie,
    Kathy Gordon, (1980) [24.9]
Furtenbach, Börje, (1987) [9.53.8]
Fury, Kathleen, (1986) [33.2.3]

Garcia, Nasario, (1989) [9.52.1.2]
Gardiner, Alan, (1936) [9.4.4.7];

(1958) [9.4.4.8]
Gardner, Martin, (1986) [45.8]
Gardner, W. R. W., (1908-09) [12.2.4]
Garfield, Eugene, (1977) [47.11];
  (1983) [47.1.13A]
Gariepy, Henry, (1974) [5.3.2]
Garraty, John A., (1986) [26.17]
Garton, Charles, (1964) [9.14.10]
Garvin, Paul L., (1947) [9.3.12]
Gasque, Thomas J., (1990) [1.14];
  [26.18]; (1991) [15.4]; (1994)
  [26.19]
Gatschet, Albert S., (1895) [9.3.13]
Gauk, Roma Z., (Compiler), &
  Slavutch, Yar, (Ed.), (1961) [9.56.2]
Gelb, I(gnace) J., (1951/52) [9.4.5.2];
  (1954) [9.4.3.2]; (1955) [9.4.1.2];
  (1960) [9.4.3.3]; (1961) [9.4.6]
Gellner, E., (1969) [9.40.7]
Genovese, Eugene D., (1974) [9.2.2.3]
Georgacas, Demetrius J., (1959)
  [9.13.6]; (1969) [9.14.11]
George, K. E. M., (1986) [47.12]
Gershevitch, Ilya, (1970) [9.4.7]
Gersuny, Carl, (1974) [1.15]
Ghosh, Jata S., (1975) [47.1.14]
Gibson, J. C. L., (1962) [5.10]
Gibson, Jeremy (Sumner Wycherley),
  (1989) [9.17.12]
Giesecke, G. Lee, (1973) [9.52.3.3]
Gifford, Edward Winslow, (1932)
  [9.3.14]; (1936) [9.3.15]
Gilbreth, F. B., (1958) [15.5]
Gillen, John, (1984) [8.1.3]
Gillingstam, Hans, (1988) [9.53.2.4];
  (1990) [9.53.9]
Gilmore, David D., (1982) [9.52.2.5]
Gilmore, Melvin R., (1929) [9.3.16]
Giorgis, Kabreab W. (1973) [9.18.1]
Gitter, Lena L., (1968) [10.6]
Glasse, R. M., (1987) [9.42.3.1]
Glazier, Jack, (1987) [9.35.11A]
Gleason, R. W., (1964) [12.7]
Glenn, Menahem G., (1961) [7.8]
Glickman, Bob, (1990) [11.1.7]
Goetze, Albrecht, (1953) [9.4.3.4];
  (1954) [9.4.3.5]; (1958) [9.4.8];
  (1959) [9.4.8A]; (1960) [9.4.9];
  (1962) [9.4.10]
Goff, J. H., (1953) [9.3.17]
Goitein, S. D., (1956) [12.1.1]
Gokhale, Shobhana, (1957) [9.29.6]

Gold, David L., (1986) [9.35.6.3]-
  [9.35.6.4]; (1987) [9.35.6.5]-
  [9.35.6.6]
Gómez, L. M., (1965) [12.8]
Gonda, J., (1952) [9.40.8]
Goode, Erica E., (1988) [29.5]
Goodman, Mary Ellen, (1970) [33.1]
Gordon, Arthur E., & Gordon, Joyce S.
  (1951) [9.14.12]
Gordon, Cyrus H., (1970) [12.9]
Gordon, E. V., (1935) [9.17.6.14]
Gordon, Lois B., (1974) [46.2.3]
Gore, Stuart, (1968) [9.42.1.3]
Gorr, Shmuel, (1992) [9.35.12]
Gottlieb, Karen, (1983) [29.7]
Gottlieb, Karen, (Ed.) (1983) [29.6]
Gottlieb, K(aren) & Kimberling, W. J.,
  (1979) [34.4]
Grabbe, Lester L, (1988) [5.11]
Grace, Virginia R., (1953) [9.13.7]
Grafflin, D., (1983) [9.12.6]
Grant, Jeff. (1986) [35.11A]
Grant, W. Leonard, (1953) [9.33.4]
Gray, John, (1953) [12.10]
Graybill, Guy, (1984-85) [26.20]
Greene, Bob, (1988) [28.13]
Greenway, John, (1961) [47.14]
Greet, W(illiam) Cabell, (1944) [30.8];
  (1948) [30.9]
Gregg, John M., (1957) [20.6]
Griest, Terry L., (1986) [9.49.4.5]
Griffiths, J. Gwyn, (1951) [9.4.4.9];
  (1953) [5.2.1]
Gross, John, (1974) [22.15]; (1986)
  [45.10]
Grosshandler, Stan, (1978) [26.3.1]
Grottanelli, Vinigi L., (1977) [9.1.3.2]
Gruffudd, Heini, (1982) [9.57.1.1]
Gruffydd, W. J., (1912) [9.57.4]
Gruita, Mariana, (1984) [3.16]
Gudeman, Stephan, (1979) [9.2.2.4]
Guggenheimer, Heinrich W., &
  Guggenheimer, Eva H., (1992)
  [9.35.6.7]
Guiteras-Holmes, C(alixta), (1961)
  [9.39.4]
Gulliver, P. H., (1952) [9.1.1.8]
Gunnemark, Erik, (1988) [9.47.3]
Guth, Gloria J. A., (1976) [8.1.4]

H., A. C., (1956) [9.17.2.2]

Haberman, Clyde, (1984) [9.34.4]
Hachlili, Rachel, (1979) [9.35.1.2]
Haden, H. Jack, (1972) [9.17.3.5]
Hager, Virginia R., (1986) [35.12]
Hagland, Jan Ragnar, (1988) [9.41.3];
 (1990) [9.48.2]
Hahn, E. Adelaide, (1969) [25.4]
Hahn, Ferdinand, (1969) [5.3.3]
Hair, P. E. H., (1976) [9.17.13]
Hajdú, Mihály, (1972) [9.27.3]; (1983)
 [9.27.4]
Hale, Leslie, (1953) [9.17.1.5]
Hallberg, Göran, (1988) [9.53.10]
Hamblen, Carol Howe, (1979) [3.17]
Hamilton, Mary, (1906-07) [36.5]
Hamp, Eric P., (1954-55) [9.10.7];
 (1968) [9.13.8]; (1978) [9.57.5]
Hanks, Patrick & Hodges, Flavia.,
 (1986) [1.16]; (1988; 1989) [1.17];
 (1990) [1.18]
Hanley-Dunn, Patricia, & McIntosh,
 John L., (1984) [33.2.5]
Hanley, J. Richard, & Cowell,
 Elaine S., (1988) [33.2.4]
Hanson, R. P. C., (1956) [5.12]
Harcourt-Bath, William, (1934)
 [9.17.9.11]
Harden, A., (1957) [9.17.9.12]
Harder, Kelsie B., (1986) [1.20];
 (1990) [9.2.4]; (1993) [24.10]
Harder, Kelsie B., (Ed.), (1986) [1.19]
Hardie, M. M., (1923) [9.23.5]
Hare, Nathan, (1962) [9.2.1.1]
Harlan, Sam, (1986) [35.13]
Harper, Richard P., (1967) [9.4.3.6]
Harré, Rom, (1975) [9.17.5.3]
Harris, Anne, (1977) [9.17.3.6]
Harris, Edward M., (1986) [9.13.9]
Harris, Huntington, (1950) [38.1]
Harris, M. C., (1960) [45.11]
Harris, Ron, (1979) [26.21]
Harrison, Cynthia M., (1982) [9.13.10]
Harrison, Simon, (1985) [9.42.3.2]
Hart, C. W. M., & Pilling, Arnold R.,
 (1966) [9.42.1.4]
Hartman, Louis F., (1963) [12.11]
Hartmann, Torsten, (1985) [9.22.3]
Hassebrauck, Manfred, (1988) [9.22.4]
Hastings, James, (Ed.), (1963) [5.13]
Hatcher, John, (1972) [47.1.16]
Hatt, D. & Parsons, P. A., (1965)
 [9.42.1.5]

Hauben, Hans, (1975) [9.4.4.10]
Haugaard, Kay, (1986) [44.12]
Haugen, Einar, (1969) [9.41.4]
Hawes, J., (1974) [11.2.4]
Hayes, William C., (Ed. & Trans.),
 (1955; 1972) [9.4.4.11]
Hazen, Barbara Shook, (1979) [1.21]
Heath, D. I., (1855) [5.14]
Hecht, Frederick, (1983) [47.1.17]
Hector, Leonard Charles, (1967)
 [44.13]
Hedblom, Folke, (1984) [9.53.1.1];
 (1985) [9.53.11]
Heider, Karl G., (1980) [26.22]
Heilman, Madeline E., (1975) [3.18]
Helfer, H., (1954) [45.12]
Hemans, T. J., (1968) [9.1.7.3]
Hemon, Roparz, (1976) [9.40.9]
Henderson, Hamish, (1962) [9.49.2.2]
Hengst, Karlheinz, (1990) [47.15]
Henley, Alix, (1979) [9.29.7]
Henley, Arthur, (1970) [28.14]
Henningsson, Per, (1993) [9.53.12]
Herbert, Robert K., & Bogatsu, Senna,
 (1990) [9.1.5.2]
Herlihy, David, (1973) [9.33.5];
 (1988) [9.33.6]
Herndon, Marcia Alice, (1971) [9.37.2]
Herndon, Marcia & McLeod, Norma,
 (1972) [9.37.1.5]
Hersey, William D., (1963) [33.2.6]
Hershberg, Theodore; Burstein, Alan; &
 Dockhorn, Robert, (1976) [8.1.5]
Herskovits, Melville Jean, (1938)
 [9.1.1.9]; (1966) [13.4]
Herzfeld, John, (1987) [30.10]
Herzfeld, Michael, (1982) [9.23.6]
Hexter, J. H., (1983) [15.6]
Hilarion, (1987) [17.6]
Hilbig, Frederick Walter, (1968)
 [9.22.5]
Hilger, M. Inez, (1958) [9.3.18]
Hill, Thomas. D., (1983) [12.12]
Hillaby, Joe, (1982-84) [9.35.13]
Hinz, Walther, (1965) [9.4.11]
Hirsch, Claus W., (1992) [9.35.6.8]
Hirschson, Niel, (1974) [9.35.14]
Hitt, Roberta Frissell, (1984) [1.22]
Hjertstedt, Ingrid, (1987) [9.17.4.7]
Hoag, Joy Marie, (1969) [11.1.8]
Hodge, Bob; Kress, Gunther; & Jones,
 Gareth, (1979) [9.17.1.6]

Hoffman, Susannah M., (1976) [9.23.7]
Hoffner, Harry A. Jr., (1968) [9.4.12]
Hogbin, H. Ian, (1943) [9.42.3.3]
Holgate, P., (1971) [29.8]
Holland, Theodore J. Jr., (1990)
  [26.23]-[26.25]
Hollander, Lee M., (1952) [9.28.2]
Holloway, David, (1978) [22.16]
Holway, Hope, (1965) [9.3.19]
Honeyman, A. M., (1960) [9.4.4.12]
Hook, Donald D., (1984) [3.19]
Hook, J. N., (1991) [1.23]
Hooker, J. T., (1989-90) [9.40.10]
Horn, Jack C., (1975) [11.3]; (1985)
  [26.3.2]
Horne, Marcia D., (1986) [33.2]
Horsley, G. H. R., (1987) [7.9]
Horsnell, Malcolm John Albert, (1974)
  [9.4.13]; (1977) [9.4.14]
Hoskins, W(illiam) G(eorge, (1984)
  [9.17.9.13]
Hourahane, Peter, (Compiler), (1964)
  [9.57.1.2]
Hoyer, Eva, (1976) [9.52.2.6]
Huffmon, Herbert Bardwell, (1963)
  [9.4.15]
Hughes, Charles P., (1963) [9.49.4.6]
Hughes, (James) Pennethorne, (1965)
  [40.1]; (1967) [9.17.9.14]
Hughes, John P., (1954) [9.17.6.15]
Hughes, Marija Matich, (1971) [46.1.3]
Hughes, Pennethorne, (1967)
  [9.17.9.14]
Humbert, Marc, (1993) [3.20]
Hume, A., (1858) [9.31.5.4]
Humphrey, Caroline, (1978) [9.40.11]
Hunnisett, R. F., (1972) [16.2]; (1980)
  [9.17.4.8]
Hunsberger, David Ritchie, (1971)
  [5.15]
Hunt, George W., (1987) [15.7]
Huntingford, G. W. B., (1951)
  [9.1.1.9A]
Hurd, James P., (1983) [29.9]
Hursky, Jacob P., (1957) [9.56.3]
Hussels, Irene, (1969) [9.54.4]
Hutchinson, J., (1898) [47.1.19]
Hyatt, J. Philip., (1955) [12.2.5]

Iivanen, Leevi, (1960) [9.47.4]
Ilan, Tal, (1989) [9.35.1.3]

Infante, Dominic A., Pierce, Linda L.,
  Rancer, Andrew S., et al., (1980)
  [42.4]
Infante, G(uillermo) Cabrera, (1987)
  [30.11]
Ingholt, Harald, (1953) [5.16]
Ingram, Marsha Jill, (1978) [42.1.3]
Innes, Gordon, (1966) [9.1.1.10]
Inscoe, John C., (1983) ([9.2.2.5]
Insley, John, (1985) [9.17.8.2];
  (1987) [9.17.4.9]
Intons-Peterson, Margaret Jean, &
  Crawford, Jill, (1985) [46.3.2]
Irvin, Maurice R., (1975) [5.3.4]
Irving, Ronald, (1973) [7.11]
Isenberg, Shirley Berry, (1988)
  [9.35.15]
Iszaevich, Abraham, (1980) [9.52.1]

Jablonski, Stanley, (1991) [47.1.20]
Jackson, Donald D., (1989) [26.3.3]
Jackson, Edward M., (1990) [9.2.5]
Jackson, Kenneth H., (1960) [9.10.8];
  (1961) [9.57.6]; (1965) [9.49.3]
Jackson, S. K., (1957) [9.1.7.4]
Jacobs, J(ohan) U., (1991) [9.1.5.3]
Jacobs, Leland B., (1953) [26.26]
Jacobs, Nicolas, (1978) [9.17.9.15]
Jacquemet, Marco, (1992) [9.33.1.5]
Jaffe, A. J., Cullen, Ruth M., &
  Boswell, Thomas D., (1980) [44.14]
James, Alice V., (1983) [9.58.2]
Jansson, Sven B. F., (1963) [9.53.5.1]
Jarman, A. O. H., (1969) [9.57.7]
Jarv, Harry, (1973) [47.17]
Jarvis, S(tanley) M(elville), (1979)
  [9.17.3.7]
Jeffreys, M. D. W., (1956) [9.1.7.5];
  (1963) [9.1.1.11]
Jell-Bahlsen, Sabine, (1989) [9.1.4.2]
Jenkins, Dan, (1986) [26.3.4]
Jennings, Brendan, (1951) [9.31.14]
Jennings, Gary, (1965) [1.25]
Jerram, C. S., (1875) [11.2.5]
Jobes, G., (1961) [1.26]
Johansen, Anfinnur, (1993) [9.19.1]
Johnson, Charles, & Sleigh, Linwood,
  (1973) [11.1.9]
Johnson, Dirk, (1990) [42.5]
Johnson, Thomas A., (1977) [9.2.6]
Johnson, William Redpath, (1971)

[9.17.9.1.4]
Johnston, Mary, (1957) [9.14.13]
Johnston, R. J., (1971) [9.17.14]
Jones, C. P., (1988) [9.13.11]
Jones, George F., (1990) [9.22.6]
Jones, Gwilym Peredur, (1926-1927)
    [9.57.8]; (1973) [9.17.15]
Jones, Malcolm, & Dillon, Patrick,
    (1987) [9.17.9.16]
Jones, P. M. S., (1984) [9.57.2.5]
Jordan, David K., (1972) [9.12.1.2]
Jørgensen, Bent, (1986) [9.15.3];
    (1988) [9.15.4]; (1991) [9.15.5]
Josephus, Flavius, (1958) [5.2.2]
Joslin, J(ohn) F(rancis), (1980)
    [9.17.16]
Joubert, Charles E., (1985) [21.3];
    [28.15]
Joyner, Charles, (1984) [9.2.2.6]
Just, Peter, (1987) [9.40.12]

K., A. D., (1966) [47.1.21]
Ka'ano'i, Patrick, & Snakenberg, Robert
    Lokomaika'iokalani, ([9.24.1]
Kaganoff, Benzion C., (1955)
    [9.35.4.2]; (1956) [9.35.6.10]
Kajanto, Iiro, (1962) [9.40.13]; (1964)
    [9.14.14]; (1967) [9.14.15]; (1968)
    [9.14.16]; (1972) [9.14.17]; (1975)
    [9.14.18]; (1986) [9.14.19]
Kalcik, Susan J., (1985) [26.27]
Kaleta, Zofia, (1987-89) [9.50.1];
    (1990) [9.50.2]
Kamm, Henry, (1985) [9.55.2]
Kane, Eileen, (1968) [9.31.15]
Kang-hu, Kiang, (1934; 1977)
    [9.12.1.3]
Kapelrud, Arvid S., (1952) [9.4.16]
Kaplan, Bernice A., & Lasker, Gabriel
    W., (1983) [9.17.9.17]
Kaplan, Justin, (1987) [7.12]
Karma, Inez, (1956) [33.2.7]
Kashyap, Lalit K., (1980) [29.10]
Kashyap, Lalit K., & Tiwari, S. C.,
    (1980) [29.11]
Kasof, Joseph, (1993) [42.5A]
Katranides, Aristotle, (1970) [9.23.8]
Katz, P., (1954) [12.13]
Kaufman, Stephen, (1970)   [9.4.2.2]
Kaufman, Stephen A., (1978) [9.4.3.7]
Kay, H. E. M., (1973) [47.1.22]

Kealey, Robert J., (1984) [26.28]
Kellett-Smith, S. K., (1984) [9.17.17]
Kelley, David H., (1962) [9.11.1]
Kendall, Martha B., (1980) [9.3.20];
    (1981) [3.21]
Kenna, Margaret E., (1976) [9.23.9]
Kenny, Michael, (1961) [9.52.2.7]
Kepsu, Saulo, (1991) [9.20.5]
Kerr, Rosamond, (1977) [6.1]
Khera, Sigrid, (1972) [9.40.14]
Kilpatrick, James J., (1985) [43.5]
Kimbrough, S. T. Jr., (1989) [12.14]
Kimenyi, Alexandre, (1978) [9.1.1.12]
Kimmerle, Marjorie M., (1945)
    [9.41.5]
King, William, (1965) [12.15]
Kingsbury, Stewart A., (1987) [31.1]
Kingsbury, Stewart, & Kingsbury,
    Millie, (1986) [26.29]
Kingston, Maxine Hong, (1977)
    [9.12.7]
Kirk, Matthew, (1979) [7.13]
Kirkpatrick, Harold, (1973) [9.49.4.7]
Kisbye, Torben, (1983) [9.15.6]; (1984)
    [9.15.7]; (1988) [9.15.8]; (1990)
    [9.15.9]
Kitchen, K. A., (1965) [9.4.5.3];
    (1972) [9.4.4.13]
Kiteme, Kamuti, (1972) [9.1.3]
Kivi, Dolores, (1985) [3.22]
Kjellmer, Göran, (1987) [4.1]
Klimas, Antanas, (1969) [9.6.1]; (1971)
    [9.6.2]
Klymasz, Robert, (1959) [9.50.3]
Kniffka, Hannes, (1990) [9.5.4]
Koenig, V. Frederick, (1956) [11.2.6]
Koertvelyessy, T., Collins, M., &
    Keeping, D., (1986) [9.9.8]
Kohout, Joan S., (1973) [46.1.4]
Kolb, Avery E., (1974) [23.6]-[23.7]
Konigsberg, Evelyn, (1957) [3.23]
Koopman, Adrian, (1979) [9.1.8.1]-
    [9.1.8.2]; (1987) [9.1.8.3]; (1989)
    [9.1.8.4]
Kopelman, Richard E., (1985) [11.3]
Kormos, Charles, (1987) [9.35.17]
Kormos, Charles; Lawson, Edwin D., &
    Ben Brit, Joseph, (1992) [9.35.6.11]
Kostka, Gail, (1988) [10.7]
Kraemer, Ross, (1989) [9.35.6.12]
Kraft, Charles E., (1986) [1.27]
Kraft, Charles H., (1976) [9.1.4.3]

Krahmalkov, Charles, (1969) [9.4.17]
Krauthammer, Charles, (1981) [3.24]
Krebs, H., (1886) [9.17.6.16]
Kristensson, Gillis, (1965) [9.17.4.10];
    (1967) [9.17.4.11]; (1969)
    [9.17.9.18]; (1975) [9.17.6.17]-
    [9.17.6.18]; (1977) [9.17.9.19]
Kristof, Nicholas D., (1990) [9.12.8]
Kruck, William E., (1986) [9.17.9.20]
Kruger, F., (1937) [9.1.1.13]
Kruken, Kristoffer, (1989) [9.41.6]
Kuchemann, Christine F., Lasker,
    Gabriel W., & Smith, Douglas I.,
    (1979) [9.17.7.5]
Kuehne, Oswald R., (1951) [10.8]
Kugelmass, J. Alvin, (1952) [9.35.2.3]
Kulikoff, Allan, (1986) [9.2.2.7]
Kupper, Susan J., (1990) [46.3.3]
Kurzweil, Arthur, (1980) [9.35.18]
Kuschel, Rolf, (1988) [9.42.2.2]
Kvillerud, Reinert, (1983) [9.53.2.5];
    (1993) [9.53.1.2]
Kyrris, P. (1967) [9.23.9A]

Lacey, Marj Frazier, (1974) [42.1.4]
Laird, Carobeth, (1976) [9.3.21]
Laird, Helene, & Laird, Charlton,
    (1957) [1.28]
Lakoff, Robin, (1973) [3.25]
Lambdin, William G., (1973) [45.13]
Lamber, Julia C., (1973) [20.2.3]
Lambert, Tom, (1960) [9.47.5]
Lanahan, William F., (1974)
    [9.17.9.21]
Landar, Herbert J., (1961) [9.3.22]
Landsman, Ted, (1984) [23.8]
Lapierre, André, (1988) [47.18]; (1991)
    [9.9.9]
Lardner, Rex, (1974) [44.15]
Lasker, Gabriel W., (1968) [9.43.1];
    (1969) [9.43.2]; (1977) [9.43.3];
    (1978) [9.43.4]; (1982) [9.17.7.6];
    (1983) [9.17.7.7]; (1988) [9.17.7.8]
Lasker, Gabriel W., Chiarelli, B., et al.,
    (1972) [9.33.7]
Lasker, Gabriel W., Coleman, David
    A., et al., (1979) [9.17.7.9]
Lasker, Gabriel, & Kaplan, Bernice,
    (1974) [9.39.5]; (1985); [9.39.6]
Lasker, Gabriel W., Kaplan Bernice A.,
    & Mascie-Taylor, C. G. N., (1985)

[9.17.7.10]
Lasker, Gabriel W., Mascie, C. G. N.,
    & Coleman, David A., (1986)
    [9.17.7.12]
Lasker, Gabriel W., & Mascie-Taylor,
    C. G. N., (1983) [9.17.7.11]
Lasker, Gabriel W., & Roberts, D. F.,
    (1982) [9.17.9.22]
Lasker, Gabriel W., & Steegman,
    Theodore, Jr., (1985) [29.12]
Latham, Joe, (1975) [28.16]
Lave, J(ean Elizabeth) C(arter), (1967)
    [9.51.1.2]
Lavender, Abraham D., (1988) [23.9];
    (1989) [23.10]; (1992) [9.25.1]
Lawson, Edwin D., (1988/89) [2.7];
    (1989) [1.29]; (1990) [1.30]; [2.8];
    (1991) [9.35.19]; (1992) [1.31];
    [42.1.5]
Lawson, Edwin D., (Compiler), (1987)
    [2.6]
Lawson, Edwin D., & Glushkovskaya,
    Irina, (1994) [9.35.4.3]
Lawson, Edwin D., & Roeder, Lynn
    M., (1986) [42.1.6]
Lawton, Robert Brooks, Jr., (1977)
    [9.35.1.4]
Layng, T. P. R., (1972) [9.17.3.8]
Layton, Robert, (1971) [9.21.3]
Leak, Gary, K., & Ware, Mark E.
    (1989) [42.6]
Lebell, Sharon, (1988) [24.11]
Lee, Mary Price & Lee, Richard S.,
    (1985) [19.2]
Lee, Motoko Y., (1976) [9.34.5]
Leeds-Hurwitz, Wendy, (1980) [3.26]
Leeson, Francis, (1964) [9.17.9.23];
    (1965) [9.17.9.24]; (1968)
    [9.17.2.3]; (1970) [9.17.9.25];
    (1971) [9.17.9.26]
Lehikoinen, Laila, (1990) [9.20.6]
Lehiste, Ilse, (1958) [9.17.6.19]
Leighly, John, (1983) [9.22.7]
Leirer, Von O., Hamilton, David L., &
    Carpenter, Sandra, (1982) [42.1.7]
Leishman, Thomas L., & Lewis, Arthur
    T., (1965) [12.16]
Lennox, Bernard, (Ed.), (1980)
    [47.1.23]
Leon, Harry Joshua, (1960) [9.35.1.5]
Leslie, D(aniel), (1962) [9.35.3.1];
    (1963-64) [9.35.3.2]; (1964-65)

[9.35.3.3]
Leslie, Paul L., & Skipper, James K.,
    Jr., (1990) [26.30]
Levine, Baruch A., (1967) [9.35.1.6]
Lewis, Geoffrey L., (1957) [9.55.3]
Lewis, Henry, (1933-36) [9.57.9]
Lewis, I. M., (1961) [9.1.1.14]
Lewis, Lionel S., (1963) [3.27];
    (1965) [3.28]
Lewis, Margaret Jane, (1970) [26.31]
Lewitter, F. I., Hurwich, B. J., &
    Nubani, N., (1983) [9.5.5]
Leys, O., (1971) [25.5]
Lieberman, Evelyn, (1985) [10.9]
Lieberson, Stanley & Bell, Eleanor O.,
    (1992) [24.12]
Light, John, (1983) [9.17.18]
Liguori, Irene, (1989) [45.14]
Limon, José, (1979) [9.52.2.8]
Linde, Gunnar, (1985) [9.53.13]
Linden, Myra J., (1986) [46.1.5]
Lindquist, E., (1967) [9.53.14]
Lindqvist, Tor-Erik, (1990) [9.20.7]
Lindskoog, Kathryn, (1984) [45.15]
Linville, Deborah R., (1982) [42.7]
Lip, Evelyn, (1988) [9.12.9]
Lipsitt, Lewis P., (1990) [17.7]
Lipski, John M., (1976) [30.12]
Lisse, Christine., (1986) [9.15.10]
Littlefield, D. F. Jr., & Underhill, L.
    E., (1971) [9.3.23]
Littmann, Enno, (1953) [9.4.18]
Litwack, Leon, (1979) [9.2.1.2]
Lloyd, Gregory, (1988) [26.32]
Lloyd, J. E., (1929) [9.57.2.6]
Locks, Gutman G., (1985) [27.3]
Lockyer, Herbert, (1958) [5.1.2];
    (1967) [5.17]
Löffler, Heinrich, (1988) [9.54.5];
    (1989) [9.22.8]
Loewenthal, Isidore, (1911) [9.29.8]
Logue, Larry M., (1987) [23.11]
Lohr, Steve, (1985) [9.44.2]
Loizos, Peter, (1975) [9.23.10]
London, Robb, (1990) [42.8]
Loomis, C. Grant, (1956) [15.8]
Lopez, Robert Sabatino, (1954) [9.33.8]
Lorayne, Harry, (1975) [33.2.8]-
    [33.2.9]
Lorchirachoonkul, Vichit, (1982)
    [9.40.15]
Lorenz, Brenna, (1989) [45.16]

Louie, Emma Woo, (1987) [9.12.10];
    (1991) [9.12.1.4]; [9.12.11]
Lowie, Robert H., (1909; 1975)
    [9.3.24]; [9.3.25]; (1917) [9.3.26];
    (1924) [9.3.27]; (1954; 1963)
    [9.3.28]
Lowry, Lillian, (1953) [45.17]
Loyd, Lewis Christopher, (1951;1975)
    [9.17.9.27]
Lu Zhongti with Millward, Celia, (1989)
    [9.12.12]
Lublin, Joann S., (1975) [46.1.6]
Lund, Niels, (1975) [9.17.6.20]
Lurie, Alison, (1983) [24.13]
Lussier, Ernest, (1956) [5.18]
Lutterer, Ivan, (1967) [38.2]
Lutz, George Winston, (1983) [26.33]
Lyell, Charles, (1849) [9.2.2.8]

Mac Giolla Domhnaigh, Padraig,
    (1975) [9.31.5.5]
MacAlister, R. A. S., (1922) [9.10.9]
MacAndrew, Robert, (1963)
    [9.49.4.1.1]
MacClintock, Lander, (1965) [30.13]
MacColl, Ewan, & Seeger, Peggy,
    (1986) [9.49.2.3]
MacDonald, Donald F., (1965)
    [9.49.4.8]
MacDougall, Priscilla Ruth, (1972/73)
    [46.1.7]
MacGregor, Alasdair Alpin (Douglas),
    (1949) [9.49.4.9]
Mackay, R. L., (1974) [9.49.1.1]
MacKay, Robert L., (1978) [9.49.1.2]
Mackenzie, W(illiam) C(arl), (1903)
    [9.49.4.10]
MacLeay, John, (1980) [9.49.2.4]
MacLysaght, E(dward A., (1969)
    [9.31.5.6]; (1970) [9.31.1.3]; (1976)
    [9.31.5.7]; (1980) [9.31.5.8]
MacMillan, Somerled, (1970)
    [9.49.4.10A]
MacNeil, Neil, (1948) [9.9.10]
Macqueen, J. G., (1959) [9.4.19]
Madron, Thomas W., (1985) [8.1.6]
Maenchen-Helfen. O., (1955), [9.22.9]
Magalini, Sergio I. & Scrascia, Euclide,
    (1981) [47.1.24]
Mai-Dalton, Renate R., & Sullivan,
    Jeremiah J., (1981) [33.3]

Jeremiah J., (1981) [33.3]
Maidbury, Laurence, (1954) [9.17.3.9]; [9.17.9.28]; (1954-56) [9.17.9.29]
Mallows, R. J., (1980) [9.42.1.6]
Mangion, Giovanni, (1978) [9.37.3]
Manley, G. T., (1962) [12.17]
Manser, Martin H., (1988) [47.19]
Mansuroglu, Mecdut, (1954) [9.55.4]; (1955) [9.55.5]
Marapara, Malakia, (1954) [9.1.1.15]
Marcus, Leonard, (1973) [15.9]
Marcus, Ralph, (1953) [9.35.20]
Margolick, David, (1991) [20.7]
Markreich, Max, (1961) [9.35.6.13]
Markrich, Max, (1958) [9.35.6.14]
Markwei, M., (1966) [9.1.1.16]
Marshall, Arthur, (1977) [7.14]; (1978) [9.17.3.10]; [45.18]
Martin, Charles B., (1987) [1.32]
Martin, Charles Trice, (Ed.), (1910; 1982) [9.17.9.30]
Martin, Edward A., (1972) [9.17.9.31]; (1974) [9.17.9.33]
Marty, Martin E., (1985) [24.14]
Mascie-Taylor, C. G. N., Lasker, G(abriel) W., et al., (1987) [9.49.3.2]
Mason, Susan E., (1986) [33.2.10]
Massarik, Fred, (1966) [9.35.6.15]
Massolo, Maria Laura, (1990) [9.51.2]
Massotty, Karen A., (1974) [7.15]
Mastoris, S. N., (1985) [9.17.19]
Mathews, Anthony, (1968) [9.31.5.1.1]-[9.31.5.1.3]; (1971) [9.31.5.1.4]; (1972) [9.31.5.1.5]; (1973) [9.31.5.1.6]
Matthews, C. M., (1963) [9.17.9.33]
Maurer, David W., & Futrell, Allan W., (1982) [26.34]
Maynard, Rona, (1990) [11.1.10]
McCarter, P. Kyle, Jr., (1888) [5.19]
McCarville, Evelyn, (1952) [9.31.5.9]
McClure, Edmund, (1883) [25.6]
McClure, Peter, (1973) [9.17.4.12]
McCracken, Alex, (1972) [9.49.1.3]
McCullough, John M., Giles, Eugene; & Thompson, Richard A., (1985) [9.39.7]
McDavid, Raven & O'Lain, Raymond K., (1976) [30.14]
McDonald, Forrest, & McDonald, Ellen Shapiro, (1980) [23.12]-

[23.13]; (1984) [23.14]
McDowell, John H., (1981) [9.51.1.3]
McGeachy, John, III, (1978) [26.35]
McGregory, Jerrilyn, (1990) [9.2.7]
McGuigan, Peter, (1984) [9.9.1.2]; (1985) [9.31.5.10]
McKenzie, John L., (1965) [12.1.2]
McKinley, R(ichard) A(lexander, (1969) [9.17.9.34]-[9.17.9.35]; (1981) [9.17.9.36]; (1988) [9.17.9.37]; (1990) [9.49.9.37A]; (1990/91) [9.17.4.13]
McLaughlin, M., (1974) [7.16]
McMurtrie, Douglas, (1982) [9.49.4.1.2]
McNaughton, D., (1981) [9.49.4.1.3]
McRobert, William, (1976) [9.49.4.1.4]
McWeeny, Kathryn H., Young, Andrew W., et al., (1987) [33.2.11]
McWilliam, Roy, (1942) [11.5]
Mead, A. D., (1958) [9.42.2.1.3]
Meaders, Daniel E., (1975) [9.2.2.9]
Meadow, Kathryn P., (1977) [22.17]
Meek, Theophile S., (1935) [9.4.20]; (1939) [5.20]
Meer, Jeff, (1983) [42.9]
Meertens, P. J., (1971) [9.16.2]
Meeter, Glenn, (1986) [22.18]
Megaw, Basil, (1976) [9.38.2]
Mehrabian, Albert, (1990) [42.1.8]
Mehrotra, R. R., (1979) [9.29.9]
Meigs, P., (1941) [9.21.4]
Meimaris, Yiannis E., (1986) [36.6]
Meldgaard, Eva Villarsen, (1983) [9.15.11]; (1984) [9.15.12]; (1989) [9.15.13]; (1992) [9.15.14]
Meltzer, Milton, (1984) [1.33]
Memar-Sadeghi, Abdomaljid, (1980) [9.30.2]
Menges, K. H., (1951) [9.8.2]
Mephisto, (1952) [9.27.5]
Mercer, A. C. B., (1954) [9.48.3]
Merrill, Arthur A., (1967) [33.2.12]
Merritt, Jesse, (1956) [23.15]
Merton, Robert King, (1973) [47.20]
Mertz, Elizabeth, (1983) [9.9.11]
Messenger, J. C., (1967) [9.31.16]
Messing, Simon D., (1974) [9.18.2]
Mewett, Peter G., (1982) [9.49.2.5]
Mezes, Basileios, (1989-90) [1.34]
Michaels, Ken, (1968) [26.36]

Mills, A. D., (1963) [9.17.4.14];
    (1966) [9.17.4.15]
Milne, J. D(orothy), (1981) [9.9.12]
Minton, A(rthur), (1958) [43.6]
Miran, M. Alam, (1975) [9.40.16]
Moeller, Henry R., (1962) [12.18]
Monagan, Charles, (1986) [26.37]
Montalbano, Frank J., (1951) [13.5]
Moore, G. A., (1972) [9.17.3.11]
Moore, John H., (1984) [9.3.29]
Moore, Robert L., (1993) [9.12.13]
Morgan, Lewis Henry, (1851; 1962)
    [9.3.30]
Morgan, Prys, (1968) [9.57.2.7];
    (1986) [9.57.2.8]; (1990-91)
    [9.57.2.9]
Morgan, T. J., (1987) [9.57.10]
Morgan, Ted, (1978) [7.17]
Morgan, T. J., & Morgan, Prys, (1985)
    [9.57.2.9A]
Morpugo-Davies, Anna, (1968)
    [9.13.12]
Morris, Percy S., (1960) [20.8]
Morris, T(homas) E(vans), (1938)
    [9.57.11]
Morrison, Lemuel & Speed, Anoona,
    (1980) [9.2.8]
Morrow, Robert D., (1989) [9.40.17]
Mors, Otto, (1951) [22.19]
Morton, Mike, & Eckler, A. Ross,
    (1986) [35.14]
Morton, Newton E., (1973) [29.13]
Morton, N(ewton)E., & Hussels, Irene,
    (1970) [9.54.6]
Moss, Robert F., (1990) [37.2]
Mossop, H(enry) R(ichard), (1970)
    [9.17.6.1.3]
Motyer, J. A., (1962) [5.21]
Moyser, P. J., (1985) [9.17.3.12]
Mueller, Dieter, (1973) [9.4.4.14]
Muhammad, Wallace D., (1976) [9.2.9]
Mundal, Else, (1990) [9.41.7]; (1992)
    [9.41.8]
Munday, J. T., (1948) [9.1.1.17];
    (1956) [9.1.1.18]
Munnecke, Tom, (1980) [8.1.7]
Murdock, George Peter, (1934)
    [9.3.31]
Murphy, Cullen, (1991) [3.29]
Murphy, Francis Xavier, (1967) [11.6]
Murphy, R(ichard) T(homas), A(quinas),
    (1967) [12.1.3]; [12.19]

Murray, James A. H., (1933) [1.38]
Murray, M. A., (1942) [9.17.6.21]
Murtonen, A., (1951) [13.6]
Must, Gusta, (1957) [9.14.19A]
Mydans, Seth, (1985) [9.47.6]
Myrc, John, (1902; 1969) [9.17.6.22]

Nader, Habibi, (1992) [9.30.3]
Nadvi, S. Salman, (1987) [9.32.3]
Nakhimovsky, A. D., (1976) [9.47.7]
Nalibow, Kenneth L., (1973) [9.45.1]
Närhi, Eeva Maria, (1987) [9.20.9];
    (1989) [9.20.10]; (1990) [9.20.11]
Närhi, Eeva Maria, (Ed.), (1990) [1.36]
Nash, Michael L., (1984) [9.17.3.13];
    (1985) [9.17.3.14]
Nathan, Carmen, (1990) [9.1.5.4]
Nau, L. T., (1988) [9.9.13]
Nau, Tim, (1991) [9.9.14]; (1993)
    [36.7]
Naveh, J(oseph), (1970) [9.35.21]
Neethling, S. J., (1988) [9.1.5.5];
    (1990) [9.1.5.5A]; (1991) [9.1.5.6]
Nelson, Lowry, Jr., (1981) [9.22.10]
Nemer, Julie F., (1987) [9.1.1.19]
Nemy, Enid, (1987) [3.30]; [26.38]
Ness, M. E., (1949) [9.9.15]
Neumann, Joshua H., (1965)
    [9.35.6.16]
Newman, David J. M., & Forrester,
    Colin D. I. G., (1986) [9.17.20]
Newman, Edwin, (1982) [26.39]
Newman, Louis Israel, (1965)
    [9.35.4.4]
Newman, Michael, (1975) [24.16]
Newmark, Peter, (1983) [47.1.25]
Nicolaisen, W(ilhelm) F. H., (1976)
    [25.7]; (1986) [25.8]; [9.22.11]
Nielsen, Karl Martin, (1987) [9.15.15];
    (1988) [9.15.16]
Nikhilanda, Swami, (1957) [9.29.10]
Nikonov, V. A., (1971) [9.47.8]
Niles, Daniel Premaseelan, (1975)
    [12.2.6]
Nilsen, Don L. F., (1987) [45.21]
Nilsson, Lars-Göran; Law, Janine; &
    Tulving, Endel, (1988) [33.2.13]
Nimuendaju, Curt, (1939;1967)
    [9.51.1.4]
Nimuendaju, Curt & Lowie, Robert H.,
    (1939) [9.51.1.5]

Nitze, William A., (1953/54)
     [9.17.6.23]; (1956) [9.21.5]
Noah, Timothy, (1986) [17.10]
Noble, (Wilfred) Vernon, (1976)
     [26.41]
Noel, Richard C., & Allen, Mary J.,
     (1976) [42.10]
Nogrady, Michael, (1990) [9.27.6]
Noon, John A., (1949; 1964) [9.3.32]
Noory, Samuel, (1965) [30.16]
Nordenskiöld, Erland, (1938) [9.3.33]
Norton, Mary Beth, ([9.2.2.10]
Nosnikrap, A. J., (1985) [32.2]
Noth, Martin, (1956) [9.4.21]
Nsimbi, M., (1949) [9.1.1.20]
Nu'Man, Muhammad Armiya, (1981)
     [9.32.4]
Nuessel, Frank, (1992) [1.37]
Nunoo, Ebenezer, (1971/1972)
     [9.1.3.3]
Nurnberg, M., (1966) [7.19]
Nurse, G. T., (1976) [9.1.1.21
Nuttin, Jozef M. Jr., (1985) [33.2.14]
Nwachukwu-Agbada, J. O. J., (1991)
     [9.1.4.4]

Ó Corráin, Donnchadh & Maguire,
     Fidelma, (1981) [9.31.2.4]
Ó Cuív, Brian, (1986) [9.31.17]
Ó Danachair, Cáoimhín, (1975)
     [9.31.5.11]
Ó Muraile, Nollaíg, (1987) [9.31.18]
Ó Murchadha, Diarmid, (1985)
     [9.31.5.12]
O'Boyle, Michael W., & Murray,
     James, (1988) [33.4.2]
O'Brien, M(ichael) A., (1956)
     [9.10.10]; (1971) [9.31.19]
O'Connell, J. P., (1952) [36.8]
O'Donnell, Richard, (1994) [14.3]
O'Laughlin, Michael C., (1993)
     [9.31.5.13]
O'Shaughnessy, Marjorie, (1962)
     [45.22]
O'Sullivan, Chris S., Chen, Audrey, et
     al., [42.11]
Oates, John F., (1963) [9.4.4.16];
     (1964/65) [9.4.4.17]
Oberlander, Frank, & Oberlander,
     Mary, (1986) [35.15]
Obermann, Julian, (1949) [12.2.7]

Odelain, O., & Séguineau, R., (1981)
     [5.22]
Oesterly, W. O. E., & Robinson,
     Theodore H., (1932) [5.2.3]
Okasha, Elizabeth, (1971) [9.17.6.24]
Okediji, F. Olu & F. A., (1966)
     [9.1.4.5]
Olesen, Virginia, & Whittaker, Elvi,
     (1968) [47.4.5]
Oliver, Revilo P., (1977) [9.14.20]
Olson, B. Lynette, & Padel, O. J.,
     (1986) [36.9]
Omijeh, M. E., (1968) [9.1.2.1]
Ontario Law Reform Commission,
     (1976) [9.9.2.3]
Orgel, Irene, (1958) [11.2.7]
Ortego Villero, Begona, (1989-1990)
     [9.13.13]
Oseni, Z(akariyau) I(drees-Oboh),
     (1981) [9.1.4.6]
Ott, Sandra, (1981) [9.40.19]
Otterbjörk, Roland, (1983) [9.53.5.2]
Otto, Julie Helen, (1994) [23.16]
Oxer, O. E., (1973) [9.17.2.4]
Oxtoby, Willard Gurdon, (1962)
     [9.4.22]

Pacanowsky, Michael & Anderson,
     James A., (1981) [26.42]
Packer, J. I., (1986) [44.1.4]
Padrnos, Dennis, (1960) [20.10]
Paetzke, H. H., & Rajk, L., (1986)
     [9.27.7]
Paffard, Michael, (1980) [44.16]
Palestine, Government of, (1931)
     [9.5.6]
Pall, Ellen, (1989) [32.3]
Palmer, L. R., (1958) [13.7]
Palmer, L(eonard) R(obert), (1969)
     [9.13.14]
Panelius, Olav, (1987) [9.53.6.3]
Papp, A. H. R. E., (1959) [40.2]
Parisi, Albert J., (1987) [20.12]
Parker, Richard A., (1966) [9.4.4.18]
Parkinson, C. Northcote, (1975)
     [9.17.1.7]
Parkinson, Dilworth B., (1982) [9.5.7]
Parman, Susan, (1976) [9.49.2.6]
Parry-Williams, T. H., (1921-23)
     [9.57.12]
Partow, Shin, (1960) [13.8]

Partridge, Harry B., (1986) [35.16]
Pascoe, W. H., (1972) [9.17.9.1.5]
Pasterczyk, Catherine E., (1985)
  [9.50.4]
Paterson, D. R., (1920) [9.57.13]
Patil, Vimla, (1990) [9.29.11]
Patterson, Joan, (1980) [9.17.22]
Pauls, John P., (1963) [9.47.9]; (1969)
  [9.45.2]
Paxton, Evelyn, (1972) [9.5.8]
Pearce, Edward, (1979) [9.17.23]
Pedersen, Birte Hjorth, (1986) [9.1.4]
Pehrson, Robert N(iel), (1957) [9.36.2]
Pehrson, Robert N., & Whitaker, Ian
  R., (1952) [9.36.3]
Pelan, Margaret, (1954) [9.21.6]
Pelteret, David A. E., (1986) [9.17.24]
Pender, Seamus, (Ed.), (1939)
  [9.31.5.14]
Pentland, David H. & Wolfart, H.
  Christoph, (1982) [2.11]
Penzl, Herbert, (1987) [9.22.12]
Perceval-Maxwell, M., (1973)
  [9.31.5.15]
Perring, Douglas, (1985) [9.17.3.15]
Peter, Prince of Greece and Denmark,
  (1954) [9.40.20]
Peterson, Lena, (1980) [9.53.15]-
  [9.53.15A]; (1981) [9.53.16];
  [9.53.5.3]; (1983) [9.53.7.1]; (1984)
  [9.53.17]; (1985) [9.53.7.2]; (1986)
  [9.53.18]; (1987) [9.53.3.4]; (1988)
  [9.53.19]; (1989) [9.53.7.3]; (1992)
  [9.53.2.6]; (1993) [9.53.5.4]
Pfaller, Benedict, (1966) [3.31]
Philippides, Marios, (1989-90)
  [9.23.11]
Picton, J. A., (1886) [9.17.6.25]
Pilcher, William W., (1972) [26.43]
Pina-Cabral, João de, (1984) [26.44]
Pine, Leslie Gilbert, (1970) [3.32]
Pinsent, R. F. J. H., (1975)
  [9.17.9.1.6]
Pinto-Cisternas, J., Castelli, M. C., &
  Pineda, L., (1955) [9.51.3]
Pitt-Rivers, J(ulian) A(lfred), (1961)
  [9.52.2.9]; (1977) [9.52.2]
Pitt, Valerie, (1971) [19.3]
Plancke, M., (1971) [9.5.9]
Pocock, L. G., (1967) [9.13.15]
Pogue, Marilyn, (1985) [47.4.6]
Pokorny, J., (1956) [9.57.14]

Pollitzer, W(illiam) S., (1983) [9.7.2]
Pollitzer, William S., Smith, Malcolm
  T., & Williams, W. Robert, (1988)
  [9.17.7.13]
Pollock, F., (1919) [9.17.1.8]
Poole, FitzJohn Porter, (1981)
  [9.42.3.4]
Porten, Bezalel, (1968) [9.35.22];
  (1971) [9.35.1.7]
Porteous, J. Douglas, (1982)
  [9.17.9.1.7]; (1985) [9.17.9.1.8];
  (1987) [9.17.9.1.9]; (1988)
  [9.17.9.1.10]
Poulsen, Jōhan Hendrik W., (1985)
  [9.19.2]
Powell, J. G. F., (1984) [9.14.21]
Powell, Mary, (1990) [24.17]
Power, Michael, & Weinberg, Eugene,
  (1991) [17.11]
Prentice, George G., (1860) [15.10]
Price, Roger, & Stern, Leonard, (1960)
  [42.12]
Price, Roger; Stern, Leonard; & Sloan,
  Lawrence, (1985) [15.11]
Priest, Anne, (1964) [9.51.1.6]
Pritchard, James B(ennett) (1955)
  [9.4.4.19]
Pulgram, Ernst, (1951) [1.39]; (1959)
  [25.9]
Pullicino, Joseph Cassar, (1956)
  [9.37.1.6]
Punch, Terrence M., (1985) [9.9.16]
Purvis, Thomas L., (1984) [23.17];
  [23.18]

Quaegebeur, Jan, (1971) [9.4.4.20]
Quick, Armand J., (1970) [47.1.26]
Quindlen, Anna, (1987) [46.1.9]
Qutub, Ishaq Y., (1963) [9.5.10]

Rabinowitz, Isaac, (1956) [9.4.2.3]
Rack, Philip, (1982) [24.18]
Raine, K., (1953) [9.17.1.9]
Rait, S. K., (1984) [6.3]
Ramirez, Antonio, (1989) [9.8.3]
Randolph, Boris, (1986) [35.17]
Ranganathan, S(hiyali) R(amamrita),
  (1988) [6.4]
Ranke, Hermann, (1950) [9.4.4.21]
Raphael, Frederic, (1976) [1.40]

Rasmussen, Carl George, (1981)
[9.4.1.3]
Raum, O. F., (1940) [9.1.1.22]
Raun, Alo, (1982) [9.6.3]
Ravitch Mark M., (1968) [47.1.27];
(1977) [47.1.28]; (1979) [47.1.29]
Rawick, George P., (Ed.), (1972)
[9.2.2.11]
Reaney, P(ercy) H(ide) (1951)
[9.17.3.16]; (1952) [9.17.6.26];
(1953) [9.17.6.27]; (1961)
[9.17.4.16]; (1965) [9.17.9.39];
(1976; 1977) [9.17.9.44]
Redmonds, G(eorge), (1972)
[9.17.9.41]-[9.17.9.43]; (1975)
[9.17.9.44]; (1985) [9.17.9.44A]
Rees, Nigel & Noble, Vernon, (1985)
[26.45]
Reilly, Dennis M., (1975) [33.1.1];
(1978) [33.1.2]; (1979) [33.1.3];
(1984) [33.1.4]
Reilly, Linda Collins, (1969)
[9.13.16]; (1978) [9.13.17]
Reinmuth, O. W., (1967) [9.4.4.22]
Reisner, George Andrew; Fisher,
Clarence Stanley; & Lyon, David.
(1924) [5.2.4]
Relethford, John H., (1982) [9.31.3.1]
Relethford, John H., & Lees, Francis
C., (1983) [9.31.3.2]
Relethford, John H., Lees, Francis C.,
& Crawford, Michael, [9.31.3.3]
Rennick, Robert M., (1968) [11.1.11];
(1969) [7.20]; (1969) [22.21];
(1985) [23.19]
Rhodes, Michael, (1987) [9.17.25]
Richards, G. Melville, (1966) [9.57.15];
(1969) [9.57.16]; (1970-71)
[9.57.17]; (1972) [9.57.18]
Richman, Daniel Avram, (1993)
[11.1.12]
Richman, Daniel A(vram), Marosi,
Stephen B., Staniec, Fran, et al.,
(1991) [11.1.13]
Richmond, W. Edson, (1974) [31.2]
Rici, Julien, (1967) [9.1.1.23]
Rigg, A. G., (1987) [9.17.9.1.11]
Riley, Morgan T., (1956) [11.2.8]
Ritzenthaler, Robert, (1945) [9.3.34]
Roberts, Brynley F., (1973) [9.10.11]
Roberts, D. F., (1980) [9.17.7.14]
Roberts, D. F., & Rawling, C. P.,

(1974) [9.17.7.15]
Roberts, D. F., & Roberts, M. J.,
(1983) [9.49.3.3]
Roberts, R. J., (1961) [2.12]
Roberts, Warren E., (1981) [44.17]
Robertson, M. G., (1972) [47.1.30]
Robinson, A. P., (1983) [9.49.3.4]
Robinson, Cardew, (1975-1976) [42.13]
Robinson, D. M., & Fluck, E. J.,
(1979) [9.13.18]
Robinson, Matthew, (1970) [3.33]
Robson, John M., (1988) [9.17.9.45]
Roche, Owen I. A., (1965) [9.26.1]
Rodrigue-Schwarzwald, Ora, (1988)
[9.35.23]
Rogers, Edward S., & Rogers, Mary
Black, (1978) [9.3.35]
Rogers, George C., (1970) [9.2.2.12]
Rogers, James, (1970) [26.46]
Rogers, L. A., (1987) [29.14]
Rogers, Mary B., & Rogers, Edward S.,
(1980) [9.3.36]
Rokeah, David, (1968) [9.35.1.8];
(1970) [9.35.1.9]
Rolleston, Humphry, (1937) [47.1.31]
Rolls, Charles J(ubilee), (1953; 1984)
[5.3.5]; (1956) [5.3.6]; (1958)
[5.3.7]; (1965; 1985) [5.3.8];
(1975; 1985) [5.3.9]
Rolnick, Philip A., (1992) [12.20]
Room, Adrian, (1986) [22.22];
(1987) [22.23]; (1989) [32.4]
Root, Eileen M., (1987) [9.24.2]
Rose, Arthur, (1951) [9.17.9.46]
Rose, Christine, (1987) [11.6]
Rosenblatt, Roger, (1980) [26.2.3]
Rosenkrantz, Linda & Satran, Pamela,
(1988) [11.1.14]
Rosenwaike, Ira, (1990) [9.35.24];
[9.35.6.17]; (1991) [9.52.3.4]
Roth, Cecil, (1962) [9.35.25]
Rothman, Anne, & Hicks, Kenneth,
(1984) [19.4]; [19.5]
Roughton, Karen G., & Tyckoson,
David A., (1985) [8.1.8]
Rovere, Richard H., (1958) [43.7]
Rowe, M. M., & Jackson, A. M.,
(Eds.), (1973) [9.17.26]
Royko, Mike, (1989) [42.1.9]
Roys, Ralph L(oveland), (1940)
[9.39.8]
Rubenstein, Carin, (1983) [17.12]

Rubenstein, Carin, (1983) [17.12]
Rudnyckyj, J. B., (1969) [46.4]; (1991) [46.5]
Rule, La Reina, & Hammond, William K., (1973) [1.41]
Rumble, Alexander R., (1984) [9.17.4.17]
Ruofu, Du, (1986) [9.12.1.5]
Russell, J. M., (1980) [9.49.2.7]
Rust, L. D., (1982) [9.17.3.17]
Ruthven, K. K., (1986) [17.13]
Ruud, Jørgen, (1961) [9.1.1.24]
Ryan, J. S., (1966) [9.42.1.7]
Rylance, T., (1980) [9.17.9.47]
Rzetelska-Felezko, Ewa, (1978) [9.45.3]

Sabine, William H. W., (1957) [44.18]
Sabourin, Leopold, (1967) [5.3.10]
Safire, William, (1989) [30.18]
Sakah, B. T., (1963) [9.1.1.25]
Salberger, Evert, (1979) [9.53.5.5]; [9.53.5.6]; (1985) [9.48.4]; [9.53.5.7]; (1986) [9.53.5.8]; (1987) [9.53.5.9]; [9.53.5.10]; (1989) [9.53.5.11]; (1990) [9.53.5.12]-[9.53.5.13]; (1991) [9.53.5.14]-[9.53.5.15]; (1993) [9.53.5.16]
Salomon, Frank, (1986) [9.43.5]
Salys, Antanas, (1951) [9.6.4]
Samet, Jonathan M., Key, Charles R., Kutvirt, Daniel M., et al., (1980) [34.5]
Samra, Myer, (1989) [9.35.26]
Sandison, Alexander, (1959) [9.49.3A]; (1968) [9.49.4.11]
Sandström, Raija, (1984) [9.53.20]
Sanford, A. J., Moar, K., & Garrod, S. (1988) [22.24]
Sanneh, L. O., (1989) [25.10]
Sarikakis, Theodore C., (1976) [9.13.19]
Sasson, J. M., (1966) [9.4.23]
Scadding, Henry, (1868?) [7.21]
Scheetz, George H., (1988) [1.42]
Scheffler, H. W., (1976) [9.51.1.7]
Scherr, Arthur, (1986) [7.22]
Schild, E., (1954) [12.1.4]
Schimmel, Annemarie, (1987) [9.29.12]; (1989) [9.5.11]

Schmemann, Serge, (1982) [9.47.10]
Schmickel, Roy D., (1983) [47.1.32]
Schmidt, Tom, (1992) [9.41.9]
Schneider, David M., & Homans, George C., (1955) [3.34]
Schomer, Jacqueline, (1980) [9.3.37]
Schonenberger, Paul, (1961) [9.1.1.26]
Schoonheim, Tanneke, (1990) [9.16.3]
Schwartzenberg, Charles, Prince, (1981) [40.3]
Schwegel, Janet, (1988;1990) [11.1.15]
Scott, Forrest S., (1986) [9.42.2.3]
Scott, Reid, (1969) [9.52.3]; (1972) [9.52.4]
Scott, Timothy, (1989) [20.1.3]
Sears, Albert D., (1952) [45.23]
Seefeldt, Carol, (1984) [10.10]
Seim, Karin Fjellhammer, (1991) [9.41.10]
Selenius, Ebba, (1985) [9.20.12]
Senior, A., (1951) [9.17.9.48]
Senn, Alfred, (1948) [9.54.7]
Sequeira, Debra-Lynn Marie, (1988) [3.35]
Serruys, Henry, (1958) [9.12.14]
Severi, Carlo, (1980) [9.33.1.6]
Sharify, Nasser, (1959) [6.5]
Sharman, Lyon, (1934;1968) [9.12.15]
Shaw, David H., (1978) [9.17.9.49]
Shaw, Richard F., (1960) [9.25.2]
Shehinski, Shelley, (1988) [9.3.38]
Shevoroskin, V., (1984) [9.4.24]; (1988) [9.4.25]
Shin, Eui-Hang, & Yu, Eui-Young, (1984) [29.15]
Shoumatoff, Alex, (1988;90) [1.43]
Sibata, Takesi, (1978) [9.34.6]
Sidi, Smadar Shir, (1989) [9.35.4.5]
Sidney, John, (1956) [45.24]
Sigmundsson, Svavar, (1992) [9.28.3]
Sijpesteijn, P. J., (1990) [9.4.4.23]
Sikström, Tomas, (1990) [9.53.5.17]
Sill, Geoffrey M., (1978) [9.17.9.1.12]
Silverman, David L., (1986) [35.18]-[35.21]
Silverman, M. H., (1969) [9.35.1.10]
Simons, Elizabeth Radin, (1984) [10.11]; (1985) [10.12]
Simpson, William Kelly, (1953) [9.4.4.24]; (1972) [9.4.4.25]
Sisam, Kenneth, (1953) [9.17.6.28]
Skeat, Walter W., (1891) [9.17.6.29]

Skeat, Walter William & Brogden,
    Charles Otto, (1906; 1966) [9.40.21]
Skinner, Alanson, (1913) [9.3.39];
    (1923) [9.3.40]; (1926) [9.3.41]
Skinner, Henry Alan, (1970) [47.1.33]
Skinner, Mary Ann Long, (1994) [5.23]
Skipper, James K. Jr., (1968) [38.3];
    (1986) [26.47]-[26.48]; (1987)
    [26.3.5]; (1989) [38.4]; [26.3.6];
    (1990) [26.3.7]; (1992) [26.3.8]
Skipper. James K., & Leslie, Paul L.,
    (1988) [26.1.1]; [26.1.2]; (1989)
    [26.1.3]; (1990) [26.49]
Skutsch, Otto, (1987) [13.9]
Slade, Margot, (1984) [46.1.10]
Slater, Anne Saxon & Feinman, Saul,
    (1985) [39.3]
Slavutych, Yar, (1963) [9.50.5]
Slorance, Andrew J., (1978)
    [9.49.4.1.5]
Smart, Veronica, (1970) [9.17.6.1.4];
    (1973) [9.17.6.1.5]; (1986)
    [9.17.6.1.6]
Smith, Antar Ibn-Stanford Ibn-Edward
    Ibn-George, (1985) [9.32.6]
Smith, Daniel Scott, (1989) [29.16]
Smith, Elsdon C., (1953) [1.44]; (1971)
    [44.19]
Smith, J. Jerome, (1981) [26.50]
Smith, Jack, (1986) [28.20]
Smith, Kenneth L., (1989) [9.22.13]
Smith, Steven M., (1985) [33.2.15]
Smith, T. H., (1892) [9.42.2.1.4]
Smithers, Janice A., (1977) [3.36]
Snowden, F. M. Jr., (1970) [9.13.20]
Sobel, Dava, (1982) [17.14]
Sofola, J. A., (1970) [9.1.4.7]
Solin, Heikki, (1987) [9.14.22]
Solomon, Jolie, (1989) [26.51]
Sommerville, C. John, (1982) [24.19]
Søndergaard, Georg, (1986) [9.15.17];
    (1990) [9.15.18]
Sorg, Marcella H., (1983) [29.17]
Sotiroff, George, (1978) [13.10]
Souden, David & Lasker, Gabriel W.,
    (1978) [9.17.7.16]
Sourvinou, Christiane, (1970) [13.11]
Speirs, Doug, (1986) [9.9.1.3]
Spencer, Margaret Eve, (1973) [20.2.4]
Spencer, Robert F., (1961) [9.55.6]
Spender, Stephen, (1981) [3.37]
Spiegelhalter, Cecil, (1940) [9.17.9.50];

(1947) [9.17.9.51]
Spiegl, Fritz, (1979) [9.22.14]
Spier, Leslie, (1928) [9.3.42]; (1930)
    [9.3.43]
Spitzer, Neil, (1988) [7.24]
Stahl, Abraham, (1992) [9.35.27]
Stanes, Robin, (1975) [9.17.9.13]
Stayt, Hugh A., (1931) [9.1.1.27]
Steckley, John, (1988) [9.3.44]
Steele, Kenneth M., & Southwick,
    Laura E., (1989) [42.1.10]
Steer, Barbara D. G., (1954)
    [9.17.9.14]
Stein, Lou, (1986) [44.20]
Steinbreder, John, (1989) [37.4]
Steiner, Mary Florence, (1953)
    [9.52.3.5]
Steinkeller, Piotr, (1982) [9.4.3.8]
Steinmueller, John E., & Sullivan,
    Kathryn, (1950) [5.24]; (1956)
    [5.1.3]
Stemshaug, Ola, (1983) [9.28.4]
Stephenson, Charles, (1974) [8.1.9]
Stern, Gladys B., (1953) [1.45]
Stern, William, (1974) [9.35.6.18]
Steuart, Bradley, (Ed.), (1990) [30.19]
Stevenson, J. C., Brown, R. J., &
    Schanfield, M. S., (1983) [29.18]
Stevenson, W. H., (1886) [9.17.6.30]
Stewart, A. I. B., (1986) [9.49.4.12]
Stewart, George R., (1952) [1.46];
    (1954) [23.20]
Stewart, Julia, (1993) [9.1.5]
Stigler, Stephen M., (1980) [47.21]
Stohlman, Martha Lou, (1971) [45.26]
Stokes, J. F. G., (1930) [9.42.3]
Stokes, Whitley, (1890) [9.31.21]
Stone, Lawrence, (1977) [9.17.27]
Stone, O. M., (1963) [9.17.28]
Strachan, L. R. M., (1935) [9.17.6.31]
Strandberg, Svante, (1989) [9.53.21];
    (1993) [9.53.22]
Strathern, Marilyn, (1982) [9.17.29]
Streshinsky, Shirley, (1967) [11.1.16]
Strid, Jan Paul, (1989) [9.53.5.18]
Stringer, Maurice, & Lavery, Collette,
    (1987) [9.31.4.4]
Stringer, Maurice, & McLaughlin-Cook,
    Neil, (1985) [9.31.4.5]
Strizower, Schifra, (1971) [9.35.28]
Strong, William Duncan, (1929)
    [9.3.45]

Stuart, Jesse, (1962) [22.25]

Sturges, Christopher M., & Haggett, Brian C., (1987) [9.17.7.17]

Sturtevant, Albert Morey, (1952) [9.48.5]; (1953) [9.48.6]; (1958) [9.48.7]

Sullivan, Robert, (1985) [45.27]; (1987) [26.3.9]

Sumser, John, (1982) [42.14]

Sundby, Bertil, (1952) [9.17.4.18]; (1972) [9.17.6.32]

Sung, Margaret M. Y., (1981) [9.12.16]

Sunners, William, (1951) [22.25A]

Super, D. E., (1985) [3.38]

Susman, M. E. Stewart, (1976) [4.3]

Süsskind, Nathan & Cohen, Gerald Leonard, (1985) [47.4.7]

Svanevik, Anne, (1990) [9.41.11]; (1991) [9.41.12]

Swan, Michael, (1953) [9.17.1.11]

Swanton, John R., (1910;1960) [9.3.46]

Swedlund, Alan C., (1971) [29.19]; (1975) [29.20]; (1980) [29.20A]

Swedlund, Alan C., & Boyce, A. J., (1983) [29.21]

Swift, Jonathan Z., & Buxton, Richard G. A., (1991) [22.26]

Syme, Ronald, (1949) [9.14.23]; (1958) [9.14.24]; (1986) [9.14.25]

Symons, W. M., (1975) [47.22]

Tabori, Paul, (1961) [22.27]

Tait, James, (1916) [9.17.4.19]

Talbert, Robert H., (1955) [9.52.3.6]

Tamony, Peter, (1985) [47.4.8]

Tashima, Charles K., (1957) [47.1.34]; (1965) [47.1.35]

Tavares-Neto, José, & Azevêdo, Eliane S., (1977) [9.7.3]; (1978) [9.7.4]

Tavris, Carol, (1983) [4.4]

Tay, J. S. H., & Yip, W. C. L., (1984) [9.40.22]

Taylor, A. B., (1966) [9.49.4]

Taylor, A. J., (1981-82) [9.57.19]

Taylor, Archer, & Mosher, Fredric J. (1951) [2.13]

Taylor, Frank C., & Climo, Percy L., (1987) [9.9.4.3]

Taylor, Isaac, (1886) [9.17.6.32A]; (1891) [9.17.6.33]

Taylor, J., (1963) [5.25]

Taylor, Vincent, (1953) [5.3.11]

Terrell, Francis; Terrell, Sandra L., & Taylor, Jerome, ([9.2.11]

Thelander, H. E., (1971) [47.1.36]

Thipa, H. M., (1983) [9.1.1.28]; (1987) [9.1.5.7]

Thode, Ernest, (1988) [9.22.15]

Thomas, Charles, (1985) [9.17.6.34]

Thomas. David, (1978) [9.57.2.10]; (1979) [9.57.2.11]; (1987) [9.57.2.12]

Thomas, Jacqueline, (1985) [10.13]

Thomas, Peter Wynn, (1987-89) [9.57.2.1

Thomas, Rosemary Hyde, (1980) [26.52]

Thompson, David W., (1962) [5.26]

Thompson, Herbert, (1932) [9.4.4.26]

Thompson, L. A., (1969) [9.14.26]; (1971) [9.14.27]

Thonus, Terese, (1991) [9.7.5]

Thors, Carl-Eric, (1971) [9.20.13]

Thrush, Paul W., (Compiler & Ed.), [47.23]

Thuresson, Bertil, (1950) [9.17.9.52]

Tibon, Gutierre, (1954) [11.2.9]

Tierney, Robert W., (1979) [9.39.9]

Till, W. G., (1979) [9.17.5.4]

Timpunza-Mvula, Enoch, (1984) [9.1.1.29]

Tod, Marcus N., (1951) [9.4.26]

Toledano, Joseph, (1986) [9.35.6.19]

Tooker, Dorothy Thomasina, (1953) [7.25]

Tooker, William Wallace, (1904) [9.3.47]

Towers, John Robert, (1935) [5.2.5]

Tozzer, Alfred M., (1907) [9.39.10]

Train, John, (1985) [45.28]

Travers, James, (1980) [9.49.5]

Treece, James M., (1968) [20.14]

Trepp, Leo, (1962) [9.35.5.2]

Trillin, Calvin, (1987) [47.24]

Trippett, Frank, (1978) [24.20]

Trujillo, Nick, (1984) [7.26]

Tscherikower, V., (1937) [9.4.27]

Tsevat, Matitiahu, (1954) [13.12]

Tsushima, Jean, (1987) [9.26.2]; (1990-91) [9.26.3]

Tuland, C. G., (1958) [5.27]

Tuleja, Tad, (1987) [47.25]; (1990)

[47.26]
Tummon, Katherine, (1986) [20.2.5]
Tura, Perez, (1956) [9.35.6.20]
Turner, Barbara Kay, (1991) [11.1.19]
Turner, Brian S., (1968) [9.31.5.16];
     (1974) [9.31.22]; (1975) [9.31.5.17]
Turner, E. A., (1956) [9.17.9.53]
Turner, Noleen S., (1992) [9.1.8.5]
Turville-Petre, J. E., (1956-57)
     [9.17.6.34A]
Tushyeh, Hanna Y., & Hamdallah,
     Rami W., (1992) [9.5.13]
Tushyeh, Hanna Y., Lawson, Edwin D.,
     & Rishmawi, George, (1989)
     [9.5.12]
Tvedt, Kevin, (1990) [9.22.16]
Tylor, E(dward Burnett (1889) [24.21];
     (1903?; 1958) [24.22]; (1903?;
     1958); [9.42.1.8]
Tynan, Kenneth, (1975) [9.17.9.54]

Umunna, Ifekandu, (1968) [9.1.4.8]
Unbegaun, B. O., (1967) [9.47.11]
Ungerer, H. J., (1988) [9.1.8.6]
Urdang, Laurence, (1985) [30.20]
US. Central Intelligence Agency, (1963)
     [9.6.5]; (1965) [9.1.4.9]; [9.18.3];
     [9.40.23]
US. Department of Commerce. Bureau
     of the Census, (1980) [9.52.3.7]
US. Social Security Administration,
     [28.22]

V., S., (1971) [47.1.37]
Valtavuo-Pfeifer, Ritva, (1983)
     [9.20.14]
Van Buren, Abigail, (1988) [18.3]
Van Doren, Barbara, (1953) [7.27]
van Gennep, Arnold, (1960) [24.22A]
van Huyssteen, P. J. J., (1988) [5.28]
van Imschoot, P., & Louis F. Hartman,
     (1963) [12.1.5]
van Son, Sol, (1990) [9.35.29]
Van Lancker, D., & Klein, K. K.,
     (1990) [33.3.3]
Van Langendonck, Willy, (1990)
     [9.40.24]
Vanek, Anthony L., & Darnell, Regna,
     (1977) [3.40]
Vannah, Thomas, (1990) [26.53]

Vasek, Antonin, (1988) [9.40.25]
Vee, Samuel, (1970) [47.1.38]
Vellender, Anne, (1989) [10.14]
Verhovek, Sam Howe, (1993) [9.3.48]
Vetter, Craig, (1985) [37.5]
Vide, Sten-Bertil, (1973) [9.53.4.3]
Viertler, Renate B., (1976) [9.51.1.8]
Villa Rojas, Alfonso, (1947) [9.39.11]
Villaume, Susan K., & Wilson, Louisa
     Cam, (1989) [10.15]
Vines, Maxwell L., (1979) [9.17.5.5]
Vlasenko-Bojcun, Anna, (1984)
     [9.56.4]
Voet, Joop, (1987) [9.35.30]
Vogt, Evon Z., (1969) [9.39.12]
Vogt, Susanne, (1991) [9.15.19]
von Feilitzen, Olof, (1965) [9.17.8.3]
Voth, Henry R., (1905) [9.3.49]

W., D., (1961) [9.49.6]
W., M. M., (1960) [9.17.30]
Wafer, Lionel, (1934; 1967) [9.3.50]
Wagaw, Teshome G., (1987-88)
     [9.35.31]
Waggoner, Walter H., (1960) [9.17.31]
Wagner, Geoffrey (Atheling), (1968)
     [1.47]
Wagner, Heinrich, (1979) [13.13]
Wahlberg, Mats, (1987) [9.53.23];
     (1990) [9.53.24]-[9.53.25]
Wainwright, F. T., (1942) [9.17.6.35]
Waitt, Robert W., (1985) [11.7]
Walker, Barbara G., (1983) [1.48]
Walker, Norman, (1951) [12.22];
     (1953) [12.23]; (1956) [12.1.6];
     (1958) [12.2.8]
Walker, R. J., (1969) [9.42.2.1.5]
Walker, Sheila, (1977) [9.2.12]
Wallace, Madeleine L., (1953)
     [9.17.1.12]
Wallman, Sandra, (1973) [9.33.1.7]
Walls, R. M., (1969) [22.28]
Walsh, Jim, (1970) [7.1.4]
Walterscheid, Ellen, (1989) [46.1.11]
Walton, Eliza Charles, (1987) [24.23]
Ward, Andrew, (1979) [11.1.20]
Warda, Mark, (1988) [20.1.4]
Ware, John N., (1956) [30.21]
Warmington, Brian H., (1991)
     [9.40.26]
Warren, B. H., (1958) [9.42.1.9]

Warren, B. H., (1958) [9.42.1.9]
Warren, Virginia Lee, (1972) [28.23]
Waterhouse, Viola, (1981) [9.39.13]
Waters, Mary C., (1989) [38.5]
Waters, Tony, (1989) [9.1.1.30]
Watson, H. W., (1889) [41.3]
Watson, H. W., & Galton, Francis, (1875) [41.2]
Watson, Harry D., (1982) [9.49.4.1.6]
Watson, James L., (1976) [9.12.17]
Watson, Rex, (1975) [9.17.9.55]
Watson, Rubie S., (1986) [9.12.18]
Watt, W. M., (1953) [9.5.14]
Weaver, P. R. C., (1964) [9.14.28];
  (1965) [9.14.29]; (1968) [9.14.30]
Weise, Lis, (1989) [9.15.20]
Weisenthal, Lee, (1956) [20.1.5]
Weiss, Kenneth M., Chakraborty,
  Renajit, Buchanan, Anne V., et al.,
  (1983) [29.22]
Weiss, Volkmar, (1980) [9.22.17]
Weissenburger, Fred D., & Loney, Jan,
  (1975) [22.29]
Werner, M. A., (1967) [24.24]
Wescott, Roger W., (1974) [9.1.2.2];
  (1975) [9.1.2.3]; (1984; 1993)
  [25.11]
West, Richard, (1977) [37.6]
West, Robert C., (1986) [9.21.7]
Westermann, Claus, (1991) [22.30]
Western, W. G., (1987) [9.17.9.15]
Westlund, Börje, (1989) [9.53.5.19]
Wettinger, Godfrey, (1968) [9.37.4];
  (1969) [9.37.5]; (1971) [9.37.1.7];
  (1973) [9.37.6]
Wheeler, Timothy J., (1987) [26.3.10]
Whitaker, Ian, (1955) [9.36.4];
  (1977) [9.36.5]
White, David, (1980) [9.17.3.18]
White, Diana, (1981) [42.15]
White, William Charles, (1966)
  [9.35.3.4]
Whitehorne, Katharine, (1978)
  [46.1.12]
Whitelock, Dorothy, (1937-1945)
  [9.17.6.36]
Whitman, William, (1937) [9.3.51]
Whyte, Donald, (1981) [9.49.4.13]
Wiktorsson, Per-Axel, (1993)
  [9.53.5.20]
Wilkinson, Beryl Marie, (1961)
  [9.14.31]

Williams, A. R., (1949) [9.57.20]
Williams, D. Elwyn, (1961) [9.57.2.14]
Williams, Franklin B. Jr., (1954)
  [32.5]
Williams, Henrik, (1991) [9.53.5.21]
Williams, Ifor, (1935) [9.57.21]
Williams, J(ames) D., (1977)
  [9.31.5.1.7]-[9.31.5.1.9]; (1978)
  [9.31.5.10]; [9.31.5.11]
Williams, Jay & Lubell, Winifred,
  (1962) [19.6]
Williams, William Morgan, (1964)
  [9.17.32]
Williamson, Jane, (1982) [46.1.13]
Williamson, Joel, (1965) [9.2.13]
Willis, Roy, (1982) [9.1.1.31]
Willoughby, W. C., (1905) [9.1.1.32]
Wilson, Brenda S., & Skipper, James
  K. Jr., (1990) [26.3.11]
Wilson, John A., (1954) [9.4.4.27]
Wilson, Monica, (1951) [9.1.1.33]
Wilson, P. A., (1976-77) [9.10.12]
Wilson, Susan R., (1981) [9.29.13]
Winchester, Ian, (1970) [8.1.10]
Winograd, Eugene, & Church, Vaughan
  E., (1988) [33.2.16]
Wipf, Karl A., (1967) [9.11.2]
Wiseman, Donald J., (1959) [9.4.28]-
  [9.4.29]
Wiseman, T. P., (1965) [9.14.32]
Wong, J. S., (1960) [9.12.19]
Wood, Florence, (1966) [10.16]
Wood, Michael J., (1985) [9.17.3.19]
Wood, Peter, (1974) [9.2.14]
Woodson, Carter G., (1925) [9.2.15]
Woolf, Henry Bosley, (1937-38)
  [9.17.6.37]
Woolf, Leonard, (1953) [9.17.1.13]
Wray, Herbert, (1982) [17.15]
Wren, Christopher S., (1984) [9.12.1.6]
Wright, R. P., & Jackson, K. H.,
  (1968) [9.17.33]
Wright, Sylvia, (1954) [15.13]
Wrigley, E. A., & Schofield, R. S.
  (1973) [8.6]
Wu, Ching-chao, (1927) [9.12.20]
Wulcko, Laurance M., (1948)
  [9.17.3.20]
Wulf, Steve, (1987) [45.31]
Wulfman, David S., (1986) [9.9.17]
Wyatt, Katherine, & Burrow, Lesley.
  (1980) [11.1.21]

Yadin, Yigael, (1973) [9.35.1.11]
Yang, Martin C., (1945) [9.12.21]
Yao, Blake, (1990) [18.4]
Yapp, Wilfred, (1974) [15.14]
Yassin, M. Aziz F., (1986) [9.5.15]
Yasuda, Norikazu, (1983) [9.34.7]
Yasuda, N(urikazu), Cavalli-Sforza,
    L(uigi)., Skolnick, M., et al., (1974)
    [41.4]
Yasuda. Norikazu & Furosho,
    Toshiyuki, (1971) [9.34.8]-[9.34.9]
Yeivin, S., (1954) [9.4.4.28]
Yetman, Norman R., (1970) [9.2.2.13]
Yeutter, Frank, (1960) [26.3.12]
Young, Andrew W., McWeeny, Kathryn
    H., et al., [33.3.4]
Young, Dariel A., (1980) [45.32]
Youtie, H. G., (1944) [13.15]
Yule, Valerie, (1979) [9.17.34]

Yutang, Lin, (1935) [9.12.22]

Zadok, Ran, (1977) [5.29]
Zawawi, Sharifa, (1993) [9.1.6.3]
Zborowski, Mark & Herzog, Elizabeth,
    (1952) [9.35.5.3]
Zei, G., Guglielmo, C. R., Siri, E.,
    Moroni, A., [9.33.9]
Zeitlin, Solomon, (1952) [9.35.1.12]
Zeldin, Arthur, (1966) [9.9.1.4]
Zgusta, Ladislav, (1961) [9.4.30];
    (1962) [9.4.31]; (1965) [9.4.32];
    (1991) [1.49]
Zonabend, Françoise, (1980) [1.50]
Zuckerman, Diana, (1985) [45.34]
Zuntz, Gunther, (1951) [9.13.22]
Zusne, Leonard, (1987) [47.27]

SUBJECT INDEX

Note: The term *name* (or *names*) is assumed to follow many of the categories such as CHANGE, ETHNIC, or UNIQUE.

The following abbreviations have been used:

anc.   ancient
is.   island
lang. language or dialect
tri.   tribe, may refer to a culture, people, or society

Major sections are in capitals and the entries in those sections have been placed first. In checking ethnic groups such as CANADIAN, check under the ethnic name as well as the type of name, i.e., CHANGE.

Aberystwyth, Wales [9.57.2.2]
aborigines, Australia [9.42.1.4],
   [9.42.1.8]
aborigines, Peru [9.43.5]
Abraham [9.35.1.1]
Abu Ghosh, Isr. [9.5.5]
abused children [18.1]
academic performance [45.34]
Acadian [9.9.5]; [9.21.4]; [9.21.7]
Acadian, Cajun [26.4]
achievement: [22.4]
   English [9.17.4]
acronyms [9.35.6.16]
Ada, tri., Afr. [9.1.1.1]
ADDRESS, FORM OF [3.1]-[3.41]
   Afghani [9.40.16]
   American Indian [9.3.3],
      [9.3.31A]
   Arabic [9.5.4], [9.5.10]
   Chinese [9.12.21]
   East African [9.1.1.11]
   Egyptian [9.5.7]

   English [9.17.32], [9.17.1.1]
      [9.17.1.13], [9.17.3.18]
   Italian [9.33.1]
   Japanese [9.34.2], [9.34.5]
   Lappish [9.36.2]
   Polish [9.45.1]
   Russian [9.47.7]
   Turkish [9.55.5]
Adonai, name for God [13.2]
AFFECTIONATE NAMES [4.1]-
   [4.4], [1.10], [3.38], [9.13.13],
   [11.13], [42.1.6]-[42.1.7]
   Hungarian [9.27.1]
   Jewish [9.35.12]
Afghani [9.40.16]
Africa, North [9.14.14]
AFRICAN:
   General [9.1.1]-[9.1.5];
   BINI, tri. [9.1.2.1]-[9.1.2.3],
      [9.1.1.7]
   cataloging [6.2]
   GHANA [9.1.3.1]-[9.1.3.3],

[9.1.1.1]
gods [13.4]; [13.14]
IGBO, tri. [9.1.4.1]-[9.1.4.9]
MISCELLANEOUS GROUPS
    [9.1.1.1]-[9.1.1.33]
REPUBLIC OF SOUTH AFRICA
    [9.1.5.1]-[9.1.5.7], [9.1.1.27]
SWAHILI, lang. [9.1.6.1]-
    [9.1.6.3]
twins [22.19]
Xhosa, lang. [9.1.5.6]
ZIMBABWE [9.1.7.1]-[9.1.7.5],
    [9.1.8.1], [9.1.8.6], [9.1.1.17]-
    [9.1.1.18]
ZULU, tri. lang. [9.1.8.1]-
    [9.1.8.6], [9.1.5.6]
AFRICAN AMERICAN [9.2.1]-
    [9.15]
CHANGE OF NAME [9.2.1.1]-
    [9.2.1.3]
SLAVE NAMES [9.2.2.1]-
    [9.2.2.13], [9.2.13]
Ahmadhiyyas, sect. India [29.10]-
    [29.11]
Ainu, people, Japan [9.34.1]
Akan, tri. Afr. [9.1.3.3]
AKKADIAN, anc. culture [9.4.1.1]
    [9.4.1.3], [9.4.20]
ASSYRIAN. See: ANCIENT
    MIDDLE EAST: ASSYRIAN
Alaska [9.3.6]
Albanian [9.40.18]
Albany, NY [8.1.9]
Alberta, Can. [9.3.24]; [9.3.38]
Algonkian [2.11]
alias:
    ENGLISH [9.17.2.1], [9.17.2.4]
    Scottish [[9.49.6]
alliteration:
    first names [11.4]
    Old English [9.17.6.32]
almanac, Danish [9.15.4]
alphabet position [22.29]
Altaic, lang. [9.8.2]
alternation [9.17.6.15]
Amandebele, tri. Afr. [9.1.7.3]
Ambivius, pers. name [9.14.25]
AMERICAN INDIAN [9.3.1]-
    [9.3.51], [9.40.2]
American Name Society [1.7]
Amharic, lang. [9.18.2]-[9.18.3]
Amish [29.9]
Amorites, anc. tri. [9.4.15]
Amoritic, lang. [9.4.17]
anagrams [35.7]
Anaitis, goddess [9.4.3.6]

Anatolia, Turk. [9.4.19]
Anatolian, lang. [9.4.23], [9.55.4]
Ancient Greek [9.4.32]
ANCIENT MIDDLE EAST [9.4.1]-
    [9.4.32], [1.48], [12.10],
    [13.6]
AKKADIAN [9.4.1.1]-[9.4.1.3]
ARAMAIC [9.4.2.1]-[9.4.2.3],
    [9.9.4], [9.35.1.10]
ASSYRIAN [9.4.3.1]-[9.4.3.8],
    [9.4.20]
Canaan [13.12]
EGYPT [9.4.4.1]-[9.4.4.28],
    [5.2.3], [9.4.25], [9.4.27],
    [9.4.2.3], [9.4.4.1], [9.4.4.28],
    [9.35.1.8]-[9.35.1.9], [13.15]
graffiti [14.1]
mythology [1.24]
HITTITE [9.4.5.1]-[9.4.5.3],
    [9.4.19], [25.4]
Samaria [5.2.4]
Ancient World [7.9]
Andersson, surn. [9.20.1]
anecdotal [22.28]
angels/devils [36.4]
Anglo-Norman [9.17.9.27]
Anglo-Saxon names [9.17.6.32A]
Anglo-Saxon Chronicle [9.17.6.19]
animal [22.26]
anonymous, reviewers [22.15]
anonyms [2.13]
anthropology [24.6], [17.4]
aphetic Name, Russian [9.47.11]
apotropaic name [9.41.8]
Aquila, translator [12.2.23]
Aquinas [12.3]
ARABIC [9.5.1]-[9.5.15], [1.32],
    [9.5.19.5.15], [9.35.8]
preIslamic [9.4.22]
ARAMAIC. See: ANCIENT
    MIDDLE EAST: ARAMAIC
Arapaho, Ind. tri. US [9.3.28]
archeology, Wales [9.57.6]
Arctic [9.36.1]
Arikara, Ind. tri. US [9.3.16]
Arizona [9.3.42]
Armenian, lang. [9.40.23]
Arnold, first name [28.8]
Arthur, legends [9.57.16]
article, definite [5.7]
Asian, Southeast, langs. [9.40.17]
Ashkenazi Jews [9.35.2], [9.35.2],
    [26.21]
Askletarion, pers. name [9.4.4.23]
Aspinall, surn. [9.17.9.44]
Assinboine, Ind. tri. [9.3.24]

ASSYRIAN [9.4.3.1]-[9.4.3.8],
  [9.4.20]
Athens, gods [13.10]
Aurispa, pers. name [9.33.4]
AUSTRALIAN *See:* OCEANIA:
  AUSTRALIAN
Austrian, housenames [9.40.14]
authors, order of [47.20]
auxiliary names [9.31.5.11]
Avestan, lang. [25.4]
avoidance, taboo [9.1.1.33]
Aymara, Chile, Boliv. tri. [9.51.1.1]

Baal, god [9.4.16]
BABY-NAMES. *See:* FIRST
  NAMES: BABY-NAMES
Babylon/ian [9.4.6], [9.4.13]-[9.4.15]
Baganda, Afr. tri. [9.1.1.20]
Bahaya, Tanzania, tri. [22.19]
BALTIC, area [9.6.1]-[9.6.5]
Bantu, lang., tri. [9.1.1.17],
  [9.1.1.18], [9.1.1.31]
baptism, Catholic [11.1.1]
baptismal names [9.56.1]
baptismal register, Method. Ire.
  [9.31.22]
Bar Kokba [9.35.1.12]
baseball [4.3], [26.3.1]-[26.3.8],
  [26.3.11]-[26.3.12]
basketball [26.3.9], [26.3.10]
Basque [9.40.19]
Bassari, West Afr. tri. [9.1.1.4]
BaVenda, South Afr. tri. [9.1.1.27]
beauty [9.22.4]
Bechuana, Afr. tri. [24.21]
Becwana, Afr. tri. [9.1.1.32]
Bedouin [9.4.22]
Belgian/Belgium [9.40.3], [33.2.14]
Bellonese, Solomon Is. tri. [9.42.2.2]
Benabarne, Sp. [9.52.2.1]
Benedictine order [3.31]
Bengal, India [9.29.5]
Beowulf [9.17.6.37]
Berber [9.40.7]
Berg, Austria [9.40.14]
BIBLE [5.1-5.29], [1.24],
  [5.15.29], [5.3.9], [9.4.21],
  [9.17.3.11], [22.28], [47.13]
  dictionary [5.22]
  figures/people [5.17], [9.29.8]
  GOD [12.1.1]-[12.1.6]
  Hebrew [9.35.10]
  Modern Israel [9.35.19]
  New Testament [5.7], [5.25]
  Old Testament [5.2.2], [5.2.3],

  [12.2.3], [27.3]
BIBLIOGRAPHIES [2.1-2.13],
  [1.29], [2.12.13]
bilateral transmission [24.2]
Bimanese, tri. Indonesia [9.40.12]
Bini, Afr. tri. [9.1.2.1]-[9.1.2.3]
BIRTH [46.1.1]-[46.1.13], [3.3],
  [3.17], [9.9.2.2]
  retention [46.2.1]
black, ethnic group [7.23], [9.13.20]
Black Bart, nickname [26.12]
Black Country, Eng. [9.17.5.4]
Bleheric, pers. name [9.57.4]
blood types [29.18]
BLUES SINGERS: NICKNAMES
  [26.1.1]-[26.1.3]
Boadicea, Brit. queen [9.17.9]
Bohemian [9.40.4]
Bolivia:
  [9.51.1.1]
  Siriono, tri. [9.51.1.6]
Boris, first name [28.8]
Bororo, tri. Brazil [9.51.1.8]
Bosotho, tri. Afr. [9.1.5.7]
bottles [47.13]
Boudicca, Brit. queen [9.17.9]
Brahman, ethnic group [9.29.4]
brain, anat. [33.3.1], [33.4.1]-[33.4.2]
BRAZILIAN [9.7.1]-[9.7.5],
  [9.51.1.2], [9.51.1.7], [13.4]
  Indian [9.51.1.4]-[9.51.1.5]
Breton, lang. [9.40.9]
Brie, Fr. [9.21.1]
Britannic, lang. [25.4]
British Armed Forces, nicknames
  [9.17.5.1], [9.17.5.2]
British Columbia [9.3.6], [9.3.12]
Buckinghamshire, Eng. [9.17.9.49]
Buddhism [12.6]
BULGARIAN [9.8.1]-[9.8.4],
  [9.55.2], [9.32.5]
Byelorusian, lang. [9.50.5]
bynames:
  British [9.17.11]
  Swedish [9.53.4.2]

Caedmon, Engl. poet [9.17.6.9]
Caesar, Roman leader [9.14.24]
Cajun [26.4]
  nicknames [26.4]
Calabria, Ital. [9.33.1.1]
calendar:
  Egy. Ptolemaic [9.4.4.26]
  Norwegian [9.41.6]
  Swedish [9.53.12]

California [9.52.3.2], [9.52.3.4]
Cambodian [9.40.17]
Cambridgeshire, Eng. [9.17.9.55]
Camden, William, Engl. author [1.12]
Cameroon, Afr. [9.1.1.25]
Canaan/Canaanite [9.4.4.28], [13.5]
Canaanite, gods [13.12]
CANADA/CANADIAN [9.9.1]-
   [9.9.17], [9.3.45], [9.56.1], [20.9]
   CHANGE OF NAME [9.9.1.1]-
      [9.9.1.4]
   Hungarian [9.27.6]
   Indians [9.3.2A], [9.3.3],
      [9.3.4]
   LAW [9.9.2.1]-[9.9.2.3], [9.9.4],
      [9.9.31]
   NAMING PATTERNS [9.9.3.1]-
      [9.9.3.3]
   NICKNAMES [9.9.4.1]-[9.9.4.3]
Cape Breton, NS [9.9.10], [9.9.11]
Cappadocia, Turk. [9.4.9], [9.4.3.6]
Carian, lang. [9.4.25], [9.4.24]
Carna, Ir. [9.31.5]
Carolinas, US states [9.2.2.5]
Carthaginian [9.40.26]
Casteldelfino, Ital. [9.33.7]
Castile, Spain [9.52.2.7]
Catalan, lang. [9.52.1]
CATALOGING [6.1]-[6.5]
   Ethiopian [9.18.1]
Catamantaloedis, pers. name [9.10.5]
Catholics, N. Ire. [9.31.4.1],
   [9.31.4.5]
Catholic law [24.24]
Catholicism [7.25]
Cavan City, Ire. [9.31.5.1]
CB (radio) [26.27], [26.50]
Celia, first name, Engl. [11.2.9]
CELTIC [9.10.1]-[9.10.12], [1.48],
   [9.17.33], [9.28.2], [9.57.1],
   [9.57.14]
CENTRAL AMERICAN [9.11.1]-
   [9.11.2]
Central & South American Indians
   [9.3.33]
Central Africa [9.1.1.3]
Chaga, tri. Tanzania [9.1.1.22]
Chalbes, Egy. myth. [9.4.4.9]
CHANGE [7.1]-[7.28], [1.39], [3.33],
   [9.8.3], [9.17.9.45], [9.22.2],
   [9.40.25], [9.49.4.9], [24.7],
   [26.39], [45.21], [46.1.3],
   [46.1.13], [46.3.2]-[46.3.3]
   AFRICAN AMERICAN [9.2.1.1]-
      [9.2.1.3]
   Albanian [9.40.18]

CANADIAN [9.9.1.1]-[9.9.1.4]
   DeFoe, author Engl. [9.17.9.1.12]
   English [9.17.16], [9.17.22]
   ENTERTAINERS [7.1.1]-[7.1.5]
   Finland/Finnish [9.20.9]-[9.20.10]
   folklore [22.21]
   German-American [9.22.1]
   Hungarian [9.27.2], [9.27.6]-
      [9.27.7]
   India [9.29.9]
   Japan [9.34.4]
   JEWISH [9.35.2.1]-[9.35.2.3],
      [7.8]
   LAW [20.1], [20.1.1]-[20.1.6],
      [20.2.2]
   marriage [46.1.7], [46.1.10]
   to wife's name [9.9.1.3]
   Muslim [9.8.4]
   Norwegian [9.41.8]
   pronunciation [30.21]
   Scottish [9.49.4.1.5]
   Slavic [9.50.3]
   South Africa [9.1.5.4]
   Swedish [9.53.1.1], [9.53.1.2],
      [9.53.1.3]
   Turkish [9.55.2]
   Ukrainian [9.56.4]
   women [46.1.1], [46.2.3], [9.27.7]
Channel Is. [9.17.12]
Chemehuevis, Ind. tri. [9.3.21]
Cheremiss, ethnic grp. Russia [24.22]
Cherokees, Ind. tri. [9.3.17]
Chesapeake Bay [9.2.2.7]
Cheshire, Eng. [9.17.4.19], [9.17.6.3
                                          5]
Chewa, tri. Malawi [9.1.1.29]
Cheyenne, Ind. tri. US [9.3.29]
Chiapas, Mex. tri. [9.11.2], [9.39.1],
   [9.39.4], [9.39.10]-[9.39.11]
Chicago [26.36]
children [10.1], [10.4], [10.6],
   [10.10], [10.14]-[10.16], [24.17]
   change of name [20.1.5]
   literature [2.5]
Chile [9.51.1], [9.51.1.1]
CHINESE [9.12.1]-[9.12.22], [1.32],
   [9.40.2], [12.6], [21.2]
   first names [9.12.1]
   Jewish [9.35.3.1]-[9.35.3.4]
   style [43.3]
   SURNAMES [9.12.1.1]-[9.12.1.6]
Chinese-American [9.12.10]-
   [9.12.11]
Chippewa, NA Ind. tri. [9.3.18]
Chontal, Mex. Ind. tri. [9.39.13]
Christian:

[12.6], [9.14.19], [11.8]
Early [9.40.13]
Cicero, Roman leader [9.14.2],
[9.14.22]
Cilicia, Turk. [9.4.10]
civil rights memorial [17.9]
Civil War [30.21]
nicknames [26.2]
Clanvowe, Engl. [9.17.9.15]
Clare County, Ire. [9.31.5.6]
CLASSICAL GREEK [9.13.1]-
[9.13.22], [1.48], [9.4.3], [9.4.26],
[9.14.1], [13.11], [25.4], [40.2]
Classical Period [39.1]
mythology [1.24]
CLASSICAL ROMAN [9.14.1]-
[9.14.32], [9.4.4.22],
[9.10.4], [9.13.20], [9.40.13]
clergymen [43.7]
Swedish [9.53.5]
CLINICAL PSYCHOLOGY
[33.1.1]-[33.1.4], [26.8], [26.33]
nicknames [26.7]
coal miners [26.47], [26.47]
coats of arms [9.40.4], [9.17.9.1],
[9.17.9.47]
Cobourg, ON [9.9.4.3]
codenames [22.10]
Cohen/Kagan, surnames [7.19]
coins, Irish [9.31.11], [9.31.12]
coins, English [9.17.6.1],
[9.17.6.1.5], [9.17.6.1.6]
coins, Old English [9.17.6.1.3],
[9.17.6.1.4]
coins, Roman [22.23]
collections of names, Finnish
[9.20.11]
Collefiore, It. [9.33.1.3]
Colombia, SA [9.51.1.3]
commercial use [22.25A
composers, pseudonyms [32.2]
COMPUTERS [8.1]-[8.6], [9.40.15],
[11.1.13], [22.20]
SOUNDEX [8.1.1]-[8.1.10]
[9.21.1], [9.35.6.1], [9.40.15],
[30.19]
Sweden [9.53.4], [9.53.10]
conductors, music [30.4]
Congress, US, names [43.5]
Connecticut [23.16]
Continental Europe [24.3], [24.4]
converts [7.25]
Islam [9.32.6]
Cook Is., Pac. [9.42.1]
Corinth, Greece [9.13.21]
Cork, Ire. [9.31.5.12]

Cornish/Cornwall [9.40.1],
[9.17.9.31], [9.17.9.1.5]
saints [36.9]
couples, nicknames [26.3]
coyote [9.3.22]
Cree, Ind. tri. Can. [9.3.3], [9.3.28]
Creeks, Ind. tri. US [9.3.17]
Creole [9.21.4], [26.52]
nicknames [26.52]
Crete, Ancient [9.40.10]
criminals [26.34]
slang [26.11]
Crow, Ind. tri. [9.3.26]
Cuba [13.4]
Cumberland, Eng [9.17.32]
Cummins, surn. [44.1.1]
Cuna, tri. Panama [9.3.50], [9.3.33]
cuneiform [9.4.28], [9.4.29]
Cuomo, Mario [30.18]
curriculum, school [9.52.3],
[9.52.4]
Cyprus [9.13.5], [9.23.9A
Cyrenica, region, Libya [9.13.5]
Czech [9.40.25]
Czechoslovakia [38.2]

Dahomey, Afr. [9.1.1.9]
Dakotas, US states [9.3.16]
Danelaw, area, Engl. [9.17.2],
[9.17.6.20]
Daniel, Book of, Bible [5.28]
DANISH [9.15.1]-[9.15.20],
[9.53.15], [9.53.18]
day-names [9.2.14], [13.4]
de, particle [9.17.9.11]
Dead Sea Scrolls [5.2]
deaf [22.17]
death [9.1.4.8]
Dedham, Essex, Engl. [9.17.3.19]
Deerfield, MA [29.19], [29.20A],
[29.21]
Defoe, Daniel [9.17.9.1.12]
delinquents [18.1]
destiny [15.3], [17.3], [45.7]
See also: INFLUENCE
developmental [10.5], [10.9],
[33.1]
devils [36.4]
Devon, Engl. [9.17.9.15]
devotional [9.7.3], [9.7.4]
diabetes [29.17]
Diana, first name [9.17.3.3]
dictionaries [9.17.9.44]
Hungarian [9.27.4]
Russian [9.47.1]

diminutives [1.10]
directories, telephone [9.19.9.4]
dissatisfaction [24.7]
Dives, pers. name, Bible [5.3]
Docnimarus, pers. name [9.10.5]
Dodge, surn. [9.17.9.1.2]
dolls' names [28.20]
Domesday Book [9.17.4.17]
Domesday, Cheshire [9.17.4.19]
Donald Duck [45.14]
Dorset, Engl. [9.17.4.15]
Dostoevsky [9.47.2]
double-names [9.10.3]
Doukhobors, sect, Can. [3.40]
Down, County, Ire. [9.31.5.4]
Dufay, Guillaume, composer [30.13]
Dunkling, Leslie [28.18]
DUTCH [9.16.1]-[9.16.3]
    Jewish [9.35.29], [9.35.30]
DuPage County, IL [28.5]

East Africa, Dorobo, tri. [9.1.1.9A]
Easter, Is. Pacific. [9.51.1]
EDUCATION [10.1]-[10.16], [1.33],
    [33.1], [44.16]
Effutu, tri. Ghana [13.14]
Egyptian [9.5.7]
    ANCIENT. See: ANCIENT
    MIDDLE EAST: EGYPT
Elam, anc. Iran [9.4.11]
elections [42.5], [42.8], [42.11]
elementary school [10.2]-[10.3],
    [10.7]
Elephantine, Egypt [9.35.22]
Elizabeth, Queen [7.28]
endearment terms [3.35]
engineering [47.2]
England, Ancient [9.17.33]
England, Jewish [9.35.13],
    [9.35.25]
ENGLISH [9.17.1]-[9.17.34], [7.11],
    [9.17.2.4], [9.40.1], [22.5]
    ADDRESS, FORMS OF
    [9.17.1.1]-[9.17.1.13]
    ALIAS NAMES [9.17.2.1]-
    [9.17.2.4]
    bibliography [2.3]
    change of name [9.22.2]
    Early English [9.17.6], [9.17.7]
    Early Modern English [9.17.6.15]
    FIRST NAMES [9.17.3.1]-
    [9.17.3.20], [9.17.4.15]
    MIDDLE ENGLISH [9.17.4.1]-
    [9.17.4.19], [9.17.6.3], [9.17.6.8],
    [9.17.6.17], [9.17.6.36],

[9.17.9.19]
    NICKNAMES [9.17.5.1]-
    [9.17.5.5], [9.17.4.4], [9.17.4.7]
    OLD ENGLISH [9.17.6.1]-
    [9.17.6.37], [9.17.9.2], [25.4]
    OLD ENGLISH: COINS
    [9.17.6.1.1]-[9.17.6.1.6]
    POPULATION STRUCTURE AND
    NAMES [9.17.7.1]-[9.17.7.17]
    saints [36.9]
    SCANDINAVIAN NAMES IN
    ENGLAND [9.17.8.1]-[9.17.8.3],
    [9.17.6.35]
    SURNAMES See: SURNAMES:
    ENGLISH
    SPECIFIC SURNAMES See:
    SURNAMES SPECIFIC
Enit, Enide [9.10.1]
ensembles, music [30.6]
entertainers [7.1.1], [7.1.2],
    [7..3], [7.14], [45.19]
ENTERTAINERS, CHANGE OF
    NAME [7.1.4]-[7.1.5]
epic poetry [13.3]
eponyms:
    [9.13.7]
    Australia [9.42.1.8]
    English [9.17.9.44A]
    Swedish [9.53.1]
Erasmus/Rasmus [9.15.13]
Eriskay Is. Scot. [9.49.3.4]
Essex, Engl. [9.17.4.16]
Estonian [9.6.3]
ETHIOPIAN [9.18.1]-[9.18.3],
    [9.4.1]
    Jews [9.35.31]
ethnic names [22.6], [28.16], [38.5]
Etruscan, lang. [9.14.3], [11.2.9]
Evans, Cleveland Kent [28.18]
ex-slaves, US [9.2.13]. See also:
    AFRICAN AMERICAN: SLAVE
    NAMES
exercises, teaching [10.2]-[10.3]
Exeter, Engl. [9.17.26]
explorers [9.1.1.2]
extinction [9.17.7.17]

Faeroe Is. [9.28.1] See also:
    FAROESE
Falkland, Is. [9.51.2]
Falkner, surn. [44.1.2]
farm names [9.53.3], [9.33.2],
    [9.41.4], [9.53.11], [9.41.5],
    [9.20.6], [9.20.12]
    Finland [9.20.6], [9.20.12]

Swedish [9.53.3], [9.53.11]
FAROESE, lang. [9.19.1]-[9.19.2]
Farsi, lang. [6.5], [9.30.2]
Faulkner, surn. [44.1.2]
feminism [43.4]
Fermanagh Cty, Ire. [9.31.5.17]
fictitious names [20.7]
Fierabrace, pers. name [11.2.6]
Fierabras, pers. name [11.2.6]
filial names [9.17.9.43]
FINNISH [9.20.1]-[9.20.14]
Fipa, tri. Tanzania [9.1.1.31]
FIRST NAMES [11.1]-[11.8], [1.16],
   [1.18], [1.21], [1.22], [1.27], [2.9],
   [3.37], [5.15], [9.2.8], [9.5.5],
   [9.12.1.6], [9.17.6.13], [9.17.9.30],
   [9.33.5], [9.39.13], [9.40.1],
   [9.57.1.1]-[9.57.1.2], [10.8],
   [11.1.11], [15.3A], [15.11],
   [22.25A], [44.10]
   address [3.30]
   androgynous See: FIRST NAMES:
      UNISEX
   African [9.1.2]
   BABY-NAMES [11.1.1]-[11.1.21],
      [9.2.1], [9.2.6], [9.47.10],
      [15.5], [42.1.9]
      Jewish [9.35.4.1], [9.35.4.4]
   Brazil [9.7.5]
   Bible [5.9]
   Canadian [9.9.13]-[9.9.15]
   Chinese [9.12.8], [9.12.21]
   Danish [9.15.5]-[9.15.7], [9.15.9],
      [9.15.11]
   ENGLISH [9.17.3.1]-[9.17.3.20],
      [1.12], [23.19]
   Finnish [9.20.5]
   IRISH [9.31.1.1]-[9.31.1.3]
   Israel [9.35.4]
   JEWISH [9.35.4.1]-[9.35.4.5],
      [9.35.12]
   Latin equivalents [9.17.3.9]
   New Zealand [9.42.2.3]
   Norwegian [9.41.1]
   popularity [28.6]
   Russian [9.47.5], [9.47.8],
      [9.47.10]
   Republic of South Africa [9.1.5.1]
   SCOTTISH [9.49.1.1]-[9.49.1.3]
   Spanish:
      [9.52.1.1]-[9.52.1.2]
      New Mexico [9.52.1.2]
   SPECIFIC [11.2.1]-[11.2.9],
      [9.53.2.3], [15.13], [28.13]
   STEREOTYPES [42.1.1]-[42.1.10]
   Swahili [9.1.6.1], [9.1.6.3]

   SWEDISH See: SWEDISH: FIRST
      NAMES [9.53.2.6]
   Ukrainian [9.56.2]
   UNISEX [11.3.1]-[11.3.2],
      [9.17.3.8], [42.1.2]-[42.1.3]
   unique [45.26]
   WELSH See: WELSH: FIRST
      NAMES
   women [42.1.1]
first cousins [9.17.7.2]
Flemish [33.2.14], [9.40.24]
floral, words [47.2.1]
Florida:
   [9.52.3.4]
   change of name [20.1.4]
folklore [17.3], [22.21], [44.17]
football [26.3.4], [38.4]
form, for cataloging [6.1]
foundling names [9.17.18]
Frassinora, It. [9.33.1.6]
freedmen, Roman [9.14.9], [9.14.28]-
   [9.14.29]
freemen, Engl. [9.17.26]
FRENCH [9.21.1]-[9.21.7],
   [8.1.1], [9.17.9.18], [47.18],
   Acadian [9.9.5]
   change of name [9.22.2]
   Jewish [9.35.9]
   Old [9.21.5]
French-Canadian [9.9.9]

GAELIC [9.31.2.1]-[9.31.2.4],
   [9.31.11], [9.49.4.8]
   Nova Scotia [9.9.10]
   Ulster [45.3]
   Welsh [9.57.4]
   See also: IRISH
Galton, Francis [41.2], [41.3]
Galway, Ire. [9.31.4]
gambling [26.9], [47.7]
Garumna, Ire. [9.31.4]
Ge, tri. South Amer. [9.51.1.2],
   [9.51.1.5], [9.51.1.7]
gematria [27.1]
GENERAL WORKS [1.1]-[1.50],
   [10.13], [44.19]-[44.21]
   juvenile [19.1]
   Spanish [9.52.3], [9.52.4]
   surnames [44.13], [44.15]-
      [44.16]
genetics [9.43.4], [29.6], [29.18],
   [41.2]-[41.3]
Geniza, Cairo [9.35.8]
geography [9.17.9.1.8]
GERMAN [9.22.1]-[9.22.17]

German-American [9.22.1], [9.22.6],
   [9.22.7]
Germanic [1.48], [9.16.1], [9.22.9],
   [9.22.12], [25.4]
GHANA [9.1.3.1]-[9.1.3.3], [9.1.1.1]
Gilles, pers. name [9.49.4.10A
Glamorgan, Wales [9.57.13],
   [9.57.2.14]
Glendi, Crete [9.23.6]
Gloucestershire [9.17.3.4]
GOD [12.1]-[12.23], [5.1.3], [5.21],
   [40.2]
   BIBLE [12.1.1]-[12.1.6]
   names of [5.24]
   YHWH [12.2.1]-[12.2.8]
GODS [13.1]-[13.15], [1.26],
   [9.4.3.8], [9.4.4.19], [9.4.4.24],
   [9.6.3], [9.35.6.2], [9.48.5]-
   [9.48.6], [17.3]
   Hattian [9.4.19]
   Norse [9.41.7]
godparents [9.23.1]
Gothic [25.4]
GRAFFITI [14.1]-[14.3], [9.13.1]
Grant, Ulysses S. [7.12]
Greece, Mycenae [9.13.14]
GREEK:
   CLASSICAL [9.13.1]-[9.13.22],
      [1.48], [9.4.3], [9.4.26], [9.14.1],
      [13.11], [25.4], [40.2]
   gods [13.7]
   inscriptions [36.6]
   MODERN [9.23.1]-[9.23.11],
      [9.4.26]-[9.4.27], [9.35.1.5]
Griqua, tri. South Afr. [9.1.1.21]
Guatamala [9.11.1]-[9.11.2]
Guernsey, Engl. [9.17.17]
Gullah [9.2.14]
Guthlac, St. [9.17.6.5]
Gwion, legend. Welsh figure [9.57.5]

Haida Ind. tri. Can. [9.3.31]
Haiti [13.4]
Halifax, Eng. [9.17.9.48]
Hampus, first name [9.53.2.3]
Hanes, slang [47.4.1]
Harvard grads [23.20]
Harvey, first name [11.2.2]
Hattians, tri. Anc. Middle East
   [9.4.19]
Hausa, lang., tri. Afr. [9.1.4.3],
   [9.1.4.9]
Havasupai Ind. tri. Ariz [9.3.20],
   [9.3.42]
HAWAIIAN [9.24.1]-[9.24.2],

   [7.11], [9.42.3]
headband [9.40.21]
health [9.35.6.17]
Hebrew [9.5.6]
Hebrew, Ancient [5.11]-[5.12]
Hebrides Is. [9.49.3.1]
Heinrich, first name [18.2]
Helen [13.3]
Helmet B [9.14.19A
Hengest, pers. name, [9.17.6.34A]
Herefordshire [9.57.2.6]
Hidatsa, Ind. tri. US [9.3.2],
   [9.3.26]
hieroglyphics [9.4.4.27]
high school [10.11]-[10.12]
Hindu [9.29.5], [9.29.7], [9.29.10]-
   [9.29.11], [12.6], [24.18]
HISPANIC [9.25.1]-[9.25.2],
   [9.52.3.7]
   first names [23.9]
   stereotypes [42.10]
   surnames [9.52.3.7], [34.1],
      [44.14]
historical
   American Name Society [1.7]
   records [8.6]
   PATTERNS [24.1]-[24.24]
   surnames [29.5], [29.20A
   Jewish [9.35.6.13]
   Swedish [9.53.6]
Hitler [7.13]
HITTITE people. Anc. Middle East
   [9.4.5.1]-[9.4.5.3], [9.4.19], [25.4]
Hodge, surn. [9.17.9.1.2]
Homer [9.13.15]
homosexual, Greece [9.13.18]
hooligan [47.3], [47.17]
Hopi, Ind. tri. [9.3.49]
hoplite general [9.13.19]
Horsa, legend. figure [9.17.6.34A]
housename [9.40.14]
Hualapai, Ind. tri. SW [9.3.20]
HUGUENOT [9.26.1]-[9.26.3]
Humberhead, Engl. [9.17.9.1.9]
HUMOR AND NAMES [15.1]-
   [15.14], [1.13], [1.33], [3.21],
   [7.2], [7.14], [9.17.9.3], [11.1.7],
   [11.3.2], [17.11], [22.27], [33.2.7],
   [35.2], [35.12], [35.15], [42.12],
   [42.1.9], [45.18], [45.24], [45.28],
   [47.1.30]
   English [9.17.3.10]
   words [47.3.1], [47.24]
HUNGARIAN [9.27.1]-[9.27.7]
Huron, Ind. tri. North Amer. [9.3.44]
Hurrian, people, Anc. Middle East

[9.4.8A]
Hutterites, sect [29.3]
hyphenated [44.2], [44.5]
hypocoristic *See:* short names

Iatmul, tri. Papua New Guinea
[9.42.3.2]
Iberian [9.40.6]
Ibo, tri. Nigeria [9.1.4.8]
ICELANDIC [9.28.1]-[9.28.4],
[9.53.17]
identity [7.26], [9.1.5.3], [9.44.1],
[9.52.2.5], [33.2]
Igbo, tri. Afr. *See: African: Igbo*
Ikhnaton, king, Anc. Egypt [13.2],
[17.1]
Illinois [28.2]-[28.4]
Imogen, first name [9.21.5]
INDEXING AND NAMES [16.1]-
[16.2], [30.19]
first names, Swedish [9.53.11]
India [6.3], [9.29.9], [24.21]
Jewish [9.35.15], [9.35.28]
India *See:* INDO-PAKISTANI SUB-
CONTINENT
Indian:
AMERICAN, NORTH (including
Canada) [9.3.1]-[9.3.51], [2.11]
Can. [2.11]
East, cataloging [6.4]
Mexican [9.39.2], [9.39.4],
[9.39.10]-[9.39.11]
South American [9.51.1.1]-
[9.51.1.8]
Indiana [44.17]
Indianapolis [9.35.11A
Indic, lang. [25.4]
Indo-European, lang. [25.4], [25.6]
Indo-Iranian, lang. [25.4]
INDO-PAKISTANI SUB-
CONTINENT [9.29.1]-[9.29.13]
Indonesia, Sanskrit [9.40.8]
Indonesian [9.40.12], [12.21]
INFLUENCE [17.1]-[17.15], [22.27],
[35.16]
initials [3.35], [22.12], [35.5]
Innin, Sumerian goddess [9.4.3.3]
inscriptions:
English [9.17.6.24]
Jordan [9.4.22]
Welsh [9.10.9]
Inuit, people, North Amer. [9.9.1]-
[9.9.2], [9.40.2]
Ioway, Ind. tri. [9.3.41]
IRANIAN [9.30.1]-[9.30.3], [6.5],

[9.4.11], [25.4]
Iraq, Jews [9.35.26]
IRISH [9.31.1]-[9.31.22], [9.9.1.2],
[9.17.12], [42.5]
FIRST NAMES [9.31.1.1]-
[9.31.1.3]
GAELIC [9.31.2.1]-[9.31.2.4],
[9.31.11], [9.49.4.8]
gods [13.13]
POPULATION STRUCTURE
[9.31.3.1]-[9.31.3.3]
STEREOTYPES [9.31.4.1]-
[9.31.4.5]
SURNAMES [9.31.5.1]-
[9.31.5.17], [9.17.7.8]
SURNAMES: SPECIFIC
[9.31.5.1.1]-[9.31.5.1.17],
[9.17.7.8]
Iroquois, Ind. tri. NA [9.3.30],
[9.3.32]
'I'sa, pers. name [9.29.8]
ISLAMIC [9.32.1]-[9.32.6], [9.5.11],
[9.30.3], [12.6]
isonymy [29.2]-[29.3], [9.34.7],
[9.43.1]-[9.43.4], [29.13], [29.16],
[29.19], [29.21]-[29.22],
Israel:
family name file [9.35.6.9],
First Temple period [9.35.7]
first names [9.35.19], [9.35.27],
[9.35.4.5] *See also:* Jewish.
ITALIAN [9.33.1]-[9.33.9]
NICKNAMES [9.33.1.1]-
[9.33.1.7]
Izzot, first name [9.17.3.2]
international [1.32]

Jack, first name [9.17.3.17]
Jakun, tri. Malaysia [24.22]
Janvier, surname, Alta. Can [9.3.38]
JAPANESE [9.34.1]-[9.34.9], [1.48],
[7.16]
style [43.3]
jazz musicians [26.48]
Jefferson, Thomas [47.4.1]
Jehovah [9.35.6.2]
Jericho, Jewish names [9.35.1.2]
Jerusalem, inscriptions [9.35.21]
Jesus [5.1.3]
JEWISH [9.35.1]-[9.35.31],
[5.15], [5.27], [7.19], [9.4.27],
[9.9.4], [9.17.9.50], [9.35.6.2],
[12.6], [13.6], [27.3], [44.1.3]
Anc. Israel [9.35.1.1]-
[9.35.1.12]

CHANGE OF NAME [9.35.2.1]-
  [9.35.2.3], [7.8]
CHINESE [9.35.3.1]-[9.35.3.4]
FIRST NAMES [9.35.4.1]-
  [9.35.4.5], 99.35.12]
Hungarian [9.27.2]
Maltese [9.37.4]-[9.37.6],
  [9.37.1.1]
Moses [5.2.1]
NAMING PATTERNS [9.35.5.1]-
  [9.35.5.3]
SURNAMES [9.35.6.1]-
  [9.35.6.20]
Jie, tri. Afr. [9.1.1.8]
Jim-Dandy , slang [47.4.2], [47.4.6]
John Hancock, slang [47.14]
John Henry, slang [47.14]
Jordan, inscriptions [9.4.22]
journalists, women, stereotypes [42.4]
journals [1.30], [1.31]
Jubbins, surn. [9.17.9.7]
Judas Iscariot [5.16]
Judeo-Spanish, lang. [9.35.23]
JUNIOR [18.1]-[18.4], [24.15],
  [33.1.1], [33.1.3]
JUVENILE LEVEL [19.1]-[19.6],
  [1.21], [1.33]

K'aifeng, China [9.35.3.1]-[9.35.3.3]
Kagan, surn. [7.19]
Kamsa, tri. Colombia [9.51.1.3]
Kashmir, India [29.10], [29.11]
Kassite period, Anc. Babylon [13.6]
Kastoria, Gr. [9.23.5]
Kelsey's nuts, slang [47.4.8]
Kent, Engl. [9.17.7.16]
Kentucky [9.22.7]
Kenya [9.1.1.9A
Kim, surn. [29.15]
King Scorpion, title/name [9.4.4.1]
King's Lynn, Engl. [9.17.4.4]
kings:
  titles [3.10]
  Engl. [9.17.6.28]
  Northumberland [9.17.6.21]
kinnui, Jewish [9.35.11], [9.35.4.2],
  [42.3]
Kintyre, Scot. [9.49.4.12]
Kirkpatrick, surn. [9.49.4.7]
Klamath, Ind. tri. Oregon [9.3.43]
Kono, tri. Afr. [9.1.1.10]
Korean:
  [1.32], [29.15]
  style [43.3]
Krikati, tri. Brasil [9.51.1.2],

[9.51.1.7]
Kutenai, Ind. tri. NA [9.3.12]
Kwakiutl, Ind. tri. BC, Can. [9.3.2A]

Labrador [9.3.45]
Lachares, pers. name [9.4.5]
Ladino (Judeo-Spanish) [9.35.23]
Lainiovuoma, Lapp ethnic group
  [9.36.4]-[9.36.5]
Lakhares, pers. name [9.13.4]
Lambas, tri. Zimbabwe [9.1.7.2]
Lancandones, ethnic group Mex.
  [9.39.10]
Lancashire, Engl. [9.17.9.44]
Lancelot, pers. name [9.17.1]
language [22.5], [22.24]
Laotian [9.40.17]
LAPPISH [9.36.1]-[9.36.5]
Laredo, TX [29.22]
Larry, first name [4.1]
Latin [9.14.15], [9.17.9.28],
  [9.17.9.30], [9.35.1.5], [25.4]
Latvian [9.6.5]
LAW [20.1]-[20.14], [7.22], [9.17.16],
  [9.41.11], [9.53.3.1]
  Australian [9.42.1.6]
    change of name [9.42.1.2]
  birth name [46.1.8]
  birth name retention [46.1.3],
    [46.1.4]
  CANADIAN [9.9.2.1]-[9.9.2.3],
    [9.9.4], [9.9.3.1]
  CHANGE OF NAME [20.1.1]-
    [20.1.6]
    women [46.2.3]
  English [9.17.3], [9.17.22],
    [9.17.28], [9.17.30]
  Finnish [9.20.4]
  Icelandic [9.28.3]
  Japanese [9.34.3], [9.34.4]
  Norwegian [9.41.12]
  Scandinavian [9.48.1]
  South Africa [9.1.5.4]
  Swedish [9.53.3.1]-[9.53.3.4]
  WOMEN [20.2.1]-[20.2.5],
    [46.2.1]-[46.2.3], [20.7], [46.1.1]
leadership style [3.1]
LEARNING [33.2.1]-[33.2.16],
  [10.5]
Lee, surn. [9.17.9.23]
legal [7.10]
Lerwill, surn. [9.17.9.1.14]
Lettermullen, Ire. [9.31.4]
letters, of alphabet [33.2.14]
Lewis, Is. Scot. [9.49.2.5]-[9.49.2.6],

[9.49.4.1], [9.49.4.10]
Libya, Ancient [9.14.27]
Lincolnshire, Engl. [9.17.4.6],
  [9.17.4.10]
Linda, first name [28.13]
linen [9.13.6]
linguistic changes, Rumania
  [9.40.5]
Lipinski, Edward [9.4.2.1]
lists [22.20]
Lithuanian [9.6.1], [9.6.2], [9.6.4]
London [9.17.4.5]
  Ancient [9.17.25]
loneliness [9.31.5.2]
longer names [22.13]
longshoremen [26.43]
Louisiana [9.21.4], [9.21.7]
Luger/Lugar/Lugger/Luggars
  [9.17.13]
Luwian, anc. group, Middle East
  [9.4.10], [9.4.31]
Lycia, country. Anc. Middle East
  [9.4.31]

Mac, suffix [9.49.4.4]
Maccabee [9.35.20]
Mackay [9.49.1.1]
Mackenzies [9.49.4.9]
MacAndrew [9.49.4.1.1]
MacLean [9.49.4.10A]
Maelog [9.57.18]
Mafia [9.33.1.5]
magic [27.1], [17.4], [17.8]
Mailoc, pers. name, Welsh [9.57.18]
Maimonides, Jewish philosopher
  [12.3]
Maine [29.17]
Malagasy [9.1.1.24]
Malawi, Afr. [9.1.1.29]
Malaysia/n [9.40.21], [24.22]
Malcolm X [1.47]
MALTESE [9.37.1]-[9.37.6]
  NICKNAMES [9.37.1.1]- [9.37.1
                          .7]
Manambu, tri. Papua New Guinea
  [9.42.3.2]
Mandan, tri. US [9.3.26]
MANX [9.38.1]-[9.38.2]
MAORI, NEW ZEALAND, tri.
  [9.42.2.1.1]-[9.42.2.1.5], [13.1],
  [24.22]
Mari texts [9.4.21], [9.4.1.3]
marriage [9.42.1]
Mary [5.1.3]
Maryland [9.2.2.7]

Massachusetts [5.23]
  change of name [20.1.3]
Massereene, Ulster [9.31.5.16]
Mathew effect [47.20]
Mattel (dolls) [28.20]
Maya/n [9.11.1]-[9.11.2], [9.39.7]-
  [9.39.8], [9.39.12]
Mayo County, Ire. [9.31.2], [9.31.3]
MaShona, tri. Zimbabwe [9.1.7.1]
McCann [9.31.5.1.6]
McClellan, General [30.21]
McGuiness [9.31.5.1.1]
McKenna [9.31.5.1.5]
McLew [9.49.4.1.3]
McMurtrie [9.49.4.1.2]
McQuigan [9.9.1.2]
McRobert [9.49.4.1.4]
meaning [5.8]
media, influence of [26.42]
Melita, first name [11.1.18]
Mell, surn. [9.17.9.1.7]-[9.17.9.1.10]
Memphis, Egypt [9.4.26]
men [7.26]
Mende, tri. Afr. [9.1.1.10]
Mennonites [29.14]
Menomini, tri. US [9.3.39]
mental illness [18.4]
Mercia, anc. Engl. [9.17.6.1]
Merlin [9.17.6.23], [9.57.7]
Metatron, Jewish relig. figure [36.3]
Methodists, Ire. [9.31.22]
methodology [9.17.4.16]
MEXICAN [9.39.1]-[9.39.13],
  [9.11.2], [9.51.1.8]
Miami Beach [9.25.1]
Michigan [28.6]
MIDDLE ENGLISH. See: ENGLISH:
  MIDDLE ENGLISH
MIDDLE NAMES [21.1]-[21.3],
  [1.21], [20.8], [24.8], [24.11],
  [24.15], [37.7]
  Danish [9.15.11]
  Sweden [9.53.2]
Midir, pers. name [9.10.10]
Midland dialect [9.17.4.5]
Middle East [9.17.6.27], [9.17.9.39],
  [9.17.9.42], [9.17.9.50]-
  [9.17.9.51]
mining [47.23]
Minor, surn. [20.1]
MISCELLANEOUS [22.1]-[22.30],
  [8.2], [47.24]
  ETHNIC GROUPS [9.40.1]-
    [9.40.26], [37.6]
Mississippi [26.31]
Moabite, anc. Middle East lang.

[9.4.4]
mobility, Engl. [9.17.5], [9.17.13]-
    [9.17.15]
modification, French-Canadian [9.9.9]
moneyers [9.17.6.1.2], [9.17.6.1.4]-
    [9.17.6.1.5]
Mongolian [9.12.14], [9.40.11]
monickers [26.9], [26.34]
Montagnais-Naskapi, Ind. tri. Can.
    [9.3.4]
Montana [9.3.24]
Mormon [23.11]
Moroccan [9.32.1]
    Jewish [9.35.6.19]
Moses [5.14], [12.2.5], [5.20]
Motaverese, It. [9.33.1.1]
mother, importance of, Anc.
    Egypt [9.4.4.2]
movement/stability [9.17.9.16]
Ms. [20.2.1]
Mt. Sinai, graffiti [14.1]
mummy labels [9.4.4.14]
Murphy [9.31.5.1.7], [44.1.1]
Museum of the Diaspora [9.35.17]
music, Maltese [9.37.2]
musicians [7.5], [15.9], [9.22.14],
    [30.4]-[30.6]
    Dufay [30.13]
Muslim [9.1.4.6], [9.2.9], [9.8.4],
    [9.29.7], [9.32.1], [24.18] See
also: ARABIC; ISLAMIC
    Bengal [9.29.5]
    Pakistan [9.29.12]
Mweenish, Ire. [9.31.5]
Mycenae, Gr. [9.13.14]
Mysore, India [9.29.4]
mythology [9.4.12]
myths [13.3]

Nabal, Bible figure [5.1]
Nabataean, anc. Arab people [9.4.18],
    [9.9.4]
name writing [10.9]
name confusion [22.1]
name-calling [26.26]
NAMES: GENERAL WORKS [1.1]-
    [1.50]
names & arms clauses [9.17.28],
    [9.17.30]
NAMING PROCESS: HISTORICAL
    PATTERNS [23.1]-[23.20],
    [44.18]
    English [9.17.15], [9.17.9.22]
    New Mexico [44.4]
    Roman [9.14.24]

NAMING PROCESS: PATTERNS
    AND PRACTICES [24.1]-[24.24],
    [9.1.1.30], [9.2.6], [9.3.1]-[9.3.2],
    [9.3.16], [9.3.18], [9.3.45],
    [9.9.3.3], [9.15.3], [9.31.1],
    [11.1.1], [11.1.6], [15.6], [19.4]-
    [19.5], [22.13], [22.18], [22.28],
    [26.26], [28.19], [46.1]
    Africa [9.1.3]
    Arabic [9.5.10]
    Berber [9.40.7]
    Canadian [9.9.3.1]-[9.9.3.3]
    English [9.17.27], [9.17.29],
        [9.17.32], [9.17.6.8], [9.17.6.22],
        [9.17.9.1], [9.17.9.19]
    Greek [9.23.1], [9.23.3],
        [9.23.7], [9.23.9]
    India [9.29.4]
    Inuit [9.9.2]
    Iroquois, Amer. Ind. [9.3.30]
    Irish [9.31.2.2]-[9.31.2.3]
    Islamic [9.32.1]
    JEWISH [9.35.5.1]-[9.35.5.3]
    Maori [9.42.2.1.2]
    Japanese [9.34.3]
    New Testament [5.4]
    Nova Scotia [9.9.7]
    Scottish [9.49.1]
    St. Lucia [9.58.1]
    Swedish [9.53.2.2], [9.53.3.4],
        [9.53.6.2]
    Swiss [9.54.5]
naming ceremonies [24.6]
NAMING PROCESS:
    THEORETICAL AND
    LINGUISTIC [25.1]-[25.11],
        [9.40.9], [23.5], [26.30], [38.1]
naming, religious aspects [25.10]
naming, magico-religious, African
    [9.1.1.25]
Naskapi, Ind. tri. Labrador [9.3.45]
Navaho. Ind. tri. US [9.3.8],
    [9.3.11], [9.3.22], [9.3.31A]
Naval Academy [26.29]
Navy [26.32], [26.32]
Neo-Assyrian [9.4.3.1]
New England [23.7], [29.16]
New Mexico [9.52.1.2], [29.4],
    [34.5], [44.4],
New York City [7.22], [28.17]
New York, Colony [29.12]
New York State [9.52.3.4]
NEW ZEALAND [9.42.2.1]-[9.42.3],
    [24.22]
    MAORI [9.42.2.1.1]-[9.42.2.1.5],
        [13.1], [24.22]

NICKNAMES [26.1]-[26.53], [1.13],
    [1.21], [2.5], [2.8], [2.10], [3.35],
    [9.1.1.29], [9.3.51], [9.4.4.15],
    [9.5.10], [9.12.5]-[9.12.1.6],
    [9.17.9.7], [9.17.9.46]-[9.17.9.47],
    [9.35.1.11], [9.39.12], [9.42.1],
    [9.49.2.3], [9.49.2.7], [9.52.2.3]-
    [9.52.2.4], [11.7], [20.4], [20.13],
    [38.4], [44.1]
  Afghani [9.40.16]
  African [9.1.1.1], [9.1.2.3]
  Arabic [9.5.13], [9.5.15]
  Australian [9.42.1.1]
  Baganda [9.1.1.20]
  BLUES SINGERS [26.1.1]-
    [26.1.3]
  CANADIAN [9.9.4.1]-[9.9.4.3]
  Chinese [9.12.13]
  English [9.17.5.1]-[9.17.5.5],
    [9.17.4.4], [9.17.4.7]
  Falkland Is. [9.51.2]
  family [9.35.1.2]
  French [9.21.2], [9.21.3]
  Ghana [9.1.3.1]
  Greek [9.23.3], [9.23.8],
    [9.23.10]
  Indian, Central America
    [9.3.33]
  Irish [9.31.15], [9.31.5.11]
  Italian [9.33.1.1], [9.33.1.5]-
    [9.33.1.7]
  Jewish [9.35.8], [9.35.11A
  Kamsa, tri. Colombia [9.51.1.3]
  Lappish [9.36.1], [9.36.3]
  Maltese [9.37.1.1]-[9.37.1.7]
  Mexican [9.39.2]-[9.39.3], [9.39.9]
  Old Norse [9.41.2]
  Philippine [9.44.1], [9.44.2]
  Portuguese [9.46.1], [9.46.2]
  PRESIDENTS [26.2.1]-[26.2.3]
  SCOTTISH [9.49.2.1]-[9.49.2.7]
  SPANISH [9.52.2.1]-[9.52.2.9]
  Specific [9.17.5.5]
  SPORTS [26.3.1]-[26.3.12],
    [38.4], [45.27], [45.31]
  SWEDISH [9.53.4.1]-[9.53.4.3]
  Ukrainian [9.56.3]
  Welsh [9.57.2.14]
Nigel of Canterbury [9.17.9.1.11]
Nigerian:
  [1.32], [9.1.2.2]
  Bini, tri. [9.1.2.1]
Ninian, pers. name [9.10.7]
Niniane, pers. name [9.17.6.23],
  [9.57.7]
nobility, Swedish [9.53.9]

nomenclature [9.15.14]
nomina sacra [40.2]
Nonconformism [9.17.3.1]
Norfolk Is. Oceania [9.42.2]
Norfolk, Engl. [9.17.9.35]
Norman names, Ire. [9.31.5.7]
norms [22.5]
Norse:
  influence [9.38.2]
  mythology [1.24], [9.41.7]
  Norse, Old [9.41.2], [9.57.8]
North Africa [9.14.26]-[9.14.27]
North Dakota [9.2.2]
Northern Ireland [9.31.4.1]-
  [9.31.4.5]
Northern Sotho, lang. S. Afr. [9.1.5.2]
Northumberland, Engl. [9.17.7.15]
NORWEGIAN [9.41.1]-[9.41.12],
  [9.53.13], [9.53.17]
Nova Scotia [9.9.5], [9.9.11],
  [9.9.16], [9.9.4.1]-[9.9.4.2],
Nso, tri. Cameroon [9.1.1.25]
Nuer, tri. Sudan [9.1.1.5]
number as name [45.33]
NUMEROLOGY [27.1]-[27.3]
numbers [22.25]
numismatics [22.23]
Nuzi, Old Akkadian, lang. [9.4.20]
Nyakyusa, tri. Tanzania [9.1.1.33]
Nzema, tri. Ghana [9.1.3.2]

O'Brien [9.31.5.1.8]
O'Flaherty [9.31.5.1.2]
O'Kelly [9.31.5.1.3], [9.31.5.1.9]
O'Neill [9.31.5.1.4], [9.31.5.1.10]
O'Sullivan [9.31.5.1.11]
occupational [9.17.9.33]
occupations [44.12]
OCEANIA [9.42.1]-[9.42.3]
  AUSTRALIAN [9.42.1.1]-
    [9.42.1.9]
  NEW ZEALAND [9.42.2.1]-
    [9.42.2.3], [24.22]
  NEW ZEALAND: MAORI
    [9.42.2.1.1]-[9.42.2.1.5], [13.1],
    [24.22]
  PAPUA NEW GUINEA [9.42.3.1]-
    [9.42.3.4]
Ogam, early Irish alphabet [9.49.3]
Ohio [9.57.2]
  change of name [20.1.2]
Ojibwa, Ind. tri. N. Amer. [9.3.35]-
  [9.3.36]
Okinawa [9.34.6]
OLD ENGLISH [9.17.6.1]-

[9.17.6.37], [9.17.9.2], [25.4] *See also:* ENGLISH: OLD ENGLISH: COINS
Old Norse [9.31.21], [9.48.6]-[9.48.7], [9.57.13]
Old Persian, lang. [25.4]
Old Testament [12.2]
older people [33.2.10]
Oldswinford, Engl. [9.17.3.5]
Omaha, Ind. tri. [9.3.2], [9.3.10]
Ontario [9.9.13]
Oraibi, Ind. tri. [9.3.49]
Origen, Christian theologian [5.12]
Orkney, Is. Scot. [9.49.4], [9.49.3.3], [9.49.4.2]
Os, prefix [9.17.6.2], [9.17.6.6], [9.17.6.16], [9.17.6.30], [9.17.6.32A]
Oscar, first name [11.2.4]-[11.2.5]
Ossian. legend. Gaelic hero [9.15.6]
ossuaries [9.35.21]
Otmoor, Engl. [9.17.7.5]
Oto, Ind. tri. US [9.3.51]
Owein, Welsh pers. name [9.57.14]
ox-names [9.1.1.5], [9.1.1.8], [9.40.16]
Oxfordshire, Engl. [9.17.9.36]
Oxyrhynchus papyri [9.35.1.8]-[9.35.1.9]
Ozark Mts. [45.26]

Packers, surn. [44.1.4]
pagan deities [36.5]
Palestine [9.4.2], [9.4.27]
    inscriptions [36.6]
Palestinian [9.5.12]
palindromes [9.9.3], [35.20]
Palmyrene, anc. inscriptions [9.4.4]
Panama [9.3.33], [9.3.50]
papponymy [9.35.1.6]
PAPUA NEW GUINEA *See:* OCEANIA: PAPUA NEW GUINEA
papyri [9.4.3]
Parliament [9.17.34]
particle [9.17.9.11], [40.3]
patients, address, form of [3.36]
Patraic, Celtic pers. name [9.10.10]
patriarchs, biblical [5.10]
patronymics [9.40.6]
PATTERNS *See:* NAMING PROCESS: PATTERNS AND PRACTICES
Pefko, Gr. [9.23.6]
Pellaport, Fr. [9.21.3]
Penarth, Wales [9.57.2.2]

Pennsylvania [23.2], [26.20], [29.9]
PERCEPTION [33.3.1]-[33.3.4], [42.6]
Perpignan, Fr. [9.35.9]
Persian [6.5]
Persian, Old [9.4.7], [9.13.10
PERUVIAN [9.43.3]-[9.43.5]
Pharoahs [9.4.4.13]
PHILIPPINE [9.44.1]-[9.44.2]
Philo, philosopher [5.11], [9.35.1]
philosophical aspects [5.11], [12.5], [25.1]
Phoenician [9.9.4]
phonemes [24.12]
PHYSIOLOGICAL PSYCHOLOGY [33.4.1]-[33.4.2], [33.3.1]
Pictish, lang. [9.49.3]
placenames:
    English [9.17.9.8], [9.17.10], [9.17.6.18], [9.17.6.20]
    Swedish [9.53.22]
Pogols. Nfld. [9.9.8]
police [26.42]
POLISH [9.45.1]-[9.45.3], [9.56.1], [30.12]
politics/politicians [9.17.34], [22.6], [26.39]
popes [36.7]
POPULAR [28.1]-[28.23], [9.9.15], [9.31.1.3], [9.31.5.4], [9.52.3.4], [11.1.15], [11.3.1], [21.3], [24.12], [45.34]
    Canadian [9.9.6], [9.9.13]
    English [9.17.21], [9.17.3.5]-[9.17.3.6], [9.17.7.8], [9.17.9.1]
    Jewish [9.35.24]
    Scottish [9.49.5], [9.49.3.1]
    surnames [23.6]
    stereotypes [42.1.8]
    Welsh [9.57.2]
popularity [9.17.9.9], [9.31.5.2], [42.2]
    Hungarian [9.27.3]
POPULATION STRUCTURE [29.1]-[29.22], [9.34.7], [9.42.1.5], [9.43.1]-[9.43.4],
    Brazilian [9.7.1]-[9.7.2]
    Canadian [9.9.8]
    ENGLISH [9.17.7.1]-[9.17.7.17]
    Germany [9.22.17]
    Griqua, tri. South Afr. [9.1.1.21]
    Hispanic [9.25.2]
    India [9.29.2], [9.29.13]
    Irish [9.31.3.1]-[9.31.3.3]
    Italy [9.33.7], [9.33.9]
    Japanese [9.34.8]-[9.34.9]

Jewish [9.35.6.15], [9.35.6.17]
Mexico [9.39.5]-[9.39.7]
Peruvian [9.39.5]
SCOTTISH [9.49.3.1]-[9.49.3.4]
Singaporan [9.40.22]
Swiss [9.54.1]-[9.54.4], [9.54.6]
Taiwan [9.12.4]
Venezuelan [9.51.3]
Wales [9.17.7.1]-[9.17.7.2],
   [9.17.7.4], [9.17.7.7], [9.57.3]
West Indian [9.58.2]
PORTUGUESE [9.46.1]-[9.46.2],
   [9.7.3]-[9.7.4], [9.35.14]
   change of name [9.22.2]
Pound, Ezra [17.13]
Powell, Colin [30.15]
Powell, surn. [30.17]
Powhatan, Ind. pers. name [9.3.47]
praenomen [9.14.21]
praise names [9.1.1.6]
prejudice [42.10]
   Can. [9.9.4]
Prentice, G. D. [15.8]
preparatory school [26.46]
preppy [26.5]
Presidents [21.1], [28.10], [35.7],
   [35.13]-[35.14], [35.16], [44.18]
   NICKNAMES [26.2.1]-26.2.3]
Prince Edward Is. Can. [9.9.1.2]
Princeton [23.20]
Probus, pers. name [9.14.7]
professors [26.35]
prohibitions [17.4]
PRONUNCIATION AND NAMES
   [30.1]-[30.21], [1.5], [3.39],
   [9.2.4], [9.17.9.20], [9.35.19],
   [17.4], [20.5]
   Bulgarian [9.8.1]
   Chinese [9.12.22]
   English [9.17.31]
   Middle English [9.17.4.10],
      [9.17.4.12]
   prophets [5.6]
   Protestant North Ire. [9.31.4.1]-
      [9.31.4.5]
PROVERBS AND NAMES [31.1]-
   [31.2], [9.1.1.6], [9.1.4.4],
   [9.1.5.6]
Prunella, first name [11.1.18]
PSEUDONYMS [32.1]-[32.5], [2.13],
   [9.1.1.2],
   Australian [9.42.1.6]
   Russian [9.47.9]
   Swedish-American [9.53.14]
PSYCHOLOGY [33.1]-[33.3], [42.7],
   [42.10]

self-esteem [9.2.11]
CLINICAL PSYCHOLOGY
   [33.1.1]-[33.1.4], [26.8], [26.33]
   identity [9.1.5.3], [9.44.1]
   LEARNING [33.2.1]-[33.2.16],
      [10.5]
   PERCEPTION [33.3.1]-[33.3.4],
      [42.6]
   PHYSIOLOGICAL PSYCHOLOGY
      [33.4.1]-[33.4.2]
psychosomatics [26.8]
PUBLIC HEALTH [34.1]-[34.5],
   [3.36], [29.17]
   Welsh [9.57.2.1]
Puerto Rico [7.7]
Punic, lang. [9.14.14]
Punjab [6.3]
Puritan/Puritanism [9.17.3.1],
   [23.19], [24.19]

Quebec [8.1.1], [9.9.13], [9.9.14]

Raetic, lang. [9.14.19A
Reading, Engl. [9.17.7.9]
Reagan, Ronald W. [35.14]
real McCoy, slang [47.4.8]
RECREATIONAL ASPECTS [35.1]-
   [35.21], [15.1],   [22.11]
Redpath, surn. [9.17.9.1.4]
reference name [9.31.16]
regional names, Denmark [9.15.17]
RELIGIOUS FIGURES [36.1]-[36.9],
   [9.32.2]
restrictions [9.33.3]
retrieval [9.50.4]
Retter. surn. [9.17.9.13]
Reuben, pers. name [9.35.1.1]
reversible names [22.25A]
Rhode Island, Jewish [9.35.16]
Rhodesia [9.1.1.18], [9.1.7.2]
Rickling, Essex, Engl. [9.17.3.15]
Ridehalgh, surn. [9.17.9.44]
Rileyed, slang [47.4.8]
Roman [1.48]
   divinities [13.10]
   Empire [9.4.4.17], [9.14.4]-
      [9.14.6], [9.14.30]
   England [9.17.6.34]
   Jewish [9.35.1.5]
Rory, first name [11.1.18]
Rose, first name [11.2.8]
roses [47.16]
Rumanian [9.40.5]
Rundi, tri. Afr. [9.1.1.23]

rune/runic [9.15.15]-
    [9.15.16], [9.17.6.10], [9.22.12],
    Norwegian [9.41.3],
    [9.41.10], [9.48.4]
    SWEDISH [9.53.5.1]-[9.53.5.21]
Russia [24.22]
    Jewish [9.35.5], [9.35.6]
RUSSIAN [9.47.1]-[9.47.10],
    [9.50.4]-[9.50.5]
    Doukhobor, sect [3.40]
Rwanda, Afr. [9.1.1.12]

Saami, Nor. [9.36.1]
Saas Valley, Switz. [9.54.4]
sacred name, Papua New Guinea
    [9.42.3.4]
saints [9.33.6], [13.4], [36.1]-
    [9.10.3], [36.5], [36.8]-[36.9]
    Irish [9.31.6]
    Welsh [9.57.17]
St. Barthelemy, West Indies [9.58.2]
St. Cadog, Welsh saint [9.10.3]
St. David, Welsh saint [9.10.3]
St. Felix, village, It. [9.33.2]
St. Helena, place & saint [9.53.13]
St. Lucia, West Indies [9.58.1]
St. Mechyll, Welsh saint [9.57.15]
St. Ninian, saint [9.10.12]
St. Ninian's Is. Scot. [9.10.8]
Samaria, West Bank [5.2.4]
SAME NAME [37.1]-[37.7], [44.13]
San José, Peru [9.43.1]-[9.43.2]
Sanskrit [9.40.8]
Sarakatsani, tri. Gr. [9.23.3]
sarcasm [3.21]
Sardinia, It. [9.33.9]
Satigenus, pers. name [9.10.5]
satire [15.7]
Sauk, Ind. tri. US [9.30.40]
SCANDINAVIAN [9.48.1]-[9.48.7],
    [9.17.10], [9.17.6.19]
    England [9.17.8.1]-[9.17.8.3],
    [9.17.6.35]
Schickelgruber [7.13]
Scotland, St. Ninian's, inscription
    [9.10.8]
SCOTTISH [9.49.1]-[9.49.6],
    [9.9.10], [9.17.12]
    FIRST NAMES [9.49.1.1]-
    [9.49.1.3]
    NICKNAMES [9.49.2.1]-
    [9.49.2.7]
    Nova Scotia [9.9.7]
    POPULATION STRUCTURE
    [9.49.3.1]-[9.49.3.4]
    Scottish, Irish [9.31.5.15]
Searle, W. G. [9.17.6.31]
self-esteem [9.2.11]
semantic differential [42.1.5]-
    [42.1.6], [42.1.10]
Semitic [9.35.1.5], [9.4.23]
Sephardic Jews [9.35.2], [9.35.3]
Serente, tri. Brazil [9.51.1.5]
serfs [9.17.24]
service areas [47.24]
Sesotho, tri. South Afr. [9.1.1.28]
several names [22.9]
sex [22.8]
sex differences [11.3.1]
sexism [33.2.7], [42.7]
Shaddai, name of God [12.18]
Shawnee, Ind. tri. US [9.3.13]
Sherbro, tri. Sierra Leone [9.1.1.16]
Shetland Is. Scot. [9.49.1], [9.49.3A],
    [9.49.4.11]
Shime'on, pers. name [9.35.1.1]
Shona, tri. Afr. [9.1.7.4]
short names [3.35], [3.38], [4.2],
    [9.39.13], [11.3], [42.1.6]-[42.1.7]
Shoshonean, Ind. tri. US [9.3.25],
    [9.3.27]
Shufflebottom, hypothesis [28.1]
Sicily [9.33.1.2]
Sierra Leone, Afr. [9.1.1.10],
    [9.1.1.16], [9.1.1.19]
Sikh [9.29.7], [24.18], [6.3]
Sikhism [12.6]
Singaporan [9.40.22]
single-letter Names [44.6], [44.8]
Sioux, Ind. tri. US [9.3.9]
slave:
    Antiquity [9.13.20]
    China [9.12.17]
    Greece [9.13.16]-[9.13.17]
    Roman [9.14.9], [9.14.28]-
    [9.14.29]
    US See: AFRICAN AMERICAN:
    SLAVE NAMES
Slavic [9.6.1], [9.6.2], [13.10]
Slorance, surn. [9.49.4.1.5]
smart Aleck, slang [47.4.3]
social behavior [22.4]
social class [38.3]
    English [9.17.20]
social Psychology [1.29]
SOCIOLOGICAL ASPECTS [38.1]-
    [38.5], [3.36]
sociolinguistics [38.2]
soldiers' names [9.20.8], [9.53.24]-
    [9.53.25]
    Sweden [9.53.8]

Solomon Is. Oceania [9.42.2.2]
Somalia, Afr. [9.1.1.14]
SOUND [39.1]-[39.3], [9.1.1.19],
    [9.55.6], [20.5], [24.12], [42.13]
SOUNDEX [8.1.1]-[8.1.10], [9.21.1],
    [9.35.6.1], [9.40.15], [30.19]
South, region, US [23.4], [45.16]
SOUTH AFRICA See: AFRICAN
    REPUBLIC OF SOUTH AFRICA
South Carolina [9.2.2.6], [9.2.14]
SOUTH AMERICAN [9.51.1]-
    [9.51.3]
    INDIANS [9.51.1.1]-[9.51.1.8]
Soviet Union, Jewish [9.35.4.3]
SPANISH [9.52.1]-[9.52.4], [7.7],
    [9.39.12], [9.52.2.9], [21.2],
    [29.22], [44.4]
    FIRST NAMES [9.52.1.1]-
        [9.52.1.2]
    NICKNAMES [9.52.2.1]-
        [9.52.2.9]
    SURNAMES [9.52.3.1]-[9.52.3.7],
        [9.52.2.2], [34.3]-[34.4], [44.14]
Spanish: Surnamed [34.2]
special collection [9.17.9.25]
SPELLING [40.1]-[40.3], [9.17.3.8],
    [9.47.4], [9.49.4.12]
    Chinese [9.12.22]
    English [9.17.4.8], [9.17.7.16]
    Huguenot [9.26.3]
    Scottish [9.49.4.8]
spirit names [9.1.1.17]
sports [26.3.1]-[26.3.12],
    [38.4],[45.27], [45.31]
stability [9.17.9.1.8]
Stanley, first name [42.1.2]
STATISTICS [41.1]-[41.4]
STEREOTYPES [42.1]-[42.15], [3.8],
    [17.10], [20.9], [35.5], [39.3]
    Canadian [9.9.4]
    English [9.17.4]
    FIRST NAMES [42.1.1]-[42.1.10]
    Flemish [9.40.3]
    German [9.22.3]-[9.22.4]
    Hungarian [9.27.5]
    IRISH [9.31.4.1]-
        [9.31.4.5]
    Walloon [9.40.3]
    women [46.4], [46.5]
STYLE [43.1]-[43.7], [3.37], [6.1],
    [9.12.11]
suffixes, French [9.21.6]
Sumerian, people, Asia Minor
    [9.4.1.2], [9.31.2.1]
Sun Yat-sen, Chinese leader [9.12.15]
supernatural [36.4]

SURNAMES [44.1]-[44.21], [1.15],
    [1.17], [1.27]-[1.28], [1.41], [2.9],
    [8.5], [9.12.1.6], [9.17.6.13],
    [9.17.9.24], [9.31.5.4], [10.8],
    [15.8], [16.2], [20.11], [24.11],
    [28.7], [30.17],
    Arabic [9.5.13], [9.5.15]
    Bohemian [9.40.4]
    Brazilian [9.7.1]-[9.7.4]
    Canadian [20.2.5]
        specific [9.9.17]
    CHINESE [9.12.1.1]-[9.12.1.6],
        [9.12.10]-[9.10.11]
    choice of [20.2.3]-[20.2.4]
    colors [44.11]
    Danish [9.15.11], [9.15.12]
    decline [41.2], [41.3]
    devotional [9.7.3]
    Dutch [9.16.2]
    ENGLISH [9.17.9.1]-[9.17.9.56],
        [1.12], [7.28], [9.17.31],
        [9.17.2.1], [9.17.4.7]-[9.17.4.8],
        [9.17.4.14], [9.17.4.18],
        [9.17.7.1], [9.17.7.12],
        [9.17.7.17], [9.48.3], [40.1],
        [41.1], [44.16]
        SPECIFIC [9.17.9.1.1]-
            [9.17.1.15], [9.17.9.14]
        evolution [9.17.9.31]
        occupational [9.17.9.33]
    farm [9.41.5]
    feminine form [46.4]
    German [9.22.11], [9.22.14],
        [9.22.17], [23.2],
    German-American [9.22.5]
    Greek [9.23.11]
    history [9.17.9.29]
    hyphenated [44.2], [44.5]
    Irish [9.31.5.1]-[9.31.5.17],
        [9.17.7.8]
    Israeli [9.35.6.11]
    Italian [9.33.8]
    JEWISH [9.35.6.1]-[9.35.6.31]
    Lithuanian [9.6.1]-[9.6.2]
    locative [9.17.9.26], [44.9]
    Maltese [9.37.1], [9.37.1.1]
    Mexican [9.39.6]
    New England [23.7]
    New Zealand [9.42.2.1]
    Norwegian [9.41.5]
    Nova Scotia [9.9.16]
    occupation [17.15]
        English [9.17.9.52]
    Old English [9.17.6.26]
    Old Norse [9.41.2]
    Polish [9.45.3]

popular [23.6]
Japanese [9.34.9]
repetition [9.49.3.2]
Republic South Afr. [9.1.5.1]
Russian [9.47.3], [9.47.11]
Scottish [9.17.7.8], [9.49.4.6],
  [9.49.4.10A]-[9.49.4.13]
skin color [9.7.2]
Slavic [9.50.1], [9.50.2],
  [9.45.2]
social class [38.3]
SPANISH [9.52.3.1]-[9.52.3.7],
  [9.52.2.2], [29.7], [34.3]-
  [34.5]
SPECIFIC SURNAMES [44.1.1]-
  [44.1.4], [9.9.1.2], [9.17.9.20],
  [9.17.9.23]-[9.17.9.24],
  [9.17.9.1.2], [9.17.9.1.4],
  [9.17.9.1.7], [9.22.10], [9.49.4.7],
  [9.49.4.1.2], [9.49.4.1.4]
  IRISH [9.31.5.1.1]-[9.31.5.1.11]
  Turkish [9.55.6]
  Ukrainian [9.56.3]
  Welsh [9.57.2.3], [9.57.2.5],
    [9.57.2.6], [5.27.2.7], [9.57.2.8],
    [9.57.2.9], [9.57.2.9A]
  WOMEN [46.3.1]-[46.3.3]
Sussex, Engl. [9.17.9.37]
Sutherland, Scot. [9.49.1.2]
Swahili See: AFRICAN: SWAHILI
Swankie, surn. [9.49.4.1.6]
Swansea, Wales [9.57.2.1]
SWEDISH [9.53.1]-[9.53.25],
  [9.20.7]-[9.20.8], [9.36.2]-
  [9.36.3], [9.20.14]
  CHANGE OF NAME [9.53.1.1]-
    [9.53.1.3]
  FIRST NAMES [9.53.2.1]-
    [9.53.2.6]
  LAW [9.53.3.1]-[9.53.3.4]
  NICKNAMES [9.53.4.1]-
    [9.53.4.3]
  RUNIC NAMES [9.53.5.1]-
    [9.53.5.21]
  SURNAMES [9.53.6.1]-[9.53.6.3]
  THEORETICAL ASPECTS
    [9.53.7.1]-[9.53.7.3], [9.53.19],
    [9.57.7.3]
Swedish-American [9.53.1.1],
  [9.53.11]
Swedish, Finland [9.20.3],
  [9.20.12]
SWISS [9.54.1]-[9.54.7]
Sydney, Australia [9.35.26]
Sylvia, first name [15.13]
Syria, Ancient [9.13.22]

taboo [9.1.1.30]
Tahiti [9.42.3]
Taiwan [9.12.1.2]
Tallensi, tri. Afr. [9.1.1.7]
Tamil, tri. S. India [9.29.3]
Tanzania [9.1.1.22], [9.1.1.26],
  [9.1.1.30], [9.1.1.31]
tartans [9.49.4.5]
teachers [26.46]
teaching [10.1], [10.4], [10.6],
  [10.10], [10.13], [10.14], [10.16]
technonyms [9.40.12]
Tecumseh [9.3.13]
teknonymy [9.1.1.9], [24.21]
telephone directories [9.49.2.1],
  [44.1.1]
Telugu, tri. India [9.29.1]
Temne, lang. Afr. [9.1.1.19]
testimonials [22.14]
Texas [9.52.3.4], [26.13]
Thai [1.32], [9.40.15]
theophoric [5.15], [9.4.4.12],
  [9.35.10], [9.35.22], [9.35.1.4],
  [9.1.1.23]
theoretical [9.53.18]
  Swedish [9.53.16], 9.53.7.1]-
    [9.53.7.2], [9.53.19], [9.57.7.3]
  See also: NAMING PROCESS:
  THEORETICAL AND
  LINGUISTIC ASPECTS.
Thessaly, Greece [9.13.12]
throne names [22.30]
Tibetan [9.40.20]
Tigre-Tigrinya, tri. Ethiopia [9.18.2]
tinkers [9.49.2.2]
Titisienus/Tisienus, pers. name, Roman
  [9.14.32]
titles [3.7], [3.10], [3.18], [3.33],
  [3.35], [9.14.24], [9.55.5]
  Scottish [9.49.2]
Tiwi, tri. Austral. [9.42.1.4]
Tlingit, Ind. tri. North Amer. [9.3.6]
Tlokwa, tri., Afr. [9.1.1.13]
tobacco [9.3.16]
Tocharian, lang. [25.4]
Togo, Afr. [9.1.1.4]
toponymic surnames [44.19]
toponyms, Italian [9.33.8]
transcription [9.47.4]
translation [9.47.2], [22.22]
  Swahili [9.1.6.2]
transposable [22.11]
Tret, It. [9.33.2]
Tswana, lang. South Afr. [9.1.5.2]
Tuogh, Ire. [9.31.1]

TURKISH [9.55.1]-[9.55.6], [9.8.3],
  [9.8.4]
  influence [9.23.2]
Tuscany, It. [9.33.1.3]
Twana, Ind. tri. US [9.3.7]
twins [9.3.2A], [22.19]
types, anc. It. [9.14.3]
Tzeltal, lang. tri. Mex. [9.39.1]-
  [9.39.2], [9.39.4], [9.39.11]-
  [9.39.12]

Uganda [9.1.1.8]
UKRAINIAN [9.56.1]-[9.56.4]
  surnames [9.45.2]
ulcers [26.8]
Ulster, N. Ire. [9.31.5.15], [45.3]
UNIQUE [45.1]-[45.34], [7.18],
  [9.3.48], [9.17.3.11], [9.47.5],
  [15.12], [17.5], [17.12], [22.27],
  [28.1]-[28.2], [33.2], [33.2.13]
  African American [9.2.8], [9.2.10]
  Australia [9.42.1.9]
  Canadian [9.9.3], [9.9.12]
  English [9.17.9.3]
  surn. [7.6]
Utah [23.11]

Vākātaka, anc. inscriptions, India
  [9.29.6]
Val Varaita, It. [9.33.7]
Valais, Switz. [9.54.3]
Valdemora, Spain [9.52.2.4]
Van Gogh, Vincent [30.10]
Vanessa, first name [11.2.3]
Venezualan [9.51.3]
Vietnamese [9.40.17]
Virginia, state of [9.2.2.7]
Vivian, pers. name [9.57.7]
Viviane, pers. name [9.10.7],
  [9.17.6.23]
vocative, seamless [3.24]
Vortigern, pers. name [9.17.6]-
  [9.17.7]
vulture, in surnames [9.39.1]

Waha, tri. Tanzania [9.1.1.30]
Wales [9.17.12], [9.10.9], [9.57.13]
Wanyamwezi, tri. Tanzania [9.1.1.26]
Wazesuru, tri. Zimbabwe [9.1.1.15]
Weagamow, Amer. Ind. [9.3.35]
WELSH [9.57.1]-[9.57.21],
  [9.10.6], [9.10.9], [9.10.11],
  [9.17.6.1], [9.17.9.53], [9.31.19]
FIRST NAMES [9.57.1.1]-
  [9.57.1.3]
Old Welsh [9.10.2]
population structure [9.17.7.1]-
  [9.17.7.2], [9.17.7.4],
  [9.17.7.7], [9.57.3]
SURNAMES [9.57.2.1]-
  [9.57.2.14], [9.17.7.1]
US [9.57.2.10]-[9.57.2.12]
WEST INDIAN [9.58.1]-[9.58.2]
West Riding, Engl. [9.17.9.41]
West Semites/ic [9.4.6], [9.4.3.1],
  [9.4.21]
West Sussex [9.17.9.25]-[9.17.9.26]
West, surn. [45.2]
Western, surn. [9.17.9.15]
Whitman, Walt [7.12]
WOMEN [46.1]-[46.5], [3.25], [7.1],
  [7.4], [7.11], [7.15]-[7.16], [7.26],
  [9.4.3.1], [9.9.2.2], [9.14.17],
  [9.17.4.15], [9.40.11], [24.1],
  [33.2.7], [42.7]
  baseball [26.3.11]
  Bible [5.17]
  BIRTH [46.1.1]-[46.1.13] [3.3],
    [3.17], [9.9.2.2]
  Canada [9.9.2.3]
  CB (radio) [26.27]
  change of name [9.9.1.3]
  English [9.17.22]
  hyphenated [44.2], [44.5]
  India [9.29.1]
  Japanese [9.34.3], [9.34.5]
  journalists, stereotypes [42.4]
  LAW [46.2.1]-[46.2.3], [20.7]
  SURNAMES [46.3.1]-[46.3.3]
  Sweden [9.53.20]
  titles [3.18]
WORDS [47.1]-[47.27], [45.21],
  [47.1.21]
  Australian [9.42.1.3], [9.42.1.7]
  criminal [26.11]
  English & French [47.12]
  MEDICAL [47.1.1]-[47.1.38]
  Pitcairn Is. Oceania [9.42.2]
  RECREATIONAL ASPECTS
    [47.2.1]-[47.2.2]
  SCIENCE [47.3.1]-[47.3.2]
  SLANG [47.4.1]-[47.4.8]
    Australian [9.42.1.3]
Wyandot, Ind. tri. NA [9.3.44]
Wynot, Nova Scotia [9.9.17]

X, beginning first names [11.2.1],
    [35.1]
Xhosa, tri. South Afr. [9.1.5.5]-
    [9.1.5.7]

Yavapai, Ind. tri. US [9.3.14]-
    [9.3.15], [9.3.20]
year-names [9.4.13], [9.4.14]
YHWH, God [12.2.1]-[12.2.8],
    [13.6]
Yiddish, change from [9.22.2]
Yorkshire, Engl. [9.17.14],
    [9.17.7.13], [9.17.9.42]-[9.17.9.44]
Yoruba, tri. Afr. [9.1.4.5], [9.1.4.7]

Yucatan, Mex. [9.39.7
Yuman, Ind. tri. US [9.3.20]
YW [12.10]

Zaire [9.1.1.17]
Zambia [9.1.1.3]
Zimbabwe [9.1.7.1]-[9.1.7.5],
    [9.1.8.1], [9.1.8.6], [9.1.1.17]-
    [9.1.1.18]
Zinacantan, Mex. [9,39,2]
zodiac [11.1.21]
Zulu See: AFRICAN: ZULU
Zuni, Ind. tri. US [9.3.5]
Zweigenhaft, Richard L. [45.32]

About the Compiler

EDWIN D. LAWSON is president of the American Name Society. He is Professor Emeritus of Psychology at the State University of New York at Fredonia and the author of *Personal Names and Naming* (Greenwood, 1987), and numerous other books in the fields of onomastics and psychology.

ISBN 0-313-28582-9

90000>

EAN

9 780313 285820

HARDCOVER BAR CODE